JONAS

Events of recent years have thrust Jonas Savimbi, leader of the UNITA movement in Angola, into the forefront of world media attention. His visit to Washington at the invitation of President Reagan clinched US government support for his cause almost at the same time as his troops were capturing yet more European hostages and marching them the length of Angola to prove how powerful his movement is.

In JONAS SAVIMBI: A KEY TO AFRICA award-winning journalist Fred Bridgland provides much more than a biography of the UNITA leader; he also portrays in vivid detail the changing face of Africa in general and Angola in particular.

About the author

Fred Bridgland is the London based diplomatic correspondent for *The Scotsman* newspaper. A former Reuters correspondent in New Delhi and then Central Africa, his work has also appeared in the *New York Times*, *Newsweek* magazine, *The Times*, *The Sunday Times*, *The Guardian*, *The Economist*, *The Spectator* and *Neue Zuercher Zeitung*. A documentary he made of the Angolan civil war in 1984 was screened by the BBC, CBS, West German Television, NHK TV of Japan and Swedish TV.

JONAS SAVIMBI:
A KEY TO AFRICA

Fred Bridgland

CORONET BOOKS
Hodder and Stoughton

For Kathryn, who also understood it
and who also suffered it; and to all
the people of Angola.

Copyright © 1986 by Fred Bridgland

First published in
Great Britain in 1986
by Mainstream Publishing
Co. Limited

Coronet edition 1988

British Library CIP

Bridgland, Fred
    Jonas Savimbi: a key to Africa.
    1. Savimbi, Jonas
    2. Revolutionists –
    Angola – Biography
    I. Title
    322.4'2'0924   DT611.76.S2

ISBN 0-340-42218-1

Printed and bound in Great Britain
for Hodder and Stoughton
Paperbacks, a division of Hodder
and Stoughton Limited, Mill Road,
Dunton Green, Sevenoaks, Kent
TN13 2YA. (Editorial Office:
47 Bedford Square, London
WC1B 3DP), by Richard Clay
Limited, Bungay, Suffolk. Photoset
by Rowland Phototypesetting
Limited, Bury St Edmunds, Suffolk.

Contents

List of Maps

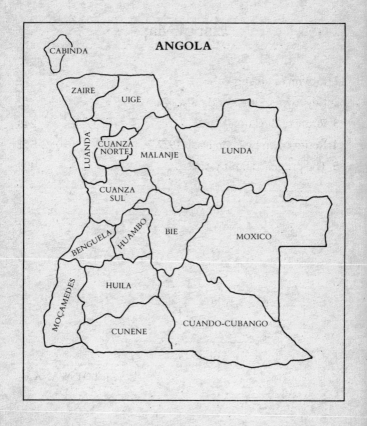

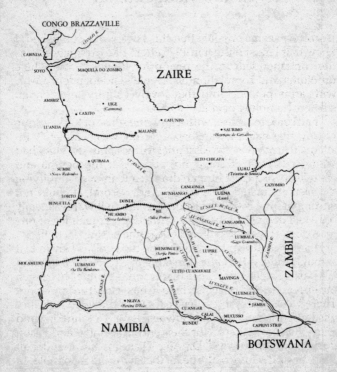

Acknowledgements

It scarcely seems possible that this book is at last finished. I knew that I must write it in 1976 after I had experienced – as the correspondent in the region for Reuters – the whole unfolding and completion of Angola's independence war, with arms pouring into that lovely country and foreign soldiers trampling over it.

I had come to realise, with a growing sense of Kafka-esque horror, that daily newspaper reporting was completely inadequate to convey two essential truths about the war I had witnessed. First, it could not cope with the depths and complexity of a great human drama, and in oversimplifying the facts it created falsehoods. And, second, it could not encompass my own conviction that the civil war was really only just beginning, because of the special qualities of one man, Jonas Savimbi, who led one of the 'losing' factions.

I finally got down to real work on the book as I lay in bed through August 1979 after breaking my leg in my first – and last – parachute jump. Since then various people have given me important and unselfish help in ensuring its completion. There were others in earlier years who provided a well of wisdom from which I could always draw. To John Rigg and Harry Ree I owe thanks for their encouragement and vision during my schooldays. Dr Alec Dickson, the founder of VSO, helped reinforce the belief that anything is possible. In the world of journalism, I owe a special debt to Eric Mackay, my editor at *The Scotsman*, who encouraged me in his own special way and printed stories about the renewed civil war in Angola years before other papers had woken up to the fact that anything significant was happening. My thanks to all colleagues on *The Scotsman*, who tolerated my quirks and eccentricities, but especially to Jim Seaton, one of the finest newspapermen in Britain, who inspires devotion among all those who work under him. Richard Harwood, of the *Washington Post*, taught me invaluable lessons in the time I spent with him in Angola. Gwynne Roberts was a cheerful companion on one expedition and gave his time generously when I was preparing for others. The BBC and *The Sunday Times* gave important financial help in preparing some of my expeditions. I have Reuters to thank for ten fascinating years of my career, much of it spent in India, the Middle East and Africa in turbulent times: without the agency's willingness to pay me to live in exotic places, I would not have discovered Angola and its people.

Though I've tried to base as much as possible of this book on personal experience, I've had to fill in lots of gaps from the work of other writers. Two in particular I would like to mention. First, Professor John Marcum, without whose two magnificent works on the history of Angola from 1950 to 1976 I would have been lost. I felt honoured when Professor Marcum, now Academic Vice-Chancellor at the University of California at Santa Cruz, generously agreed to find time in his hectic schedule to read and criticise my draft, even though he disagreed with my conclusions. He saved me from making some basic errors of fact and guided me towards gentler judgements on people on whom I had pronounced harshly. Special thanks also to Leon Dash of the *Washington Post* who made two extraordinarily brave journeys through Angola in the early and late 1970s: without his accounts, we would be almost completely ignorant of important events in the country's history. I am grateful to the *Washington Post* for permission to quote his work at some length.

My thanks to my publishers, Bill Campbell and Peter MacKenzie, whose energies, enterprise and cheerful encouragement ensured that the project would be completed. I owe lots of thanks to Angolans who have looked after me and shared their lives with me and taught me much during my time in their country. I single out Tito Chingunji, Jimmy Muecalia, Marcus Samundo, Jaka Jamba, 'Antonio', Ben-Ben Arlindo Pena, Geraldo Nunda, John Celas and Smart Chata for special thanks, but there are many others who for me have made Angola a rich and rewarding discovery.

There are many others who have given invaluable help whom I cannot name here: they will know who they are.

Finally, Violet Bridgland deserves special thanks for her unrelenting hard work over many years and for passing on her belief that things can be different. To Fred Bridgland senior my love and thanks also. To Kathryn Kane I owe a debt that goes beyond words: the book would not have been researched or written without her. To my three daughters, Annwen, Samantha and Rebecca, I owe lots of time that should ideally have been theirs: their cheerful love, tolerance and irreverence helped me keep things in perspective.

* * *

I've striven to ensure that this book is factually accurate. But the trouble with Angola is that practically every fact is in dispute. I take all responsibility for factual errors and omissions, and of course the interpretation of the 'facts' is all mine. Because the facts are so contentious I have supplied plenty of notes, but they are kept at the back of the book for those who want to use them so that the flow of the narrative will not be interrupted for others.

Explanatory Note

For European readers, the strange names and great array of acronyms used in Angola can cause confusion. I have therefore simplified issues by cutting many of them out, and I hope this does not cause too much offence to Angolans and other Africans, who continually have to endure Europeans who oversimplify their societies and cultures. The Ovimbundu tribe, for example, speak the umBundu language; and the Mbundu tribe speak the kiMbundu language. I refer to them as the Ovimbundu and Kimbundu tribes who speak Ovimbundu and Kimbundu: ethnolinguistically this is wrong, but I think that in this context it makes for clarity. UNITA and MPLA have armies which are called FALA (the Armed Forces for the Liberation of Angola) and FAPLA (People's Armed Forces for the Liberation of Angola). Wherever possible, I avoid FALA and FAPLA, and simply refer to the UNITA army and the MPLA army. Another source of confusion is the wholesale renaming of towns after independence; in the chapters before independence I use the old names, but as the changes are made I introduce them in brackets and thereafter stick to the new names. Thus Nova Lisboa becomes Nova Lisboa (renamed Huambo after independence); then Huambo (formerly Nova Lisboa); and finally the transformation is completed with just plain Huambo.

*   *   *

When I first set out to write the book I resisted suggestions from some publishers that I write an overall history of Angola over the past ten years. That, I believe, is an impossible task when civil war is still raging. I therefore stuck to my original plan to tell the Angolan story as it has been lived and seen by one of the major players in the drama. It is therefore a partial story, and I myself am not impartial, though I have tried to be as intellectually rigorous as possible. I have only let my opinions really hang out in the final chapter, but no doubt readers will spot my prejudices in passages where I believed I was being a model of objectivity and fairness.

To make sure readers are adequately protected against my biases, and those of others, I would like to remind them before they set out through the thickets of Angola of one of the many splendid passages in George Orwell's account of the Spanish Civil War, *Homage to Catalonia*:

> It is difficult to be certain about anything except what you have seen with your own eyes, and consciously or unconsciously everyone writes as a partisan. In case I have not said this earlier, I will say it now: beware of my partisanship, my mistakes of fact, and the distortion inevitably caused by my having seen only one corner of events. And beware of exactly the same thing when you read any other book on this period of the Spanish war.

Ditto for Angola.

Brussels, September 1986.

Prologue

God's Men

1975

'That people fighting for their independence will take aid from wherever they can find it is clear. To win our independence we should even take aid, as they say, from the Devil himself.'
Agostinho Neto, in a broadcast, August 1969.[1]

On 20 August 1975 a man of God landed at the airport in the small town of Silva Porto in central Angola. He wore black – shirt, trousers, moustache, sideburns, heavy sunglasses. A big silver cross on a long black chain flapped on his chest, and he was a top CIA agent.

John Stockwell, a case officer for the American secret intelligence agency in Saigon until the South Vietnam capital's fall to the Viet Cong in April that year, had now been appointed chief of the CIA's Task Force in Angola, where another Third World civil war was being absorbed into the East-West global conflict.

The man of God was in Silva Porto to see Jonas Savimbi, black African, graduate of Lausanne University, leader of the Angolan guerrilla movement UNITA, and friend of the late Che Guevara. He wanted to study UNITA's strengths because, in the previous month, the President of the United States, Gerald Ford, had approved and signed the expenditure of 14 million dollars for the covert supply of arms by the CIA to UNITA (the National Union for the Total Independence of Angola) and another black nationalist movement, the FNLA (the National Front for the Liberation of Angola).

On 29 July the first planeload of arms for Angola left the United States. On the next day, at the end of his leave following the Vietnam debacle, Stockwell was appointed to run the Angola operation.[2]

It was the brainchild of Henry Kissinger, the US Secretary of State, who wanted to establish a military balance between UNITA, the FNLA and a third Angolan movement, the MPLA (Popular Movement for the Liberation of Angola), a Marxist-Leninist group whose soldiers were being armed by the Soviet Union and trained by Cuban military officers.

Angola's independence was due on 11 November, after nearly five centuries of Portuguese colonial rule. The Portuguese had fought the three nationalist movements in a rather desultory civil war since the early sixties; but after the Portuguese revolution of April 1974, which ended 42 years of right-wing dictatorship, Portugal planned to hold multi-party elections in Angola before relinquishing control of its colony. The plan was abandoned when the FNLA and MPLA began a civil war which eventually encompassed UNITA; but the Portuguese said that even without elections they would still leave Angola by 11 November.

As the movements fought among themselves, the MPLA consolidated control in its natural hinterland among the Kimbundu, Angola's second largest tribe, eastwards from Luanda, the capital, to the Zaire border.

The MPLA also took control of all the coastal towns south of Luanda; though in the two biggest, Benguela and the magnificent port of Lobito, UNITA claimed the support of the majority of the citizens, who were members of the Ovimbundu, Angola's largest tribal grouping. UNITA claimed the loyalties of the majority in Luso, a strategic town at the eastern end of the Benguela Railway; but Luso too was overrun by the MPLA, which in August 1975 seemed set to take over the whole of central and southern Angola.

Kissinger kept his plan to prevent an MPLA takeover in Angola secret from the American people because he knew that so soon after the painful and humiliating finale in Vietnam they would not support involvement in another far-off foreign war.

*   *   *

Before visiting Savimbi, Stockwell had been with the leader of the FNLA, Holden Roberto, whose power base was in the north of the country among the Kikongo, Angola's third largest tribe. It was Roberto who enjoyed most favour from Kissinger, for the FNLA leader was openly anti-Communist and pro-free enterprise. Savimbi, by contrast, had trained as a guerrilla in China, was an admirer of Mao Tse-tung, and was depicted by some American journalists as the most radically Marxist of all the Angolan nationalist leaders.[3] But if he was not seen by Washington as a reliable ally, at least he was opposed to Moscow's men in Angola.

Travelling with Roberto, Stockwell saw that the FNLA had thrust southwards from its northern tribal stronghold to within 32 kilometres of the MPLA bastion in Luanda.[4] For Kissinger it was good to hear news of his pliant ally's military advance. But Stockwell sensed a frailty about the FNLA which contrasted with his first impressions of Savimbi's movement: 'It was immediately clear that UNITA was an organisation of very different calibre than the FNLA.'

When Stockwell arrived in Silva Porto he was taken to a cinema hall where Savimbi was about to address the UNITA faithful at a party congress. The CIA priest noted that the UNITA leader's skin was very black, his beard full and shiny, his eyes wide, prominent and flashing: 'As Savimbi began to speak, the assembly stilled to hear a master of a speaking style once popular in our society but now as rare as the deep-throated belly laugh and the bar-room brawl.'

Savimbi's voice was rich and well modulated. He turned his whole body to different parts of the audience and leaned forward and reached his hands towards the people before drawing them back to his chest: 'The crowd's reaction was spiritual, more like a prayer meeting than a political gathering.'[5]

In restrained, downbeat fashion Savimbi described to the CIA man how the MPLA had been driven out of Silva Porto at the beginning of August when UNITA entered the civil war. His account impressed Stockwell: 'Roberto would have exaggerated and called it a major victory.'[6]

Savimbi then took Stockwell by plane and Land Rover to

within one kilometre of Luso, which was being besieged by UNITA troops under the command of Colonel Samuel Chiwale, the number three man in the movement who had also received his guerrilla training in China. On the journey to and from Luso Savimbi spoke of his philosophy, and Stockwell grew reflective and pondered the empty cynicism of his own life: 'Savimbi was impatient to move on. For a moment I resented him, with his clear objectives and clean conscience. He was that rare coincidence of history, a throwback to the great tribal leaders of Africa – Tchaka Zulu, Msiri, and Jomo Kenyatta[7] – a far cry from the conflicting values and goals of America, and of the CIA in its middle-aged mediocrity.'

Stockwell was in Angola with UNITA for only 24 hours, but he left convinced that Savimbi was 'a good man by any standard'. Together he and the UNITA leaders calculated the movement's strength – 4,000 troops ready for combat plus 6,000 trainees – to be reported to CIA headquarters in Langley, Virginia. 'Here was the most significant finding of my trip. We had understood that UNITA was the weakest militarily of the three liberation movements; in fact, Savimbi's army was several times larger than the FNLA's, better led, and supported by a political organisation of some depth. This would be good news at headquarters, an unexpected asset in our war against the MPLA.'[8]

Savimbi never saw the Angola Task Force chief again. He dealt with lesser CIA operatives, though with some reluctance because he had sought open, not covert, American government assistance: 'My only request was through the US Ambassador to Zambia, Jean Wilkowski, and I gave her reports in Lusaka asking for American help. It was America which chose to give that help through the CIA. If they chose to give it that way I was not going to be apologetic, because I needed support for my struggle. But I was not given the money for giving information, so I was not on the CIA payroll. I addressed myself to the American government, and it is a domestic matter about the way they decided to help me.'[9]

*   *   *

The CIA's Man of God had returned to his command centre when I set foot in Angola for the first time on 21 September 1975. I too landed in Silva Porto, where the wall slogans in Portuguese read *'Deus no Ceu; Savimbi em Angola'* (God in Heaven; Savimbi in Angola).

What God preferred for Angola was hard to judge, but what was obvious was UNITA's total control of the beautiful little administrative and railway town high on the Angolan plateau. The small airport terminal was festooned with UNITA and pro-Savimbi slogans and colours: on top of it were silhouetted a UNITA soldier with an anti-tank rocket launcher and others carrying machine guns. Mauve jacaranda and red flame of the forest trees lined the wide streets, from which were set back the Mediterranean-style pink and white stuccoed villas the Portuguese had built.

I had spent 1975 following convoluted developments in the Rhodesia problem from my base in Lusaka – the assassination of the Zanu leader Herbert Chitepo; intra-Zanu massacres in Zambia; the release from prison in Rhodesia of black nationalists like Joshua Nkomo, Ndabaningi Sithole and Robert Mugabe; the historic handshake of black Zambian President Kenneth Kaunda and white South African Prime Minister John Vorster at the Victoria Falls conference on Rhodesia that August.

Very little attention was being paid to Angola. Rhodesia, the aftermath of Vietnam, Mrs Indira Gandhi's suspension of democracy in India, and the ever-simmering Middle East attracted international media attention. There were scarcely ever more than about four foreign correspondents in Luanda at any one time, and from neighbouring Zambia I had given Angola only passing attention. But when a UNITA representative in Lusaka offered a flight into the country, it sounded like an interesting diversion from Rhodesian nationalist politics. From Lusaka Airport two Danish pilots flew Nicholas Ashford, southern Africa correspondent of *The Times* of London, and myself in a luxurious Lear executive jet into Savimbi's territory.[10]

It was a surrealistic way to get involved in a civil war, and the surrealism did not end there. Ashford and I were lodged in the sumptuous former official residence of the Portuguese governor of Bie Province, of which Silva Porto was the capital. We were served at table by the departed grandee's servants, and we ate off his exquisite bone china and silverware. Of the many paintings in the residence, there was one I remember as the most stunning I have ever seen. It was of an open-sided African *django* (meeting hut) at night, with people gathered around a blazing fire, and the artist had depicted the scene with skill and exquisite beauty, using only red and black paints. I often wonder, in the light of subsequent history, whether the painting now graces Fidel Castro's official residence in Havana.

The next day Ashford and I were driven to a secondary school in which Savimbi had his headquarters. It was a scene straight from a Graham Greene novel: a cardboard sign written in runny red paint proclaimed it as the *Quarters of the Dragons of Death*, while a young guard draped with belts of cartridges for his heavy machine-gun completed an image of sadness verging on farce.

Soon we were ushered into Savimbi's office, which was hung with maps of Angola. Savimbi's greeting was warm, his handshake firm, and his magnetism immediately apparent. His manner was open and unaggressive and his English fluent – an interesting discovery because Savimbi had never lived in an English-speaking country. He wore commando camouflage uniform, brilliantly polished boots and a green beret with a general's three gold stars.

At this time UNITA was confined to two main towns – Silva Porto and, 120 kilometres to the west, Nova Lisboa, the second largest city in Angola. The MPLA was probing the western defences of Nova Lisboa with armoured cars; it had had an assured supply of arms from the Soviet Union for more than a year, whereas UNITA had received very few and only on an irregular basis. It was therefore a surprise to us to find Savimbi in an optimistic frame of mind. 'We control the most densely populated areas,' he said. 'The majority of the population is in the countryside. That is why we are optimistic. Definitely the movement that has the ability to mobilise the countryside is bound to win.'[11] In the UNITA-controlled areas at that time lived perhaps 2.5 million of the country's 6.5 million people.

Savimbi predicted that within another month there would be a tremendous increase in military activity by the three liberation movements: 'Each one would like to reach 11 November (Independence Day) in a position of strength.' UNITA's main objective was to recapture Lobito from the MPLA: an assault on the port would begin very soon.

We asked Savimbi how he would get the necessary arms to lay siege to Lobito. 'We are getting all sorts of military equipment,' he said. 'We are much better off than we were three weeks ago.'[12]

He declined to specify where the arms were coming from, but said that some Western democracies were among the suppliers. Ashford and I had no way of knowing then that the CIA air-bridge was bringing arms to the Zairean airbase of Thysville, where they were loaded onto other planes for delivery to the FNLA and UNITA. Some of the weapons for Savimbi came overland from Zambia, which was party to the CIA operation.[13] CIA case officers, including 'disinformation' experts, were sent to Lusaka, where they were based in Wilkowski's embassy.[14]

Savimbi had told Stockwell repeatedly, during the Task Force chief's 24-hour sojourn in UNITA territory, that the only real hope for Angola lay at the conference table, not on the battlefield.[15] Savimbi had been at the forefront of the preparations for multi-party elections before Angola sank into chaos and civil war in mid-1975.

UNITA continued to prefer a peaceful solution of political problems, Savimbi told Ashford and me. 'We argued that there should be elections, but now there will be no elections because one group had more weapons for imposing its will on the others. Without that steady flow of Soviet arms, the MPLA could not have won their victories. The Angolan situation is like that in Portugal after the revolution in 1974 where the Communists, through the Armed Forces Movement, tried to control the country even though they were a minority.'

He said he did not think the world would just watch the Soviets supplying arms and taking over Angola without a word: 'We have a democratic and moral stand, so we look to other countries to help us with arms.'

Savimbi added, so casually that we hardly noticed, that
Cuba had entered the civil war. There were Cuban commanders with the MPLA forces and Cuban military instructors in the training camps. And he added that his rival
Agostinho Neto, the leader of the MPLA, always 'used to
say that he wanted to build here a sort of Cuba. But we don't
think we have anything in Common with Cuba. The cultural
background is so different.'

*   *   *

I travelled to Nova Lisboa and watched some of the saddest
death throes of the 500-year-old Portuguese empire. The
empire was not ending with dignified ceremonial, but with a
rush to the airports. After the fighting intensified in July
1975 some 400,000 or more Portuguese left Angola by land,
sea and air within a couple of months.

After Luanda, Nova Lisboa was the main point of escape
for Portuguese refugees. At the airport thousands were
waiting for special international flights to evacuate them.
Some had been there for many days, sleeping on the stone
floors of the hangars. The more far-sighted had brought
mattresses or canvas chairs which had seen service on
verandahs during balmy tropical evenings. Some sat in
family groups comprising three generations, the children
clutching dolls and teddy bears and the adults munching
cold chicken. The toilets had long ago overflowed and were
in an unspeakable condition. There was no longer an airport
administration to supervise care and maintenance. A black
nun dressed in white was trying to give practical help and
boost morale.

While the airlift went on, more Portuguese were arriving
all the time in trucks and cars from across central Angola. As
they abandoned their vehicles, Africans tried to start them
and drive them away. But often the Portuguese had taken
the keys with them or dropped them down drains.

There were still Portuguese soldiers in Nova Lisboa, surly
and slovenly youthful products of their country's revolution, whose role was limited to shepherding batches of
refugees to the two or three aircraft which arrived each day.
Savimbi had ordered the departure of the Portuguese

military as soon as the last refugee was gone. UNITA soldiers controlled the city, the approaches to the airport and the control tower.

The Portuguese abdication was near complete. The villas were emptying, the banks were closed, dozens of factories had stopped production, and only a handful of shops, with fast diminishing stocks, remained open. By 11 November there would be no Portuguese presence in the bright modern city they had proudly named New Lisbon.

All the doctors from Nova Lisboa's civil hospitals had left. There were ten Portuguese Red Cross doctors looking after the refugees and feeding some 3,000 Africans who had come into the city to escape fighting in the north. These doctors too planned to leave before Independence Day.

Otherwise there was only one doctor in the whole of Savimbi's territory – George Burgess, a Canadian missionary with the Protestant United Church of Christ at a hospital at Dondi, the site of several mission institutes where Savimbi attended school in the early fifties. It was at Dondi, near the small town of Bela Vista between Nova Lisboa and Silva Porto, that I caught up again a few days later with Jonas Savimbi.

*　　*　　*

Several thousand people had gathered to greet Savimbi in a forest glade. The singing, dancing crowd had covered the path leading to the speakers' platform with palm leaves for about half a kilometre. Savimbi arrived clad in a bright yellow toga, and as he advanced along the palm path the crowd scattered white, sweet-smelling frangipani flowers at his feet. The toga was in the style of traditional African chieftains, with one shoulder bared. But it was possibly in homage to a hero of Savimbi's youth, Kwame Nkrumah, the Ghanaian pan-African nationalist, who also liked to wear togas. On Savimbi's right wrist was a yellow bead bangle and on his left a yellow gold watch.

He spoke first in Portuguese and then in Ovimbundu, his own tongue and that of the people of Dondi. It was in the latter that his charisma was most apparent as he used proverbs, irony and traditional jokes to make his points.

'We've lost everything there was to lose,' he told the crowd. 'Now the time has come for the MPLA to start losing. The MPLA controls the capital, but in Luanda they produce only sand. Here we produce food.'

The MPLA had started the 'criminal' war: 'All we can do is fight back and hope for a just peace. The MPLA talks of peace and democracy when it means dictatorship . . . Even though the MPLA has the arms advantage now, the weapons haven't got brains: with people we can win.'

*   *   *

I stayed in Silva Porto until 7 October before deciding to return to Lusaka because UNITA had refused to take us near the fighting. The war seemed to be in a stagnant phase.

Before leaving I took a quick look at UNITA's military training camp at Nhunha, near Silva Porto. Recruits were completing their basic training inside 45 days instead of the six months it had earlier taken to train an infantryman. Captain Armando Chau, the camp commandant who had once been a black soldier in the Portuguese colonial army, had 700 men in training. The marching, obstacle course and weapons drill all looked fairly professional, but conditions were tough – hundreds of glass huts and one concrete building which served as a hospital, though without electricity or a doctor.

In Nhunha camp sat six Panhard armoured cars and two jeep-mounted rocket launchers, none of which worked and all of which lacked spare parts. I was told they had been left by the departing Portuguese though years later Savimbi said they had been given by Zaire. Anyway, it was hard to see how these clapped-out machines could help reverse the MPLA tide.

Of more use might be the old DC-4 without identity markings which I saw make several landings at Silva Porto and disgorge small arms. No one would say where the plane came from. The pilot and co-pilot seemed to speak with British and German accents, but they moved away whenever a journalist tried to speak to them – except for 'Skip'.

'Skip' had been introduced to me as an American journalist. But he stayed in a separate building from the others – five more reporters and photographers had flown in – and none of us could find out who he worked for, though he said he had once been a marine in Vietnam. Other Americans joined him. One announced himself as another Man of God, a missionary checking on the fate of his parishioners. Another was straight out of an American nightmare – a black Texan hat, high-heeled boots, studded jeans, a mean swagger, and a sour, gum-chewing face which carried the message: 'Look at me, admire me, but don't speak to me.'

Though I didn't know it at the time, 'Skip' was the CIA's resident liaison man with Savimbi. The new Man of God and the Texan were military specialists who were part of a CIA team which had arrived to train UNITA officers.[16]

The day I went to the airport to leave, a giant camouflage-painted C-130 transport plane was on the tarmac. It was heavily guarded by UNITA troops, and light weapons were being carried from it. 'Skip' was there observing the operation, probably unaware that the little war in which the US and others were getting involved would become a very big one which, more than a decade later, would still be laying waste to Angola and its people.

1

Origins

1934–58

Jonas Malheiro Savimbi was born on 3 August 1934 in Munhango, a small town on the 3,000-kilometre-long Benguela Railway. His father, Loth Malheiro Savimbi, was a man of strong and independent mind, from whom Jonas inherited the determination and perserverance which would shape both his own future and that of his country.

Loth's special qualities resulted in his eventual appointment as the first black station-master on the railway, which in its journey eastwards from the Atlantic towards the copper mines of Central Africa neatly cuts Angola into northern and southern halves.

As a boy, Loth, who was born at the turn of the century, had been determined to obtain an education to escape the oppressive Native Law and forced labour which were special features of the 'magnificent certainty' of Portugal's 'civilising mission' in Angola.[1] For four hundred years, until the late nineteenth century, the foundation of the Portuguese system in Angola had been the slave trade. Some four million Angolans were exported to the Americas; but during the same period it has been estimated that nine million blacks died during the slaves' march to the coast and while waiting to be herded on to ships.[2] Portugal and the state Roman Catholic Church, which closely followed the flag, argued that the slave trade in Angola was spiritually beneficial. Both insisted that slaves be baptised before crossing the Atlantic in chains: 'On the wharfs at Luanda as late as 1870, there could still be seen a marble chair in which the bishop had sat and baptised by boatloads the poor wretches as they were rowed alongside the ship. The Government collected its tax, the pious ecclesiastic received his fee, and the slaves had their first introduction into the white man's religion.'[3]

The effects of the trade were pernicious and long-lasting. Whole African communities were destroyed, and the Portuguese had to range deeper and deeper inland to find the *pombos* (markets) where African chiefs, or their agents, bartered men and women, often captured in local wars, as slaves. Not only was the population drastically reduced, but those taken away were young people in the prime of their lives: 'The strongest men and some women (in Brazil one out of four slaves was a woman) were drained off from an economy which depended primarily upon the physical energy of hunters, warriors, traders and farmers. Articles bartered for slaves were non-productive: trinkets, textiles, tobacco, brandy, wine, firearms, powder, and lead shot . . . Each article of trade either undermined some local Angolan industry or introduced destructive or disruptive commodities. Therefore the slave trade was doubly pernicious economically – it diverted human energy from productive enterprises and fed non-productive items into the economy.'[4]

After the abolition of slavery, an 1899 decree stated that blacks had a duty to work for whites in menial jobs that the Portuguese considered to be beneath them. From this grew a system of forced labour that was more draconian than any implemented by the French, British or even Belgian colonial powers in Africa. At any one time up to half a million Angolans might be under compulsory recruitment and receiving miserable wages in a system that continued into the second half of the twentieth century.[5] A missionary nurse who approached the Portuguese district administrator's headquarters at Chitembo, in Bie Province, in October 1959 wrote: 'We heard the sounds of blows and screaming. We passed into the building and through an open door saw an African lying on the floor being beaten by a *cipaio* (African policeman). The administrator sat behind his desk watching.' Onlookers explained that the reason for the beating was that 'the man, a village chief, had been unable to collect enough men for contract labour.'[6]

The Native Tax, applicable to all adult males, was introduced to raise revenues for the government and to force Africans into the money economy. Since they were obliged to pay in Portuguese currency rather than the traditional means of exchange such as shells, salt or cloth, they had to enter the cash economy to obtain the money. Those who did not pay were the most liable to be contracted for forced labour: in 1928 each African male in central Angola paid an annual tax of 80 angolares, which was the total pay received for 100 days of contracted labour.[7] Thousands of Angolans in the east fled to the Belgian Congo and Northern Rhodesia in the 1930s and 1940s to escape the tax. A later generation among these exiles would play an important role in the liberation struggle to overthrow Portugal's rule in Angola.

There was, however, one very thin loophole through which the really bright native could wriggle away from the Native Tax and forced labour. Under the Native Policy (known as the *Indigenato*, which translates literally as 'the quality of being a native') Africans in Angola constituted the lesser of two distinct classes. The 'natives' were consigned menial occupations. Their lives were mainly regulated by native custom and law, but also according to special Portuguese decrees. Europeans enjoyed full rights as Portuguese citizens, which guaranteed opportunities for them in the bureaucracy, education and commerce that were closed to Africans.

These apartheid-like policies were based more on a concept of civilisation than on colour of skin. The Europeans were known as *civilizados* (literally 'civilised people') who were steeped in European culture: this was no barrier to sexual liaisons, or even marriage, with blacks, and their *mestico*, or half-caste, offspring were classified as Portuguese citizens. Their numbers grew to more than 50,000, concentrated mainly in the coastal cities of Luanda, Lobito and Benguela. Later they came to play an important but contentious role in the politics of independent Angola: *mesticos* wrestling with 'problems of identity (were they primarily Europeans, African, or an élite apart?) were understandably attracted by the political arguments of European Marxists who stressed the importance of class as opposed to racial conflict'.[8]

One of the duties imposed by the *Indigenato* on *civilizados* was to 'uplift' the natives so that they could be gradually integrated into citizenship in the European sector. A fully 'uplifted' native was one who had assimilated Portuguese customs and values so thoroughly that he had in all ways, other than skin colour, became a Portuguese and been fully alienated from his tribal and village culture.

But strict formal tests had to be passed by Africans who desired to spring free of the restrictions of the *Indigenato* and throw away the *caderneta* (identity card) and passbook that non-assimilated Africans were required to carry. Among the many standards set for assimilation were these: the African had to be at least 18, be able to speak and write Portuguese fluently, have a clean police record, exercise a profession which brought in enough income to support a family, and 'have acquired the enlightenment and habits presupposed for Portuguese citizens.'[9]

If a petition to become an *assimilado* was approved, the successful applicant was issued with a special identity card (*o bilhete de identidade*) confirming that he had made the transition from African to *assimilado*. But the pitiable level of educational opportunity provided by the Portuguese authorities for Africans was a formidable obstacle to those wanting to escape from helotry. As late as 1956 only about one per cent of the African school-age population was attending school, as compared with a figure of 11 per cent for neighbouring Northern Rhodesia, where the British were not trying to assimilate Africans;[10] the illiteracy rate among Angolan Africans was put at 97 per cent in 1958 by UNESCO; and by 1960 only 38,000 blacks out of an African population of 4,600,000 had *assimilado* status – less than nine in every thousand.

The Portuguese had applied *Catch 22* long before Joseph Heller brilliantly elaborated the concept in the book of the same name in the 1960s: an African could have full citizenship if he got an education, but at the same time an African could not get an education because the Portuguese

provided no primary schools. There was, however, one way
of dodging *Catch 22*. Protestant missionaries, mainly from
North America, had established several primary education
centres because they needed followers who could read the
Bible and evangelise in the villages.[11] They offered official
certificates and even training opportunities to Africans who
wanted to become teachers. One of these centres was run by
Canadian and United States Congregationalists at Dondi.
Loth Savimbi applied and was admitted.

But there was another difficulty. Loth's father and Jonas'
grandfather, Sakaita Savimbi, was a traditional chief who
had been stripped of his powers and much of his lands by
the colonisers because he had fought in the Bailundo Uprising of 1902. This small war, in which the Africans were
armed only with muzzle-load rifles against the sophisticated
artillery of the Europeans, erupted as a result of two factors.
First, the price collapsed for a low-quality rubber that had
been traded by the Ovimbundu people of Bailundo. Second,
many Portuguese and Boer farmers had begun to settle in
the Bailundo area, the most densely populated part of
Angola to the north of Nova Lisboa. The Ovimbundu resented the competition and increased demand for contract
labour from the whites, especially at a time when the basis
for their own prosperity had collapsed.[12] It took a two-year
war of 'pacification' and some 2,000 casualties before
the Ovimbundu resistance was broken and the Portuguese
established their domination.

So when Sakaita, who for the rest of his life brooded with
resentment at his treatment by the Portuguese, heard that
Loth planned to go to mission school he forbade what he
saw as a sell-out to the whites and their religion: Sakaita
was an animist, not a Christian. Loth nevertheless went
ahead and thus became estranged from Sakaita for 20
years.[13]

Loth completed his primary and teacher training education, converted to Christianity, and married a fellow
student. Henry Curtis MacDowell, a black American who
arrived at Dondi in 1919 with his wife, Ruth, and infant son,
Curtis, to begin a career as a Protestant missionary in
Angola, met Loth: the black American and the black African

established a deep friendship that lasted more than 50 years until Loth died in 1973.

In a tribute written to Loth after his death, Dr MacDowell said: 'In his inner self, he was a completely free man, whatever the outward circumstances. He was the Ovimbundu epitome of struggle, ever seeking to be a dedicated Christian whatever the exigencies of life. He bore more than his share of political persecution and through it all his Christian integrity was intact.'[14] This was a reference to the prison sentence Loth would serve late in his life when his son, Jonas, having won the patronage of Mao Tse-tung and the friendship of Che Guevara, became the guerrilla leader of a liberation movement operating from bases in eastern Angola.

After graduating from Dondi, Loth and his wife were appointed teachers at a village primary school funded by the American Protestant mission centre at Chilesso, about 100 kilometres north of Silva Porto, where both had been born. Sakaita too lived in Chilesso where, until his death, he was the *Mwekalia* (Attorney-General) to one of the Ovimbundu paramount chiefs.

In 1922 Loth's wife, M'Bundu, fell seriously ill. There were no local hospitals, so he had to pay for her to be treated by an African healer using traditional medicine. To meet his debts, Loth asked for a loan from the Chilesso missionaries. They refused. He could not approach his father, who still owned many cattle, because Sakaita had said: 'With the missionaries you will always remain a pauper. They will give you the Book while they get the land. It will always be the same. Either you stay with me where we have our land, or you go to those people for ever. If you go, I will not see you again.'[15]

Crippled with debts, Loth decided the time had come to apply for *assimilado* status which would enable him to enter better paid employment on the railway. But the education given by the missionaries was conditional on students agreeing to work after their graduation as Christian teachers in the villages. 'Senhor Loth agonised greatly before making his final decision,' said Dr MacDowell. 'He knew that if he took work on the railroad the attitude of the missionaries would be that he was abandoning the work of the Church. Well do I remember an all-night discussion with him about the practice of assimilation and its implications for Ovimbundu culture and tribal solidarity. Assimilation was the custom of blacks adopting, for all intents and purposes, the Portuguese language and culture: Loth was not at all convinced, to begin with, that it was a good idea.

'However, I explained to him that he did not necessarily need to renounce his culture and his people. He was intrigued by the story of American blacks and their adjustments and the fact that in so many ways they had to be parts of two cultures. As best I could, I stimulated him to think in terms of Christian witness from day to day on the job. The very next day he decided to become assimilated and take a railway job. He signed up (the necessary documents) and registered his property and did it in a manner and with the determination that, whatever happened, it would not diminish his devotion to his own people and that he would advance their welfare, the good points of their culture, in every possible way. At the same time, he would in full candour and integrity take advantage of every opportunity that the Portuguese culture offered.

'His decision created quite a furore in the Church and, being a young missionary, it put me in a very difficult position. However, Senhor Loth was faithful to his religion in every respect. Patrons of the railroad noticed his courtesy and gentlemanly ways. They saw very much of a Christian in him; and in every place where he worked there was soon a Christian movement, not only among blacks but among the Portuguese.'[16]

Loth's first posting to a railway station was as a low-grade clerk, and although his salary was small it was still twenty times the amount he had received from the missionaries. He paid his debts and used some of the rest of his money to establish a small church in a grass hut; it served as a primary school during the rest of the week, staffed by one of the Dondi graduates. Protests by Portuguese Catholic priests against Loth's Protestant enterprise led to his transfer to another station. Local people continued nevertheless to support the first church, and at his next post Loth founded yet another church and another school.[17]

Once more he was moved on. Once more he established a church and a school. But Loth was also moved on regularly as he obtained promotions in recognition of the quality of his work, and 20 years later, in 1942, he was appointed as the first black station-master. Eventually there were 'Savimbi' schools and churches all along the Benguela Railway in central Angola, earning for Loth's family a prominent and respected position among their fellow Ovimbundu. It gave young Jonas an early lesson in the need for any successful 'native' movement to be rooted firmly among the ordinary people.

Loth Savimbi's thirst for self-improvement was seldom channelled into demands for political liberation. In his younger days and up until 1961, when the first modern uprising against the Portuguese took place, political freedom seemed an impossible dream under the harsh system which the colonial power saw continuing for ever. Loth's power and passion were poured into religion, which promised to Africans more prospects in the hereafter than were offered in Angola by political action in the foreseeable future.

Loth was highly self-disciplined, a trait that Jonas noted and emulated – 'If I decided to complete the study of a book within a week, I would do it: even if I had to spend two days without sleeping, I would do it.'[18] Loth also raised his son's sights. When Jonas said he wanted to be a steam locomotive driver, Loth said he must aim to be a doctor, impossible though that seemed for an African; he had, said Loth, to tell himself every day that he was going to achieve the impossible. Loth also told Jonas that he had to think of the Portuguese as oppressors and that he must never accept humiliation at their hands.

By the time Jonas was six, in 1940, and he went to a missionary primary school at Lutamo, near Dondi, the idea had already formed that one day he would fight the Portuguese.[19] In 1942 he moved to the Protestant school at Chilesso, where Loth had decided his wife should live and bring up their children while he was posted from station to station. Loth by this time was reconciled with Sakaita; and in his final years the old pagan chief established a close relationship with Jonas. Speaking in 1980, Jonas said: 'My grandfather told me that although he had a big soul, it was in great pain because of the humiliation imposed upon him by the Portuguese. He kept ten old flintlock muzzle-load rifles in his house: they were his pride. He had a barrel of gunpowder left over from the days when he was part of the resistance against the Portuguese in the Bailundo Uprising. He used to say: 'The Portuguese overran us because we ran short of powder – if we had powder today, the Portuguese would not be here.' Sometimes he would get so angry and frustrated about what the Portuguese had done to him that he would load his flintlocks and go outside and fire them wildly in the air. I use my grandfather's story about running short of powder to this day. I tell people we lost the civil war in 1975 and 1976 because we ran short of powder. The lesson for today is that if we get materials and support – and, inevitably, many of our materials will come from outside – we should use them intelligently so that UNITA will never run short of powder again.'[20]

An invaluable gift Jonas gained from old Sakaita was an ability to speak the traditional form of Umbundu, the language of the Ovimbundu. Classic Umbundu is a rich brew of allegorical proverbs and folk tales: the language is not direct but allusive, demanding patience and courtesy from participants in a conversation. *'Etu tua tunga vovipembe viovopakulu'* (We have roots in the fields of our ancestors) and *'O pipia onganji; o malapo osoma'* (The advocate speaks; the king concludes or decides) are just two of the shortest and more straightforward Ovimbundu proverbs.[21] As a leader of rebellions against the Portuguese and then against Angola's Marxist government and its Cuban allies, Savimbi used his fluent traditional Umbundu to court and win chiefs and elders.

The year Sakaita died, 1949, was also the year Loth retired from the Benguela Railway Company and returned home to Chilesso to become director of the Protestant mission. Jonas was a pupil at Chilesso until 1950, and he began to clash with Loth. Though his father had encouraged Jonas to think of the Portuguese as oppressors, he urged his son to conform at school so that he could obtain a good education, become a doctor and then help his people. Jonas recalls: 'I told him there was a terrible conflict in his advice. He said I should not accept humiliation, and I said that sometimes the white missionaries had humiliated me to an extent I could not accept. Then he would say that I had to be careful, but I went on questioning many things.'[22]

On one occasion the Chilesso missionaries arranged a football match between their black pupils and a team of white children from nearby Andulo. The Andulo team included the son of the local Portuguese chief administrator. 'They brought their own referee, a Portuguese, and he was cheating. When we scored he disallowed it. My father had bought me a football and it was the only one at the mission – so we were using it for the match. When the referee cheated I told him he would need to get his own ball. I began walking away with the ball, and my own team shouted that I could not do it because the administrator's son was playing. I shouted back that the administrator should buy a ball for his son rather than think of arresting me. I carried on walking and the game had to be abandoned.'[23]

* * *

After his father retired, Jonas began to hear stories of Daniel Ekundi, a friend of Loth's who in the 1920s had been among the first blacks permitted to leave central Angola and attend secondary school in Luanda. There were no secondary schools in central Angola at the time. On returning, Ekundi at first taught at one of the missions before leaving in 1943 to set up his own private primary school at Chiumbo, near Dondi, which he named *Salvaterra* (Save the Land). Ekundi gave schooling to older pupils who had previously had no educational opportunities. His reputation grew, especially when he gave places to children of underprivileged families who could not afford the fees.[24]

Ekundi was one of the earliest Angolan black nationalists of the modern era. He was very politically aware. Though it was forbidden by law that history and the Portuguese constitution be taught to blacks, Ekundi subtly wove them in with the teaching of other subjects. For years the Portuguese either ignored or did not understand the implications behind the name of Ekundi's school and the hidden curriculum he was teaching. 'He just taught the subjects factually, without comment, and left the pupils to think about it,' said Savimbi. 'He was sowing seeds, and he was doing it with sacrifice because the fees he was asking were barely enough to pay his licence fee to the Portuguese and buy the food for the boarders.'

By the fifties Ekundi's nationalism was more overt. He began writing letters to the United Nations about political conditions in Angola. He protested to the Luanda authorities that a local Portuguese administrator, Joao Vaz Monteiro, had confiscated land owned by black peasants for himself. Then when he wrote in 1953 to the Portuguese government in Lisbon demanding self-determination for Angola he was arrested and tried for subversion. *Salvaterra* school was closed.[25]

By the time of Ekundi's arrest, Savimbi, nearly 19, was a pupil at Dondi. A collection was held there for a lawyer to defend Ekundi. 'I understood then that this man was more than a teacher. I started to admire him. We wanted to rally behind him but we did not know how. We saw him as a hero: he was defending something we did not fully understand but at the same time we knew we wanted it to materialise.'

Ekundi was imprisoned for more than 10 years, first in the *Baia dos Tigres* (Bay of Tigers) prison camp, on the desert coast of southeastern Angola, and then in Luanda. In prison he continued giving lessons, to Portuguese as well as Africans. As the first African in Central Angola to be arrested for political crimes, he achieved celebrity and local fame. When he was released from prison in 1964 he reopened the *Salvaterra* school and resumed his favourite relaxation as a church organist.

Savimbi recalls meeting Ekundi again for the first time in 20 years when he returned to Dondi in January 1975 at the end of the nationalist war against the Portuguese: 'I never thought that I would find him alive. Before, when I was young, I did not really talk to him properly even though he was a friend of my father. When I went to study in Europe he just gave me the kind of advice that older people give: "Go ahead, concentrate on your studies, but look forward also to other objectives." So when I saw him again I had a long, long talk so that he could tell me how he started, why he had taken such a bold stand as a pioneer in the struggle against the Portuguese. Then in July 1977 Ekundi was killed by the MPLA because he refused to renounce his support for UNITA.'[26]

In 1976, after Angola had achieved independence and Savimbi and his UNITA guerrillas had retreated into the Angolan bush, Ekundi stayed behind at Chiumbo, which was now under MPLA control. Since he was old and retired, he did not think he would be victimised for his UNITA sympathies. But MPLA troops went to Chiumbo, according to reports UNITA received from villagers, and demanded that Ekundi sign up as a member of the MPLA. Ekundi refused. He was interrogated and accused of organising food in the area for UNITA's guerrillas.

'He was very bold in his replies,' said Savimbi. 'He told them: "When you three liberation movements came [out of the bush before independence in 1975], we were told that each one of us was free to join any movement. So it was a free choice. I joined UNITA because I knew the backgrounds of those people, and I agreed with everything they were saying. I took my choice, I am not MPLA, I am UNITA. But I am too old to play any role, so I will just stay UNITA and die peaceably.' The MPLA said that he was not really being intelligent and that he had to sign. He said they were his children and they had no right to talk to him in such a brutal way.'

Ekundi, then aged 73, was taken away with his wife to jail in Huambo (formerly Nova Lisboa) and, without having been charged or tried, both were shot dead by the MPLA on 27 August 1977.

*   *   *

In 1950 Jonas transferred school from Chilesso to Dondi. At one of Dondi's missionary establishments, the Currie Institute, Savimbi began the four-year course of secondary education, which equipped its graduates as primary school teachers but did not give them qualifications for university entrance. The missionaries were deeply puritanical: they banned smoking and drinking, and, less reasonably, forbade European-style ballroom dancing, of which Savimbi and his friends were keen exponents. The ban was especially irksome because the Portuguese had forbidden traditional tribal dancing to any African with aspirations to become assimilated into Portuguese society. 'They banned everything, and that led me into revolt. Even though I remained a believer in the Christian God, increasingly there were many things that I could not accept.'[27]

While Savimbi studied hard and successfully at the Currie Institute, he frequently went out dancing. 'I used to tell the other pupils openly that they should dance because there was nothing wrong with it and there was no good reason why it sould be forbidden.' But in 1954 Savimbi was punished by the missionaries for his defiance. They suspended his scholarship and ordered him to return home for a year to Chilesso to work as a teacher before resuming his studies.

Loth was furious with his son. He agreed there was nothing wrong with dancing, but urged Jonas to dance only at home with his sisters;[28] outside he should conform with the missionaries' wishes because their scholarships offered the only passport to success for a black who desired to become a doctor. 'I said that I could not accept that I should only dance with my sisters and not with other girls outside. The principle should be either no dancing at all or freedom to dance anywhere.'

The friction increased greatly between Loth and his son, and by 1955 Jonas had decided he would not return to Dondi. Instead he resolved to go to Silva Porto and ask to be admitted there to the *Liceu*, an exclusive fee-paying government school which had never admitted blacks. If he gained admission he could escape the burden of the *Indigenato* more surely than if he returned to Dondi.

*   *   *

It was a worried but determined Jonas Savimbi who trekked into Silva Porto in the mid-1950s. It was then the home of a

Portuguese military garrison and about 12,000 civilians. A market town, it lay at the eastern extremity of Angola's economic heartland, a belt of rich agricultural land stretching 400 kilometres to the sea.

Savimbi knocked on the front door of Senhor Corte Real, headmaster of the Silva Porto *Liceu*, and pleaded for a chance to study. Real told Savimbi to go away: the African had no money to pay the high fees; he had presented himself in the middle of the school year; and, at 20, he was older than any of the school's white pupils. But Savimbi's intelligence and ambition must have been apparent, for the headmaster's wife pleaded with her husband to give him a chance. Corte Real relented. Savimbi passed a written test and the headmaster agreed to waive his fees for a trial period until after the year-end examinations. To earn his keep, Savimbi worked in Corte Real's kitchen and washed his dog. He shared sleeping quarters with the Reals' cook.

'The wife was very kind to me. Sometimes she would excuse me from working in the kitchen in the evenings so that I could study. One month before the exams she persuaded Corte Real to excuse me from afternoon work in the kitchen. They put a lamp in my room so that I could study more easily. She coached me in mathematics and French – she was also a teacher at the school. For the final month she helped me so much that she was like my mother. She gave me money to buy notebooks and when it was time for the exams she bought me a new suit so that I would be clothed like the white pupils. She also promised to try to get me a scholarship to continue my studies if I passed my examinations.'

Savimbi passed, but disaster struck. The school had run out of funds. It closed in 1956 and the Portuguese pupils transferred to another school in Nova Lisboa. Savimbi had neither the funds nor sufficient patronage to make the transfer. 'Senhora Corte Real called me. She was weeping and said she had really wanted to help. That lady had no children of her own. She said she and her husband were returning to Portugal and they knew of no way they could help me.'

The Reals' cook (later to become a member of UNITA)

obtained a new job in a Silva Porto hotel. He told Savimbi he could share his shelter. While Savimbi waited to see what might turn up, the school secretary, who was finalising the school's accounts, told him of a rumour that the Silva Porto *Liceu* might be taken over by Roman Catholic missionaries.

By the end of January 1956 the Catholics had arrived and begun to admit pupils. Savimbi went to Father Armando Cordeiro, a Brazilian priest who was the new headmaster, and told him that although he had no money he wanted to continue his studies: 'Cordeiro told me his job was to teach; he had not come to Angola to dispense charity. If I wanted to earn money I could help him build a volleyball court. I said OK. It took us two months of digging and fetching stones, and I used to mutter to myself that this man was just another colonialist: here I have asked him to help by giving me money to study, and he is making me work like this. But I looked, and he was working as hard himself.

'At the end of the two months Armando Cordeiro said he would pay me and I could go. I broke down and cried. I told him that I thought he was testing me when he set me to work on the volleyball court to see if I was serious or not, so that he could decide whether or not to give me a scholarship. I told him I was shocked that he thought I had worked with him just to get money. He comforted me and told me to return the next day.'

When Savimbi went back Father Cordeiro told him he could have a scholarship, but there was a condition. It was obvious that Savimbi was a good labourer; it was less obvious that he would be a good student. The scholarship would be only for six months: if Savimbi studied well it would be extended for another six months. If at the end of a year Savimbi was still proving a good student it would be extended for another year.

Savimbi proved a brilliant pupil, completing the three-year course at Silva Porto in two years. There were new experiences. He moved into the school boarding-house where the rest of the pupils were whites: for the first time in his life he wore pyjamas. (In the villages people wrap themselves in skins at night.) A deep friendship was formed with Armando Cordeiro: 'That man saved my life. Although my relations with my father were badly strained, I still wanted to make him happy by becoming a doctor. If Armando Cordeiro had not given me a scholarship, I do not think I would have been able to continue my studies. He changed my life; although the things my father and grandfather taught me remained the basis of my life, he did things for me that they could not do. Also he reminded me all the time that I should prepare myself to serve my people. He used to point to the trucks full of forced labourers going north to the coffee plantations and say that they were like slaves. Although I was being treated like a Portuguese I should never forget that I belonged to them (the blacks). He said that if I became a doctor and never did anything for my people my life would have been a waste of time.'

Armando Cordeiro opened up new dimensions in the thinking of Savimbi, black and Protestant. 'Armando was white and Catholic. How was it then, I asked myself, that he had become as my father? Let me examine what my father and grandfather told me: all the whites are enemies – you cannot trust them. My father used to say all the time that when you are dealing with a white man you must take two steps backwards for each one you take forward. I decided then that not *all* white men are enemies: from that time I said no, some are good.'

Savimbi was persuaded by Cordeiro's arguments that he should seek to serve his people. He would do it as a doctor. Under Cordeiro he also developed a philosophy which would serve him well in the future: 'Sometimes you get very depressed if you put all that you have into an undertaking and it fails. But after failure you simply have to start again.'[29]

When Savimbi completed his examinations at Silva Porto, Father Cordeiro said his missionary society would help him to go through medical school in Lisbon. First Savimbi had to spend a few months at a senior secondary school in Sa da Bandeira, in south-west Angola: in 1958 he graduated at the top of the class and was awarded the treasured Portuguese high school graduate certificate which could open up new worlds.

In September 1958 Savimbi's mother and Dr Henry and Ruth MacDowell accompanied him on the journey along the

Benguela Railway to the port of Lobito, from where he was to sail to Portugal to begin his medical training. He had said goodbye to his father in Chilesso; they could not know it, but they would never see each other again.

At the harbourside he embraced his mother and the MacDowells. On board ship he fell into conversation about politics with a black American sailor before the vessel had even sailed: 'He told me: you people have to fight. Kwame Nkrumah [leader of newly independent Ghana, the former British colony of Gold Coast] is interested in helping any black people to get their independence. He said don't go to Lisbon, come to Ghana. He said that in Ghana they were helping a group of Angolans[30] to organise an uprising in Luanda to get rid of the Portugueses. I was near going, because I would have joined a freedom movement immediately. But then I thought how it would grieve my mother and father and that the missionaries would see it as conclusive proof that I was not a serious person, just a troublemaker. But the sailor gave me books on Marxism and by Marcus Garvey [the early American black consciousness leader], and after I had read them I was really burning to join a freedom movement. On the ship I already knew that my studies would be a secondary matter for me.'

Angola faded on the horizon. It would be almost a decade before Savimbi returned, not openly but as the leader of a dozen guerrillas trained in China. They would be armed only with knives and one Soviet-made Tokarev pistol given to Savimbi in Dar-es-Salaam by Sam Nujoma, the leader of SWAPO, the black liberation movement in South African-ruled South West Africa (Namibia), which neighbours southern Angola.

2

Portugal and Switzerland
1958–61

In October 1958 Savimbi gained his first sight of Europe as his ship entered the wide estuary of the Tagus River to dock at Lisbon, capital of an empire which looked untroubled and which the Portuguese believed would never end.

1958 was an important transitional year for Europe. It marked the launching of the European Community, a commitment among nations who had fought each other in the Second World War to reinforce their post-war democracy and co-operation. Synonymous with their moves towards European union was an increase in the momentum to wind up their empires in Africa, as expressed at the time by a leading expert on colonial administration: 'The end of colonial power is in sight. The three major powers in Africa have declared their objective. All French colonies except Algeria are free to choose independence or membership of the French Community. The Belgian government has declared the aim of freedom for the Congo, though in that vast region the fulfilment of the promise may be slow. Britain has already recognised the independence of the huge territory of the Sudan and the small one of Ghana. Nigeria will take her freedom in 1960 and become Africa's most populous state. Tanganyika has started on the road to freedom. In Kenya, as a white-settled country, the way forward is complicated but the corner has surely been turned.'[1]

By contrast, Portugal had not participated in the World War. It remained a dictatorship; recognised no duty 'to train its African subjects for a self-government it denies to its own people';[2] and it showed no sign of surrendering a colonial empire on which a precarious prosperity had been built. By staying out of the 1939–45 conflict Portugal benefited from the sale of colonial raw materials marketed at high wartime prices. Angola's resources, such as coffee, sisal, cotton, maize and diamonds, were brought into the world economy and they provided Portugal with the foreign exchange to maintain a financial balance at home.

Savimbi remembers a holiday visit in early 1945 to Munhango, where his father was the station-master. Loth, who by then had white Portuguese under him and was entitled to a chauffeur-driven car to take him home for his annual leave, was lamenting the fact that Portugal was not in the war. 'Why?' asked Jonas. 'Because afterwards they would be so tired that they would not have the will to dominate us any more,' replied Loth.[3]

In Lisbon, as he stepped off the ship, Savimbi saw the trappings of the capital of a great empire: palaces, wide boulevards, triumphal arches and statues, and warehouses of colonial trading companies lining the quayside. But the wealth was built on the sweat of African forced labour in Angola and other territories such as Mozambique, Guinea-Bissau and East Timor. And the riches were concentrated in the hands of a narrow élite; the people of Portugal were the poorest in Europe. In 1961 the $US 270 average annual income of Portugal's nine million people was one-quarter the average for Western Europe as a whole.[4] With Portugal's dictator, Dr Antonio de Oliveira Salazar, aware of his country's pre-industrial economic dependence on territories like Angola there was scant chance of Lisbon joining the decolonising mainstream. Instead, Salazar continued to assert that Angola was an inalienable part of the Portuguese 'homeland'. Salazar found support from the dictator of neighbouring Spain, General Francisco Franco, who intended holding on to his country's small African colonies of Rio Muni, Fernando Po and Spanish Sahara. While Salazar and Franco continued to rule, there was no prospect that Lisbon would relinquish its overseas territories.

Savimbi was undeterred. He immediately began looking for a way to fight Portuguese rule in Angola. And very soon he began to hear that a man called Agostinho Neto might help him to do it.

Neto was by far the most prestigious black Angolan nationalist. Born in 1922 at Katete, near Luanda, the son of a Methodist pastor, he was one of the few blacks to have graduated from Luanda's top secondary school, the *Liceu Salvadore Correia*. He left Angola in 1947 on an American Methodist missionary scholarship to study medicine at the universities of Lisbon and Coimbra. From 1952 he was in and out of Portuguese prisons because of his activist role in opposition politics and because of his radical writing, especially his verse. Just before arriving in Portugal he wrote one of his most famous poems, *Farewell at the Hour of Parting:*

My Mother
  (all black mothers
    whose sons are gone)
you taught me to wait and hope
as you hoped in difficult hours

But life
killed in me that mystic
  hope
I do not wait now
I am he who is awaited[5]

When Savimbi arrived in Portugal Neto was nearing the end of yet another jail sentence: after 11 years of interrupted studies he had still not completed his medical degree. Savimbi heard from other students from Portugal's colonies that Neto's aim was the independence of Angola; but his strategy was to participate in Portugal in the movement against Salazar, believing that a democratic government in Lisbon would concede independence. Neto was therefore a secret member of the anti-Salazar Communist Party-oriented youth organisation, the *Movimento de Unidade Democratica-Juvenil* (MUDJ). Savimbi later asked him why he was not fighting directly for independence and Neto replied that it could not happen without change in Portugal.[6] His prophecy proved accurate nearly two decades later when the overthrow of the Portuguese dictatorship by the Army led directly to Angola's independence.

In Lisbon Savimbi began receiving leaflets from the Communist Party. They impressed him because the Communists seemed to be the only people attempting to fight the dictatorship. When he asked his friends from Portugal's colonies how he could contact the Party, they directed him to the Club Maritime, at the docks, which was ostensibly an association for sailors from Angola, São Tomé and Cape Verde. In fact it was a Communist Party cell and its President – unknown to the Portuguese and, until much later, Jonas Savimbi – was Agostinho Neto.

Savimbi made contact and began to distribute Communist pamphlets within the university. His loyalty was reinforced when the Communist Party immediately denounced the Portuguese army after it began a crackdown in August 1958 on striking dockworkers in the West African colony of Guinea-Bissau and shot dead 50 dockers.[7]

The young Ovimbundi told only one fellow student about his clandestine political activities – Jose Liahuka, who had been a pupil at the Currie Institute, Dondi, and whose father was a close friend of Loth. Liahuka, who was nearing the end of his medical studies met Savimbi on his arrival from Angola with good news. American missionaries from the United Church of Christ, who had watched Savimbi as he progressed outstandingly under Armando Cordeiro, were now offering a better scholarship than that secured by Cordeiro. Savimbi accepted.

Liahuka, five years old than Savimbi, gave the new arrival two warnings. First, medicine was too demanding to permit distractions such as politics. Second, the dangers of arrest were great because the student community was riddled with informers. Liahuka advised Savimbi to give up politics because his father and Armando Cordeiro would be greatly disappointed if he did not complete his medical studies.

Nevertheless Savimbi pursued both his studies and politics. All went well until April 1959 when he was summoned to the offices of the PIDE (*Policia Internacionale de Defesa de Estado*), the ruthless political police who were the guardians of the dictatorship. They thrust in front of Savimbi a letter addressed to him from Angola and asked him to read it. It was from Savimbi's friend and Dondi schoolmate, Arao Kunga, a 22-year-old African in his final year at Nova Lisboa *Liceu* who planned to travel to study law in Portugal. The choice of law was unusual enough to attract the attention of the PIDE. Keenly interested in what was happening in

Portugal, Kunga had exchanged letters regularly with Savimbi.

Savimbi read out loud one of the letters intercepted by the PIDE, and managed to avoid choking on one sentence which went: 'Look, you must open your eyes and see what these people are. We are going to fix them.'[8]

So which people are you going to fix? – the PIDE interrogator asked. 'I said that we had studied together under American Protestant missionaries in Angola and that the Portuguese authorities did not approve of many of the missionaries' activities.[9] Maybe Kunga was referring to the missionaries and was suggesting that I watched carefully to see if they behaved the same way in Portugal as they did in Angola.'

The PIDE interrogator suggested that Kunga was talking about the Portuguese. 'No,' said Savimbi, 'he can't be because we are all Portuguese, unless you are thinking that because we are black we are not Portuguese?'

They let Savimbi go. He immediately wrote to Kunga, urging him to drop controversial subjects. He sent the letter with a returning student. Kunga went underground after helping another student, Julio Cacunda, to plan an insurrection in central Angola based on a political party they had formed with its own flag. Kunga was eventually persuaded to come out of hiding by an American missionary who assured him he would not be accused by the PIDE. But Kunga was arrested and died, aged 24, in Mombaka prison, Lobito, on 14 April 1961 after a series of beatings. Cacunda was also arrested and was never seen again. Their deaths coincided with reports by missionaries of mass arrests by the Portuguese in areas north of Nova Lisboa and Silva Porto. 'According to Africans present at the time, the police shipped a boatload of persons presumed to be infected with nationalist sentiments to sea, and that was the last that was heard of them. European vigilantes, *dragões de Angola*, backed by the army, hunted down educated Africans, raided villages, and killed untold hundreds suspected of nationalist sympathies.'[10]

Another of Savimbi's correspondents who got him in trouble with the PIDE was Dr John Mallory, a former missionary in Angola who had returned home to California shortly before Savimbi sailed for Portugal. Mallory stopped off in Ghana. He wrote highly of Nkrumah, though naïvely because the 'Redeemer' was already building gigantic statues of himself which would be smashed when he was overthrown in 1966 after impoverishing the most prosperous state in black Africa. Mallory said Nkrumah had been educated in the US but had not forgotten the needs of his own people: Savimbi's studies abroad were only a preparation to help relieve the suffering of his fellow black Angolans.

This time the PIDE rejected Savimbi's excuses. Nkrumah may have been handed power peacefully by the British Empire, but in Portugal he was regarded as a Communist. Savimbi was arrested but he denied any contacts with opposition groups. In fact, although he was distributing pamphlets, he could have told the PIDE very little of any use to them: he knew about the Club Maritime, but did not know of its connection with Neto, whom at this time he had yet to meet. After a week the PIDE released Savimbi on condition that he infiltrate opposition movements and inform on them. They wanted information about Neto and on American Protestant missionaries working in Portugal. But Savimbi's first job would be to join and inform on 'subversive' Jehovah's Witnesses.

Savimbi says he refused. When the PIDE accused him of being a Communist he denied it, especially as he was beginning to question Marxist philosophy despite his involvement with Communist Party pamphleteering. The PIDE placed wads of money on the table in front of Savimbi and said he could complete his studies without problems if he cooperated, and have his own car and apartment. 'I said no . . . but they told me to go away and think about it.'[11]

When Savimbi was released in May 1959 Liahuka told him he was finished in Portugal: he was in deep trouble because the PIDE would never leave him alone. Savimbi had never mentioned that he knew of Neto, and Liahuka now spoke of Neto as though it was a name unheard of by his friend. Neto, said Liahuka, was a medical student who should have become a doctor long ago, but he got involved in politics and had spent a long time in jail. Neto was, however, now completing his qualifications because he had only become politically active in his fourth year of studies. Savimbi could never qualify: he was in trouble before his first year had been completed. Preparations would have to be made to smuggle him out of the country, said Liahuka.

*   *   *

Meanwhile, in June 1959, Kwame Nkrumah planned a transit stop at Lisbon Airport on his way to the United Nations in New York. The impending presence of the man who symbolised pan-African freedom was not announced, but word nevertheless spread among Lisbon's African student community.

On the day, Savimbi made his way alone to the airport where hundreds of Africans had gathered to greet Nkrumah. He presumed there would be arrests since the PIDE would want to know how news had got out about Nkrumah's secret stopover. Immediately after getting a glimpse of Nkrumah, who waved his white handkerchief to the Africans before being ushered to the VIP lounge, Savimbi left in a taxi for his quarters in the city. Nearly all the other Africans stayed on to try and meet Nkrumah: when the Ghanaian leader left, more than 100 of the students were immediately arrested.[12]

Though they missed him at the airport, the PIDE turned up shortly afterwards at Savimbi's rooms and took him to their headquarters. He was beaten and accused of having been at the airport to greet Nkrumah. Savimbi denied it and after three days he was again released.

For Liahuka the incident emphasised the need to get Savimbi out of Portugal. One of Savimbi's friends, a Portuguese academic who edited a radical magazine called *Seara Nova* (*New Field*) and who had been arrested by the PIDE several times and lived for periods in exile, said he could obtain for the young Angolan a PIDE declaration saying he was free to leave Portugal. He would get the document and an illegal passport through his contacts in Oporto, in northern Portugal, where the PIDE was unlikely to know of the suspicion surrounding Savimbi in Lisbon.

In July, as he waited, Savimbi met Neto for the first time. He was introduced through a contact and shared a meal with the mysterious Angolan nationalist whose courage and poetry he had come to admire. Neto referred to his many spells in jail as times spent 'on holiday'. By now he had completed his medical studies and was determined to finish a year's apprenticeship as a junior hospital doctor before returning to Angola. Savimbi recalls Neto saying: 'The way you have been working is correct. Remember, after this we will never meet. If one of us is forced to go 'on holiday' he never admits he knew anyone else.'[13]

Neto was sympathetic when Savimbi said his studies were going badly because of the PIDE. But Neto made a mistake which would contribute to an eventual estrangement from the young Ovimbundu and grow into an epic enmity. The assumption of many Kimbundu people, like Neto, from Luanda and its hinterland, was that the Africans of central and southern Angola were comparatively backward: they also regarded them as collaborators with the Portuguese because the Ovimbundu formed the majority of contract labourers on the coffee plantations of the north. When Savimbi said he came from near Nova Lisboa, Neto said it was impossible that a militant as bright and brave as he could have emerged from the south: surely his family originally came from the north?

Savimbi was hurt by these remarks of Neto, who then commented on the good marks that students from central and southern Angola were getting in their studies in Portugal. 'He said: "But they do not get involved in the liberation movement. Maybe it's the effect on them of the missionaries." Then he started laughing, the special way he used to laugh. And he said: "I am also with the missionaries. My father also is a pastor, but those missionaries are liars – my father told me that – they don't want us to see clearly. And your friends from the south will never participate in the struggle if they believe everything the missionaries tell them. That is why I do not believe that someone like you who is participating in the struggle can be from the south." But I assured him I really was from the south and he did not talk about it any more.'[14]

Despite these wounding remarks, Savimbi was greatly
impressed by Neto's quiet strength and determination. He
accepted him as a leader.

Just before the hour-long meeting ended, Neto told
Savimbi it would be good if he could combine his studies
with political struggle. But if he was forced to choose, he
should leave the studies and concentrate on the struggle.
With hindsight, Neto must later have regretted that advice.

*   *   *

The PIDE continued to harass Savimbi. They asked him to
deliver a speech to the Geographical Society of Lisbon on
15 August, a public holiday marking the restoration of
Portuguese rule in Luanda by force in 1648 after a temporary
Dutch takeover. It was considered an honour among Portuguese academics to be invited to address the Society. The
prepared speech Savimbi was asked to make praised colonial rule at a time when it was under heavy attack at the
United Nations.[15]

There was a passage which said the Portuguese had cut
off the tails of the Ovimbundu and raised them from backwardness. 'When I asked what they meant by this they said
they were referring metaphorically to the "tail of ignorance". They wanted me to say that the Ovimbundu were the
most backward in Angola but that my presence in Portugal
to study was evidence that that ignorance had been cut
away.'

Despite threats of arrest Savimbi refused to deliver the
speech. Escape had become even more urgent. But there
was another meeting with Neto a few days before Savimbi
took flight.

Neto was studying in Oeiras, a small town outside Lisbon. Word reached black Angolan students that Neto was
planning to marry a white Portuguese woman. The students
felt it important that he marry an African: ordinary people
back home would not be able to understand or accept it. So
five students, including Savimbi, made their way – separately and carefully – to Neto's house despite injunctions
against contacting him and despite risks of being picked up
by the PIDE. When the delegation arrived, Eugenia, Neto's

fiancée, was there. The students asked her for tea so that they could talk to Neto alone. They had not been able to meet beforehand to discuss their strategy for the confrontation, so they were looking round at each other to see who would be the spokesman. Seeing their hesitation, Neto reminded them that it was dangerous for them to be there: they should say what they needed to say quickly and then go.

'By the time one of us, Pinto Sobrini, Neto's cousin, had begun to speak, Eugenia had come back in with the tea,' Savimbi recalled. 'Pinto dried up, but Neto realised her presence was an inhibition and he asked her to leave us. Then Pinto began, but it was a really bad speech: he said that Neto was our leader but that our fathers and old people in Angola might take it badly if he returned home with a white woman.

'Neto said nothing while Pinto spoke. When Pinto had finished he looked directly at us and said: "Look, first of all politics has nothing to do with whether or not you marry a Portuguese. And you have to learn that not all Portuguese are against us. Some are with us in our struggle for independence. Second, when I was in jail she was the only person who came to visit me and comfort me. She used to take away my soiled clothes and wash them. She is as militant for Angola as you are, so I reject your advice.' Then he stopped and said nothing more. We were embarrassed and could think of nothing more to say. We hadn't even drunk the tea. It was cold. We just said yes, thank you very much, and left very meekly.'[16]

* * *

Towards the end of September 1959 the editor of *Seara Nova* contacted Savimbi and told him that PIDE documents and a forged passport had been obtained. He should prepare to leave on 29 September: at a fixed time in the early morning he was to go to the Park Setubal and wait near the statue of King Don Jose. If there was anyone standing around, the escape was off, and Savimbi should return home. If the area was clear he should enter the first car that stopped on his left.

In Savimbi's apartment block he reckoned there were four people reporting his movements to the PIDE. To distract attention he threw a party on the eve of his departure to which the informers were invited. Before the party he told Liahuka, and no one else, of his imminent departure. His friend wished Savimbi God's blessing and urged him not to concentrate on political activity alone: 'Get a degree. It is part of your struggle and it is something of which you will feel proud.'

The party went well. Everybody drank a lot and at 3.30 a.m. on 29 September Savimbi slipped away with only the clothes he was wearing. At the Park Setubal the way was clear: a large Citroen drew up and Savimbi got in. The driver was a young European: with him were his wife and two children. No one spoke for two hours until the car approached Spain.

A few kilometres short of the border the driver stopped the car, announced himself as a Dutch doctor and asked Savimbi if his passport was a forgery. When he learned that it was, the doctor said Savimbi would have to hide in the boot for the frontier crossing in case Portuguese officials detected the fake. 'He told me the frontier authorities knew him as a doctor and had never searched his car. When he closed the boot it was terribly cramped and gasoline fumes were coming into my nostrils. We stopped for five or ten minutes at the frontier. They did not search the car, but I had to force myself not to cry out – for a moment I thought I was going to die so that it would be better to cry out and be able to breathe.' But then the car started to move and after driving about five kilometres into Spain the doctor stopped and let Savimbi out of the boot.

After crossing from Spain into the French border town of Hendaye, the doctor told Savimbi that both he and the editor of *Seara Nova* were clandestine members of the Portuguese Communist Party. The doctor said he understood that Savimbi also was a Party member and that was why he had agreed to help him to flee.[17] He suggested that the best place for Savimbi to continue his studies would be Lumumba University, the special university for Third World students in Moscow: he could get him a scholarship there if Savimbi travelled on with him to the Netherlands. Savimbi took the Dutchman's address, opted to stay on in Hendaye and never did write in search of the scholarship to study in the Soviet Union.

The first letter that Savimbi wrote from Hendaye was to the PIDE in Lisbon. It said: 'You people have been nothing but trouble to me and I have failed in my studies because of you. Now I am out, and when we meet again it will be with fire. We are not going to shake hands.'

* * *

From Hendaye Savimbi moved to Toulouse where he was given shelter by members of the French Communist Party who were heavily involved in Algeria's struggle against domination by the French settler minority: a million people died in the war before President Charles de Gaulle conceded independence in 1962.[18] As a matter of principle, Savimbi did not want to stay in France because of its military and security links with Portugal through the North Atlantic Treaty Organisation (NATO). Instead he had decided to head for Switzerland: its neutral international stance suggested that he would be free to engage in political activities without harassment by the authorities. The French Communists also tried to persuade him to go to Moscow, arguing that Switzerland was capitalist and reactionary. But when Savimbi insisted, they still gave him money and clothes for his journey into exile in the Swiss mountains.

In Zurich he went to a Protestant missionary society, the Institute of Emmaeus, and asked for help, giving as referees two Swiss medical doctors who had worked as missionaries in Angola. A scholarship was granted[19] and in October 1959 Savimbi again began studying medicine, this time at the University of Fribourg in the Alps.

One of his first priorities was to decide how best to pursue his political goals. There were two fledgling liberation movements operating in exile outside Angola – the MPLA, founded in December 1956, with its roots among Luanda's urban intellectuals and slum dwellers and, to a lesser extent, among the Kimbundu people of the capital's hinterland; and the Union of the Angolan Peoples (UPA), the forerunner of the FNLA, whose roots were among the Kikongo of the far north.

The only propaganda Savimbi could obtain was from the MPLA, so he began to correspond with the movement's leaders who were based in Conakry, capital of Guinea, a former French West African colony. In 1958 Guinea was the first Francophone territory to become independent – outside de Gaulle's proposed French Community[20] – under its Marxist-oriented leader Sekou Toure, a recipient of the Lenin Peace Prize. Toure was strongly sympathetic to the MPLA, whose Conakry-based leaders were Viriato da Cruz, Mario de Andrade and Lucio Lara. All three were *mesticos*. Da Cruz was the party's first Secretary-General; de Andrade, a social science graduate of the Sorbonne and a poet, contributed most towards the MPLA's intellectual image and became President of the movement for a time; Lara, the son of a wealthy Portuguese merchant, was a founding member of the MPLA who had close ties to Moscow and was still the party's chief ideologist until 1985. Da Cruz and de Andrade resigned from the party in later years after disagreements with other leaders.

The UPA was led by Holden Roberto, who lived in exile in Leopoldville, capital of the Belgian Congo. Roberto's hopes of securing Angola's independence soared after the decision in mid-1960 by the Brussels government to give freedom to its huge African territory, which neighboured Angola.[21] Roberto was urged by Dr John Tucker, a missionary who had known Savimbi in Angola, to recruit the young exile in Fribourg. In August 1960 Roberto turned up unannounced at the home of the Sprengers, former missionaries with whom Savimbi was lodging.

Savimbi was away in Lausanne, but Mrs Sprenger contacted him and he arranged to meet Roberto in the early evening at the Hotel du Pays, near Lausanne railway station. They talked until four in the morning.

'Very little that Roberto said impressed me. He took a persistent anti-Communist line, but he could not tell me what the policy was of his own organisation. He had no programme: he could not even give me a small booklet or leaflet describing it.[22] When I asked him about the way the

UPA was organised, I discovered that *he* was the organisation. There was no Central Committee. He also told me that the MPLA was a Communist organisation. I did not know at that stage whether or not it was true. I had already decided that I did not want to be a Communist: but I knew that the MPLA's programme was a *progressive* one, and I wanted to be progressive. I did not want to be on the right wing.'[23]

Roberto tried to persuade Savimbi to align himself against the MPLA because his father was a Christian pastor. Savimbi said the matter was not whether his father was a pastor, but which organisation was most capable of launching an effective struggle against the Portuguese.

However, Savimbi admits that he was interested by Roberto's allegation that the MPLA was controlled by *mesticos*. If Roberto was unconditionally for the blacks, that was a point in his favour; and if the MPLA was dominated by *mesticos* Savimbi doubted whether he could join the movement. 'It may sound like racialism, and it is certainly not the way we feel today because we have learned a lot. But it is a fact that it was very difficult at that time for blacks to understand why *mesticos* should be leading a liberation movement to fight the Portuguese. It was not clear to us that *mesticos* were suffering in Angola; they were privileged people.'

Otherwise, Savimbi found that Roberto made a very poor impression compared with Neto. In October 1960 Roberto travelled to New York to address the United Nations General Assembly: while in America he told former missionaries to Angola that Savimbi was involved with Communists. Savimbi received letters from them urging him to join the UPA. He ignored them.

Savimbi wanted to meet some of the MPLA leaders and he was disappointed when Viriato da Cruz passed through Geneva and wrote to Savimbi only to say he was too busy to see him. However, towards the end of 1960, the MPLA sent Savimbi a one-way air ticket to Conakry suggesting that he come for talks and see how the movement worked. He declined because he feared that difficulties might be put in the way of his return to his studies in Switzerland. He continued, though, to read MPLA publications: he found the philosophy attractive and saw nothing in it to support Roberto's allegation that the MPLA were Communists.

Savimbi's sympathies were with the MPLA more than the UPA. As a step towards making a commitment, he considered joining the MPLA's student wing, UGEAN (the General Student Union of Black Africans under Portuguese Colonial Domination).[24] He started to exchange letters with the UGEAN leader, Luis D'Almeida, who was studying at Frankfurt am-Main in West Germany. D'Almeida, as part of the attempt to bring Savimbi into the organisation, asked him to travel to Uganda in September 1960 to deliver a speech on behalf of UGEAN at a big international student gathering sponsored by the Western-oriented International Student Conference (COSEC). Savimbi agreed and caught a train to Frankfurt to meet D'Almeida before flying to Uganda.

He had never met the UGEAN leader before, and at Frankfurt station he was expecting to be met by a black African. But he saw no one. Then two men came up behind him, one *mestico* and the other white, and asked if he was Savimbi. The *mestico* was D'Almeida, whose Portuguese father owned a number of hotels in Luanda, and the other man was a white Mozambican who held one of UGEAN's top posts.

At D'Almeida's home Savimbi was given a typewritten speech to deliver at the conference at Makerere College in Kampala, Uganda's capital. He was told how to read it, and he noted a passage which said the MPLA was the *only* representative of the Angolan people and that the UPA was a reactionary, CIA-backed organisation. It reminded him somehow of the occasion when the PIDE had asked him to deliver their speech to the Geographical Society of Lisbon. Savimbi told D'Almeida that he thought UGEAN should take a more neutral stance, using what influence it had to bring the MPLA and UPA together and to propagandise among the world student community the suffering of *all* the Angolan people. While accepting D'Almeida's longer acquaintance with international politics and large-scale conferences, Savimbi nevertheless wanted to discuss the contents of the speech.

'I had my own particular experience of how the Portuguese oppressed the people in my part of Angola, and I had my own special experience in Portugal. I wanted to talk about these things, but D'Almeida said they would not be valuable: UGEAN had already explained the suffering of the Angolan people, and he said the politics of it all had moved beyond my understanding. I concluded that UGEAN was just using me as a black face to be paraded at Kampala. At this time the Union of Students in Ghana had just severed its relations with UGEAN because it was dominated by *mesticos* while the majority of people in Angola were black.'[25]

Before Savimbi caught his flight to Kampala he took a bag containing his speech and MPLA propaganda into the toilet at Frankfurt airport and left it there. He boarded his plane with not even one small fragment of the official speech in his luggage.

* * *

Savimbi was returning to Africa at a tumultuous time: in the two years he had been away the pace of change had accelerated dramatically. Seventeen African states were born in 1960 alone, though nothing changed in Portugal's territories where Lisbon's grip remained firm.

The year had begun with a prophetic and, later, famous speech by the British Prime Minister, Harold Macmillan. Addressing South Africa's whites-only Parliament in Cape Town, he said: 'The most striking of all the impressions I have formed since I left London is of this African national consciousness. In different places it takes different forms, but it is happening everywhere. The wind of change is blowing through this continent.'

In British East Africa, into whose heart Savimbi was heading, Tanganyika was moving smoothly towards independence; the British were working towards a self-governing and democratic Uganda, and trying to discourage the secessionist tendencies of the powerful Baganda tribe. Even in the difficult case of Kenya, where the Mau Mau revolt had led to 14,000 deaths before it was suppressed, Britain had convened a constitutional conference in London at which the powerful white settler minority had been told that black rule was inevitable.

The Kampala conference was to prove of enormous importance to Savimbi's future. He delivered his own speech, in French, which simply appealed for scholarships to be given in other countries so that Angolan students who had fled from Angola or Portugal could continue their studies. He established contacts with some of the leading African nationalists of the day: Ben Kiwanuka, who was to become the first Prime Minister of Uganda; Mwai Kibaki, then a lecturer at Makerere, 'the Harvard of Africa', but later to be Vice-President of Kenya; Ben Mkapa, a Makerere student who later became Foreign Minister of Tanzania (as Tanganyika was renamed) and a very close friend of Savimbi.

The most important contact, however, was with Tom Mboya, the strong-willed and clear-minded president of the Kenya Trades Union Congress who had already become a big name in African politics and would serve in the cabinet of the first government of independent Kenya. After delivering one of the conference's major speeches, Mboya asked Savimbi to visit him at his hotel, where he urged the Angolan to join the UPA and invited Savimbi to travel with him and meet the Kenyan nationalist leader, Jomo ('Burning Spear') Kenyatta.

Savimbi was thrilled by this opportunity. Kenyatta was a living legend in Africa. He had been struggling since the 1920s for improved rights for Kenya's blacks, appearing in leopard skins in London in 1931 to press their case, and spending several months in Moscow in 1933 studying the strategy and tactics of revolution.[26] In London he helped form the Pan-African Federation, which demanded equal rights for all Africans. Kenyatta returned to Kenya and was arrested in 1952, accused of being the Mau Mau leader, and sentenced to seven years hard labour. He was released in 1959 but was put under house arrest in the small outpost of Lodwar in the remote north-western Turkana district, where he lived with his third wife and was able to receive visitors. (Kenyatta was freed in 1962 and became the first Prime Minister of independent Kenya in 1963.)

Savimbi had been impressed by Kenyatta's book, *Facing Mount Kenya*, calling for African freedom;[27] and by Kenyatta's account of how, as a boy working in a mission in Kenya, one of his tasks was to put clean cloths on the pews when the Africans had left their service and before the whites arrived for theirs. He was impressed, too, by the similarity of one of Kenyatta's favourite aphorisms to that of old Sakaita Savimbi's[28] – 'When the missionaries arrived the Africans had the land and the missionaries had the Bible. They taught us to pray with our eyes closed. When we opened them, they had the land and we had the Bible.'

Fired by the contacts he had made in Kampala and excited by the prospect of a meeting with Kenyatta, Savimbi must surely have been inspired further to serve the liberation of Africa as he drove with Mboya the 650 kilometres eastwards from Uganda to Nairobi through some of the world's most beautiful scenery. As they travelled through the fresh air of the Kenyan Highlands, with trout streams fed by mountain snows, and dark pine forests alternating with neat European farms on which fat cattle grazed and tea, coffee, wheat and maize grew abundantly, Mboya used a simplistic argument to influence Savimbi in his choice between the MPLA and UPA: 'The MPLA are *mesticos* and Communists, so you cannot play any useful role there; the UPA is the organisation for black people, so that's the one you should join.'[29]

While waiting to meet Kenyatta, Savimbi followed Mboya to rallies and took to wearing the small pillbox Luo tribal hat which had become one of the symbols of the Kenyan nationalists. Savimbi met another of the black Kenyan leaders, Oginga Odinga, a brave and fiery anti-white individual who maintained close contact with Communist governments[30] and became Kenyatta's main opponent after independence. Odinga's advice was: 'Join the MPLA. They are good and progressive. You can work with them and fight for your country. Don't get involved with Mboya. He is a reactionary and a CIA agent.'[31]

The personalities of Mboya and Odinga were crucial elements in the choice Savimbi was soon to make. He disliked Odinga's severity, burning indignation and ferocious intensity: less rationally, he took objection to Odinga's

eccentric habit of dressing in knee-length shorts and carrying a big stick. By contrast, he liked Mboya's urbanity and
relaxed charm. 'My own inclination was towards him. He
was young and had power within him. I felt he was a good
man.'

When eventually Savimbi and Mboya travelled to Lodwar, on a permit issued by the British, Kenyatta asked
Savimbi to leave while Mboya briefed him on Angola.
Kenyatta then summoned Savimbi and told him to join the
UPA. 'I protested that Roberto had no programme and
seemed to be a very ignorant man. "OK," Kenyatta said,
"that's one very good reason to join because you have ideas
and can produce a programme." That's when I decided to
join the UPA. That's how it was.'[32]

Savimbi returned to Nairobi with Mboya, who was due
to leave to lobby the October 1960 session of the United
Nations General Assembly. Holden Roberto was also due in
New York, so Mboya took with him a letter from Jonas
Savimbi applying for membership of the UPA.

In December 1960 Roberto sent Savimbi an air ticket so
that he could travel to the headquarters of the UPA in
Leopoldville (later renamed Kinshasa). Savimbi decided not
to travel immediately to the capital of the former Belgian
Congo, which had descended into chaos after becoming
independent on 30 June 1960. In January 1961 the radical
Congolese leader, Patrice Lumumba, was beaten to death by
Congolese politicians with alleged close connections to the
CIA's chief of Technical Services Division, Sid Gottlieb.[33]
The civil conflict on the newly independent country grew
bloodier, and the internal betrayals more tragic. But Savimbi
could not postpone his meeting with Roberto indefinitely,
and on 1 February 1961 he flew to Leopoldville and was
inducted into the UPA.

Savimbi did not know it, but African uprisings were about
to begin in Angola – on a scale far larger than the Mau Mau
revolt in Kenya – which would jolt the Portuguese out of
their complacency and demonstrate to Africans their potential power. 1961 was to prove a watershed in Angolan
history.

3

The Angolan Uprisings

1961

On 4 February 1961, three days after Savimbi's arrival in Leopoldville to join the UPA, there was an uprising in Luanda. Africans from the *musseques* (slums), armed only with clubs and knives, attacked the capital's jails in an attempt to release political prisoners. Perhaps 14 Portuguese were killed, but the response of the colonial authorities was awesome in its scale and disregard for constitutional niceties. The police helped white civilian vigilantes to organise nightly attacks on the *musseques*, where they dragged Africans from their flimsy, densely packed huts made of packing cases and corrugated iron, shot them and left the bodies in the streets. The full scale of the reprisal massacre will never be known, but it is certain that several hundred Africans were killed.

It is not clear who organised the uprising. The MPLA at that time had two organisations – one outside Angola in Conakry, 'a head without a body, and one inside, a body without a head'.[1] The MPLA leadership in Conakry considered the attack, not unreasonably, as suicidal, but as time went on the MPLA claimed full credit. The Angolan national anthem, introduced by the MPLA after independence in 1975, begins: 'O Fatherland, never will we forget the heroes of the fourth of February.' In fact, the uprising was more a nationalistic expression not only by MPLA supporters but also by small groups loosely affiliated to the UPA, various Christian movements and other organisations, as well as by individuals incensed by the continued imprisonment of relatives taken in a wave of mass PIDE arrests that had begun in 1959.[2]

Savimbi's first question to Roberto following the Luanda uprising concerned when the UPA intended launching its own co-ordinated resistance inside Angola. Roberto's response was to assure him that the UPA was preparing 'something bigger and better'[3], and to appoint Savimbi as secretary-general of the movement with responsibility for reorganising its administration.

On 15 March the UPA launched a multi-pronged attack in northern Angola in which European farms, trading settlements and government posts were overwhelmed. Some 250 to 400 Portuguese civilians were killed in the first few days and 750 within three months. Ordinary Africans, who had learned from centuries of received wisdom to say respectfully *'Sim, Senhor'* (Yes, Master), turned their work *catanas* (cutlasses) on their white employers, overseers and traders and their women and children. They also slaughtered *mesticos* and *assimilados*, living symbols of Portuguese domination of blacks, as well as many Ovimbundu contract labourers on the coffee plantations.

The UPA leadership seems to have hoped that the Portuguese, faced by the ferocity of the revolt, would cut and run, as the Belgians had in the Congo the previous year. But they reckoned without the tenacity of the Portuguese dictatorship which was immune to the pressures of press and democratic public opinion that had led France, Britain and Belgium to make concessions to their African colonies.

Instead, planes and ships ferried paratroopers and other special forces from Portugal to Angola and an army of about 17,000 soldiers, supported by fighter-bombers and settler militias bent on vengeance, was unleashed against the Africans of the north. Villages were machine-gunned and planes dropped fire bombs on them. One estimate puts the number of African casualties at 20,000 by October 1961: by the end of the year 150,000 of the half-million Africans living in the north had fled into the Congo as refugees.[4]

Savimbi was not given any detailed advance information about the UPA's military uprising, but he comforted himself with the fact that he now held a senior position in a liberation movement on which international attention was suddenly being focused and which seemed to have the best chance of combating the Portuguese in Angola. There had been no momentum or follow-up to the 4 February Luanda revolt which the MPLA had claimed for its own.

Holden Roberto left Leopoldville a few days before the UPA uprising to attend a UN Security Council debate on Portuguese colonialism; he announced in New York on 15 March that a revolt had begun. The UN soon afterwards formed an investigatory committee on Angola which was denied entry to the country, but it nevertheless went ahead and produced a report unfavourable to the Portuguese. Roberto also won valuable open support from Algeria's National Liberation Front (FLN), which was fighting a furious war for independence from France in which a million would die, and from Frantz Fanon, the fashionable philosopher of African anti-colonialism whose books, *Black Skin*, *White Masks* and *The Wretched of the Earth*, became Bibles of the freedom movements.[5]

Savimbi felt a general satisfaction with the UPA revolt, even though Roberto had not closely confided his plans and despite the murder of Ovimbundu people. 'Here at last we were involved in an armed struggle, which I saw as the only way forward. And it was being conducted from the bush inside Angola, where we needed to stay and organise in order to ensure the continued support of the people. I believed the excesses were bad, but I thought they could be brought under control once I had had time to create a better organisation and we had trained officers of a higher calibre.'[6]

Among the flood of refugees moving into the Congo from the Portuguese counter-offensive Savimbi met many men who would become long-term comrades in the fight against the Portuguese, and later against the Cubans and Soviets. They included Tony Fernandes, a *mestico* who fled from Cabinda, Angola's tiny oil-rich northern enclave, dressed as a priest; Miguel N'Zau Puna, from one of the royal families of Cabinda's Woyo tribe; and Joseph N'Dele and Ernesto Mulato, both Kikongos. All joined the UPA.

The UPA uprising continued throughout 1961, but at the end of March Savimbi had to return to Switzerland to prepare for examinations. By July he had decided to give up medical studies. It was a big decision because he and his family had always dreamed of him becoming a doctor. But the heavy load of practical work demanded by the Fribourg professors meant Savimbi had to choose between a commitment to medicine or his political struggle. Medicine was sacrificed, but Savimbi was still determined to get a degree: 'I would have considered it a failure not to complete a university course after coming through so many difficulties.' So in December 1961 he enrolled as an undergraduate in the Department of Law and International Politics at Lausanne University, Switzerland.

Savimbi's pattern of life for the next four years was to consist of alternate three-month periods spent in Switzerland, on studies, and in Africa and elsewhere on political work. Immediately after enrolling at Lausanne, for example, he travelled with Roberto to attend a United Nations General Assembly debate in New York. To succeed in these twin tasks on different continents required immense intellectual rigour, self-discipline and versatility – qualities Savimbi had learned from his father and which he would badly need in the difficult years to come.

His new academic supervisor, Professor Henri Rieben, a distinguished expert on the movement for European unity, was struck immediately by his new pupil's special qualities of charisma and intelligence, courage and honesty. In a conversation with the author in 1984, Professor Rieben recalled his thoughts when Savimbi told him, in mid-1962, that the reason for his many absences from lectures was because of his work with an African liberation movement, but that he was serious about his studies. The Professor, for whom amateurism is unacceptable but much too common within his fields of research, believed he was being told the truth: 'I just thought, well, we shall see how much he knows in his first examinations. I was amazed and excited by Savimbi's papers. He showed remarkable insight and a grasp of the geopolitical scene which was very rare indeed.'[7]

4

Savimbi and Che Guevara Plot Revolution

1962–64

As Savimbi set about reorganising the UPA he discovered that most of the executive posts were held not merely by Roberto's own Kikongo tribe but by Roberto's own family. To widen representation, Savimbi drew up a proper constitution which gave the party a Central Committee which had to be elected every four years.

He believed also that victory over the Portuguese could not be achieved only by the kind of mass attacks that had attracted world attention from 15 March 1961. They had to be complemented by intensive political recruitment and indoctrination; efficient health, welfare and educational provision for civilians; and a highly organised and sustained guerrilla warfare campaign, less dramatic than the original attacks but more enduring. To be successful, the leaders of the movement would have to begin moving into Angola to live with the peasantry.

Savimbi founded a new Angolan student movement, UNEA (the National Union of Angolan Students), which was funded by the UPA and operated in rivalry to the MPLA's UGEAN.[1] In its first year, 1962, fifteen scholarships were organised by UNEA for young party followers at universities in Western Europe and North Africa.[2] 'UNEA was the first means the UPA had of intellectual expression to the outside world, and UNEA was more progressive than the party,' according to Savimbi. 'We became known as the Young Turks and we gained many propaganda coups for the UPA. UNEA for a time became stronger than UGEAN and was recognised by more African student movements.'[3]

Savimbi also established UPA youth and trade union wings[4], and a medical service, SARA (Social and Medical Assistance to Angolan Refugees), led by Jose Liahuka who had completed his medical training.

In March 1962 Savimbi achieved a merger between the UPA and a smaller nationalist group from the north, the PDA (Democratic Party of Angola).[5] The movement was christened the National Front for the Liberation of Angola (FNLA), though it was 'national' in name only since its components were both Bakongo-based.

One week after its formation, the FNLA announced on 5 April 1962 the creation of the Revolutionary Angolan Government in Exile (GRAE), with Holden Roberto as President, Emmanuel Kunzika, the leader of PDA as Vice-President, and Savimbi as Foreign Secretary. Savimbi had argued against this development: he thought it important first to step up the fighting and begin moving leaders into Angola rather than take on the trappings of government in a foreign land. Roberto circumvented Savimbi's opposition by proclaiming the GRAE while his foreign secretary was in Switzerland.[6] Roberto was encouraged in his action by the achievement of the FLN (National Liberation Front) earlier that year in winning a ceasefire to end the Algerian civil war: this culminated in independence for Algeria on 1 July 1962. During the war the FLN had proclaimed its own government-in-exile, the Algerian Provisional Government (GPRA).

Having lost the argument with Roberto, Savimbi nevertheless threw himself into winning official recognition for the GRAE from African governments. With nearly thirty countries now independent, the Organisation of African Unity came into being in Addis Ababa on 22–25 May 1963. Savimbi attended as the GRAE delegate. He won an influential position as chairman of a group of liberation movement representatives advising on the formation of a committee which would co-ordinate fund-raising to support nationalist movements in countries remaining under colonial rule. Among Savimbi's committee members were Kenneth

Kaunda, seeking independence for Northern Rhodesia from Britain; Joshua Nkomo, leader of the ZAPU movement in white-ruled Southern Rhodesia; and Luis Cabral, leader of the PAIGC liberation movement in Portugal's Guinea-Bissau. On their recommendations, the OAU Liberation Committee was created and based in Dar-es-Salaam with Tanganyika's Foreign Minister Oscar Kambona as Chairman.

Savimbi's part in forming the Liberation Committee helped in his diplomatic battle for the GRAE. The first breakthrough came when the Congolese government gave *de jure* recognition to the GRAE on 29 June 1963. This was a stunning blow to the MPLA which was seeking equal freedom to organise on Congolese territory, to train guerrillas there and transport arms into Angola. Worse followed for the MPLA when, on 2 August 1963, in Dakar, OAU foreign ministers accepted Liberation Committee advice, officially recognised the GRAE and recommended that all independent African states do the same. The foreign ministers also recommended the absorption of the MPLA into the GRAE. Soon the GRAE had been recognised by nearly every independent state in Africa except Ghana, Guinea and Congo-Brazzaville. The Liberation Committee was influenced by the disarray it found within the MPLA as the result of a series of personal and ideological splits. After the initial uprising in Luanda of 4 February 1961 there had been no sustained MPLA resistance.

Agostinho Neto had become a political legend because of the long years he had spent in Portuguese jails. In July 1962 he escaped from his latest spell of detention across the Straits of Gibraltar to Morocco. He made his way to Leopold-ville: the MPLA had moved its headquarters there from Conakry in October 1961 to have ready access to the zone of rebellion in northern Angola.

The arrival of the 'Crown Prince' in Leopoldville to be elected as the President of the MPLA in December 1962 coincided with the ousting of Viriato da Cruz from the post of Secretary-General. Da Cruz, who had a reputation as one of the most disciplined Marxists in the MPLA,[7] formed his own breakaway MPLA/Da Cruz: he was supported by several others, including Matias Migueis, who had just been elected first Vice-President to Neto. The rival groups argued bitterly: the Congolese police intervened in a knife and chair-throwing fight for control of the MPLA's Leopoldville offices, which ended with 43 arrests and two people being taken to hospital with stab wounds.[8]

The OAU's verdict on the MPLA was harsh because it failed to take into account that the movement's attempts to launch guerrilla activity in Angola were blocked by FNLA/GRAE control of the Angola/Congo border. MPLA patrols which did manage to get across were sometimes wiped out on Roberto's orders. For example, 21 MPLA soldiers were intercepted by Roberto's troops on 21 October 1961 while crossing the M'Bridge River in northern Angola and taken away and executed.[9]

In November 1963 the Leopoldville government ordered Neto's MPLA to stop all activities on Congolese soil. Neto led his remaining followers across the Congo River to Congo-Brazzaville, where the left-wing regime of President Alphonse Massamba-Debat felt an ideological compatibility with the MPLA. Massamba-Debat's personal dislike of Prime Minister Cyrille Adoula of the Congo also helped.

As the dejected MPLA men straggled into Brazzaville, the British writer and historian Basil Davidson, one of the MPLA's leading Western sympathisers, said Neto's claim to leadership had ended: his movement, 'fractured, split and reduced to a nullity' had 'ceased to count'.[10] In fact, it was far too soon for anyone to write Neto's political obituary.

Despite winning breakthroughs for the FNLA/GRAE, Savimbi had deep misgivings about the direction in which Roberto was taking the movement. Though journalists were taken to 'liberated areas' of northern Angola in 1961 and 1962, the Portuguese quickly reorganised and struck against villages identified in foreign press reports. The FNLA/GRAE was past its peak when it was recognised by the OAU. Its new status disguised fundamentally serious problems.

As FNLA/GRAE forces were driven back and fragmented in Angola, Roberto sat in Leopoldville and was unreceptive to ideas on halting the decline. 'Ministers and functionaries within the GRAE came to view themselves as members of a real government. They all confused form with substance, ceremony with function . . . Aggravating this malaise, Roberto accepted the gift of a black Mercedes from an anonymous (rumoured German) benefactor.'[11] Ignoring the requirement for a leader to identify with the hardships of his people, Roberto took to driving about the Congolese capital in his shiny new status symbol.

Savimbi knew the initial fervour which sustained the 1961 assaults could not ensure success unless the people learned some of the theories and sophisticated skills of guerrilla warfare. Algeria, China, Egypt and Indonesia all offered to train guerrillas – but Roberto turned them down in case recruits became contaminated by 'Communism'.[12]

Savimbi's followers in the FNLA/GRAE came to form a distinct unit known as the 'Opposition Group' because it challenged Roberto on many issues. It comprised several different tribes and opposed Roberto's continued bias towards his own Bakongo.

Many Ovimbundu had joined the FNLA/GRAE along with some Chokwes, Nganguelas and Seles tribesmen and OAU recognition had raised their expectations that Roberto would extend the war beyond the north and penetrate their areas in the centre and south. When they perceived a 'slowdown of the war imposed by Roberto',[13] 325 of them tried to desert from the FNLA/GRAE's training and logistics camp at Kinkuzu, in the Congo to the south-west of Leopoldville; they were forced to return by Congolese troops. Another 65 Ovimbundu deserters managed to reach Leopoldville. They angrily confronted Roberto, who responded by having them thrown into prison by Congolese forces.[14]

Savimbi's relationship with Roberto deteriorated as he pressed for deep reforms. Savimbi particularly wanted to extend the FNLA/GRAE's friendships beyond the narrow range of contacts with Congolese, Tunisians and Americans favoured by Roberto. Roberto disagreed, but the 'Opposition Group' independently forged relationships with Ahmed Ben Bella, the first President of independent Algeria, and Egypt's President Gamal Abdel Nasser.

When Roberto's relationship cooled with Kwame Nkrumah, Savimbi maintained his own links with the Ghanaian leader. He made contact with Co Liang, one of China's leading agents in Africa, who was working as a Hsin-Hua News Agency correspondent in Ghana. Co Liang gave Savimbi the complete works of Mao Tse-tung.[15] Savimbi's contacts were thus ready for the day when he would need the Peking connection for the training of his own guerrillas.

Savimbi says he argued with Roberto the need to make contact with the Chinese and ask them to train FNLA/GRAE officers. 'I said we needed their techniques because they had fought the most successful guerrilla war. But Roberto said the Chinese would teach our people Communism and they would bring Communism to Angola.'[16]

The 'Opposition Group' was also concerned about the poor education of field commanders. They argued that more high school graduates should be given military training. 'Roberto preferred to send people who had no academic background because they could be more easily controlled and were less likely to revolt against the leadership.' They were also concerned about Roberto's own limited education and scant knowledge about Angola. Born in São Salvador, northern Angola, in January 1923, Roberto was taken to the Belgian Congo at the age of two and finished his education at the age of 17 after attending a Baptist mission school in Leopoldville. His deepest friendships were with Congolese politicians, and later he married a relation of Mobutu Sese Seko, who took power in the Congo in a 1965 coup.

'In the "Opposition Group" we believed it was a mistake to elevate the principle of military resistance above all others. We needed to grasp that although it would be necessary to use weapons, any real permanence would be achieved through political struggle. But we could not make Roberto see our point of view.'[17]

*   *   *

Che Guevara entered Savimbi's life when his confidence in the FNLA/GRAE as a vehicle to achieve his ideals was at a low ebb. The meeting with the Argentine-born Cuban revolutionary in January 1964 was even more seminal for Savimbi than his encounter with Jomo Kenyatta.

Guevara and Stokely Carmichael, of the American Black Power movement, were guests of honour at a conference of African liberation movements in Dar-es-Salaam. Among those represented were the FNLA/GRAE, with Savimbi as its delegate, the MPLA, FRELIMO, SWAPO, ZAPU, ZANU, the ANC and PAC of South Africa,[18] and two Dar-based Congolese groups which, with at least nominal Sino-Soviet support,[19] were involved in a growing insurgency in the eastern Congo.

After Guevara, an international cult figure among youthful leftists in the sixties, had given his speech, punctuated by frequent applause, Savimbi rose and said he disagreed with his arguments. This created uproar and some delegates, especially the Congolese rebels and delegates of FRELIMO (the Mozambique Liberation Front), shouted at Savimbi that he was a CIA stooge: they also yelled abuse at the representatives of SWAPO (the South-West African Peoples Organisation), with whom Savimbi had established warm friendship. Guevara intervened and said Savimbi should be heard.

Guevara's speech, according to Savimbi, had dwelt on the need for the working class – the proletariat of the Marxist-Leninist lexicography – to be the 'vanguard' in any liberation struggle: like Fidel Castro, he did not believe in a long-term mobilisation of the peasant 'masses'. Guevara also argued that the Congo, huge and rich in minerals and agricultural potential, was the key to revolution in central and southern Africa. If the capitalist-orientated régime there could be replaced with a revolutionary government, a blow would be struck against Western imperialism in the very heart of Africa. Subsequently it would be easier to break through in more peripheral places like Angola and Mozambique.[20]

In a tactical sense, Savimbi responded, Guevara was right: it would undoubtedly be a major breakthrough if the Congo could be removed from imperialist control by a combined effort of all African nationalists. But strategically it could turn out to be a big mistake: if everyone was crushed while making a joint endeavour in the Congo, who would be left to continue the struggle elsewhere?

The Congo should not be the major issue for African revolutionaries, said Savimbi. As it was independent, it was free to develop according to its own internal dynamics, regardless of whether they were to Che Guevara's liking. The greatest priority for Africans was to fight colonialism. If Guevara wanted to promote revolution in the Congo he should help liberation movements intensify their wars in Angola, Mozambique and elsewhere: that way the 'imperialist enemy' would have to spread its forces and would be more vulnerable.

After the public session, Guevara asked Savimbi if he would meet him at eight the next morning. A car took him to the Cuban Embassy, where he and Guevara exchanged ideas for five hours. Savimbi did most of the talking. First, he challenged one of the principles that Guevara had expounded during the conference – of guerrillas establishing a fixed base camp on somewhere like a farm. This flew in the face of Mao's principle of avoiding settled bases: instead, guerrillas had to swim freely like fish in the sea among people whose confidence they had won. Perhaps a set base had been acceptable in a small country like Cuba when Guevara and Fidel Castro were fighting from the mountains to overthrow the Batista dictatorship, but in the vast bush of Angola with its scattered villages, it was not necessary – the guerrillas could live with the people.

A different political analysis was needed for Africa, Savimbi told Guevara. In Angola the working class could not be the 'vanguard' of any struggle. The people who mattered there were the peasantry, the 90 per cent of the population who survived on subsistence agriculture and hunting and trapping: they might seem weak and easygoing to an eager, well-educated revolutionary, but they would endure prolonged suffering if they could be won for a cause. In Angola it was from the very small working class that there was emerging a bourgeoisie, precisely the class that had to be overthrown by the working class in Marxist-Leninist terms. Thus, the theories evolved by Marx and Lenin in nineteenth-century and early twentieth-century industrial Europe, with its large and oppressed working class, were burdened by a fundamental contradiction when any attempt was made to fit them to African realities.

Savimbi told Guevara he disagreed profoundly with the OAU Liberation Committee's apparent desire for leaders of liberation movements to base themselves outside of the countries their guerrillas were fighting to free. 'I argued that the leadership has to go inside and live with the people, even if it means risking death. More people would rally around the cause if they saw their leaders suffering alongside them. Also it was the only way for leaders to make a realistic assessment of the strengths and weaknesses of their people.'

Guevara also needed to accept that Africa could produce revolutionaries of its own, Savimbi told the Argentine-Cuban revolutionary. He had to come with an open mind: 'If outsiders like you bring along all their formulas of revolution and try to impose them on us, then you are coming with the same kind of superiority complex as the colonialists in Africa.' But Angolans were different historically and culturally from Cubans: the armed struggle would be practised in a different way in Angola than it had been in Cuba.

Before coming to the Dar-es-Salaam conference Guevara had spent a month in Brazzaville with the MPLA, but had not been allowed to visit areas of Angola's Cabindan enclave that Neto claimed to have liberated. Guevara told Savimbi he had heard from him what he wanted to hear on the need for leaders to establish bases alongside the people. It fitted with ideas he himself was developing concerning the 'liberation' of Latin American countries beyond Cuba.

According to Savimbi, Guevara said: 'I went to Brazzaville to see the MPLA, and nothing is happening. They are just bourgeois. From now on you are my friend. I am going to Fidel to make a report on you, and he will give you assistance through our friend Ben Bella in Algeria.'[21]

In February 1964 Guevara and Savimbi travelled together to Algiers to attend an 'Afro-Asian Solidarity Seminar' on economics. There they held talks with Ben Bella, who offered his help to both men to establish bases among the peasantry. But Ben Bella never did become a conduit of Cuban arms for Savimbi. In 1965, before Savimbi had entered Angola to launch his idea of revolution, Ben Bella was overthrown by Colonel Houari Boumedienne, who threw Algeria's support behind the MPLA.[22]

As for Che, he died before the end of the decade while putting into practice the ideas he had discussed with Savimbi. He chose Bolivia as the Latin American country in which to launch his revolution, fighting and living alongside the peasantry. Bolivian troops, armed and trained by the United States, trapped Guevara in a forested ravine. There he was riddled by bullets and fell dead.[23]

*   *   *

The FNLA/GRAE insurgency continued to disintegrate beneath its governmental pose; Roberto's movement had become an organisational fiasco.[24] On 15 March 1964 Savimbi was absent from the FNLA/GRAE celebrations in Leopoldville of the third anniversary of the 1961 uprising. And from April, after Roberto admitted the MPLA dissident Viriato da Cruz into the FNLA/GRAE without consulting Savimbi, the two men ceased to be on talking terms.[25]

By May, Savimbi had decided that his position was impossible. He slipped quietly out of Leopoldville for Switzerland to consider when and how to announce his resignation decision. There he discussed with Tony Fernandes, who was studying economics at Fribourg University on a UNEA scholarship, the possible shape and policies of a new liberation movement. But they went no further at that stage: 'I had no wish to cause any further harm to the FNLA struggle because I knew that in the beginning they meant well. I was sad about their limitations.'[26]

Through May and June Savimbi concentrated on his studies at Lausanne under Henri Rieben. But the FNLA started to attack him. *The Banner of Socialism*, a Trotskyist journal published in Algeria, reported inaccurately that Savimbi had been expelled from the FNLA/GRAE because of connections he had with the CIA and Israel. Trotskyist publications in Brussels and Paris made similar allegations.

Ben Bella, who was still in power in Algeria at this stage,

and Gamal Abdel Nasser sent messages to Savimbi saying he had to defend himself or the allegations would stick. They reminded him that he was still Foreign Minister of the GRAE and advised him to attend the July 1964 OAU heads of state summit in Cairo. 'I was given an official reception as the GRAE Foreign Minister. I sat next to the other GRAE ministers. They said nothing to me, but they made no move to expel me. Perhaps they thought there was a possibility of reconciliation.'

On 15 July Savimbi announced his resignation. At a press conference he denounced the FNLA's tribalism, the inefficiency of its administration, and the inadequacy of support for the guerrillas inside Angola. Pledging that he would dedicate his life to liberating Angola, Savimbi said: 'Our war has stopped for the time being. Resistance is less than at any time since the beginning of the fighting in 1961 . . . For from intensifying military action and regrouping the popular masses – the only way to hasten the liberation of Angola – the GRAE has limited itself to empty speeches.'[27]

Savimbi also attacked Roberto's weak and secretive leadership and his failure to seek *entente* with the MPLA. In the months preceding the OAU summit Savimbi's followers in the FNLA/GRAE had denounced Roberto's failure to open a new military front into central Angola from the Katanga region of the southern Congo. They also accused Roberto of diverting funds into his foreign bank accounts.[28]

Ironically, the African heads of state – with strong objections from Nkrumah and Congo-Brazzaville's Massamba-Debat – chose the Cairo summit to confirm the OAU's official recognition of the GRAE by foreign ministers the previous August.

The day after Savimbi resigned he received a telegram from Agostinho Neto asking the newly unemployed nationalist to visit him in Brazzaville.

5

UNITA is Born – Disaster Follows

1964–67

Savimbi flew straight from the OAU summit in Cairo to Brazzaville to talk to Neto. There Neto offered him the post of Secretary of Foreign Affairs in the MPLA.[1] He declined.

Savimbi was received warmly by Neto at the house provided for the MPLA leader by President Massamba-Debat. Dr Neto's followers also helped 185 of Savimbi's supporters to cross the Congo River from Leopoldville for safety, and welcomed them to Brazzaville with financial help. The group included Liahuka and Jose Kalundungo, the Chief of Staff of the FNLA/GRAE army. In the group were Cabindans and members of the Bakongo tribe from the far north; Ovimbundu, Nganguela, Selas and Chokwe tribesmen from Central Angola, and Cuanhaunas from the far south.[2]

Savimbi wished to do more than talk with Neto. There were rumours of a recovery in MPLA morale and activity. Cuban military instructors, perhaps a thousand, had arrived to train the Congo-Brazzaville army at its main base just outside the capital; some of the Cubans were also training MPLA guerrillas alongside the host state's regular soldiers.[3] Cuba would remain a staunch friend of the MPLA through many difficulties for more than the next two decades. At the same time, the Soviets began supplying light weapons, and young MPLA supporters began going to Eastern Europe for studies and military training.

The MPLA had also been given its own training base at Dolisie, near the enclave of Cabinda, the only part of Angola with which Congo-Brazzaville shared a common border. To get into the main part of northern Angola from Dolisie required crossing a strip of Congolese (Leopoldville) territory, where the government was hostile and FNLA/GRAE forces blocked the way.[4]

Savimbi asked to visit Dolisie to see the techniques the guerrillas were being taught. If he was impressed by what was happening, he said, he and his whole group would join the MPLA. But he was gravely disappointed by what he saw at Dolisie: 'The MPLA had only 30 men there, and between five and ten of them might go into Cabinda at a time. They might ambush a Portuguese car and then run back immediately to Dolisie: they never stayed to mobilise the people. Though the FNLA was disorganised and Roberto was politically inarticulate, it was clear to me that the FNLA was doing more than the MPLA.'

When Savimbi returned to Brazzaville he told Neto that his views were totally negative: 'There was no real fighting going on and Daniel Chipenda [commander of the MPLA forces] was drinking too much and so were all his men. I told Neto that Chipenda might be reporting to him that fighting was going on in Cabinda, but his men really spent most of their time on Congo-Brazzaville soil.'[5]

Neto reminded Savimbi of the difficulties that the MPLA had faced in Leopoldville: it took time to reorganise. Savimbi acknowledged this, but asked why the MPLA's communiqués did not say there were problems instead of claiming to be killing hundreds of Portuguese. 'Propaganda is also a weapon,' Neto replied.[6]

Savimbi was not isolated in his criticism. Professor John Marcum, the West's most assiduous student of Angola, wrote that the rural people of Cabinda were resistant to political mobilisation by the MPLA, whose operations 'were modest in scope'.[7] A Leopoldville-based magazine which had dismissed the FNLA/GRAE leaders as ineffectual, self-enriching and corrupt said the MPLA's *assimilado* leadership 'invented' Cabindan war stories while frequenting the French bistros and fashionable shops of Brazzaville. 'One hears on the radio about a portion of Cabinda having been liberated, whereas it is a public scandal that MPLA guerrillas scarcely dare cross the Cabindan frontier.'[8]

And many years later an account by two British journalists, both supporters of the MPLA, endorsed Savimbi's view of Chipenda, his fellow Ovimbundu. 'Chipenda was ebullient, hard-drinking and a womaniser, notorious at the front for his non-military exploits,' wrote Michael Wolfers and Jane Bergerol in their book *Angola in the Front Line*.[9].

*   *   *

Savimbi concluded that the MPLA was not ready to set up bases inside Angola. He left Brazzaville, where his followers faded into the labyrinth of a big refugee community typical of most capitals in black Africa. His mind turned towards forming a new liberation movement through which he could put his ideas into practice. He travelled to Dar-es-Salaam, where his old friend Co Liang was now based. The Chinese agent contacted Peking and negotiations began which would end eventually with followers of Savimbi attending courses in guerrilla warfare at Nanking Military Academy.

From Dar, Savimbi travelled to Zambia and made contact with a network of small Angolan exile associations, organised on a fragmented tribal basis mainly for recreational and mutual support purposes: nearly all were based on the northern Copperbelt, where their members worked in the mines. Savimbi described his ideas for a new kind of freedom movement. A small group, led by Smart Chata of the *Ukwashi Wa Chokwe* (Angolan Chokwe Association), agreed to start organising for when Savimbi could return with arms, money and trained guerrillas.

Stopping next for a short time in Switzerland, Savimbi then began a journey to the Soviet Union, Czechoslovakia, Bulgaria, Hungary, China, North Korea and North Vietnam in search of international support. He was received icily in Eastern Europe: 'Unfortunately for us they were not as interested as we were in new experiences in Angola, but were only interested in recruiting new members for the MPLA.'[10]

The Chinese expressed real understanding of his aims but they found it difficult to trust him because of reports that the FNLA/GRAE had been pro-American.[11] Nevertheless, they promised to train some of Savimbi's men and to distribute

1,000 dollars through the Chinese Embassy in Brazzaville to his supporters stranded there.

After his return from China in October 1964 Savimbi threw himself into his studies, but at Christmas he and Tony Fernandes went to a hotel at Champay in the Swiss Alps. There they finalised their new party's programme which they had been working on since May. They decided that the time had come to launch the party, but that it was essential for the official inauguration to take place inside Angola. They decided a constitution and that the party's name would be UNITA. 'It symbolised the unity we believed was necessary among all Angola's peoples if we were to have any hope of defeating the Portuguese,' said Savimbi.

* * *

In the first three weeks of 1965 Savimbi made another trip to China to arrange dates for guerrilla training for UNITA's first recruits. The Chinese gave Savimbi 15,000 dollars, the first donation received by UNITA for party funds. Fernandes flew to Tanzania and Zambia to reveal the decisions made at Champay and to prepare the ground for the launch of the movement. In Tanzania Fernandes spoke to ministers who were friendly to Savimbi and whose help would be essential in getting men and supplies across Tanzania and Zambia into Angola: they included Foreign Minister Oscar Kambona, Planning Minister Abdulrahman Babu, who was a close associate of Co Liang, and Ben Mkapa, then a junior minister running the influential magazine *Uhuru* (*Freedom*). Fernandes also established close contacts with leaders of SWAPO, who were waiting for permission to enter Zambia and establish bases to launch guerrilla raids into Namibia. He also secured a commitment from the Angolan exiles in Zambia that they would provide 11 people to go to China later that year to train as guerrillas.

On 15 July 1965 Savimbi completed the final examinations at Lausanne for his *licence* in political and legal sciences. 'Then I said I am leaving Switzerland. Europe for me is over . . . So on 22 July I left for good.'[12] He then went to Nanking for an intensive guerrilla leadership course which lasted until early November. In September Savimbi welcomed to

Nanking the group of 11 chosen as UNITA's first guerrilla
commanders. Their training would last until early May 1966.
They were Jose Kalundungo, the former Chief of Staff of the
FNLA/GRAE army, Samuel Chiwale, who by the 1970s rose
to General Commander of the UNITA forces, David
'Samwimbila' Chingunji, destined to become a legendary
UNITA hero, Tiago Sachilombo, destined to become a
traitor, Jeremias Kussiya, Nicolau Chiyuka, Mateus Banda,
Paulino Moises, Samuel 'Mwanangola' Chivala, Isaias
Massumba and Jacob Inacio. Of the founding 11, only five
were still with UNITA 20 years later in 1986 – Kalundungo,
Chiwale, Kussiya, Chiyuka and Banda. Of the others, two,
Samwimbila and Moises, died in combat with the Portu-
guese and one, Inacio, against the MPLA. Three defected –
Sachilombo to the Portuguese in 1969, Mwanangola to the
FNLA/GRAE in 1969, and the third, Massumba, to Zambia
where he became a member of the Zambian Air Force.[13]

The 'UNITA Eleven' were joined in Nanking at the beginning of 1966 by 11 Rhodesian African nationalists of the
ZANU (Zimbabwe African National Union) movement.
The Rhodesians were led by Josiah Tongogara, later to
become commander of Robert Mugabe's guerrillas fighting
the white government of Mr Ian Smith.[14]

Before he left China, Savimbi wrote to former missionaries in Angola of the US United Church of Christ setting out
his political thinking. Considering he had just undergone an
intensive course of Maoist ideology, it was a surprisingly
tolerant and broad-minded document. It started from his
fundamental premise that only Angolans inside Angola
could free the country. Exiles had to return home to fight:
'George Washington could not have freed the British colonies of America by fighting from a base of exile against an
army superior in numbers and equipment.'

A problem of the liberation struggle to that date, he wrote,
was that the MPLA was an essentially Kimbundu tribal
movement and the FNLA/GRAE was fundamentally
Bakongo, leaving outside more than half the population
belonging to such groups as the Ovimbundu, Chokwe,
Lunda, Nganguela, Nyaneka-Humbe, Herero and Bushmen. The MPLA had become 'pro-Communist' under

Moscow and the FNLA/GRAE was 'supported by Western forces'. A new political movement had to work for the majority of Angolans and the total independence of all Angolans from outside political forces.

In arguing for the inclusion of all sections of Angolan society in the liberation fight, he cautioned prophetically against an 'ideological struggle' which might lead to 'a direct or indirect confrontation of the great powers'. He went on: 'This struggle is not ideological because it cannot exclude anybody. It has to unite all . . . It is a democratic national struggle of a popular nature. This struggle has to incorporate everyone from the sincere chief who dislikes the odious Portuguese colonial system up to the most enlightened revolutionary . . . from the isolated peasant in the valley and the mountains who only gets from his work poverty to the contract labourer who does not even know the warmth of home.'

He turned to a theme – the importance of respecting the traditions of the peasantry – which was central to his philosophy and set him at odds with *dirigiste* and anti-religious trends within the MPLA: 'Political and economic theories which are supported in atheistic attitudes do not fall in line with the feelings of Africa. The African believes in a higher Being, whatever his name may be or whatever the place where he is worshipped. There is an ancestral force which transcends man.' Anyone who alienated the peasantry from their deep spiritual convictions would also divide the forces available to fight colonial domination.[15]

*   *   *

Savimbi left his recruits in China in November 1965 and flew to Cairo where, during earlier visits, he had formed a friendship with Zambia's young Ambassador to Egypt, Rupiah Banda. Zambia had become independent in October 1964 and early in 1965 it threw its official support behind the MPLA, permitting it to set up offices in Lusaka and to prepare to open a new military front in eastern Angola where Savimbi also intended launching war. Despite Lusaka's backing for the MPLA, Banda gave Savimbi a visa to enter Zambia to prepare among exiles there for UNITA's founding meeting inside Angola. In later years Banda would play a crucial role in switching Zambian sympathy from the MPLA to UNITA and he would rise to become Foreign Minister.

In Zambia Savimbi found that Smart Chata and his contacts inside Chokwe territory, on the eastern edge of Angola's Central Plateau, had mobilised a number of village chiefs prepared to support a new movement using their territory as a base area in resisting the Portuguese. The FNLA and the MPLA had never been active in this part of Angola.

In early 1966 Chata entered Angola with two assistants, Moses Kaniumbu and Solomon Njolomba. On 13 March at a big Chokwe village called Muangai, 250 kilometres inside Angola from the border with Zambia, UNITA was officially born at a congress of 67 chiefs and other delegates. They elected a provisional Central Committee and adopted the constitution prepared by Savimbi and Fernandes which called upon UNITA to educate 'all Angolans living outside the country to the idea that real independence for Angola will only be achieved through an armed struggle waged against the Portuguese colonial power inside the country'. Chata stayed on in Angola after the proclamation to continue securing recruits and food supplies and to establish party cells for when the Chinese-trained guerrillas arrived later in the year.

With UNITA launched and rudimentary support networks being organised, Savimbi worked on plans to smuggle the Chinese Eleven into Angola. Help was offered by Sam Nujoma, the President of SWAPO, and his Defence Secretary, Peter Nanyemba. Though Zambia was officially for the MPLA, Savimbi had made friendships with Vice-President Simon Kapepwe and three other Zambian government ministers who were ready to assist UNITA. President Kaunda knew of Savimbi's presence in Lusaka and, perhaps aware of UNITA's pledge at Muangai to struggle for 'the formation of a real *United Front* of all the Angolan nationalist forces',[16] invited Holden Roberto to Lusaka and brought him together with Savimbi at State House for reunification talks. Roberto laid down tough terms: Savimbi must publish a written apology for his 1964 walkout from the FNLA/GRAE; dissolve UNITA; and bring all his members back into FNLA/GRAE membership as individuals, not on a collective basis. Savimbi refused, no doubt partly in the awareness that Roberto maintained a prison camp for dissenters where executions took place and which one escapee described as an African Buchenwald.[17]

In July and August 1966 Savimbi also met the MPLA representative in Lusaka[18] to propose an MPLA-UNITA *entente*, not a merger, in which he and his followers would have a 'free hand to work for ourselves'.[19] MPLA headquarters in Brazzaville rejected Savimbi's overtures.

*   *   *

The Chinese Eleven flew into Dar-es-Salaam from Peking in early June 1966. With the co-operation of Savimbi's friends in the Tanzanian government, they were taken to a guerrilla camp allocated to SWAPO outside Dar. The plan was to move them into Zambia as SWAPO fighters. But Zambia, independent for less than two years, was economically and geographically vulnerable to the militarily powerful white governments of southern Africa. It was still working out ground rules under which African liberation movement guerrillas would be allowed to operate from its soil: liberation movement officials were welcome to come and go in Zambia, but not as yet their fighters.

The Eleven were stuck in the SWAPO camp throughout July and August and into September. This had its own dangers. SWAPO was part of a loose alliance of southern African movements who received help from the Soviet Union,[20] and nearby were the guerrilla training and transit camps of other members of the alliance – the ANC of South Africa, FRELIMO and the MPLA. UNITA noted 170 MPLA recruits from Zambia pass through the Dar-es-Salaam camp in summer 1965 *en route* for training in the Soviet Union.[21] Another 90 passed through Dar a little later on their way to Cuba for seven months of military training.[22]

By late August the MPLA suspected there were men loyal to Savimbi in the SWAPO camp and complained to the OUA Liberation Committee, which from March 1965 had extended official recognition to the MPLA as well as the FNLA/GRAE. The Liberation Committee ordered SWAPO to hand over Angolans in their camp to the MPLA. The UNITA men believed this would mean certain death – not without reason. Exile politics were murderous. At this time two followers of Viriato da Cruz, who had joined him in resigning from the MPLA – including former MPLA First Vice-President Matias Migueis – passed through Brazzaville on their way to Leopoldville from a conference in Indonesia. At the MPLA's request, the Congo-Brazzaville police arrested the travellers and transported them to the local MPLA headquarters. MPLA/Neto officials then drove them to Dolisie where they were executed by firing squad.[23] Their ten-minute 'trial' was presided over by Lucio Lara, by now the Organising Secretary of the MPLA.[24]

Sam Nujoma pleaded cleverly to the Liberation Committee that the 'suspected Angolans' were genuine members of SWAPO. He said, truthfully, that a confusion of tribes overlapped the border between Namibia and Angola. Inevitably some SWAPO members spoke Portuguese because they had been born or brought up in southern Angola.

The Liberation Committee accepted Nujoma's plea, but the time had come for emergency action. It was decided to smuggle four of the UNITA guerrillas into Zambia and pass them more than 1,500 kilometres across that country to Angola through the clandestine network of exiles. In early September Jeremias Kussiya, Nicolau Chiyuka, Isaias Massumba and Mateus Banda crossed the border from Tanzania. Kussiya was soon arrested by the Zambian police and sentenced to nine months hard labour, but the others reached Savimbi in Lusaka. He immediately despatched them into Angola.

On 1 October 1966 Zambia finally raised its restrictions on African liberation movement guerrillas. On 2 October SWAPO commanders began arriving from Dar-es-Salaam, and the other seven UNITA men arrived later with the rank and file SWAPO guerrillas. They too were immediately sent into Angola by Savimbi.

Then, on 26 October, Savimbi himself crossed the border into Angola, setting foot on his native soil for the first time since he had set sail for Portugal more than eight years earlier. To take on 50,000 Portuguese soldiers in Angola, Savimbi and his Chinese Eleven had between them only knives, *pangas* and one Soviet Tokarev pistol, a personal gift from Sam Nujoma to Savimbi.[25]

*   *   *

Savimbi and his band split up into four areas of south-east Angola, slotting into the organisation prepared by Smart Chata. Savimbi went to a forested area near Cassamba, about 200 kilometres from the Zambian border. A few recruits were waiting to be trained, but there were no weapons. Savimbi had asked the Chinese for arms, but they refused because of the difficulties in getting them across Tanzania and Zambia. 'Instead they gave us money. Their theory of guerrilla warfare, anyway, was that the best source of arms was from the enemy.' Chata was sent to the Congo to buy some rifles. He returned to Angola with ten standard NATO 7.62 mm FN rifles.

Portuguese intelligence quickly picked up information about Savimbi's arrival and his recruitment of local peasants. After a few minor clashes between two-man Portuguese patrols and Savimbi's raw recruits the Portuguese began issuing First World War-vintage Mauser sub-machine-guns to the villages – 15 to each chief – for protection against the *fantoches* (bandits). Since several chiefs had been mobilised by UNITA, many of the Mausers ended up with the guerrillas.[26]

The first major attack attempted by UNITA was on 4 December 1966 against Cassamba – a small timber outpost with a couple of hundred Portuguese soldiers, a score of Portuguese lumberjacks and their families and several hundred Angolans. Savimbi planned and led the attack, and: 'It was a failure. It was a disaster.'

All the theories of warfare learned in China were forgotten as bullets started flying. 'Real war was very different. It was just luck that UNITA did not die in that first attack, because half the commanders trained in China took part of it.' First, reconnaissance had been inadequate. Savimbi had relied only on intelligence given by Africans living in

Cassamba. And yet he and his followers had been taught in China that even though the people might be well mobilised and understand the policy of the movement, still only 10 per cent of what they said could be relied upon. The rest would be exaggerated. 'But we had accepted 100 per cent of what they told us. From then on we never forgot that intelligence from the people is just a starting point. What you have to do is send in your own troops clandestinely to verify whether the information is correct.'

For the Cassamba attack, which took place in the early hours of a Sunday morning, the only correct information UNITA had been given was that the Portuguese soldiers would be asleep: they always drank too much on Saturday nights. The post was surrounded by a barbed wire fence more than two metres high. The UNITA force reached it at about 3.30 a.m. The information Savimbi had received said there was more than one entrance, but there was one only. David 'Samwimbila' Chingunji told Savimbi that the intelligence was wrong and, according to what they had learned in China, the attack should be called off. 'Samwimbila' said the attack force would be safe only if they killed all the Portuguese: and he pointed to the fence and the single entrance and said retreat would be very difficult if the attack failed. 'Then he started to quote Mao Tse-tung to me on the subject,' said Savimbi. 'I told him to forget about China, we were back in Angola, and that if he didn't want to go I would be the first to enter.'[27]

Savimbi and his men got through the entrance easily: the Portuguese were all sleeping. Inside, the group of 60, largely composed of poorly trained villagers, divided into two – one to attack the Portuguese administrative post and the other to attack two shops. Savimbi reckons that his force had been firing for two minutes before the Portuguese, roused from sleep, began replying with machine-guns. 'It was the first time we had come under real fire, and the bullets had several colours – red, yellow, blue. We were really in a mess. One of our men was killed and we had to leave him. Two were wounded. We took them with us. We were all lying flat and had to crawl out through the wire.'

It had been Savimbi's hope that the Cassamba attack

would be a signal to the outside world that UNITA's resistance had begun. But when he reviewed the evidence it showed that no Portuguese had been killed.

It is interesting to compare Savimbi's account of the Cassamba attack, recalled in a conversation in the 1980s, with an earlier version that appeared in May 1967 in a British missionary magazine, *Africa and the World*. The Reverend Trevor Bush, a South African priest who had left his homeland because of his sympathies with the cause of black liberation, quoted 'one of the Savimbi's top officers' as telling him: 'The Doctor's (Savimbi's) unit immediately opened fire on the enemy, the Doctor being helped by some of his most highly experienced commanders. Some delay was caused by enemy use of heavy machine-guns mounted in well-prepared positions, but later a further attack with hand grenades resulted in the capture of the *boma* (post). Forty Portuguese soldiers were killed in this engagement for the loss of one freedom fighter dead and two wounded.'

It is an apt illustration of how perilous are the problems of reporting, or analysing, a continent as tumultuous and with such poor communications as Africa. Unless you can be a witness to what actually happened, it is hard to discern what precisely is true.

* * *

The Cassamba attack was an ignominious failure. But another UNITA group, led by two of the Chinese Eleven, Samuel Chiwale and Samuel 'Mwanangola' Chivala, was preparing a big attack on Teixeira de Sousa, a border town on the Benguela Railway where it crosses from Angola to Zaire (as Congo-Leopoldville had been renamed following the accession to power in November 1965 of President Mobutu Sese Seko).

There are varied accounts of the Teixeira de Sousa attack at dawn on Christmas Day 1966. At one extreme, Savimbi claims UNITA achieved major success by inflicting important damage on the Portuguese for low guerrilla losses. The UNITA command gave its attack force, many hundred strong, three targets – the Portuguese barracks; the airport; and the jail where African political prisoners were held and the PIDE had their headquarters. 'We succeeded to liberate all the prisoners, to kill the local PIDE chief and to take some guns from his quarters. We burned a Dakota [aircraft] which was standing on the runway, but we did not get to the airport terminal or into the barracks. But it was a tremendous effort. It is possible we lost 25 killed, though not one commander was lost.'

On the day after the attack the Portuguese said on Luanda Radio that they had killed 600 attackers. According to Savimbi, the following day they said it was 100, and on the third they reduced it again.[28] 'They admitted that some of the people they killed were black civilians living in the town. The black people had never expected fighting, and when it began they ran to get refuge in the Portuguese barracks. The Portuguese soldiers shot at them because they could not distinguish them from the guerrillas.'[29]

Other accounts suggest that UNITA, using untrained, poorly armed Chokwe recruits, launched a mass attack and lost about 300 dead against only six or seven Portuguese killed, includng the PIDE chief.[30]

The Governor-General of Angola, Lieutenant-General Rebocho Vaz, flew to Teixeira de Sousa immediately to lift white morale. He arrived there on 26 December, the first-ever Governor-General to visit the remote town, more than 1,000 kilometres from Luanda. And Portugal's President Americo Tomas said in his 1967 New Year message to the Portuguese people: 'In the recent history of the nation there are two days to remember, one the 15 March 1961 (the day the UPA uprising had begun in the north), which we are learning to forget, and the second the 25 December 1966, which we have just experienced.'

By casualty count, Teixeira de Sousa was a defeat and a foolhardy venture for UNITA. The attack breached all Mao's rules for the early stages of guerrilla warfare – mount rapid hit-and-run raids on vulnerable targets when you know your attacking strength is greater than that of the defenders, and do not attack big urban targets where you are certain to sustain heavy losses. But the assault had propaganda, not military, objectives. It had tremendous psychological impact on the Portuguese who for a week closed the Benguela

Railway to Zambian and Zairean copper shipments, thus forcing the world to take note of UNITA's entry into the Angolan war. Subsequently, the raid became a landmark in UNITA lore in the same way as 4 February 1961 and 15 March 1961 were milestones for the MPLA and the FNLA/ GRAE. If Teixeira de Sousa had not happened, some other spectacular, or reckless, attack would have been necessary as a strong reference point in UNITA's early development.

*   *   *

After Teixeira de Sousa, it became one of Savimbi's cardinal rules to avoid futile assaults on well-defended towns. UNITA now concentrated on smaller scale operations – ambushes of Portuguese patrols to capture weapons, and ripping up or dynamiting lengths of Benguela Railway track – while Savimbi prepared reluctantly for a visit to Zambia. The Central Committee had decided by nine votes against Savimbi's own dissenting vote that he should seek further publicity and drum up more support in the outside world following the Christmas Day attack.

Savimbi wanted to stay in Angola for at least another year, organising UNITA into an effective fighting force. But among those who had sent messages asking to see him was Gamal Abdel Nasser, and on 27 March 1967 Savimbi crossed back into Zambia. He was warmly received in Lusaka by President Kaunda and Zambia's Prime Minister Mainza Chona, who said they were now convinced of UNITA's serious intentions and that they were willing to provide support . . . on three conditions.

The first was that UNITA stop disrupting the Benguela Railway: the line was of critical economic importance for Zambia's copper exports following the closure of the southern African route in November 1965 after Rhodesia's Unilateral Declaration of Independence from Britain. The Benguela Railway was also crucial for Zambia's manufactured imports; following one dynamite attack on the line, Italian equipment for Lusaka's new international airport had been badly held up.

Second, the Zambians said UNITA could maintain an office in Lusaka provided it was not staffed by Angolans who had worked for years as exiles in Zambia. Lusaka regarded them as Zambians because they had become involved in domestic trade union affairs. Smart Chata fitted this category. The third condition was linked with the second. UNITA should not open party committees of its own among Angolan exiles. Zambia's ruling party, UNIP (the United Independence Party), itself wished to recruit among the exiles in its struggle for political power with the opposition Zambian ANC (African National Congress).

Savimbi agreed to all the conditions, though he asked for a grace period of three months on the first to give enough time for messengers on foot to get word to his commanders. The Zambians in return gave him a special travel document so that he could go abroad to seek support.[31]

In Cairo President Nasser gave money to Savimbi for UNITA and told him that he was considering giving arms also, provided President Kaunda would permit them to pass through Zambia.

Savimbi flew on to China where, in May 1967, he had an hour-long meeting in Yunnan with Mao Tse-tung. Mao stressed the importance of winning peasant support; encouraged Savimbi in a new plan to establish UNITA's base area 100 kilometres south of the Benguela Railway among the hill ranges and thick forests of the headwaters of the Lungue Bungu River, a big tributary of the Zambezi; and he urged the UNITA leader to be persistent and enduring because he would face many problems.[32] The Chinese gave more money and were also now prepared to ship arms to UNITA: they said they knew Tanzania's President Julius Nyerere would accept them and hoped that Kaunda would allow them to be transported across Zambia.

Savimbi returned to Lusaka, through Cairo, in early July. There the situation had changed completely. In his absence, his guerrillas had twice dynamited the Benguela Railway, derailing trains and closing the line to Zambian copper traffic for several weeks. The managing director of the British-owned line, Senhor Augusto Bandeira, had travelled to Lusaka to tell the Zambians that if they intended to shelter UNITA the Portuguese would ban Zambian traffic. Landlocked Zambia could not afford that.

Savimbi arrived on a Friday expecting a warm welcome. 'But it was cool. I called Mainza Chona and said I would like to see him. He told me to come on Monday, but on the Saturday morning the Immigration Department asked me to come to their office. They told me I had to leave Zambia and return to Cairo. When I protested and said I had no return ticket they put me in [Lusaka's] Kamwala Prison for six days. Some of the officials said I would be handed over to the Portuguese.'

Smart Chata was in Zambia at the time. He sent word of Savimbi's arrest to Tony Fernandes in Switzerland, who contacted the Egyptian President in Cairo. Nasser cabled to Kaunda asking that Savimbi not be put into Portuguese hands but returned to Cairo. President Nyerere and Oscar Kambona also pleaded for Savimbi's release.

Nasser's plea was heeded, but before Savimbi was expelled to Egypt he met Mainza Chona and the head of the Zambian CID, Vernon Mwaanga, later to be Zambia's Foreign Minister. They apologised and told Savimbi he should not interpret it as a hostile act against UNITA. 'They even asked what they could do for my supporters in Zambia. I laughed and said I only wanted to say that I would be back inside Angola within a year and that I would pass through Zambia to get there. So Chona was laughing and he asked sarcastically: "How will you do it? Are you going to fly?" I said: "Maybe, but I am just telling you that I will go back home because I am not a Zambian and I am not an Egyptian. I have to live in my own country." So they did not believe me. We shook hands and I was deported to Cairo.'[33]

Cut off from their leader and with UNITA outlawed in Zambia, the guerrillas inside Angola were now faced with a crisis. They had been deprived of their communications route with the outside world and supplies of arms, medicines and clothing that had begun to move through Zambia dried up. Savimbi himself, despite his bluster in front of Chona and Mwaanga, was in deep despair.

6

Exile and Return

1967–68

Savimbi flew from Cairo to Switzerland to talk with Tony Fernandes. He told his UNITA co-founder that the movement looked doomed: if he could not return quickly to Angola the fragile organisation would disintegrate.

Fernandes offered to give up his studies and go to Cairo, where Savimbi intended setting up temporary headquarters, to help his leader. 'I said no, we have no future, it is all dark,' recalled Savimbi. 'Tony said it was precisely because it was dark and the problems were big that I should not do things alone: we had to do it together. He said that anyone who wanted to help had to come in then, not when the difficulties were overcome.'[1]

Fernandes flew with Savimbi to Cairo and went onwards to Tunisia to talk to another Savimbi supporter from the FNLA/GRAE days, N'Zau Puna, who also abandoned his studies and joined Savimbi in Cairo. A third Angolan, Jorge Sangumba, joined the others in Egypt following completion of his degree at Manhattan College, New York.

The four had all gathered in Egypt by September 1967, at the time of the Ten Day War against Israel, and there they created what they called the External Mission of UNITA. Nasser gave it equal status with other liberation movements represented in Cairo.

One of the first decisions taken by the External Mission was to send Puna to China for guerrilla training. He arrived at Nanking Military Academy in December 1967. And although years later he spoke of how he had rejected attempts by Chinese instructors to indoctrinate him in Communist ideology,[2] Puna, like Savimbi before him, absorbed Mao Tse-tung's teachings on guerrilla warfare and the necessity for fighting to be married to clear political objectives. Mao had written: 'Without a political goal guerrilla warfare must fail, as it must if its political objectives do not coincide with the aspirations of the people – and their sympathy, co-operation and assistance cannot be gained.'[3]

Puna and Savimbi closely studied Mao's *Selected Military Writings* and considered how their general lessons could be applied to the African situation. Mao's essential tenets were that the countryside and rural populations must be won first, and the towns then gradually surrounded; that the enemy should never be engaged in conventional or pitched battles; that in any military engagements the guerrillas must always deploy numerically bigger forces than those of the enemy; that time is on the side of guerrilla insurgents. In one of his tracts on guerrilla warfare Mao said: 'Guerrilla tactics must deceive, tempt and confuse the enemy. They must lead the enemy to believe that they will attack him from the east and north, and they must strike him from the west and the south. They must strike, then rapidly disperse. They must move at night.'[4]

After a long period of small-scale operations, during which a rural base is secured, the people's support mobilised and the tactical initiative retained, Mao taught that the enemy could then be challenged on a larger scale. Finally, with liberated zones secured, conventional positional warfare and attacks on towns would become possible.

Puna, Savimbi, and the original Chinese Eleven were trained on both Western and Communist weapons. They were instructed on how to establish revolutionary bases in rural areas and how to carry out ambushes. Some were taught how to plan a sabotage operation; how to manufacture mines and incendiary bombs; and how to use explosives against houses, railway lines, bridges, tanks, trucks and locomotives.

* * *

While Puna was in China, Savimbi, Fernandes, and Sangumba worked on extending and strengthening UNITA's contacts. Towards the end of 1967 Savimbi spelled out some of his political thinking in a published interview. Photographs of the then 33-year-old UNITA leader show a well-built but lean man with a goatee beard, a tight mat of African hair, very black skin, broad nose and flashing eyes. He spoke of the need for elections in Angola when independence was achieved. He did not envisage a day when the Portuguese would suffer total military defeat. 'I think we will reach a situation when the Portuguese cannot maintain their position. We are aiming to create such pressure that the Portuguese will have to negotiate.'

He felt that tribal loyalties were not so strong in Angola that it was impossible to unite the people. Conversely, he warned that if a government was imposed that was purely tribal it could not unite the country. He felt also that an independent Angola should achieve a balance in the aid it took from East and West.

He developed a theme that would be consistent down the years: 'Angola is an agricultural country. People need food so we want to develop agriculture in order to make Angola self-sufficient.' That would involve vocational training for farming combined with mass literacy campaigns: therefore Angolans going abroad to study should be encouraged to take up technical subjects rather than law and the social sciences.[5]

*   *   *

Puna returned to Cairo from China in March 1968. The time had come for Savimbi to attempt to return to Angola. He would go with Puna, and together they would stay inside the country permanently. Fernandes would stay outside as UNITA's representative in Cairo and Sangumba would go to Britain as representative in London.

To lay a false trail concerning his return, Savimbi made a highly visible visit to Switzerland where he saw old friends and discussed the possibility of taking up further studies. On leaving he flew directly to Dar-es-Salaam. Puna had meanwhile left Cairo for Addis Ababa where he pleaded with the OAU secretariat not to dismiss UNITA's struggle in Angola. He got an unsympathetic hearing, but it provided him with the cover he needed to fly from Addis to Dar-es-Salaam and link up secretly with Savimbi. From Dar Savimbi and Puna were taken across Tanzania by their old SWAPO friends: they crossed into Zambia at a remote border point.

By now the MPLA, which had suffered an embarrassing failure in Cabinda, was developing its front in eastern Angola and had already lost two top officers in combat with the Portuguese.[6] MPLA headquarters were transferred from Brazzaville to Lusaka and a base was set up near Kalombo, in western Zambia. Officially, the base was somewhere inside Angola, but this was a diplomatic fiction to prevent embarrassment to the Zambian government.[7] (MPLA leaders imprisoned by the FNLA/GRAE in Zaire suffered badly at this time: two of them, Deolinda Rodrigues and Joao Goncalves Benedito, were tortured and killed.)

Although Zambia was now committed to the MPLA, there were still many UNITA sympathisers among the big Angolan exile population in Zambia. UNITA committees existed, despite the ban on them by Lusaka. Moving on foot, except for one short journey in a supporter's car, Savimbi and Puna were passed along a string of exile homes. Smart Chata met them at one point, and Savimbi asked him to stay in Zambia to liaise between Angola and Fernandes and Sangumba.

On 28 July 1968 Savimbi, with Puna, again set foot on Angolan soil – one year and four months after his reluctant departure.

7

Savimbi Rebuilds UNITA

1968–69

On his return, Savimbi found his guerrilla forces dispersed over a vast area. There was no central command and the scattered units were unco-ordinated as there was no attempt at co-operation among the different regional commanders. Several hundred suspected UNITA supporters in the towns had been picked up and imprisoned by the Portuguese. Key men had been killed in attacks by both the Portuguese and the MPLA, now established in eastern Angola and well armed by the Soviet Union. Among those who had died was Paulino Moises, one of the Chinese Eleven and UNITA's only expert on explosive mines.

Savimbi spent the whole of August, September and October 1968 travelling on foot to assess the state of UNITA morale and organisation. He discovered there had been a series of personality clashes, with each commander wanting to prove he was better than the others. Paulino Moises had been killed when another commander refused to help him in a defensive action against the Portuguese.[1]

To put an end to the differences, each commander was called in for a course of political training with Savimbi and military training with Puna. Savimbi taught that an undisciplined army was a threat to the peasantry. Without a sense of responsibility and maturity the soldiers 'would not be working for the people, but rather the people would be working for them. If the man who has the gun in his hand does not understand why he has the gun, he is going to abuse the power of the gun against the people.'[2]

Savimbi discovered that there were about 1,500 guerrilla

recruits, of whom only 60 were sufficiently well trained to carry arms. Five hundred were divided among four groups operating along different parts of the Benguela Railway; but the strongest unit was one of 1,000 under Samuel Chiwale, based in the Ninda area some 500 kilometres south of the Benguela Railway and near the Zambian border. Chiwale had a stockpile of 300 guns to give to the guerrillas once they were adequately trained.

This was perhaps the most critical stage in the development of UNITA. By sheer force of personality, Savimbi set out to rebuild an organisation which had virtually collapsed and to regain loyalties and restore morale for the struggle against the Portuguese. Once revived, this morale would last and grow, enabling UNITA to continue the fight into the late 1980s against the latest foreign army in Angola, the Cubans. As Savimbi worked on revitalising his fledgling movement, he could sometimes pause and stand on one of the undulating hills of the Central Angolan plateau and look out on forest that seemed to go on for ever. Before him stretched one of the greatest but least known wildernesses in the world, prowled by leopard, browsed by antelope and dissected by clear, fast flowing streams and rivers teeming with fish. There was only a scattering of small towns and a thinly spread African population living in remote villages which were self-reliant at a low level of subsistence. The endless expanses of forest were his best ally, his guarantee of survival. He and his colleagues could disappear into them at will.

By returning to live with the peasantry Savimbi established a reputation that would serve him well for many years to come. Noting the different leadership styles of the three main Angolan liberation movement leaders, one historian wrote: 'Jonas Savimbi was the first Angolan leader to return from exile to lead his movement from inside, in conformity with UNITA doctrine which criticised over-reliance on outside help and stressed the need to mobilise for a people's war inside . . . Neto and other top MPLA officials did make occasional treks into the country but were more often outside than in . . . Holden Roberto never ventured across the Zaire-Angola border.'[3]

*   *   *

The first step in UNITA's revitalisation took place at Chiwale's base after Savimbi and Puna had re-entered Angola. Commanders who could reach the base were ordered to attend a conference. Having discerned some of the problems, Savimbi promoted Chiwale to the new post of General Commander of UNITA's army, which was named FALA (Armed Forces for the Liberation of Angola). The General Commander's role would be to co-ordinate all the guerrillas into a single, centrally commanded force.

Samuel 'Kafundanga' Chingunji, commander of a guerrilla group in the Leua area, north-east of Luso, was appointed Chief of the General Staff. His role, until his death six years later, was to move between Angola, Zambia and Zaire finding supplies, particularly weapons and ammunition. Kafundanga, who had been trained inside Angola by Savimbi in 1966–67, was replaced as commander in the Leua area by one of the Chinese Eleven, Samuel 'Mwanangola' Chivala. Puna was appointed as both Secretary-General of UNITA and 'General Political Commissar' of its guerrilla forces, effectively the deputy leader, a position he would still hold almost 20 years later.

One of Chiwale's first acts as General Commander was to issue a military communiqué, dated 10 September 1968, through the Cairo office. It detailed 10 clashes with the Portuguese in August in which 86 of the enemy were killed, four trucks destroyed, and numerous rifles, ammunition and hand grenades captured.[4] It was pure propaganda, but some of the international press could be relied upon to publish a paragraph or two. (Exaggeration was not confined to UNITA. In 1967 the MPLA claimed to have destroyed the coastal city of Benguela and in another five engagements to have killed 280 Portuguese for just one wounded MPLA guerrilla. In 1968 the MPLA said its guerrillas had killed 2,760 enemy soldiers for the cost of only 80 MPLA killed and wounded.)[5]

From Chiwale's base Savimbi and Puna trekked westwards to see the UNITA group which had penetrated deepest into Angola to the area of the Cuanza River, some 600 kilometres inside Angola. In the third week of September 1968, Savimbi called local villagers to a Sunday rally near the banks of a tributary of the Cuanza to explain UNITA's new aims and organisation. Villagers said the Portuguese might attack, but Savimbi did not take them seriously. In fact, the Portuguese were camped on the other side of the river and at six o'clock on the Sunday morning they made a ground attack, supported by South African helicopters, on the bivouacs of Savimbi's guerrillas and the villagers. (South Africa operated an air unit in eastern Angola composed of Alouette III helicopters and Cessna light aircraft. A Portuguese-South African command centre was established in the town of Cuito Cuanavale for operations against both Angolan nationalist and SWAPO guerrillas.)[6]

In the attack 35 people were killed. Most were villagers, but three UNITA guerrillas died also. 'We tried to control the troops, but they were really panicking and they ran away,' said Savimbi. 'It took us two days to reorganise them. Puna and I led a counter-attack, but it was not very successful.'[7] Savimbi and Puna moved back eastwards, and by the end of October 1968 they had reached the Lungue Bungu River where Savimbi had told Mao he intended establishing his base area. Chokwe tribespeople lived there, subsisting through hunting, fishing, shifting agriculture and honey gathering among the forested hills. The Portuguese did not bother to occupy the area, driving only rough tracks through it for logging purposes and, later, for raids against the guerrillas.

Military and political training at the two camps Savimbi established in the Lungue Bungu valley continued until February 1969. 'The key problem was that although our men were very brave, they were also very amateur. We lost a lot of men because of that. We had to teach them how to hold their fire, how to make ambushes, how to take advantage of the terrain.' At first, Savimbi and Puna tried to train everybody themselves, but this proved impossible. Instead they began organising courses for leaders who in turn could train others.[8]

Savimbi was encouraged at this time by the prospect of change in Portugal when Antonio de Oliveira Salazar suffered a massive heart attack in September 1968 and was replaced, after 36 years of dictatorship, by Marcello Caetano.

But Dr Caetano soon showed that he was equally determined to retain the African colonies as part of the Portuguese Homeland. 'Portugal cannot gamble away the values that, in the shade of her flag, have turned barbarous lands into promising territories on the high road to civilisation,' he wrote. 'We cannot let up our efforts when faced with an adversary who would reveal himself to be true to the African tradition in being intolerant and implacable, who would unearth all old racial hates, and would not hesitate to sacrifice lives and property.'[9] As for Angola, Caetano said: 'Angolan Portugal has a brilliant future before it . . . Angola is quite firmly determined to remain Portuguese . . . The secret of triumph lies in the strength of one's will to conquer.'[10]

By February 1969 Savimbi believed that some of the groups in training were ready for combat and decided to put them to the test. A group of 125 guerrillas under Sub-Lieutenant Gaio Kakoma was sent to the Luando area, 150 kilometres north of the Benguela Railway, with instructions to ambush a Portuguese military convoy. They were to join up near Luando (not *Luanda*) with a small advance party led by Sub-Lieutenant Kafuna who went ahead to gather intelligence.

The early signs were that the mission had failed. The return journey from the Lungue Bungu to Luando is about 300 kilometres. Savimbi thought it would take two weeks. More than a month passed and there was no news. Savimbi and Puna were deeply worried. 'We had trained all those people in new techniques, and if they were killed we would lose credibility among the soldiers and the people. We were really demoralised and desperate and we stopped our training programme.'[11]

There were other major setbacks which seriously undermined UNITA's morale. There had been constant clashes with the MPLA since Neto's movement entered eastern Angola from Zambia. 'Wherever they went they met people who had been mobilised by UNITA, and at first they were attacking the civilians more than our soldiers because they wanted them to turn to the MPLA,' said Savimbi. 'But although they had the guns, they had no technique for mobilising the people. Theirs was a Russian type of organisation; our Chinese type was winning more support. The MPLA killed a lot of chiefs because they thought that to make a revolutionary movement they had to get rid of the chiefs so that they could build up the youth to become revolutionaries. They said the heads of villages were feudalists. But by doing it they turned the people against them.'[12]

The main problems with the MPLA were in the immediate border area with Zambia, but Savimbi claims that the MPLA never penetrated as far as the main UNITA bases, 300 kilometres into Angola.

In March 1969, as Savimbi waited anxiously for the Luando attack group to return, his problems were compounded by a mass desertion of guerrillas commanded by Samuel 'Mwanangola' Chivala in the Leua area. The MPLA, penetrating from its bases in Zambia, was surprised to find UNITA well established in that area. 'They began attacking UNITA people, killing them and destroying all our local committees.'[13] Mwanangola was a Chokwe from the area. Frustrated by shortages of weapons, he took 144 of his followers, of whom about 40 were armed, to Zaire where he was welcomed by the FNLA/GRAE. The FNLA/GRAE sent him back to establish its own main fighting force in eastern Angola, but it never developed into a major military front, and UNITA eventually forced Mwanangola back into Zaire.[14]

Mwanangola's desertion was a big blow. At the same time Savimbi was receiving news from the area of Gago Coutinho that UNITA supporters were giving themselves up to the Portuguese. These reports indicated that the people, members of the distinctive and heavily localised Mbunda, a sub-tribe of the Nganguelas, were disillusioned because Savimbi had not supplied them with enough arms to confront the Portuguese.

In April 1969 Savimbi sent Tiago Sachilombo – himself a Mbunda and, like Mwanangola, one of the Chinese Eleven – to the Gago Coutinho area to urge the people there to continue struggling until guns arrived. 'I sent Sachilombo because he was a man who really understood what the revolution meant. I believed he would be able to explain.'[15] But Sachilombo too gave himself up with his small band of soldiers and their guns, apparently demoralised by the hopeless odds presented by the strong Portuguese military presence. UNITA claims also that local PIDE agents lured Sachilombo with promises that he would be made President of a 'Republic of the Bundas' and then killed him.[16]

There were two more desertions from among the Chinese Eleven at this time. Isaias Massumba and Mateus Banda had spent most of their lives as the children of Angolan refugees in Zambia. Disillusioned by the hardships of the Angolan forest, they returned to Zambia, where Massumba took up a career in the Zambian Air Force. Banda rejoined UNITA in 1974, and by 1986 had risen again to the fighting rank of Major in command of a battalion of 800 men.

With the Portuguese and the MPLA already attacking UNITA, Mwanangola's desertion raised the spectre of UNITA being attacked also by the FNLA. Chiwale had been sent on a clandestine expedition to Lusaka to try to obtain arms from SWAPO. There he discovered that SWAPO had moved all their weapons into Cuando Cubango, Angola's most extreme southeast province, in preparation for in-filtrating Namibia. He made a long detour back through Cuando Cubango and was able to get only 26 rifles to bring back to the Lungue Bungu. To add to the dejection, Kakoma and Kafuna were still long overdue from Luando.

On a Sunday in late April 1969 sentries around the UNITA bases noticed a big group of soldiers approaching with guns. The first thought among Savimbi's low-spirited men was that they were Portuguese soldiers: the colonial army was composed, at the non-commissioned level, mainly of blacks. But surveillance by scouts showed that Kakoma and Kafuna had returned. Better still, they had been successful: 'They had ambushed a column of five Portuguese Army trucks. It was the first successful attack on a convoy since Puna and I returned. They destroyed three trucks and the other two turned back. They captured 43 guns and a lot of ammunition. We were really happy, especially with Kafuna because we had trained him from scratch over the previous few months.'[17] By 1987 Kafuna had risen to the high UNITA

rank of Lieutenant-Colonel, but Kakoma was killed in a
Cuban and MPLA ambush in May 1976.

* * *

UNITA's fortunes continued to improve throughout the rest
of 1969. More guns were captured in small ambushes. By the
year-end the flow of guns had made it possible to increase
Savimbi's personal bodyguard to 400 men from a level of 100
at the beginning of the year. The bodyguards were chosen
from among the most able of the guerrillas. They were
organised so that in case of attack 100 would engage the
enemy while 300 shepherded Savimbi away from combat.

In 1969 Savimbi participated in an attack for the last time.
It was on 4 August against a Portuguese patrol near the
village of Chicala, near Luso. 'I had sent a large group to
attack a train on the Benguela Railway. I remained near
Chicala with only seven of my security guard. Then we
heard that a small Portuguese patrol was taking people from
the village. I had been there just the previous day giving a
speech, so I said if we didn't go back we would lose face and
next time the villagers wouldn't listen to us. So we made an
ambush on ground which looked down on the patrol and we
captured one or two guns.' Savimbi had already come under
pressure from colleagues to give up battle duties because his
death would create serious problems for UNITA. Now they
insisted that he avoid combat.[18]

From 24 to 30 August UNITA held its second policy-
making Congress. Fifty-five civilian and 25 military delegates elected a 30-strong Central Committee, the first 12
members of which formed a top-level decision-making Political Bureau. Savimbi was confirmed as President; Puna as
Secretary-General; Chiwale as General Commander of the
Armed Forces; and Samuel 'Kafundanga' Chingunji as
Chief of Staff. The Congress reaffirmed that it would
carry out 'a protracted people's war for national liberation
relying on its own efforts'. It affirmed UNITA's desire to be
independent of any power bloc, and condemned both the
'continuation of American aggression against the heroic
people of South Vietnam' and the 'naked invasion of Czechoslovakia by the Soviet Union'. It called for the formation of

a 'Democratic United Front' of all the Angolan liberation
movements and urged the OAU not to favour one
movement over any other.[19]

At the Congress Savimbi – who had been given the
nickname 'Molowini' (Son of the People) – gave proof of his
belief in unity across tribal lines when he accepted in marriage a beautiful young girl offered to him by a group of
villages. Vinona Savimbi, from the Nkankala sub-tribe of the
Nganguela, stayed in the bush with her husband throughout the fight against the Portuguese and the Cubans. She
bore Jonas Savimbi four children, but died tragically in 1984
when lightning set fire to a tree which crashed onto the
thatched hut in which she was sleeping.

*   *   *

By the end of 1969 Savimbi was confident enough in
UNITA's recovery to begin inviting journalists to visit what
he described as the Freeland of Angola. A British journalist,
Mike Marshment, walked for 45 days into Angola and
interviewed Savimbi after reaching UNITA's central bases.
Subsequently, Marshment wrote a five-page letter to the
OAU Liberation Committee urging the appointment of a
commission of inquiry to visit UNITA and MPLA zones in
Angola with a view to promoting a united front. Marshment
also urged OAU recognition and support for Savimbi's
movement. 'I can't help feeling that if UNITA has come this
far without support, then how far could it go with support?'
he wrote.[20]

The most vivid eyewitness account[21] came from Steve
Valentine, an Australian reporter based in Lusaka with the
Times of Zambia. Valentine was met in Zambia on the banks
of the Zambezi River by Samuel 'Kafundanga' Chingunji.
They then marched westwards towards Angola. No frontier
posts marked the 1,400 kilometre straight-line boundary
between Zambia and Angola. As they trudged along a forest
trail, Kafundanga announced to Valentine out of the blue
that they were now in Angola. Two kilometres further on, in
a dense patch of forest, they met with about 40 soldiers led
by Samuel Chiwale. Half had standard NATO FN rifles
made in Belgium and American-designed G3 rifles made

under licence in Portugal – the two standard weapons of the Portuguese Army. Valentine also noted Mauser rifles, of the kind Savimbi said had been distributed by the Portuguese to tribal chiefs, and Italian hand-grenades which were standard issue in the Portuguese Army. Indicative of UNITA's clashes with MPLA, there were four Soviet sub-machine-guns. The guerrillas said the guns had been brought by MPLA defectors.

Valentine penetrated 400 kilometres into Angola in 13 days of walking. An intended rendezvous with Savimbi never took place. A small advance party sent to Savimbi's base to tell him that Chiwale was on the way with a reporter found that he had moved deeper into Angola towards the Benguela Railway. But, with Chiwale, Valentine was able to see some of the organisation Savimbi had rebuilt in the year since his return.

From the Zambian border the guerrillas carried only limited food supplies – dried fish, dried antelope, a little rice and a bag of mealie meal (maize flour). Within a few days of crossing into Angola they had to begin living off the land, existing almost entirely on cassava roots, dug up from secret plots in forest clearings, and wild bee honey. Some bee colonies had been established by the guerrillas in big hollowed logs placed in tree tops.

At one point, 150 kilometres into Angola, shooting broke out and Valentine thought the party had walked into the Portuguese because the guerrillas all dropped to the ground. In fact, five eland – the biggest antelope in the world – were being killed, and loud cheering broke out when the shooting was over. Valentine noted incredulously: 'The diving on the ground was part of the drill on such occasions, because the game was between us and the hunters and the bullets were coming our way.' The barrage which frightened Valentine consisted of five shots, one for each eland. Two, shot by the same man, were hit in the eye from a range of more than 100 metres. No more marching was done that day. Everyone worked furiously on butchering the animals. The meat was dried over fires and hung in trees. Later, the word was spread among people in the forest villages to come and get their share.

For the guerrillas a gargantuan feast began: 'I have never seen so much eaten. After being without meat for many days they gorged themselves until many were ill. Next morning it continued and after only two hours marching we had to stop to let the sick recover. This I was told happens about once a fortnight.'

One of the secrets of UNITA's survival over the years has been its guerrillas' ability to keep moving, covering great distances on foot for day after day after day. Valentine gave a useful picture of the never-ending trekking. Each day's pattern was similar. Rise at 5.30 a.m. and start on a ten-hour, 50-kilometre march at six. Lunch and rest for two hours at noon and walk again until 6 p.m. The guerrillas then sat around fires talking and eating until eight before fanning out through the bush for up to a kilometre, to sleeping places appointed by the 'Dragons'.

The 'Dragons' were the UNITA military police. Their nickname had been given to them by the ordinary soldiers. They had wide powers and were as hated by the troops as military police in any other of the world's armies. At night the Dragons really came into their own, exercising complete security control. Several guerrillas assured Valentine that the Dragons, chosen from the toughest UNITA recruits, would shoot dead anybody approaching a camp after dark unless his response to a challenge was instantaneous. Guerrillas caught away from the main party by the African night, which falls rapidly, always opted to sleep in the bush rather than run the gauntlet of the Dragons.

Walking patterns were systematic. Three men with automatic weapons fanned out about a kilometre ahead moving quickly between cover. Next, in single rank, came the main party, including people like cooks and porters, with fighting men evenly distributed down the line. At the rear was a guard of three, again fanned out, and on each flank of the column an officer marched parallel a few hundred metres away.

Everywhere were signs of Portugal's policy of trying to empty the countryside of people to deny food, support and information to the guerrillas. There were many abandoned villages, some rotting, others burned. In some all the treasured household goods of the departed occupants remained intact. Many had fled to Zambia as refugees. Others had retreated deep into the forests to establish new villages – 'They live in the woods, almost naked but determined to stay,' Valentine reported. The information these people supplied was invaluable to the guerrillas, as Valentine saw on one occasion. A few days after crossing the border the guerrillas camped within ten kilometres from the point where a Portuguese patrol, led by an Angolan officer called Kamanga, had laid an ambush. But many hours before the UNITA party pitched camp an old villager had intercepted the guerrilla column and described the exact location of the ambush.

The younger guerrillas wanted to attack the ambush. Chiwale refused to be diverted from getting Valentine deep into Angola for the rendezvous with Savimbi. Though he was already behind schedule, Chiwale made a day's detour around the ambush. Chiwale was beside himself with rage: 'This man Kamanga goes too far. I've warned him not to play about like this. Now look what he does. He sends in these people to annoy me, to make life difficult. I must teach him a lesson. As soon as this trip is over I'll have to come back and do something about this.'

Kamanga's name came up again and again during Valentine's four weeks of marching with UNITA. It occurred to the journalist that the relationship between Chiwale and Kamanga was similar to that between Robin Hood and the Sheriff of Nottingham, and that after many adventures shared with his adversary Chiwale might be genuinely upset if Kamanga were killed. Perhaps also Chiwale hoped one day to lure Kamanga over to the guerrillas. It was not unimaginable. Valentine's guide across the border, Kafundanga, had served for four years in the Portuguese Army and had been decorated after being wounded fighting FNLA guerrillas.

Kafundanga, tall, lean and bearded, was an *assimilado* who lost the chance of taking up a scholarship at a Portuguese university because he was conscripted into the Portuguese Army. He told Valentine: 'I could still have been fighting on the other side, I suppose. After I got shot the

Portuguese made me a bit of a hero, an example to other Africans of what they should be like. I enjoyed it. Then one day I heard that my father (a teacher) had been arrested for political organising. I went to see my commanding officer. He was very sympathetic. He said he was sure he could do something. But he couldn't. Quite suddenly I realised I was black. I stopped fighting hard and when my term was over I joined up with UNITA. My training has helped me to train others.'

The most guerrillas Valentine saw in any one group was 70 – half with firearms and the rest with bows and arrows. UNITA told Valentine that it controlled half the country. This was invention of the wildest kind, though Valentine seems to have failed to realise it, possibly because of the ease with which he saw the guerrillas wandering through bush that the Portuguese contested only sporadically.

In the course of his 800-kilometre round trip Valentine was told that 'liberated' areas had been divided by UNITA into zones and sub-zones, each with their own number. Each zone camp had a base permanently lived in by between 50 and 100 guerrillas; each sub-zone had a number of huts, staffed by a handful of sentries, which served as look-out and staging posts. Around each zone were groups of villages, and each zone was administered by a committee of villagers ultimately answerable to UNITA's Central Committee. Valentine himself passed through one zone and a sub-zone. At the zone camp he found 25 guerrillas, who said others were out on a mission. About 300 tribespeople emerged from the forest into the zone camp to attend a political rally at which they sang for about an hour. Chiwale told them to grow food for the guerrillas and not to pay their taxes. In 1969 the Portuguese admitted, in a document submitted to the United Nations, that tax revenues in Angola were decreasing as attacks on their forces by guerrillas increased.

The guerrillas told Valentine that deeper inside Angola the zones and sub-zones were bigger. He saw no reason to disbelieve them: they urged him to visit them and only lack of time prevented him from doing so. (Marshment's accounts suggested that such belief was justified.

Marshment reported to the OAU Liberation Committee that crowds of more than 1,000 greeted him in Savimbi's central base area.)

Though Valentine failed to rendezvous with Savimbi, he saw enough of the UNITA guerrillas, their supporters and their methods to conclude: 'Jonas Savimbi's only failure has been to convince the world that the organisation I have seen exists.'

That would continue to be a problem for Savimbi as UNITA's resistance continued into the 1970s.

8

The Black Chinese

1970–74

When President Richard Nixon came to power in 1969 he initiated a major review of United States policy towards southern Africa. The review concluded that African insurgent movements were so ineffectual that they were not 'realistic or supportable' alternatives to white rule. The review, in which the then White House adviser Henry Kissinger played a major part, questioned 'the depth and permanence of black resolve' and ruled out a black victory 'at any stage' in the Portuguese colonies, Rhodesia or South African-ruled Namibia.[1] The US Administration, deeply involved with Vietnam, failed to understand the basic truth that for rebels to win it was only necessary for incumbents to lose confidence, as Washington would in Vietnam and Portugal would in Angola by the mid-1970s.

However, the US analysis looked justified in Angola in the early 1970s. The Portuguese were having a busy time with the guerrillas in eastern Angola, but this thinly populated vast reserve of nature was regarded as of minimal importance compared with the developed coastal belt and the Central Highlands around Nova Lisboa. The Portuguese accepted that they could never hope to patrol the whole area effectively and that it was necessary to tolerate a certain minimum level of guerrilla activity while resettling the population in fortified villages.[2] In ten years of war up until 1971 it is doubtful whether the guerrillas of the MPLA, FNLA and UNITA between them inflicted more than one thousand deaths on the Portuguese. This, for an army of 20,000, rising to 70,000 over a decade, constituted a statistically negligible rate.[3]

The MPLA, free to move Soviet arms through Zambia and maintain bases there, reached the peak of its strength in eastern Angola in 1970–71 and was then the strongest of the liberation movements. Professor John Marcum estimated that the MPLA outgunned and outnumbered UNITA roughly 4,500 to 800 in eastern Angola. There it 'sought with possibly more dedication, though no more success, than the Portuguese to wipe out UNITA',[4] which clung on to its Lungue Bungu heartland. The MPLA, which had obtained OAU recognition, also achieved a diplomatic victory when it persuaded the OAU to withdraw recognition in June 1971 from the FNLA's Revolutionary Angolan Government in Exile (the GRAE), though not from the FNLA itself.

However, despite its superiority in numbers and its diplomatic successes, the MPLA had only limited success in winning local support. The *mestico* and *assimilado* leadership of the MPLA, most of whom were from Luanda, made remarkably little effort to gain real devotion from the Chokwe peasants of the east. What support they did get came mainly as a result of the peasantry being thrust into the MPLA's arms by the fortified villages programme and the brutality of the Portuguese Army. (One notorious set of photographs in 1970 shows Portuguese soldiers gleefully beheading an African and holding his severed head aloft by the ears.)[5] In the uneasy Chokwe-MPLA alliance, one academic noted that the peasants constantly suspected that they were being 'manipulated for ends which were not theirs by the urban creole leadership'.[6]

UNITA communiqués at the time said executions of chiefs by MPLA leaders who wanted to destroy tribal structures in the cause of a crude form of Marxism-Leninism inevitably alienated support.[7] And though Agostinho Neto said that south-eastern Angola constituted a firm base for the political and military training of MPLA guerrillas and that villagers there were giving great support to the MPLA combatants,[8] one leading expert on the liberation movements wrote: 'This simply was not true. At the end of 1970, despite patrols roaming over large areas of Angola, and holding firmly several zones near the Zambian base, its [the MPLA's] headquarters were in Lusaka, not inside Angola.'[9]

*   *   *

As UNITA entered the 1970s changes were being made by Savimbi. Until mid-1970 the biggest operational unit was a guerrilla company of 100 men. But at a ceremony on 10 July the first UNITA battalion of 300 men was formed. A UNITA communiqué said it was equipped with FN, G3 and Mauser rifles and with 40mm and 60mm mortars. But the battalion operated only sporadically against special targets, and most of the time was dispersed in its component companies. Savimbi also renamed one company the Black Panthers in solidarity with the black consciousness movement of the same name in the United States. Three years later UNITA began to receive money from a black American group, the African Liberation Support Committee.

There was a series of clashes with the Portuguese in 1970. In one, David Samwimbila Chingunji, one of the Chinese Eleven and a member of the Political Bureau, was shot dead after he led an ambush on 18 July on a military railcar west of Luso. The Portuguese returned the fire, killing two other guerrillas as well as Samwimbila. It was a grievous loss. Samwimbila, a younger brother of Kafundanga, was re- garded by Savimbi as potentially the most outstanding officer UNITA ever had.

There were other losses. Collins Luciano, a member of the Central Committee, was arrested while on a clandestine mission in the small town of Chicala, near Luso, and later executed. And one of UNITA's first guerrilla recruits inside Angola, Mine Kapwepwe, was drowned on a military mission while crossing a river.

There were also military successes. In early August local villagers passed word to UNITA of a 120-strong Portuguese Army company moving on foot from the Benguela Railway town of General Machado towards Luando, 100 kilometres to the north-east. The Black Panther Company was sent to intercept the Portuguese. The attack, on 17 August 1970, was made after the Portuguese pitched camp. Many enemy were killed and armaments, tents and uniforms were captured, said UNITA 15 years later.[10] But, again, this UNITA version of the attack demonstrates the problems of interpreting events in Angola, for in its communiqué at the time UNITA made much bigger claims: a moving convoy of Portuguese trucks was attacked, 55 Portuguese soldiers were killed and 65 rifles, 3,000 rounds of ammunition and 40 grenades were captured.

There was one sure way for guerrillas to overcome the necessary scepticism of the outside world about their exploits, and that was to capture prisoners. By 21 September 1970 UNITA had three Portuguese prisoners, taken in an ambush of four military trucks on the main road running south from Luso. They were a 29-year-old Portuguese Army sergeant and father of seven, Francisco da Silva Maia; Mrs Maria Adelina Curval Neto, 28, whose husband, a senior police officer, was killed in the ambush; and seven-year-old Maria Luisa Alves, whose policeman father was also killed.[11]

Mrs Neto and little Maria Alves, who was carried on the shoulders of the guerrillas, were taken on a 45-day march to Zambia. There they were handed to the Zambian Red Cross which in turn passed them on to the ICRC, which flew them home to Lisbon amid much publicity. The *Guardian* quoted London-based Jorge Sangumba as saying he hoped the Portuguese would draw a moral lesson from the incident and release thousands of Angolans imprisoned in Luanda and the *Baia dos Tigres* (Bay of Tigers) prison fortress on Angola's extreme southwest coast.[12] Sergeant da Silva Maia was kept prisoner for a little longer at one of UNITA's camps. After photographs of him with his captors had been distributed to the international press he too was released through the ICRC.

Recognition came from the World Council of Churches which, in October 1970, gave UNITA 10,000 US dollars from a special fund to combat racism. The WCC also gave money from the same fund to the MPLA, FNLA[13] and the Netherlands-based Angola Committee, a pro-MPLA movement which asked its supporters throughout Europe to provide information which could be used for propaganda attacks against UNITA.[14]

*   *   *

In 1971 another foreign journalist, Fritz Sitte of Austria, journeyed into UNITA territory. In two months of walking he reached Savimbi's General Headquarters in the Lungue Bungu valley and filmed guerrillas astride the Benguela Railway. He christened UNITA the 'black Chinese'. Describing the camps of Savimbi's general headquarters, Sitte wrote: 'It is a big and neat town, with huts arranged in an ordered fashion in the forest, the military camps strictly separated and, over and above that, huts with baths and lavatories.'[15]

Sitte attempted to describe the UNITA leader's political philosophy. 'Savimbi does not want a communist doctrine for UNITA. He has chosen a tendency which is of the radical socialist left. He wants Angola's total independence from Portugal, but he will accept any aid offered as long as it is not bound by political or commercial conditions. He also knows full well that if Angola was liberated he would be dependent on special technical aid from abroad.

'He has adopted the same method of revolution as Fidel Castro in Cuba, Mao in China, or Grivas in Cyprus which involves beginning a Long March with a small, close group of guerrillas and with the civil population in the remote heart of Angola. The essential point about this method, which makes UNITA different from the other Angolan movements, is that the guerrilla chiefs live with their men in the combat zones, and enter combat themselves, contrary to Agostinho Neto and Holden Roberto who act and give their orders from safe places (outside Angola). Dr Savimbi has studied the history of revolution in an almost scientific way and has tried to apply more than one method to UNITA. His mentors are Castro and Che Guevara, Grivas and Mao, but equally he admires Moltke.[16] It is this adopted road, and because of parallels with Mao's Chinese revolution, that explains why the name "black Chinese" is merited by UNITA; however, Mao's political doctrines are not Savimbi's.'

Sitte noted that in UNITA's base camps there were schools based on boarding principles. Agriculture was organised on a kibbutz-like basis, with cassava and millet as the main crops. Provisions, including reserves for the military, were stored in huts raised on piles deep in the forest.

There was a grave lack of medicines and surgical instruments. Amputations on soldiers wounded in combat, particularly in mine explosions, were carried out without anaesthetics in 'lamentable conditions' by male nurses who had trained in missionary hospitals.

The rebel areas were bombed 'day after day' by the Portuguese. Though Sitte does not seem to have witnessed such an attack himself, there are corroborating accounts of crop defoliant attacks by Portuguese Air Force planes.[17] To counter the effects of these toxic chemicals, Sitte said Savimbi and Puna advised peasants to cut off the upper parts of their cassava plants immediately to prevent the poison reaching the fleshy roots. Peasants who carried out this operation suffered skin irritation and had to wash their eyes out afterwards.

The Austrian journalist filmed his trek and hoped that the most spectacular section of his documentary would be the blowing up of a train on the Benguela Railway. He reached the line, but the main objective was not achieved, and many years later Savimbi explained what went wrong: 'When Paulino Moises was killed in battle we lost our only explosives expert and we were unable to replace him. However, Chiwale had been given some anti-tank mines by SWAPO, so we were going to use them to blow up a train for Sitte. We prepared the ambush. It was between Cangonga and Cangumbe. When I arrived with Sitte everyone was very excited: this was to be the first time a foreign journalist had seen one of our attacks.'

The mine was a traction, not a pressure, mine. That meant the detonator had to be pulled on a rope from a distance. 'We set the mine and further down the track our troops were waiting to attack the damaged train with rifle fire. Everything went well, and Sitte was ready to film. When the train came the soldier pulled the rope – and nothing happened! The ambush group opened fire, but Portuguese soldiers poured off the train and we had to retreat. When the ambush group joined up with us they were very upset. Sitte kept asking Chiwale to explain to him how the mine worked. We didn't tell him because we didn't know; but we didn't tell that we didn't know. We didn't want him going back and writing anything like that which would make us look foolish.

'But when he had gone we got the mines out in the forest – we had only four of them – and practised using the same technique as we had done at the ambush. We attached a grenade detonator. Nothing happened. So we gave up attempting to use the mines. It took us another four years before we got someone who knew you couldn't detonate a mine with a grenade detonator. The explosive force of a grenade detonator was not enough to make the five kilos of TNT in the mine explode. But we didn't know.'

There were other farcical incidents. One combined farce with tragedy. 'Our techniques of rifle ambush, learned from the Chinese, were very good, but on some other things we were amateurs. We captured an RPG-7 rocket shell from the MPLA, but we had no RPG-7 launcher tube. But we had an RPG-2 tube. We adapted the RPG-7 shell and gave it to a soldier to test fire.' The tube disintegrated and the soldier with it. 'It was two years before we got RPG-7 shells and tubes from SWAPO and we saw then that it had been crazy to mix the RPG-7 and the RPG-2.'[18]

Despite the events at the railway line, Sitte gave a good account of UNITA. 'Savimbi is certainly one of the most remarkable African leaders I have met,' he wrote. 'Within the borders of their republic, these leaders (Savimbi, Puna, Chiwale) are virtually deified. After all, unlike some freedom fighters, they actually live with the victims of colonialism, share their privations, eat the same food and live the same dangerous life. The luckier guerrillas have uniforms, but the majority live and die barefooted and dressed in rags. But they are disciplined – more so than any other guerrilla group I have come across.'

*   *   *

In 1971 UNITA pulled off a small publicity coup when it gave 2,000 kilogrammes of maize to Zambia, which at the time was suffering food shortages. These resulted from a Portuguese decision to ban maize shipments to Zambia through the Mozambique port of Beira because of President Kaunda's support for FRELIMO rebels in Mozambique. The maize, brought from UNITA's grain stores inside Angola on the heads of porters, was handed over to the governor of the western Zambia district of Kalabo. Though Zambia was providing bases for the MPLA, its attitude towards UNITA was clearly undergoing another change, for Samuel Chiwale was permitted to visit Lusaka and announce the food gift. While in the Zambian capital he invited the UN Decolonisation Committee and the OAU Liberation Committee to visit UNITA inside Angola.[19] They never responded. Chiwale also issued an appeal for the three liberation movements to come together, an appeal repeated in March of the following year, 1972. In a document sent to Lusaka by Savimbi, he warned: 'Do not wait for history to teach us a severe lesson. A platform must be set to urge the Angolan movements to join forces and fight Portuguese colonialism. UNITA is prepared and will be proud for such a genuine move towards independence of our motherland.'[20]

And indeed there was a movement towards unity in 1972 – but between the FNLA and MPLA, with UNITA excluded because it was not officially recognised by the OAU.

On 8 June 1972 President Mobutu of Zaire and President Marien Ngouabi of Congo-Brazzaville announced the reconciliation of Holden Roberto and Agostinho Neto. The FNLA-MPLA engagement ended in marriage on 13 December 1972 when Roberto and Neto signed an agreement in Kinshasa (formerly Leopoldville) which merged their followers into one movement, the Supreme Council for the Liberation of Angola (CSLA). It was a strange union because of the movements' very different political orientations and their history of fighting each other with as much vigour as they spent in combating the Portuguese. But by 1972 both the FNLA and the MPLA were very weak, and both believed there were advantages to be gained from the OAU's reconciliation efforts.

The MPLA had suffered in the Portuguese military's 'Operation Attila' in eastern Angola in 1972. The Portuguese used napalm and defoliants in scorched earth assaults against villages suspected of harbouring nationalists, and 10,000 refugees fled to Zambia. By the end of 1972 the MPLA was finished as an effective fighting force in eastern

Angola.[21] To get access to its areas of support behind Luanda, from its other bases in Congo-Brazzaville, it needed access across the intervening strip of Zairean territory. The merger with the FNLA would, theoretically, win co-operation from the Zairean government.

The FNLA had suffered a series of setbacks from 1969 onwards, when the Portuguese wiped out one of its bases in Zaire. In 1972 its military strength was struck another blow when troops mutinied at the FNLA's main camp at Kinkuzu, in Zaire: 25 FNLA soldiers died in the fighting, and Zairean forces had to intervene to rescue Roberto from overthrow; 13 of the officers who challenged Roberto's leadership were executed. The FNLA, weakened in status by the OAU's withdrawal of support from the GRAE the previous year, was also ready to appear co-operative in order to assure future OAU and other external support.[22]

The CSLA made little progress. Negotiations to implement the agreement continually broke down. Even more serious for the MPLA were the setbacks against the Portuguese, and the failure of the CSLA precipitated internal dissent. Daniel Chipenda and other MPLA leaders on the eastern front – who became known as the Eastern Revolt faction – felt they had not been adequately consulted about the union with the FNLA and attacked Neto's leadership. The OAU effort to promote Angolan unity had resulted only in further divisions. Alarmed by the growing internal strife within the MPLA, the Soviet Union withdrew support for Neto's movement from 1972 onwards.[23]

UNITA also suffered badly in 'Operation Attila'. Many of its fighters were killed. Savimbi was therefore angered by the 'discriminatory' exclusion of UNITA from the CSLA. He had asked for admittance in letters to Roberto, Neto and the four OAU leaders involved in promoting the merger, Presidents Mobutu and Ngouabi and Presidents Nyerere and Kaunda. Savimbi said he was prepared to multiply his efforts to achieve unity with the other movements. 'We wish to join the CSLA, to infuse it with new life, and to be part of a united democratic front,' he said. 'We look forward to meeting our brothers of the other movements. They know, our Portuguese occupiers, that once we achieve unity they will be defeated. Let us, however, be discreet. Let us refrain from idle gossip before tangible results are achieved. We Africans, far too often, talk before we act.'[24] This expressed barely constrained contempt for Neto and Roberto, living in comfort outside Angola and officially recognised by the OAU, while Savimbi was fighting inside without OAU help.

*   *   *

UNITA began 1973 still unrecognised by the OAU. In that year a *Washington Post* reporter, Leon Dash, trekked into Angola to attend UNITA's third policy-making Congress. A vivid series of articles by Dash, a black American whose great uncle was born in Angola, shed much of the veil of mystery that had shrouded Savimbi's followers.[25]

Dash and four UNITA representatives from overseas crossed the Zambian border into Angola in late June with an escort of 28 guerrillas. They marched for five days across a no-man's-land of empty swamp, forests and fields which the peasants had left because of Portuguese bombing. About 200 kilometres into the country Dash entered UNITA's 'Zone Zero', the movement's first camp west of the Zambian border.

Several weeks later, Dash arrived in the Lungue Bungu valley to attend UNITA's third policy-making Congress which was held in a grass-walled amphitheatre and lasted from 13 to 19 August. About 150 huts had been built to house the delegates from several tribal groups. There were constant meetings lasting far into the night as new goals for the 'liberated areas' were hammered out. The delegates discussed tribal antagonisms and ancient traditions such as tooth-filing and arranged marriages. They socialised and exchanged views at a dance and banquet where tender slices of roast antelope and chicken were washed down with *ovingundo*, a beer made from maize and wild honey. They speculated about their growing strength, about Portuguese military strategy and their own relationships with the other two Angolan guerrilla groups.

Savimbi talked to Dash about the philosophy, drawn from his Chinese experience, that he tried to impart to his commanders. The core of it concerned recruitment of the peasantry. It was very difficult to convince a peasant to participate in a guerrilla war. It was necessary to persuade him to leave land that might have been in his family for generations. So, the first time that UNITA guerrillas went into a village seeking recruits they looked for peasants who had had contact with the Portuguese: 'That contact will have always left some smouldering resentment with them.' More than half of the population of a given village might have had no contact with the Portuguese and saw no reason to fight them. The guerrillas got the village men who had done forced labour on the coffee plantations to explain how they were treated.

Once peasants began to listen it took only time and patience to change their minds. 'Shouting and screaming and telling them that they must join us would accomplish nothing. You must never talk down to them or go into some revolutionary theory about how their plight can be changed overnight. We always talk in concrete terms and repeat constantly that the road to success is long and hard, and though they may never see the end of the struggle their children's children might. It may take us months and even years to convince one particular set of villagers to come and join us. But the test is whether or not they tell the Portuguese we have been to their village. If they don't, then we know they are listening.'

Mesticos and *assimilados* were even more difficult to recruit than peasants. 'The others have to mull theories of revolutions around in their heads or, having bitten off a piece of the good life, they are more difficult to convince,' said Savimbi. 'Once you've convinced a peasant, he will not be divided in his loyalty. You've written on a clean sheet of paper.'

During the Congress a courier arrived from Zone Zero to report a Portuguese attack on the camp on 8 August. One of UNITA's representatives in Switzerland, Francisco Talanga, had been killed. The delegates observed a minute's silence, and as they lifted their bowed heads to prepare to elect a new Political Bureau and 24-member Central Committee Savimbi told them: 'Many of us will fall before this war is over. The struggle must go on. A military struggle is also a political one.'

Later, on his way out of Angola, Dash reached the place where Talanga had died. The grey-barked trees were splintered and broken from the firefight, and on the eastern edge of the camp was a circular mound of burnt wood and ashes marking the remains of the hut Talanga had been using when he was killed. It was a custom to burn the hut of a dead man.

The attack by an élite airborne commando unit of Portuguese and African troops had come at 8 a.m. as Talanga sat reading outside his hut. The African soldiers captured him and dragged him some 15 metres from the hut, while the four guerrillas on duty in the camp harassed them with gunfire from the edge of a clearing. Then they shot Talanga through the side before retreating to a field where helicopters pulled them out. The UNITA men tried to staunch Talanga's bleeding but he died in about 10 minutes without uttering a word.

A 20-minute walk away from the camp was a rectangular mound of dark grey sand without a headstone in a cool, tree-shaded glade. Joseph N'Dele, UNITA's other representative in Switzerland, stood with Dash before the grave and said: 'When we were coming in together, Talanga told me he was tired of Europe, where he had lived most of his adult life. He said this time he wanted to stay in Angola.'

*   *   *

After the Congress, Dash walked with Savimbi to the Benguela Railway. From behind bushes they watched a small green armoured rail car with six soldiers aboard scoot past. It was followed by a two-engined freight train with about 30 wagons, including two for passengers. Soldiers could be seen walking around the inside of the passenger wagons.

'They use two engines on the trains,' said Savimbi, 'so the trains can stop completely and go into reverse if they hear gunfire from the armoured car. But in the four minutes between the armoured car passing and the train arriving we can cut the line so the armoured car cannot back up to harass us.' UNITA did not attack freight trains, he said, only troop trains which provided ammunition and weapons. They were tougher to attack because they had two larger twelve-man armoured cars, one in front and one at the back of the train.

While waiting for the train, Savimbi pointed out a small culvert that ran underneath the tracks. There were hundreds along the railroad so that it would not be washed away during the rains. When UNITA blew-up culverts it took the Portuguese a week to repair one. 'The railroad is very vulnerable,' said Savimbi. 'We can make it unusable at any time we wish.' But UNITA had refrained from hitting the railway since 1967 because of the negative way in which Zambia had reacted. The restraint paid off because the Zambian government was again allowing UNITA people to pass freely through Zambia on their way in and out of Angola.

However, UNITA soldiers and peasants who lived near the line had begun to argue that the Portuguese were using taxes from the railroad to buy arms to shoot Angolans. Although it had been a political decision not to destroy the railway track (as opposed to military trains), Savimbi said military considerations were beginning to overtake the political one. 'The railroad must be destroyed. I can see no other way,' he told Dash.

After the train had passed, Savimbi and his guerrillas strode with Dash onto the track to take photos at kilometre marker 906, the distance from the railway's terminal at the Atlantic port of Lobito. After two minutes they took off into the forest at speed.

*   *   *

UNITA had four hospitals and ten elementary schools in Freeland Angola at the time of Dash's visit. The principal of one of the schools, Captain Rodrigues Wandalika, showed Dash round his school, which was built of grass huts beneath the trees. There were small two-bed dormitory huts arranged in straight lines. In the centre of the school grounds was a long, one-roomed schoolhouse: inside were log benches, a teacher's desk made from poles lashed together with strips of bark, and two ink-blackened boards on tripods. On the desk was a Portuguese elementary textbook entitled *Caminhos Portugueses* (Portuguese Paths).

'We reinterpret the book for the children,' said Wandalika. 'All we have to do is point out to them how the Africans in the book are portrayed as inferior to the whites – the pictures say the rest.' On page 146 was a photo of a smiling black Angolan wearing a top hat and tails, with his left chest bedecked with good citizenship medals. The man, Luis Gomes Sambo, an Angolan musician who lived from 1874 to 1946, was famous for playing Portuguese folk music. Under his photo was the caption *Um Homen Notavel de Angola* (a notable man of Angola). A large *X* and the word *nao* (no) was pencilled over the picture. 'He was an Angolan Uncle Tom,' said Jorge Sangumba, who had travelled from London to attend the Third Congress. 'The Portuguese try to make an African believe that he is a Portuguese, and with some of us they have succeeded.'

Near Wandalika's school was one of the hospitals. It had four long wards in huts made of dry yellow grass. A nine-year-old boy lay on a bed of rushes with a huge bump of gauze covering his mouth. The hospital director, Garcia Vinuko, lifted the gauze to show where the boy's upper palate, swollen with pus, filled his mouth and pushed his teeth out horizontally. He had been like that for three months after breaking his jaw. Vinuko had been treating him with UNITA's limited range of drugs, but the swelling had not gone down. The boy was being fed a watery maize gruel which was being forced between his gums with a syringe. Vinuko said he would die a slow and painful death.

There were four recent amputees in the hospital. One was a 23-year-old female guerrilla, Desiana Mussole, whose left foot had been amputated in 1969. Her right hand was withered and closed, paralysed by a bullet that cut a nerve in her right arm. It had taken the guerrillas four days to carry her to the hospital in a *kipoia*, an African palanquin, after she was wounded. 'The left foot was gangrenous and I could just pull the flesh off,' said Vinuko, who amputated the foot and cauterized the stump to stop the bleeding. 'She didn't scream. She was unconscious. Those who are conscious when we have to cut off a leg scream for five or six hours after the operation.' Nearly all the operations were done without anaesthetics.

*   *   *

Dash noted Savimbi's Maoist orientation towards capturing the countryside by converting the peasantry and isolating the cities; conversely, the UNITA leader considered backing that had been given by the Soviet Union to Neto to be paternalistic and demanding of allegiance in power-bloc politics.

Savimbi declined to estimate the number of people under his control, but he said of the exaggerated claims made by all the Angolan liberation movements: 'If all three groups claimed to control a third of the country (as they did), the war with the Portuguese would be over by now and we would be fighting it out among ourselves.' In his ten weeks and 1,300 kilometres of walking Dash counted 600 guerrillas and 5,000 peasants, but noted that he had not been in all UNITA's operational areas. He had been told by respected 'informed sources' in the US that UNITA operated among the Ovimbundu because this was Savimbi's tribe: the entire top leadership was Ovimbundu, and since Savimbi's movement was a tribal organisation it could not expect to draw support from other tribes. 'I found this to be the stereotyped linear vision with which so many African "experts" treat Africa,' wrote Dash, who accepted Savimbi's claim that UNITA was working to eradicate tribalism. The American journalist reported that UNITA's bases were not among the Ovimbundu but among the Nganguela, Chokwe and Lunda people of eastern Angola. As well as N'Zau Puna, Savimbi's number two and a Woyo from Cabinda, many others in UNITA's top leadership were non-Ovimbundu.

As the *Washington Post* man prepared to leave UNITA's central bases on his long trek back to the Zambian border, Savimbi told him: 'We are used to the charges of tribalism, but all we have ever said to those who make the charges is "Come and see for yourself".'

*   *   *

UNITA reported a number of successes in small attacks on Portuguese posts in early 1974, but the publication of a book on 22 February did more in one stroke to damage the Portuguese in Angola than the three liberation movements had achieved between them in more than a decade of struggle.

9

A Coup in Portugal
1974

'Angola e nossa. Angola e Portugal.' ('Angola is ours. Angola is Portugal'.) – A Portuguese patriotic song in the days when Angola was a colony.

* * *

General Antonio de Spinola was known as an arrogant, hardline Portuguese Army officer who sported a monocle and carried a swagger stick during his tour of duty in Angola from 1961 to 1964, directing offensives against the FNLA and MPLA.

It therefore came as a surprise to Angolans when Spinola, who had risen to Deputy Commander of the Army, published a book on 22 February 1974 which was to cause an upheaval in Portugal and its overseas territories. *Portugal and the Future* was a slim volume which angered the 48-year-old dictatorship and the most reactionary of the military hierarchy.[1] Two arguments in particular caused offence. First, Spinola said that there must be free debate within Portugal on all issues, which amounted to a call for parliamentary democracy. Second, he affirmed that Portugal faced certain defeat if it tried to win the wars against insurgents only by military means.

Although he had taken an uncompromisingly tough stand in Angola and become a military hero, Spinola was conditioned for his about-turn during his time from 1968 to 1973 as commander of Portuguese forces in Guinea-Bissau. Faced there by the most effective of the anti-colonial armies in Portugal's territories, Amilcar Cabral's PAIGC (African

Party for the Independence of Guinea and Cape Verde), Spinola took an unorthodox line and introduced a degree of local political autonomy. By the time of the publication of his book, military expenditure on the war in the colonies was absorbing 50 per cent of Portugal's budget. He said the proportion would continue to rise and lead to grave problems: 'The Portuguese economy must be adapted in order to be able to survive in the [European] common market conditions. The nation's survival also implies, in the military sphere, the quick establishment of peace.' The response of the dictator, Prime Minister Caetano, was to dismiss both Spinola and the Chief of Staff, General Francisco da Costa Gomes, who sympathised with Spinola's views. But this could not prevent an enthusiastic public response to the myth-shattering *Portugal and the Future*: its first two editions of 50,000 were a sell-out, but a third edition was banned.

The dismissals of Spinola and Costa Gomes strengthened the Movement of the Armed Forces (MFA), a clandestine group of career officers formed in August 1973 to protest against the lowering of standards at Portugal's Military Academy. With the unpopularity of the overseas wars, draft dodging had increased dramatically, and by 1973 only 72 cadets were attending the 423-place Military Academy.[2] The MFA soon widened the scope of its dissent and plunged into criticism of the dictatorship's politics and of the wars in the overseas territories. 'We must end, once and for all, this damned colonial war, which is consuming everything, including the dignity of military professionals of a civilised nation,' said the dissident officers.[3]

On 25 April 1974 the MFA staged a coup and overthrew the government with the loss of only five lives. Prime Minister Caetano and other politicians closely associated with the dictatorship were sent into exile, first in Madeira and then Brazil. With the end of almost half a century of fascist-style nationalism, barracks commanders were arrested and the government radio and television stations seized. Red carnations stuck into the barrels of soldiers' rifles became the symbol of the coup as enthusiastic citizens gave flowers to patrolling soldiers. Spinola became the new

President of Portugal at the head of a Junta of National Salvation.

The significance of the Portuguese coup was not immediately clear in Angola which, paradoxically, was on the crest of an economic boom. A record 6.25 million tonnes of iron ore were exported from the Cassinga mines in 1973. Coffee exports in 1973 reached a new record of $US 175 million, but were surpassed for the first time by oil, from the new Cabinda fields, as the number one export earner. Industrial output in the year rose by 26.5 per cent, and Angola had a record trade surplus for 1973 of $US 235 million. Angola's internal airline celebrated prosperity by ordering three Boeing Advanced 737-200s. As the coup was taking place, Angola's national brewery, Cuca, was winning a gold medal at the Brussels international brewery exhibition and Luanda Golf Club's new course in the suburb of Corimba-Belas was officially opened.[4]

The Governor-General of Angola, Santos e Castro, was dismissed and replaced temporarily by his constitutional deputy, the Secretary-General, Lt.-Col. Soares Carneiro, until a leftist Vice-Admiral, Rosa Coutinho, took over a few weeks later on a permanent basis.

Spinola had not argued in his book for independence for Angola and the other overseas territories. He envisioned a 'Lusitanian Federation' linking the territories and the former Portuguese colony of Brazil with metropolitan Portugal: each federal component would be autonomous, but there would be specific ties for mutual benefit under a common flag and language. However, the younger MFA officers wanted to give independence to the overseas territories. They recognised the extent to which Portugal's African wars, particularly in Guinea-Bissau and Mozambique, had drained the country's spirit and resources. Some 11,000 Portuguese soldiers had been killed and 30,000 disabled in more than a decade of conflicts. Crippled economically by the costs of its overseas wars, tiny Portugal was running a 400-million-dollar-a-year trade deficit, experiencing Europe's highest rate of inflation at 23 per cent, and had lost so many people abroad that its population had been reduced from more than 10 million at the beginning of the 1960s to only 8.6 million. Paris became the second-largest Portuguese city in the world, with more than 600,000 emigrés. Sabotage by anti-war groups at home had increased so significantly that Caetano had given the political police powers to detain people without charge.[5]

At the beginning of May 1974 General Costa Gomes flew into Luanda and announced that the Angolan nationalist groups would be accepted as legitimate political parties as soon as they stopped fighting. The Portuguese said that on 3 May UNITA had killed 34 African civilians in three attacks in Moxico Province, and in another attack on 6 May had killed six Portuguese soldiers and wounded 14.[6]

The pro-independence views of the younger officers gradually overrode Spinola's federationist sentiments. In June the new Portuguese régime lurched sharply to the left when the radical wing of the MFA managed to have their candidate, Vasco Goncalves, appointed as Prime Minister. On 27 July Spinola proclaimed the right of Mozambique, Guinea-Bissau and Angola to independence: a few weeks later he resigned and was replaced as President by General Costa Gomes.

In Angola the real problem became how to negotiate an orderly transfer to African rule. The way forward was comparatively simple in Guinea-Bissau and Mozambique, which became independent in September 1974 and June 1975 respectively, because in each country there was only one effective liberation movement with which to negotiate. In Angola there were three. On 19 May the Portuguese commander of the 50,000 troops in Angola suspended all military operations to allow the guerrillas to emerge peacefully into the open in the hope that a ceasefire could be agreed. At the same time 1,200 political prisoners were released from Angola's notorious São Nicolau penal colony in the desert north of Mocamedes.

Savimbi was the first liberation movement leader to take advantage of the suspension of offensive actions by the Portuguese Army. Through a Catholic priest, Father Antonio de Araújo Oliveira, UNITA supporters released from São Nicolau had re-established contact with the movement. In late May UNITA's Central Committee met with

Father Oliveira near Luso. As a result, the priest arranged a meeting between UNITA and local Portuguese officers which led to a truce on June 17.[7]

This brought down upon Savimbi a storm of abuse from the other movements, though he had sent N'Zau Puna to Lusaka to try to avoid it. Puna appealed to the FNLA and MPLA to form a common front with UNITA to demand that the Portuguese hold elections in Angola, and he told correspondents in the Zambian capital: 'Let us emphasise the fighting against Portugal and after the liberation of Angola let the people choose which political programme they prefer.'[8] The need for some kind of front between the rival movements and for elections were from now onwards to become Savimbi's constant themes.

The FNLA said Savimbi's early move to suspend hostilities was an act of high treason: he was described as a 'vile creature of colonialism'.[9] But the most damaging attack was launched in *Afrique-Asie*, a pro-MPLA, Paris-based magazine. It published four documents purporting to be letters exchanged between Savimbi and the Portuguese military prior to the attempted MPLA-FNLA merger of December 1972.[10] *Afrique-Asie* noted the Portuguese-UNITA ceasefire of 17 June and sneered at the Portuguese Army Chief of Staff in Lisbon, who said at the time: 'Of the three freedom fighting forces, UNITA put up the fiercest fight in the east.' But, said *Afrique-Asie*, the documents it had obtained were evidence that Savimbi had, at least since 1972, been an agent of the Portuguese.

The letters demonstrating his treason concerned joint UNITA-Portuguese plans to identify and attack MPLA and FNLA bases; requests from UNITA to the Portuguese for ammunition; and a request for a medical examination for Savimbi for suspected heart and liver trouble. The contacts between the two sides were made through a pair of Portuguese timber traders. In one letter, dated 26 September 1972, to General Luz Cunha, the newly appointed Commander-in-Chief of the Portuguese Armed Forces in Angola, Savimbi was alleged to have written: 'I ask your Excellencies [the letter was addressed through General Bethencourt Rodrigues, commander of the Eastern military zone] to supply me with at least 1,500 7.62mm calibre bullets, because our actions against the FNLA always involve the use of these arms . . . I cancel my demand for hand grenades, because we have enough for the time being.' Savimbi requested commando camouflage uniforms for N'Zau Puna and himself. He also asked for free passage for his forces along the Luanguinga River in south-east Angola to Zambia, where UNITA had attacked external MPLA camps in April and May 1972.

A letter to Savimbi from Lt.-Col. Ramires de Oliveira, a senior Portuguese commander in the Eastern zone, dated 4 November 1972, said: 'The national authorities agree that in this contingency (the achieving of an MPLA-FNLA agreement) the most worthwhile activity for UNITA is to keep the region of the High Lungue Bungu [the UNITA base area] out of the war and to strengthen its co-operation with our forces. It is our opinion that the destruction of the MPLA's bases outside this country is of extreme importance.'

There was no joy for Savimbi on the completely free use of the Luanguinga River corridor. Oliveira wrote: 'The secret character of these contacts [between the Portuguese military authorities and UNITA] unfortunately involves certain inconveniences. One is that it is impossible to give a general authorisation for the use of the corridor . . . Each time it is to be used, the [Portuguese] command must be notified so that it can send our troops away from the region on some pretext for the necessary period. If this is not done it is impossible to ensure your safety in using the corridor.'

UNITA denounced the letters as forgeries and demanded the formation of an international commission of inquiry, on which would be represented the UN, the OAU, the MPLA, the FNLA and the Portuguese Government, to determine their origin.[11] Nothing came of the demand by UNITA, which said the forgeries were an attack on the only movement which had fought within Angola by those 'who had never grasped the feasibility of fighting inside'.[12] The forgeries, if that is what they were, may have been carried out because UNITA's secure bases blocked the passage between the MPLA's increasingly unsuccessful eastern operational area and its traditional centre of resistance to the north-east of Luanda.[13]

Savimbi noted that before the 25 April coup in Portugal, *Afrique-Asie* and other 'progressive' and liberal news media in Europe had dismissed UNITA as an insignificant, ultra-radical, Maoist movement. But now, because these same organisations could no longer deny UNITA's popular base of support, they had moved to re-label it as a 'moderate or reactionary movement in possible collaboration with the Portuguese'.[14]

But the most important reason for the forgeries, said Savimbi, was to cover up the MPLA's debilitating internal difficulties: 'tribal antagonisms, rifts between leadership based outside and cadres pressing to have the headquarters moved inside, executions without trials and no real participation of the life of the organisation in the liberated areas, differences in standards of living among militants, cadres and leaders'. Confirmation of the MPLA's divisions and fratricide emerged in July 1973 when Daniel Chipenda, commander of the MPLA's 'Eastern Front', publicly denounced the common use of executions without trial from 1967 onwards to eliminate dissent within the MPLA.[15]

Most commentators were unable to reach firm conclusions about the truth or falsehood of the *Afrique-Asie* allegations. Some degree of Portuguese-UNITA collaboration against the MPLA cannot be ruled out, given the history of UNITA-MPLA rivalry and Savimbi's anger at being excluded from the 1972 MPLA-FNLA merger into the CSLA. However, the MPLA itself was not averse to collaboration with the Portuguese. The hatred between competing MPLA and FNLA forces in the Dembos forests, north-east of Luanda, was so intense that MPLA informers often disclosed FNLA positions and let the Portuguese wipe out FNLA units, according to Portuguese officers.[16] And in 1972, UNITA bitterly noted, the MPLA successfully sought permission from the Portuguese for Agostinho Neto's mother to leave Angola to see her son in Italy at a time when Savimbi's father, Loth, languished in jail.[17]

Lucio Lara claims that the MPLA has copies of the original exchange of correspondence between Savimbi and the

Portuguese, but he has never produced them publicly. 'He can't produce them because they don't exist,' says Savimbi.[18]

Co-operation between the Portuguese military and UNITA, if it existed at all, could only have been limited, for between 1972 and the signing of the 17 June 1974 truce UNITA communiqués listed many soldiers and key officers killed in fighting. Among the last recorded UNITA deaths in action against the Portuguese were those of Privates Yeta and Kavwanda in an attack on barracks at Luando in January 1974: UNITA claimed that in the attack 60 enemy troops 'were put out of combat'.[19]

In a tragedy unconnected directly with the fighting, Savimbi lost his highly regarded military Chief of Staff, Samuel 'Kafundanga' Chingunji, at the beginning of 1974. On one of his arms-buying trips into Zambia, Kafundanga caught cerebral malaria and died there.

Discounting MPLA allegations of collaboration between Savimbi and the Portuguese, the OAU gave UNITA official recognition, putting it on a par in black African eyes with the FNLA and MPLA. UNITA's biggest diplomatic triumph thus far was achieved at the eleventh OAU heads of state summit meeting on 12–15 June 1974 at Mogadishu, where the movement was given an initial OAU grant of $US 32,000.

*　　*　　*

Savimbi justified his truce with the Portuguese on the grounds that UNITA's leadership, based entirely inside Angola, needed to be able to launch the kind of preliminary talks that MPLA leaders, all based outside Angola, had already begun with the Portuguese in Belgium and Canada.[20] A UNITA statement said: 'UNITA did not sign a ceasefire with the Portuguese Armed Forces. A "truce", or, rather, suspension of military hostilities, was signed which enabled us to expand deeply into the country. Other liberation movements must begin entering Angola and actually organising and mobilising the people rather than losing time in neighbouring countries squabbling for leadership positions.'[21]

Savimbi convened UNITA's annual conference for 1974 at

a forest site near the Benguela Railway from 16 to 19 July. The conference called for the immediate formation of a broad National Democratic Liberation Front of all three movements to negotiate for independence. Stressing the need for reconciliation between the nationalists, the conference said UNITA would not negotiate separately with the Portuguese. It also rejected the possibility of serving in a provisional Angolan government without the participation of the MPLA and the FNLA.[22]

Despite their original condemnation of Savimbi's truce with the Portuguese, both the FNLA and the MPLA followed suit.

After the Lisbon coup the FNLA at first stepped up its military activities inside Angola. In June an advance party of 10 Chinese military instructors arrived at the FNLA's Kinkuzu base in Zaire to train an Angolan army of 15,000 men for Holden Roberto.[23]

The FNLA moved soldiers into northern Angola during July and August, brushing aside the Portuguese who were now committed to a passive role standing between the three opposing Angolan forces. By late September the FNLA had established an occupied zone in the north-west in the district of Uige. FNLA commissars toured villages recruiting men for military training at Kinkuzu. Some 60,000 Ovimbundu contract workers, most of them UNITA sympathisers, were expelled from northern coffee plantations to their home areas in central Angola. Harassed by the FNLA, the MPLA and UNITA managed to retain their organisations in the north only in the larger towns such as Carmona. With control of his Bakongo tribal area established, Roberto then signed a ceasefire with the Portuguese in Kinshasa. He sent a 94-man delegation to open an official FNLA headquarters in Luanda and began a political campaign. There the FNLA could count on initial support within a local Bakongo community of 5 to 10 per cent of the capital's African population of nearly 500,000.[24]

The MPLA caused no trouble militarily for the Portuguese. Beset by internal feuds and schisms, the movement had been defunct as an effective fighting force since 1972. Moscow had withdrawn its support.[25]

According to Portuguese intelligence, the MPLA had only a few dozen guerrillas inside Angola at the time of the coup in Lisbon.[26] In the months following the coup the MPLA continued to expend all of its energies on internal squabbling, torture and murder. Three factions were contesting power – Agostinho Neto's 'true' MPLA; the Eastern Revolt, led by Daniel Chipenda; and the Active Revolt, led by former MPLA President Mario de Andrade and his brother, MPLA 'Honorary President' Father Joaquim Pinto de Andrade, who was released by the Portuguese in June 1974 after 14 years in prison for opposition to colonial domination.

Just 16 days after the Portuguese coup, at a time when the MPLA needed to demonstrate unity if it hoped to take power, the Active Revolt accused Agostinho Neto of arbitrary and undemocratic 'presidentialism'. It blamed the MPLA's political and military decline on insensitive and secret leadership which had inspired fear and cynicism within the movement. From Brazzaville the exiles of the Active Revolt called for a party congress to resolve the leadership issue.[27] Under pressure from Presidents Ngouabi of Congo-Brazzaville, Kaunda of Zambia, Mobutu of Zaire, and Nyerere of Tanzania, all three factions agreed to hold an MPLA congress. On 12 August 1974, 400 delegates gathered at an MPLA military base near Lusaka for the MPLA's first electoral congress in 12 years. There were 165 delegates for the 'true' MPLA, 165 for the Eastern Revolt, and 70 for the Active Revolt.

The Congress was marked by bitter wrangling, and after eleven days Neto and the Andrade brothers walked out with their followers. This left the Eastern Revolt in charge of a rump Congress which proceeded to elect Daniel Chipenda as President of the MPLA. The Neto faction repudiated the result and announced plans to hold its own Congress inside Angola.

Alarmed by the divisions, Ngouabi, Kaunda, Mobutu and Nyerere summoned the leaders of the feuding MPLA factions to Brazzaville from 31 August to 2 September. The factions signed a pact officially reunifying the movement. The presidency reverted to Neto, and Pinto de Andrade and

Chipenda became Vice-Presidents pending another Congress to be held after independence. But the Brazzaville compromise began to fall apart almost immediately. On leaving Brazzaville, both Pinto de Andrade and Chipenda repudiated Neto's leadership, and Chipenda took with him to Zaire two to three thousand Chokwe and Mbunda guerrillas who had been under his command on the eastern front.

From September 12 to 21, just inside Angola from the Zambian border, Neto presided over a conference of 250 of his supporters who elected him MPLA President, along with a Political Bureau and a 35-member Central Committee. As in the past, the leadership were primarily *mesticos* and *assimilados* of Luanda or Kimbundu tribal origin.[28]

Jonas Savimbi accepted Neto as the legitimate leader of the MPLA: 'In UNITA we concluded that Neto was the most representative of the three MPLAs, and we persuaded the FNLA to rally to our position. With three MPLAs it would complicate any negotiations with the Portuguese.'[29] Portugal and the Soviet Union also accepted Neto as the authentic MPLA chief and on 21 October the Portuguese signed a ceasefire with Neto.[30] The ceremony took place at a temporary camp 70 kilometres inside Angola from the Zambian border, but Savimbi was quick to note that Neto had negotiated beforehand with the Portuguese at places outside Angola, indicative of his lack of a secure internal military base. 'Neto had to be flown in by helicopter from Lusaka to sign the agreement in Angola,' said Savimbi.[31]

* * *

Though Neto was now established in many people's eyes as the MPLA leader, the legacy of division would plague his movement into the future. Kenneth Kaunda had become particularly disillusioned by the MPLA. He had given the movement camps in western Zambia and near Lusaka, but from the early 1970s he had witnessed the rapid rundown of its fight against the Portuguese and the development of the bitter and bloody struggle between its factions on Zambian soil.

Zambian intelligence told Kaunda during the MPLA Congress in August that 12 to 15 Chipenda supporters had been executed in one of the distant camps in western Zambia. Fighting and killing between the factions were not unusual, and Lusaka residents remember one particularly big infantry and light artillery duel at the camp outside Lusaka in 1974. But the manner of these particular executions badly upset Kaunda. Five-sided wooden frames had been fitted to the heads of the victims and tightened very gradually until their skulls cracked. Kaunda privately vowed that Neto would never again set foot on Zambian soil.[32] And although Kaunda was soon afterwards one of the African leaders involved in the Brazzaville compromise, he refused Neto's request to return on his plane from Brazzaville to Lusaka.[33]

A rift had opened up between the MPLA and Kaunda which would be crucial to the subsequent shape of events in Angola.

10

Agreement on Independence
1974–75

Following the settlement of the MPLA's internal troubles and the signing of the Portugal-MPLA ceasefire, Jonas Savimbi launched a major political initiative to achieve agreement on Angola's independence between Lisbon and the three liberation movements.

He convened a conference of UNITA from 26 to 29 October 1974 which endorsed his proposal that the movement work towards the formation of a united front – though not a unified party – with the MPLA and the FNLA. The 650 delegates gathered at Cangumbe, on the Benguela Railway; they agreed that Savimbi should embark upon a diplomatic tour of black African states to meet heads of state, and also Neto and Roberto, as part of the effort to forge the front.[1]

The Governor-General, Vice-Admiral Coutinho, seemed to endorse the UNITA initiative when he arrived in Cangumbe on the second day of the conference to meet Savimbi for the first time. Photographs of the time show Coutinho, a stocky man with thick hairy arms in white uniform, smiling and shaking hands with a bespectacled and bereted Savimbi carrying a hand-carved ebony and ivory walking stick.[2]

However, despite Coutinho's presence, the conference rejected participation by UNITA in an Angolan transitional government under terms Lisbon had offered two months earlier. Portugal's proposals were that the transitional government include – as well as UNITA, the FNLA and the MPLA – representatives of 50 or so political and ethnic groups which had sprung up after the Lisbon coup, including some representing Angola's half million-strong white population. These proposals, said the Portuguese, would pave the way to free elections after about two years.[3]

In stressing the need for reconciliation between the nationalist movements, UNITA said it would neither negotiate separately with the Portuguese, nor would it serve in a provisional government without the participation of the FNLA and the MPLA. The Portuguese proposals were dismissed also by the MPLA and FNLA. But they alarmed some 'ultras' among Luanda's whites so greatly that when MPLA militants in the *musseques* began attacking white shopkeepers and murdered a white taxi driver, white vigilantes retaliated. In the pillage that followed more than 50 people were killed. Within a few weeks another 40 people died in new MPLA–FNLA clashes, and in early August more than 50,000 Africans left the *musseques* for the comparative safety of the countryside.[4]

On Friday 15 November 1974 Savimbi left to promote his initiative for three-party unity. He flew into Lusaka with a 20-man delegation to see Kaunda for the first time since 1967, and he was given an official greeting at the airport by Zambia's Deputy Foreign Minister Greenwood Silwizya. Savimbi said on arrival that Angolans were tired of the liberation movements' petty differences: the movements had no right to delay independence for the people. Emphasising that the FNLA, the MPLA and UNITA had to work together to speed up the decolonisation process, he said: 'There is a great and urgent need for us to unite . . . The time for accusations and counter-accusations is gone.'[5]

As Savimbi arrived in Lusaka yet another wave of violence broke out in Luanda, leaving more than 100 dead. An FNLA patrol detained and handed over to the Portuguese military a white carpenter who was said to have shot dead two Africans attacking his shop. Gangs wearing MPLA badges attacked FNLA positions, drove whites out of the suburb of Catambor and burned their houses: Lucio Lara condemned the attacks and dissociated the MPLA leadership from the violence.[6]

On 17 November Savimbi held several hours of talks with

Kaunda in one of the ornate drawing rooms at State House, Lusaka, formerly the residence of British governor-generals. That Sunday evening he saw Kaunda off on an official visit to the Soviet Union, having secured the Zambian leader's commitment to promote unity among the liberation movements; to help secure black Africa's backing for early Angolan independence; and, through diplomatic channels, to ensure co-operation from the Portuguese. Kaunda seemed already to have received a message from Lisbon, because the following day Savimbi said that Portugal's military government would welcome an FNLA-MPLA-UNITA coalition as a helpful development in bringing a peaceful end to the colonial era.[7]

Now Savimbi was ready to lock in one of the first big pieces in the jigsaw puzzle that he hoped would lead to elections and independence for Angola. After a meeting with OAU officials in Lusaka, he flew to Zaire where he had meetings with President Mobutu Sese Seko and with the man he had fallen out with more than 10 years earlier, Holden Roberto. On 25 November UNITA and the FNLA signed a reconciliation agreement: Savimbi and Roberto were photographed walking hand in hand through one of the ministries in Kinshasa, Savimbi smiling and Roberto impassive and mask-like behind his habitual dark glasses. Savimbi told Roberto he now intended seeking reconciliation between UNITA and the MPLA and that an FNLA-MPLA agreement would also be necessary before serious negotiations could begin with Portugal.[8]

Savimbi next travelled to Abidjan to obtain backing from Ivory Coast President Felix Houphouet-Boigny. He returned to Lusaka to prepare for a meeting, arranged by Zambia and Tanzania, with Agostinho Neto. The fact that Zambia and Tanzania had persuaded Neto to talk was good news for the UNITA leader. Two months earlier Neto had refused to consider any conversation with UNITA, despite pressure from several African nations. Of the planned meeting with the MPLA President, Savimbi said: 'As we are bound to work together to form a new government in Angola, we must cease attacking each other and mobilise the people for freedom. We want to prepare the ground for

talks with the Portuguese so that we go to meet them not as
rivals but as equals.'

Julius Nyerere was in Lusaka for talks with Kaunda,
ostensibly on the situation in the rebel British colony
of Rhodesia, and on 7 December Savimbi flew with the
Tanzanian leader to Dar-es-Salaam, where Neto maintained
his headquarters. On 8 December Savimbi began two days
of talks with his bitter adversary, whom he had last met
more than ten years earlier in Brazzaville when Neto tried to
persuade him to become Foreign Secretary of the MPLA
after his defection from the FNLA.[9] Details of the talks
were not revealed, but Savimbi said afterwards: 'It was
really a brotherly meeting. The spirit of the talks was
encouraging.'[10]

Savimbi again returned to Lusaka to prepare for momen-
tous developments in the saga. On 15 December he
gathered a corps of international pressmen in the Zambian
capital and flew back to Angola. The plane landed at Luso
where Savimbi had become a folk hero among the townsfolk
during the years of his struggle in the bush. Now Portuguese police and soldiers stayed discreetly in the background as Savimbi went on a motorcade into the centre of
Luso with cheering crowds lining the route and car-horns
sounding. Draped from windows and over cars was the
UNITA flag of red and green with a black cockerel and rising
sun. The celebrations went on into the night, and the
following morning Savimbi flew with the pressmen to his
bush headquarters, 160 kilometres from Luso, aboard the
very Portuguese army helicopters which until earlier that
year had combed the forests in search of the rebel leader.
Some 6,000 people, including about 1,500 soldiers carrying
automatic weapons, greeted Savimbi, who told them about
the journey he had made to the outside world to try to form a
transitional government.

On 18 December Neto flew from Lusaka to Luso and held
talks with Savimbi. Then, after both had held separate talks
with Rosa Coutinho, they embraced and signed an agreement binding them to a common front in negotiations with
the Portuguese to form a transitional government. They
also agreed on the necessity to include the FNLA in the

front. The next day Savimbi and Neto returned together, on a plane provided by the Portuguese military, to Lusaka to report their progress to Kaunda and to prepare for another round of diplomacy to pave the way to independence.[11]

As 1974 reached its close, Savimbi announced that the Portuguese had agreed to convene talks in Portugal from 10 January 1975 with the MPLA, FNLA and UNITA to decide a timetable for independence. 'UNITA, long ignored and attacked by the other movements, has emerged as the binding force in the new nationalist union,' wrote the *Guardian's* Africa correspondent. 'Dr Savimbi in particular is striving to dampen the tribal and personal animosities that divided the liberation movement so deeply during their 13-year war with the Portuguese.'[12]

Praise was showered on Savimbi for his peace-making role. Peter Kayser, then Reuter's Central Africa correspondent, filed to his agency: 'Dr Savimbi has been a tireless traveller over the past few weeks holding meetings with both Dr Neto and Mr Roberto aimed at getting all three movements together around a table and hammering out a common platform for their talks with Portugal. But he declined today (29 Dec 1974) to be described as a mediator – "A mediator is a disinterested party. We [UNITA] are interested. We want independence for Angola."'[13]

Savimbi's labours were not over. Reconciliation between the FNLA and MPLA still had to be achieved. Savimbi suggested three possible places where they could meet to patch up old differences. Roberto picked Mombasa; Neto agreed; and as 1975 began all three liberation movement leaders headed for Kenya.

In Mombasa, with Savimbi's old mentor President Kenyatta in the chair, Roberto, Neto and Savimbi agreed a common position on negotiations with the Portuguese. By the end of their talks, from 3 to 5 January 1975, they had signed the trilateral accord that Savimbi had been seeking since he left Angola seven weeks earlier on his diplomatic marathon. The movements recognised each other as independent parties with equal rights and responsibilities. They also agreed they were not ready to take over Angola immediately and that a period of transition in co-operation with Portugal was necessary before independence.[14]

Savimbi recalled that Kenyatta told the three Angolan leaders at Mombasa: 'In the African tradition, you carried rifles and you fought the Portuguese, but you have also fought each other for many years. Now we have agreed that you will work together in the future, so, in the African tradition, let us plant a tree to symbolise your friendship.' According to Savimbi, Neto argued that planting a tree would have no significance for his life because Kenyatta was a reactionary. 'But Kenyatta forced us to do it anyway, and we planted the tree, and he said that every time we came back to Mombasa we would have to water it and cement our peace for ever. But Neto said "I'm not going back to Mombasa", and he left.'[15]

The nationalists now moved on to the Penina Golf Hotel at Alvor, on Portugal's Algarve coast, to discuss an independence timetable with the Lisbon government. Savimbi was returning to Portugal for the first time since he fled the country 15 years earlier. By 15 January at the Alvor talks the Portuguese and the three Angolan movements had hammered out and signed an agreement which set 11 November 1975 as the date for independence after the holding of elections in October for a Constituent Assembly. Until that date power would be vested in a Portuguese High Commissioner and a transitional government. The FNLA, MPLA and UNITA would have three ministerial posts each in the transitional government, and each would hold the premiership on a rotating basis. The Portuguese would hold three ministerships as well as the High Commissioner's post. The Alvor Agreement also called for the formation of a joint Angolan Defence Force consisting of 8,000 combatants each from UNITA, MPLA and FNLA to be combined initially with a 24,000-strong Portuguese force. Portuguese soldiers in excess of 24,000 would be evacuated from Angola by 30 April 1975. The Portuguese troops designated to the Angolan Defence Force would also eventually be sent home: their evacuation would begin on 1 October 1975, six weeks before independence, and be completed by 29 February 1976, 11 weeks after independence.[16]

Angolans were euphoric when the transitional government was inaugurated in Luanda on 31 January 1975. The path to independence and unity in a multi-party democracy looked smooth. Intensive campaigns for the pre-independence elections began.

But even before the Alvor Agreement was signed moves were well under way which would ensure that independent Angola would be born in blood and chaos.

11

The Plunge into Disaster

1974–1975

In June 1974, two months before Portugal announced that it intended giving independence to Angola, Chinese arms and instructors began arriving in Zaire.

Peking must have been confident that it had picked a winner. When the last of its 120 instructors arrived in August with 450 tonnes of weapons – including AK-47 rifles, rocket-propelled grenades and mortars[1] – the MPLA was in the middle of its bitter, three-way leadership struggle and was militarily impotent. In August the pro-Peking Rumanian President Nicolae Ceausescu sent weapons to the FNLA to supplement the Chinese effort.[2]

China's support was one of the bizarre consequences of the Sino-Soviet dispute. Moscow traditionally had backed the MPLA, so Peking now threw its support behind the FNLA, despite Roberto's strongly proclaimed anti-Communism. The initiative for China's involvement came from President Nyerere of Tanzania. Temporarily disillusioned by the MPLA's murderous infighting and the collapse of its war effort – which enabled the Portuguese to switch troops from Angola to fight in Mozambique – he asked Peking to help the FNLA.[3]

But with independence promised, and with the Chinese building up the FNLA, it would have been asking a lot of the Soviet Union to stay out of the struggle for Angola. Moscow resumed arms aid to its long-standing client, the MPLA, from late August 1974, precisely at the moment when the struggle against the Portuguese was over and preparations were being made for the creation of a sovereign, independent Angola. The generally agreed estimate is that about six million dollars worth of Soviet weapons were given to the MPLA in the last four months of 1974.[4] The first consignments were shipped through Dar-es-Salaam and later through Congo-Brazzaville,[5] from where the weapons were ferried into remote parts of northern Angola by small vessels and light planes.

Agostinho Neto, having emerged as leader of the 'true' MPLA, moved rapidly to establish the movement in the race for the independence prize. Having regained Soviet backing and signed a ceasefire agreement with the Portuguese, Neto opened an MPLA office in early November in Luanda, the party's traditional centre of support, just one month after the FNLA had moved into the capital. Neto had an ally there in the Portuguese Governor-General appointed after the April coup. Vice-Admiral Coutinho was known as the 'Red Admiral' because of his open leftist sympathies with Neto's 'progressive ideas', and he turned a blind eye to the Soviet weapons deliveries.[6]

The *Observer's* correspondent in Luanda wrote: 'Portuguese officials here concede that the MPLA, once thought to be by far the most important of the liberation movements, is not so well supported as they thought. Admiral Rosa Coutinho and most of the other Portuguese officials here appear to be still backing the MPLA, and this has led to suspicions among the other two movements and most of Angola's whites that the administration plans to prop up the MPLA.'[7]

Ominously, there was a number of small clashes in November between FNLA and MPLA supporters in Luanda, presaging later killings. But, despite these clashes, most people were probably still hedging their bets, as evidenced by one African seen at a rally wearing a cloak emblazoned with the names of all three liberation movements.[8]

In December 1974, as Neto and Savimbi embraced after signing their agreement, a large contingent of MPLA officers was flown to the Soviet Union for intensive military training.[9] According to William Schaufele, the then US Under-Secretary of State responsible for Africa, the Soviet arms shipments 'continued up through the January 1975 independence talks among the Portuguese and the three liberation movements which culminated in the Alvor Accord'. These Soviet actions, he said, effectively destroyed the agreements reached at Alvor. And he noted that prior to the Soviet re-arming of the MPLA the US had rejected requests for military support to the FNLA.[10]

Schaufele was not being strictly truthful. As early as July 1974 the CIA had begun to give money to the FNLA without informing the working group – known as the '40 Committee' – of the National Security Council, to whom the CIA was answerable. It also began lobbying in Washington in support of the FNLA. Cash handouts were small at first, 'but enough for word to get around that the CIA was dealing itself into the race. In August the Communist Party of the Soviet Union announced that it considered the MPLA to be the true spokesman of the Angolan people.'[11]

When, with the ink hardly dry on the Alvor Agreement, the 40 Committee itself authorised a covert grant of $US 300,000 to the FNLA – while at the same time rejecting proposed aid of $US 100,000 to UNITA, the movement most often on record as committed to open elections to solve the independence problem – the US government joined the Chinese and Soviets in helping doom democracy in Angola.[12]

*   *   *

The inauguration of the transitional government on 31 January 1975 was the high point of Portugal's efforts to guide its colony towards independence and democracy. From then onwards it was downhill all the way. The government got off to a bad start because neither Savimbi nor Neto nor Roberto opted to serve in it, preferring to concentrate on rallying support and increasing their strength before the elections.

Savimbi and Neto also shared a common problem. The clause in the Alvor Agreement calling for each movement to contribute 8,000 of their men to the integrated Angolan Armed Forces left them embarrassed by their own earlier propaganda, for neither had anything like this number of trained and armed guerrillas. Only the FNLA could respond, though its men were notoriously ill-disciplined. Savimbi recalled that at the time of Alvor he had only 1,500 trained guerrillas. 'We had a lot of people who came to inflate our army without training. We issued arms to them when we could, but they were not real soldiers.'[13]

To bridge the gap Savimbi sought help elsewhere. One man who came to the rescue was President Nyerere. He accepted 120 UNITA soldiers on a nine-month officer training course in Tanzania. Nyerere also gave Savimbi 100 'old Chinese carbines, some mines and quite a big amount of money'.[14] A bigger supply of arms and money came from President Ngouabi of Congo-Brazzaville – a surprising source in view of his channelling of Soviet arms to the MPLA. But Ngouabi was playing a complex game. He was also supporting FLEC (the National Front for the Liberation of Cabinda) in its attempt to make a secessionist takeover of the oil-rich enclave. When Neto protested, Ngouabi said Congo-Brazzaville rejected the MPLA's claimed right to impose itself by force in Cabinda. 'The MPLA protested about the support Ngouabi was giving us,' said Savimbi. 'But he told them we were progressive, and that it was unfortunate that they could not get along with UNITA.'[15]

At the same time as Nyerere accepted the UNITA officers for training, the Chinese told Savimbi they were sending him 70 tonnes of arms which would be delivered through Dar-es-Salaam.

* * *

There were two immediate outcomes of the CIA's $US 300,000 contribution to the FNLA. First, Roberto grew more confident and, second, through its embassies in Luanda and Kinshasa Soviet intelligence learned of the American commitment.[16]

The FNLA bought Luanda's leading daily newspaper, *A Provincia de Angola*, and one of the capital's television stations. Then Roberto began moving more troops from Zaire into areas of northern Angola the FNLA had occupied the previous September. On 23 March 1975 FNLA soldiers attacked MPLA posts in Luanda, and three days later attacked an MPLA training camp at Caxito, to the north-east of Luanda, killing more than 50 recruits. Another 500 FNLA soldiers arrived in Luanda on 30 March, and fighting raged on for days in the Luanda *musseques*.[17]

But the aggression was not one-sided. Daniel Chipenda set up offices in Luanda, still claiming to be the real MPLA. On 13 February 1975 they were attacked by Neto's followers. Fifteen Chipenda followers were killed. Chipenda fled from Luanda and joined the FNLA, taking with him perhaps 3,000 soldiers.[18] Periodic orgies of bloody reprisal killings between the FNLA and MPLA from now onwards made Luanda a terrifying place. One Western journalist estimated that by June 1975 more than 5,000 people had been killed and many others wounded and left homeless.[19]

The FNLA had given the screw of violence another turn. The Soviet Union twisted it even more powerfully. The flow of Soviet arms began again, increasing in parallel with the fighting. The arms went to Brazzaville and were then transported to the coast to be sent southwards by small boats to Angola. In April planes were flying the arms directly into Angola. Finally they began to arrive on Greek, Yugoslav and Soviet ships. By May 1975 the MPLA had large mortars and armoured cars.

General Antonio Silva Cardoso, who took over in January 1975 from Admiral Coutinho in the new post of High Commissioner of Angola after the signing of the Alvor Accord, attempted to stem the flow of Soviet weapons. In April he ordered Portuguese forces to impound a Bristol Britannia aircraft which arrived at Luso carrying 32 tonnes of arms, manifested as medicines, for the MPLA.[20] In the same month the Yugoslav freighter *Postoyna* carrying weapons for the MPLA was turned away from Luanda by General Cardoso. She sailed northwards to the port of Pointe Noire in Congo-Brazzaville. She unloaded, and the armaments were ferried to Angola by smaller boats.[21] In May Cardoso told Savimbi he wanted to attack the MPLA's Massangano camp near Luanda because Cuban military instructors were doing training there: 'He told us he wanted to bomb that fort, so we said "OK, go and do it." But there were pro-Soviets in the Military Council. They warned

Cardoso that if he did it they would tell Lisbon and he would be dismissed. The next day we found him very demoralised. He couldn't do anything, even though he wanted to. Portugal was divided, and its will and that of its soldiers in Angola had virtually collapsed.'[22]

Other African leaders grew alarmed by the escalation of arms deliveries and of FNLA-MPLA violence. They included Kaunda, whose country has a 1,300-kilometre border with Angola. On 19 and 20 April the Zambian President visited Washington and was received by President Ford. While public attention was drawn by a White House speech of Kaunda's, criticising American policy in South Africa, Namibia and Rhodesia, privately he was warning Ford and Henry Kissinger of Soviet intentions in Angola and encouraging them to react effectively and give assistance to UNITA and the FNLA.[23]

Preoccupied with the imminent collapse of the government of South Vietnam, the Ford administration dallied. It saw no need for an urgent diplomatic effort to save the fleeting chance that an election rather than a war would determine who governed Angola. It made no move to work through the OAU and UN, or bilaterally with the Soviet Union, to end the growing arms race.[24] Indeed, to the contrary, it would soon make another contribution to the acceleration of the race.

*   *   *

As the arms race and the killing escalated, the politicking went on. Neto returned to the capital on 4 February 1975, the 14th anniversary of the 1961 uprising. He was greeted by big crowds in the MPLA's fiefdom as he drove in military convoy, with representatives of Cuba and the Soviet Union, to a rally in the São Paulo stadium.

Savimbi timed his first-ever visit to Luanda for 25 April, the anniversary of the Portuguese coup. 'I had been given good receptions in places like Luso and Nova Lisboa, but there we had expected it. We were nervous about how we would be received in Luanda. Because it was an MPLA stronghold it was a test for us, and it was important that everything was successful. The propaganda beforehand was that we would be received only by the whites [who increasingly saw in Savimbi's moderation their best hope for a tranquil Angola in which they would have a place]. That wouldn't have been good. I was not ashamed of support from the whites: I wanted it, but I wanted also the Africans in.'[25]

But tragedy struck Savimbi. His first child, four-year-old Ngongoyavo, became very ill with fever at one of the UNITA camps. Savimbi sent his son to Chissamba mission hospital, near Silva Porto, with Vinona. It was at Chissamba that Savimbi's father, Loth, had died in 1972. The person who had tended Loth in his last hours was a Canadian medical missionary, Dr Betty Bridgman. Now Dr Bridgman watched Ngongoyavo die too, on the evening of 24 April.[26]

Savimbi was faced with one of the most difficult decisions of his life – whether to continue with the entry into Luanda, or go to Chissamba to bury his son. 'Ngongoyavo was a real friend. Often in the bush, with all the difficulties, I used to play with him. Sometimes if Puna and I were depressed, he would understand and say: "You are worrying; let us go and play." The news that he had died was more terrible than I can tell you, because I was gathering all my strength for Luanda. I was in a state of shock and struggled for two hours about my decision. Then I decided I was not going to bury my son. I had to get myself into a mood so that when I addressed the people my face would not show that I was suffering deeply inside. So, it was a difficult day, but I went.'[27]

Before leaving, Savimbi wrote to Dr Bridgman: 'My heart is sore tonight. My son, though still so young, had become a companion to me in the woods. I cannot think that he is gone. We used to talk and we understood one another. I shall miss him. Now, you have seen both my father and my son pass from this life. Thank you for what you have done for them . . . I must go on. The people are expecting me in Luanda, and I cannot let them down. I have dedicated my life to the liberation of my people, and I cannot let personal grief come between me and my people.'[28]

As well as rallying support for UNITA, Savimbi wanted to present himself in Luanda as a peacemaker and to give momentum to the transitional government which was making little progress, spending its time having 'big squabbles about small matters'.[29] On the morning of 25 April he flew to Luanda. The same morning Ngongoyavo was buried in a coffin draped with a UNITA flag next to his grandfather in the ancestral village.

In Luanda Savimbi received an enthusiastic reception in a city regarded by the MPLA's leaders as their exclusive patch. A big crowd greeted him at the airport. Many months later, after the MPLA won total power, Betty Bridgman was imprisoned in Luanda with other missionaries. She recalls MPLA supporters among some of the common criminal inmates talking about Savimbi's visit to the capital: 'They told us of the great crowds of people who were out to see and hear him and cheer him. And every time they discussed it they said that had there been elections there was no doubt that Savimbi would have been chosen as the President of Angola, even by the people of Luanda. They differed on many things, but they were all agreed on the popularity of Savimbi.'[30]

Tragedy continued to stalk Savimbi in Luanda. On the night of 28 April, heavy fighting broke out in the city between the FNLA and the MPLA. It continued for three days, leaving more than 700 people dead and more than 1,000 wounded. Fighting spilled over into the towns in eastern and northern Angola. There was a big exodus of Africans from the *musseques* to their villages in the bush, and foreign consulates began evacuating wives and children as fears grew of all-out civil war.[31]

High Commissioner Cardoso, Neto, Savimbi, and the FNLA's number two, Johnny Eduardo, together toured the *musseques* as the fighting died down. General Cardoso was asked by journalists how the others had reacted: 'Savimbi was shocked. He feels for the people . . . but Neto was cold. After the tour Savimbi turned to the MPLA leader and the FNLA representative and said: "You have no place in Angola." '[32]

A news agency correspondent described the uneasy peace in the *musseques* after the fighting: 'In the townships armed men from FNLA and MPLA parade nightly before their headquarters and their flags fly proudly above the remains of their strong-points. Attempts are being made to control the numbers of armed men in the *musseques*. Each movement is allowed to occupy 15 buildings with no more than 15 armed men (per building). The rest of the MPLA and FNLA troops must stay in barracks . . . The first attempts at promoting a truly national army are being made. When I went on patrol with a mixed group, I saw that troops from the FNLA or the MPLA are never mixed on one patrol, although UNITA soldiers are mixed with troops from the other two. The Portuguese captain in charge told me: "If we go to investigate trouble in an MPLA area, we can send in MPLA and UNITA men. If in an area which supports FNLA, we can send in only FNLA and UNITA. We cannot send MPLA into FNLA country." '[33]

Savimbi was dismayed to discover that the transitional government had made little progress towards preparing for pre-independence elections. A provisional constitution, which according to the Alvor Accord had to be ready by 31 March, had not been drawn up. The electoral law was supposed to be ready by April, but work on it had not even begun. The registration of voters was far behind schedule.[34]

Savimbi said there was no hope of real independence for Angola unless it was brought in by elections. 'We need one flag, one anthem, one army,' he said in a speech. 'How can the Portuguese give us independence with three flags, three anthems and three armies? The liberation movements inside the government are still operating as independent groups. We [all] will have to make concessions so that we can make independence possible and society viable.'[35]

Before leaving Luanda, Savimbi, noting the extent to which China was helping the FNLA at Nyerere's bidding, warned against making Angola an arena for confrontation between the super-powers. He recalled Jomo Kenyatta's old adage: 'When two elephants fight, it is the grass that gets trampled.'[36]

He flew back to Nova Lisboa, and immediately went to the grave at Chissamba to pay homage to his dead son. Then he began again the task of trying to get Angola back on the path of a peaceful transition to independence through elections.

He called for a summit of the liberation movement leaders 'before it is too late'.[37] But despite Savimbi's diplomacy the fighting between the MPLA and the FNLA intensified. Soviet weaponry continued to arrive for the MPLA, which recruited a mercenary force of 3,500 Katangese gendarmes who had fought on behalf of the anti-Soviet Congolese leader Moise Tshombe in his secessionist bid in the 1960s. Only a few months earlier the Katangese had been fighting as mercenaries with the Portuguese against the MPLA and UNITA.

The recruitment of the Katangese incensed the FNLA's patron, President Mobutu, and by mid-May 1,200 Zairean soldiers had moved across the border into Angola with French-made Panhard armoured cars to fight alongside the FNLA. Tens of thousands of Portuguese civilians now began to leave the country as Angola descended deep into civil war.

* * *

Savimbi aimed to get the sides together again at a conciliation conference outside Angola, under the auspices of a respected leader, to reaffirm the agreement made at Alvor. 'UNITA has kept its troops almost entirely outside the violence,' wrote Jane Bergerol, the *Financial Times*' specialist on Angola. 'Dr Savimbi is increasingly seen as the mediator who can bring together the three movements . . . [His] original claim to fame as the single leader to have spent the war entirely inside Angola has been overtaken by his immediate popularity on the hustings. He also impressed African leaders as a man of compromise leading a party of peace.'[38] Even the fiercely pro-MPLA Angola Solidarity Committee in Western Europe conceded that UNITA had stayed out of the fighting.

In a new round of fighting, the capital's São Paulo hospital was abandoned after being hit by rocket fire. Then UNITA itself became a victim of the violence. On 4 June MPLA troops in Luanda killed a big group of young UNITA recruits in what became known, in UNITA folklore, as the Pica-Pau massacre. Estimates of the numbers of dead varied between 50, according to some independent accounts, and 260, according to Savimbi. Bodies were mutilated by the MPLA in acts of 'pure barbarism', said a communiqué of the Armed Forces, whose soldiers helped collect the bodies.[39]

The young men had gathered at UNITA's 'peace offices' in the suburb of Pica-Pau to travel to central Angola to be trained as recruits for UNITA's contribution to the national army. There was speculation that black radicals loyal to Nito Alves, one of the fiercest of the MPLA leaders, had staged the attack independently in an attempt to force Savimbi's hand.[40] Savimbi declined to be intimidated and did not retaliate, although many of his followers demanded reprisals. However, Pica-Pau destroyed any immediate hope the MPLA may have had of persuading UNITA to join them in an alliance against the FNLA. Lucio Lara had been on a special mission in May to Brazzaville to see President Ngouabi: together Lara and Ngouabi asked Prime Minister Abdou Diouf of Senegal to persuade UNITA to join the MPLA, saying Savimbi's movement had no future if it tried to act alone.

'The MPLA in their contacts with us told us we were good people, not reactionaries like the FNLA,' said Savimbi. UNITA declined the invitation because it believed the MPLA was only seeking help to eliminate what it saw as the bigger danger, the FNLA. 'After that they would get rid of us. Everybody was struggling for power. The FNLA also was thinking to use UNITA to destroy MPLA, and after that get rid of UNITA because UNITA was not strong militarily.

'But after the MPLA surrounded our young recruits at Pica-Pau and massacred all 260 of them and cut them into pieces our members were crying for us to attack the MPLA. They advocated that we join the FNLA and crush the MPLA once and for all. But in the leadership we knew that the FNLA, despite its numbers, was a hollow movement. Politically they were weak and badly organised. We said we could not form an alliance with them because they were going to lose. Some of our people accused us of being cowards for refusing to confront the MPLA, but after the massacre even those who argued that the MPLA had something to offer us said it was no longer possible to think of forming a front with them.'[41]

On 6 June – two days after Pica-Pau – Savimbi flew to
Zambia to discuss with Kaunda arrangements for the meeting between the Angolan leaders. Savimbi was in an understandably pessimistic mood. He told reporters in Lusaka
that the promised elections seemed unlikely to take place
before Independence Day. Thousands had died in the
fighting between the MPLA and the FNLA. 'The situation
inside Angola is very difficult. People cannot understand
why they should continue to die even when our independence is near.' It was therefore essential, he said, to restore
the possibility of a peaceful transition to independence.[42]

Nakuru in Kenya's Great Rift Valley was chosen as the site
of the reconciliation meeting. It was to take place from 16
June 1975 under the chairmanship of Kenyan President
Jomo Kenyatta. Before they went, Savimbi and his senior
colleagues had admitted to themselves that the chaos in
Angola meant they could not expect to take immediate
power following an election. So they changed their
approach: 'We said it was absolutely obvious that any
election organised in Angola would be won by UNITA, but
this presented a problem for the FNLA and the MPLA. So
we said let us work out a compromise. Let us say that for five
years, from 1975, we all agree on a coalition government so
that all the animosities can cool down – then only after five
years let us organise elections so that we know who will rule
the country with the support of the people.'[43]

After five days of talks at Nakuru the Angolan leaders
signed a new agreement renouncing force and reaffirming
support for the Alvor Accord, the transitional government
and the creation of a unified army. But there was no support
for Savimbi's proposal that there be a five-year coalition
before the holding of the first election: 'No one wanted to
admit that they had no majority, so they had to say they
wanted elections. But we knew from Nakuru onwards that
no one wanted elections. Neither the FNLA nor the MPLA
could compete with us at the ballot box.'

The Nakuru Agreement said: 'The holding of elections in
Angola is the most adequate form of guaranteeing a peaceful
transference of powers at the moment of independence.' A
new timetable was drawn up to ensure that elections

preceded independence, now less than five months away. Clause 7 of the 7,000-word agreement called for the elections to be held in October and for the constituent assembly to meet at the beginning of the following month before the November 11 Independence Day.

The agreement was signed under the paternal gaze of President Kenyatta, and there was much smiling and embracing in front of international cameramen. Clauses 1 and 3 called for an end to the fighting between Angolans, but they had little impact. In the first few weeks after Nakuru the transitional government drew up a draft constitution and the first 120-man company of an Angolan National Army was formed. But on 9 July the heaviest FNLA-MPLA fighting yet broke out and the MPLA drove the FNLA out of Luanda after three weeks of killing. The British consulate closed in July and an RAF plane was sent to evacuate Britons. Amidst the bloodshed there were bizarre pockets of normality. At weekends people watched the shooting from the end of Luanda Island, as they bathed and fished. And the local press got extraordinarily excited by a letter which had been mailed in Portugal on 25 September 1961 and had finally been delivered . . . to the wrong address.[44]

When the new fighting began Savimbi decided to withdraw his people from the capital, believing that the logic of the MPLA build-up of arms was that they would again be turned heavily on UNITA.

And so, with the FNLA's expulsion from Luanda, and UNITA's decision to leave, the transitional government collapsed. Savimbi was not surprised by the government's failure, but he was nonetheless bitterly disappointed. 'People tended to think that UNITA was naïve to believe that elections really would be held,' he said. 'It was not that. We knew that what was at stake was so big that nobody was prepared to lose the battle. Our philosophy had always been that if we failed, at least we tried. But after eight years of fighting inside Angola with many difficulties we were dismayed by the failure.'[45]

Some 10,000 UNITA supporters prepared to leave Luanda for the central Angolan towns where UNITA's strength was concentrated. They were to travel in a column of 180 trucks. Savimbi obtained from the Portuguese High Commissioner and the MPLA written guarantees of safe conduct for the column.[46] His first instinct was that senior UNITA officials should travel with the column to maintain morale, but he was suspicious of the guarantees and on second thoughts he ordered the leaders to travel by ship and plane.

The truck column moved slowly. On 12 July it reached Dondo, an important bridge-point across the Cuanza River 200 kilometres south-east of Luanda. The bridge was controlled by MPLA troops. According to Savimbi, the MPLA stamped the safe conduct papers and the atmosphere was relaxed. People at the head of the convoy were asked to wait for a few more minutes while other formalities were completed. An ambush had been laid, and suddenly the column was attacked with bazookas and automatic rifles. 'It was a massacre again. Only 12 people reached us in Nova Lisboa to tell us the story. They said it was a dramatic thing they had seen. They had run eastwards from Dondo along the north bank of the Cuanza until they reached a point where they could cross.'[47]

It was impossible to tell how many died at Dondo. Most survivors trekked directly to their villages and towns in the centre and south. But it increased pressure on Savimbi to declare war. 'People were saying after Pica-Pau and Dondo that it was impossible to say the MPLA was not at war with us. But I told them to hold on. We needed to be cool because I was still consulting with my friends among the African heads of state. We were still waiting for arms from China and Rumania. It was no good committing ourselves to a war with the MPLA unless we were strong enough to fight them and keep them out of our areas. But after Dondo the people were all the time crying for war.'[48]

Elsewhere the FNLA eliminated all remaining MPLA representation in the northern districts of Uige and Zaire. The FNLA accused the Portuguese of backing the MPLA and launched an assault towards Luanda, warning Lisbon's troops not to interfere. On 24 July FNLA troops, led by a former Portuguese anti-guerrilla commando officer, Lt.-Col. Gilberto Santos e Castro, captured Caxito, within 50 kilometres of the capital. The MPLA's Nito Alves declared: 'We are one hundred per cent enemies and can never come to any agreement. Our fight must go on until FNLA is defeated as the American imperialists were in Vietnam.'[49]

The MPLA consolidated its hold in its Kimbundu hinterland. On 24 July and 1 August rival secessionist groups declared the independence of Cabinda, but the MPLA established control despite the protests of President Ngouabi of Congo-Brazzaville.

The OAU, at a bizarre and chaotic heads of state summit in Kampala in late July, chaired by the notorious Idi Amin, deplored the Angolan fighting and asked the Portuguese to assume properly and impartially their responsibility for the future of their colony. The OAU sent a 10-member fact-finding commission to Angola from 10 to 20 October 1975. It presented a report a fortnight later saying that public support was greater for UNITA than either the MPLA or FNLA. The OAU team again called for a ceasefire, the termination of foreign arms deliveries, the cessation of external interference and the establishment of a government of national unity. The MPLA, growing in military confidence, rejected these ideas and also a proposal to create an OAU peace-keeping force.[50]

MPLA, UNITA, and FNLA troops lived very uneasily alongside each other in the centre and south while the fighting escalated in the north. But when, towards the end of July, the FNLA were driven out of Luso by the MPLA, Samuel Chiwale, based in Luso, asked to be allowed to join with the FNLA to crush the MPLA garrison in the little railway town. Savimbi refused permission, but on 30 July the MPLA turned on UNITA and killed 30 of its soldiers at Lucusse, just to the south-east of Luso. Chiwale ordered a UNITA evacuation of the town. 'From there, people said that was the end,'[51] Savimbi recalled. He flew to Lusaka for another meeting with Kaunda. On 3 August, before leaving Zambia, he told reporters of his country's 'grave and tragic' situation and he called on the OAU to intervene and try to establish peace.[52]

*   *   *

On 4 August UNITA entered the war.

After returning from Lusaka, Savimbi spent the early part of the day in Silva Porto working on documents. His personal jet, provided by Kaunda's close friend, Tiny Rowland, chief of the British trading company Lonrho, was waiting on the tarmac at Silva Porto airport. Savimbi was meant to leave again for Lusaka for another meeting with Kaunda at 10 a.m. He was still working at 1 p.m. He had a security guard around his plane, and at 12.30 a section had come to tell him that the MPLA had laid a long ambush behind bushes on one side of the airstrip. 'I was annoyed with my men. I told them they were just trying to create problems and that I wanted restraint. I ordered Mateus Katalayo to go to talk with the Portuguese commander in Silva Porto so that he could advise the MPLA to leave the airstrip. The commander was a good man and he said he would talk to them.

'The MPLA must have discovered that there was contact between UNITA and the Portuguese, because as Katalayo returned into town to report to me the MPLA started shooting at the plane. I heard it and picked up my gun and went in a jeep to the airport. There was firing all over the place, and I was worried about the plane because it had been loaned to me. I ordered one section to push the MPLA back towards their barracks, and they succeeded in less than half an hour. But the MPLA had other soldiers in the town and they too started attacking us. I personally conducted that battle and by 6 p.m. it was all over. While it was on the British pilots got in the plane and flew away.

'We drove the MPLA out of town, and from that day onwards we were in the war, though nobody in the outside world knew immediately.'[53]

Savimbi's jet later returned and took Jeremiah Chitunda, who had been UNITA's Minister of Natural Resources in the transitional government, to Lusaka: there he accused the MPLA of planning to declare unilateral independence on 11 November and said this would solve nothing unless it was supported by the majority of Angolans. Chitunda added: 'We are now in the phase of total war. All hope for a peaceful solution is gone.'[54]

12

Prelude to Independence

1975

There is this turbulent land,
a storehouse of pain and trouble,
confused mother of fear,
Hell in life.
Seventeenth-century Portuguese poem about Angola[1]

*　　*　　*

It was as the civil war grew, through August and September 1975, that I made my first visit to Angola and met Savimbi.

Through that period UNITA controlled the central section in Angola of the Benguela Railway and the MPLA dominated the eastern and western ends. This caused big problems for Savimbi's ally, Kaunda. In 1974 the railway had carried 55 per cent of Zambia's exports, mostly copper, and 45 per cent of its imports.[2] But by mid-August 1975 Zambia was forced to declare *force majeure* (unforeseen circumstances outside one's control excusing fulfilment of contract) on most of its copper exports because traffic on the Benguela Railway had been stopped.[3]

A director of the Benguela Railway, owned by the British company Tanganyika Concessions Ltd, visited both the MPLA and UNITA to see if it was possible to run trains with MPLA armed guards on the MPLA sections and UNITA guards elsewhere. Savimbi ruled it out. 'When we are fighting it will be very difficult to stop soldiers shooting at one another as one group leaves the train and the other boards it,' he said in late September. 'We would very much like to help Zambia and Zaire, but in practical terms I do not see how it could be organised.'[4] But, according to John Stockwell, head of the CIA's new Angola Task Force, Savimbi was under tremendous pressure to get the railway working again by 11 November. 'If Savimbi controlled the railroad by Independence Day Kaunda could rationalise continued support, even recognition,' said Stockwell. 'Otherwise, Kaunda would have to deal with the MPLA.'[5]

There was a lull in the fighting in the first half of October. But it was deceptive. Angola was like a volcano waiting to erupt, with molten lava building up under pressure inside. High Commissioner Silva Cardoso retired in despair to Portugal, exhausted by his efforts to prevent civil war, and was replaced by Commodore Leonel Cardoso. Between 25 September and 12 October three ships docked in Congo-Brazzaville with nearly 1,000 Cuban troops who were immediately flown to Angola to fight with the MPLA.[6] Then, on 26 October, UNITA announced that its people had captured Sa da Bandeira, a provincial capital in the southwest about 250 kilometres north of the Namibian border.[7]

Savimbi arrived in Lusaka on 30 October for one of his periodic consultations with Kaunda and said that on the previous day UNITA forces had taken control of the southern port of Mocamedes, giving UNITA access to the sea.[8] Mocamedes was the third largest port in Angola, after Lobito and Luanda, and Savimbi stressed the significance of its capture: 'Friendly countries know that we have a port through which to get supplies . . . We are going to take things very seriously so that we do not lose it.' He added that some UNITA troops had advanced to within 40 kilometres of Lobito. Savimbi nevertheless continued to argue for talks between the liberation movements. With arms deliveries to each of them escalating, he asked: 'Where are we going to end? We will be the instruments of those who manufacture guns. I will be better for us to become the instruments of our independence, and not the instruments of the killing of our own people.' He was still insistent that the MPLA had started the war, and said that, although he was a Christian, one tenet he could not subscribe to was that which required a believer who had been given a beating to turn the other cheek . . . 'If the MPLA beats me once, I will beat them twice.'[9]

At the beginning of November I returned to Angola to try to discover what had turned the tide in UNITA's favour. Along with several other foreign journalists I was cooped up in an evil-smelling Nova Lisboa hotel which had no running water because the town's pumping plant had stopped working through lack of spare machinery parts.

We were kept waiting by Savimbi until 4 November when we were summoned to his Nova Lisboa headquarters, the mansion of a departed Portuguese industrialist. UNITA intelligence reports from inside Lobito, Savimbi said, showed that MPLA political and military leaders were leaving for Luanda by sea as UNITA troops moved towards the great Atlantic port. UNITA might take Lobito within another two or three days. 'We have a force of 5,000 men and 55 armoured cars advancing on it from three directions.' He said a thrust by 2,000 UNITA soldiers had also resulted in the capture from the MPLA of the town of Cela, about 200 kilometres north of Nova Lisboa. UNITA's thrust therefore seemed to be two-pronged – one along the coastline, and the other parallel, some 250 kilometres inland and already further northwards.

UNITA had found aid to match that supplied by the Soviet Union to the MPLA. However, Savimbi pointed to obvious dangers in the growing scale of the fighting: 'It will be more serious than the Congo (civil war of the early 1960s) if a political solution cannot be found.'[10]

There were no telephone, telex or commercial transport services in central Angola, so on 5 November – six days before Independence – I decided to fly on a UNITA plane the 2,000 kilometres to Lusaka to file a story about the impending fall of Lobito. As we waited at the airport for the plane to refuel, Savimbi was driven up to the terminal in a Range Rover. He leapt out waving a piece of paper: UNITA forces were entering Lobito. UNITA now controlled most of the Benguela Railway, from Lobito on the coast to Luso high on the plateau in the east. Savimbi said a military strategy had to be devised to clear the MPLA from the 300-kilometre eastern stretch between Luso and Teixeira de Sousa, the border town where the railway crosses into Zaire.[11]

I returned again on 7 November to Nova Lisboa where in the central plaza UNITA had felled the statue of Jose Norton de Matos, a former Governor-General in Angola. Norton de Matos was remembered best for his 1921 decree prohibiting the use of native languages in schools.[12]

On 9 November I again flew to Lusaka to telex a pre-independence story. Early on 10 November, the eve of independence, I returned to Nova Lisboa and was invited to join other correspondents on a trip to newly captured Lobito. We flew across the spectacular African escarpment, which plunges dramatically towards the Atlantic, in a Beech-craft plane, one of three aircraft in the UNITA 'airforce'. (The Beechcraft was owned and flown by a Portuguese business-man who lived in Luso. The other planes were Savimbi's Lonrho-supplied jet and a Fokker Friendship of Angolan Airlines which sympathetic Portuguese pilots had flown to the UNITA side after the break up of the transitional government.) We landed at Benguela, on the coast to the south, and were driven by mini-bus the 35 kilometres into Lobito, where we were greeted by the new UNITA 'governor' of Lobito, Jorge Valentim.

Valentim had studied at university in Belgium. A veteran of the movement, he had given invaluable support to Savimbi in the difficult days of transition from the FNLA to UNITA but had not fought inside Angola. He was now back in his home town for the first time in 17 years, and he began by taking us to the little concrete house in the African quarter where he had grown up. It had been stripped of whatever modest furniture it had had, and there were anti-UNITA and anti-Valentim slogans scribbled crudely on the walls from the MPLA's occupancy.

A huge warehouse and bunker in central Lobito had been blasted into ruins by the attacking UNITA forces. The bunker was still burning and there was a sickly sweet smell of rotting human flesh coming from beneath the rubble. Around the battle site were light Soviet-made machine-guns which had been bent almost double in the inferno which had consumed the warehouse. Rockets and mortar casings used by the MPLA in their defence were scattered all around.

A visit to the massive natural harbour showed why UNITA prized it so highly and why the big powers were rumoured to covet it for strategic purposes. A series of low cliffs formed the landward side. On the seaward side it was bounded by a long sand and shingle spit on which the Portuguese had built the beautiful suburb of Restinga. There was only one ship at anchor in the middle of the harbour, where all work had stopped. Of the 200 Portuguese managers, clerks and foremen who had run the port, more than 150 had left Angola and most of the documentation had gone with them. Crates of personal belongings labelled for addresses in Lisbon and Rio de Janeiro stood on the quays at the southern end between the cliffs and the spit: these belongings would never leave. Also stranded, waiting for the Benguela Railway to reopen, were tracked vehicles for the Zambian copper mines and turbines for the great Kariba hydro-electric project on the Zambezi between Rhodesia and Zambia.

The African shanties on the steep hillsides behind Lobito contrasted sharply with the beauties and comforts of Restinga. Here people were living in wooden and corrugated iron shanties. There was no electricity and water had to be drawn from wells. I had not seen these kinds of dwellings inland. I imagined they must be similar to the *musseques* of Luanda, which I had never seen.

UNITA's were not the only soldiers in town. There were also FNLA troops, and many of their officers seemed to be Portuguese. It was not clear where they had come from, and their relationship with UNITA seemed to be uneasy.

There was a kind of manic quality about Jorge Valentim which was faintly disturbing. He told us there had been some looting by the local people after the UNITA takeover, but . . . 'I called a meeting of the population yesterday, and I told them that anyone we find stealing will be shot on the spot, no matter what their colour.'

On that note we returned to Benguela and flew back to Nova Lisboa through towering black anvil-shaped storm clouds. The midnight hour of Independence was approaching fast.

* * *

That same day, 10 November, the Portuguese brought five centuries of colonial rule to a pathetic, whimpering end. The High Commissioner, Leonel Cardoso, and his staff scuttled out of Luanda, leaving their former subjects to shoot things out among themselves.

Cardoso, dressed in the ceremonial uniform of an admiral, appeared before the press at midday in the High Commissioner's palace and read a short statement in which he handed sovereignty to 'the Angolan people'. No Angolans were at the ceremony. The departing High Commissioner rejected any Portuguese responsibility for the situation in the country, but expressed regret that the three liberation movements had been allowed to arm themselves in the run-up to independence. He ended by saying '*Viva Angola. Viva Portugal*'. He got no response.

Cardoso immediately left the palace with his entourage, and under heavy guard went down to the port quarter of San Miguel to fold the red and green Portuguese flag. They drove to a naval base on Luanda Island and the road behind them was sealed off by Portuguese military police while a helicopter hovered overhead. The Portuguese then boarded a waiting convoy of frigates and transports which left the harbour in daylight and stayed just off Luanda until a little before midnight when they weighed anchor and passed out of Angolan territorial waters.[13]

'There is no excuse for the manner in which decolonisation took place, namely a complete abdication by the Portuguese,' lamented the editor of *Angola Report*. 'The already very difficult situation in Angola was damned from the very moment when the provisional government under Rosa Coutinho allowed the movements into Luanda without giving up their arms. People who had no political experience were allowed to play politics with their fingers on the triggers of Kalashnikovs.'[14]

As the Portuguese fleet steamed away, Agostinho Neto, in Luanda, proclaimed a People's Republic of Angola with

himself as first President. A handful of African governments, along with the Soviet Union, Yugoslavia, North
Vietnam and other Communist states, recognised Neto's
administration as the legitimate government of Angola. But
at independence the MPLA was in deep trouble in its
Luanda stronghold. By 10 November an FNLA force from
the north had advanced as far as Quifandongo, just 20
kilometres from Luanda, and was preparing its final push
into the capital.

Meanwhile the coastal UNITA column had moved on far
beyond Lobito and was attacking the port of Novo Redondo,
250 kilometres south of the capital. The inland column had
pressed north of Quibala and was attacking Santa Comba,
just 200 kilometres south of Luanda. And at the eastern end
of the Benguela Railway line a UNITA force was laying
heavy siege to Luso.

In Nova Lisboa heavy firing broke out in the hours before
midnight. Most of it was in celebration. Even a western
television reporter joined in, knocking out all the street
lights in the big boulevard outside the press hotel. But
among the merriment was some fighting between UNITA
and the small FNLA contingent based in the city. At least
one FNLA officer died.

It was enough to dissuade any more than 2,000 people
from attending the midnight independence ceremony in
Nova Lisboa football stadium. At 33 minutes past midnight
a group of African children sang the Portuguese national
anthem as the Portuguese flag fell to the ground. Not a
single Portuguese was present. Then the desultory ceremony ended as a lowly officer in the UNITA military police
took the salute while the UNITA flag was raised. None of the
UNITA leadership was present. Around the city there was
firing everywhere.

13

Independence

1975

Jonas Savimbi began his Independence Day peroration before an audience of 20,000 in Nova Lisboa football stadium
with a ferocious attack on his own soldiers. The firing of the
previous night had stopped only after 12 hours.

'Listen well,' he said. 'If tonight, or at any other time from
now onwards, any UNITA soldier fires a shot without an
order, it will be his last shot . . . if we catch you firing your
gun, you will not move again from that very spot.

'You have no shame. You do not represent the spirit of
FALA but that of bandits. You should not be under the
illusion that a gun is to be used for exerting personal
authority, to steal or to drink . . . We prefer to have two
hundred soldiers who treat the people well, rather than one
million who are thieves and delinquents.

'I felt sickened when I heard the firing. This will only
make the former colonialists happy because they will say it
proves what they have always said, that a black man is
incapable of keeping a gun in his hand without causing
confusion.

'In the forests we survived because we had discipline. We
cannot lose it here. We are going to enforce it here. We
will not have you irresponsible and drunken hoodlums
shooting in the air when other soldiers are suffering at the
war fronts and the people are here to celebrate the decline of
colonialism.'

After berating his soldiers, Savimbi turned on the MPLA,
accusing it of having caused the civil war. He said he was

still willing to talk to Agostinho Neto, and yet again he called for elections to decide Angola's future. 'The day that MPLA decides to consider other liberation movements as patriots, when the MPLA holds the people's interests in its heart, then we will say to MPLA: "Come here brother." While the MPLA goes on thinking that only through Russian arms can they offer an ideology, we will say "no" and we will continue to fight.'

Savimbi announced the renaming of Nova Lisboa (New Lisbon) as Huambo, after a local chief who reigned in the region before the Portuguese established control. Then he launched an attack on the departed Portuguese rulers, now steaming along the West African coast towards Lisbon: 'Admiral Leonel Cardoso fled like a fox. And the only one responsible for the situation that we face today is Portugal. If Portugal had had the firmness to guide the process, today we would not have war. But Portugal wished to decolonise by leaving us here with its godchild named Antonio Agostinho Neto, and today we find ourselves in a civil war.'

Actors entertained the crowd with mocking skits on the former colonialists. Two Africans carried a white *senhor* in a *kipoia* – an African palanquin of netting slung between two poles – which they constantly dropped clumsily: the *senhor*, an African with his face painted white, lost his temper and beat his bearers with his fly whisk as he chased them, which caused great hilarity among the crowd. Elsewhere one man representing the millions of Angolans the Portuguese had sent into slavery in the New World trudged around the stadium with a big bundle on his head and shackles on his feet.

Savimbi spelled out his ideas about 'people-oriented socialism' by saying leaders had to ask what people wanted, rather than dictate what they should have. 'What they want is to live well. They want jobs, schools, sanitation. We depend on the people. From the institutions here they deserve respect, kindness and consideration. The people must be cherished.'

He spoke of an idea that had been agreed – to form a joint UNITA-FNLA government of combat that declared by the MPLA. Due to 'various circumstances' the form of a UNITA-

FNLA government could not yet be announced and, furthermore, Savimbi cautioned: 'When this government comes into being, it will be provisional. It cannot be definitive. Only through general elections, when peace returns to the country, will we be able to decide definitively who will be the leaders of the nation. Anything other than this we cannot accept.'

The distance between the FNLA and UNITA was emphasised by the fact that Roberto's movement celebrated Angolan independence at Ambriz, 700 kilometres north of Nova Lisboa.

At the end of the Nova Lisboa ceremony the UNITA flag was raised again in a repetition of the previous night's low-key event. This time there was loud cheering and whistling. It was time for the celebrations to begin, but first Savimbi ordered his soldiers back to their barracks . . . 'We want to build a big family and tonight we want only civilians singing, eating chicken and dancing in the streets . . . not one soldier. Soldiers who get caught in the streets will be severely punished. Tonight I myself will be the policeman.'

The next day, when all the merry-making was over, Savimbi produced a propaganda coup in the shape of a Cuban prisoner-of-war. Private Samuel Ducentes Rodriguez, a thin, white and frightened 17-year-old, was brought before the press. A Spanish-speaking *New York Times* journalist interpreted. Savimbi told Rodriguez not to be afraid; he was not about to be killed.

Rodriguez said he was from Cuba's Matanza province, and when asked what he was doing in Angola, the boy said: 'I don't know. I don't know how to explain that.' Had his government sent him? – 'No.' Who then? – 'I don't know.'

Rodriguez had a big wound on the left side of his face on which new scar tissue was forming. Asked how he got hurt, he said: 'Some mothers did this to me when I was captured. They attacked me with a stone.'

At that point Savimbi ended the interview and said thousands of Cuban soldiers were now arriving in Luanda with crates of heavy Soviet weapons to fight with the MPLA.

But Cuba's was not the only foreign army busy entering the Angolan war, as I had been finding out.

14

South African Invasion

1975

'If you are a drowning man in a crocodile-filled river and you've just gone under for the third time, you don't question who is pulling you to the bank until you're safely on it.'

Jonas Savimbi, 14 November 1975

* * *

On 1 November 1975, on my second journey into Angola, I was surprised by what I saw as I stepped from Savimbi's Hawker-Siddeley 125 executive jet on to the tarmac at Silva Porto (now renamed Bie by UNITA). Two trucks crossed the parking area towing spick-and-span armoured cars decked in camouflage and with the word 'UNITA' and a crowing cock, UNITA's symbol, painted crudely on the sides in red.

The trucks halted, so I wandered across to one of the armoured cars. In it sat a slight teenage white man with a thin, light brown, scraggy beard. He could almost have been Rodriguez's brother.

A greeting in Portuguese brought no response, so I asked him in English what language he spoke. 'English,' he said – except that the thick guttural accent was a product of southern Africa, not some English country. I asked him where he came from, and he replied grudgingly: 'I am from England.'

I moved to the second armoured car where another young white sat in the driving compartment. He was equally unanimated, but when I asked him where he came from, he said 'I am a mercenary.' Fine, but from which country? – 'I

cannot say.' However, the accent, obviously formed south
of the Orange and Limpopo Rivers, spoke for him.

How long had he been here? – 'Two or three weeks.' Had
he fought as a mercenary before? – 'Yes, in several places.' In
the cabs of the trucks sat three more whites. A polite 'Good
morning' produced from one of them a heavily South
African-accented 'Good morning'.

Before I could ask more questions a fawn Range Rover
drove up and out stepped 'Skip' (see Prologue), accompanied by a tall, flaxen-haired man in khaki shorts and a blue
shirt. The newcomer issued orders in Portuguese to a couple
of UNITA soldiers. Then, turning to English, he courteously
ushered me to the Range Rover and I was driven off to the
luxuries of the former Portuguese Governor's palace.
Again, the accent had been South African.

At Bie on 7 November, during a short stop *en route* to
Huambo, I again saw the flaxen-haired white man with a
group of black and white soldiers gathered round a Panhard
armoured car aboard a road transporter. I was driven away
into town, and when I was brought back again to begin the
second leg of the flight the Panhard was on the ground and
the transporter gone.

It was beginning to look clear what had made Savimbi's
phenomenal advances possible. But two or three armoured
cars whose white drivers declined to confess they were
South African soldiers were insufficient evidence to back up
a story for my international news agency of an invasion of
another country by Pretorian hordes. So I waited and got on
with telling the story of Angola's independence as seen from
UNITA's territory. However, when I flew to Lusaka on 9
November, on board Savimbi's jet, with me was a British
television journalist, Mike Nicholson, who had recently
arrived in Huambo. I told him of my encounters with
mysterious whites and armoured cars.

Mike was a convivial soul. In Lusaka I went home while
Mike, away from his London base, struck up a friendship
with the British pilots of the Lonrho jet over drinks into the
small hours at the Intercontinental Hotel.

The pilots warmed to him, and as a result they invited us
to stay aboard the aircraft after it landed at Huambo early in

the morning of 10 November following our return from Lusaka. There was no jet fuel in Huambo, and since Savimbi had to be flown that day on an urgent pre-independence visit to a neighbouring country, they were heading south to refuel. The pilots said they were sure that what we were about to see would interest us greatly. The conditions were that we agreed not to report directly either the flight or anything we saw or ask the pilots too many questions.

First, we had to persuade a *Newsweek* man who had travelled with us from Lusaka that he needed to go into the centre of Huambo to get his accreditation before he could begin reporting. We helpfully told him where to go and who to see. Then we were off.

The plane had flown some 650 kilometres south over the immense forests and bush of southern Angola before it began to lose height. Now the tree cover was very much thinner: the crowns of the trees did not overlap, they were more stunted and there were stretches of open, sandy soil between each one.

A pilot beckoned me to the flight deck and pointed to a silver river winding through the dry forest. The radio crackled into life and the subsequent conversation showed that the river we were crossing was the Cubango, marking the international frontier between Angola and South African-ruled Namibia. The woman's voice over the radio had the clipped sound of South African English. She was ground control at Rundu, on the south bank of the Cubango, one of the Republic of South Africa's main forward military bases for operations against black guerrillas of SWAPO fighting for Namibia's independence.

We touched down on a runway lined by sand-bagged machine-gun emplacements. Mike and I crouched on the floor of the plane for we had been told to keep our heads down and stay away from the exit door until we were in the air again. The plane taxied through a narrow entrance into a vast tarmacadamed area totally surrounded by a wall of sandbags seven metres high. There we saw the pot of gold at the end of UNITA's rainbow, the explanation of Savimbi's change of military fortunes.

Peeping over the bottom edge of the window, as the pilots

supervised the refuelling and talked on the tarmac to South African officers, we saw that we were at the centre of what could only be Pretoria's military staging post for Angola. Lined up were columns of Panhard armoured cars of the kind I had seen hundreds of kilometres inside Angola: there were white men in the gunnery and driving positions. The Panhards were in too immaculate a condition to have just returned from patrol in the local bush. Their immediate destination was a distant parking area, where we could see waiting Hercules C-130 transport planes in exactly the same camouflage – black and green with other indentification marks obliterated – as I was about to see later that same morning deep inside Angola. Next stop for the C-130s and the Panhards *had* to be Angola.

Soon we were flying back to Huambo. Savimbi's plane had landed, apparently routinely, at one of South Africa's most sensitive military bases. We had been given a view of the heart of the South African operation. It seemed slightly unreal: for some reason best known to themselves, for we never asked them, the pilots had guided us directly to the firmest evidence possible of South Africa's involvement in Angola.

In Huambo we joined up with Mike's camera team and flew by Beechcraft plane to Benguela for an eve-of-independence visit to neighbouring Lobito (as described in Chapter 12). Three interesting sights greeted us which I deliberately did not refer to earlier. As we landed at Benguela we saw a handful of light-haired white soldiers, stripped to the waist in khaki shorts, slip furtively out of sight into a big hanger just to the left of the small airport terminal.

Then, as we were entering the terminal, a Hercules C-130 came in to land. It had exactly the same markings as those we had seen just a few hours earlier in Namibia.

We were hustled into a mini-bus, but as we drove away we passed on the narrow road a Panhard armoured car guarding the approaches to Benguela Airport. Its camouflage paint was the same as that we had seen on Panhards earlier in the day: it was the same also as that I had seen on the Panhards at Bie airport on 1 and 7 November.

The Panhard at Benguela was surrounded by young white soldiers in shorts lolling in the African sun.

Mike's immediate problem was how to obtain television evidence of the South African presence without alerting the South Africans to the fact that they were being filmed. If they discovered it, the consequence would have been confiscation of the film – for the South African invasion was still a secret. The MPLA had made vague allegations that South African troops were involved in the fighting, but they had not been taken seriously.

After being shown around Lobito by Jorge Valentim, Mike's cameraman prepared for the return bus ride to Benguela. He sat in the front next to the driver, his camera held casually on his shoulder, finger off the trigger and eye away from the viewfinder. He had lined up the camera at an angle he thought would frame the armoured car. As the bus passed the Panhard we all waved to the soldiers, and the cameraman casually depressed the operating trigger.

As we approached the airport terminal we again saw white soldiers running out of sight into the hangar – only this time there were 30 to 50 of them.

We flew to Huambo for Independence Day, and the following evening Mike and I flew back to Lusaka – again in Savimbi's plane – to file our Angolan independence stories, some 24 hours after similar stories had been filed from MPLA territory in Luanda. We touched down at Lusaka airport in darkness. The daily British Airways flight to London was preparing to leave. Mike just had time to run across the tarmac and toss the bag containing his precious film through the front door of the jetliner with instructions to the stewards to deliver it to his Independent Television News studios. Then as the plane began to taxi towards the runway, the front door reopened slightly and someone tossed the bag out again, presumably on the instructions of the captain or chief steward as a security precaution. Mike stood dumfounded on the tarmac, but as the plane moved away he shook his fists and shouted in impotent rage: 'I hope you crash, you bastards.'

I was secretly glad that Mike's film had been delayed. For, although he had agreed not to usurp any details of the story I had found out for myself, I had been given another 24 hours to flesh out my narrative before Mike's film of the armoured car broke on international television.

I decided that before I telexed my story to London I needed to question Savimbi. So, on 13 November, Mike and I again returned to Angola and caught up with the UNITA President in Lobito, where he was due to address a mass rally. As we stepped from the plane I noticed two uniformed white soldiers with rifles on the balcony of the airport terminal. Before I had time even to reach for my camera they had moved inside.

Savimbi's rally in the main square was attended by some 50,000 people. He spoke from a balcony while people clambered over rooftops to hear him. Afterwards, at a press conference in a hotel, Nicholson and I put to him our conviction that South African troops were the secret of his successful advances. We did not tell him the evidence for our beliefs.

Savimbi's replies were understandably ambiguous: 'There are no South African troops committed by the South African government here. I agree that we have some white troops – not soldiers, but technicians – working for us here doing things that we don't know how to do. I need people to fight with armoured cars that we cannot operate ourselves. The MPLA had the Russians with them. We had to address ourselves to people who could match them.'

There were other journalists present who picked up the drift of our questions. Someone asked Savimbi whether the white troops fighting with him were mercenaries. Defensively, but nevertheless with intense passion, he replied: 'The one you saw, a Cuban [Rodriguez], is he or is he not a mercenary?'

He said it was obvious that the MPLA could not have achieved for themselves what the Cubans were achieving for them. 'So in my own mind if I have to get support from anyone, I will do it without any heavy conscience. It does not raise questions of morality . . . I am doing it to save the fate of my country.'

Now the questions were raining down. When I said I believed there were armoured units of the South African

Army spearheading the advance on Luanda, Savimbi replied: 'If those armoured columns are converging on Luanda, as you say, they are not our troops . . . and, if they are our troops, they are not converging on Luanda at all. *We* are thinking in terms of consolidating what we have won and cleaning up the countryside. I need people to fight with armoured cars that we cannot operate ourselves. Maybe they are South Africans, Rhodesians, but there are more French. Mercenaries who fought in Biafra are here.'

Savimbi was upset by the pointed questions on South Africa, and later as we all returned to Lobito airport he grabbed the *Newsweek* man's arm and said emotionally: 'You journalists from Western countries, you say you want to oppose Communism, but you are the ones who just help Communism by the way you act. Why? You are weakening your democracy and giving a chance to the East to come up. We could not accept that the Communists will come here, but we knew that MPLA was building up a strong army.

'Back in November 1974 I went to see every embassy of the Western countries in Lusaka. I told them the danger is this one, the danger is this one, the danger is this one . . . Everybody said "We understand you, we are with you" . . . but they did not act until the MPLA got us.'

This failure of the West to respond in kind to the Soviet build-up was at the heart of Savimbi's personal conflict. Faced with a choice between helpless submission to the MPLA or surviving to fight another day, he had accepted help from the sworn enemy of black Africa. And in that Lobito hotel, without openly admitting to receiving South African help, he told us a parable which summed up his dilemma: 'If you are a drowning man in a crocodile-infested river and you've just gone under for the third time you don't question who is pulling you to the bank until you're safely on it.'

Then, in a gesture that has impressed me ever since, Savimbi put his plane at our disposal to fly the 2,500 kilometres from Lobito to Lusaka, knowing that stories would be filed that would help to destroy him. It would have been entirely within his power to keep us in Angola as permanent 'guests'. Without telephone or telex, and with no independent road, rail or air services, our only means of communication with the outside world was by UNITA plane.

I wrote my story during the UNITA flight to Lusaka on the 14th of the month. I filed the copy that day and it became front page news around the world. However, Reuters were still nervous about stating categorically that South Africa had invaded Angola. So the story that the agency's international subscribers received began this way: 'Columns of armoured vehicles manned by white personnel are slicing across great tracts of Angola through the defences of the Marxist-oriented MPLA, informed sources said. The major unanswered question is the origin of the white soldiers.'

For days afterwards the story was reworked. On 22 November I finally persuaded the agency to name the South Africans and the next day the story appeared on the front page of the *Washington Post*.

A Marxist philosopher, Jean Ziegler, said my report in the *Post* was instrumental in persuading the most powerful country in black Africa to change sides and support the MPLA – 'On 22 November 1975, Fred Bridgland published an unambiguous report about the presence of South African troops on Angolan territory. Nigeria, the leading political power of black Africa and supplies of petrol to the United States, changed camp, rejected UNITA and gave an immediate grant of 20 million dollars to the government of Agostinho Neto.'[1]

John Stockwell subsequently wrote that my story undermined the South African effort in Angola and fatally weakened the limited CIA support for Savimbi: 'The propaganda and political war was lost in that stroke. There was nothing the Lusaka (CIA) station could invent that would be as damaging to the other side as our alliance with the hated South Africans was to our cause.'[2]

15

Savimbi Treads a Tightrope

1975

'Without any memos being written at CIA headquarters saying "Let's co-ordinate with the South Africans," co-ordination was effected at all CIA levels and the South Africans escalated their involvement in step with our own.'

John Stockwell, *In Search of Enemies*

*   *   *

After independence, UNITA – or, rather, the South Africans – continued to make dramatic progress through Angola. On 14 November the coastal column, code-named 'Zulu' and led by an Afrikaaner colonel who was nicknamed 'Rommel' by his comrades because of the spectacular speed of his advance,[1] took Novo Redondo, a port 275 kilometres south of Luanda.

'Rommel' then joined up with the inland column, known as 'Foxbat', and by the beginning of December they had advanced to the Queve River – south of a line of three towns, Porto Amboim, Gabela and Quibala – 750 kilometres inside Angola and just 225 kilometres from the capital. 'Foxbat' was led by the mysterious flaxen-haired man I had seen at Silva Porto airport, a South African paratroop colonel who became known to UNITA as Commander Kaas – which in Afrikaans means 'Commander Cheese' – because of his fair hair.[2]

Then, on 11 December, Luso was taken by another South African column code-named 'X-ray'. For a while it seemed possible that the column might be able to push eastwards

from Luso to the Zairean border and thus free the Benguela
Railway again for use by Zairean and Zambian traffic.

But the military edifice that was being built for Savimbi
was illusory. It was like an elaborate pie with no filling. Once
it began to crumble its hollowness would be exposed.

The original directive by South Africa's politicians to
the military was that 'Zulu', 'Foxbat' and 'X-ray' should
take as much 'traditional' UNITA territory as possible by
11 November, and then prepare to withdraw.[3] Some high-
level administrators and politicians in Pretoria had always
been more cautious than their military officers on the
ground in Angola. They argued: since it had been possible to
come to terms with a left-wing FRELIMO government in
Mozambique, why not accept the inevitability of MPLA
victory in Angola and do business with the resultant
government?[4] Others argued that South Africa could not
tolerate the emergence of the Soviet-backed MPLA as victors
because every other African country would conclude that
any interest group receiving Soviet backing in any set of
circumstances was bound to triumph: therefore it was
necessary to heed appeals to correct the military imbalance
in Angola. These arguments continued throughout South
Africa's sojourn in Angola, and beyond.

*   *   *

After Savimbi's Lonrho jet had taken Nicholson and me
clandestinely to Namibia on its 10 November refuelling trip,
it flew the UNITA leader that same afternoon to Pretoria for
his first meeting with South African leaders, including the
then Prime Minister John Vorster.

Savimbi wanted the South Africans to delay their tenta-
tive 11 November withdrawal until at least 9 December. That
was the date that OAU heads of state were due to meet in
Addis Ababa for an emergency summit on Angola. The
ostensible reason given by Savimbi for the South African
presence in Angola had been that it would give him territory
with which he could bargain for a share in a coalition
government: if UNITA and the FNLA could hold on to major
towns outside Luanda it might be possible to get a majority
OAU vote in favour of such a coalition. Other opponents of

MPLA hegemony, including Presidents Ford, Kaunda and Mobutu, were making similar requests to Savimbi's and asking Pretoria to keep its military forces in Angola.[5]

South Africa temporarily reversed its withdrawal decision pending the OAU vote. But Vorster had some bad news for Savimbi in Pretoria on 10 November: that very day, the eve of independence, a concerted effort by the West and South Africa was being made to put the FNLA into Luanda by Independence Day.

Savimbi was shocked by Vorster's news. If he had not gone to Pretoria he would not have learned of the plan, though he did know that the FNLA had pushed to within 50 kilometres of Luanda. (The Pretoria trip was the reason for Savimbi's absence from the eve-of-independence ceremonies in Huambo. And the news he was given probably accounted for his unusually severe mood on Independence Day.)

Savimbi learned years later, from Western intelligence, that the plan was that, if the FNLA took power, UNITA would be offered three or four minor portfolios such as Water Supplies . . . 'The main part of the 2,000-man South African force was in our area, and yet they [the South Africans and the West] had planned to take over Luanda and give it to the FNLA without telling us. What sort of friendship was that?'[6]

The authors of the MPLA's official account of the war subsequently supported Savimbi's contention. They wrote: 'If the South Africans had pushed ahead [from the south], Angola might have been theirs. But the West's plan was for taking Luanda by the northern black force.'[7]

The closure of the US Consulate-General in Luanda and the evacuation of all staff on 3 November 1975, just one week before the FNLA attempt to take Luanda, may not have just been coincidental. And an American political scientist, noting that just before independence the CIA deputy director Vernon Walters visited Angola at least twice and also Zaire, observed: 'The CIA may have been linked with an FNLA attempt to seize power in November 1975.'[8]

Other evidence that such a Western plan existed lies in the composition of the first South African armoured column to strike into Angola. There were no UNITA troops in the 'Zulu' column led by 'Rommel', though Savimbi's soldiers did occupy towns after the column had cleared them of MPLA military. When 'Rommel' led his force across the border at Cuangar on 14 October he had thirteen other white South African soldiers with him – six officers and seven NCOs. They had under them a bushman battalion of 800 men – first-class trackers and deadly close-quarters fighters – and a battalion of about 1,000 black FNLA troops loyal to Daniel Chipenda, who had established himself as a kind of warlord with headquarters in the southern town of Serpa Pinto where his men received training from South African instructors. Within a week 'Rommel', who had invaded Angola with a transport fleet of civilian trucks, cars and Land Rovers, was reinforced by about 20 armoured cars and their crews, and a mortar unit from the South African Army.[9]

*   *   *

The FNLA assault on Luanda – under the 'Western Plan' – began two hours after first light on 10 November 1975. About 1,500 soldiers began advancing in a single column across the broad and marshy valley of the Bengo River, 30 kilometres north of Luanda. The FNLA forces were supported by two regular battalions of the Zairean Army and 100 Portuguese Angolan soldiers.[10]

South African Army gunners on a ridge to the north of the river aimed their three 17-kilometre-range artillery pieces across the river, where some 800 Cubans were dug in on hilltops around the village of Quifandongo. CIA officers, South African advisers, and French and British intelligence agents together watched the beginning of the push into Luanda, whose outskirts, dominated by petrol storage tanks, were just visible in the distance.

Holden Roberto was also on the ridge. He had never been to Luanda, having chosen to stay in Kinshasa even during the time of Angola's transitional government, against the advice of his top lieutenants. They had urged him to visit Luanda on 15 March 1975, the anniversary of the 1961 FNLA rebellion against the Portuguese. Roberto feared assassination and stayed away.[11] But now the capital, and absolute power, seemed to lie within his grasp, just a few hours away.

As the FNLA advanced across the swamp along a narrow metalled road, on top of a dyke, a devastating barrage was laid down from Quifandongo by the Cubans and supporting MPLA troops. Heavy mortar shells rained down on the column and salvos of 122mm rockets, fired from 40-barrelled launchers known as 'Stalin Organs', screamed into the midst of the soldiers. The South African artillery was no match for the Cubans' brand-new Soviet hardware. And a big Zairean 130mm field gun, obtained from North Korea, exploded the first time it was fired, killing the Zairean crew. Most of Roberto's dozen armoured cars and a half dozen jeeps mounted with anti-tank rockets were knocked out within an hour. The CIA men watching the debacle from the ridge estimated that some 2,000 rockets had landed among the FNLA forces. Three South African warplanes, probably Mirages, which attacked Cuban and MPLA positions, were of no real help to the FNLA. Because of the need for secrecy, they flew so high that two missed their targets and the third failed to release its bombs.

Roberto's men panicked and got bogged down in the swamp. Cubans dashed forward in jeeps to fire RPG-7 and anti-aicraft guns along the dyke among the demoralised Africans, compounding their terror and misery. Hundreds of FNLA men and Zaireans died, and also five of the Portuguese. The 26-man South African contingent escaped with a million dollars' worth of radio and decoding equipment from a beach near the small port of Ambrizete. There they made a night rendezvous and were helicoptered to the South African Navy frigate *President Steyn* waiting three miles offshore.[12]

The disaster, which became known as '*Nshila wa Lufu*' (Death Road), broke the FNLA. They never recovered, retreating in ill-disciplined alarm from one town to the next, as and when the Cubans and MPLA decided on a methodical push forward.

*   *   *

With the FNLA virtually out of the war, Savimbi was confronted with a serious problem. As he prepared his diplomacy for the emergency OAU summit on Angola, the MPLA and their Cuban allies were bound to turn their full attention to the UNITA enemy in the south.

And on 5 November a decision had been taken in Havana by Cuba's President Castro which would add to the problems of Savimbi and the South Africans.[13] By that date there were probably already some 1,100 to 4,000 Cuban troops in Angola in support of the MPLA;[14] and by then Castro's troops retreating in the south would have told him they were up against South Africans. The Cuban leader boldly calculated that once the South African presence became known it would be internationally condemned, regardless of the rights and wrongs of Angola's internal situation. He also reckoned astutely that, following the withdrawal from Vietnam earlier that year and the loss of trust in their political leaders as a result of the 1974 Watergate Affair, the US public would be in no mood for fresh adventures in a little-heard-of country called Angola.

On 7 November, two days after making his decision, Castro launched 'Operation Carlota', named after a black woman who had led a revolt by slaves in Cuba in the mid-nineteenth century. It was an air-bridge which boosted the Cuban Angolan Expeditionary Force to 7,000 by December and to 12,000 by January 1976.[15] Russian-made Ilyushins and British-built Britannias, which refuelled in Barbados, the Azores and Guinea-Conakry, transported the Cuban troops. The Russians supported the Cubans – described by one journalist as the 'Gurkhas of the Soviet Empire'[16] – by flying in tanks, armoured cars, trucks, helicopters, MIG-21 jet fighters, rocket launchers and small arms. This was no half-hearted effort to maintain their client's hold on 'traditional' territory. Havana and Moscow had seen that outright political and military victory was possible for the MPLA, and they made sure they gave their clients the means with which to achieve it.

The Angolan civil conflict had become the first Cuban-South African war, though neither had yet admitted publicly that their troops were involved.

Militarily the South Africans continued to make gains. However, they were fast losing the political battle . . . and even on the military front they began to run into trouble. They suffered their first heavy casualties south of Novo Redondo on 12 November – 28 days and 700 kilometres after 'Rommel' had entered Angola. Crossing flooded marshes on an exposed stretch of road similar to that where the FNLA had been destroyed, the 'Zulu' column was hit by a heavy mortar shell. One South African died and 17 were wounded.[17]

The casualties among his men led 'Rommel' to ask for reinforcements. He was given a battery of 25-pounder field guns but was denied a paratroop company to drop behind entrenched enemy positions. He therefore asked permission to withdraw to Lobito: it was refused and he was recalled to South Africa on 29 November and relieved of his command.[18]

From late November onwards the South Africans were encountering Cuban troops in much bigger numbers, and better organised and equipped than when their first contingents arrived from across the Atlantic. The South Africans, now numbering more then 2,000, found themselves confronting Soviet-made T-34 and T-54 tanks, PT-76 light amphibious tanks, missile-firing helicopters, and 122mm anti-tank cannon.

West European intelligence officials operating in southern Africa estimated that between November 1974 and November 1975 the Soviet Union supplied \$US 110 million worth of arms to the MPLA – about twice the amount sent during the previous 14 years when the MPLA was fighting the Portuguese.[19] By February 1976 it was estimated by the CIA that the value of the weaponry sent by Moscow to its MPLA clients and Cuban allies had reached \$US 400 million.[20]

At independence the majority of African members of the OAU had backed the organisation's stance favouring a ceasefire and the establishment of a transitional coalition government, to be followed by the holding of free multi-party elections. But nine[21] of the 46 OAU states recognised the MPLA as the legitimate government of Angola, enough to embolden the Soviet Union and Cuba to give their own recognition and step up the supply of arms, more or less openly.

Weaponry poured in from all directions, even through Tanzania which had not recognised the MPLA but which was deeply disturbed by reports that Savimbi, some of whose officers had been trained by the Tanzanian Army, was receiving help from South Africa. By late November 600 tonnes of Soviet military equipment were in Dar-es-Salaam awaiting transhipment to Luanda for the MPLA. Also in Dar-es-Salaam harbour was the Soviet ship *Valery Mezhlauk* carrying 785 tonnes of arms for SWAPO, according to the ship's manifest. Western intelligence believed these arms were in fact intended for the MPLA.[22] The Tanzanians were also holding 100 tonnes of arms sent by China via Dar for UNITA: President Nyerere eventually diverted these weapons to the MPLA, causing immense UNITA bitterness.

Despite the weapons superiority of the Cubans/MPLA the South Africans continued to achieve remarkable military successes: for example, at the 'Battle of Bridge 14', across the Nhia River north of the town of Cela, where the biggest action of the 1975–76 civil war raged for three days from 9 to 12 December. The South African force was attacking Cela from the north, having previously moved eastwards inland from Novo Redondo along the southern bank of the Queve River. The South Africans claim to have taken on an entire battalion of 1,000 Cuban troops, killing some 200 of them for only four South Africans dead.[23] The Cubans admitted their heaviest casualties in any single battle of the war, and the dead included the commander of their expeditionary force, Commandant Raul Diaz Arguelles.[24]

At another battle north of 'Bridge 14', on 14 December, another 50 Cubans were killed; the seriously wounded were flown to East Germany for treatment. And in the battle for Cela itself on 17 December the South Africans 'out-manoeuvred the cannon, knocked out the tanks and killed scores of MPLA soldiers'.[25]

But the South Africans never solved the problem of how to capture Teixeira de Sousa, at the eastern end of the Angolan stretch of the Benguela Railway, which would have given UNITA control of the entire line. If Savimbi had been able to open the railway to international traffic from Zambia and Zaire his status, credibility and chances of military and political success would have been greatly enhanced. However, the Cubans put a strong defensive force into the town and blew up a major rail bridge about 20 kilometres to the west of it. This made Teixeira de Sousa difficult to attack overland; and the big bridge was so comprehensively destroyed that the South Africans decided it would take several months to repair, even under peacetime conditions.

This highlighted a special problem the South Africans faced in Angola – a lack of pontoons and other bridging equipment. This deficiency had also prevented the South Africans crossing the Queve River after the capture of Novo Redondo on 14 November and pushing onwards along the coast without further obstacle to Luanda. The following day the Cubans blew up all the bridges on the Queve's lower reaches, and the South Africans were forced to skirt inland against their will.[26]

*   *   *

One of the key countries that the Angolan liberation movements needed to win in their diplomatic struggle was Nigeria, the most populous country in black Africa and rich in oil. Just three days before Angolan Independence Day Nigeria was condemning support for the MPLA and calling on Moscow to stop all further interference in Angola. 'Nigeria does not understand or appreciate the support given by the Soviet Union to one of the liberation movements to declare independence unilaterally,' said Lagos Radio.[27]

Less than three weeks later, on 27 November, Nigeria reversed its stand and recognised the legitimacy of the MPLA government, giving as its reason South Africa's intervention. This marked the beginning of UNITA's diplomatic downfall. Nigeria's recognition of the MPLA was followed by Tanzania, whose government-owned newspaper, *The Daily News*, had carried on 16 November my report of South Africa's invasion of Angola under the headline 'Savimbi Admits Betrayal'. Ghana, Sudan and other states joined the Nigerians and Tanzanians, and by 10

December 14 of the 46 member states of the OAU had recognised Agostinho Neto's administration as the legitimate government.

In an attempt to stem the diplomatic tide running for the MPLA, the FNLA and UNITA had on Independence Day declared their intent to set up a Government of the Democratic People's Republic of Angola (DPRA), to be based in Huambo in direct rivalry to the MPLA's People's Republic of Angola (PRA). The DPRA was to comprise nine ministers from each of the movements, with two nominated prime ministers holding office in alternate months. It was a totally unnatural alliance, urged upon reluctant partners by the CIA and other clandestine foreign allies. Savimbi quickly expressed reservations about forming a government with the FNLA, saying he believed the way had to be left open for negotiations with the MPLA.[28]

Because of the hostility between the two movements, they were unable to agree on the composition of the government until 1 December. Neither Savimbi nor Roberto served in the Huambo-based administration. The FNLA leader stayed in Kinshasa. Within a month of forming their coalition government, the FNLA and UNITA would be fighting each other with as much vigour as they had the MPLA.

The DPRA failed to gain recognition from anywhere, whereas the South African intervention had had the effect of legitimising Soviet and Cuban support for the MPLA.

*　*　*

As the argument about whether to prolong involvement in Angola went on among government officials in South Africa and as more and more of black Africa recognised the MPLA, so also a crucial shift of opinion on Angola had begun in the United States.

At the beginning of August 1975 Dick Clark, a US Democratic Senator from Iowa who had espoused the radical form of liberalism spawned by the anti-Vietnam War movement, set out on a major fact-finding trip to Central Africa in his role as Chairman of the important Senate Foreign Relations Subcommittee. He was briefed beforehand by CIA Director William Colby, who told the Senator that as President

Mobutu sent arms to the FNLA and UNITA so the US was replenishing Mobutu's weapons stores. Colby said no Americans would be involved in the Angolan conflict and no American arms would be sent into that country.[29]

Clark was a spirited and determined academic type, with a puritanical streak. He turned up in early August at the Victoria Falls conference where Presidents Kaunda and Vorster held a series of historic, and very friendly, meetings as Rhodesia's white rulers and black nationalist opponents sat in a railway carriage parked midway across the spectacular Victoria Falls bridge and talked, with great acrimony, about their country's future. Clark questioned those of us who were there as journalists with great seriousness, intensity and intelligence about the dramatic developments in the region.

He journeyed to Lusaka, Dar-es-Salaam, Kinshasa, Luanda, Bie and Ambriz talking to American ambassadors, heads of state, journalists and to Neto, Savimbi and Roberto, about the Angolan situation. He returned home believing he had been misled by the CIA; that Americans were involved in the war; that Washington was sending arms directly to Angola; and that the CIA was co-operating directly and illegally with South Africa.

Clark was unable to speak out about his belief that the CIA was conducting a misleading campaign. There was a tacit understanding that any Congressman who received a CIA briefing about Angola could not make public the information.[30]

'Quietly, Clark continued to watch the Angola programme, trying to discern the truth through our shields of secrecy and falsehood,' wrote the head of the CIA's Angola Task Force. 'In early November he queried the State Department about the Angola conflict and was told that Mobutu was not using United States aid to support the Angola factions. On December 12 Colby reassured the House [of Representatives] Intelligence Committee that there were no Americans involved in Angola.'[31]

In fact, they were deeply involved. For example, CIA paramilitary officers in Ambriz and Bie were training FNLA and UNITA recruits in the use of infantry weapons.[32]

Savimbi, seeing diplomatic victory surging towards the MPLA, left in early December on another trip to Zambia to argue for OAU support in favour of the formation in Angola of a national unity government to be followed by elections. He got backing from Kenneth Kaunda, who said Africa should not pretend it did not understand the forces at work in Angola, a reference to his belief that the Soviet Union and Cuba were more to blame than the US or South Africa for the Angolan civil war.

'It would be unrealistic to think that one political party can rule Angola and still maintain the country's territorial integrity,' said Kaunda. Unless the three liberation movements agreed to a solution, foreign forces would not leave Angola, and history would pass a very severe judgement against the leaders of Africa if they feared to face these facts.

Kaunda appealed to the OAU to call for an immediate ceasefire in Angola and work towards a political solution which would create unity and peace. 'We strongly condemn outside intervention in Angola, from whatever quarter,' he said. 'We demand that all foreign military personnel must quit the country. We believe in a government of national unity as still the best solution which will end the war and guarantee the territorial integrity of Angola.'[33]

Savimbi himself met foreign correspondents and blamed the Soviet Union, Cuba and the MPLA for starting the civil war. But just as South Africa had not told its population that its troops were fighting a war in Angola; just as William Colby had lied to Congressmen about America's direct involvement in Angola; just as Cuba would not admit publicly its own embroilment in the Angolan civil war until 21 December 1975;[34] so Savimbi denied that UNITA had acquiesced in taking help from South Africa. 'We have to make our diplomatic offensive now because African countries are getting emotionally aroused over allegations that South Africa is fighting with us. We reiterate here that we are not being helped by South Africa.'

He went on to say: 'The civil war was not started by South Africa. The people who have intervened in Angola are the Soviet Union. The first armoured vehicles to appear in the war were T-54s from the Soviet Union. The first foreign troops to appear in Angola were from Cuba. Why are people refusing to see this?'

This would be the central point of the argument that raged, through December 1975 and January 1976, between those African states which supported outright recognition of the MPLA as the rightful government of Angola and those which supported the formation of a transitional coalition government to be followed by multi-party elections. The former argued that the Cubans arrived in Angola only after the South African invasion; and the latter said South Africa became involved only in response to the Soviet Union's and Cuba's prior intervention on behalf of the MPLA.

Savimbi said African people were very emotional, and it was from that perspective that they interpreted reports of South Africa's interference in Angola: 'No one will sit down coolly and examine who came in first. The Soviet Union started pouring in arms when the transitional government was operating, but no one listened to us. We could have solved Angola's problems through elections, but the MPLA knows that if elections had been held UNITA would today be ruling the country.'[35]

Savimbi was particularly distressed by Nigeria's switch of camps. 'I think they show ignorance, or they trust very much the lies of the MPLA. By recognising the MPLA they are only encouraging the continuation of our civil war. Instead of encouraging the civil war, they should do all they can to bring this war to an end through political negotiation.'

Savimbi tried to play on fears of what might possibly happen to other African states if the Soviets and Cubans, or the South Africans, achieved their aims in Angola. 'The OAU has to condemn all foreign intervention in Angola because if the foreign troops are allowed to intervene freely no one can guarantee that tomorrow they will not intervene in another independent country. The face Russia is showing in Angola should be a warning to the continent. It should remind us of those Soviet interventions in Czechoslovakia and Hungary. If it had not been for the Russian tanks, the democratic and liberal systems the Czechs and Hungarians wanted could not have failed.'

A similar theme was being taken up by the United States

in the United Nations, where on 8 December its flamboyant and robust Ambassador, Daniel Patrick Moynihan, warned the General Assembly that it should not settle for the 'big lie' that only one country, South Africa, had intervened in Angola: 'At just the moment, with the European colonisers of the seventeenth, eighteenth, and nineteenth centuries departing, at just that moment, a new European colonising, colonial, imperial nation appears on the continent of Africa – armed, aggressive, involved in the direct assault upon the lands and the people of Africa.

'Which of the great powers has not condemned *all* intervention in Angola? We know very well which has not. It is the Soviet Union which has not, the European power now engaged in colonial expansion in the continent of Africa. The Soviet government, far from condemning intervention, has acknowledged it, saying it is assisting its friends in Angola and saying that it would continue to do so . . .'

Andrew Young, the black American leader destined to become US Ambassador to the United Nations in the Carter Administration, joined in the condemnation of the Soviet Union. At the opening of a new 'Martin Luther King Library' in Lusaka, he praised President Kaunda's daring in meeting President Vorster and said Luther King would have done the same thing. He also called on the United States to stop sending grain to the Soviet Union unless Moscow halted the flow of arms to Angola.[36]

Hilgard Muller, the South African Foreign Minister, on a visit to London, denied the presence in his country's troops deep inside Angola, but he went on: 'Let me say . . . I can't understand why so much fuss is being made about the possibility of South Africa's participation since it's no secret the Russians and several thousand Cubans are in there.'[37]

But despite this verbal onslaught against the Soviets, the tide was inexorably turning their way. The FNLA had become a 'demoralised, undisciplined rabble, out of control of their officers'[38] and was in headlong flight before the steady advance northwards of the Cubans and the MPLA. By mid-December the MPLA had captured Roberto's headquarters at Ambriz and the FNLA retreated to the inland town of Uige (formerly named Carmona) and to São

Salvador (since re-named Mbanza), in the far north-west near the Zaire border. President Mobutu's élite Zairean battalions broke and ran even faster than the FNLA, looting villages *en route* and leaving behind unused American and other Western arms which were a propaganda gift to the MPLA.

As the FNLA fell apart, the Cubans and the MPLA were able to turn more and more attention to the south. And though the small South African columns continued to make progress it was now much slower and at far greater cost.

The cost was greatest at the end of the first week of December. Four South African Army mechanics sent forward to repair a vehicle north of Cela accidentally drove into enemy territory and were taken as prisoners. Within a few days they were displayed before television cameras in Luanda, a major propaganda victory for the MPLA.

South Africa's general policy objective of withdrawal from Angola after the special OAU summit was progressively postponed. This was because the summit itself was twice delayed as competing OAU member states struggled to win supporters for their point of view. First, the summit was set for 9 December; then 18 December; and finally 10 January 1976.

But on 5 December Senator Clark set in motion a process which would make South Africa's withdrawal absolutely inevitable. He recommended to the Foreign Relations Subcommittee that all covert US aid to liberation movements in Angola be terminated. The Committee voted its agreement.

Senator Hubert Humphrey summed up the dominating trend in the Senate. Just as a British Prime Minister in the thirties had dismissed Czechoslovakia as a small, far-away country of little concern to Britons, so Humphrey explained why his vote would be cast against further arms for Angola: 'The United States had better start taking care of things it knows how to take care of. We know so little of Africa, the 800 and some tribes that make up Africa . . . I say it is like a different world.' On 19 December the Senate voted in favour of the Clark Amendment by 54 to 22. Of the $US 31.7 million originally approved by the 40 Committee for the CIA's Angola Task Force, only nine million dollars remained to be spent before the operation would have to be wrapped up. President Ford angrily denounced the stoppage as an 'abdication of responsibility' unbecoming of a 'great nation' and inviting 'more crisis tomorrow'.[39]

Though Kenneth Kaunda and senior American officials continued to appeal to South Africa to hang on,[40] the die had been cast. South African officials in Pretoria believed that their country's intervention in Angola was based on an understanding with Washington that the US would match any weaponry sent by the Soviet Union or other countries to the MPLA.[41] The Senate had betrayed that understanding, and now just as surely as the supply of American arms to UNITA would dry up so would South African troops withdraw from Angola. This would ensure victory for the MPLA and their resolute Soviet and Cuban allies.

It spelt disaster for Jonas Savimbi.

16

Emergency African Summit
1975–76

Savimbi's reaction to the 19 December US Senate vote cutting off aid to the Angolan movements was to fly to Pretoria once more on 20 December. He asked Prime Minister Vorster not only to keep his forces in Angola but to advance on Luanda.

'The whole of December had just been a bargaining with the South Africans. I told them that if I had had the choice I would not have chosen them.

'But they had come in and we had been made dirty. I said that since we already had a bad name let us go, let us move to Luanda. Let us go on because when you win a winner can explain himself, a loser cannot explain. You cannot really say "I lost, but I am an honourable man". Winners write history. But they said no, they were not moving north of Cela, and they did not move from there.'[1]

The South Africans did agree to hold the territory they had already gained until the 10–12 January 1976 extraordinary OAU summit was over, in the hope that a diplomatic solution to the Angolan civil war could be produced.

Governments which had encouraged South Africa's Angolan venture with nods and winks were now alarmed at the extent of Pretoria's political and diplomatic exposure. 'Some frenzied backroom diplomacy took place, involving numerous trips back and forth between black African capitals – notably Lusaka – and Pretoria. There were renewed pleas for South Africa to hold the ring for a bit longer.'[2]

The small band of Lusaka-based foreign correspondents

were kept constantly guessing about which top-level South African official, perhaps Foreign Minister Hilgard Muller or Brand Fourie, the top civil servant in the Foreign Ministry, was in Zambia on yet another liaison mission. Between July and December 1975 Fourie made more than 20 clandestine trips to Zambia to see Kenneth Kaunda.[3]

Alternatively, speculation turned to whether Mark Chona, the bright and wily special adviser to President Kaunda, was in South Africa on another of his special missions. Chona became known as 'Zambia's Kissinger' because of the similar Machiavellian role he played in the conduct of his country's foreign policy to that played by Dr Henry in America's. He travelled to a similar degree, and towards the end of December and in early 1976 visited Washington, Paris and London as well as Pretoria.

Following the US Senate vote, I asked for a briefing from Chona on the line Zambia would be pursuing at the extra-ordinary OAU summit. As I waited on the morning of 23 December 1975 in one of the outer rooms of the Presidential office suite at State House, Jean Wilkowski, the big, bossy US Ambassador, who always reminded me of an English Girl Guide leader, was bustling around the place as if she owned it. She clearly had been at home there for some time.

Chona, a thin, bespectacled man with an enigmatic smile, took a militantly anti-Soviet line on Angola: 'The Soviet Union made elections impossible in Angola. It was the first foreign power to interfere, and there are more troops from Cuba in Angola than from any other power.

'Why now that Angola is independent should the Russians supply SAM-7s for blacks to kill blacks when they did not provide such sophisticated weapons before? The people running from their battered homes in Angola are blacks.'

Chona said that at Addis Ababa Zambia would demand the withdrawal of *all* foreign troops from Angola and the establishment of a government of national unity. President Kaunda had just returned from Kenya, where he had obtained support for this line from President Jomo Kenyatta.

The Kaunda-Kenyatta line was immediately attacked in Tanzania by the government newspaper, *The Daily News*,

which said the MPLA was already the legitimate government of Angola: to ask it to join with UNITA and the FNLA
was 'tantamount to indulging in a collective sellout of
Africa'. In a reference to the assistance given to the
FNLA/UNITA by South Africa, the paper said: 'There cannot be a government of national unity between patriots and
self-confessed traitors.'[4]

Africa needed to make a less emotional, more rational
analysis of the South African involvement, said Chona. The
origin of the Angolan conflict did not lie in South Africa.
'The South African presence is an effect of the civil war, not a
fundamental cause.'

The OAU at its previous summit in Kampala in July 1975
had called for the establishment of a government of national
unity, he said. And right up till the moment of independence the OAU had recognised the legitimacy of all three
Angolan movements. Thus, he continued, the Zambian line
was that of the OAU, and the Soviet Union had therefore
been wrong to recognise the MPLA as the legal government.

'The internal affairs of Angola are for Angolans to decide.
The OAU must therefore take very strong action to persuade
the Soviet Union to withdraw from Angola along with
troops from Cuba.'

Not least of the tragedies caused by Angola was the
opportunity it had given the South African military to
deploy heavily in Namibia, which black Africa wished to see
brought to rapid independence.

But while Zambia was opposed to the racism practised by
South Africa, it was equally opposed to the neo-colonialism
being practised by the Soviet Union in support of the MPLA.

Zambia, said Chona, made no apologies for the web of
contacts it had established with South Africa. These were
consistent with the Lusaka Manifesto on southern Africa
signed by the independent black states of east and central
Africa in 1969, which asserted: 'We have always preferred,
and we still prefer, to achieve liberation without violence.
We would prefer to negotiate rather than to destroy, to talk
rather than kill.'

But, though Chona and Kenneth Kaunda were preparing
to do battle at Addis Ababa for an Angola where multi-party

elections could be held, they were pessimistic about what 1976 held. 'The coming year looks like being the most difficult in our history,' said the President's adviser, who added with prophetic accuracy: 'We don't see the Russians and Cubans withdrawing. The South Africans will withdraw, but the civil war will continue.'

*   *   *

There could be no doubt where Zambia stood. Savimbi had won the admiration and support of Kaunda, who said just prior to the Addis Ababa summit: 'The UNITA-FNLA coalition had every right to request arms from the USA when the MPLA received such arms from the Soviet Union.

'If the United States aid is asked by any Angolan party, who am I to say the USA should not respond? . . . Once Portugal was out of Angola, there was no justification for Soviet support of the MPLA. I feel we must speak plainly on Angola. We must be morally and politically courageous and tell the Soviets: "You are wrong".

'We in Africa must look at Angola in a sober, cool way, not emotionally. And much as we condemn South Africa's presence in Angola, we cheat ourselves if we think by condemning South Africa we are settling things.'[5]

*   *   *

Elsewhere other actors in the drama were putting out their own signals.

In Johannesburg Pieter Botha, South Africa's Defence Minister (and future Prime Minister) responsible for the Angolan strategy – which he still had not revealed to his own electorate – said of the US Senate vote: 'If the West does not want to contribute its share for the sake of itself and the free world, it cannot expect South Africa to do it . . . South Africa is not prepared to fight the West's battle against Communist penetration on its own.' Reuter's chief correspondent in Johannesburg interpreted Botha's speech as indicating that South Africa was preparing to withdraw its forces from Angola if open Western support was not forthcoming.[6]

Henry Kissinger said in Washington that the United

States favoured the removal of both Cuban and South African forces from Angola. 'The issue is whether the Soviet Union, backed by a Cuban expeditionary force, can impose on two-thirds of the population its own brand of government,' said the US Secretary of State. 'Without outside support, the war would end on the basis that the OAU has proposed, through some sort of coalition among the local forces.'[7]

The pre-Addis diplomatic frenzy also saw Savimbi leave Angola to travel to Lusaka, Kampala, Kinshasa, Yaounde, Abidjan and Dakar to coordinate with the Presidents of Zambia, Uganda, Zaire, Cameroon, Ivory Coast and Senegal a strategy for the OAU summit which would condemn Soviet, Cuban *and* South African involvement in Angola.[8]

William Schaufele, the US Under-Secretary of State for African Affairs, left Washington on Christmas Day for an eleven-day tour of Africa to drum up support for the Savimbi and Kaunda line. Meanwhile, Henry Kissinger went on holiday to Jamaica.[9] In Brussels Britain's Foreign Secretary James Callaghan, attending a NATO meeting, urged support for the creation of an Angolan government of national unity.[10] President Ford sent letters to 32 African heads of state on the same theme. And the CIA was gathering every available agent and sending them to Addis Ababa to bolster the US behind-the-scenes efforts to influence the crucial vote.[11]

Despite this diplomatic onslaught, Fidel Castro's confidence grew. In Havana, at the annual congress of the Cuban Communist Party on 21 December he told delegates that Cuba would grant the MPLA all the necessary military support – the first public admission by Cuba of its involvement in the civil war.[12] Lucio Lara, the MPLA's chief ideologist, told the Havana congress that the MPLA thanked the Soviet Union and Cuba for their 'concrete acts' of assistance which had enabled the MPLA 'to face French and American tanks and cannon used by South African expansionists to invade Angola'.

In late December 1975 Mr Pik Botha, the South African Ambassador to the United Nations, returned home for talks with the Prime Minister and defence chiefs on the implications of the US Senate vote. South Africa's leaders were dismayed by the Senate decision, but they were infuriated and felt even more betrayed by the US Government's failure to block a United Nations Security Council resolution calling on South Africa to pay war damage reparations to the MPLA.[13] It was at this meeting, at a retreat called Oubosstrand, that the final decision on withdrawal from Angola seems to have been taken.[14]

On Christmas Day the South African commander in Angola, Major-General van Deventer, told Savimbi that his troops were pulling out of Cela, the forward South African position 200 kilometres north of Huambo, for good. The withdrawal would begin as soon as the vote had been taken at the OAU emergency summit. Savimbi immediately flew to Lusaka and arranged, through Kaunda, a third visit to South African territory, this time to Windhoek, the capital of Namibia. There Savimbi pleaded with the South Africans to carry the fight to Luanda. No, they said, the decision was irrevocable.[15]

As Savimbi returned to Angola on the eve of New Year 1976, President Kaunda summoned Brand Fourie from Cape Town to his ancestral home in eastern Zambia. As the old year went out, Kaunda told the South African Foreign Ministry chief, whom he had come to know well, that South Africa should either go forward all the way to Luanda or pull out of Angola entirely. But, Kaunda said, his preference was for South Africa to go forward. Fourie told the Zambian leader that it was impossible for South Africa to make that kind of commitment because countries like France and the United States, which had backed South Africa clandestinely, were now 'getting off the bandwagon'.

Back in Angola Savimbi attended the end of UNITA's annual party conference in Bie. On Christmas Eve the artificial FNLA-UNITA coalition had begun to fall apart when soldiers of the two groups in Huambo engaged in a major battle. Estimates of the number of dead ranged between 28 and 200.[16] Now, on New Year's Eve, the UNITA conference passed a mass of resolutions reiterating all the party's past demands for the formation of a coalition government to be followed by elections. It also condemned the MPLA for trampling on the Mombasa, Alvor and Nakuru agreements.[17]

But by now UNITA was tilting at windmills.

On 5 January 1976 South African Defence Headquarters announced what must have been for Pretoria the absolute final straw. Three more of its soldiers had been taken as prisoners by the Cubans/MPLA – the second time members of the South African Defence Forces had been captured, bringing the total to seven.[18]

It only remained for the final *dénouement* in Addis Ababa.

*   *   *

I had been banned by Savimbi from entering UNITA territory following my revelation of the South African invasion. But on 5 January 1976 the ban was lifted and I managed to get back into Angola before the Addis Ababa summit. Savimbi wanted publicity on three Cuban prisoners UNITA was holding and whom he was considering taking to the summit.

The three, wrists bound and feet clad in laceless shoes, were brought before foreign correspondents in grey prison uniform outside the small former Portuguese jail in Bie. Among them was Samuel Ducentes Rodriguez, the 17-year-old white boy whom Savimbi had told, back in November, that he was not about to be killed. The others were Lieutenant Selso Caldez, a black man, and Private Jose Durudi, a *mestico*.

Caldez, from La Sierrita, near Cochinos Bay (the Bay of Pigs), had arrived on the Cuban ship *Vietnam Heroica* in October 1975. He had been left in a Lobito hospital, where he was being treated for dysentery, when the Cubans retreated from the port in November.

Durudi, from Guantanamo, near the site of the small US naval station on Cuba, had arrived in early November aboard the Cuban ship *Coral*. He was a mechanic and had been shot in the thigh during the South African advance on Lobito. At first, he said, he was beaten by his captors, but then treated well because of his wound.

Rodriguez had obviously become a mascot to his guards.

A cheerful and warm little man, he had begun to speak Portuguese and the local Ovimbundu tribal language. He added a little to his earlier story: when he had been captured he had been tied to a tree through one night and beaten by soldiers. He said: 'The MPLA and UNITA seem to be fighting for practically the same cause. UNITA seem to be the Angola people, so I don't know what the fighting is about.' But, of course, what prisoners-of-war say in front of their captors is wide open to interpretation.

Before he left Bie Savimbi repeated his hopes for the Addis summit and appealed to the US Senate not to abdicate 'its responsibilities'. He said: 'The history of this century and the next one should not be made around Vietnam. In Vietnam the United States was on the side of the minority. In Angola it is the opposite. The majority of the people are with us and the MPLA wants to impose its will by force on the majority.'

Savimbi said that whatever the final US congress decision on aid to UNITA and the FNLA, his movement would continue to fight.

* * *

Savimbi's party arrived in Addis Ababa on 9 January without the Cuban prisoners. He had been advised against bringing them by the Ethiopian authorities for security reasons. However, the MPLA turned up with two young white South African soldiers who became the propaganda hit of the summit when they were paraded before the international press.

On the final day, 12 January, of the extraordinary summit Kaunda made a brave speech outlining Zambia's view of the crisis: 'We are not an electoral college. We have not come here to confirm any one political party as the government of Angola . . . Zambia wants a progressive and non-aligned Angola completely free from external pressures.'

And in a scarcely veiled allusion to the Soviet Union, he said: 'Africa must understand that imperialism is imperialism. It knows neither race nor colour nor ideology. All nations which seek to impose their will on others are imperialists. Africa must not permit those Trojan imperialist horses which come under the guise of furthering the cause of liberation to divide us.'[19]

But divide Africa they did: 22–22 to be exact, with two abstentions, on two motions – the first by Senegal's President Leopold Senghor calling for an Angolan ceasefire, the withdrawal of foreign troops, and reconciliation of the three movements in order to form a government of national unity; and the second by Nigeria's military leader, Brigadier Murtala Muhammed, which called on the OAU to recognise the MPLA as the legitimate government of Angola.

The summit failed to produce a resolution condemning South Africa. Many of black Africa's leaders, for whom hatred of the South Africans was a political imperative, had demonstrated by the way they had cast their votes that their distrust of the Soviets and Cubans was even greater.

But the split was illusory. The two abstainers, Ethiopia and Uganda, soon afterwards gave recognition to the MPLA, and thereafter there was an avalanche in the Popular Movement's favour. Within six weeks it had been recognised by 41 of the 46 OAU members, and on 10 February Agostinho Neto's government became the 47th member of the pan-African grouping.

Kaunda returned to Lusaka knowing he had lost. On 16 January he addressed Zambia's parliament at the opening of its new session. 'History will pass a harsh judgement on Africa if we fail to strengthen our unity and hand the continent over to former colonial masters or new imperialists,' he said.

On the same day, two South African generals flew into Bie and then drove northwards to their troops' front with the Cubans and MPLA at Cela. There they told Jonas Savimbi that in six days time South African forces in Angola would begin withdrawing, never to return.[20]

17

South Africa Withdraws:
Savimbi Faces Oblivion

1976

Also at Cela on 16 January for the meeting with the South African generals were Holden Roberto and his semi-autonomous lieutenant in southern Angola, Daniel Chipenda. The South Africans were adamant about their decision to withdraw,[1] despite Savimbi's protests and those of Roberto and Chipenda that the FNLA and UNITA would be left with nothing other than bad names by association with Pretoria.

The FNLA, who were now in terrible trouble in the north and had begun to recruit British and American mercenaries in an attempt to reverse their fortune, started to panic. 'Chipenda began crying in front of the South African officers. I said no, it is just that: they came in, they want to go out, so let them go,' said Savimbi.

'Then when we went outside Roberto asked me what made me so confident that I had troops who could replace the South Africans. I said I didn't have any, but I wasn't going to cry in front of the South Africans. If they want to leave us, they leave. If we have to die, let us die; this is our country; what can we do? We were not part of the arrangement when they came here, so we have no power to persuade them to stay.

'The one who sent them in is sending them out, so we have to accept it.'[2]

*　　*　　*

I got a glimpse of the two generals during a return trip I made to UNITA territory with other foreign correspondents from 13 to 19 January. I spotted them in the front of a Land Rover as they were whisked through Bie. They were short-sleeved khaki shirts. But UNITA officials would not even admit that the two white men were present, let alone say who they were or what they were doing. The nearest I got to the truth at the time was information from a Portuguese journalist[3] close to Savimbi who said they were a South African general and an American general carrying out an inspection of the military situation.

Since visiting correspondents knew nothing of the news brought to Savimbi by the generals there was a phoney nature to our coverage of the war. But it was not the usual kind of phoney war – one that is about to begin – but one that was about to end.

Savimbi met us briefly and told us defiantly: 'I have been seven years in the jungle. I did not spend them there to be dominated after independence by the Russians.' Then he sent us along the Benguela Railway on the wonderful 400-kilometre trip which at the time seemed divorced from reality and which, with hindsight, was indeed so. A big and beautiful steam locomotive built in Glasgow more than 50 years earlier pulled a column of freight cars filled with UNITA soldiers, and at the back we reclined in an ornate private passenger carriage with a rear viewing platform of the kind on which 'goodies' and 'baddies' wrestled desperately in Western movies.

We correspondents stood on the platform and gazed across the great African plateau at a breathtaking sunset as fiery in its redness as the war which none of us had managed, or would manage, to see at first hand. We laughed when the sombre *Wall Street Journal* man, newly arrived from his London base to have a look at the Angolan conflict, was unmoved by the glories of the sinking sun. Instead, he complained: 'What a goddamn country. Do you know you can't get a single statistic in this place? No figures on coffee production, no banana tonnages . . .'

Through the night red hot embers flew past from the wood-burning engine furnace. The locomotive's spotlight lit up the bush for many kilometres ahead. At every little station soldiers stood over little fires cooking their maize porridge. There was lots of laughter and talking because everybody on the train seemed to know everybody at each station.

We reached Luso and packed aboard a little electric rail inspection car to travel a further 100 kilometres eastwards to see the remains of a rail bridge across the Lumege River blown up by the MPLA on their retreat from Luso. It turned out to be a more dramatic tour of inspection than any of us had expected.

We approached the twisted wreckage of the bridge at what seemed far too high a speed. We needed people of demonstrative temperament aboard to yell at the young Portuguese driver to slow down. Instead, the party was composed mostly of Britons indoctrinated in the virtues of the stiff upper lip: we said nothing. At the last moment the driver slammed on the brakes. It was much too late. The rail-car skidded on at great speed, and we plunged down the remnants of the broken rails on the bridge towards the river bed. We were halted in mid-dive towards oblivion by a twisted girder. We hung precariously in mid-air, above the water, before crawling silently out of the debris and clambering back up the hanging rail line towards safety.

It was the first of four rail and road crashes we would have within 24 hours, and led us to christen UNITA's territory *The Land With No Brakes.*

*   *   *

In the Luso area we travelled with Samuel Chiwale and Smart Chata.

'At each village, the crowds of schoolchildren had been assembled to sing for us with that wonderful rhythmic cadence that makes the propaganda lyrics irrelevant,' wrote one journalist. 'The villagers came solemnly forth to greet Colonel Chiwale, each in his aged solar topee, the headman wearing a yachting cap and the oldest wing collar and tie in Africa.'[4]

At six foot, three inches, with long arms swinging close to hip-level revolvers, Chiwale looked like a black version of Hollywood 'tough guy' Jack Palance. He took us southwards 340 kilometres to Gago Coutinho across vast tracts of forest interspersed by lush and marshy river valleys. UNITA had only established control of the area in recent weeks, and on the return journey Chiwale's convoy picked up 13 dishevelled MPLA stragglers meandering through the forest alongside the road.

In Gago Coutinho, which had lost its electricity and running water in the course of the war, Chiwale was showered with rose petals by local people, and in the evening, in a villa formerly occupied by the Portuguese, they laid on a meal in our honour consisting of glutinous rice, boiled goat and a rough wine made from local fruits. From a shelf in the villa I picked up a colour photo which showed UNITA soldiers and young whites in shorts – obviously South Africans – unloading crates of small arms ammunition from the back of a lorry in a forest clearing. The message on the back of the photo was 'To my *camaradas*,' and I couldn't help wondering to what extent real bonds had been established between some of these men from the land of apartheid and the black people of Angola with whom they had become so closely involved.

I slept the night in an abandoned house. I thought I was alone, but as I struggled to find the toilet by moonlight I bumped into an African who was also sleeping there. He said he was a Zambian police official 'just paying a friendly visit'. But since we had been told by UNITA soldiers that lorries travelled regularly between Gago Coutinho and the Zambian border town of Kalabo, and since we had seen boxes of small arms ammunition in Luso with Zambian Army markings, it was not hard to guess he had some kind of liaison role. And he also would have known about UNITA's white *camaradas*.

Before we left Luso to return to Bie Chiwale spoke to us and, though we were not able to see it at the time, his remarks reflected the new and serious problems that UNITA faced following Savimbi's meeting with the South African generals at Cela: 'UNITA was created through difficulties and will go through more difficulties. But we have the people with us. If the Cubans drive us back we can raise a million men to fight them in the bush . . . The Russians and the Cubans can never win in the long term because they do not know the people, they do not know the countryside.

*   *   *

Since the reports by Mike Nicholson and myself two months earlier, no other reporters had seen South Africans in UNITA territory. But all correspondents who arrived subsequently wanted to make their own sightings, not least the BBC television team who had travelled with us to Luso. So when, on the return journey to Bie, we crossed a big railway bridge on the River Cuanza, near Camacupa, and we saw that it was guarded by a score of rifle-carrying South African soldiers, the BBC producer was naturally very excited. Unfortunately for the BBC it was early morning: the cameraman was asleep and by the time he was roused and ready the train had slipped past and UNITA officials refused requests for it to go back.

And once back in Bie – where our rail-car crashed into the back of a train – we met an American NBC television crew who were as surly and morally outraged as only an American television crew can be when they have been frustrated in the pursuit of their objective. The previous afternoon they had been walking the streets of Bie shooting atmospheric scenes when a convoy of South African troops drove through the centre of the town. The South Africans waved cheerfully at the townspeople, who waved back equally cheerily. The cameraman merged into the crowds and shot the scenes. Nobody bothered him, and the team went to bed at the former governor's mansion happy with their scoop. But at 4.30 a.m. a squad of UNITA soldiers entered their rooms and at sub-machine-gun-point confiscated all their film.

*   *   *

The UNITA military training camp at the former Portuguese prison colony of Kapolo, near Bie, was another feature of the phoney war. Four companies of 108 men were being trained each fortnight and put into battle. They were being instructed on American-made 120mm, 81mm and 60mm mortars; 12.7mm heavy machine-guns; 106mm recoilless rifles; and hundreds of US World War II .30 calibre carbine rifles, which Savimbi later said were so useless that they had to be thrown away.

According to one of the camp commanders, instruction

was in the hands of UNITA officers. But, although we never saw a white face in the camp, where there was a well-maintained aistrip, another UNITA officer told us confidentially that 15 'American mercenaries' were there – which was confirmed later by the head of the CIA Task Force who said American paramilitary officers had been sent to Bie to train UNITA.

The Americans were therefore at Kapolo along with military trainers from South Africa, for when 'Commandant Kaas' arrived at Bie in September 1975 he established his 18-strong team of infantry instructors at the old Portuguese prison. Their number eventually grew to 40.[5]

*   *   *

Ron Gooday of the Lusaka-based firm Aeradio was another personality in the phoney war. Gooday was an engineer, and he was in Bie to supervise the installation of a long-range radio transmitter for UNITA supplied by the British electronics company Racal, for whom Aeradio were agents. Similar Racal transmitters for UNITA had been set up in Lusaka, Huambo and Mocamedes and another three were planned. Gooday said he did not know who would operate them, but he probably knew who had arranged their delivery – Britain's MI6 intelligence service, through its Lusaka station, from where its employees were frequent visitors to UNITA territory. According to one writer with good contacts in the intelligence community, the British MI6 men and their counterparts from America, France, West Germany, Italy, Spain, South Africa and Israel met frequently – sometimes at remote airstrips inside Angola – to compare inventories of equipment they had sent to UNITA to ensure they were not duplicating each other's efforts.[6] But a British intelligence officer involved in the campaign told me this account gave an impression of high-powered co-ordination that simply did not exist.

*   *   *

On 20 January 1976 Savimbi flew to Lusaka to speak with President Kaunda and left the same night for Kinshasa to meet the deputy director of the CIA, General Vernon Walters. There was speculation that Zambia was promoting

a compromise between UNITA and the MPLA and that the
two sides would soon meet in Kenya. As Savimbi left his
Lusaka offices to fly to Kinshasa, he declined to say anything
about his talks with Kaunda. But when he was asked
whether he would be meeting an MPLA representative
within the next few days, he replied bitterly: 'I will not be
meeting with the MPLA. I wish it were possible.'[7]

Savimbi was justifiably bitter because, at this time, the
Americans had begun putting him under great pressure to
reach agreement with the MPLA. He pointed out that it was
too late: he was now in a state of maximum weakness, and
the MPLA was looking only for total victory. Immediately
after the OAU Addis summit, on 12 January 1976, the MPLA
Information Minister, Joao Filipe Martins, had said: 'We
have always stated that the FNLA and UNITA are our
enemies. There is only one movement in Angola and that is
the MPLA.'[8]

Savimbi felt especially distressed because the Americans
had discouraged a series of peace feelers he had put out to
the MPLA between June and September 1975, before the
really large-scale interventions of Cuban and South African
troops had begun. Between mid-June and late August 1975
the MPLA and UNITA Prime Ministers in the transitional
government, Lopo do Nascimento and Jose N'Dele, held a
series of talks in Lisbon, under Portuguese mediation but
arranged by Congo-Brazzaville, in an attempt to form an
MPLA-UNITA coalition. The CIA warned Savimbi that
America wanted no 'soft' allies in its 'war against the
MPLA'. But Savimbi says he ignored this threat, and the
main reason for the breakdown of the talks was resistance
among MPLA hardliners against any accommodation with
UNITA.[9]

*   *   *

On the day Savimbi flew to Lusaka and Kinshasa, the South
Africans began their withdrawal from Angola. By 23 January
they had totally evacuated their forward logistics at Cela and
Novo Redondo, the most northerly port on their coastal
advance, and Cuban forces had entered the towns without a
fight.[10] On 24 January, South Africa's Defence Minister

Pieter Botha appeared before parliament in Cape Town and said: 'I have on various occasions stated that South Africa's involvement in Angola is part of the involvement of the free world. But I also stated that South Africa is not prepared to fight on behalf of the free world alone. Furthermore, South Africa will defend with determination its own borders and those interests and borders we are responsible for.'[11]

The South Africans had formed heavy defensive lines north of Lobito to cover their carefully planned and orderly retreat. By the beginning of February they had withdrawn to the far south and were holding a strip of Angola 80 kilometres deep to the north of the Namibia-Angola border. In this buffer zone there were between 3,000 and 5,000 troops.

South Africa, waiting for the Cubans to roll southwards into the vacuum that its withdrawal had left, was bitter about the failure of the West and secret black African allies to give open support. Pieter Botha, John Vorster and 'high officials' in Cape Town began to tell senior South African journalists that South Africa had intervened in Angola at the urging of the United States and certain black African countries, particularly Zambia and Zaire. The *Washington Post*'s Bernard Nossiter met Botha, who spoke of several black African states and at least one 'free world' power giving their blessing to Pretoria's Angolan adventure. The nearest Botha came to identifying directly that 'free world' power was when he told Nossiter enigmatically: 'I would be the last man to destroy our diplomatic relations with the United States.'[12]

And an interview at the time between Vorster and senior *Newsweek* journalist Arnaud de Borchgrave went like this:

> *de Borchgrave*: 'Would it be accurate to say that the US solicited South Africa's help to turn the tide against Russians and Cubans in Angola last fall?'
>
> *Vorster*: 'I do not want to comment on that. The US Government can speak for itself. I am sure you will appreciate that I cannot violate the confidentiality of government-to-government communications. But if you are making the statement, I won't deny it.'

de Borchgrave: 'Would it also be accurate to say that you received a green light from Kissinger for a military operation in Angola and that at least six moderate black African presidents had given you their blessings for the same operation?'

Vorster: 'If you say that of your own accord, I will not call you a liar.'[13]

Barry Goldwater, the right wing Republican US Senator, was more blunt than Vorster. He said: 'There is no question but that the CIA told the South Africans to move into Angola and that we would help with military equipment.'[14] And in 1978 Pieter Botha said he personally had watched as US planes delivered arms in 1975 to anti-MPLA forces in Angola. They were unloaded under the supervision of American personnel in the presence of South African troops, who were asked to help distribute them.[15]

Henry Kamm of the *New York Times* reported that South Africa pushed into Angola on the understanding that the United States would rush sufficient supplies to make possible an effective resistance to an MPLA takeover. 'A high official said in an interview that the South African hope that the weapons superiority of the Soviet-backed forces could be balanced was based on contacts with American officials. He did not name them as he made this statement, but at another point he expressed special disappointment with Secretary of State Henry Kissinger. "We had been in touch," the official said. "We felt that if we could give them a lapse of time they could find ways and means . . . We accepted the utterances of Mr Kissinger and others. We felt surely he has the necessary pull to come forward with the goods." '[16]

In fact, Kissinger, the joint architect with Kaunda of the US-South African strategy, had managed to wriggle clear of direct involvement himself. The American support had been delivered by Daniel Patrick Moynihan, US Ambassador to the United Nations, to his South African counterpart, Pik Botha, and also by the US Ambassador to South Africa, Mr William Bowdler, to Prime Minister John Vorster.[17]

Kamm of the *New York Times* was also told by his 'high

official' in South Africa that both before and after the extraordinary OAU summit in Addis Ababa Presidents Kaunda
and Mobutu had pleaded with South Africa to strengthen its
military presence in Angola. And annoyed as Pretoria was at
being let down by Washington, the official said it was as
nothing compared with the chagrin felt by the Zambian and
Zairean leaders over the American betrayal and collapse of
will.

*   *   *

The blows now rained thick and fast on Jonas Savimbi. The
South African retreat would assure quick military victory for
the Cubans and their MPLA clients. And in Washington on
27 January the US House of Representatives confirmed by
323 votes to 99 the Senate decision to halt covert aid to
UNITA and the FNLA. Democratic Congressman John
Burton summed up the mood of the House when he said:
'Angola does not mean a damn thing to the future of this
country.'[18] President Ford angrily signed the decision into
law in the Defence Appropriations Act and accused
Congressmen of having 'lost their guts'.[19]

Senator John Tunney (Democrat, California), one of the
main architects of the Clark Amendment cutting off aid to
the Angolan movements, was almost gleeful about the final
Congressional decision and the fact that Savimbi and
UNITA would have to return to the bush as guerrilla
fighters. 'Savimbi has no illusions about how swiftly the
end is coming,' said Tunney. 'The war in Angola beyond
guerrilla fighting is almost over.'[20]

In his meeting on 21 January in Kinshasa with General
Vernon Walters, Savimbi had anticipated the final Congressional outcome. He told the deputy CIA chief: 'The Clark
Amendment is a bad thing because UNITA is fighting for a
cause that is also America's cause. Eventually Americans
will realise that by not helping UNITA, UNITA will lose and
the Americans also will lose. If one day you change your
minds you will find us still in the struggle'.[21]

*   *   *

With the South Africans gone, Savimbi began making
morale-boosting visits to his troops on fronts south of the

towns of Novo Redondo, Cela, Mussende and at Bucaco, just to the north of Luso. The Cubans and the MPLA were probing southwards only gingerly, but Savimbi, knowing that his enemies' offensive would gain momentum, told a party of 30 visting reporters that he had ordered the civilian population in some of the more northerly towns held by UNITA to evacuate into the bush. Their instructions were to form groups not more than 20-strong and to be prepared to live that way for the foreseeable future.[22]

But for a while UNITA directed its aggression not against the Cubans/MPLA but aginst its putative 'ally', the FNLA. There had been a series of clashes with the Chipenda-led forces since the major Christmas Eve battle in Huambo between the two movements. Chipenda's forces, based mainly in the southern town of Serpa Pinto and including many whites of Portuguese origin, had become virtual warlords, robbing banks and looting shops and villas in areas where UNITA was weakly represented. Then a lightning raid on a bank in Huambo, where N'Zau Puna had his headquarters, enraged UNITA.

On 27 January the party of 30 journalists was flown out of UNITA's territory and told that reporters would not be allowed to return for some time. As they departed heavy fighting was breaking out in the city between UNITA and remnants of the FNLA. The fighting had begun after the 200 or so FNLA troops based in the Huambo area had refused an order from Puna to go north and join UNITA forces on the Cela front. Savimbi told the reporters that he had moved 400 of his troops to the Novo Redondo front after FNLA soldiers abandoned their positions under Cuban artillery fire. By the end of January it was being reported that Chipenda had fled with many of his followers to Namibia.[23]

One of the journalists summed up the stark dilemma Savimbi faced: 'There can be no doubting the personal appeal of Dr Savimbi, the enthusiasm of his soldiers and the general support he excites . . . but if the South Africans have now decided that they cannot make the commitment it would need to contain the Russians, Cubans and MPLA, if they have decided their own front line is not the northern half of Angola, is the support of the people going to be

enough to keep Savimbi's movement afloat? Political support of the masses is no defence against Russian tanks.'[24]

By 5 February Jorge Sangumba was telling the big corps of
foreign journalists gathered in Lusaka, desperate for news
of the Cuban advance, that MPLA warplanes had gone into
action for the first time and bombed UNITA front line
positions. And Soviet ships carrying Cuban troops had
appeared 30 to 50 kilometres off Lobito, which was still in
UNITA hands.

On 7 February I managed to join Jorge Sangumba on a
flight going back into UNITA territory. We were nervous
passengers in view of reports that MPLA fighter planes were
now in action: the lumbering Fokker Friendship was an easy
target. We landed at Luso where Savimbi, intense and
preoccupied, was waiting: tension was palpable among his
senior officers. Savimbi went straight into conversation with
Sangumba, and afterwards the portly Foreign Secretary
staggered away with his head in his hands saying: 'Oh, my
country, it is in trouble.'

We waited in one of Luso's streets while Savimbi discussed strategy in a house with Chiwale. The main piece of
gossip I picked up was that Huambo was expected to fall to
the Cubans within 48 hours. N'Zau Puna had radioed that
he had woken up that morning at his Huambo headquarters
to find half the civilian population gone: Cuban armoured
columns were pressing on Alto Hama, just 70 kilometres
north of Huambo. They were being harassed by two battalions of UNITA forces, totalling 1,600 men, who were
blowing up bridges and attacking troop carriers and supply
trucks at the rear of the Cuban column.

Earlier that day a South African brigadier in full uniform
had flown into Luso to assess the military situation and to
pass on a message from Washington – the Ford Administration remained committed to help UNITA in every remaining
way possible, but there could be no overt assistance until
after the Presidential election at the end of the year.

There was talk full of hatred for Senators Tunney and
Clark. Just the previous day, in Washington, Clark had
proposed that the US begin negotiations with the MPLA and
acknowledge that 'the tide of history' was on their side – a

particular American verdict that 'was a much more confident one than that given by many of Africa's leaders'.[25]

Piled in the streets of Luso were weapons and materials UNITA had captured in a battle 48 hours earlier at Lumege, 60 kilometres to the east. They included two brand new Chinese 75mm recoilless rifles. UNITA officers fingered the Chinese weapons and looked through the prismed sights and speculated tartly that they were part of the Peking consignment sent through Dar-es-Salaam for UNITA but diverted to the MPLA by President Nyerere.

Jorge Sangumba picked up the diary of a Cuban killed in the Lumege action. Folded into the diary was a mimeographed letter from Fidel Castro saying that by fighting in Angola Cuban troops were advancing Cuba's revolution. Sangumba fingered the writings of the dead young Cuban and said for the benefit of my press ears: 'He died a glorious revolutionary death in Africa fighting blacks.'

* * *

We flew onwards from Luso to Bie, from where Savimbi left immediately with Chiwale to make an overnight assessment of the situation at fronts to the north of both Huambo and Bie. A trickle of refugees was arriving in Bie from Huambo, including members of the fruitless coalition government with the FNLA.

The following day, 8 February, Savimbi returned and, in the by now very familiar surroundings of the former Portuguese governor's palace, he told me his forces faced a critical situation. An estimated 7,000 Cuban troops had moved southwards. Some 3,500 of them were advancing on Huambo in three columns. Alto Hama had fallen and the UNITA High Command was considering giving orders to evacuate both Huambo and Bie, UNITA's administrative capital and military headquarters respectively. Two hundred and fifty kilometres to the west of Huambo, Cuban columns were also closing on Lobito. And 550 kilometres east of Huambo Cuban columns were pushing towards UNITA's Luso stronghold.

The Cubans advancing on Huambo were supported by jet fighters; 30 armoured vehicles, helicopters, and several batteries of 'Stalin Organs' which had begun the rout of the FNLA in the north.

Strafing by the jets and pounding by Cuban artillery had caused high casualties among Savimbi's front line troops, but he was particularly bewildered about how to counter the Cubans' use of helicopters to put down large numbers of troops behind UNITA lines. Part of the UNITA defensive strategy was to blow up every bridge on the Cuban line of advance, but two important bridges across the River Queve, north of Huambo, were abandoned unblown when UNITA sappers panicked as Cuban troops arrived by helicopter as the explosive charges were being placed.

UNITA troops defending Luso were suffering similarly. One encounter left Savimbi 'stoically incredulous at the Cubans' use of helicopters in a vertical envelopment. At night the UNITA force had been facing several hundred Katangese troops, and the next morning they found a full battalion suddenly behind them, attacking from the rear and blocking their retreat.'[26]

Savimbi spoke more with regret than bitterness about the US Congressmen who had opposed help to UNITA, and particularly Senators Tunney, Clark and Humphrey and Representative Charles Diggs: 'We deplore that they want to defend democracy and freedom for themselves in the United States, but want dictatorship for us . . . . They are working a contradiction . . . It is too simple reasoning for Senator Humphrey to say that Angola is too far away . . . They are defending an undemocratic society for us. For Angolans they want the Cubans and their Russian tanks and jets to impose on us a system.'

He said UNITA would never give up fighting and the MPLA would never win acceptance. 'If they really had the support of the people they would not have resorted to armed struggle instead of going a democratic way.'

UNITA had fought for liberty from the Portuguese – 'Now we are fighting again for the liberty of our people. We will fight until one day the world consciousness will understand that between justice and injustice there is no choice. The Russians and Cubans are slaughtering our people. The South African presence was just a pretext for the Russians for the invasion of our country using the Cubans. Now there are no South Africans at any of the fronts, why are the Cubans continuing to advance and kill our black people? Why don't they stop?'

I could not know it at the time, but I would not see Savimbi again for many years and 8 February 1976 would be my last day on Angolan soil for more than half a decade to come.

Before I left to fly one last journey from Angola to Lusaka, the UNITA President reiterated his old theme, that which he had hammered for 18 months before independence and had stressed when I met him for the first time in September 1975: 'We stand for elections because we think in a situation like this they are the only way to determine the leadership of this country, as in Britain, France, West Germany and in America itself. Only free elections can determine which one of the three liberation movements commands majority support. Even if we have to go back into the bush the four million people who support us will continue to hope that UNITA will come back one day.'[27]

*   *   *

In the early hours of 9 February 1976 Cuban tanks started rolling into Huambo. They met no resistance. Some 5,000 UNITA troops had left the city and pulled back to the small town of Vila Nova, about 50 kilometres to the east, and to heights a few kilometres to the south.

No independent observers witnessed Huambo's fall. Correspondents in Lusaka, who gave the news to the world, relied on the account of Jorge Sangumba who, in turn, had received his information by radio from UNITA's military headquarters at Bie. Sangumba said 6,000 Cubans entered the city, though just 24 hours earlier Savimbi had said only 3,500 Cubans were on the Huambo front.

Sangumba also said the Cubans were killing women, children and elderly people indiscriminately in Huambo. The MPLA, in turn, claimed that UNITA, before retreating, had shot dead hundreds of MPLA prisoners in jail in Huambo.[28]

On 10 February Savimbi and eight other UNITA leaders signed an order for the movement's followers to leave the towns to return to the bush and begin a new guerrilla war –

this time not against the Portuguese, but against Cuba and the Soviet Union.

The seven-point communiqué said UNITA had decided to convert its army into a guerrilla force to save it from annihilation: 'No army in Africa outside Egypt has had to face a war machine of such dimensions as those of the army now dividing our country.' It said UNITA's allies had lacked political courage and that unfulfilled promises caused it to sacrifice hundreds of the movement's best soldiers. It expressed gratitude to black African states which had supported the formation of an Angolan coalition government of national unity, singling out for special thanks Egypt, Gabon, the Ivory Coast, Morocco, Senegal, Zaire and Zambia.[29]

Savimbi also wrote letters to every African head of state telling them he would never go into exile.[30]

As Savimbi led his defeated forces away from the towns, Max Hastings, a British television and radio journalist, published a lament. 'In any internal power struggle in Africa the personal risks for those involved of execution or exile have always been high,' he wrote. 'So when entering a struggle the message of Angola is that it pays to be on the side the Russians are on. They win. Whatever amiable mutterings the American Ambassador whispers into receptive ears, when it comes to the crunch he cannot deliver the cash, votes or guns from Washington to back them . . . And so now (in Angola) the Russians can confidently prepare to rake in their huge winnings, staked successfully upon the resounding apathy of the West.'[31]

On 10 February UNITA's misery was compounded as MPLA forces retook Lobito and Benguela. And on the following day the OAU hammered another nail into UNITA's coffin when its secretariat announced from Addis Ababa that the MPLA's People's Republic of Angola had been admitted as the 47th full member of the organisation.

UNITA's response to the OAU's recognition of the MPLA was to issue a statement saying: 'We were here before the Russians and Cubans invaded. We will be here when so much Russian and Cuban blood has been spilled on the soil of Africa that the new imperialists will also be forced to withdraw.

'We will never accept a minority regime imposed by a racist European colonial power. We will fight in the jungles, we will fight in the mountains. We will infiltrate the cities. Let the Russians and their Cubans come by their tens of thousands, let them stay for years. In the end the people of Angola will win.'[32]

* * *

The allegation in Savimbi's 10 February communiqué that broken promises by UNITA's allies had cost the lives of hundreds of soldiers was more than propaganda rhetoric. Through late January and early February Jorge Sangumba had been arguing that UNITA would soon be able to launch air strikes of its own against the MPLA. And on 8 February when I had asked Savimbi if he had any hopes of outside military aid, he replied: 'I don't think we are without promises. I think that within a few days we will know what is going to happen.'

What prompted the question was something one of his officials had told me as we stood gossiping in the street in Luso on 7 February while waiting for Savimbi. The official said UNITA was hoping for the arrival the next day of a C-130 aircraft with technicians, back-up equipment and ammunition to enable four Israeli-piloted Mirage fighters that had arrived in Zaire to go into action with UNITA in Angola. UNITA would soon receive delivery of American Redeye ground-to-air missiles. And Jorge Sangumba would be sent out of Angola to speed up the delivery of 24 heavy 120mm field guns that had been promised.

It took years to find out whether there was any truth to this careless gossip – and there was. When John Stockwell, chief of the CIA's Angola Task Force, published his account of America's involvement in the war, he revealed that France had contributed four missile-firing Alouette helicopters to the UNITA cause, which US Air Force C-141 planes transported to Kinshasa in early January 1976. The CIA was debating sending Redeye missiles and heavy artillery, said Stockwell, and in addition it had negotiated an agreement with the US Air Force to repaint one of its C-130 transport planes for delivery to South Africa so that its forces could support the Alouettes at the battlefront. When Savimbi visited deputy CIA chief General Vernon Walters in Zaire on 21 January he was shown the helicopters and their West German HOT air-to-ground missiles.[33]

'Since early January my feeling had been that the conventional war was over,' Savimbi told me during a conversation in Morocco in 1980. 'It was not possible for us to continue because we were not being given the right kind of arms, and even if we did begin to get them we did not have enough people trained to use them effectively.

'I called in Chiwale and Puna and said we should consider the (conventional) war as over. What we are doing is foolish. Let us give the order to our people to disperse into the bush so that we can save men and arms. Then we can begin to reorganise again.

'But we hesitated. It was difficult to leave the people and the towns behind. And we were misled by our friends among the black African heads of state. I went out and told them (the heads of state) I considered the conventional war as lost and that I was going back to give orders to my people to regroup in the bush and start a guerrilla war. So they said: "No, no, no, no – in a guerrilla war you won't be able to resist beyond six months. You can't do that. We have got the promises that they will send us helicopters with HOT rockets; you will get this; you will get that."'

Here Savimbi's voice became heavy with a weary irony: 'I told them they would not reach us in time to defend Huambo, and once the Cubans had entered Huambo it would be too late. Then they said: "Look, the helicopters will be here tomorrow with all the pilots."

'And the helicopters did get to Kinshasa with the HOT rockets that would have destroyed the Stalin Organs which made a noise like thunder and demoralised our people. I saw the helicopters and I saw the rockets, but they had not brought any pilots. They (the heads of state) said: "Why do you feel you don't have any hope? The helicopters are there, the rockets are there, and now we are only looking for specialists to operate them."

'I conceded that it gave us some hope, and instead of giving the order to disperse I said we would try and hold on a bit longer. We would try to do something until the helicopters and pilots arrived.

'But the Cubans approached and the pilots did not come and as a result 600 of our people were unnecessarily killed defending the road from Cela to Huambo.'

Even after the loss of Huambo, Jorge Sangumba continued to assert that aircraft would soon be thrown into the battle on UNITA's side. On the evening following Huambo's fall one foreign correspondent heard Sangumba making an international telephone call to an unidentified person from Lusaka's Intercontinental Hotel. 'Please tell them to move,' he said. 'The whole of our Motherland is at stake.'[34]

As late as 18 February Henry Kissinger was still telling Savimbi, through the US Embassy in Kinshasa, that as long as UNITA demonstrated that it could resist the MPLA effectively the US would continue to give it support. But, said the CIA's Angola Task Force chief: 'By that date Kissinger knew full well that we could provide no more support to UNITA.'[35]

Years later Savimbi told me of a meeting he had in December 1979 with James Schlesinger, then US Secretary of Defence, who asked whether Kissinger was UNITA's friend. 'Yes,' said Savimbi, who recalled that Schlesinger replied with a sardonic grunt: 'Good luck.'[36]

*   *   *

Through January 1976 the rout of the FNLA continued. Its soldiers had fled without fighting from nearly every encounter since the debacle at Death Road on 10 November 1975. The FNLA's backup forces from the Zaire Army also retreated quickly, stripping entire areas as they went of refrigerators, furniture and anything else of value. On occasions they even unloaded their own wounded from trucks to make way for the booty.[37] And although instructed to take all military equipment with them, they took only their own artillery and left behind FNLA weaponry, much of it with US markings.

And then correspondents began to notice the arrival at the Intercontinental Hotel, Kinshasa, of young Britons who 'sport tattoos, effect a self-important swagger and seem quite lost'.[38]

The contribution by Western governments to the Angolan imbroglio had plumbed its most distasteful low. Unable, or unwilling, to commit themselves publicly to a particular cause in Angola, they now turned a blind eye as Holden Roberto, in his desperation, recruited mercenaries in Britain, the US and Holland with crisp new hundred-dollar bills, courtesy of the CIA, to beef up and reorganise the FNLA.[39]

The quality of the mercenaries was exceptionally low. They were not the tough, professional adventurers who had made the word 'white mercenary' something to be genuinely feared in the Congo of the sixties. They were the new young unemployed of the mid-70s, and for the most part they were the most socially ill-equipped of their genera-tion – poorly educated and from poorer homes, many of them real intellectual innocents in an African country that had been robbed of its own innocence.

Most had very little combat experience. Some had no military training at all, and two were London street sweepers recruited with the lure of $US 300 a week and sent from their jobs straight to Angola. 'They are not the hard, tough, experienced personnel needed in this war,' observed one Western military attaché in Kinshasa. 'Some may have had experience in Northern Ireland, but I don't think most of them realise what they are in for.'[40]

That was an understatement. The raw and unversed mercenaries were unable to halt the FNLA's disintegration, and reports began to emerge of the appalling psychopathic actions of a former British paratrooper called Costas Georgiou, also known as 'Colonel Callan', who had been appointed Roberto's Senior Field Officer in Angola. Worst of these was the execution of 14 mercenaries, mainly Britons, by other soldiers of fortune on the instructions of Callan.[41] After the 14 men had been gunned down, Callan stripped their bodies and left them to rot unburied. His demented intent seemed to be to discourage others from repeating the errors of the dead men. On a reconnaissance patrol they had attacked one of their own posts, wrongly identifying a

French armoured car as a Soviet tank and mistaking fellow mercenaries for Cubans.[42]

The mercenaries now joined FNLA and Zairean soldiers fleeing from Angola into Zaire as the Cubans cleared up the remaining FNLA pockets near the Zaire border.

Robin Wright, a young woman reporter, then with the *Christian Science Monitor*, brilliantly described the FNLA's dramatic end in San Antonio do Zaire, Angola's most north-westerly town, situated on the Atlantic coast at the mouth of the Congo River, opposite Zaire: 'The surprise assault began at 8.45 a.m., Feb 6, with the sound of T-54 tanks and the crash of mortars falling on the hospital and airfield on the outskirts of town. At first many people thought the sounds were thunder from the gale-force of the rainy season that was drenching this steamy little town located six degrees below the equator . . .'

But then the town degenerated into chaos. 'The 350 deployed FNLA soldiers merely fled as the assault moved closer. People and troops fled down the street towards the river, the only exit on the peninsula. At the port, where half a dozen fishing boats were docked, women and children were fighting and pulling each other out to get a place.

'The MPLA tanks were immediately backed up with heavily equipped troops who started firing randomly at everything in sight. The five British mercenaries who had administered the town for the last three weeks made an effort to organise men and check the strength of the opposing forces. But it was clear within minutes that nothing could be done to save the small town with the meagre 20 minutes of firepower available.

'This reporter and one mercenary headed for the single small motorised boat that had just been repaired the night before. Approaching the vessel – smaller than a tiny tugboat – we saw it, too, was swarming with people clawing for space.

'Fifteen minutes later, the remaining four British mercenaries ran through the pouring rain to the boat while African troops and civilians on all sides were being shot down by machine-guns. One T-54 was close behind them, manned by a bearded Cuban.

'Shortly before they reached the dock, the boat, under

pressure from the overload, and rocking from the heavy waves of the storm, capsized, dumping most of the Africans into the rough water. Many went down after being hit by machine-gun fire that was blasting into the water on all sides.

'The boat, once turned upright, veered off the dock and only two of the British mercenaries were able to board. As it pushed off, the other two Britons were still standing on the dock under fire.

'The approximately 20 who left on the boat – three mercenaries, this reporter, and 16 Africans – headed for Banana in southern Zaire, an hour's journey away. During the escape and throughout the day from Banana we could hear the sound of mortars and tanks blasting away at the defenceless city.'[43]

In Angola, Callan and twelve other mercenaries were captured and sent to Luanda to be put on trial by the MPLA for war crimes. For months they became the focus of international media attention, inevitably distracting analysis from the deeper issues involved in the Angolan conflict. And though Savimbi's forces had no links with Roberto's mercenaries, UNITA, already tainted by its South African connections, was further damaged by the mercenary scandal.

Callan and his men were a propaganda gift to the MPLA. For Savimbi, though not as much as for Roberto, they were a public relations disaster. For years afterwards UNITA representatives spent a lot of time trying to explain why theirs was not the movement which had been helped by the mercenaries who were tried in Luanda.

* * *

Savimbi's friend, Kenneth Kaunda, was in deep trouble too as a result of the South African withdrawal and President Ford's signing of the Defence Appropriation Bill. Only ten months earlier in Washington he had appealed to Ford 'to reverse what he considered to be a tide sweeping the MPLA to victory'.[44] He had campaigned vigorously for the establishment of a government of national unity in Angola to be followed by multi-party elections, only to see his ideas gradually rejected by fellow African heads of state. He had argued that Soviet and Cuban intervention, not South African, was the main cause of the civil war. He had co-operated with the CIA and the South Africans to save Savimbi, whose courage and intelligence he had come to admire, from annihilation.

Now Savimbi's destruction seemed inevitable – and there was little that Kaunda could do about it. The Zambian President would have to accept as his neighbour an inevit-ably hostile MPLA government, supported by an exultant and confident Cuban Army whose future course of action could not be predicted and whose capacity for interference in Zambia might be great.

In his isolation Kaunda got support from Zambian Parlia-mentarians, one of whom, Nalumino Mundia, a future Prime Minister, told Parliament: 'I cannot understand how anyone can argue with a stand such as the one chosen by Zambia, which allows the indigenous Angolans to decide their own future by universal vote.'[45]

Zambians like Mundia believed that Kaunda's Angola policy had been honourable, courageous and entirely con-sistent with the twin pillars of OAU philosophy: no intervention by foreign powers in African affairs, and no interference by OAU members in the internal affairs of other independent states.[46]

But there were others in Zambia who took a more hostile stand to their President. One was Robinson Makayi, a senior journalist on the *Times of Zambia*, owned by Kaunda's own ruling party. Makayi, the paper's features editor, travelled to Luanda and wrote a series of articles sympathetic to the MPLA in contradiction to his paper's editorial line. Makayi was later arrested and detained without trial.

Another centre of hostility was a small group of politicians centred around Reuben Kamanga, a tough member of the ruling United Independence Party's Central Committee, who argued – behind closed doors but not in public – for alignment with the MPLA. Also strongly opposed to Kaunda's policy on Angola was the students' union at the University of Zambia. Union representatives accused the President of treachery in a fiery document[47] issued on a day of demonstrations during which university signs were painted over with MPLA slogans. Battle-helmeted riot police with rifles, sub-machine-guns, clubs and shields surrounded the campus.

A statement by the students' union described Savimbi as a 'bearded quisling, pseudo-revolutionary, professional traitor and cunning fox', employed by the secret services of Portugal and South Africa. It said camps stocked with weapons sent by the United States for UNITA had been set up in Zambia, and it went on: 'It is indisputable that the Zambian government supports UNITA, a movement whose long-standing treachery has been made explicit. This compels us to charge the Zambia ruling clique headed by Dr Kaunda, 'our beloved President', with criminal treachery.'

Such tirades by students in North America or Western Europe would sink into oblivion, but, given the realities of African politics, they were dynamite in Zambia and were bound to provoke a reaction.

The reaction was slow in coming. The demonstration had taken place on 15 January, but it was not until 25 January that Kaunda began to range in. Addressing some 800 members of the youth wing of the United Independence Party (UNIP), he said that a Russian based in Lusaka had told Zambia it would have only itself to blame if the MPLA government denied Zambia access to the Benguela Railway to punish it for its failure to recognise the Luanda government.[48]

'What cheek of the Russians,' said Kaunda. 'Should MPLA shut the route it will be a pity, but Zambia will not be a puppet to the MPLA and will not be cowed into doing wrong things because of routes.'

It was all very well for the MPLA to crush the other Angolan movements with Cuban and Soviet force – 'but will that make Dr Neto's government a representative government?' To which the UNIP youths were reported to have shouted 'No'.

On 26 January one of Kaunda's closest lieutenants on UNIP's Central Committee, Frank Chitambala, accused foreign lecturers at the university – 'misled Marxists who are bent on confusing Zambian students' – of having organised the anti-government demonstration.[49]

Then on 28 January – after the South Africans had begun their Angolan withdrawal and the US House of Representatives had cut off any further aid to UNITA and the FNLA – the Zambian President went on television and radio and declared a full national state of emergency. It was necessary, he said, to counter a deteriorating security situation on Zambia's borders and growing evidence of internal subversion.

In a now-famous allusion to the Soviet and Cuban intervention in Angola, Zambia's leader said: 'We have witnessed imperialism at work in all its manifestations. Africa has fought and driven out the ravenous wolves of colonialism, racism and fascism from Angola through the front door. But a plundering Tiger with its deadly Cubs is now coming in through the back door. The effects of foreign intervention are now being felt in Zambia.'

Grim-faced and seated before the Zambian flag, Kaunda said the state of emergency was 'designed to defend the Constitution and the nation . . . I want the country to be put in a state of full preparedness to counter any move calculated to destroy our country. We as a nation must prepare for the worst. We are at war. Make no mistake.'

Then Kaunda used Chinese terminology to accuse the Soviets of fomenting trouble at the university: 'Some of our institutions of learning have been infiltrated. Some student groups are like an orchestra with an invisible conductor on the payroll of a socialist imperialist power.'

The following day six Marxist foreign lecturers at the University of Zambia, four of them from the Department of Politics, were arrested by police and detained in Kabwe Prison, north of Lusaka, without charge or trial. At least 19, and perhaps more than 40, students were also imprisoned without being tried.[50] The students' union declared a protest strike. Kaunda responded by closing the university and sending riot police to herd the students into fleets of buses which returned them to their homes throughout the country.

*   *   *

As the Cubans pushed towards Angola's border with Zambia, so Zambian verbal attacks on the Soviet Union became more vehement. On 6 February Foreign Minister Rupiah Banda said: 'Any foreigner fighting in Angola is a mercenary. All foreign intervention in Angola is condemnable and mercenary.

'After they have killed the South Africans in Angola, who will the Cubans and Russians be remaining there to fight? The Soviet Union knows very well that it is not in Angola because of the South Africans. If they're supposed to be in Angola to help us (black Africans), why don't they go and fight in South Africa and Namibia? Haven't they heard of Cape Town?'

Banda, speaking at a Lusaka Press Club dinner, became more and more emotional as the evening progressed. By the end he was clearly urging UNITA to continue resisting: 'There is nothing much you can do against a power like the Soviet Union, and the Soviets know it. Only if the people of Angola rise up against the Soviet Union and give them a hard time, like the Americans in Vietnam were given a hard time, will the Soviet Union know what they have done is wrong.'[51]

* * *

By mid-February the Cubans/MPLA had pushed southwards in the wake of the South African retreat as far as the port of Mocamedes and the inland towns of Sa da Bandeira and Serpa Pinto. As the South Africans retreated, they blew up bridges and destroyed runways. The Cuban advance was cautious. Before several hundred soldiers were put ashore at Mocamedes from a seven-ship flotilla on 12 February, three Soviet Alligator-class landing craft spent the previous day firing shells on the port from 12 kilometres offshore.[52]

Though Kaunda's Angola strategy was in disarray, he continued to condemn Soviet policy. He also permitted a clandestine airlift of CIA arms through Zambian airspace to Savimbi's temporary redoubt at Gago Coutinho, near the Zambian border. Savimbi had retreated there, via Luso, with thousands of his followers after giving his 10 February order to return to guerrilla warfare. Three planes were involved in this airlift – Savimbi's own Fokker Friendship-27;

an F-27 of Zaire Airways; and a Viscount hired by the CIA Lusaka station from a Grenada-based company, Pearl Airways, for $US 106,000 plus operating costs.[53]

The airlift of arms was able to continue to Savimbi despite the Congressional ban because not all of the $US 32 million allocated to the CIA for the Angola Task Force had been spent. It was the last nine million dollars in the programme that the CIA was now utilising to give Savimbi the capacity to survive.[54] The consignments flown in from Kinshasa included US Law-66 anti-tank missiles, 60, 82 and 102mm siege mortars, 76mm anti-tank cannon, and 105mm recoilless rifles.

The lowest ebb of Zambia's relations with the Soviet Union came on 20 February when the Czechoslovak Ambassador to Zambia, Mr Stanislav Kouhousek, seated next to the Soviet Ambassador, ostentatiously walked out of a meeting between Kaunda, the press corps, diplomatic representatives and the ruling UNIP Central Committee. Kaunda accused the Soviet Union of fomenting the disturbances at the university and recalled Zambia's condemnation of the Soviet Union's 1968 invasion of Czechoslovakia. On these remarks the Soviet Ambassador, Mr Dimitri Belokolos, nodded almost imperceptibly to Mr Kouhousek, who rose and left. It caused a stir in Mulungushi Hall, the big auditorium built for the 1972 Lusaka non-aligned conference, but Kaunda waved dismissively towards the Czechoslovak Ambassador and said: 'Let him go, let him go.'[55]

Mr Belokolos stayed on and sat stony-faced as Kaunda said the MPLA could not control Angola unless they negotiated with the FNLA and UNITA: 'A military victory has not come through MPLA but through Russia and Cuba. Now let all foreign forces withdraw so that there can be peaceful negotiations.

'We don't see any country on earth where a power can sit on a people, oppress a people and expect to get away with it. Sooner or later, the people who are being oppressed are bound to rise.'

Dunstan Kamana, Zambia's Ambassador to the United Nations, heavily criticised Moscow's post-independence Angola policy in an article he wrote for the *New York Times*:

'Zambia believes that it is one thing to help Angola with its independence but quite another to help any group of Angolans impose a government over the people of Angola . . . Even if the MPLA overruns all of Angola, as appears to be the case now, and defeats the other parties in a conventional war, this would be no proof of the popularity of the victor or the unpopularity of the vanquished.'[56]

But Zambia was now in an exposed position, and the Luanda government made it pay for its criticism of the MPLA and its support for Savimbi. After the MPLA retook Lobito it ordered a ship, just before it sailed, to unload 1,200 tonnes of Zambian copper it had taken aboard. The load was part of a large stockpile of Zambian copper, lead and zinc which had been stuck in the port for seven months together with 72,000 tonnes of Zambian imports, mainly mining and electricity generating equipment, and six new American diesel locomotives and 800 wagons belonging to Zambian Railways.[57]

Kaunda's exposure was made more stark when articles appeared in the British and South African press quoting Savimbi as saying that, at all stages of its military intervention in Angola, South Africa had acted 'painfully correctly' and with the approval of Zambia, Zaire and the Ivory Coast. The articles, quoting the records of a meeting between Savimbi and Mr Bill Coughlin, an assistant to Senator John Tunney, said Zambian, Zairean and Ivorien presidents Kaunda, Mobutu and Houphouet-Boigny had asked South Africa to intervene militarily to counteract the Cubans and Soviets. They also said Kaunda arranged the 20 December 1975 meeting between John Vorster and Savimbi.[58]

Savimbi was summoned from Angola to Lusaka for three days by Kaunda. The clandestine foray to Zambia by the beleaguered UNITA leader was not officially announced, but afterwards UNITA paid its dues by issuing an unconvincing statement in Lusaka saying it was untrue that Kaunda had arranged the Vorster visit: 'Russian and Cuban propagandists cooked up a story claiming that Dr Jonas Savimbi of UNITA visited South Africa at the suggestion of Zambia. And to make such slander and malicious propaganda more effective the Russians and the

Cubans used Mr Bill Coughlin, an aide to United States Senator John Tunney.'[59]

With hindsight, Jorge Sangumba was undermining the credibility of the statement as he issued it by telling correspondents that, the allegations concerning Kaunda apart, Savimbi had never visited South Africa. Years later Savimbi talked quite freely to the author about the visits he had made to South Africa at that time.

Things were changing rapidly now. On 13 March MPLA MIGs bombed Gago Coutinho, forcing Savimbi to surrender the last town held by UNITA and retreat deep into the forests.

On 15 March the Pearl Airways Viscount, now unable to fly into Gago Coutinho, made a routine touch-down at Lusaka Airport and its Austrian and British pilots were surprised when the Zambian authorities impounded the plane.[60]

The following day an executive jet belonging to a Swiss-registered company – and hired, according to Zambian officials, by the same Lonrho Company which had earlier provided Savimbi with an executive jet for his travels around Africa – flew into Lusaka from Luanda. Aboard was Senhor Jose Eduardo dos Santos, Foreign Minister of Angola's MPLA government. Intense security was enforced at Lusaka Airport. Reporters were turned away, and also diplomats, including Cuba's Ambassador to Zambia, Senor Eduardo Morejon Estavez.[61]

Dos Santos and his seven-member team met a Zambian delegation led not by Rupiah Banda but by Reuben Kamanga, the pro-MPLA chairman of the foreign policy sub-committee of UNIP's Central Committee. No communiqué was issued at the end of the talks, but Zambian government officials said privately that both sides had made proposals for normalising relations.

A glum-looking Rupiah Banda was at Lusaka Airport in the interests of protocol on 18 March to say goodbye to Senhor dos Santos. The Angolan Foreign Minister declined to speak to reporters, and Banda, who just the previous month had encouraged the MPLA's enemies to turn Angola into Russia's Vietnam, said only: 'I would rather not say anything at the moment.'[62]

18

Mutiny in Zambia

1976

There are many unanswered questions surrounding the war in Angola. Two major ones arise from the period January-February 1976.

Why did President Kaunda *really* feel obliged to declare a full state of national emergency on 28 January, apparently in response to unrest among less than 1,000 students at the university and when the Cubans advancing through Angola were still far away from the border with Zambia?

Who was UNITA's Foreign Secretary Jorge Sangumba referring to when he told reporters in Lusaka, after the Zambian state of emergency had been declared, that warplanes had bombed MPLA forces in the eastern Angolan town of Cazombo, within 150 kilometres of the Zambian border? 'MPLA forces have definitely been bombed. I cannot say by whom,' said Sangumba.[1]

By itself, Sangumba's vague assertion could be ignored. But it ties in with other snippets of information which, together, perhaps make an interesting whole. They certainly make a working hypothesis.

Jonas Savimbi, President Kaunda, Zaire's President Mobutu and the South Africans did not always share objectives during the Angolan war. But one thing they *all* had in common was a desire to clear the MPLA from all 1,300 kilometres of the Benguela Railway in Angola and to reopen the line, under UNITA control, to Zairean and Zambian imports and exports.

For Savimbi it would have reinforced his credibility in a world where economics is usually the key imperative: for Mobutu and Kaunda it would have meant they had access again to their cheapest and most important land route to the sea: and for South Africa it would have reinforced the strength and morale of three of its most important black African allies of convenience.

Kaunda stressed to Savimbi the importance of reopening the Benguela Railway: and, with the help of the South Africans, UNITA gained control of the whole line, except for a short stretch at the eastern end near the border town of Teixeira de Sousa. The South Africans and UNITA laboured mightily to take Teixeira de Sousa (renamed Luau after independence), approaching it across Angolan territory from the west. But the Cubans/MPLA strongly defended the town, and after they blew up a major bridge on its western approaches the South Africans abandoned the attempt to approach it from that direction.

Instead they turned their attention to a possible attack from the east, through Zairean territory. The Kinshasa station of the CIA relayed to its headquarters in Langley, Virginia, requests from South Africa for aircraft fuel, more sophisticated weapons, trucks and air support – 'Then it reported a South African plan to fly a task force into southern Zaire to attack Teixeira de Sousa from the border,' wrote John Stockwell. 'Kinshasa station was encouraged in its policy towards the South Africans by cables from the CIA stations in Lusaka and Pretoria.'[2]

The former chief of the CIA's Angola Task Force leaves his readers tantalisingly in the air with this piece of information. He does not say what, if anything, came of the plan. But it does emphasise the importance in the conflict of Teixeira de Sousa.

And in Zambia, which desperately wanted Teixeira de Sousa prised from the MPLA's grip, stories spread that the Air Force had been scrambled to attack the town. A Zambian Army lieutenant-colonel whom I met at a lunch in Lusaka with foreign friends said that a flight of four Yugoslav-made jet fighters of the Zambian Air Force were ordered in late January 1976 to bomb Teixeira de Sousa. One can only

speculate whether it had any connection with the South
African plan.

The Zambian planes, whose flight path from Lusaka
would have taken them close to Cazombo, had begun their
approach to Teixeira de Sousa when one of them disintegrated, apparently struck by a missile, said the lieutenant-
colonel. The other planes turned back and landed at Lusaka.
There was a phone call from State House, President
Kaunda's official residence, enquiring about the outcome of
the mission. On being told that the attack had not been
pressed home because the defences were too sophisticated,
State House ordered the Air Force to return to the attack.
The pilots refused and they were supported by the commander of the Zambian Air Force, Air Commodore Peter Zuze. A
gunfight then broke out in the militarised area of Lusaka
Airport between 'loyal' and 'disloyal' airmen in which seven
men died. The planes did not go back into the attack.

Western intelligence officers confirmed at the time that
they had information concerning a gun battle at Lusaka
Airport between members of the Zambian military, but they
declined to say what lay behind it.

One small piece of corroborating evidence was contained
in one of the letters which arrived at my office from one of
the rebellious students at the University of Zambia.[3]
Addressed to Reuters and signed, it gave details of arrests
on the campus and of the activities of Zambian secret service
agents. It said that the students' union executive had concluded at an emergency meeting that Zambia's advocacy of
an Angolan government of national unity was a mask for its
support of UNITA. And it went on: 'At this meeting also
students gave evidence about the government's support for
UNITA, which included a small mutiny by the Zambia Air
Force which refused to go and fight on behalf of UNITA'.

The evidence is too incomplete to reach definitive conclusions, but if the Zambian Air Force did try to attack
Teixeira de Sousa it seems possible that its planes also
attacked nearby Cazombo, as described by Jorge Sangumba.
And if the airmen mutinied because they did not like what
they were being commanded to do, that seems a better
reason for declaring a full state of national emergency than

any of those that President Kaunda gave on 28 January 1976.

There are other possible explanations of both the Cazombo attack and the Zambian Air Force mutiny. The semi-official MPLA account of the civil war, by Michael Wolfers and Jane Bergerol, says that Zairean Air Force bombers flew a sortie into eastern Angola in early 1976, and they therefore might also be the bombers to which Jorge Sangumba was referring.[4]

Some Western intelligence officials believe the mutiny was partly inspired by resentment at Zambia's growing military co-operation with South Africa. In a long defence of Kenneth Kaunda's policies during 1975–76, two Canadian academics wrote that 'vague reports of mysterious night flights through remote airports in the Western Province (of Zambia) gave rise to allegations that South Africa had been accorded transit rights in Zambia to support UNITA and possibly her own military activities in Angola'.[5] But there was nothing vague about the reports United Nations officials in Lusaka were sending to their New York headquarters confirming sightings of South African troop movements by land and air through western Zambia to Angola. Justified as Kaunda might have been, in terms of wider strategic perspectives, in co-operating militarily with Pretoria, it takes little imagination to see that it could have caused immense resentment among young and idealistic officers in his military forces who were expected to co-operate with, or turn a blind eye to, the South Africans.

* * *

Later in 1976 President Kaunda announced that the Zambian Air Force had been stripped of its independent status and was being merged into a single Zambian military command. Air Commodore Zuze would henceforward be directly answerable to the Army Commander.

19

Human Reckoning

1976

Hoorah for Revolution
And more cannon shot:
The beggar on horseback
Lashes the beggar on foot.

Hooray for Revolution
The cannons come again:
The beggars have changed horseback
But the lash goes on the same.

W. B. Yeats

*　　*　　*

As the Cubans/MPLA established their control across
Angola and UNITA began its retreat into the bush, both
sides began exchanging allegations of atrocities.

According to UNITA officials, there was a 'tremendous
massacre' of civilians as the MPLA and the Cubans took
control of Huambo: 'Innocent women and children, old
people who cannot run, are dying by the thousands.'[1]

Savimbi sent a communiqué to Lusaka, by one of the
flights from Gago Coutinho, which said he had received
confirmation of more than one hundred UNITA sympathisers being executed by the MPLA in Lobito, Benguela and
Huambo. Peasants in towns just to the north of Huambo –
the area where forced Ovimbundu labour was gathered for
the coffee estates during the Portuguese era – were being
rounded up and sent to northern Angola to reactivate the
plantations which had been badly neglected during the civil
war.[2] Amnesty International, the world's leading human

rights organisation, later reported that UNITA guerrillas and their suspected supporters had been executed extrajudicially by the MPLA in Central Angola.[3]

By the beginning of March 1976 more than 45,000 Angolan refugees had fled into Zambia and continued to come across at a rate of about five hundred a day.[4]

Savimbi gave details in his communiqué of what he claimed were the first two major engagements by UNITA troops since his order to return to guerrilla warfare. In the first, near Serpa Pinto on 22 February, three Soviet-made armoured cars and five trucks had been destroyed and an unknown number of Cubans killed for the loss of two UNITA dead and three wounded. In the second, in Moxico Province at the beginning of March, three Cubans had been captured and five killed when guerrillas ambushed their Land Rover, one of many from which they had been 'raping women and raiding food stocks'.[5]

The MPLA, for its part, alleged that atrocities had been carried out by UNITA in Lobito in early February before it evacuated the port. The dead had been buried on a hillside behind the city. Two British writers close to the MPLA later dubbed the hillside the 'Hill of Death', saying UNITA had begun summary executions there in the final weeks of its rule, under orders from the 'Governor', Jorge Valentim: 'More than 500 were killed, children as well as adults, of all colours and all classes.'[6]

A BBC television correspondent, Martin Bell, was one of the first foreign reporters to visit Lobito after the alleged killings and the MPLA had taken over. He was taken to the 'Hill of Death', but MPLA officials on the spot told him there had been 36 people executed under Valentim. Bell reported in his film despatch: 'Wartime atrocity stories are, of course, notoriously unreliable . . . On the ground, where the bodies had lain, were some gruesome human remains, not anything like proof in themselves but circumstantial evidence that something terrible did happen here, and it certainly wasn't suicide.

'UNITA as they retreated left behind a legacy if not of atrocities then at least of atrocities stories, both here and at Silva Porto (Bie) and elsewhere. And there is evidence to suggest there may be some substance in some of these stories. At least, all of them are believed as facts by the MPLA, and that itself makes national reconciliation a bit more difficult to achieve.'[7]

The accuracy of the MPLA case was impossible to gauge in view of the paucity of first-hand evidence. But at some time in late 1976 Jorge Valentim was disciplined by UNITA for unspecified misdemeanours during his time in charge of Lobito which had alienated many members of a population seen as naturally pro-UNITA. Valentim was removed from the Central Committee and sent into five years of 'internal exile' as a low-rank 'information official' operating with guerrillas in the forests of the central province of Bie.[8]

In Huambo a French journalist, René Lefort, visited the alleged mass grave of 235 MPLA prisoners killed by UNITA just before the city was entered by the Cubans on 9 February.[9] Again it is impossible to say how accurate the allegations were, but Amnesty International, whose impartiality and restrained reporting of the horrific things that people do to other people is widely feared and respected by governmental and rebel authorities around the world, felt they had sufficient basis to include them in one of their reports.[10]

I believe that one person who may have died in Huambo was Senhora Fernanda Carolina Rodrigues Vargas de Freitas, a Portuguese woman who had lived in Angola for 25 years since settling there in her early twenties. I was asked to try to trace Senhora Vargas de Freitas by her daughter, Maria Goncalves de Freitas Christ, who wrote to me from her home in West Berlin after reading articles I had published on UNITA.

Senhora Vargas de Freitas became separated from her husband and three adult children during the tumult of 1974–75. She worked as a nurse with the MPLA but had UNITA friends. Her daughter said of her: 'All her life she loved to help people in bad situations. For the same reason she became involved with the MPLA as a nurse. She treated the ill and wounded people.

'In October 1975 she stayed with MPLA troops in Matala (290 kilometres south of Huambo). One day she heard outside of one of the nursing blocks a man crying. While she helped him (a UNITA soldier), suddenly appeared another UNITA soldier and captured her. She was transported to Huambo and imprisoned near the city in a former animal slaughter-house named ACMOL.'[11]

Maria Goncalves de Freitas Christ had managed to get out of Angola on a refugee flight on 7 September 1975 with one small suitcase of belongings. She heard nothing about her mother until March 1976 when a Portuguese woman nurse who had worked in Huambo with UNITA arrived in Portugal, where Maria was then living, with a bundle of letters from her mother written from prison on Red Cross notepaper and toilet paper. The nurse, who had befriended Senhora Vargas de Freitas, left Huambo with UNITA as the Cubans approached.

The final letter was dated 24 January 1976. Nothing has been heard since of Senhora Vargas de Freitas. Maria's inquiries through the International Committee of the Red Cross were fruitless, and UNITA representatives in Europe said they had no records of her mother or knowledge of her fate.

* * *

Before UNITA began its retreat on 13 March 1976 from Gago Coutinho deep into the forests, it issued a communiqué saying 17 Cuban military prisoners had been executed by an all-woman firing squad.[12] In what sounds as if it must have been a drumhead court-martial, five of the Cubans were convicted of rape and the rest of murder.

A statement in Savimbi's name was issued with the communiqué. It said thousands of people were fleeing as refugees as the Cubans/MPLA set about destroying the structures of UNITA and killing and torturing the families of UNITA officials. 'People are suffering very much. We don't have the means to take care of the women and children, but I am confident that UNITA has started on a new path which will lead to true freedom for our people.

'It is very hard for me to imagine that the same Castro who fought an invasion of his country (at the Bay of Pigs in 1961) is now himself invading a far-away country. It is not with

pleasure that I report the execution of Cubans because I was
one of the closest friends of Che Guevara. I don't think if
Che was in Cuba today there would have been a Cuban
invasion of Angola.'

Years later I learned that among the 17 Cuban soldiers
who had been executed was Samuel Ducentes Rodriguez.

Rodriguez. The slight 17-year-old boy who had been sent
to Angola and was captured before he ever fired a shot in
anger; whose cheeriness and efforts to learn the local languages won the affection of his captors; and whose nerves
were calmed when Savimbi assured him he was not about to
be killed. Now he was part of the Angolan soil, along with
many hundreds of other Cubans, many British mercenaries
in the north, some 30 to 40 white South Africans, and
thousands of Angolans unknown and uncared about in
Havana, Washington, Moscow, London, Paris or Pretoria.

The knowledge of his death stirred and depressed me
greatly. It somehow crystallised all the futility and wicked-
ness of the war. My wife too was deeply upset. Although
she had never met Rodriguez, I had told her about him. She
wrote a poem which I think captures the poignancy and
symbolism of his death and which I hope ensures that
somewhere *all* the unsung or anonymous casualties of this
war will be remembered:

Rodriguez

The green time has come
The rains
invade

Smitten earth yields dust
comes lush
alive

Streamlets form columns
surround
'high ground'

Earth redoubt crumbles
into
fresh moat

The citadel's laid bare

Ribcage whitely gleams
through flood-force rising
a one-man *Mary-Rose*

The listing masthead
tilts and tilts again
surrend'ring eighteen years

Heeling beneath mud
final arms laid down
rebuke life's brevity

No dry dust remains
Nor sign
Nor shallow mound

Angola's reclaimed

Unsung
The boy from Cuba dies again[13]

20

The Long March

1976

'The Long March has provided the Chinese People's Republic with its greatest source of patriotic inspiration . . . Only 30,000 of the original 100,000 communists survived the 8,000-mile march, although they were joined by further "Route Armies" over the following twelve months. Once in Yenan it was possible to establish a stronger position for challenging Chiang (Kai-shek) and, from 1937 to 1945, for engaging the Japanese invaders.'[1]

*　　*　　*

August 3 1976. Jonas Savimbi, black African, sometime medical student of Lisbon University, licentiate of Lausanne University, guerrilla leader, sat near the west bank of the Cuito, deep inside Angola, some 800 kilometres north of where that big river ends its long journey in the Okavango Swamps of Botswana.

It was the southern African midwinter when night temperatures plunge below zero. In his arms Savimbi cradled a delirious teenage guerrilla dying from exposure and exhaustion after a body-racking, bone-numbing crossing of the Cuito.

There could hardly have been a more depressing way for the guerrilla leader to spend his 42nd birthday. The cause for which he had fought for more than a decade looked finished. For six months he had been chased ceaselessly through Angola's vast forests and grasslands by Cuban troops, planes and helicopters: the enemy was closing in even as he comforted the dying soldier. Savimbi had lost contact with other groups in his fragmented army. His outside allies in Africa and on other continents had deserted him. If death came now it would mean ignominy: Savimbi would be no more than a small footnote in history, depicted as a quisling character of minor relevance in the tempestuous unfolding of the African continent's late twentieth-century history.

Savimbi stopped comforting the stricken soldier to check on the rest of his party. Half an hour after he had left, a close aide, Captain Pedro 'Tito' Chingunji, brought news that the young guerrilla was dead.

Soon, another two guerrillas had died. The crossing of the 400-metre-wide main channel had been bad. Hippos, which claim more human life than any other African wild animal, had threatened to overturn the single canoe running shuttle crossings: despite the risk of the explosions being heard by enemy patrols, precious hand grenades had been tossed into the water to frighten off the snorting beasts. But the worst part of the crossing had been on foot, through 300 metres of chest-high muddy swamp lining the east bank of the Cuito. Freezing temperatures and sheer toil had sapped the three exhausted men of their last reserves.

For Savimbi's 350-strong band it seemed as though only death and oblivion lay before them. They had covered some 2,000 kilometres on their long march, and now they were trapped in the middle of Angola – a country twice the size of France – far from any international border which could be crossed in the hope of finding sanctuary. It looked as though the march would all have been for nothing: no one would ever know, let alone care, that it had ever happened.

*   *   *

The long march of Jonas Savimbi, devotee of Mao Tse-tung's theories of warfare, began on 9 February 1976, the day the Angolan civil war (or, more accurately, its first phase) effectively ended. That was when Cuban armoured columns entered Huambo, which for the previous six months had been UNITA's political headquarters. With the capture of Huambo, victory was virtually complete for the Cubans and the MPLA.

After the South Africans had begun their withdrawal

ANGOLA

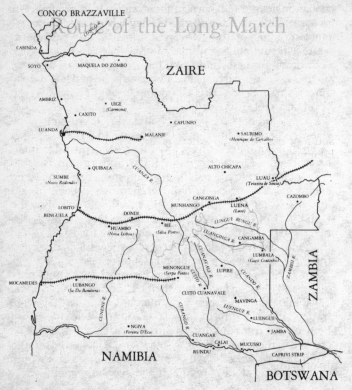

Route of the Long March

from Angola, UNITA tried to stop the Cuban advance on Huambo, vainly hoping that help might still arrive from the United States and other Western democracies. Their light rifles and light mortars were no match for the Cubans' tanks, helicopters and Stalin Organs. About 600 UNITA guerrillas, including two experienced commanders, were killed in the futile defence of Huambo.

There was no resistance when the Cubans entered the city. On the following day Savimbi abandoned his military headquarters in Bie and flew eastwards aboard a Fokker

Friendship to Luso, having first ordered his soldiers to disperse to their old forest bases and advised UNITA's civilian followers to return to their relations in villages. As far as possible, the enemy must be left with empty towns to conquer.

In Luso Savimbi began planning UNITA's new guerrilla war against the Cubans and MPLA.

* * *

With Savimbi on the flight to Luso were N'Zau Puna and Samuel Chiwale. Together they decided there must be two centres of initial resistance – one in the forests immediately south of Luso and the other around Serpa Pinto, some 400 kilometres to the south-west of Luso.

The Luso resistance would be easier to organise. There were 3,000 guerrillas in the area and they had not come under such severe attack as the forces around Huambo. Chiwale would control this front.

Puna was to go to Serpa Pinto with several officers to co-ordinate the scattered, demoralised UNITA groups who had moved south to the area from Huambo and Bie. He was also to survey the forests north-east of Serpa Pinto to see if they were suitable for the establishment of a new central base for guerrilla resistance.

Puna flew out of Luso on the morning of 10 February for Serpa Pinto. (The Cubans were well to the north of the town at this stage.) As the Fokker Friendship took off there was an MPLA light spotter plane over Luso which UNITA opened up on with rifle fire. And before the sun had set the Cubans, advancing from the north, had begun shelling and strafing the town.

* * *

In the early afternoon of 10 February Captain 'Bok' Sapalalo heard Cuban and MPLA trucks approaching the last bridge north of Luso. Sapalalo, UNITA's explosives expert, supervised the dynamiting of the Lumege River bridge, ten kilometres from town, and then withdrew. Cuban engineers moved up to throw a temporary bridge across the Lumege while their artillery directed 120mm and B10 rocket fire on Luso.

Savimbi was sleeping for the first time in 70 hours as the first shells crashed on Luso at 4 p.m. He was shaken from his deep sleep by Chiwale. The population was in panic. Savimbi rapidly organised a meeting to tell them that UNITA would retreat and organise a new guerrilla war. Within half an hour of the first mortar shells falling, three MIG planes strafed and bombed the town. About 50 people died.

Immediately after the planes had attacked the order was given to evacuate Luso. By 5.15 p.m. the first UNITA vehicles were leaving town: in the convoy of assorted cars and Land Rovers there were about 1,000 guerrillas whom Chiwale had managed to collect together. Several thousand civilians with their belongings were moving along the roadsides. The procession headed south towards Gago Coutinho, 350 kilometres away. Some guerrillas were left with orders to contact other troops and tell them to regroup near Gago Coutinho.

Savimbi's column stopped for a short time during the night at the small town of Lucusse, 135 kilometres south of Luso. Since the road to Gago Coutinho was also a route to Zambia, Savimbi was worried that many of the people might believe he was on his way out of Angola into exile. 'The people were in panic,' recalled Tito Chingunji, who accompanied Savimbi on UNITA's long march. 'I was astonished how the President reassured them and organised a calm evacuation. He told them that he was not going to leave Angola and that he was going into the bush to fight on.'[2]

Savimbi reached Gago Coutinho on the afternoon of 11 February after crossing a dozen big east-flowing tributaries of the Zambezi River.

*   *   *

Until he was driven out by the Cubans a month later, Savimbi used the time in Gago Coutinho to reorganise. Soldiers were sent back towards Luso to blow up every road bridge, but with orders to leave each one intact until the latest possible moment before the Cubans advanced. Local people fleeing south had to be allowed time to make the river crossings.

Savimbi made quick flights from Gago Coutinho to Lusaka and Kinshasa to tell Presidents Kaunda and Mobutu that he intended to fight on. He also wrote a letter of gratitude and farewell to Kaunda:

UNITA lost 600 men in the battle for Huambo. The machine of war that Cuba and the Soviet Union have assembled in Angola is beyond the imagination. To prevent the total destruction of our forces we have decided to revert immediately to guerrilla warfare. The friends [i.e., the CIA and the United States] that have promised to help us did not fulfil their promises and we must face our own fate with courage and determination.

I have two requests for Your Excellency: (1) No one is responsible for this disaster but the big powers. That is why with my humble and limited understanding I beg Your Excellency that my brother for years, Zambian Minister for Foreign Affairs, Rupiah Banda, be spared so that UNITA can be sacrificed [i.e. that Kaunda abandon his support for UNITA rather than for Banda, who had been a vociferous advocate for Savimbi]. Rupiah is a big African, though very young. (2) I am sending with this my mother who is seventy-one years old so that she will be able to die in Zambia. My sister and (her) three children and my two (youngest) children are with my mother. Accompanying them are the wife of our Secretary General with two children and the wife of our Commanding General with four children.

The Political Bureau of the Central Committee of UNITA joins me to thank you once more for everything. Whatever stand your government takes on Angola, we will accept with resignation. It is paramount that Zambia survives and the love and the admiration we have shared with my colleagues for your leadership will be sufficient to comfort us in the dark days of our country.

I would like to end this letter by asking Your Excellency to convey my greetings to Mwalimu Julius Nyerere [the President of Tanzania]. I have read his interview concerning me. It is a pity that President Nyerere did not believe and know me. I have always tried to the best of my ability

and courage to serve the interests of Angola and Africa. I
am not a traitor to Africa and the hard days that we expect
ahead will prove to the world that I stand for my principles. In Angola might has made right but I will remain in
the bush to cry for justice.

God bless your beloved country.

God bless you.

Savimbi, Jonas.

Kaunda at first resisted Savimbi's suggestion that he abandon UNITA in Zambia's self-interest. Zambia held off longer
than most African states, but on 15 April 1976 the Lusaka
government fell into line and announced its official recognition of the MPLA. On 10 May Kaunda buried Savimbi's
plea for Rupiah Banda to be spared: the Foreign Minister
was sacked and sent abroad on 'study leave'.[3]

*   *   *

In Gago Coutinho Savimbi was sending US Law anti-tank
missiles northwards towards Luso as soon as they arrived
from the CIA stockpile in Kinshasa (see Chapter 17). The
intention was to delay the Cubans' advance by hitting their
armoured cars. Twenty French mercenaries, hired jointly by
the CIA and the French Secret Service, the SDECE, flew into
Gago Coutinho to instruct UNITA troops in the use of these
weapons.[4]

As guerrillas who had been left behind straggled into
Gago Coutinho, Savimbi began reorganising and rede-
ploying them. The period in Gago Coutinho was one of
intense work. Arms arriving on the flights from Zaire were
quickly moved to dumps in the forests. For the most part
they went to the heads of village people. All food, except for
bare necessities, was also moved out.

There was a setback to morale at the beginning of March.
Though Lonrho had withdrawn its executive jet from
UNITA's service following the South African decision to
withdraw from Angola, Savimbi still had a Fokker Friendship and a light Beechcraft plane at his disposal. One day,
the Portuguese pilot of the Beechcraft took off from Gago
Coutinho's gravel strip on a routine flight but never

returned. UNITA later learned he had landed in Namibia and asked for asylum in South Africa.

A puzzling feature of this period was why the Cubans did not attack Gago Coutinho with MIG fighter-bombers or make an assault with helicopter-borne troops. The Cubans certainly knew what was going on in the town because they sent several light spotter planes over the area.

The lull ended suddenly and decisively.

*   *   *

March 13 1976 marked the tenth anniversary of the official founding of UNITA. People began to assemble on the school football pitch at Gago Coutinho for a parade and a commemorative speech by Savimbi, who at breakfast had told his senior aides that the town would eventually be bombed and that they should therefore prepare to begin the evacuation.

On 13 March at 10 a.m., shortly after the anniversary celebrations had ended, MPLA MIG-21 fighter-bombers struck. In the first attack three planes bombed and strafed the last intact river bridge, 35 kilometres to the north of Gago Coutinho. Some of the guerrillas guarding the bridge, over the Luanguinga River, were killed and others wounded.

The second MIG attack was against the Gago Coutinho airstrip. On the ground was the Zairean Airways Fokker Friendship which had arrived with arms from Kinshasa. It was destroyed. Savimbi ordered every guerrilla to fire freely in the general direction of the attackers. Three Browning-50 machine-guns augmented the Kalashnikov and rocket fire. The aim was to make the MIGs fly high rather than hit them, but one plane was struck and crashed in the direction of the Zambian border.

Just before the sun went down, the two surviving MIGs returned and strafed Gago Coutinho's houses. No one was injured, but Savimbi ordered preparations for a complete evacuation the following day, 14 March.

The MIG attacks concentrated the minds of the French mercenaries. Their commander, a French Army colonel, told Savimbi they were leaving because UNITA's cause was hopeless. He said they had radioed contacts in South Africa for a plane to be sent the following morning to a bush airstrip at Ninda, 75 kilometres to the south, to fly them out of Angola. They left by truck that same night – 13 March – for their rendezvous. Savimbi and his followers were now entirely alone, without any outside support, in the resistance they planned against Fidel Castro's Soviet-equipped army.

Before the French colonel left, he tried to persuade the UNITA leader to go with him. 'He said to me: "You cannot remain here. You have no chance whatsoever. If you stay you will be dead within two months,"' is how Savimbi recalls their final conversation. '"If you come with us it will be valuable to the West. We can arrange for you to stay in an African country until the situation changes, then you can return to start your struggle again."

'I said: "No, I am not going. The situation will not change if I wait in some other part of Africa, but it may change if we stay here. If I am to die, that must be my fate, but I am not leaving."'

After the French mercenaries left, their $US 425,000 payment from the CIA scarcely earned, Savimbi summoned his senior officers and spoke to them about what the immediate future was likely to hold. The MIGs would come again, but in double the numbers, and the Cubans would also bring helicopters and Antonov bombers.

'He tried to put us in the picture about the great courage and the suffering involved in guerrilla war,' said Tito Chingunji. 'But he said we should not accept capitulation. We were starting a new kind of life. It would be hard, and it was impossible to know how many people would still be willing to continue the fight six months onwards.'

At sunrise on 14 March a UNITA column of 4,000 guerrillas and civilians began moving out of Gago Coutinho. Though the safety of the Zambian border was just 70 kilometres away to the east, Savimbi's people headed due west towards the heart of Angola.

*   *   *

The evacuation went on all day long: explosives experts were left behind to blow up key buildings. Savimbi took with him three trucks and five cars. The MIGs now diverted their attention to machine-gunning the column. The drivers of the vehicles kept the doors open as they moved slowly forward, and whenever they heard aircraft noise they drove into the shade of the roadside forest. After the MIGs returned to base the drivers would push forward again, their vehicles crudely camouflaged with tree branches, to gain distance before the next attack.

Some people were terribly wounded in the attacks, but miraculously no one was killed. 'That day was a very valuable lesson to everybody,' said Tito Chingunji. 'They realised the MIGs were only a psychological threat. Once the trucks moved under the trees we couldn't be seen.'

Late that night Savimbi's column reached Sessa, a small Portuguese forestry centre – just a timber mill, four or five big Portuguese stuccoed villas and some local people living in traditional huts. There Savimbi continued dispersing his people which he had begun earlier that day by sending 150 troops and three trucks southwards from Gago Coutinho to organise a regional command at Ninda. From Sessa, Savimbi sent another 1,750 soldiers to prepare for guerrilla warfare along, and to the north of, the Benguela Railway. He told them to try and paralyse the roads with ambushes. But, above all, they had to show the population that UNITA was capable of launching guerrilla warfare again. Some guerrillas were sent back towards Gago Coutinho to mobilise villagers in the surrounding countryside. A group of about 200 under Lt.-Col. Smart Chata were sent due southwards to Muie, 70 kilometres away, to explore its suitability as an alternative base area to that being surveyed by N'Zau Puna around Serpa Pinto.

Savimbi had decided his own next move would be northwards to the headwaters of the Lungue Bungu River, the vast area of dense forest in which his central base was located during the war against the Portuguese. From there he hoped to begin establishing contact with guerrilla groups who had become isolated to the west of the Cuanza River – around Lobito, Huambo and Bie – during the Cuban advance.

On 15 March Savimbi ordered the vehicles to be soaked in petrol and burned, overruling pleas from some of the guerrillas that they should be hidden for future use. Savimbi realised that for a long time to come his would have to be an army that relied entirely on its feet.

*   *   *

The guerrilla redeployment took 10 days. By 24 March Savimbi was ready to move, and his foot column which left Sessa was about 1,000-strong. Some 600 were guerrillas and the rest civilians, including women, children, several African Protestant pastors and three black Catholic priests. Though Savimbi had urged people to abandon most of their possessions, many clung to their best town clothes, platform-heeled shoes so beloved by Africans at that time, and items like pillows. The first few days of the march over apparently endless forested hills were exhausting. Soon, some of the marchers wanted to abandon everything and Savimbi lectured them on the need to choose essentials and retain them.

Each guerrilla carried at least two weapons and ammunition as well as personal equipment and food, including mealie flour, beans and some canned meat and fish.

After about a fortnight's marching, the column was spotted crossing a dirt road by a four-man MPLA patrol, which retreated quickly. Savimbi knew he would now have to begin a rapid march because the MPLA soldiers would return with reinforcements. First, however, he allowed the column to rest at an abandoned village where they ate from old stocks of cassava. But the MPLA returned within 30 minutes in company strength of 150, cutting off the UNITA rearguard which had to retreat, only joining up again with Savimbi many weeks later. As the MPLA encountered the UNITA pickets, Savimbi divided the column and the MPLA was thrown off the trail after a brief firefight in which no one was wounded.

The column was now entering a Chokwe tribal area of long-standing UNITA support. Villagers helped to carry the baggage, but also demanded of Savimbi an explanation of how he had managed to lose the war. They said it was his fault that the leaders of the MPLA and FNLA had re-entered Angola after Portugal had conceded the principle of independence in 1974; and it was his fault too that the MPLA had taken power. 'But they were the kind of people who were not easily shaken once they had given their loyalty,' said Tito Chingunji. 'Once these people are with you they are really strong. They won't give a secret away or betray you.'

*   *   *

After a month the column reached Sandona, an old UNITA base in the Lungue Bungu valley. There, preparations were made for a four-day conference to assess UNITA's plight and make plans for the future. Savimbi was joined by N'Zau Puna and the soldiers the Secretary-General had taken to the Serpa Pinto region. Savimbi had sent him an order to try and link up with Smart Chata in the alternative base area near Muie. But Puna found it impossible to cross the Cuito River, between Serpa Pinto and Muie, so he struck northwards instead to join Savimbi.

The conference produced on its final day, 10 May, the River Cuanza Manifesto, in which UNITA pledged that it would never give up the fight against the MPLA, Cuba and the Soviet Union. When the Manifesto reached the outside world, via Lusaka, it was largely ignored by the international news agencies who assumed, not unreasonably, that the civil war was over.

In the light of subsequent developments, parts of the Manifesto are worth re-examining. 'There will be no peace in Angola. No economic development,' it threatened. 'No railroad traffic. No working harbours while the Luanda regime hangs on to power thanks to Cuban soldiers and the Russian armour and fighter planes.

'We know that we will triumph. Those that doubt our possibilities are those that never believe in man's creative capacity when inspired by noble and just collective ends . . . Those that have the people are never small, even faced with the giant imperialist Russian invaders. With the people you always win. Against the people you always lose.'

As well as the guerrilla rhetoric, the River Cuanza Manifesto contained a detailed analysis of why the MPLA could not establish control over Angola, even with Cuban and Soviet support.

First, Angola was a vast territory, which the Portuguese had never been able to control completely during their 500 years of colonial rule. Two-thirds of the six million people were loyal to UNITA. (A gross exaggeration.)

The extended system of roads and railways in remote areas would make sabotage and ambushes easy, said the Manifesto. With the economy already destroyed by civil war, with resistance continuing, and without reconciliation, conditions in the country would continue to deteriorate. The inexperienced Angolan civil service which had replaced the Portuguese would be unable to cope with the serious conditions. The Cubans, if they stayed on, would in due course come to be regarded by Angolans in the same light as the former Portuguese rulers: the blame would fall on them as unemployment grew and essential products became scarce.

UNITA, for its part, would be able to build upon the support it had developed over the years in rural areas, where it had always had its bases and where 90 per cent of Angola's people live.

For UNITA, the Sandona conference was a real turning point. Many civilians trekked in from areas along the Benguela Railway: about 2,000 guerrillas who had been left behind in February in the Huambo and Bie areas also made their way to the conference. For these people the meeting with their leader was important: MPLA pamphlets and broadcasts had said that Savimbi was dead or that he had fled abroad with his family. They said Puna had been caught and executed. In Lobito, a former hotbed of support for UNITA, a funeral procession had been held with three coffins announced to be those of Savimbi, Chiwale and Puna.

Many of the soldiers who trekked into Sandona were very demoralised. Until then they had no real idea what was going on. But when they realised Savimbi was still alive it gave them new impetus and determination to fight.

Tito Chingunji recalled one village elder telling the conference: 'I have only my arrow and axe, but these will be enough to fight the Cubans. These people did not come from here. Who planted these trees under which we are talking? Not the Cubans.'

But, good as the forest cover was, the Cubans were about to locate Savimbi and force him to flee for his life.

* * *

From Sandona Savimbi ordered about 2,000 guerrillas to disperse westwards and north-westwards to the countryside around Lobito, Cela and Bela Vista to begin guerrilla operations. He himself intended heading south to Muie with a party of about 900 to work from the base camp being prepared by Smart Chata. But before leaving Savimbi wanted to tour the villages in the Lungue Bungu region, to explain to the people what was happening and urge them to continue the struggle.

Immediately after the conference Savimbi and his personal group of about 1,000 moved a few kilometres northwards to visit a village called Samasseka. Here he received radio reports that the Cubans were attempting a big encircling movement of the Lungue Bungu region. Convoys were moving westwards from Gago Coutinho and southwards from Munhango in a major military operation. As the convoys moved they were dropping reconnaissance patrols at various points along the 500 kilometres of laterite road between Munhango and Gago Countinho which skirted the south and west of the Lungue Bungu area. To the north, Cuban and MPLA troops took up positions along the railway. The rapid deployment was completed within three days.

On the morning of 21 May Savimbi and his comrades heard distant gunfire to the north-west of Samasseka where UNITA guerrillas had encountered an MPLA patrol. At 8 a.m. two MIG-21s and three lumbering Antonov-26s started bombing the forest in the area of Savimbi's radio position about 30 minutes marching time to the north of Samasseka. One Antonov sprayed machine-gun fire from a hatch in its belly. Another UNITA radio position nearly 100 kilometres to the south reported that it too had been bombed at 6 a.m.

No one was killed in the bombings, but Savimbi concluded from the attacks in the specific areas of the radio stations that the Cubans had monitored messages and pinpointed the radio positions.

Savimbi ordered his own group to begin a rapid march immediately the Samasseka bombing raid ended. The natural way to move was due south, away from the line of rail, but reports from villagers and Savimbi's own scouts said Cuban and MPLA foot patrols were thick on the ground in that direction. More convoys of Cuban and Katangese mercenary troops were pouring down from Munhango to lay ambushes for people moving westwards and southwards from the conference. So Savimbi headed due east.

As the Savimbi column pushed on over the next few days, messages arrived saying that many UNITA people, including two senior commanders, had died in the Cuban-Katangese and MPLA ambushes.

*　　*　　*

For the next few days Savimbi's column did not stop moving, day or night, except for very brief rests. His followers were receiving a frighteningly practical lesson in the art of guerrilla survival. Savimbi lectured them at each rest point and constantly moved up and down the column explaining what they must do.

First, they had to march at speed, much faster than the enemy could imagine was possible.

Second, they were not to leave a trail that could easily be picked up by MPLA trackers. Every effort had to be made to confuse their pursuers. For 10 to 15 minutes after most halts the column would double back in the direction from which they had just come. Then, as they turned again to head in the right direction, everybody would spread out over a broad front for a kilometre or two before joining up again in a single column. From Samasseka a herd of about 60 cattle had joined the column to provide food on the hoof. Savimbi instructed the drover to use the cattle to cover the guerrillas' tracks. Weaving and circling through the forests, the UNITA column often recrossed its own tracks and crossed those of its pursuers.

Third, they had to be as quiet as possible. 'There were children in the column,' said Tito Chingunji. 'When we first left Samasseka they cried often, but the tension was so great that they soon stopped. After that, the remarkable thing is that they did not cry again on the march.'

Fourth, they had to camouflage themselves and discard even more of their possessions. Everybody wore a shroud of twigs and leaves over their heads and shoulders. Women with bright dresses had to abandon them.

Fifth, tight discipline was essential. Savimbi insisted that when things were discarded they should not be buried haphazardly. Everybody made up parcels and got help from those who could write to put slips of paper inside them listing their name and the contents. Then a pit was dug and a low platform built at the bottom of it. Ashes were scattered at the bases of the four posts supporting the platform to discourage termites. The pit was covered by a thick closely-woven framework of logs and branches which in turn was covered with earth and sand. Logistics officers recorded the location in their daily log.

On the march selected soldiers were made directly responsible for four other individuals. A soldier was given a sheet of paper by senior officers with the names of his four special wards, and at each stop he had to ensure they were counted. If people disappeared search parties had to be sent out to find them: it was essential that no one was captured, for they would endanger the rest of the column by giving away information. As a safeguard, in case anyone was captured, only four senior commanders knew where the column was heading – Savimbi, N'Zau Puna, Chiwale and Ernesto Mulato, UNITA's senior civil administrator during the 1975–76 war.

As the days passed, several people started getting left behind through sheer exhaustion. They would simply stop walking because they were desperately tired. Others fell into deep sleeps at rest halts. On nights when there was no moon everyone had to stay close together or people got lost. It was so dark that they could hardly see their hands stretched out in front of their faces.

By mid-May the nights on Angola's Central Plateau begin to turn very cold. Fires therefore had to be made at each night halt. Officers had to make sure that all traces of ashes were eliminated and that every scrap of unused food and paper was buried. A jungle craft that came into its own was the making of blankets and ropes from the bark of a forest tree, the *chimwanji*. When the bark lining was removed, the exposed white pith of the tree trunk was smeared with sand and ash to disguise it from anyone looking at it from a distance. When the *chimwanji* bark was used for making ropes and blankets, thin strips would be taken from high in the tree, or, if a small tree had been used, the whole trunk would be cut down and the stump buried.

*   *   *

Within a couple of days of the move eastwards from Samasseka, villagers told Savimbi that Cuban helicopters were putting troops down in that direction. Savimbi turned south, with the intention of crossing the Gago Coutinho-Munhango road 60 kilometres away. It would be highly risky, but if he could cross it he would have broken through the cordon the Cubans had thrown around the Lungue Bungu region. A few days later the column reached a small UNITA guerrilla camp, where the soldiers said the position had been bombed just two days earlier. Savimbi reasoned that the Cubans would ignore the area for a few days after the attack, and this gave him confidence to continue heading southwards.

As the column approached the road Savimbi decided to cross it in darkness. Two hundred of the guerrillas were from Savimbi's élite personal bodyguard, soldiers who had proved themselves exceptionally brave and loyal in combat. Fifty of them formed the rearguard, fanning out for several kilometres behind the main column. About 100 were with Savimbi, walking in front, behind and to the sides of him. A vanguard of 50 scouted several kilometres ahead and reported back that a large armoured and motorised column was passing along the road. They were laying ambushes, but were concentrating on an area east of a small bridge crossing the headwaters of the Cuando River.

Savimbi knew that once he had crossed the road it would be too dangerous to spend time covering up the trail. And since MPLA trackers would soon know that a large column had passed he ordered non-stop marching to take his people far from the crossing point as quickly as possible. The only comfort was that the MPLA and Cubans could not know for certain that Savimbi was in this column and would not be able to transfer all their forces from the Lungue Bungu encirclement.

After three days and nights of continuous marching Savimbi ordered a halt at a point about 60 kilometres south of the road, just north of a village called Chissimba. The column spent a night at the position to allow its exhausted followers to sleep, then Savimbi sent the women and children onwards towards a 'safe' village several kilometres south-east of Chissimba where they were to be left while he continued his march deeper into Angola. A guerrilla escort sent with the women and children, under a Captain Chivinga, was ordered to try to replenish the column's food stocks from the villagers. Grain was running low and the cattle herd seemed to have been lost because there had been no contact with the drove for several days.

Chivinga safely escorted the women and children, including Jonas and Vinona Savimbi's own surviving three children, through the Chissimba area to the village where they were to stay. (The two youngest Savimbi children had not, after all, gone with Savimbi's mother to Zambia.) Chivinga obtained some cassava and began returning to Savimbi's post.

Meanwhile, Savimbi was having a difference of opinion with Vinona, who had opted to go with the column rather than stay with her children in the village. Some time after the children left she suddenly announced that she was going to pack her possessions and join them. She had been born near Chissimba in a village of the Nkankala sub-tribe, and she said that up until 1970, when UNITA became the dominant force in the area, many of the locals had supported the MPLA: some of the young men had joined the MPLA guerrillas. 'I feel we are going to be attacked,' she told Savimbi. 'If the MPLA and the Cubans are in this area the villagers will not warn us.'

Vinona's was not a voice that could be ignored easily. She was a decisive woman of few words, able to mobilise and discipline other women by her example. 'However, Savimbi laid down no special privileges or terms of address for his wife,' said Tito Chingunji. 'She was just part of the column.'

Savimbi called Puna and Chiwale and told them of Vinona's warning. Savimbi did not dismiss premonitions lightly: 'It is true, when you have been in a war as a guerrilla for a long time, you develop a flair, a feeling, for whether there is going to be an attack.' But neither Chiwale, Puna nor Savimbi himself believed the MPLA could be so far south.

Nevertheless, Vinona insisted that she intended leaving and joining the children. Meanwhile, her parents arrived from their home village to greet their daughter and son-in-law. Vinona asked Savimbi to come and speak to them before they returned home.

Savimbi had hardly said farewell to his parents-in-law when Chivinga and some of his soldiers came running back with news that they had been ambushed by MPLA troops just north of Chissimba. One UNITA guerrilla had been captured and he was virtually certain to admit that Savimbi was nearby. 'I hardly believed the MPLA's presence possible,' said Savimbi. 'But my wife had been right in her insistence, so I immediately gave orders to prepare to leave.'

Savimbi's column could not go south towards the ambush site. They dared not return northwards, and any retreat eastwards was blocked by the Quembo River. So they had to strike westwards across a two-kilometre-wide area of cultivation which had been cleared of trees.

Savimbi gave Captain Chivinga reinforcements, boosting his force to about 50, and sent him south again to Chissimba to hold the MPLA for as long as possible. About 30 minutes after Chivinga left, rocket and mortar shells began falling on Savimbi's position, so he ordered his party to leave too. They had just crossed the cultivated area and reached forest when two helicopters appeared in the distance. 'I took personal command because I realised we were in a very serious position,' he said. 'I told everyone to lie down. I said no one else was to give any orders for the time being, not even Puna or Chiwale. I didn't want any confusion.'

There was a UNITA guerrilla outpost 20 kilometres north-west of where he was hiding that Savimbi wanted to reach. Good food supplies were essential for the break-out he was now planning, and messengers had brought news that the outpost had built up plentiful stocks of dried antelope meat.

Savimbi took his group deeper into the forest across a small river and sent officers with instructions for the commander of the outpost, a Major Samalambo. As they lay up during daylight Savimbi's people saw the helicopters moving from Chissimba in the direction of Samalambo's outpost. Then towards dusk came alarming news. A messenger from the officers sent to contact Samalambo said a helicopter had flown over them as they were crossing open ground: they were sure they had been spotted.

There was no time to waste. The strategy Savimbi had devised to confuse the MPLA and Cubans must be completed before the night ended. In the darkness he divided into three entirely new groups his own followers, those of Samalambo, and those of a Captain Chimbijika, who Savimbi's officers discovered had established a UNITA base a few kilometres to the north-west of Samalambo's. There would be 350 people with Savimbi, 400 with Samalambo and 100 with Chimbijika. Each would break out during the night in different directions. The hope was to fool the MPLA's trackers that the biggest column, Samalambo's, was the one protecting Savimbi.

All three groups would head into deep forest as far away from rivers, roads and villages as possible. Savimbi's officers had noted that the Cubans patrolled fairly rigidly along the lines of rivers and roads in their search for UNITA. They ventured little into the intervening tracts of forested countryside, with which they were inevitably unfamiliar.

In the early hours of the night men and equipment were shuttled between the three groups through the forest undergrowth. Savimbi transferred his radio and radio operator to Samalambo, who would have greater need of them: he was to head into an area of clearly greater enemy control and set up a guerrilla base near the Benguela Railway.

Savimbi told his rank-and-file guerrillas to sleep, but he spent the night giving instructions to senior officers from all three columns. 'He said that, as military men, they might desperately want to fight the enemy. Instead they had to motivate their soldiers to walk strongly and quickly away from trouble,' recalled Tito Chingunji. To achieve maximum effect they would have to reconcile the need for strict

obedience from their men with the need to show them
compassion in a desperate situation. He told them there was
plenty of reason for hope. The enemy had shown that their
strategy was poor. They were acting as foreigners; they did
not know the terrain or have the support of the people, or
Savimbi would by now have been captured. It should be
clear to the officers by now that the people were with
UNITA.

Chingunji went on: 'And Savimbi said: "If the people are
not giving up why should I give up, why should you give
up?" He gave us very big lessons that night.'

While Savimbi was lecturing his officers the drover re-
appeared, as if by some miracle, with the cattle. Savimbi
immediately sent him off in the south-westwards direction
he intended taking with his own column.

When all was ready Savimbi ordered Samalambo's and
Chimbijika's columns to start moving out, the former to the
northeast and the latter to the northwest. By 4.30 a.m. both
columns and everybody in Savimbi's, except for Savimbi
himself and his 50-man rearguard, had gone: now he
ordered the rearguard also to go. Savimbi's column did not
stop moving until 3.30 p.m., but shortly after daybreak the
marchers heard explosions and gunfire from the direction in
which they had lain up in the forest. Scouts said the Cubans
had flown over the position, firing heavy machine-guns
from the helicopters. Crucially, they later reported, the
Cubans were shifting their search in the direction of the
decoy columns.

*   *   *

The result of the encounter with the MPLA and Cubans had
been to splinter Savimbi's original column into five groups.
The women and children and their guerrilla escort stayed
undetected and unharmed for several weeks in the 'safe'
village, which was never visited by enemy troops. Captain
Chivinga's 50-strong group kept the MPLA troops just to the
north of Chissimba pinned down for several hours until
Chivinga was wounded in the thigh: then they dispersed
with their commander, but were unable to join either the
main columns or the women and children. It was only many

months later that Savimbi received messages that the
women and children and Chivinga and his men were safe.
As for Major Samalambo and Captain Chimbijika, they led
their columns safely away from danger. In 1986 both men
were still fighting.

*   *   *

For a week Savimbi's column encountered no problems,
except for a tricky crossing of the Cuanavale River: there
they had to fell several trees to form a chain of logs to help
them cross the central deep water channel. This left them
exposed in the open for several hours, but no enemy
appeared. The tension gradually eased. By the time the
column approached the banks of the Gunde, a tributary of
the big Cuito River, everyone felt relaxed: the MPLA and
Cubans seemed to have lost their trail and no planes had
been seen since the day of the breakout.

The banks of the Gunde, like most Angolan rivers, were
lined by belts of *anhara* (elephant grass) four metres high,
and in some places 500 metres wide. Savimbi halted the column in the forest and sent ten guerrillas across the *anhara* belt
and across the river to ensure that the western bank was safe.
N'Zau Puna also took five men across the *anhara* to the eastern bank to find the easiest crossing place for the column.

A helicopter was heard approaching from the south.
Savimbi ordered everyone in the main column to spread out
under the trees. N'Zau Puna's group began to run back from
the riverbank towards a small clump of forest standing like a
small island in the surrounding *anhara* within 200 metres of
the Gunde. Puna and two of his men reached the trees
before the helicopter arrived overhead, but the other three
were still in the open. They were spotted and the craft began
strafing from a low altitude. The three replied with small
arms fire and the helicopter crashed and exploded some
three kilometres along the river.

From his position in the forest, Savimbi watched the
pattern of the helicopter's descent. It flew beyond the three
stranded guerrillas, seemed to dip towards the ground,
began rising again, and then fell earthwards. Savimbi reckoned the pilot had retained control of the craft until the last

moments: he had, therefore, perhaps had time to radio to his base his position and other brief details of what had happened. Within a short time more helicopters would be at the scene.

'Everyone was in confusion,' Savimbi recalled years later. 'Each one was giving his own separate orders. Go back, Chiwale was saying. Go north along the riverbank, Puna was saying. I said we must go forwards, never backwards, and I ordered an immediate crossing of the river. We had hoped to find a small wooden foot-bridge, of the kind built by village hunters, but now there was no time. I told people to cross anywhere. They were in water up to their necks and my wife lost her shoes in the river.'

Savimbi sent a patrol to check the wrecked helicopter: it reported that three Cubans aboard were all dead.

Having crossed the Gunde, Savimbi's 350-strong column reached thick forest beyond half a kilometre or so of *anhara*. He ordered everyone to stop just inside the forest border. 'I could have ordered everyone to continue, but I wanted to check whether the pilot had managed to radio a message,' he recalled, 'If the Cubans did not come it would be clear they did not know where the helicopter had disappeared; in that case, we would be safe. If they came in a short time, then they knew where the helicopter had been fired upon and we would know they would be on our heels in a big way again tomorrow.'

Within 30 minutes helicopters arrived and immediately found the crash site. Darkness was falling, so they did not linger. Knowing the helicopters would return by first light, Savimbi ordered a rapid night march westwards.

Thick forest in the area was to the guerrillas' advantage, but everything was dark because there was no moon. Eventually Savimbi had to call a halt against his will because it became too dark. He ordered Ernesto Mulato to go ahead to tell the vanguard troops to halt also and form defensive ambush positions. The cattle herd, whose strength was down to a dozen from its original size of about 50, did not move with the guerrillas in case too big a trail was left. The drover was ordered to spread the cattle out over a wide front and rendezvous later with Savimbi.

After resting, Savimbi moved the main party up to join the vanguard. Mulato was not there and the vanguard had not seen him. Savimbi was acutely worried. The Cubans could arrive at any time and Mulato would be in danger of capture. This was especially dangerous because Savimbi had made a decision, shared only with N'Zau Puna, Chiwale and Mulato, to abandon any idea of Muie as the area for the future central base camp and instead establish it in the Cuelei area to the west of Serpa Pinto. If Mulato were to be captured he would be tortured and it was assumed he would eventually give the secret away.

Savimbi decided to press on westwards: there would be no change in plan for four days, by when it would be clear whether or not Mulato was hopelessly lost. Scouts would report whether Cubans were being dropped behind. If so, Savimbi would have to assume that Mulato would be captured, necessitating entirely new plans.

Another day's march brought the main column to forest within sight of the *anhara* lining the banks of the Cuito. Savimbi had sent an advance party of three men on a high-speed march to try to find a canoe for the crossing of the 400-metre-wide river. (Villagers in Angola leave canoes at frequent intervals in reed banks along rivers near good crossing points.) There were problems, they reported. They had only been able to find a canoe which accommodated three people: this meant that only two persons could be ferried across at a time. On the near, eastern, side of the river was a 300-metre-wide stretch of deep mud swamp. This meant the cattle could not cross the river: cattle will swim rivers from firm banks, but they panic and get stuck in swamp. Savimbi ordered the twelve cattle to be slaughtered and cut into hunks of meat that could be carried. It was now the beginning of August and the cattle had been the only source of food for the past month. There had been no grain because, after the incident at Chissimba, Savimbi concluded that his security was best served in that region by avoiding settlements.

People were ferried across the Cuito throughout the night. But when Savimbi called a halt at about 4 a.m. many of the party were still on the east bank. Savimbi sent orders for them to hide in the forest and begin crossing again the next night. He feared that the Cubans and the MPLA would be in the area the following day. Grenades tossed into the river to frighten off hippos were likely to have been heard by enemy patrols.

On the west bank Savimbi led his own truncated band across the *anhara*, leaving clear trails through the frost dusted grass. The soldiers had no changes of clothes, so they had to march onwards in shirts and trousers soaked in water deeply chilled by the freezing nights. The single blankets each carried, and which they wrapped around themselves, were also wet as well as being thin and torn.

Many were so cold after wading through the swamp and crossing the river that they could not speak. 'They were exhausted, malnourished and their cheeks were sunken,' according to Tito Chingunji. 'Savimbi kept marching between the front and the rear of the column urging people to march hard towards the forest before the sun rose. He ordered his batman to give all his spare clothes to the soldiers, but his senior officers hid one spare set from him for his own use.'

Savimbi had estimated that the march across the *anhara* would take half an hour. It took three hours because of the column's weakened condition. By 6.30 a.m., when the sun began to rise, they were still in the grassland, so they had to start running. Later that morning, two Soviet-made MI-8 helicopters arrived over the spot where the river crossing had been made. They hovered a short distance above the ground as 15 to 20 Cuban troops leapt from each. Fortunately for Savimbi's people, the sun in the cloudless skies had dried out the frost which earlier had made the UNITA trails through the grassland very obvious.

'We couldn't move. We had no choice. My troops were exhausted after the crossing and some were already dying,' Savimbi recalled. 'My people were separated – some on the west bank and others on the east, and Mulato lost. I said we would take defensive positions and if they came our way we would fight. By the time the fight began we might have gathered strength; then most of the column could run into the forest while others held off the enemy.'

Again Savimbi was lucky, for the Cubans stuck with their familiar tactics and did not leave the line of the river. Another two helicopters arrived in the afternoon and set down more men – one of them landing within 500 metres of Savimbi's pickets on the edge of the forest – so that there were perhaps 60 to 80 enemy soldiers patrolling the river grasslands. Before nightfall the Cubans began laying ambush positions.

Savimbi decided his people had to move away from trouble fast, but first he sent a scout patrol of three men through the darkness to the previous night's crossing point. None of the three ambushes made by the enemy were there, but Savimbi was worried that the rest of the column would stick rigidly to his previous night's orders to recommence the crossing and that they would be discovered. A two-man patrol from the other side had crossed the river and was lying in wait just north of the crossing point. New orders from Savimbi were delivered to them for the mass crossing to be abandoned: the eastern column was instead to head northwards along the Cuito River to the Bie region, link up with any UNITA guerrillas there and spread news among the people that Savimbi was alive and reorganising resistance. But if Mulato had been found, he was to attempt to cross with about 20 others and rejoin Savimbi.

Mulato had been found by a search party. He had got lost by following antelope paths which he had thought were those of a vanguard. So Mulato crossed, and he caught up with Savimbi 24 hours later.

'When Mulato rejoined us, it lifted our spirits,' said Savimbi. 'He was our comrade in arms and we loved him. And because he was safe we no longer needed to change our plans.'

Savimbi needed something to raise his spirits. Three men had died from exposure and exhaustion, and food was now a critical problem. Meat from only nine of the twelve slaughtered cattle had been brought across the river. Everyone was beginning to feel weak. They could not afford the time to trap game, nor could they risk being heard shooting for the pot.

The party was now some 250-strong, consisting mainly of

soldiers but also about 15 women and 10 male civilians, mostly skilled administrators. The reduced size of Savimbi's own column held certain advantages. The group was easier to control, it left less distinct trails, and it would be able to manoeuvre and weave more adeptly out of trouble.

There were also many serious problems. Savimbi's next target was to cross a major north-south road, from Bie to Serpa Pinto, about 120 kilometres to the west. But he was moving into an area of territory of the Nganguela tribe with which no one in the column was familiar. Without local guides or a compass, Savimbi's officers had to rely entirely on their maps and on sun and star positions.

Soon the meat ran out and the rate of progress slowed to a crawl. After about a week of marching everyone was so weak that Savimbi had to call a halt. For the sake of the guerrillas' morale contact would have to be re-established with villages to obtain food: contact was also necessary politically. Patrols were sent out from the resting place in a forest glade to make contacts with villages. But the area was sparsely inhabited and because the men were weak, and therefore could not patrol deep, they were initially unable to find any settlements.

There was little game available, but guerrillas from the Chokwe tribe who had been skilled traditional hunters managed to kill a bush pig. As well as its flesh, the starving column ate its skin and bones. The bones were boiled and the thin soup was drunk: then the softened bones were crushed and devoured.

The only other source of food was red-coloured, wild *kmussequele* (bushmen) beans, which were gathered from trees and boiled; then the skins were peeled away and the poisonous insides thrown away. The skins were boiled again with leaves from another tree. The resulting liquid soup was like vegetable oil, and after half an hour it left the emaciated diners very weak and bloated. But it was food of a sort.

One guerrilla knew how to collect wild honey and he brought in a small supply. Vinona Savimbi, an expert on edible forest fungi, collected some for the pot. But five soldiers died of poisoning after collecting and eating fungus without consulting Vinona.

Tito Chingunji, who himself felt he was going to die, said Savimbi gave a pep talk in which he urged soldiers that they should not surrender to death because people were waiting for them to fight. 'That was a really shocking and frightening moment because some of the soldiers just didn't have the physical ability to respond to his call, although you could see they wanted to. Most did manage to stand and say they would fight on, but several collapsed moments later.'

Despite the rest, Savimbi's group grew weaker and weaker through lack of food. They sprawled on the forest floor and by the sixth day most were unable to drag themselves to their feet: but on that same day a patrol brought life-giving news. They had discovered a village 15 kilometres away, and its inhabitants were long-standing UNITA supporters. The village was just over on a hill from the furthest point the soldiers had been patrolling to: they had not crossed the hill because they were weak and feared being ambushed. Desperation had pushed them into crossing it on the sixth day.

*   *   *

News of the village acted like a life-saving injection. The soldiers were desperate to make contact again with the ordinary population. Though they found hidden strength, the 15-kilometre journey, which would have taken them just two hours when they were fit, took twelve.

The villagers came out to meet Savimbi and help bring the column to their huts. They said they had been visited by UNITA guerrilla commanders who had told them Savimbi was being pursued by the Cubans and MPLA. The village chief drew diagrams in the dust to show Savimbi how he had sent patrols in several directions to help find the President's column. 'He was behaving like a general,' said Tito Chingunji. 'It was typical of many chiefs who like to show the President that they are as good as the full-time guerrillas.'

The villagers did not have big stocks of food, but they gave maize, cassava and antelope meat. Savimbi, drawing on his medical training in Portugal, gathered his officers and explained to them the dangerous consequences of taking solid food after a long period of starvation. Sketching the digestive system in the dust, he explained how intestines deprived of food simply shrivelled and shrunk: introduce solids while they were in that state and their owners would go into spasms which could result in death. The maize first had to be ground to make a thin gruel. This would be the only food eaten for the first two days: after that a little meat could be taken. Even the thin gruel would at first cause severe stomach cramps. Savimbi then ordered the officers to repeat the advice to the people they were responsible for, using the same diagrams.

The village was an isolated one. No Cuban or MPLA patrol had ever reached it, but after about five days, when most of the party were taking solid food again, a Cuban helicopter flew high overhead. 'It was just bad luck,' recalled Savimbi. 'Although the Cubans could not know we were there, they would plot the village on their map and eventually return. So I ordered the villagers to disperse and find a new place to build.' His intuition was that the Cubans and MPLA would attempt to cover as many villages as possible to force him to rely entirely on the bush.

More than half of Savimbi's party, now down to less than 250, were still suffering severely from exhaustion, fungus poisoning and debilitation. They would have to remain with the villagers. For the rest, Savimbi ordered a rapid march in the direction of the Bie-Serpa Pinto road, and then across it towards the planned base area.

*   *   *

Everyone was to travel as lightly as possible. Tito Chingunji buried the records he had made, in three thick notebooks, of the long march – every name of the participants, their special skills, their illnesses and deaths. Bok Sapalalo buried his records too: he had been required to give an account to Savimbi at every halt of all the arms and ammunition carried by each guerrilla.

The villagers gave Savimbi two guides to take him to a small UNITA guerrilla encampment some 36-hours march away across a headwater tributary of the Cuanza River. The aim was to pick up fresh guides at the camp for the road crossing.

About 30 minutes marching time from the camp they saw two Cuban helicopters machine-gunning the position and landing troops. Savimbi immediately switched direction and headed straight for the road: the news later reached him that more than 30 people, mainly women, had been killed in the attack.

A day later Savimbi ordered about 20 soldiers who had quickly lost strength to return and join the people dispersing from the column until they had convalesced. He was now down to about 110 people. Within another day they came within sight of a friendly village on the main road.

During the night the chief and his elders brought food and joined Savimbi in the forest. The chief told him to lie up in the forest during the day and move through the village when the conditions were right.

They stayed for two days being briefed about potential crossing points along the heavily patrolled road. The crossing would have to be made at night: the safest place might be where the Cubans would least expect it and where they would be least likely to have their trackers and scouts at work. The decision was made to cross directly through the big roadside village of some 500 inhabitants with a stockaded post containing about 10 Cubans and MPLA soldiers on its outskirts.

'We could see the Cubans and MPLA moving around with their guns,' said Savimbi. 'But the chief said they were fools. They never moved into the bush on foot and they would not suspect anything, provided we made no noise. We trusted him because he was an old member of our party.'

Savimbi's column in the forest watched Land Rovers move occasionally from the Cuban base, about 500 metres west of the village, down a track to the main road. Between the base and the central cluster of village huts were a few trenches dug by the Cubans, which were unmanned.

Within an hour of nightfall on the day of the crossing, 22 August, the chief returned and said he had arranged entertainment in the village that night for the Cubans in the garrison and also for the local schoolteacher, an MPLA activist who had been posted to the school by the government. Eight would be drinking in huts to the east of the road and three in huts to the west. Savimbi's men were to cross in groups of four or five, guided by village militiamen whose pickets would give warning if the Cubans left the huts.

*   *   *

The chief, unknown to the Cubans, was president of the village UNITA civilian committee. From the centre of the village, huts straggled for about two kilometres along the main road.

On 22 August Savimbi's column was joined by a group of 50 soldiers led by a Major Bandua who had fled from Lobito in February and had been heading for the Lungue Bungu valley. With Bandua was Jorge Valentim, the former 'Governor' of Lobito.

The route from the forest took the UNITA column across the road among the central cluster of huts and others straggling along the road to the north. To have crossed further northwards, beyond the outskirts of the last huts in the village, would have set the village dogs howling and attracted the attention of the Cubans; movement through the village with the local militiamen armed only with bows and arrows, would not arouse the dogs to any unusual degree.

Once across the road, to the west, the groups of UNITA men walked between the main body of huts and the empty trenches to a rendezvous in the forest about one kilometre to the south-west of the village outskirts.

When the crossing had been completed, a group of about 20 villagers – the chief, elders and their wives – joined Savimbi in the forest. The column and the villagers moved another two or three kilometres into the forest so that Savimbi could have discussions with the chief and elders and explain his future plans and how the villagers could help. He then spoke to a larger gathering, including a few other villagers and his own officers. Tito Chingunji recalled it this way: 'The President lectured that UNITA had no prospect of success unless the people were with the movement. They would ask awkward questions and there was no way those questions could be avoided. They would ask, for example, whether the war would finish soon or whether it would be long.

'The President said it would be long. There would be no

quick victory. He told the chief that one day the enemy would discover that his village was helping UNITA and it would be attacked. The village should start building up food stocks in the bush for when the day came that they needed to flee.

'He said he could not hide that all UNITA's friends would think we were incapable of resisting, that we were finished. The President said UNITA no longer had any active allies. We would have to rely on our own efforts, support from the people, existing weapons stocks and captured guns. He wanted to dispel any notion that help would come from outside before the people helped themselves. He said: "We have to fight first, and then you will see that people on the outside will want to get in touch again."

'The President said the Cubans had a clear advantage in terms of the quality of their weapons and in terms of the ruthlessness with which they were prepared to act; but they were at a real disadvantage in terms of knowledge of the countryside, the people and the language.'

Savimbi said goodbye to the chief and elders a couple of hours before daybreak on 23 August. Guides from the village moved ahead and behind the column, communicating in traditional birdsound codes. For a while the column moved northwards through forest parallel with and within sight of the road. At 9 a.m. a convoy of armoured cars and trucks carrying MPLA and Cuban troops started passing southwards down the road within sight of Savimbi's men who could hear the enemy singing. The village guides told the column to keep moving, assuring Savimbi that his men could not be seen from the road.

Savimbi intended making rapid progress towards the new base area. He knew he was about to move through a chain of pro-UNITA villagers. He could have crossed the road far to the north where the terrain was unpopulated, but the country was mountainous and deeply ravined and progress would have been too slow for his now compelling purpose of getting the central base established. Also he wished to establish a high profile so that word would spread that he was alive.

Savimbi established a higher profile in these villages than he intended. Guerrilla patrols from the area he was heading towards, about 120 kilometres west of the main road, were making contact with his column and spreading word ahead of his impending arrival. People were coming out in daylight with banners, singing and dancing.

'We were worried that a helicopter might pass over,' said Savimbi. 'I said this was no way to conduct a guerrilla war; we want no risks. But the people said don't worry, we've not been disturbed here.

'At one village, just two days walk from the base, there were thousands of people dancing and singing. They said they would walk with us to the base. I told the chief that this was no good, that if the people behaved like this there would be no security. One day they would be discovered and they would be attacked by the MPLA and Cubans.

'I told the chief I didn't want the people with me. I would call them in one week to the base for a big rally. But I failed; they just followed us, singing all the way. I gave in and said let us take the risk. So they came with us to Cuelei and that was the end of the long march.'

The Cuelei base was about 150 kilometres south-east of Huambo. It was under the command of Major Katali, who has assembled in his camp about 800 guerrillas and 200 women and children.

The long march ended with Savimbi's entry into Cuelei on 28 August 1976, some seven months and 3,000 kilometres after he had fled Luso with 1,000 followers. Of these, only 79, including nine women, were still with him at the end, others having died, been separated, sent elsewhere or left behind.

'The march was the most profound experience of my life,' Tito Chingunji, recalled years later. 'You felt you needed to love your brother as yourself. Alone, you couldn't survive. When colleagues died you truly felt diminished. All of us who were on the march believed by the end of it that the war really could be won.'

It had been a traumatic few months but, against all the odds and outsiders' expectations, Jonas Savimbi had survived. The war which most commentators pronounced finished with the Cuban victory in February 1976 would continue.

21

Savimbi Disappears

1976

'Life is a terrifying experience, but oblivion is sadder.'
Tennessee Williams

For a while, after his friends had vanished into Angola's depths, Kenneth Kaunda continued to speak out on behalf of Savimbi. The people of Africa had scarcely begun to understand the consequences of events in Angola, he said. 'Independence is impossible with Big Brother hanging over your shoulder. He is overbearing and will overpower you. It's a real puzzle to me how people can talk of independence when they are unable to govern a country without Cuban and Russian soldiers.'[1]

At a breakfast meeting with foreign correspondents at State House, Lusaka, on 29 March 1976, Kaunda spoke of the need for majority rule in Rhodesia. When he was asked whether it was his principle that majority rule was as important in Angola as it was in Rhodesia, he replied: 'Precisely. It's the only way peace can come. Majority rule applies everywhere.'

But though Kaunda was revealing where his heart lay, a fortnight later, on 15 April, he obeyed what his head told him. Zambia announced its official recognition of the MPLA as the legitimate government of Angola. It came in the form of a one-sentence statement, with no elaboration, from a Foreign Ministry spokesman: 'The Minister of Foreign Affairs Mr Rupiah Banda today announced Zambia's recognition of the People's Republic of Angola.' Twenty-five days later Banda, who had been one of UNITA's staunchest advocates, was dismissed from the government.[2] Anti-MPLA rhetoric ceased. The price of principle had become too high, and *realpolitik* reigned.

* * *

Rupiah Banda was retained in office long enough to act as host to Dr Henry Kissinger when he arrived in Lusaka on 27 April for the most important stop on an African safari designed to staunch the wounds inflicted on his battered African policy.

Kissinger faced a formidable task in restoring American credibility. 'It is two and a half months now since Henry Kissinger learned the hard way that he didn't know enough about Africa – which is precisely why he is there now,' wrote one prominent American columnist, Joseph C. Harsch.[3]

'The faction backed by Moscow with arms and Cuban troops is the complete winner. The whole of Angola is now in its hands . . . It was a case where the Kremlin had decided long ago to back one faction in a three-cornered competition to see who would be the future rulers of Angola. The Kremlin planners did a first-class job. They chose the tribal group which was dominant in and around the capital and throughout the central part of the country. They gave it weapons and training before Washington even recognised that Angola was on the way to independence and black majority rule. By the time the Portuguese pulled out of Angola last November the Russians had the situation under firm control.

'In theory Dr Kissinger could still have frustrated the Russian plan. A division of US Marines could have been landed at or near Luanda, backed by the entire US Atlantic fleet. The Soviet Union could not have moved enough strength to the South Atlantic to balance the American forces which were potentially available.

'But Congress in Washington and American public opinion in general were in no mood for any such adventure. The country then was in a post-Vietnam condition – and still is.[4] It was impossible for Dr Kissinger to send to Angola the force which could have changed the outcome . . . The plain fact is that Congress and the American people have had enough military intervention in far away places to satisfy them for some time.

'All of which means that Dr Kissinger has learned a bitter lesson the hard way. In the Angola story he miscalculated the readiness of the Portuguese to leave, the determination of the blacks to take over, the firmness of Soviet support and – most important of all – the determination of Congress to have nothing to do with far away adventures now. He made just about every mistake which could be made . . . The operation gets the prize as being the worst bungled of its kind in at least a quarter century.'

The residual question was whether Kissinger could help rebuild the prestige of his ally in the Angolan war, Kaunda, by unfolding a new American policy which would help bring about a solution of the problems in another neighbouring country of concern to the Zambian leader – the rebel British colony of Rhodesia.

Publicly, Angola ceased to be the issue. Savimbi was gone. The focus of attention had shifted southwards. The Secretary of State outlined a 10-point programme to bring within two years black majority rule in Rhodesia. He also called for a definite timetable for Namibian independence, warned South Africa to end its racial policies, and pledged a new US aid programme for the continent.[5]

The Kissinger programme raised high expectations in Zambia and neighbouring black states of major changes in southern Africa.[6] In the United States he was mercilessly criticised by the right-wing of the Republican Party and their candidate for the Presidency, Ronald Reagan, for threatening Rhodesia's white minority rebel government and for offering aid to 'Communist-dominated' Mozambique.[7] (In 1985 there would be the irony of Reagan, as US President, *supporting* President Machel of Marxist Mozambique and receiving him in the White House).

Not all African leaders were impressed by Dr Kissinger's damage limitation exercise. Nigeria, which pursed a strongly anti-Western policy after it decided to back the MPLA, persuaded Ghana's head of state General Ignatius Acheampong to cancel the US Secretary of State's scheduled visit to Accra.[8]

But further along the West African coast, President Felix Houphouet-Boigny of the Ivory Coast, a firm supporter of Savimbi, was 'constantly amazed by the West's levity of approach' towards the Soviet Union in Africa.

The former European colonial powers in Africa should have acted to stop what the Ivoirien President described as the Soviet advance: 'But you didn't do it. You didn't even think of it. Do you still exist? Are you not now fascinated and paralysed by the Soviet Union? The Soviets only advance when they have nothing before them. In Angola, believe me, they took their precautions. They hesitated for months.'[9]

*   *   *

As Savimbi suffered hardship and obscurity on his long march, as Kenneth Kaunda reoriented his regional foreign policy, and as Henry Kissinger tried to restore American prestige in black Africa, so the MPLA set about governing the vast and rich land of Angola.

Dissent was quickly stamped on. Having outlawed UNITA and the FNLA, the MPLA arrested and detained without trial other opponents, among them the former MPLA honorary President and leader of the Active Revolt faction, Joaquim Pinto de Andrade, and Gentil Viana, a former personal adviser to Agostinho Neto. Both were founding members of the MPLA.

Portugal's Socialist Party leader Mario Soares sent a message to President Neto expressing surprise at the arrest of Andrade and Viana and of 'other comrades in the struggle against fascism' and asking for their 'rapid liberation'. The appeal followed a series of reports in Lisbon newspapers which said Angola's Interior Minister Nito Alves was cracking down on moderate and Maoist opponents of the government. The others arrested were members of the tiny Maoist-oriented Communist Organisation of Angola, founded in 1975, which in its *Journal Communista* attacked the MPLA as a bourgeois party, condemned Soviet imperialism, and asked for withdrawal of all Cuban forces.[10] UNITA representatives in Lusaka alleged that Andrade was being tortured by East German security police who had been brought in to head the MPLA's intelligence service. UNITA also accused the East Germans of firing in one incident into a crowded cell of protesting prisoners, killing four people and wounding 13.[11]

It is difficult to assess the precise truth of the UNITA allegations. Amnesty International reported that during 1976 the MPLA held on average about 300 political prisoners in Luanda's São Paulo prison. But it also said the MPLA government had not answered many questions about long-term or missing detainees; nor had it responded to 'appeals against the use of torture or the death penalty'.[12] However, MPLA police chief Andre Petroff said publicly after returning from a mission abroad that East Germany, Yugoslavia and Algeria had promised 'technical assistance and training help' to combat 'delinquency and banditism'.[13]

Amnesty International further reported that in June 1976 MPLA troops carried out extra-judicial executions at Chissamba, in the central province of Bie, of both captured guerrillas and civilians suspected of helping UNITA. In July more executions took place of UNITA guerrillas and supporters at Cassemba in Huambo Province. It is not known how many people were killed.[14]

Once in power, the MPLA did hold elections of a kind, but only in Luanda. There was little interest in the poll, on 27 June 1976, to elect members of the one-party 'local people's councils'. Only about ten per cent of Luanda's residents voted.[15]

*　　*　　*

Meanwhile, South Africa had continued its slow withdrawal from Angola. Its troops pulled out from their final position at the Calueque dam, on the Cunene River hydro-electric project, in late March 1976.[16] Calueque had been occupied on 9 August 1975 by the South Africans 'for the purpose of protecting the lives of the (South African, Portuguese, Angolan and Namibian) workers and of safeguarding the installations'. The $US 63 million installation at Calueque was one of a string of dams that South Africa had been financing, in co-operation with the Portuguese, on the Cunene, which forms the Angola-Namibia border along the last 250 kilometres of its journey to the sea.

South Africa also withdrew from two camps it had been running in Angola at the border towns of Calai and Cuangar for thousands of refugees who had fled from the fighting to the north.

The Cuban/MPLA forces, which for two months had inched forward slowly enough to avoid combat with the withdrawing South Africans, finally reached the Namibian border on 1 April 1976 to stamp MPLA sovereignty over the whole of Angola.[17]

At the end of May Angola's Prime Minister Lopo do Nascimento began a week-long visit to Moscow, where he signed a declaration with Soviet Prime Minister Alexei Kosygin which virtually guaranteed Soviet responsibility for the security of Angola. To strengthen the MPLA's defence capabilities, Kosygin and Nascimento said Soviet defence and armaments specialists would be sent to work in Angolan 'government offices'.[18]

The MPLA furthered its international respectability when it was admitted to the International Labour Organisation in Geneva.[19] At this time also, Agostinho Neto went to Brazzaville and met his bitter enemy, Zaire's President Mobutu, whose country was in the throes of what bankers were calling undeclared bankruptcy.

Like Kaunda, Mobutu had backed one of the losing sides in Angola and was in the position of supplicant. He needed to regain access to the Benguela Railway to export his copper and cobalt. Angola agreed to carry Zairean goods, though the railway was unlikely to be ready to resume operations before the end of 1976 because of rebuilding work on bridges destroyed in the war.

As his side of the bargain, Mobutu agreed to shut off all aid to the FNLA and UNITA. FNLA bases in Zaire were immediately closed down after the Brazzaville meeting. And when Roberto reacted by issuing a statement blaming Mobutu for his defeat in Angola, the Zairean President sent 300 armed police to sack the FNLA's offices in Kinshasa and burn its records. Roberto was permitted to stay on in Kinshasa but he was finished politically.[20]

Mobutu's hope was that the 6,000 Katangese gendarmes, who had fought effectively for the MPLA against UNITA in eastern Angola, would not now be turned back into Shaba, Zaire's richest and southernmost province, from which they had been driven in the mid-sixties when it was known to the world as Katanga.

Meanwhile, Kaunda was rebuilding his bridges with the Soviet Union by accepting as Moscow's ambassador to Lusaka a leading Soviet Africanist, Vassily Solodovnikov, Director of the African Institute in Moscow. Solodovnikov was the author of a classic text on Soviet strategy in Africa entitled *Political Parties in Africa*, published in 1970.

He also was an experienced diplomat who had served at the UN headquarters in New York. He was clearly expected to exercise his knowledge and experience and his sympathy for Africa to enable the Zambian government to move with dignity towards the MPLA.

Savimbi understood Kaunda's position, as his letter of 12 February 1976 to the Zambian leader showed (see Chapter 17). Many years later, in one of my conversations with Savimbi, he still said of Kaunda: 'He is my friend and I respect him. I don't believe that Kaunda is with the MPLA. He is forced to. He cannot help me, but I believe his heart is with me. I will never hurt Kaunda, because the time I have been dealing with Kaunda in 1975 has marked me deeply. He's a good man. He is the one who has backed UNITA, and we lost, so he has to join with them (the MPLA).'[21]

*　　*　　*

The trial of the 13 mercenaries caught fighting with the FNLA further strengthened the MPLA's standing in the world community. The MPLA knew they were on to a propaganda winner and opened the doors to the world's press to witness the proceedings in June 1976 before a People's Revolutionary Tribunal.

It became a spectacular media event, and, although its legal validity was deeply questionable, the bestiality and futility of the crimes of the leading defendants shocked people and won sympathy for the MPLA.[22] The more fundamental issue of the aborted Angolan elections and the question of whether the MPLA was a legitimate government got buried by the immediacy and high drama of the trial. For the reporters in Luanda, Savimbi and his supporters, marching for their lives some 750 kilometres to the south-east, were virtually non-people.

Angola's People's Prosecutor, Manuel Rui Monteiro, described the mercenaries as 'professional murderers in the pay of imperialism'. The West took a non-stop drubbing, especially when it became clear that the United Kingdom Labour government had turned a blind eye to recruitment in Britain, and that the mercenaries had been given VIP treatment when passing through London Airport without passports.

'As one watched the 13 men on trial in court during nine harrowing days of testimony, one could not escape the conclusion that others should have been in the dock with them,' wrote a British correspondent. 'Most of the mercenaries were poorly educated. Many were out of work. They came from societies where violence, war and avarice are accepted and often encouraged. The "dogs of war" told the court that they had been motivated by money and the chance of adventure.'[23]

It was publicity of a value that the MPLA could never have conjured or bought for itself.

A team of 48 international observers were invited to the trial by the MPLA. Less than half of them were from Western democracies, and nearly all of these were of various forms of socialist persuasion whose sympathies were with the MPLA – for example, Wilfred Burchett, the Australian Communist journalist, and Michael Wolfers, a British Marxist and former African correspondent of *The Times* of London, who had taken a job in the MPLA's Ministry of Information. Their function was to give a stamp of international respectability to a trial that was essentially political. The verdicts were virtually pre-ordained. And, looked at from the MPLA's point of view, it was hard to condemn the government's action. The mercenaries had, after all, been recruited in sophisticated Western democracies to kill black African peasants in the ranks of the MPLA's soldiery. Somebody should have warned them of the potentially severe consequences if things went wrong.

The ten British and three American defendants were

accused of various offences, including the newly created crime of 'mercenarism'. One prominent jurist observing the trial – not as a member of the official observers team – later argued that no such crime existed in Angolan law at the time the mercenaries were captured.[24] Costas Georgiou, under the alias 'Colonel Callan', was charged with the murders of three Angolans and with ordering the executions of 13 of his fellow Britons.

All of the accused were convicted. Three of the Britons – Georgiou, Andy Mackenzie and 'Brummie' Barker – were condemned to death, along with a young American, Daniel Gearhart, who was selected less for judicial reasons than for the fact that the MPLA felt the need to make a political example of the United States.[25] On 10 July 1976 the four were executed by firing squad at Grafanil military base outside Luanda.

*   *   *

Though the MPLA was gaining international sympathy from the mercenary issue, trouble had begun within its own ranks. While the mercenary trial was in progress, a big strike at a coffee bag factory was ended when MPLA troops occupied the premises. And Prime Minister Nascimento alleged that workers on coffee and sugar plantations around Carmona in the north had been idling because they thought the Cubans had now taken control. 'You, comrades, know better than us that this is not true,' said Nascimento in a speech at the 'Heroes of Caxito' sugar plantation. 'Direction is in the hands of Angolan comrades with Cuban comrades there to help and teach us.' Nascimento warned that the government would 'have to detain people in Luanda and send them for the sugar and coffee. It is one thing for people not to work because there are no jobs. But it is another for them not to work because they do not want to. Those who do not want to work we have to oblige to work.'[26]

It is not clear whether Prime Minister Nascimento appreciated the irony of the similarity between his own policy and that of forced labour system which the Portuguese had imposed and which had helped inspire nationalist revolt (see Prologue and Chapter 1).

Cuban advisers had taken prominent posts in the Angolan civil service, particularly in the Interior and Education Ministries and on Neto's personal and security staff. The Cubans were also supervising the MPLA's programme of 'political mobilisation' to drum up support for a 'mass Marxist-Leninist party'.[27]

There were also rumblings of a fundamental split within the MPLA between 'moderates' committed to careful and gradual growth, grouped around Neto and Nascimento, and a radical, extremist faction led by Nito Alves, the black Interior Minister, who objected to the predominance of *mesticos* and whites in the government. 'There are racial tensions within the Popular Movement government of Agostinho Neto,' wrote one correspondent. 'The white and mixed-blood people play a disproportionately heavy role in running the government of what is predominantly black nation. Neto has insisted that his new government be multiracial. But there are blacks in his cabinet who know the power they could gain from a frankly racist appeal to the black masses. Signs scrawled on walls in Luanda call in Portuguese for "power to the blacks".'[28]

It threatened a storm – but it would not break *yet*.

22

Cuelei – Savimbi Reorganises Resistance

1976

'You in Europe have a tendency to underestimate the role in history of great personalities.'
Armando Hart, Castroist leader in Cuba[1]

*   *   *

On reaching the end of his long march, on 28 August 1976, at Major Katali's Cuelei base in central Angola, Savimbi immediately set about reinvigorating and reorganising his traumatised followers.

After the South African withdrawal most of his soldiers had returned to their villages, either with or without their arms, accepting with resignation the MPLA victory; and loyalists who had continued fighting were in small, scattered and unco-ordinated bands, most of which had no recent news of the fate of their leader.

From Major Katali, Savimbi learned where some UNITA groups were located. Messengers and scouting groups were sent out to try to locate others and strengthen the network of communication.

The fundamental message of Savimbi's teaching at this time was the necessity of having the will to endure: 'Let us avoid set battles with the MPLA so that we can avoid being crushed. Let us survive. And if we do survive the situation will change (in areas held by the MPLA) in such a way that the people will realise that they need to support UNITA.'[2]

Surviving did not mean passivity. It meant preparation,

training, the rejection of Quixotic heroic gestures. 'We need to employ very flexible tactics which do not provoke the enemy unnecessarily so that we are broken. But we will have to make attacks so that our soldiers get used to being under fire. We will have to have contacts with the enemy to enable the leadership to plan its strategy and study the thinking of the Cubans and Russians – how they attack, how they withdraw, how they encircle our forces. We want to know how they *act*.

'When we have understood the tactics of the MPLA, Cubans and Russians we will try to test ourselves further. We will have to confront them more often, in bigger groups. But there will be no all-out large offensives. The aim of this new stage will be to confuse the enemy and see how they *react*. If we pass the test of confusing the enemy then we will gain plenty of time to plan major attacks and offensives.

'What we have to achieve in all these stages of military tactics is to cripple the economy. No war can be successful if it is not backed by a strong economy, so we have to blow up bridges, to make ambushes so that the roads will be unsafe for transport, and to stop the railways.'[3]

Savimbi's first survey showed that a number of UNITA groups had continued to struggle on autonomously, hoping their leader had survived and would eventually make contact. As well as the 800 men under Katali and several thousand left scattered in the east under the overall command of Smart Chata, another senior commander, Major Arão Chingufo, had established bases and organised troops to the north of Huambo.

Two interesting young organisers of resistance were Demostenes Chilingutila and Arlindo Pena. Chilingutila was leading a small band of guerrillas in the difficult open country of the coastal province of Benguela, and Pena was at the head of a group with bases in the forested hills just to the south of Huambo.[4]

Unlike Chata and Chingufo, Chilingutila and Pena represented a new trend within UNITA. They had not fought with Savimbi against the Portuguese. They were high school graduates, products of the educational opportunities expanded rapidly in the late sixties by the Portuguese.

Chilingutila and Pena had joined the Portuguese Army, rising to become sergeants, the highest rank permitted to blacks. Others of their generation had left high school (the *liceu*) or university and set up rural education and health networks, become auto mechanics, telephone engineers or agricultural technicians. They joined UNITA during the 1975–76 civil war and continued to come over from 1977 onwards.

'It is this group which came into UNITA which is making new life and organisations possible,' Savimbi said in one interview. 'They did not participate in the first war. There were highly trained engineers and basic mechanics among them, the people who do the small, unglamorous things which make a nation move. They started training other people in our bases.

'We have scarce materials, but when the means are limited and you have skilled technicians, then you can achieve great things. But when you have the means without the skilled people, you can't do anything.'[5]

Another interesting centre of resistance was Cunene Province, in the far south of Angola opposite Ovamboland, the most densely populated region of neighbouring Namibia. Cunene was the region of the Cuanhama tribe, fierce and proud horse-riding warriors who were the last of Angola's tribes to be suppressed by the Portuguese and who were still at war with the colonial power as late as 1928. The Cuanhamas were part of the Ovambo tribe across the border in Namibia. The links between the two were almost inextricable, and they moved freely across the border between each other's settlements.

The Namibian Ovambos formed the core element of SWAPO, the liberation movement seeking to end South African rule in their territory. When Antonio Vakulukuta, the leader of the Angolan Cuanhamas, took his people into UNITA it was natural that the closest of links be consolidated between the two movements.[6] Vakulukuta had enormous prestige on both sides of the border because he was a direct descendant of the senior tribal family of the Ovambos.

After the fall of Huambo to the Cubans in February 1976, Vakulukuta had walked south with some 100 Cuanhama

members of UNITA and about 400 head of cattle. When they
reached their home province they were greeted with suspicion by the headmen, who wanted to know whether it
was true what local MPLA commissars were saying about
Savimbi having fled from Angola. It took Vakulukuta some
weeks to persuade them of his conviction that UNITA's
leader was still in Angola. After that, hundreds more
UNITA soldiers who had returned to their Cunene villages
and hidden their guns rejoined Vakulukuta. The headmen
gave him more cattle with which to retreat into the bush and
set up bases from which his men began attacking small
MPLA posts.

Fighting with Vakulukuta's UNITA forces were some
elements of SWAPO with whom Vakulukuta had long been
intimately allied. But – and this is one of the bitterest twists
of the whole Angola-Namibia saga – among those they were
fighting was the main body of the SWAPO military, the
People's Liberation Army for Namibia (PLAN).

Though UNITA and SWAPO had for years been blood
brothers,[7] the outcome of the Angolan civil war had confronted both with cruel dilemmas in their mutual relationship and in each of their desires for their own country's
freedom. UNITA had allied itself with SWAPO's enemy.
And now that UNITA had been defeated, SWAPO's leader
Sam Nujoma, who had given UNITA its first weapon back in
1966, allied his movement with UNITA's enemies.

In mid-June SWAPO opened its new headquarters in
Luanda, having been promised arms by the Soviet Union,
military training by the Cubans, and Angolan soil by the
MPLA from which to launch raids against Namibia.[8]

According to Vakulukuta, the MPLA put a SWAPO unit
in charge of security at Calueque. A chain of other SWAPO
bases was established along the border just inside Namibia.
SWAPO then began identifying the location of UNITA bases
in Cunene to the MPLA. Vakulukuta's forces, including
those SWAPO men personally loyal to him, responded by
attacking and routing the SWAPO base at Calueque.[9]

Geography, history and culture had made UNITA and
SWAPO close. Now the unwinding of local and international politics had put them in opposing camps, and the

enmity would grow. In Cunene/Ovamboland there was the grimmest consequence of the 1888 Treaty of Berlin under which Europeans drew the colonial frontiers of Africa. Tribal clans who had remained united by deep kinship, despite the straight-line border drawn through their traditional territory, had been finally divided and were killing each other.

In late 1976 Savimbi declared: 'Now that the Nujoma faction of SWAPO has decided to side with our implacable foes, that is, the Soviet Union, the Cuban forces in Angola and the so-called *Faplas*[10] of MPLA, UNITA has no alternative but to regard Nujoma and his exile followers as the fourth enemy.'[11]

It was inevitable that the Cubans/MPLA would strike back at Vakulukuta. The MPLA launched an offensive in August 1976 during which some 5,000 Cuanhamas, mainly women, children and old men, fled across the border into Namibia.[12] But the main assault, a combined one by the MPLA and Cubans, followed in early November. Thousands of Cuanhama refugees crossed into Namibia to escape the fighting and told reporters that the MPLA/Cubans were using scorched earth tactics to destroy crops and livestock over a wide area of Cunene. MPLA troops tried to seal the border to stop the exodus. Refugees said people were being shot as they tried to cross the border; bodies were being buried in mass graves one to two kilometres inside Angola.[13] South African troops in Ovamboland said they had watched through binoculars as Cuban/MPLA troops took over small border towns and villages; the sounds of rifle and artillery fire were clearly audible.[14]

The reports of the November battles were the clearest indications in months to the outside world that UNITA was still intact as a fighting force. But a Reuter journalist near the border noted: 'There has been no confirmation that Dr Savimbi has survived the recent government push against his forces.'[15]

In fact, Savimbi was some 450 kilometres to the north in his Cuelei base planning his long-term military strategy; and preparing to hold UNITA's fourth Congress, the four-yearly policy-making forum and electoral college of the movement.

And at this time, as the journalists at the border speculated whether or not Savimbi was still alive, a French journalist, Dominique De Roux of the Paris-based Gamma News Agency, emerged from Angola with photographs of Savimbi in a forest clearing and with an interview. The photographs appeared around the world as the first real evidence that Savimbi was still alive and fighting on inside Angola.

De Roux did not identify where in Angola he met Savimbi, but the photographs showed a camp consisting of a few huts and a rectangular conference table made of split logs in a clearing. De Roux's interview was unspectacular. He served up some of the UNITA leader's windier rhetoric, but amongst it Savimbi hammered his key theme of the need for elections and a secondary one of how Angola could not be developed on the Cuban model: 'Our aim is not to be beaten. The people want to taste freedom in peace. For that they need a democratic government, elected and representing the three liberation movements, MPLA, FNLA and UNITA. The building of African socialism cannot be the same as the Castro model. We have our past, our customs. Let people stop seeing us, the Negroes, as irresponsible men.'[16]

Luis Rodrigues, a Portuguese journalist who was close to UNITA and worked for the BBC, set out from Lusaka in April 1976 on a trek into the interior of Angola to find Savimbi. After walking for seven months and shedding 30 kilos from his normally corpulent frame, he finally caught up with Savimbi on 14 November 1976 at a UNITA base 70 kilometres south of Menongue (as Serpa Pinto had now been renamed by the MPLA). Savimbi had come south from the Cuelei central base to attend a rally of supporters. 'The day Savimbi arrived there was a colour guard consisting of a full battalion,' Rodrigues wrote in his diary. 'For ten days beforehand people had been told he would be coming, so some three to four thousand people had come from several places to see him and they were camping around the base.

'Then we heard the shouting and the songs. They had laid down a carpet of green leaves for about two kilometres, and women came racing along that track singing welcome songs. Then there was the advance guard, the captain of the bodyguard and then came Savimbi wearing a big straw hat. He was carrying a big Weston six-shooter strapped to his waist and a Kalashnikov rifle. N'Zau Puna was with him. Behind them were two donkeys loaded with supplies they had picked up from one of the arms dumps.

'Everybody went mad, but there was no shooting in the air. UNITA are a very disciplined group. Whoever shoots a gun not in combat gets 20 strokes with a cane. There was just singing, shouting and throwing of leaves. When Savimbi saw me he rushed to embrace me. We hadn't seen one another for many months.'

Savimbi, Puna and Rodrigues were led to some big thatched huts which had been newly prepared for the rally. After three days of non-stop marching from the north, which involved crossing the main tarmac road from Menongue to Lubango (formerly Sa da Bandeira), Savimbi's feet were bleeding. In the huts they swilled five gallons of maize beer, chewed roasted chicken and swapped yarns about their respective marches. Savimbi ragged Rodrigues about his flat stomach – 'He asked if I had sold my big one to the MPLA.'

Savimbi was particularly pleased about an attack UNITA troops had made on an old PIDE prison at Missombo, near Menongue, where about 100 UNITA soldiers and officials were detained. The assault was inspired by Israel's raid on Uganda's Entebbe Airport at the beginning of July 1976. After that, the UNITA commander in the Menongue area had called for volunteers, and in a dawn attack on the prison they had quickly wiped out the MPLA mortar crews. The rest of the MPLA troops fled: the prisoners were released and two light mortars and five machine-guns were added to the UNITA armoury.

Luis Rodrigues described to Savimbi details of some of the adventures on his own march, particularly of two attacks on trains on the Benguela Railway near Munhango in September. In one of them the driver of the wood-burning locomotive had to bring his train to a halt because guerrillas had ripped up the tracks ahead. The locomotive was blown off the tracks with a Laws missile while the carriage were raked with machine-gun fire until people began emerging with hands above their heads. The train had been carrying 150 MPLA activists to Teixeira de Sousa for a planned formal reopening of the Benguela line. They were marched off to a UNITA base near Nharea, 100 kilometres north of Bie, to work on cassava plantations. For a couple of days after the attack the guerrillas continued to rip up stretches of rail and blow up culverts. The train yielded great quantities of tinned cheese and fish and Caritas relief agency rations for UNITA's food stocks.

(Journalist allowed into MPLA territory also reported UNITA attacks on the railway. In a despatch from Huambo on 3 June, Marvine Howe of the *New York Times* said that during April and May UNITA guerrillas had destroyed three locomotives and derailed another, as well as cutting the line in several places. These attacks would have been carried out by groups acting independently of central control by Savimbi, who at that time was fleeing from Gago Coutinho towards the Lungue Bungu valley.)[17]

Luis Rodrigues stayed with Savimbi for ten days before he began his trek back out of the country and the UNITA leader headed back northwards to Cuelei. 'Our aim at this moment is simply to protect our people,' Savimbi told him. 'A lot of them are hoping that foreign help will come again. What we must teach them is that they cannot depend upon it, otherwise they will end up the same as the FNLA. They must be prepared to fight this war against the Cubans and Soviets without outside help.'[18]

*   *   *

As Rodrigues left Savimbi, another foreign journalist joined the UNITA leader – Leon Dash, the black American whose reports brought Savimbi's movement vividly alive during the war against the Portuguese. Now Dash had once more trekked from Zambia to rejoin UNITA. From the base south of Menongue he went north with Savimbi at the beginning of what is the most extraordinary and courageous journey yet undertaken by a reporter with forces in the Angolan conflict.

23

Dash's Journey
1976–77

'I do not get frustrated with blows or conceited with victory. It does not help to have hatred or resentment. They are two bad emotions that will cut off the light to think clearly.'

Jonas Savimbi[1]

* * *

When future historians come to the daunting task of writing a definitive history of the Angolan wars, they will have to refer to the work of Leon Dash. Without his daring and endeavour there would be no reliable, independent account of UNITA's activities during the crucial months after Savimbi completed his long march and as he prepared for another protracted war against the Cubans/MPLA.

Dash crossed the border from Zambia into Angola's Moxico Province on 4 October 1976 with an escort of 100 UNITA guerrillas. He would emerge again seven-and-a-half months later, on 22 May 1977, having walked 3,400 kilometres; watched UNITA forces go into battle; fallen seriously ill; eaten honey-coated grubs; talked at length to UNITA guerrillas and their MPLA prisoners; and attended UNITA's fourth Congress, 750 kilometres inside Angola, as the sole journalist observer. By the time Dash came out of Angola, his friends back in the United States were deeply worried: they had expected him to be gone for only two to three months.

To enter Angola Dash made a two-hour crossing of the Ninda River swamps – he and the guerrillas waded naked, their clothes on their heads, through tangled roots and razor-sharp grasses which left their legs, arms and hands covered with tiny cuts that streamed blood. Across the river, Dash was greeted by Smart Chata who told the American: 'It takes tough men to live in these conditions and that is why it will be difficult for the government to defeat us. Their soldiers don't like to come into these areas.'[2]

Three hours' walk through the forest into Angola Dash hit UNITA's first camp. 'The guerrillas' bases are all built similarly, with the grass huts scattered under trees for cover. The green canopy keeps the camps from being spotted by the occasional single-engined reconnaissance planes the government uses. In the camps live female guerrillas and children – some of the men have their entire families with them. The children begin military training as soon as they can walk.'

By 13 October, after crossing several swollen rivers in bark canoes, Dash reached a base where a baby had been born 15 minutes earlier. In the traditional African manner of marking events, the baby was named Neto Dash – after the *Washington Post* man and his guerrilla escort, Captain Neto Epalanga. The baby was not expected to live: his undernourished mother had no milk, and the only food available in Moxico's uncultivated wilderness was wild honey and antelope meat.

Deeper into Angola the food situation improved, and on 28 October Dash recorded a meal of roasted corn, river catfish, antelope, honey and honey-coated bee larvae.

On 4 November Dash's party came across 23 foxholes dug into the bank of a river. The site, littered with empty tins bearing labels of *Salva* brand Russian stewed beef and South African *Koo* green peas, had been an ambush site of MPLA soldiers during Savimbi's long march. 'They knew that Savimbi was due to pass here,' said a guerrilla officer who had been on the march with the UNITA president, 'but we knew they were here and passed through another river valley north of here.'

On 8 November Dash reached a base of 200 guerrillas where he was told that the *Voice of America* had reported the election of Jimmy Carter as the next President of the United States. The cuts on Dash's legs inflicted by the sharp grasses at the Ninda River had stubbornly refused to heal and several had turned to large running sores. It was decided he should rest at the base for several days to allow scabs to form, and, while waiting, the guerrillas held an independence festival to celebrate the first anniversary of the end of Portuguese rule on 11 November 1975: 'A large T-shaped table was built from saplings. The women dished out huge helpings of boiled antelope meat and mounds of boiled corn meal, which had the consistency of bread dough. That night there was a dance under the trees, with married and unmarried female guerrillas mingling with men on the dusty earth dance-floor. A truck battery, captured in an ambush against government forces the week before, powered the guerrillas' phonograph, which ground out Zairean and Angolan music which I found monotonous. No one else seemed to share this feeling, however, for the dance went on until dawn when it was ended by a cloudburst.'

With the base political commissar, Kawendima Chipipa, Dash listened to the live broadcast of the MPLA's celebration of independence in Luanda, during which President Neto praised the Cubans for having fought with the MPLA against UNITA and the FNLA. Neto's speech was greeted with loud applause by the Luanda crowds. 'We have fought many enemies,' Chipipa laughed. 'First the Portuguese and now the Popular Movement and the Cubans. I don't know when the fighting will stop.'

After 800 kilometres of walking Dash finally caught up with Savimbi, and Luis Rodrigues, at the rally south of Menongue – '"Welcome, welcome," Savimbi greeted me with the traditional Angolan bearhug. "There is lots for you to see. There is a lot of fighting going on in Angola."'

* * *

From Menongue, Dash went north with Savimbi to his Cuelei base area, where Savimbi said he was once again, in November 1976, applying the Maoist tenets of guerrilla warfare spelt out to him and the first eleven UNITA guerrillas when they trained in Nanking in 1965:

engage government troops only when you have massed twice their number of soldiers or more, to kill as many as possible and demoralise the army by never giving them a victory;

destroy all means of communications, make road transportation unsafe with numerous ambushes and destroy all railroads;

sabotage the economy and create psychological instability among the civilian population that supports the government through acts of urban terrorism;

disperse when attacked by large government forces, causing frustrated government soldiers to retaliate against the civilian population and thereby cement the ties between peasant supporter and guerrilla.

Savimbi also explained four different Cuban/MPLA military offensives against UNITA that his officers had identified since May of 1976.

First, there was Operation Tigre in eastern Angola, launched as UNITA held its Sandona conference in May 1976. Then came Operation Cacuenha in the south-east; and finally Operation Huambo in central Angola and Operation Vakulukuta in Cunene Province which were just ending.

'They bombed and strafed us with their MIG jets,' said Savimbi, 'but we just dispersed or moved our bases to another area of the forest. I love this forest. Without it, things would be very difficult for us.

'The Cubans and the Russians don't know how to fight an anti-guerrilla war. The bigger the military machine, the easier it is to escape. They should use smaller groups, but they don't have the morale. The Cubans will not accept 20 of their men to be dropped here in the bush (on a search and destroy mission). The (MPLA) soldiers are too poorly trained to do it.

'When they come with (Soviet T-34 and T-54) tanks, it is true, we will run away. But we will return when they have passed. They've just wasted petrol.'

There were no battle lines in this war, Dash noted. The guerrillas attacked wherever government troops were concentrated. When the guerrillas were attacked in their forest bases they quickly ran into the bush and regrouped later to build another base.

There was precious little reporting of the war either. From July 1976 – after the mercenary trial was over – the MPLA closed its door into Angola for Western journalists. Such news as emerged came from the state-owned National News Agency of Angola (ANGOP), the state-owned Luanda Radio, and two resident freelance journalists who were politically 'committed' to the MPLA. Frustrated by the near-disappearance of Angola's troubles from the foreign pages of the overseas press, Savimbi sent a statement to the outside world in which he said: 'It is not in their (the MPLA/Cubans/Soviets') interest to publicise the continuation of a war they thought they had won.'[3]

* * *

Following the government's Operation Vakulukuta in November 1976, UNITA noticed that the Cubans were withdrawing from the countryside to the major cities and towns of south and central Angola – Huambo, Bie, Luena (formerly Luso), Menongue and Lubango. 'Too many of them were dying,' Samuel Chiwale told Dash.

The retreat of the Cubans to their city barracks resulted in harsher retaliatory measures against UNITA's civilian supporters by MPLA troops and their SWAPO allies. 'There is a difference between the Cubans, government soldiers and SWAPO,' Savimbi told Dash. 'The Cubans are not so savage and will usually not kill our supporters. The government soldiers are more savage and the SWAPO are the most savage. Now we will never let them operate against the South Africans in Namibia again. Never! Not unless we are defeated.'

Savimbi's observation then, on the Cubans' treatment of the civilian population, matches that he made to the author some years later about their attempted hearts-and-minds campaign: 'In 1976–77 the Cubans were being a little bit more lenient towards the people. When they captured people and accused them of being UNITA or anti-government, they did not ill-treat them, they did not imprison them. They wanted to win them over, particularly in the traditional areas of UNITA around Huambo and Bie and Luena.'[4]

The MPLA, however, killed villagers suspected of giving UNITA food and providing the guerrillas with information about government troop movements, Dash was told. On 14 December the *Washington Post* man reached the village of Kavango in the western province of Huila, and there . . . 'The stench of death choked me as the wind shifted suddenly, carrying the smell of dead cattle to the eastern edge of the burnt and deserted village. Chief Jacinto Seven guided me and an escort of 50 guerrillas past the 45 dead cows.

'A short distance away Chief Seven pointed to the scattered bones of a leper sticking up from the red mud – symbols of the savage, fratricidal civil war. 'He and the other lepers were too weak to run when the government soldiers came here,'' said Seven, chief of the now-deserted village of 300 peasants. ''The soldiers burned him and another leper alive,'' Seven continued unemotionally while pointing to the dead man's jawbone, a thighbone and a forearm lying among the fast-growing weeds in front of the dead man's fire-blackened house.

'''The soldiers threw another man down a well and shot the other nine. It was the fifth time they had come here, but the first time they had done this. They were angry because we support the guerrillas.'''

Kavango had been the site of a small American Baptist mission which had founded the small leper colony and built a hospital, a church and an elementary school. The small, red-brick houses of the lepers and the thatch-roofed mud huts of the peasants in the main village had all been gutted by fire. The hospital was smoke-blackened and littered with the charred remains of medical texts on the treatment of leprosy and other tropical diseases. The homes of the former American missionary and an American doctor had been ransacked.

Chief Seven dated the beginning of the deterioration of his villagers' relationship with the MPLA from the time of a government rally in Kavango in May 1976: 'They told us UNITA was finished and Savimbi was dead with his legs cut off. We didn't believe them because there were UNITA guerrillas there in the crowd listening to them.' While the villagers listened to the speeches, Seven said, MPLA soldiers were going through their houses taking blankets, radios, salt and money. 'They said theirs was the only real liberation movement, but they were thieves.'

In June the soldiers returned again and took all the blankets from the hospital. Soon afterwards the villagers moved into the forest because they heard rumours that people were being shot by the MPLA in a neighbouring settlement. On 22 October 1976, during Operation Huambo, MPLA soldiers came again to Kavango without the Cubans. 'I had returned to the village to weed my corn,' said Chief Seven. 'It was about noon and I heard the shooting begin around the hospital. I ran away back to the forest.'

There were eight wounded guerrillas recuperating at the hospital when the MPLA soldiers attacked. A male nurse told Dash: 'All of them managed to escape because the troops began firing and making a lot of noise before they reached the hospital. Only the lepers were caught. They were too weak to run.'

Angola was now firmly into that cycle of horrific violence which civil war breeds, for the guerrillas too admitted killing unarmed civilians, often accidentally, but sometimes with callous deliberateness.

Lt.-Col. Mario Chilulu Cheya was a UNITA leader whose base was close to the government-occupied town of Chitembo, in Bie Province. He met Dash in December 1976, and told him: 'I had to attack Chitembo several times before the peasants would leave the town. But then some of them went back.' And so, when they left the town to go to their fields to cultivate corn, 'we would attack them and kill some of them'. The purpose, said Cheya, was to prevent them taking food to the MPLA soldiers in Chitembo.

Finally, after Operation Huambo, Cheya said he massed a big force of guerrillas from several bases and attacked Chitembo for the seventh time, killing everyone caught in the line of fire, civilians and soldiers alike. 'The people then left Chitembo because they no longer felt safe,' added Cheya. 'They have now moved into the bush with us.'

* * *

The tit-for-tat quality of the fighting was again noticed by Dash as he passed through the central plateau town of Ringoma, just 30 kilometres south of the Benguela Railway, on 13 January 1977, one month after a force of 300 UNITA guerrillas had attacked it. Hundreds of spent cartridges, their brass colouring turning grey, littered the centre of the town along with empty green boxes with Russian lettering that had once contained 82mm mortar shells. The red clay-tile roofs of all the cement houses, shops and the church had been smashed by the guerrillas with the butts of their rifles. The intent was to make them uninhabitable during the long rainy season and thus deter MPLA soldiers from returning.

The struggle for the town had begun on 22 November 1976 when UNITA's Major Jose Kanjundo had ambushed a column of five trucks carrying MPLA soldiers southwards from the Benguela Railway town of Camacupa (called General Machado before independence) to Ringoma. Kanjundo's guerrillas bivouacked in ambush positions, twelve men to a truck, and killed 30 of the MPLA government troops, said the Major: 'In retaliation the government soldiers attacked one of our villages and killed 40 peasants the next day.'

To avenge the slaying of the villagers and drive government troops from his area, Kanjundo attacked Ringoma at dawn on 13 December 1976: 'I also wanted to teach the *soba* (chief) at Ringoma a lesson. He had been a UNITA supporter but changed sides when the government troops came to Ringoma in October during the offensive.'

Kanjundo's 300 men attacked the 90 MPLA soldiers and 120 trainee cadets from the east and south. The first to open fire were the guerrillas on the south side. After two hours, when the guerrillas began to run out of ammunition, the government forces began to advance on them. Then the eastern wave of the guerrillas opened up and the town was overrun. Kanjundo's claimed count was 51 MPLA soldiers and 30 civilians dead; one UNITA soldier dead and two wounded; and 26 civilians taken away to live in a UNITA 'liberated area'.

The *soba* ran with the MPLA troops to the MPLA garrison at Camacupa. 'The people are now very angry with their *soba,'* said Major Kanjundo. 'Before the attack we told them it would be dangerous to stay here with the soldiers. Now they believe us.'

One of Kanjundo's officers pointed to the brand-new brown Soviet combat boots he was wearing and told Dash he had taken them from the body of a dead MPLA soldier: 'We take anything we can use. We are *guerrilleros.'*

* * *

From Ringoma, Dash crossed the Benguela Railway and walked some 100 kilometres to a guerrilla base near Andulo, due north of Bie. There he intended joining the local guerrilla commander, Lt.-Col. Sabino Sandele, to observe an assault on Andulo planned for 27 January 1977. But as the guerrillas streamed out of Sandele's base for the attack, Dash was bed-ridden with a high fever and could not go: 'At 5.10 a.m. 27 Jan., however, I was startled awake by the noise of explosions and small-arms fire. I was also drenched in perspiration. The fever had broken.'

A gleeful Sandele reported that it had taken only 20 minutes to overrun the 500-strong MPLA battalion defending Andulo. He claimed that his men had counted 97 dead – MPLA soldiers, civilians and the only Cuban in town, a journalist caught in crossfire as he ran to his car.

Sandele refused to say how many men he had sent into the attack, but Dash counted 1,110 guerrillas who returned to the base in small groups the following day. They said two of their men had been killed and were buried outside the town. Three wounded guerrillas were carried back to the base in blanket litters.

Of the three prisoners taken only two, a civilian woman and a soldier, were brought back to the base. 'The other soldier tried to escape on the march back here, was recaptured and executed,' said Sandele.

Dash noted, during his epic journey, that it had become UNITA policy to execute all captured MPLA officers. He was told by a UNITA officer: 'We keep some of the soldiers (i.e., privates) for re-education – they have not been indoctrinated into the Marxist line of the goverment. The commanders are hard-line Marxists – there is nothing else to do but kill them.'

Of those MPLA personnel who were taken prisoner, most were intimidated by their captors and were anxious to ingratiate themselves with UNITA, said Dash, who conducted long interviews with ten prisoners at different times and different places.

Nineteen-year-old Celeste Cango Antunes was the first of the two surviving prisoners from the battle at Andul to be led into the guerrilla camp. Blindfolded and apparently composed, the only signs of her terrifying ordeal were a swollen left cheek and drops of dried blood on her green-striped yellow pullover.

A young soldier whipped off the towel wrapped around her eyes. She blinked and looked slowly around at the jeering, bearded faces of the guerrillas. 'Fear gradually replaced her bewildered look, her legs began to quiver, and urine trickled down to her ankles and into her dirty white sneakers. The guerrillas laughed harder.'

When she raised the partly clenched fist of her left hand and said weakly '*Viva* UNITA', the guerrillas shouted, 'THE RIGHT ARM, THE RIGHT ARM'.

She quickly raised her right arm, dropped her left, and made another whispered attempt at the slogan. When the guerrillas shouted, 'No, very bad. Very weak,' she abandoned her feeble effort and began to stroke the scab on her left cheek where a guerrilla's rifle butt had struck her the morning before, knocking her to the ground.

Celeste Antunes had married her childhood sweetheart just a month earlier in their home town, Mussende, to the north-east of Andulo: 'MPLA soldiers came to our town in January and took us and three of my brothers to Andulo. They were forced to join the army. They were given training, but no weapons.'

She and her husband and a girl were put in a small house near the town's church. 'We used to eat badly prepared rice, a small plate for each of us, twice a day. Nothing else.'

On the day of the attack, Celeste and her husband had been in Andulo for two weeks. 'When the attack began my husband ran away and left me. I ran out of the house towards the UNITA men and shouted, "Brothers, don't shoot me" with my hands up.' Then, a guerrilla ran at her and smashed her to the ground.

* * *

Maravilha Mbaka was another MPLA prisoner taken by UNITA. When Dash met her in January 1977 she had been a captive in a guerrilla camp in an isolated area of Bie Province for six months with her two young daughters – Elsa Maria, aged five-and-a-half, and Augusta Luzia, two-and-a-half – and 34 other female prisoners.

The dignified Mbaka, described by Dash as a 'feisty 22-year-old widow', said that for the first few days in the forest she was afraid, but had since adjusted and enjoyed the company of the other women. Then she glared at the commander of the base, Major Eugenio Ngolo, and said: 'My most important problem here is food. Every day I go to the stock and some days there is no food. That is a problem for my children.'

Dash said the 'normally unflappable' Ngolo swallowed hard, turned towards the American reporter and defensively answered the proud woman's implied question: 'There has been a food problem in this area since the offensive. The offensive disrupted the planting.'

Mbaka interrupted Ngolo and pointed to the open sores caused by malnutrition covering her daughters' arms and legs: 'I'm afraid for them, but what can I do? There is no medicine. I pray every day for strength and help from God.'

* * *

Abel Ngere, 23, and Luciano Sangungo, 23, were two MPLA soldiers whom Dash met at their place of imprisonment, a bare concrete storehouse 20 kilometres south of the Benguela Railway town of Nova Sintra. They had been bound hand and foot with coarse hand-made ropes and their faces were swollen and bruised by beatings.

Both had been captured in an ambush near Nova Sintra. Throughout their two-hour interview with Dash they knelt in front of him with an armed guerrilla standing behind them.

A UNITA captain who had escorted Dash to the makeshift jail from a nearby civilian rally, leaned forward, looked both men in the eye and said in a low voice: 'I will keep you to see if you can be re-educated.' Then, enunciating each word slowly and purposefully, he added: 'If I do not think I can trust you or I feel you are too stupid to learn, then I will personally shoot each of you in the head.' Ngere and Sangungo anxiously applauded his words with loud claps and thanked him for the opportunity to be 're-educated'. Dash noted drily: 'They assured him they would be eager students.'

Dash was obviously nauseated by what he had witnessed, and as he walked the five kilometres back to the rally through drizzling rain with the captain, the guerrilla protested at the American's profanely-expressed disbelief in 're-education'. 'No, no, it works,' he said. 'I'll let them sit in jail for a month or two. Let them think a little.'

They would be given a lesson in Angolan history – how, why and when the Portuguese came; Angolan resistance to Portuguese rule. 'They've never heard this before,' said the guerrilla. 'The Portuguese never taught it.' Then he would examine with them what they had seen when they were sent from their homes in southern Angola for military training in Luanda – Portuguese civil administrators,[5] Cuban soldiers and Soviet advisers, all supporting the MPLA government.

'So what if it is one-sided? I'm on *one* side,' he said to the quizzical Dash. 'When I'm finished they'll have received information they never heard of before, never thought of and I'll have two new warriors.'

*   *   *

Dash was finally able to watch UNITA go into battle on 9 February 1977. More than 100 kilometres north of the Benguela Railway, in Huambo Province, the attack on the small town of Mungo began in the half light of a grey and cloudy dawn.

There were 100 MPLA troops in the town. UNITA attacked with a force of 250. First, at 5.40 a.m., 25 guerrillas opened fire from the north with automatic rifles and mortars, immediately killing two sentries who had been smoking cigarettes as they patrolled the town's northern edge.

The defenders were awoken. They poured out of their houses and directed their fire towards the flashes of the guerrilla positions. Then 125 guerrillas began firing from the south at the backs of the MPLA soldiers. As half of the defenders turned to meet the unexpected attack from the south the original 25 attackers broke off their firing to join another 100 guerrillas lying silently in the grass on the town's eastern side. Rising in unison, they filtered noiselessy into the town to close a trap. As they began to link up in an *L* with their comrades moving in from the south, they too opened fire and the government troops were caught in a vicious crossfire.

Watching from a low mountainside about one kilometre from the town, Dash calculated that it had taken the guerrillas four minutes to ensnare the MPLA. With the trap closed, Dash descended the mountain with two majors and 50 more guerrillas to get a closer look at the fighting. He noted the guerrilla weaponry – American mortars, Belgian automatics, American M-79 grenade launchers and World War II vintage M-1 carbines delivered by the CIA in 1975–76. The guerrillas also had Kalashnikovs.

After crossing a small log bridge across a river to the south of the town, Dash heard the deep cough of the guerrillas' American Browning machine-gun – captured from the FNLA during one of the clashes that had marked the end of their so-called coalition. 'Suddenly, in the dim light, we saw a group of peasants running from the southern end of the town – civilians who had been accused by the government of supporting UNITA and jailed to await execution. The guerrillas had released them.'

With Dash was Major David Wenda Catata, who pointed to the fleeing peasants and said: 'I don't know if all of them were our supporters, but they are now.' Catata, Dash and their guerrilla group reached the edge of the forest and were preparing to cross open ground, towards the town's white-washed and orange clay tile-roofed buildings, when two guerrillas appeared carrying a wounded comrade and shouted, 'Go back, go back'. Minutes beforehand, government reinforcements had entered the town from the north-east and the guerrillas were withdrawing.

In a fit of over-confidence the UNITA commanders had ignored one of their movement's own fundamental battle rules – they had failed to lay ambushes on the roads into town, and the government reinforcements were able to enter Mungo unchallenged.

The guerrillas claimed to have achieved their major aims of inflicting heavy casualties to weaken MPLA morale; of destroying the town to prevent its future use by government forces; freeing UNITA supporters from jails; and capturing peasants for transportation to their own bases. Major Catata was content with the balance of casualties: three UNITA wounded against a claimed kill of 50 of the enemy, including seven wives of the MPLA men who died when a mortar shell hit the house in which they were hiding.

But the oversight on the ambushes had cost the guerrillas their secondary goal: the capture of arms and ammunition. It had also left the UNITA attackers terribly exposed. Dash said that only the MPLA soldiers' display of poor morale had saved UNITA from being trapped. He was told by a guerrilla commander to retreat at a walk, not a run; the government soldiers would not leave the town: 'His confidence proved justified. After a 15-minute walk we were back in the flood-plain, bathed in early morning sunlight and in full view of the town. Recrossing the river, we continued at a slow gait for half an hour. The troops did not pursue us.'

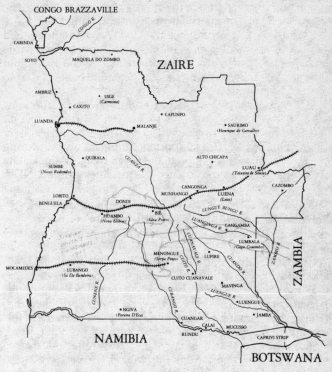

ANGOLA
Route taken by Leon Dash 1977

CONGO BRAZZAVILLE

CONGO R.

CABINDA

SOYO

MAQUELA DO ZOMBO

ZAIRE

AMBRIZ

UIGE
(Carmona)

CAXITO

CAFUNFO

LUANDA

MALANJE

SAURIMO
(Henrique de Carvalho)

QUIBALA

ALTO CHICAPA

SUMBE
(Novo Redondo)

CUANZA R.

LUAU
(Teixeira de Sousa)

CAZOMBO

CANGONGA

LOBITO

MUNHANGO

LUENA
(Luso)

BENGUELA

DONDI

LUNGUE BUNGU R.

HUAMBO
(Nova Lisboa)

BIÉ
(Silva Porto)

LUANGINGA R.

CANGAMBA

Sierra del
Congresso
1977

LUMBALA
(Gago Coutinho)

ZAMBIA

ZAMBEZI R.

MENONGUE
(Serpa Pinto)

LUPIRE

CUANDO R.

MOCAMEDES

LUBANGO
(Sá Da Bandeira)

CUITO CUANAVALE

MAVINGA

CUNENE R.

CUITO R.

CUBANGO R.

LUENGUE R.

LUENGUE

JAMBA

NGIVA
(Pereira D'Eça)

CUANGAR

CALAI

MUCUSSO

NAMIBIA

RUNDU

CAPRIVI STRIP

BOTSWANA

24

Chief Ephrai

1977

'If you don't know the fables, you can't reach the peasants.'
Gina Chinosole, a UNITA political commissar

*　　*　　*

The time had come for Dash to return southwards across the
Benguela Railway to attend the Fourth Congress, but first he
spent some time with a traditional *soba* who was a supporter
of UNITA.

Chief Carvalho Ephrai's village was near Bailundo, 60
kilometres north of Huambo. Dash arrived with guerrilla
major Arao Chingufo to be greeted by several thousand
peasants who danced behind them as they approached the
village gaily singing songs and clapping their hands rhyth-
mically. The village men, some puffing on long iron-
stemmed pipes which glittered like tiny reflectors in the
sunlight, stood apart from the women to perform their
traditional duty of greeting visitors.

Chingufo and Ephrai hugged each other in warm greeting
and the singing and dancing temporarily stopped as Dash
was introduced to the chief. Then the singing resumed, and
there was drumming as the women brushed Dash's
and Chingufo's shoulders with leafy branches in another
traditional greeting.

Watching the chief and the UNITA officer walking
through the throng, Dash was impressed by the contrast of
the customary *soba* and the twentieth-century guerrilla who
had somehow blended: 'The chief, 50, his full head of white
hair highlighting his regal bearing, would stiffly acknowledge the crowd's cheers and shouted comments with a

slight bow of the head. An illiterate peasant, his head was
filled with the oral lore of the Ovimbundu covering history,
legends, spirits, witchcraft, property rights and criminal
law. He was the final mediator in any dispute.

'The guerrilla, 28, exuberant and informal, would plunge
into the excited crowd to shake hands with a friend long
missed, banter with a pretty girl and continually adjust the
captured 10-pound Kalashnikov rifle dangling from his left
shoulder. A high school graduate in a land where more than
90 per cent of the population is illiterate, his head was filled
with thoughts of nationalism, anti-communism, war and
the political necessity of keeping the peasants' support. He
was the contemporary warrior.'

There followed a four-hour rally at which guerrilla officers
and civilian leaders made speeches covering the 500-year
history of Portuguese rule, its shameful end, the civil war in
1975–76, and the new conflict against the Cubans and the
MPLA.

At the end of the rally, *Soba* Ephrai told Dash: 'We talk a lot
because that is our way. It is the way we pass on information
from father to son to grandson. It has always been this way
with the Ovimbundu.'

The overwhelming majority of African societies had no
written languages until they were colonised by Europeans.
UNITA understood the importance of oral tradition, Dash
observed. They used it and followed tribal customs while
proselytising among Angola's many ethnic groups, of
which the two million-strong Ovimbundu was the largest.

Savimbi had told Dash that when he was trying to convert
a new tribe to his cause he would send in their fellow tribesmen who were already with UNITA. 'These men already
know their customs, how they look at the world outside
their tribe, how to approach the chiefs and elders. When you
don't follow this procedure you make costly mistakes,'
said Savimbi, reinforcing his point with an example. In the
1950s the Portuguese colonial administration ordered the imperious Cuanhama people of Cunene to cut their cattle's
weighty horns to improve meat production. 'What the Portuguese did not understand,' said Savimbi, 'is that the Cuanhama measure each cow's worth by the length of its horns.

'The Cuanhama thought the Portuguese wanted to steal the cattle's worth by cutting the horns. They rebelled. Many people were killed on both sides and the Portuguese didn't find out until afterwards why they had rebelled.

'We don't make those kind of mistakes.'

After winning a tribe over, then the process began of trying to persuade them to perceive events in national terms. 'It requires a lot of patience and hours, days, weeks, months of endless discussions and meetings. You are trying to get a man to switch from thinking of himself as a Cuanhama to thinking of himself first as an Angolan. It's very complicated.'

*   *   *

In Chief Ephrai's village UNITA political commissar Gina Chinosole, aged 20, was worrying about the divided support in the villages for UNITA and the MPLA. At a nearby village one informer had recently caused the death of many people by telling government soldiers that UNITA had held a rally there. She told Chief Ephrai's villagers: 'And at this village (Chief Ephrai's), I know there are informers and their work results in soldiers coming here and killing the people, whether they are informers or not.'

Then she told the crowd a parable about a rabbit who wanted to marry a bear's daughter. The bear told the rabbit that the only creature his daughter would be allowed to marry was one who could build a house in one day. The rabbit then called all of his look-alike relatives – careful to let the bear see only one at a time – who rapidly helped the suitor build the house. The bear gave his daughter to the rabbit.

At the end of the story the villagers applauded. 'When we work together,' Chinosole told them, 'things that seem impossible can be possible. We must remember this and apply it concretely.'

Fables, she later told Dash, are the surest tools for winning the attention of the peasants. 'From childhood onwards,' she said, 'everything is taught traditionally in stories. Each animal has a characteristic. The rabbit is always wise and the bear slow-witted. If you don't know the fables, you can't reach the peasants.'

25

UNITA's Fourth Congress

1977

On 24 March 1977 Fidel Castro, President of Cuba, arrived in Luanda and laid wreaths on the graves of Cuban and MPLA soldiers who had died in Angola's fighting during the previous two years. Casto was greeted on his state visit to the People's Republic by Agostinho Neto.

Some 700 kilometres to the south, at a forest site within 80 kilometres of Angola's second city, Huambo, Samuel Chiwale was telling delegates to UNITA's Fourth Congress: 'Neto must die . . . Today, everyone in the bush, soldiers and civilians, are fighting Neto's friends, the Cubans, so everything will be better for black Angolans.'

On 27 March, Dash and his interpreter, Major Mateus Katalayo, listened to a live speech on Radio Luanda by Castro, who criticised the FNLA and UNITA for having used 'white mercenaries' during the civil war.

'Who is he to talk about white mercenaries?' spat Katalayo angrily. 'He's a white mercenary. He should take his soldiers out of here.'

*   *   *

On the opening day of the Congress Savimbi made his keynote speech. His theme was that Angola, having rid itself of the Portuguese, was saddled with new Soviet colonial masters: 'We must not be colonised again. The Portuguese, who knew all the ways of the people, went out, and do you think Neto, who is also Portuguese, can win this war? The Russians are using Neto and the Cubans to rule Angola. They must be defeated.

'The country is living a moment of decision, and that is why you are here. To make decisions that will free our country from Soviet imperialism.'

At this point, reported Dash, the delegates rose to their feet and cheered wildly for five minutes. He noted how Savimbi, dressed in immaculately pressed camouflage uniform, highly polished red-tan boots, green silk cravat, and red beret at a jaunty angle, waited in a stately and imperious manner for the cheering to end: 'Seemingly, it did not matter what he said just as long as Savimbi spoke – telling them what to do, how to do it and how long it would take. They would follow.'

Savimbi urged a philosophy of self-sufficiency, which could hardly fail to have been reinforced by the stark realities of UNITA's total isolation: 'Some people are saying, "Why don't the South Africans come and fight for us so we will pay them later?" That is wrong. If they fight for you, you will be colonised again. You must fight for yourself.'

His speech was interrupted for prayers led by a Protestant minister and a Catholic priest, both Angolans, who sanctioned the war against the MPLA 'in the name of God'. Then there was hymn singing before Savimbi resumed his opening address, and castigated the delegates, about two-thirds of whom were civilians, for timidity in criticising the guerrillas. Such diffidence, he said, ultimately weakened the guerrillas' efforts: 'You people, when you see something wrong among the soldiers, you are afraid to go to the guerrilla commander and tell him because you think he will kill you and throw you in a river. He will not kill you. You must not be afraid to talk to the commanders when they are wrong.'

The Congress was attended by 1,600 peasant delegates and their families and guerrillas who had travelled on foot from all over central and southern Angola. Many had travelled hundreds of kilometres, crossing rivers which had been swollen by the March rains. Some were sick and exhausted on arrival and spent the whole Congress recuperating. Several thousand more people had heard the Congress was being held and had turned up uninvited. They were turned back, despite their weeks of travel, because the site was already overcrowded and was creating sanitation problems.

The footpaths were churned into a muddy morass on the first day, and by the end of the third day the outskirts of the camp were an obstacle course of faeces, which swept a stench over the site as the sun rose. 'Many of our soldiers and most of our peasants don't know anything about hygiene,' Katalayo complained to Dash. 'That's just one of the areas we have to work on.'

* * *

The Congress broke up into four study committees: Strategy and Tactics; the Masses; Administration; and Conflicts. Dash was allowed to listen to the deliberations of three of them. The exception was Strategy and Tactics.

Savimbi, who chaired the forbidden committee, responded with a smile but negatively to Dash's appeal to lift the ban: 'We are discussing the lifeblood of UNITA, our future tactics as a guerilla movement. The officers would be intimidated if you attended, and they don't want you to attend.'

So Dash headed for the largest committee, the Masses meeting, with about 200 delegates. When Dash and Katalayo entered, the chairman, Chiwale, asked Katalayo what Dash was doing there. 'This *espiao*[1] has been given permission,' Katalayo said in Portuguese with a straight face. Chiwale laughed hard and waved them to one of the log benches.

Proceedings were painstakingly translated between four languages – Portuguese, Chokwe, Ovimbundu and Cuanhama. A civilian delegate criticised political commissars – or political organisers – who preferred to work in their own tribal areas. However, he also said that in some areas UNITA civilian assemblies, usually comprising four villages, did not want political commissars from other tribes.

Chiwale angrily responded: 'This will not be tolerated. That is tribalism and we don't want it. The main problem between the political commissar and the masses is that when he arrives at a village he acts as if he is the god, the king.' This was greeted with loud applause. 'The people resent this and it gets translated into tribalism if he is from a different tribe. There is fault on both sides.' The applause died.

Dash and Katalayo moved on to the Conflicts Committee, which proved the liveliest of the three the American was allowed to attend.

A civilian assembly president rose and complained that too many guerrillas in his area were drunk all the time: 'They're using the corn and sweet potatoes we give them to make moonshine when other military bases could use the food. This is a waste and it is also dangerous.'

A guerrilla private said he had been trying to get married for more than a year: 'We want freedom of marriage, but what type of freedom is it when one officer is marrying four or five women at a time and everyone keeps quiet?'

'And some officers,' another soldier added, 'are sabotaging the efforts of the soldiers. When they see a soldier has a pretty girl, they have him transferred so that they can steal the girl.'

An elderly peasant man shouted: 'And the girls want to marry only officers.' But a female guerrilla leapt to her feet and said: 'Wait a minute. Not all the fault is on the side of the girls. Sometimes a commander will talk to you and when you reject him because you don't like him, then he will accuse you of tribalism or indiscipline and have you beaten as well as persecute you.'

A woman peasant delegate said: 'There is also a problem of classes. The girls want only boys who are educated. The guerrillas make the uneducated girls pregnant and leave them. This is not true love.'

The committee chairman, Lt.-Col. Antunes Cahale, had been wincing through all these proceedings as he watched Dash making notes. Several times he asked Katalayo if he was sure that Savimbi had given permission for the American to attend. Now Cahale turned to Katalayo and said: 'Hasn't he heard enough?' as more guerrillas and peasants rose to make their points on relations between the sexes. Katalayo told the chairman that Dash had not, and the discussion went on.

Four secretaries on Cahale's left noted all the points to be presented at the closing plenary debate of the Congress.

When Dash finally left, Katalayo told him: 'Cahale is not used to allowing journalists see our dirty linen. He's from the old school. What happens at the committee meetings isn't so secret. It's just human.'

As the Administration Committee Secretary-General N'Zau Puna was leading a much calmer discussion on the establishment of bush schools for children and adults. 'We may be in the bush for a long time and we will need these schools,' Puna told the hundred or so committee members, a quarter of them Christian clergymen.

A census would have to be taken, he said, 'so during a government offensive we will know how many people have been either captured our killed or run away. It is also a measure of our success to know the numbers of new persons leaving the towns and coming into the forest or UNITA-controlled villages.'

Puna also urged UNITA guerrillas and supporters to collect the new Angolan currency, called the kwanza, which the MPLA had begun issuing in January 1977, and to send it to UNITA's central bases.

After the Congress Puna showed Dash a large pile of kwanzas that had been collected in little more than three months. 'This amounts to five million kwanzas,' he said. 'We collect it, create a paper shortage of money, force the government to print more and then put what we have collected back into circulation. Inflation will follow.'

* * *

On the final day of the Congress the delegates, meeting in plenary session, passed a long list of resolutions. They included:

> guerrillas and civilians exhibiting tribalist attitudes were to be transferred from their home regions to other tribal regions;
>
> soldiers and civilians caught drunk would be jailed and/or beaten severely;
>
> boards of inquiry, made up of soldiers and peasants,

would be established to resolve social conflicts in military camps and villages.

A resolution proposing a new coalition with the FNLA was defeated overwhelmingly by acclamation.

The major recommendation to emerge from Savimbi's Strategy and Tactics Committee was the formation of a semi-regular army. 'From this day 70 per cent of our time will be spent on the structure of the army,' Savimbi said in his final address. 'We must have a conventional army to fight the Cubans. It must be politicised, disciplined and well-structured to be able to defeat the Cuban enemy.'

Later, Savimbi told Dash privately: 'I am pleased with our guerrilla operations so far, but the price has been too high. Too many men and officers have been killed when we attack the towns. Many of our guerrillas are just thrown together momentarily to attack a town and it is too unco-ordinated, too undisciplined.

'A guerrilla army itself cannot defeat a regular army. The government is a puppet government of the Soviet Union and the Cubans, but it is an Angolan government. They will not give up like the Portuguese.

'The Cubans will not leave here because of pressure from America or anyone else. They will leave here because Neto lied to them and told them he was the most popular. The Cubans are dying, so they know it is not true. And if Castro leaves them here too long, they will become counter-revolutionaries when they return home. The Russians mean business in Angola, and so do we. The Cubans are only the Russians' lackeys.

'The Russians think they will expand throughout the South African subcontinent, but no one in the West will sacrifice South Africa. Not France, nor Britain, not the American Republicans, not the American Democrats.

'None of them will sacrifice South Africa. Geopolitics will force them to come back to me.'

*   *   *

During the Congress, UNITA troops attacked the small town of Mbunjie to the south of the conference site. Three soldiers captured there were paraded on the final day of the Congress. But it had adverse consequences. There were attacks on UNITA villages after the Congress broke up and civilians were killed by MPLA troops.[2]

Despite this setback, Savimbi looks back on the Congress as an important landmark in UNITA's recovery: 'From there the people and soldiers started again to have faith in UNITA. And the leaders felt that the people were moralised again for the struggle.

'During this time we were completely alone in terms of help from outside. Nobody was prepared to help us, not even the South Africans who were supporting some small FNLA groups to the south of Menongue which were hostile to UNITA.'[3]

*   *   *

But in that same month, an outside event occurred which would change UNITA's fortunes. The Kantangese gendarmes, who had served the Portuguese and then the MPLA and Cubans against UNITA in eastern Angola, invaded their southern Zaire home province of Shaba, and Zairean troops fled before them. It was the first stark reminder of Kaunda's warning: 'The consequences of events in Angola have scarcely begun to be understood in Africa.'[4]

26

Contact Re-established with Outside World

1977

The invasion of Zaire's Shaba province from Angola began on 8 March 1977. Several thousand Kantangese gendarmes and other Kantangese exiles crossed the border and pressed hard towards Kolwezi, a major copper mining town some 350 kilometres inside Zaire.

President Mobutu's numerically superior army fled, but Moroccan paratroopers, led by French military instructors, airlifted by French Air Force transport planes, and supplied with American weaponry, turned the tide after twelve weeks of fighting. Mobutu accused the MPLA of having instigated the attack, and President Neto angrily responded by accusing Mobutu of continuing to harbour FNLA and FLEC (Front for the Liberation of the Cabinda Enclave) guerrillas and preparing them for renewed assaults against Angola.[1]

Savimbi identified the Shaba invasion as another important turning point in UNITA's fortunes: 'From February 1976 up to March 1977 the African heads of state were not only unwilling to see us, they discounted us totally. But immediately Shaba was invaded by the Katangese, organised and armed by the Cubans, African states and Mobutu started to realise that the Cubans were not only a threat to us (UNITA) but were a threat to the whole area.

'This is when I got a call from African states that they wanted to see me. They had not wanted to know anything at all about the resistance of UNITA, but after the Shaba invasion they were interested. The problem was how to get to Zaire.'[2]

Savimbi sent an envoy to Namibia to ask the South Africans for safe passage for himself through Namibia to black Africa. This was a hazardous venture at the time because the South Africans had thrown their support behind surviving elements of Daniel Chipenda's wing of the FNLA. Groups of Chipenda fighters were being trained in camps in remote parts of southern Angola: they had clashed several times with UNITA guerrillas and there had been deaths on both sides. 'We faced the Cubans and the MPLA and at our backs we had the FNLA,' said Savimbi.[3]

From among Chipenda's FNLA the South Africans had tried to create what they christened the 'Anti-Communist Party of Southern Angola', under the leadership of a Chipenda follower, Vita Kambuta. Kambuta had been with Chipenda in the MPLA, and then followed him into the FNLA. In 1979 the South Africans flew Kambuta to Kinshasa in an attempt to revive Holden Roberto's wing of the FNLA. But Kambuta quickly gave up what he judged to be a futile struggle and deserted to the MPLA in Luanda.

The South Africans agreed to Savimbi's request, and in September 1977 he flew from the South African Defence Force's base at Rundu, in Namibia, to Kinshasa. For two months he used the Zairean capital as a base as he made clandestine trips across Africa seeing many of the heads of state who had voted against the MPLA in the 22-22 OAU summit vote on Angola in January 1976.

'Mobutu's first question to me concerned what was happening with the Kantangese in Angola. Then we gave him all the information we had collected, and told him it was bad that we had had no contact because we could have told him about all the preparations to invade Zaire. We said: "We could have alerted you. Even now we can be of use to you because we can give you intelligence about the movements of the Katangese and, if need be, we can ambush them and cut them off from their bases in Angola."

'I told him that we understood that the presence of the Cubans in Angola was not only a threat to our independence but to him also. So he understood and said he was prepared to help, but he could not give us arms or money. He could only put us in contact with others who might help.'[4]

From Kinshasa, one of Savimbi's first trips was to Dakar to see President Leopold Senghor of Senegal, who had given UNITA open support in 1975–76. He now told Savimbi that UNITA representatives would be given Senegalese passports and identities so that they could travel freely around the world. He also contacted King Hassan of Morocco and asked him to meet Savimbi.

Savimbi travelled on to Morocco in October 1977: 'I think the meeting between King Hassan and me changed completely the situation of UNITA because King Hassan has conducted our diplomatic struggle. From there UNITA was no longer isolated. The King made his friends our friends.'[5]

The precise details of the deal offered to Savimbi by Hassan may never be known. Nor perhaps the exact nature of the international coalition which encouraged, cajoled and supported the Moroccan king in his support for UNITA. However, a number of facts emerged from my conversations with Savimbi.

First, UNITA obtained a secure external headquarters in Rabat, the Moroccan capital, from which to conduct its diplomatic activities. UNITA was established in a big colonial-era house in a Rabat suburb with Moroccan security men guarding the entrances. Visitors to see UNITA officials passed quickly through VIP channels at Rabat and Casablanca airports.

Second, Morocco offered Savimbi military training facilities at Benguerir, near Marrakesh, for up to 500 men at a time. A wide range of military instruction was proposed, from basic infantry techniques, through radio and explosive skills, to parachute warfare. Savimbi accepted the offer and for several years his men passed through Morocco.

Third, Morocco gave arms and other equipment. For example, ten thousand uniforms were sent to Angola from Morocco in 1978 for UNITA's newly developing semi-regular army.

Fourth, Morocco was an ideal point of contact for Western and Middle Eastern governments who either wanted to help UNITA or gather intelligence about the situation in Angola.[6]

Between 1977 and 1979 Savimbi admits to having received some ten million dollars in cash contributions for UNITA from unnamed countries.[7]

*   *   *

The Morocco connection with Angola is a complex one, but the roots of it lie in King Hassan's own war with the Polisario Front. The Front, a guerrilla liberation movement, had been fighting Morocco since early 1976 over the former Spanish territory of Western Sahara. King Hassan had annexed Western Sahara into Morocco after Spain's withdrawal, despite a UN mission's conclusion that the majority of Sahrawis wanted complete independence and that they supported the Polisario Front, and despite an advisory opinion by the International Court at the Hague recommending self-determination for Western Sahara. Polisario fought fiercely, with the backing of Algeria which provided the Sahrawis with a secure base and sanctuary at Tindouf in Western Algeria.[8]

Algeria was, in turn, one of the leading African OAU supporters of the MPLA in Angola and had good relations with the Soviet Union, who provided perhaps 600 military advisers to the Algerian army between 1970 and 1975 and some 90 million-dollars-worth of weapons. The Soviet Union had also given more economic aid in the same period to Algeria than to any African country other than Egypt.[9] Polisario's weaponry was Soviet. King Hassan thus saw the Soviets, through the Polisario and Algeria, as a major threat to his interests. The Soviets and their close allies, the Cubans, were therefore to be opposed at all possible points of their intervention in Africa. Thus Morocco had despatched troops to help fight back the Katangese invasion of Zaire, and now it was beginning to train UNITA officers.

UNITA officers I have spoken to over the years have told how they were trained by French as well as Moroccan officers near Marrakesh. The French have been one of Morocco's two major arms suppliers, and Jaguar ground attack fighters of the French Air Force joined in attacks on Polisario positions in Western Sahara.[10]

The other important source of weapons for Morocco has

been the United States. The flow in and out of Morocco in the late 70s and through the 80s of American armed forces officers and Defence Department officials, as recorded by international news agencies, has been of a remarkably high volume. By helping America's ally, Zaire, beat back the Katangans and by supporting an anti-MPLA movement in Angola, several writers noted that Morocco had done all that could be desired of it if it wanted to receive a stream of sophisticated weaponry to beat back Polisario.[11] Those weapons – F-5 fighter-planes, Bronco counter-insurgency planes, M-60 tanks, Maverick ground-to-air missiles, radar and electronic detection equipment, Bell helicopters, cluster bombs – began to arrive, and in 1982 a joint US-Moroccan military commission was set up in Rabat by the US Secretary of State, General Alexander Haig, to help the Royal Moroccan Army defeat Polisario. By 1984, Morocco – supplied also by France with Mirage-1 jets, Puma and Gazelle helicopters and armoured vehicles – had pushed 100,000 troops into areas of Western Sahara that had been roamed freely by the guerrillas for almost a decade.

In 1984 also, a magazine published a report which said: 'There are American "experts" who train UNITA rebels at Benguerir base, near Marrakesh.'[12]

The object of dwelling at length, at this point, on Morocco's close connections with UNITA, Zaire, the United States and France, and on its bitter war against Polisario, is to emphasise the *probable* inter-relations. Great novelists, a Graham Greene or perhaps an Umberto Eco, would have the artistic freedom to bring this byzantine plot to a conclusion. Laymen coping with the few known truths, without being flies on walls at meetings and in the absence of confidential documents, nevertheless *have* to make intelligent guesses about what is being done secretly in their names by people of power.

*   *   *

Having obtained a commitment of help from King Hassan, Savimbi now needed a channel for arms and materials from Morocco to UNITA and a route out of Angola to Marrakesh for officers chosen for the Moroccan-based training courses.

The South Africans agreed to let Namibia be used for transit traffic between UNITA and its outside 'friends'.[13] At the same time, the South Africans appointed a young military intelligence officer from Natal, Lt.-Col. Philip du Preez, to the role of full-time liaison officer with UNITA.

Savimbi denies that he was offered any help other than transit facilities by the South Africans at this stage. *The Daily Telegraph*, however, was reporting by July 1977 that UNITA had three bases in northern Namibia from where guerrillas were able to move freely back and forth across the border.[14] And Professor John Marcum alleged that South Africa was helping to train UNITA troops at the giant Grootfontein base in Namibia.[15]

From July 1977 a new pattern of skirmishes between the MPLA and UNITA along the border became apparent. On 27 July UNITA forces attacked the small border town of Cuangar, on the Cubango River. Accounts of its capture are sketchy and entirely one-sided. UNITA claims to have crippled an MPLA Soviet-made Antonov-26 transport plane as it taxied for take-off; to have captured four Soviet B-10 75mm recoilless cannons and more than 200 Kalashnikov AK-47 rifles; and to have destroyed the town's infrastructure.[16] The MPLA returned in force with Cuban troops on 9 October 1977 and recaptured the town.[17]

But shortly after UNITA had lost Cuangar again, its forces captured a small border trading post, Mucusso, across the Cubango from Namibia's Caprivi Strip, to which the MPLA was never to return and which became UNITA's main point of contact with the South African military authorities.[18] The MPLA never admitted publicly that UNITA had taken Mucusso, and later local MPLA forces told Luanda falsely that Mucusso had been retaken.[19] This was a pattern which would be repeated by the MPLA in the future as UNITA took more towns and garrisons: UNITA intelligence officers noted it as indicative of poor MPLA morale and discipline.

Not only did Savimbi begin sending soldiers for training in Morocco (and probably Namibia) in 1977 as part of his long-term military strategy, but he also sent an elegant young UNITA girl, Anna Kulipossa, and other young

women to Paris on two-year secretarial and language training courses. The UNITA he was building would need many
more secretaries and translators than the handful who had
trained in Senegal and the Ivory Coast in 1975–76. He also
sent a number of science graduates of the Portuguese *liceu*
system in Angola to medical schools in France, Switzerland
and Portugal and to agricultural universities in the United
States. This represented thinking in even longer terms, for
they only began to return to UNITA territory as doctors and
agricultural scientists from late 1984 onwards.

Meanwhile, there was an influx in mid-1977 of highly
qualified nurses from MPLA-held areas of central Angola
into UNITA's camps. They helped make up for the
guerrillas' total lack of doctors.

The influx was largely inspired by a crackdown that the
MPLA began against foreign missionaries. After a period of
absence during the height of the fighting in 1975–76, the
Canadian missionary Dr George Burgess (see Prologue) had
returned to the Dondi Institute in central Angola in November 1976 to carry on his medical work under MPLA rule. The
Dondi complex was the grandest of all the United Church of
Christ institutions through central Angola and was perhaps
the biggest in Africa. Situated between Huambo and Bie,
near the Benguela Railway, it covered some 32 square
kilometres. There was a primary school, a secondary school,
the offices of the Protestant Church leadership in central
Angola, a domestic science training school, a leper sana-
torium, a printing press, a seminary for training church
pastors, a nursing school, and a 35-bed hospital run by Dr
Burgess.

Dr Burgess must have known he was facing risks, for he
was the last white Protestant missionary operating in central
Angola – and was based at Dondi, where so many of
UNITA's leaders had received part of their education. Just a
short while before he returned, the then two remaining
Protestant missionaries in central Angola, Dr Betty Bridgman and Nurse Edith Radley, were arrested on the night of
19 October 1976 at their hospital at Chissamba, some 120
kilometres from Dondi. They had been subjected to constant
interrogations and searches since the MPLA had come to

power. On one occasion several local people, including hospital staff, had been rounded up and executed near the hospital on the grounds that they still continued to support UNITA.[20] Immediately after Dr Bridgman's and Nurse Radley's detentions, the 30 or so African nurses at Chissamba fled with their families to join up with UNITA groups in the bush. Dr Bridgman and Nurse Radley were detained without trial in prison in Luanda for three months before they were expelled without any of their possessions to Canada, where they were awarded government decorations for courage and service to humanity.

An anti-Church campaign, reflecting the Marxist and anti-religious sentiments of powerful factions within the MPLA, was being waged at this time by Ambrosio Lukoki, the party Secretary for Ideological Affairs. The campaign underestimated the importance of missionary-founded Protestant churches in the development of all strands of Angolan nationalism. Lukoki was sacked in December 1982, but in late 1984 Lucio Lara, the MPLA's chief ideologist, said no Angolan citizen could be both a party member and a church member; a candidate for MPLA membership could be a church-going believer, but when it came to the final decision to become a full MPLA member he/she had either to leave the church or give up the candidacy.[21]

When Dr Burgess was summoned to Luanda in May 1977, ostensibly to renew his visa, he suspected he would not be allowed to return and that the MPLA would molest his staff. He advised his senior nurse, Dachala Morais, to leave and join UNITA in the bush, taking with him other nurses and as much equipment as possible.[22]

The MPLA raided the hospital the night Dr Burgess left. 'Morais was not able to save anything,' Savimbi recalled. 'He just had to run with the others. The MPLA ransacked Dondi of all its equipment. Then they occupied it and turned it into a military training camp.' There was sadness in his voice as he went on: 'They want to make it into a military training centre so that people forget about the values that Dondi represented. The missionaries at Dondi did a good job. The Portuguese didn't like it, and the MPLA didn't like it because it was the heart and mind of the intellectuals in the

centre and south. All the time when we think about Dondi,
it is a rallying point. Many of us were educated there at some
point. Since it is a rallying point, the MPLA want people to
forget about Dondi.'

From the MPLA point of view, it was not surprising
(though not excusable) that there was a crackdown on
centres like Dondi, Chissamba and others which were un-
reconstructed centres of UNITA support. The MPLA could
have no confidence that UNITA guerrillas were not
harboured within them.

Morais and other nurses who fled with him into the bush
had helped in surgical operations at Dondi for many years.
The same applied to Manazes Kawanga, senior nurse at
Chissamba. In the bush with UNITA, they joined colleagues
from other sacked missionary centres in setting up hospitals where they themselves did the operations, mainly
amputations and appendix removals, without supervisions
by doctors. They also began training para-medicals. 'In the
first war (against the Portuguese) we had none of these
highly trained mission nurses with us,' said Savimbi. 'Until
they came to join us in 1977 we had few good nurses. People
just died when they had appendicitis, but they don't die any
more.'[23]

Along with the nurses, the leadership of the Evangelical
Church Council for Central Angola, which had its administrative headquarters at Dondi, also fled and set up bush
churches in UNITA-controlled territory.

Dr Burgess was expelled when he reached Luanda. He
returned to Canada and took up a post with a church
medical centre in Newfoundland. In due course he learned
of the MPLA's occupation of Dondi and that his own house
had been ransacked. Of Savimbi, Burgess felt it was now
safe to write: 'He has a brilliant mind; he is an outstanding
leader; he is a man of great compassion. My African associ-
ates felt they could count on the truthfulness of his word and
that he was a man of integrity . . . I feel sure that his motives
are worthy and noble and that he should be encouraged and
supported to carry on his very difficult job of seeking true
independence and justice in Angola.'[24]

Just as Savimbi has acknowledged the UNITA leadership's debt to the church network of rural schools and hospitals, so perhaps Dr Burgess identified something of the essence of UNITA when he wrote: 'The Church worked as a democratic organisation and this is why the Ovimbundu people have a much better orientation to elections, majority decisions, debate, etc than other groups. This comes out in UNITA's attempts to bring peace by discussion and vote in the days of transition.'[25]

*   *   *

The sacking of Dondi was the beginning of a new trend in the struggle between UNITA and the MPLA. Through 1976 and the first part of 1977 the Cubans and MPLA had tried to conduct a hearts-and-minds campaign to win over the people. 'They did not ill-treat them, they did not imprison them,' said Savimbi. 'They tried to give some sort of religious freedom in order not to antagonise everybody. And in 1976 the MPLA were able to mobilise their sympathisers against us around the slogan "fighting the South Africans". And it did work for a while. But then even the MPLA followers realised the South Africans had left and the foreigners who remained were the Cubans. They saw the Cubans start to bring their families, and even those people who in the beginning were sympathetic to the MPLA began to see this as neo-colonialism.

'During 1977 and 1978, when the MPLA realised those people who had supported UNITA were incurable, that they did not want to change, that they wanted to stay with UNITA, they started repression, they started to massacre people in the villages.

'Instead of intimidating the people, it galvanised them. They saw that the government was not their government.'[26]

Besides the nurses and pastors, teachers and administrators also fled into the bush as other mission centres, such as Elende, Chilesso and Camundongo, were sacked and closed down by the MPLA. By the end of 1977 only the Bailundo mission, north of Huambo, and the Dondi leprosarium were continuing to operate out of about 25 Protestant mission centres active in central Angola up to and just after independence.[27]

In late 1977 the MPLA's Director of Agriculture for Huambo Province, Daniel Catata, the brother of a UNITA commander (see Chapter 23), deserted to UNITA and became the rebels' Director of Agriculture. He brought with him every one of the agricultural experts in his department, and the exodus was joined by telephone, water and electrical engineers from the MPLA administration in central Angola who set to work installing electrical generators, pumped and piped water, and internal telephone communications systems in the UNITA base camps. Railway administrators from the Benguela line came to join the guerillas and were absorbed into the growing UNITA administrative service.[28]

As MPLA policy turned from persuasion to oppression, Daniel Ekundi, the 73-year-old 'father' of black nationalism in central Angola, and his wife were executed in Huambo jail on 27 August 1977 without having been charged or tried. The Ekundis were supporters of UNITA, but were too frail to join the movement in the bush. They seem to have been killed for refusing to renounce their loyalty to UNITA (see Chapter One).

*   *   *

One of the key elements of Savimbi's philosophy was that if UNITA managed to survive, events around them in Angola and on the international scene would eventually change to their advantage. Now there was encouraging news for UNITA from within the ranks of the MPLA.

On 27 May 1977 a radical MPLA faction, apparently orientated towards the country areas rather than Luanda and resentful of the predominance of *mesticos* over blacks in the Neto government, tried to seize power in a coup.

It was led by Nito Alves, who began fighting with the MPLA in 1961 after the movement's first uprising failed. By the time of the 1974 coup in Portugal he was the military and political leader of the MPLA in the difficult and densely forested Dembos region just to the north-east of the capital, cut off and therefore considerably independent from other leaders based in sanctuaries outside the country. During the time of the transitional government he became the leader of

MPLA militants in the Luanda slums where he organised committees called *Poder Popular* (people's power) who fought first against the white Portuguese before turning against the FNLA and driving them from the city.[29]

He was regarded by some as second in power only to Neto, and was appointed Minister of the Interior when the MPLA formed Angola's first government. But Alves' discontent with Neto's alleged orientation towards urban *mestico* intellectuals, such as Lucio Lara, Foreign Minister Paulo Jorge and Defence Minister 'Iko' Carreira, was the focus of division within the government, and in October 1976 Alves was condemned for factionalism and sacked from his Ministry.

Alves retained his place on the policy-making Central Committee, but rumours continued that Alves was plotting against the government with other *Nitistas*, as his supporters were called. Clandestine leaflets appeared attacking, in racist terms, white Portuguese who worked as expatriates for the Angolan government. A commission of inquiry was set up to investigate allegations that Alves and another Central Committee member, Jose van Dunem, political commissar of the Angolan armed forces in southern Angola, and their *Nitista* loyalists within the MPLA had deliberately engineered food shortages in order to stir up discontent.

The Central Committee met on 20 and 21 May 1977 and expelled Alves and van Dunem. Six days later the coup attempts began when *Nitista* troops attacked Luanda's São Paulo prison and other key points with mortars and automatic rifles. Ten senior government and military leaders were killed, including three Central Committee members and Finance Minister Saydi Mingas. The Cubans did not remain neutral. They rallied to President Neto and by midday the radio station, which the *Nitistas* had taken and from which they broadcast appeals for mass demonstrations outside the presidential palace, was retaken and the rebels fled into the slums with a number of hostages.

With government power precariously re-established in Luanda, a dusk-to-dawn curfew was imposed with roadblocks throughout the city. Cubans in tanks and armoured cars guarded public buildings. On 31 May Neto delivered an emotional speech in which he said the rebels had followers in the provinces and in such mass organisations as the MPLA Youth (*Juventude do MPLA*), the Organisation of Angolan Women (OMA), the Army Women's section, and the Military Police.

Although Neto initially indicated that some clemency would be shown to the plotters, a massive purge was soon underway. MPLA commissars and directing committees in eight provinces who had been appointed by Alves were removed. Thousands of people were arrested and thousands of *Nitistas* removed from their jobs.

The coup leaders initially escaped, but van Dunem was captured in June. Alves was captured in July, when Neto publicly announced the formation of a Special Military Tribunal to try those arrested for complicity in the coup attempt. The official investigation into the coup referred to the success of Alves, a champion of closer ties with Moscow and a frequent visitor to the Soviet Embassy, in misleading 'friendly' states. The Soviets failed to provide Neto with advance warnings of Alves's intentions, and the Soviet Ambassador was subsequently obliged to leave quietly.[30]

The Special Military Tribunal's proceedings were conducted in secret and its verdicts and sentences were never officially announced. It is not known how many cases were brought before the Tribunal and how many were dealt with summarily by the security police.

On 1 August 1977 Neto indicated that some of the coup leaders had been shot when he said tersely at a public ceremony: 'Once assassinations were begun, particularly here in Luanda, of comrades who were killed for clear tactical objectives, those individuals were also shot.' In 1978 the Australian Communist writer Wilfred Burchett confirmed that Alves had been executed by a firing squad.[31] Others executed are believed to have included van Dunem, Internal Trade Minister David Aires Machado, Sitta Valles (Jose van Dunem's wife), two senior Commanders of the MPLA army, Jacob Joao Caetano (known popularly as '*Monstro Imortal*' or the 'Immortal Monster') and Ernesto Eduardo Gomes da Silva 'Bakaloff' (one of the judges in the British mercenaries trial), and other senior MPLA leaders.

* * *

The *Nitista* Revolt had reduced the MPLA's Central Committee by a third – three murdered in the coup attempt, five conspirators subsequently executed, and two suspended for failing to disclose fore-knowledge of the plotters' intentions.[32] It led Neto to tighten control over the party. When the MPLA held its Congress from 4 to 11 December 1977, Lucio Lara announced plans to replace it with a new 'vanguard working class party', the *MPLA-Partido de Trabalho* (the MPLA-Workers Party). This, Neto said, would move Angola close to Marxist government. The party would strengthen workers' participation and exert supreme control over state institutions according to classical Leninist doctrine.[33]

27

The Art of Surviving

1978

'If we survive, then things will begin to change around us.'
                                                    Jonas Savimbi[1]

*   *   *

The Year 1978 was a diffficult one for Savimbi, though it began well enough.

By the end of 1977 the FNLA's Chipenda Squadron had been virtually driven out of its remaining Angolan bases between Menongue and the Angolan border by the MPLA/ Cubans. Chipenda's men filtered across the border with their leaders and sought refuge in Namibia. There some of them were intensively retrained to become the nucleus of the South African Defence Force's 32 Battalion (Buffalo Battalion) operating under South African officers on the Namibia-Angola border.

'That was when the South Africans finally came to terms with the fact that the FNLA were not a card to be played because they could not organise anything. So they began to take a more lenient line towards us,' said Savimbi. 'The FNLA had many South African instructors and advisers in Angola with them, but when the big Cuban and MPLA assault against the FNLA positions came (in late 1977) there was no FNLA resistance at all. They were cleared out completely. Not one of them was left, and the MPLA managed to capture a South African officer working with the FNLA.'[2]

According to Savimbi, the first help that South Africa gave was medical, with seriously wounded UNITA soldiers being taken into SADF military hospitals in Namibia for

Dr Jonas Savimbi

A UNITA instructor with a class learning how to handle a
SAM-7 anti-aircraft missile

Savimbi instructing his guerrilla officers in a bush camp in
1971, during the war against the Portuguese

UNITA officers stand in front of an MPLA government light Antonov transport plane destroyed by mortar fire on the runway at Munhango

UNITA soldiers in northern Angola dance and sing before going into battle

A local UNITA primary school in Angola – 1970

A clothing workshop run by UNITA in the bush of southeast Angola

MPLA government soldiers, bound and blindfolded, await
questioning by intelligence officers

Colonel Ben-Ben stands on the wreckage of Cangonga
station, destroyed by UNITA guerrilla forces after the
defeat of the MPLA government garrison on 11 February
1983

Brigadier Geraldo Nunda, commander of UNITA's Northern Front, briefs some of his troops before a battle for the town of Alto Chicapa

UNITA guerrillas crossing the Cuando River

A graveyard of steam engines at Munhango in Angola on the Benguela Railway

UNITA soldiers get themselves into the mood for battle in Angola with a traditional spirit dance

treatment. In due course, UNITA built a transit hospital on an island in the Cubango River, between Mucusso and the Namibian shore. The hospital could not be sited in Mucusso itself, because UNITA had planted the settlement so liberally with landmines and anti-personnel mines before recapturing it from the MPLA that it became a no-man's-land.

'Nevertheless,' argued Savimbi, 'the truth is that the South Africans wanted the FNLA here in southern Angola as a force they could control. And the South Africans have never dropped the idea of rebuilding the FNLA. We know that, even though they try to hide it from us.'[3]

It is difficult to be precise about the nature of the relationship between UNITA and South Africa at the beginning of 1978, but it was sufficiently relaxed for Mike Nicholson, by then ITN's reporter based in Johannesburg, to be permitted by the SADF to cross the Namibian border in early March in search of Savimbi.

Unknown to Nicholson, Neto had since February been meeting senior South African officials, in the presence of representatives of President Carter's Administration, on Sal Island in Cape Verde, off Africa's west coast. They were trying to reach a Namibian independence agreement which would lead to a cessation of SWAPO attacks into Namibia from bases in southern Angola where SWAPO's guerrillas were being trained by Cuban troops and supplied with Soviet weapons.[4]

South Africa's Prime Minister John Vorster announced his acceptance of proposals for Namibia by five Western countries, Britain, Canada, France, West Germany and the US, who formed the so-called Contact Group, on 25 April 1978. The agreement provided for the withdrawal of all but 1,500 South African troops from Namibia within twelve weeks of the arrival, to administer the territory, of a United Nations Transition Assistance Group (UNTAG). Under the agreement, SWAPO's forces would be confined to their bases in Angola. UNTAG would monitor observance of the ceasefire by both the South Africans and SWAPO and organise the election of a Namibian Constituent Assembly to prepare an independence constitution.

Savimbi saw Neto's cooperation with the Contact Group

as part of the MPLA leader's new general policy of seeking cooperation with the West in an attempt to boost the Angolan economy: 'Our information and analysis showed differences starting to deepen between Neto and the Cubans and the Russians in 1978. He was a man of outstanding intelligence and he knew that as well as fighting against guerrillas with soldiers you also had to fight them on economic and social territory. Neto knew that that was the way to get the people out of the bush to support the government. He wanted to get the economy off the ground and be able to tell the people: "Look, there is no need of following UNITA because you have this and you have that." It is my belief that by 1978 he had realised that the Cubans were not capable of doing this for him.'[5] In part, Neto's disenchantment with the Soviet Union probably also went back to the Alves coup attempt.[6]

In mid-1978 the MPLA made overtures to Portugal, France, the United States and the Scandinavian countries which resulted in more trade and technological aid and paved the way for the gradual return of Portuguese technicians on contracts to work in nearly every sector of the economy.[7]

Savimbi said that in 1978 UNITA made propaganda advantage of the economic shortcomings of the Cubans: 'There had been a Portuguese agricultural and small-scale processing settlement near Cela before independence, for example. The MPLA sent Cubans with their families to restart that project again in 1978. They gave up because the hostility of the local population was total because they saw the Cubans as a new kind of Portuguese. And those Cubans did not know how to work the machines of that area. When the project began our commissars told villagers: "Look, the Cubans are here to stay permanently."'[8]

Soon after Nicholson had crossed the border into Angola his truck was ambushed by MPLA forces. He fled on foot with UNITA soldiers deep into the bush. At about the same time, South African military liaison officials contacted UNITA to tell Savimbi of the consequences of the Sal Island understanding with Neto: 'They said that from then onwards we could not send anyone through Namibia or receive materials through it because they were going to give Namibia to the United Nations and they would leave. We said we had friends in the (Arabian) Gulf and Africa who had materials they wanted to get to us, but they said, "no, too late". So we said: "Alright, we have got used to friends who desert us. You South Africans have to look after your own interests; the MPLA has to look after its interests; each of you is fighting his own struggle. But we will carry on too. We will not give up because of difficulties, because of the desertions of friends."'[9]

Following the closure of the border Nicholson was stuck inside Angola, wandering hundreds of kilometres through the bush with guerrillas, trying to avoid capture in an MPLA offensive. It was four months before South Africa agreed, under pressure from Nicholson's employers in London, to send patrols to make contact with UNITA and arrange for the TV reporter and his crew to be collected by a small plane from an isolated bush airstrip in south-eastern Angola.

The March-April MPLA offensive was followed by another in August which forced UNITA to surrender the small border posts of Calai and Dirico in the south-east which Savimbi's soldiers had taken at the same time as they secured Mucusso in late 1977.

Savimbi also became concerned about the number of UNITA soldiers who were being killed in attacks on fixed MPLA targets: 'Captains of 200-men companies in their enthusiasm were attacking MPLA posts and having 20 or more of our men killed without capturing the posts. So I put out an order saying no local commander could attack a post without first consulting me by radio. Then before I said yes or no, I would examine with the Chief of Staff what manpower and firepower any one group had and what mastery of military techniques. Minor actions like ambushes and laying mines they could continue without referring to anybody.'[10]

Despite these difficulties, especially near the border areas with Namibia, UNITA was continuing to harass the MPLA deep inside Angola. Gerald Buthaud, a photographer, returned in September 1978 from a two-month visit to Angola with UNITA and described the ambush he had photographed of an MPLA truck on the road between Menongue and Longa about 300 kilometres north of the Namibian border:

'We got to the ambush site at 4.30 on Friday afternoon and hid along the road. There were 70 UNITA soldiers and five porters. They had automatic rifles, bazookas and grenade launchers.

'We heard a truck grinding along the road at a quarter to six. It was a Mercedes. There was a major from Longa aboard and 19 soldiers to look after him. Plus a driver. And, oddly, a woman and child.

'The firing started at five to six and lasted ten minutes. There were 21 killed – a couple of soldiers ran off into the bush. At the end there was a guy under the truck with a Russian light machine-gun. Everyone thought he was dead, but he opened up and gave us our only casualties – a guy with his jaw blown off, another hit in the leg and one scratched on the shoulder . . . but we got the machine-gunner.

'UNITA were over the moon with the weapons haul. They got a lot of AK-47s and Portuguese G3 rifles, the Russian machine-gun, a bazooka and a pile of ammunition. They stripped all the bodies of shoes and uniforms. Most of UNITA go barefoot; their clothes are in tatters.'

The guerrillas did not stay long to celebrate. 'We were frightened of aircraft and helicopters. There was no defence against attack from the air. The tactic is to walk. And so we did, without stopping, for 34 hours. No sleep, just some dried meat and manioc. Then we got to a hidden camp and just crashed out.'

Buthaud indicated that by this time UNITA had established an air link with the outside world. He arrived at a bush airstrip deep inside Angola in a DC-4 propeller-driven aircraft on what he described as a regular UNITA run, presumably from Kinshasa. He noted that UNITA was running a few small Mercedes Unimog trucks (popular with the SADF) in its territory and reported that he had stayed in ten different big permanent camps, some with more than 2,000 people. He also visited 15 smaller camps, bases for regular patrols, and a half-dozen smaller hunting camps.[11]

A specialist periodical on Africa noted that on 31 October 1978 a major bridge on the Benguela Railway had been blown up by UNITA, further reducing the possibility of traffic reopening to Zaire and Zambia, and that in the same month a Bulgarian, travelling along a road 11 kilometres from Huambo, had been killed by guerrillas.[12] Tanganyika Concessions, the British company which co-owned the railway with the Angolan government, privately confirmed reports that there were, on average, three guerrilla incidents each week along the line in 1978.

In 1978 UNITA also noted a withdrawal of the Cubans from the front-line fighting. 'Up to 1978 most of the fighting was being done by the Cubans and not by the MPLA,' said Savimbi. 'They had trained many MPLA soldiers and they began to concern themselves mostly with logistics, intelligence, protecting the MPLA military convoys, and flying helicopters and MIGs.'[13]

*　　*　　*

The MPLA-South African peace initiative did not go smoothly. SWAPO objected to several features of the Contact Group's plan and delayed making a formal response. On 4 May the South African Air Force and paratroopers carried out a devastating attack on a SWAPO base at Cassinga, 250 kilometres inside Angola, and killed some 600 Namibians. Many of them were guerrillas, but there were also a large number of women and children among the dead. South Africa justified the attack, the first full-scale raid into Angola since South Africa's involvement in the 1975–76 civil war, on the grounds that SWAPO had stepped up its abductions and killings of civilians inside Namibia precisely at a time when delicate negotiations concerning Namibian independence were being held.[14]

The instability of the region was highlighted within a few days of the Cassinga raid when, on 11 May 1978, the Katangese again attacked across the Angolan border into Zaire's Shaba province. This time several thousand Katangese reached the mining centre of Kolwezi. The degeneracy of the Mobutu regime was emphasised when an élite Zairean Army unit protecting the town collapsed, allowing the Katangese force to capture Kolwezi after only a few hours of fighting. Nearly one hundred European mining technicians and members of their families – out of the 2,000 white expatriates stationed in the town – were killed, along with several hundred Africans. The Katangese held on to Kolwezi for a week before they were driven out by 2,500 French and Belgian paratroopers, airlifted from Europe, backed up by Senegalese, Moroccan and Egyptian troops.[15] President Mobutu accused the MPLA, Cubans and Soviets of involvement in the Katangese invasion; and his denunciation was backed by President Carter whose ambassador to the United Nations, Andrew Young, had earlier said on US television that Cuban troops had in a sense brought 'a certain stability and order' to Angola.[16]

Urged on by the Carter Administration, Mobutu received Neto in September 1978 in Kinshasa, where they signed a mutual peace treaty ending support for the opponents of each regime.[17] The FNLA was heavily pushed down, but not totally closed down, by the expulsion of Holden Roberto to France and of his top lieutenants to the United States.[18] Neto, for his part, settled the 250,000 Katangese refugees in Angola further away from the Zairean border: he promised to prevent further Katangese offensives into Shaba, and none have occurred since 1978. However, because of the intensity of UNITA activity, Neto was unable to fulfil a promise to Mobutu to reopen the Benguela Railway, and Mobutu had no real intention of curbing guerrilla activity against Angola in the long run. And though a regular airline service began between Angola and Zaire as a result of the peace accord, it had a grand element of farce: the Angolan Airlines flight from Luanda would often touch down at Kinshasa's Ndjili Airport immediately before or after the UNITA plane came in from rebel-held areas of Angola. Their passengers would disembark within 50 metres of each other on the tarmac apron in front of the international terminal, the Luanda passengers passing through official immigration channels and the UNITA personnel through a side gate under the supervision of Zairean intelligence officers.

'I know that Mobutu made that agreement against his will,' said Savimbi. 'Carter was worried that if Neto continued to back, re-arm and train the Katangese the result would be the loss of Zaire also to the Cubans and to the

Russians. And the Americans were not the only ones. Some of our friends in Africa were saying that Mobutu should be forced to make all the concessions possible to Luanda so that the Katangese were not sent to attack again. Some of them thought too of abandoning us. They reasoned. "Neto is being wise, he is becoming a good man. The best way is to reach an agreement which controls UNITA and the Katangese. Neto needs peace in his country to build up his economy with the help of the West. Mobutu is too fragile to confront the Cubans and Russians, so it's best that we hope to change Neto since he is being open towards the West."

'But other friends warned us that a deal was being considered that would sacrifice UNITA. They told us to beware of it. They didn't agree with it and they would struggle against it.'[19]

*   *   *

The negotiations between South Africa and the MPLA eventually broke down in September 1978 and Pretoria again unsealed the Namibian border to UNITA. N'Zau Puna and the logistics chief, Lt.-Col. Samuel Epalanga, established high level contact once more with the SADF through the Mucusso border post. New Mercedes trucks were delivered to UNITA, and diesel fuel, ammunition and tinned food for the guerrillas began to move again across the border.

Through 1978 Amnesty International reported that the MPLA continued to carry out extra-judicial executions of UNITA supporters and MPLA dissidents. Others arrested for political reasons simply 'disappeared' in custody.

In the final month of the year the MPLA launched a new policy of deterrence – public executions. On 13 December five men suspected of supporting and aiding UNITA – Arthur Albino, Armando Kapitiya, Noe Kessongo, Eliseu Martinho and Alberto Salomao – were paraded before a crowd, which UNITA said had been mustered by force, in Lobito stadium. They were not tried but they had been denounced by someone who said they were UNITA activists and were shot dead before the crowd as an example of what might happen to others.[20]

'By the end of 1978,' said Savimbi, 'the people had come to understand that we faced a long struggle.'[21]

28

Beyond Survival

1979

The year 1979 began badly for Savimbi. On 4 February six UNITA activists were publicly executed without charge or trial in Cacilhas Stadium, Huambo,[1] where Savimbi had delivered his 1975 Independence Day address and rebuked his troops for undisciplined firing of their guns.

But also at some time early in 1979 China began delivering 550 to 600 tonnes of arms to Savimbi for use by his new battalions who would train under UNITA officers returning from courses in Morocco.

The Chinese deal is shrouded in considerable mystery. It is not clear how or when it was concluded, but what seems certain is that the weapons were transferred to UNITA through Namibia with South Africa's co-operation. It is inconceivable that so large a quantity of weapons could have been airlifted by Savimbi's then fragile, irregular and hazardous airlink with Zaire on planes no bigger than Fokker Friendships and DC-4s. A French journalist, Edward Girardet, who has followed UNITA developments closely, wrote quite categorically of the Chinese arms that 'they were channeled into Angola via Namibia'.[2]

Savimbi himself has emphasised the speed with which the arms – rifles, 82mm mortars, 70mm cannons and 12.7mm anti-aircraft guns – were moved into his sanctuaries in southeast Angola: 'The Chinese material was decisive for our struggle. If we had got so many arms during 1975 we could have put up more resistance than we did.

'In 1979 we decided we had to transfer the Chinese arms into Angola as quickly and efficiently as possible so that if there was another MPLA deal with the neighbouring countries, depriving UNITA of access to them, we would be able to continue fighting until one day a situation would be created where they (the neighbouring countries) would need us again'.[3]

On another occasion Savimbi said: 'If I get 100 tonnes of equipment I don't need to go to South Africa, I fly it directly into my areas. But if I get 1,000 tonnes I can't fly them, so I have to ask them (the South Africans) to pass them through South Africa. That's the position.'[4]

The probable instigator of the Chinese arms deal was Dr Zbigniew Brezinski, President Carter's hawkish National Security Adviser. Writing a profile of Brezinski in the *New Yorker* after interviewing scores of officials, Nancy Drew said the National Security Adviser had occasionally suggested that the US should cause trouble for the MPLA by supporting Savimbi.[5]

And when Brezinski visited China in May 1978 – the same month as the Soviet-armed Katangese struck across the border from Angola into Zaire – he asked the Chinese to supply arms and equipment for Savimbi's fight against the MPLA/Cubans, according to memoranda obtained by the Washington press. During a trip to the Great Wall, reporters with Brezinski heard him joking with the Chinese as to whether he or they would be the first to keep the Russians out of parts of Africa.

The memoranda obtained by the press related to conversations held between a senior National Security Council official, Michael Oksenberg, and John Carbaugh, an aide to the conservative Republican Senator Jesse Helms, about Dr Brezinski's policy discussions in Peking. The memoranda said that Dr Brezinski talked with his Chinese hosts about a number of ways of countering Soviet activities in Africa. The National Security Council did not deny that the conversations mentioned in the memoranda had taken place, although it said accounts of the confidential conversations seemed 'somewhat garbled'.[6]

It would have been a logical way for the Carter Administration, concerned by events in Angola and Zaire, to have got around the Clark Amendment of December 1975 which banned all future US military aid to movements in Angola. In the spring of 1978 Dick Clark, author of the amendment and chairman of the US Senate's Africa sub-committee, himself accused the Carter administration of considering sending secret supplies to Savimbi.

If this linkage between Brezinski, China and South Africa and the supply of arms to Savimbi was made, it is especially interesting since the US at that time was committed to a policy, in public at least, which involved the withdrawal of South Africa from Namibia; which said nothing about a reciprocal withdrawal of Cuban troops from Angola; which said nothing about any possible political role for Savimbi in the future of Angola; which was committed to peace between Zaire and Angola; and which was bound by the Congressional arms supply ban.

* * *

No journalists entered Savimbi's territory in 1979. For most of the year UNITA scarcely warranted a mention in the world's newspapers, although here and there, in obscure corners and specialist publications, details of the UNITA resistance did appear. Thus in January an internal memo in the London headquarters of Tanganyika Concessions said that part of Huambo station had been blown up in a UNITA bomb attack. And later Tanganyika Concessions noted that the number of sabotage attacks along the 1,100 kilometre railway increased to an average of one a day in 1979 compared with an average of three incidents a week in 1978.

Nevertheless, in March and April 1979, the first trains since 1975 managed to travel the whole length of the line in Angola from Zaire to Lobito. Six ore-bearing trains completed the trip on a completely uneconomic basis. Under massive military protection they moved at a snail's pace from one heavily guarded point to the next. But another ore train was blown up west of Luena on 2 April, and in early May a train was blown up by remote control about 80 kilometres from Benguela.

Though special army units guarded the bridges, helicopters with rockets patrolled the line, and advanced techniques for speedily replacing damaged or lifted rail were introduced, the line was effectively paralysed. By March 1979 the railway's 24 diesel locomotives had been reduced to two by guerrilla activity. From May 1979 to February 1980 only 133 loaded wagons completed the journey from Zaire to Lobito: under normal conditions, 40 wagons made up a full cargo train.[7] In desperation the Benguela Railway's MPLA-appointed general manager proposed dispersing the Ovimbundu, who were seen as a massive pool of UNITA intelligence, from areas along the line and bringing in other tribal groups to work on it. The Cubans dismissed the proposal as completely impractical.

In August 1979 UNITA blew up the 60-metre-long Luavava Bridge on the railway near Cuemba. Savimbi used one of his new semi-regular battalions of 500 men to do the job. He described the planning which went into the attack: 'We wanted to blow up that bridge so that we could forget about the railway for a while and concentrate on other matters. But that bridge was guarded heavily by the Cubans and MPLA. We collected intelligence for a long time, and we knew that relations between the Cubans and the MPLA at the bridge was bad. The MPLA were guarding the eastern end of it and a Cuban company the west.

'Then the Cubans got orders from Luanda to move to new duties in Lobito. And here I'm stressing that there was not one unified command system – the Cubans got their orders from Cubans and the Angolans got their orders from Angolans, even when they were guarding the same bridge. It happened at that bridge that only the Cubans had bazookas and recoilless cannons; the MPLA had no support weapons, only individual weapons.

'When the Cuban company got orders to move, the MPLA asked them to leave their support weapons. The Cubans refused, and the minute we got the information that the Cubans were leaving the MPLA without any support weapons, then we said: "Let us make an effort."

'We grouped our forces. The MPLA did not resist even 15 minutes and we blew up the bridge. It took them six months to rebuild it.'[8]

Thus the tide which had run against Savimbi since 1975 just perceptibly began to turn in 1979. Through 1976, '77 and

'78 he had thought purely in terms of survival. Now he began to think in terms of winning.

* * *

During 1979 about 500 of Savimbi's officer-class soldiers left for training in Morocco as paratroopers, anti-tank specialists, administrators, logistics experts, intelligence personnel, communications specialists and reconnaissance commandos. There were qualitative improvements not only in arms deliveries, but also in diplomatic and financial support. Senegal provided open support in black Africa, leading a small clutch of other black African nations, such as Zaire, who gave covert encouragement.

As well as maintaining UNITA's external headquarters in Morocco, Savimbi enjoyed support from other Arab countries, including Egypt, Saudi Arabia, the Gulf States, Sudan and Tunisia. Financial support was particularly important from Saudi Arabia and the Gulf States.

By the end of the year South Africa's support for Savimbi, which since early 1976 had varied from the non-existent to the unpredictable, had become a substantial commitment. Notwithstanding Savimbi's denials and the inability of his enemies to furnish much hard evidence to prove otherwise, it is impossible to believe that the SADF was not involved in the training of UNITA officers in specialist military skills either in Namibia or in UNITA's bases in southeast Angola.

A three-way connection between Morocco, South Africa and UNITA (which brought in also the US, France, Saudi Arabia and a number of other states) was established. In May 1979 Prime Minister Pieter Botha made a secret visit to Morocco at the invitation of the King Hassan. He was accompanied by his Defence Minister, General Magnus Malan, Foreign Minister 'Pik' Botha, and Commandant Piet Marais, Chief of Armscor, the burgeoning South African arms manufacturing enterprise.[9] By the early 80s South African arms were being delivered to Morocco.

* * *

A *New York Times* columnist perceived that Savimbi may have begun the process of driving the MPLA into a corner.

In her column from Paris on 19 September 1979, Flora Lewis wrote: 'Mr Savimbi is supplied and stiffened by South Africa which is understood to have sent in a black unit of its own army, so there is reason to accept UNITA's argument that the military stalemate is indefinite and that only a political deal can end it. It is hard to see how an economic collapse [in Angola] can be reversed while the civil war goes on.'[10]

UNITA also began in 1979 a programme of sabotage in the main cities, including Luanda itself. Bombs were planted in the capital in the East German Embassy, in the offices of the Soviet airline Aeroflot, the Labour Ministry and the Luanda terminal of the Luanda-Malanje Railway. Many members of UNITA's clandestine cells in Luanda were eventually executed for these acts of urban warfare.[11]

Cells were set up in other cities: in Lobito petroleum storage tanks were blown up and at Huambo airport the control tower was destroyed by a bomb. UNITA managed also to penetrate the administrative system, and on 20 April Agostinho Neto announced the sacking of Garcia Vasco Contreiras, Benguela's provincial commissioner, for alleged collaboration with UNITA.

As the UNITA campaign intensified, the Cubans began to gather people into strategic villages. These consisted of rows of native huts close to the military barracks and administrative blocks in the towns. The peasants in these strategic settlements were given plots within immediate walking distance of the towns so that UNITA was cut off from its sources of supply and support.[12]

'Then the MPLA dug into trenches around the towns and the strategic villages,' according to one of Savimbi's senior aides.[13] 'But eventually the Cubans saw that this didn't work because people kept running back to the bush. So then the Cubans started concentrating on training a big MPLA army.'

Savimbi estimates that in early 1978 there were some 30,000 MPLA soldiers, but that their numbers had increased to 80,000 by the end of 1979 as a result of the Cuban crash training programmes. This process went on alongside the Cubans' gradual withdrawal from mass involvement in front-line fighting, so that by early 1980 UNITA's intelligence officers reckoned that 70 per cent of the fighting was being done by the MPLA.[14]

The Cubans' lower profile had more to do with their own reluctance to become more deeply embroiled in the civil conflict than with their confidence in the MPLA's abilities to cope with the insurgency. Western intelligence obtained a report presented to Angola's State Secretariat for Co-operation on 20 August 1979 which contained the minutes of a meeting between officials and a team of Cuban economic advisers. It said that 337 Cuban technicians had had to be withdrawn from 30 small municipalities in Angola because – in the opinions of the Cubans themselves – their security in those areas could no longer be guaranteed.

Savimbi's orders of battle were designed to exploit the differences between the Cubans and the MPLA. For example, for a large part of 1979 UNITA guerrillas mounting ambushes on road convoys were under orders to single out Cubans and shoot *only* at them with the aim of exacerbating perceived Cuban-MPLA tensions.[15]

The shift in emphasis from the Cubans to the MPLA meant that UNITA began to capture more enemy arms because the MPLA were simply less efficient. 'Where you had the MPLA they made noise during the night, they made fires,' said Savimbi. 'There was confusion; you could even hear them firing their guns. But where the Cubans were, there was discipline. Sometimes if they created a new post we would run into it (unawares) because they were quiet and disciplined. It was also very difficult to get information about the Cubans. They used different radio transmissions from the MPLA and a different code which was very difficult to break. And if the Cubans were in country posts they didn't mix much with the local population because they suspected them of being UNITA agents. But the MPLA mixed with the people. They went drinking with them and had girlfriends, so then we got more information. The MPLA codes were easy to break, and when we fought the MPLA there was confusion among them.'[16]

The rapid increase in the number of MPLA recruits carried its own problems. The officer corps did not expand pro-portionately, so that UNITA intelligence teams noticed that there were problems of control, especially in some MPLA posts in the heart of UNITA-held areas where the enemy logistics lines were as long as 300–500 kilometres. Shortages of food, lack of uniforms and boots, and slow deliveries of wages sapped the morale of the MPLA recruits.

'We concluded that the more they recruited the more problems they would have, and by the end of 1979 there was a marked increase in the number of MPLA desertions to UNITA,' said Savimbi.

Another morale-sapping factor noted by UNITA intelligence was the lack of adequate medical treatment for the MPLA wounded. Savimbi said guerrilla insurgents could bear these kind of hardships more easily because they understood the kind of war they were fighting and had clearly opted for it. However, troops fighting for a government had higher expectations of material support than their guerrilla opponents, and if it was lacking their spirits were disproportionately depressed.

Savimbi also claimed that increasing pressure on the MPLA civilian militias known as the ODP (Organisation of People's Defence) caused dissension. At first the young men in the villages receiving arms thought their ODP duties would be light: 'But gradually they were fully mobilised to help the army. They had no time to do jobs of their own. As the fighting increased they were put under greater pressure to get more deeply involved in the fighting. But they were not well trained, and when they began to take casualties in clashes with us they began to inform on the MPLA for their own protection.'

There were also adverse consequences for UNITA of the increasing pressure that was being put on the MPLA. On 10 August fifteen members of a UNITA underground cell in Menongue were shot publicly, without charge or trial, in front of the Town Hall. They were given away by another UNITA activist in whose house a mine he had been given to plant was found by an MPLA search party.[17]

Savimbi claims that a number of village massacres were carried out by the MPLA in 1979. One of the worst involved the killing in September of more than 800 peasants in a group of three villages in the Sambo area about 70 kilometres southeast of Huambo. The villages – Savitanganyala, Sakachokwe and Samboto – were on the line of a UNITA communications and penetration route across the Benguela Railway.

'The Sambo massacres were ordered by the new Governor of Huambo Province, Lt.-Col. Santana Petroff. He had taken over the job only two months earlier. We heard later that many of the senior Cuban commanders had disagreed with the Sambo massacres. Not for humanitarian reasons, but for political reasons because they realised that news of what had happened would drive even more people towards us.'

Petroff's arrival was partly inspired by a local revolt at Bailundo, north of Huambo, where on 6 July ODP militia-men attacked an MPLA unit. More than a hundred MPLA and ODP men died before the revolt was quelled. But there was unrest in all the provinces of central and southern Angola and at the end of July – when Lt.-Col. Petroff took up his post – civilian provincial governors were also being replaced in the war-torn provinces of Moxico, Bie, Benguela, Cuanza-Sul, Cunene and Cuando Cubango.

'Up until 1979 the MPLA could just regard us as an irritant element,' said Savimbi. 'But by the second half of that year they realised we had become a force to be reckoned with. We held liberated sanctuaries in the southeast and they had failed in their efforts to take them back.'

On 3 October UNITA grouped two of its three fledgling battalions for its biggest military operation yet – an attack on Mavinga, a beautiful little trading and administrative town 250 kilometres north of the Namibian border in Cuando Cubango Province. The attack by the 1,200 UNITA men began at midnight. UNITA had established that there were two MPLA 300-men battalions in the town.[18]

'The fighting went on until 4 a.m. on October 4,' said Savimbi, who directed the assault. 'At 5 a.m., as the sun began to rise, our field commander called off the attack although he already held half of the town. We had heard the MPLA calling for helicopters, and we knew there were three Russian MI-8 helicopters based at Cuito Cuanavale (150 kilometres away). We accepted that the attack had failed.

'But then we realised from our radio intercepts that the

Cubans were saying no, they could not send helicopters. So we regrouped and attacked again at five in the afternoon. It lasted only 20 minutes and we took the town.'[19]

Mavinga was only temporarily occupied. The town was stripped of all useful equipment and then abandoned. The MPLA later re-entered it.

*   *   *

Agostinho Neto grew increasingly concerned about the UNITA recovery, and this must have been part of the inspiration behind his signing of a 20-year Friendship Treaty with the Soviet Union in 1979. At the same time he contacted President Senghor of Senegal to see if it was possible to set up talks with UNITA about a possible settlement. Savimbi believed that Neto was deeply disillusioned by the inability of the Cubans to end UNITA's resistance or do anything about the crumbling economy. Neto's opening towards the West – which was less paradoxical than his treaty with Moscow suggests – depended to some extent on his being able to demonstrate that the military situation was stable and that there was a possibility of a withdrawal of Cuban soldiers, who by 1979 were beginning to attract the kind of resentment that any foreign army in another's country inevitably has to endure.

But Neto had no time left to develop his new policies. In the late summer he visited the Soviet Union, and on 10 September the unexpected death of the Angolan leader, still only 56-years-old, was announced. Angola's most famous liberation leader, the country's strong-man President, and Savimbi's deadly rival, was suddenly gone. It was a further proof to Savimbi's followers of their leader's dictum that if they retained the will to survive things would change around them.

29

Transition in Angola

1979

Before Neto died, Savimbi believes, the Angolan President was having to cope with rifts in the MPLA's policy-making Political Bureau and Central Committee. These resulted from his 'opening to the West', his desire to move from a war footing to peaceful economic development, and a reluctant acceptance of the need to compromise with Savimbi.

'Neto was made of cold but strong steel,' said Savimbi. 'Cold but strong steel. He was not easy to bend. He was my adversary – I prefer not to call him an enemy – but he was a man of outstanding intelligence and I respected him.

'From 1978 Neto did not have the whole of his Central Committee behind him. But his personality was so strong that not one of them would dare to contest Neto directly before the masses. But they disagreed internally with him when he sought *rapprochement* with Mobutu and the West. Neto knew that the Cubans could not be the motor for the economic development of Angola. For that he needed an agreement with the West. To obtain Western cooperation he needed peace, and that involved making peace with his neighbours and within the country.'[1]

Savimbi gave as an example of Neto's stubborn temperament his relations with President Nyerere of Tanzania in the grouping of the five so-called Front Line states – Angola, Tanzania, Zambia, Botswana and Mozambique – who met regularly to consider the problems of white-ruled Rhodesia, Namibia and South Africa.

'Neto was a man of outstanding character and he did not accept humiliation. Nyerere had that idea that he was a teacher[2] and he liked to have a club of heads of state to whom to teach politics . . . And relations between Neto and Nyerere were very bad in the last months of Neto's life. I have my information from a very reliable source who says that sometimes Neto was invited to a meeting of the Front Line states and he refused to go because he didn't want to listen to the lessons of Nyerere.'

To meet the aspirations of his people, to move away from the Cubans and Russians towards the West in an attempt to repair the economy, Neto told President Senghor during the July 1979 OAU summit in Monrovia, Liberia, that he was willing to meet Savimbi to discuss a possible accommodation with insurgents. Senghor sent messages to Savimbi saying Neto wanted to meet him in September in Dakar, Senghor's Senegalese capital. There could be no publicity. Neto could promise nothing in advance, but he would come with an open mind.[3]

But just six weeks after the Monrovia summit Neto went to the Soviet Union to seek medical advice about an internal complaint later described as cancer. 'On arrival in Moscow he was separated from his personal doctor (his wife had not accompanied him) and taken to hospital for investigation,' wrote former British Cabinet Minister Lord Chalfont in *The Times* of London. 'When his doctor next saw him, two days later, he was dead.'[4]

Western intelligence officials leaked their scepticism about the circumstances of Neto's death. They suggested that Neto was assassinated by a deliberate bungling of the operation so that a more pliable man, less likely to flirt with the West, could be installed in Luanda.[5]

Savimbi himself speculated that Neto had been killed on the operating table, though he admitted he had no evidence to prove it. He said that even the MPLA regarded the whole episode as sufficiently disturbing to have set up a commission of inquiry.[6] .

Certainly Neto's death ended any possibility of talks between the MPLA leadership and Savimbi. A new Angolan leader trying to establish himself could not afford to be seen talking to rebels immediately after coming to power.

It also brought to an end talks between President Carter's

US Administration and the MPLA. Richard Moose, Carter's Assistant Secretary of State for African Affairs, and Don McHenry, the US deputy Ambassador at the UN, had proposed to Luanda an accommodation which would have involved US recognition of the MPLA government and the withdrawal of some of the Cuban troops in Angola.[7]

Neto and Savimbi had come to know each other well after 20 years of mutual toil both against the Portuguese and also between their movements. The steel of the older Neto against the will and charisma of his young rival had been an integral part of the Angolan independence struggle. Now a younger man than Savimbi, Jose Eduardo dos Santos, born in 1942 and educated in petroleum engineering and military communications in the Soviet Union, became President of Angola.

Savimbi had never met dos Santos and knew little about him. Early appraisals in Western capitals were that he might reverse Neto's latterly comparatively conciliatory approach to international politics and follow a line more ideologically committed to his Soviet benefactors.

Western fears such as these must have contributed to Savimbi's next breakthrough.

30

A Day in the Life of Jonas Savimbi

1979

After Savimbi established UNITA's new central base at Cuelei in August 1976, it had to be moved every few months for security reasons. While the bases were being shifted Savimbi went on two long treks through central Angola to mobilise support and show himself to the people. UNITA finally established a permanent central base camp at Jamba, near the Luiana River in southeast Angola, in December 1979. It remains there to this day.

In one of our conversations, Savimbi described to me a typical day in his life in 1979, before a permanent base camp had been established:

'I sleep on elephant grass laid on a rope bed. The first rule of guerrilla warfare is not to be caught in bed. It's a habit which was reinforced in 1976 when we were liable to be attacked anywhere by the Cubans and MPLA. They'd move into position between four and six in the morning, so we had to avoid being caught asleep.

'Immediately I go to see the 500 soldiers in my base camp, and sometimes to see the 700 in one of our training camps nearby. This is to boost morale, to talk with the sick and wounded. Then reconnaissance and firewood parties leave.

'At 5.30 my daily cabinet meeting begins in the general office – a big, open-sided grass hut under the trees. We consider urgent messages received during the night by our Chief of Communications, Lt.-Col. Andrade Chassungu. We review the previous day's programme to judge how far it has been fulfilled. Then we plan the coming day's work, as well as weekly and three-monthly strategic plans.

'By 9.30 the patrols are returning and advanced posts have been contacted by radio. If there is no emergency, then by ten I have begun dictating memoranda and letters to my secretary, Anna. This never takes me less than three hours. My heaviest work is on the political side – mobilising the people and seeking diplomatic and material support abroad. We are receiving a lot of arms from China, and several Arab and black African states back us. I leave the military side to my army chief, Brigadier Chiwale, but if there is a really big operation the final word has to be with me.

'In 1978 we had too many examples of losing men for no gain in hopeless assaults on enemy posts. Now when we attack fixed positions it is in battalion strength (more than 500 men) and the planning comes right from the top.

'I also direct all operations along the Benguela Railway because that is a major target. We have kept it closed since Fidel Castro imposed the MPLA on our country. I also liaise closely with Lt.-Col. Bok Sapalalo, who is in charge of intelligence gathering and sabotage in the towns. Bok lost his left arm in an explosion in 1978, but his department has been so successful that we have now penetrated as far as Luanda.

'Nobody eats in the morning. At noon, if the area is safe and we can make fires, we eat cassava with antelope meat and maybe cabbage or tomato from one of our farms. There are many animals in our areas. We export ivory, rhino horn and leopard and antelope skins to help pay for our war, but we have declared some conservation zones where hunting elephant, giraffe and black sable is banned. The black sable is a rare species and it is a UNITA symbol on our coat of arms. Myself, I never eat until the evening, when my personal nurse usually insists.

'In the afternoon I hear petitioners for three hours. They bring many problems. For instance, a village leader will travel hundreds of kilometres to say the local UNITA military commander is not respecting local property. Then I have to find out what is happening, and act on it, because a struggle like ours cannot succeed unless the people are with us.

'At 5 p.m. I go to the villages near the base camp to talk to the people. At six, without fail, I listen to the BBC News and *Focus on Africa* to keep up with outside events. I also listen to French Radio and *Voice of America*. But the BBC is the best. It does not generally make propaganda, though we get very upset with the Luanda correspondent because most of the time she gives misinformation about UNITA.

'At 7.30 I am back in my hut. I look at messages that have come in during the day from our 22 military regions. Then I see my wife and four children for half an hour if they are in the same camp. My last born, Chofeka, is a real trouble-maker. He is four and he will often run away from his mother and start tearing up my papers – but I don't get annoyed because I only get a short time with him.

'I sit in a chair made by our people with animal skins to write plans for the next week or month. I use the light from the wood fire or candles made by our soldiers from wild beeswax.

'UNITA officers are returning from training in Morocco, and there are many others there now: there are others in a black African country and another African Arab state. They have improved our performance: some are skilled in anti-tank warfare and others have been on commando courses, so we use them to lead missions behind and between Cuban and MPLA lines.

'I work really hard because I feel if UNITA does not succeed in forcing the MPLA to negotiate by 1990 it has no chance to succeed at all.

'I stop at one or two in the morning, and when I go to bed I am so tired I don't need a pillow to sleep. After some weeks I am exhausted. Then I like to go hunting for two days. If I kill an elephant, outside one of those conservation zones, we have meat for 500 for a week. We dry it in the sun or by fires. The hunts are my only relaxation and the only time I can read my books. I've just finished Field-Marshal Montgomery's autobiography. He said leadership is about having the capacity and will to rally men for a common cause. I like that very much.

'But the rest of the time a typical day is administration, administration, administration. We have lots of files, typewriters, secretaries. We have a secretarial school. We find we cannot do without paperwork, though we try to keep it down because we need to move every few months. When we move we put the papers in metal trunks and bury them. When we are sure the new base is secure we send soldiers back to collect the trunks.

'I also find time to visit our Protestant and Catholic churches in the bush. We have many ministers and priests with us, all black Angolans. Religion is part of my life. It is something I was brought up with, so I cannot do away with it: my father was a Protestant pastor. In times of depression and difficulties religion gives me an extra hope, a strength that comes from inside. If I die the struggle here in this world will not have been for nothing: there are other things to hope for.

'We have come a long way since we began fighting the Portuguese in 1966 with that pistol which Sam Nujoma gave to me. We have suffered a lot, but we are determined to stay in this struggle until we die. It is our country and we will not give up. The MPLA will eventually have to negotiate with us because the Angolan economy is falling deeper into ruin all the time. But our price for a political settlement will be that the Cubans return across the Atlantic.'

31

America and Europe

1979

In late October 1979 a trip was arranged for Savimbi outside Angola to meet clandestine supporters, talk to potential sympathisers and see his officers in training in Morocco.

Only after Savimbi boarded his DC-4 plane on an Angolan bush airstrip called 'Point Delta' was he told by his Washington-based Secretary for Foreign Affairs, Jeremias Chitunda, that arrangements had been made for him to spend eleven days in the United States.[1]

Savimbi stopped off in Morocco to prepare for his US visit: just a few weeks earlier, Zbigniew Brzezinski had won approval, against the opposition of other members of the Carter Administration, such as Andrew Young, Richard Moose and Don McHenry, to begin a massive supply of arms to Morocco's King Hassan for his war against the Polisario Front. Brzezinski's move, together with a Washington statement that the US no longer intended opening diplomatic relations with the MPLA government as long as Cuban troops remained in Angola, represented a clear strengthening of US policy on the Soviet-Cuban challenge in Africa.[2]

Savimbi told a *Newsweek* correspondent, who joined him on the flight out of Angola, that he wanted to urge the Carter Administration to give a signal that would encourage black states in Africa already sympathetic to UNITA to begin giving the movement greater backing.[3]

Savimbi stayed in the United States from 3 to 14 November 1979 as a guest of Freedom House, a New York-based organisation which monitors political freedom around the world. And though he was not invited to talk to senior Carter Administration officials, Savimbi regarded the trip as having been fruitful. He had 80 hours of speaking engagements and gave 23 interviews to newspaper, television and radio correspondents. He met James Schlesinger, former Defence Secretary in the Ford Administration during the 1975–76 Angolan war; Henry Kissinger; Senators Henry Jackson, Charles Diggs, Sam Nunn and Daniel Patrick Moynihan; Lane Kirkland, the newly appointed head of the giant, fiercely anti-Communist AFL-CIO trade union; and Alexander Haig, Presidential hopeful and future Secretary of State for Foreign Affairs.

I met Savimbi at UNITA's external headquarters in Rabat some two months after the end of his US visit. It was my first contact with him in the four years since I had seen him in Bie, just before he ordered the evacuation of the town at the start of his long march. Of his American trip, he said: 'I considered it was a success in the sense that most Americans now have a different view of UNITA, what we stand for, why we are fighting. The position before was that we were just stooges of South Africa and that we had no effective fighting force inside. Before, the only information they were getting was from the angle of the MPLA. The sensitive issue in America, with the Administration and especially with black Americans, was that of South Africa and I think that to most we succeeded in explaining that we were not agents of South Africa.'

Savimbi also hoped his message had been reinforced in American eyes by the major event of the following month, the Soviet invasion of Afghanistan which began on 27 December 1979. Savimbi argued that the weakness of the US response in Angola in 1975 to the Cuban/Soviet 'takeover' had encouraged subsequent Cuban/Soviet boldness in Ethiopia, Vietnamese confidence in invading Cambodia, and now Soviet certainty that its move into Afghanistan would not be opposed.

'I think the drama in America is that the technocratic decision makers are for the most part liberals who are unwittingly selling out their own principles in order to avoid confrontation with the Russians,' said Savimbi. 'The best thing a general can do is to win a war without fighting the war. If you destroy the will of an adversary to fight, that is a much better way of taking strategic territory, bit by bit, than physical confrontation.

'I don't believe Russia will give up Afghanistan. The West will have to combat this kind of Russian strategic advance by unconventional means, and we are one of the peoples who can do it. We know how to do it, we are doing it. The West must think how we can be given more support, not only through arms and money but by fitting our struggle into their own overall struggle against the Russians.'[4]

Savimbi gained most publicity on his trip with his allegation that 1,300 Angolan schoolchildren had been sent to Cuba without their parents' approval, into what he described as a form of 'neo-colonial slavery'. Preparations were being made to send another 5,000 children to the special Cuban international school on the Isle of Pines. 'But the parents are resisting,' said Savimbi. 'They are calling on the UNITA guerrillas to challenge this atrocity . . . The school is for indoctrination.' He described the children as 'victims of a most vicious cultural imperialism of our times'.[5]

William Safire, the right-wing *New York Times* columnist, backed Savimbi on his Isle of Pines protest, and said: 'After classes on this former penal colony off south-west Cuba, the children are said to work in the sugar fields. Does anybody care? This forced bussing on a grand scale is surely worthy of investigation by children-protectors at the United Nations, by private foundations and by journalists who find Mr Castro such a winning figure.'[6]

But John Stockwell, by then a private citizen in Austin, Texas, wrote a letter to the *New York Times* describing Savimbi's allegations about the forced removal of schoolchildren to the Isle of Pines – rechristened the 'Isle of Youth' by Fidel Castro – as 'preposterous'.

Stockwell went on: 'In April 1979, accompanied by a respected television producer and a private citizen, I visited the Angolan schools complex on the lovely Isle of Youth in Cuba – Safire's "former penal colony". We were impressed with the students' morale and enthusiasm . . . Too many

Congolese[7] and Angolan mothers cannot teach their children the three Rs because they are themselves illiterate, and the Cubans are proud of their international school system. I suggest Mr Safire fly to Cuba and see for himself. If it offends us that Cubans are educating Africans, we might try to compete, to build comparable schools in the United States for young Angolans, Congolese and others.'

Stockwell also described UNITA's leader as a 'perennial loser', and added: 'Savimbi has no ideology. He believes in nothing beyond his own selfish ambitions, and fighting has become his way of life.'[8]

During his US visit, in the most extensive and profound of the interviews he gave, Savimbi replied to Stockwell's charge: 'I have heard people in the West say: "It's true, the MPLA is Marxist-Leninist, but at least they have a political doctrine, and that's more than their opponents have."

'This is a foolish statement for two reasons. First, it assumes that Marxism-Leninism is the only respectable and effective ideology in the world – and that is simply not true. Second, it assumes that Marxism-Leninism is equally relevant in all times and in all situations – and that is also untrue.

'If our aim is the liberation of our people, our first and highest priority must be the working out of a political doctrine that is inspired by the values of our people. We cannot be effective in our struggle unless our goals and our language and our ideas are shared by the common people.

'No writer can escape the fact that he is a creature of his own time and place. When Marx wrote, he was speaking as a man of German origin, in an era dominated by French philosophy, living in Britain and dealing with the economic problems of Britain at that time.

'My own doctrine is this: why don't we go back to our own African roots and analyse them? It is true that we have to work for progress, and in modern times we cannot apply all our traditions without changing them or adjusting them, but we have to keep an *essence* of our values in order to remain a people with an identity. If we cannot do this, as a political party, we are going to speak a language that our people will never understand.

'No ideological system exists in a vacuum. And you cannot hurry people along a road that they do not want to follow. That is why a genuinely African revolution requires a willingness to learn from the peasants, and a patience as well, because – how can I put it – peasants are naturally *reluctant*. When you bring them a new idea they are reluctant to change. They say that the life they are living – well, it is not very good, it is not very pleasant, but they are afraid to change because they say the future is unknown. So if you want to transform their lethargy into action you must understand their aspirations.

'You cannot impose a political programme that no one understands. The Angolan peasant is not a statistic in some book of economic theories – he is not a machine. And if you attempt to treat him that way, he will reject you.'[9]

Of the effects of the war on young people, Savimbi said: 'When we see them playing with guns it is not what we want. We want them to grow up in a world where their education is political and not military, because a militarised mind is a narrow mind.

'The distinction between a soldier and a political activist who just occasionally resorts to armed struggle to achieve political goals is a difficult one for a child to make. But it is a critical distinction. Some day the war will be over, and when it is over we cannot remain a militarised people and be free at the same time.'

Savimbi also said he thought the religious faith of the Angolan people had been an element that had enabled them to resist the Cubans. As for his own continued professed Christianity, he said: 'My answer is: politics is too difficult to survive on all the time – too painful. There has to be something else.'

*   *   *

Savimbi spent more than another two months outside Angola at the end of his US visit. His movements were largely veiled in secrecy, but behind the walls of his Rabat house he received a constant stream of visitors from Africa, Europe and the Middle East. During this time, Savimbi also spent five days in West Germany clandestinely meeting a variety of politicians. He limited himself to speaking of the 'positive' nature of the German trip, which was followed by the appointment of a permanent UNITA representative, Charles Kandanda, in Germany.[10]

One set of meetings Savimbi had in Rabat was with representatives of the states, mainly Arab, who had provided him with ten million dollars worth of funds between 1976 and 1979. They said they were happy to continue providing funds to help Savimbi survive but would prefer to give him more to enable him to win. But they were unwilling to provide large sums unless Savimbi could demonstrate that he had the support of the United States or key powers in Western Europe.

'They said to me: "To give you $US 250,000 at a time, as we have been doing, so that you can survive does not interest us very much. We have money and we think in commercial terms. We are happy to give you $US 45 to 50 million if you are going to win, so that tomorrow you will be our friend. But if we carry on giving you $US 250,000 at a time just so that you can survive, then perhaps we're only encouraging you to live with an illusion, in which case it's maybe better that you die." It was clear that if other powers began to indicate that they had decided to support us then the cash will flow again from our Arab donors.'[11]

Savimbi concluded his stay outside Angola with an unpublicised visit to London, in February 1980, to brief sympathetic politicians and businessmen on events in Angola and on the outcome of his visit to the United States. He also briefed the directors of Tanganyika Concessions, who have always stayed in close communication with Savimbi, on what he was doing to their railway.

32

The Thrust North Begins

1980

The latest batch of UNITA military recruits being trained in Morocco were badly needed. In December 1979, while Savimbi was in Rabat, a UNITA attack on a Benguela Railway bridge across a river called the Cuiva had gone badly wrong. Thirty-five UNITA soldiers were killed and the MPLA retained control of the bridge for minimal losses.[1]

New artillery groups in training in Morocco would permit more accurate mortar fire to be put down in support of the infantry during attacks. 'In the past it happened that our mortars were falling on our own infantry because of the lack of co-ordination between infantry and artillery,' said Savimbi.[2]

A more professional army had become a necessity because by early 1980 there were more Cuban soldiers – possibly 19,000 – in the country than at independence to counter UNITA. East German military men had also arrived in Angola.[3] Some were helping to build up the MPLA's air force, and a unit from the Felix Dzherzhinsky Parachute Regiment,[4] named after the founder of the Soviet state security police and composed of East German internal security troops, were training a new MPLA parachute division even as Savimbi's parachutists were practising far to the north over Morocco's Atlas Mountains.

The increased commitment from Cuba and East Germany coincided with the return of Eduardo dos Santos from his first visit to Moscow as President of Angola. It also marked a hardening of the party's attitude towards dissidents within the MPLA. Announcing a sweeping purge of the party, the

Commissar for Luanda province district, Mendes de Carvalho, said the aim was to 'eliminate all elements disagreeing with the party's Marxist line'. He made his declaration in mid-January 1980 as a big Soviet military mission arrived in the Angolan capital.[5]

The war was now bigger and nastier than ever. Amnesty International reported further extra-judicial executions of UNITA supporters and torture of UNITA prisoners. It gave as one example reports from 'independent sources' – almost certainly the International Committee of the Red Cross which was by then the only independent international organisation permitted to operate in central Angola – that 27 men and boys from Chitiquengue village, near Chipapa, north of Huambo, were shot dead on 27 February 1980 after being rounded up by MPLA soldiers.[6]

UNITA itself claimed that in February, after a Cuban soldier was found murdered in the Huambo suburb of São Pedro, more than 30 civilians, including women and children, were immediately rounded up and executed without trial. In the same month, 37 MPLA soldiers from a company that mutinied against its Cuban instructors at Alto Hama, 60 kilometres north of Huambo, were executed.[7]

UNITA responded with a wave of more than 20 urban bombings in February and March 1980, in which it claimed more than 40 people were killed, including a Soviet military adviser in Mocamedes named Andre Chevchenko and the station master at Bie on the Benguela Railway.[8]

*　　*　　*

Savimbi was now ready to begin a push northwards. Up until the end of 1979, whenever UNITA had overrun small MPLA-held towns its policy had been to destroy their infrastructures before surrendering them again to the enemy. However, the decision reached at the 1977 Congress to create semi-regular battalions was intended eventually to permit UNITA to defend and hold territory it had won from the MPLA. The move north from the south-eastern bush sanctuaries would necessitate not only taking small settlements but also denying re-entry to the MPLA.

The strategy effectively began with the capture on 14 April

1980 of Cuangar, which had changed hands four times over the previous three years. The battle was watched by South African military officers across the other side of the Cubango River at Kurin Kuru in Namibia. They said UNITA attacked the town with rockets before sending in troops. The town fell after more than one hour of fighting.[9]

Savimbi identified Cuangar as a landmark. After the 900-man MPLA garrison disintegrated and withdrew, it became the first town (as opposed to small settlements) to fall under permanent UNITA control. The MPLA has never returned. UNITA captured its first SAM-7 ground-to-air missiles in the battle for Cuangar along with six Soviet 14.5mm anti-aircraft guns and hundreds of thousands of rounds to rifle ammunition.[10]

UNITA was now ready to clear out MPLA forces from a clutch of other small south-eastern towns. Its Moroccan-trained experts were scheduled to enter action for the first time in the battle for Luengue, and a group of eight foreign correspondents were flown into Angola from Zaire in early May to observe the UNITA operation.

Luengue was a former Portuguese big game hunting base, 135 kilometres north of the Namibian border, and had a big, well-prepared landing strip which could take medium-sized transport planes. The journalists found Savimbi at Camp Likua, a dispersed encampment of thatched huts nestled beneath the trees, hidden from Cuban spotter planes, about 30 kilometres to the west of Luengue.[11]

The best account of what turned out for many of the journalists to be a very testing visit came from Jack Foisie of the *Los Angeles Times*.

Savimbi's command of English and his willingness to answer the most controversial of questions impressed Foisie. When the *Los Angeles Times* man asked whether the UNITA leader's association with South Africa weakened his position in the rest of Africa, Savimbi replied: 'No. Look at the Mozambicans, who are supposed to be Marxists. Those are the people who are dealing with the South Africans in a big way. Machel would not live a month without South African trade.

'Of course, a black man like me will not say that apartheid

is a good thing. How are we going to get rid of the mistreatment of blacks in South Africa? I don't know, because I'm busy with my own problems.'

How did he feel about the United States now? – 'You Americans deserted us in 1975. You left us in the cold when the Russians sent in the Cubans. It is insultingly contradictory to condemn the Russian invasion in Afghanistan, only politely criticise the Russian interference in the Horn of Africa, and yet keep a complete silence on the Soviet and Cuban occupation of Angola.'

Foisie also identified the diplomatic and political motivation behind Savimbi's drive to capture and hold a cluster of towns in south-east Angola. (Following the capture of Cuangar, UNITA had also taken such small towns as Savate, Rito, Chirundo and Dirico.) Proposals by the United Nations – backed by the five Western members of the Contact Group (see Chapter 27) – for bringing independence and democratic rule to Namibia included the establishment of a demilitarised zone (DMZ) along the 1,200-kilometre Angola-Namibia frontier. It would be 80 kilometres deep on either side to prevent infiltration into Namibia by SWAPO guerrillas and incursions by South African troops in the opposite direction.

Savimbi said he favoured the idea of a DMZ but, since he controlled a large part of the territory where it would have to be established, the Secretary-General of the UN, Kurt Waldheim, would have to consult with him. This would, of course, have involved the UN in giving Savimbi implicit international recognition, and that was a diplomatic impossibility. Nevertheless, Savimbi invited Waldheim to visit UNITA's territory: but he warned that any international force that tried to establish the DMZ without UNITA approval would be treated as hostile.[12] Savimbi was able to assert rights in the UNITA zone in the confident knowledge that a real diplomatic reawakening on Angola was beginning. The West, worried by the Soviet invasion of Afghanistan, began to acknowledge that perhaps Angola was an earlier Afghanistan which could have been prevented by a more determined and open diplomatic and military stand in favour of free elections. Addressing the West European

Union Assembly in Paris on 3 June 1980, Mr Douglas Hurd, Minister of State in the British Foreign Office, said: 'We believe that if the West had reacted more vigorously on Angola or the Cuban military move into Ethiopia with Soviet backing – if there had been a stauncher response – the Soviet Union might have thought more carefully before invading Afghanistan.' Savimbi gained sympathetic ears in France, Portugal and West Germany, where Chancellor Helmut Schmidt was particularly enthusiastic about the UNITA leader. And in the United States the Republican Presidential candidate, Ronald Reagan, said that if elected in November 1980 he would resume US assistance to Savimbi.

To pass time while waiting for the battle of Luengue to begin, Foisie and his colleagues made a 400-kilometre return journey to see newly captured Cuangar. Savimbi said the return trip could be done in two-and-a-half days. It took ten days: 'Vehicles frequently broke down, overheated or suffered flat tires as they struggled through the sandy waste or plunged into deep brush to hide when the drone of aircraft was heard,' wrote Foisie. 'The time we spent with the guerrillas showed off to advantage their remarkable endurance, patience, self-reliance, humour, dedication, discipline and ability to improvise.

'In one ten-hour stop due to an engine breakdown, the driver and the cook chopped out the top of an empty 50-gallon drum and pounded the metal into a radiator fan to replace the broken one. When fan belts broke, UNITA soldiers were lined up and the one with the narrowest belt sacrificed it as a replacement.'

Foisie and the other journalists grew impatient waiting for the battle of Luengue, and flew out of Savimbi's territory at the end of May.

The battle came on 8 June, and for the first time the reconnaissance commandos and artillery experts trained in Morocco entered battle.

'Before we took Luengue our commandos had entered the MPLA camps several times, seeing exactly where they had their trenches; where they had their big guns,' said Savimbi. 'We wanted to capture Luengue because it would open our logistics route north towards Mavinga. We had two battalions (together totalling 1,000 men) trained to fight for up to five days. We had prepared new techniques to use over a long battle period. But unfortunately – or fortunately – the battle lasted only 30 minutes, so some of our follow-up groups were not tested.

'The artillery groups co-ordinated their fire with the advancing infantry by radio. When the infantry needed to clear up a pocket of MPLA resistance they could stop the mortar fire. And the fire was accurate because the infantry could direct it. So, technically, we knew from then onwards that we could co-ordinate infantry advance with support artillery. Before, there would be an artillery bombardment, and then the infantry would advance and have to fight it out without artillery support.'[13]

*   *   *

In July 1980 Savimbi again left Angola. His destination was London, where he and his delegation were put up under tight security on one of the top floors of an Edgware Road hotel belonging to the big multinational company Lonrho, which had given Savimbi the business jet for his use during the 1975–76 war. There Savimbi prepared the speech he had been invited to give to the influential International Institute for Strategic Studies on the theme 'Prospects for Security in Southern Africa'.

About 50 demonstrators from the Anti-Apartheid Movement and the Mozambique, Angola and Guinea Information Committee (MAGIC), financed by those three governments, greeted Savimbi outside the Institute and two people broke into the meeting and shouted 'murderer' and 'traitor' at the UNITA leader before they were escorted out.[14]

Savimbi told the Institute that the West needed to create and implement a strategy for the defence of its long-term economic and political interests in Africa. In part, that involved making an all out effort to persuade South Africa to change its internal policies. 'The policy of apartheid only makes easier Soviet penetration in Africa,' he said. 'It accelerates tension and racial confrontations, all of which can readily be exploited by the Soviet Union. Therefore, all countries which maintain friendly relations with South Africa should help persuade the South African régime to speed up change in order to avert catastrophic consequences from racial tensions. It is important, however, to point out that such action should be applied in a way that will not lead to isolationism and unco-operativeness on the part of South Africa. The situation in South Africa is infinitely delicate and requires a very wise and careful approach by Western strategists.'

Savimbi argued that the Namibian and Angolan problems had to be solved together within a regional framework. The extraordinary OAU summit on Angola in January 1976 had shown that it was no longer valid to expect that African problems could be settled solely within an African context and by Africans alone. In 1976 the OAU had decided that *all* foreign forces should leave Angola: 'Encouraged by the West, South Africa withdrew immediately; but the Cubans stayed and within four years tripled their forces. Were Africa capable of dealing with the problem alone, the Cuban expeditionary force would have been compelled to abide by the OAU edict.

'The problem of Soviet expansionism transcends African boundaries and must therefore be dealt with by a concerted effort of the international community . . . The main danger of *détente* is that the West's quest for peace at any cost is permitting the Soviets to conquer more and more strategic positions without confrontation.

'The lessons from Munich are still clear in the minds of the West. Often, to seek peace at any cost is to facilitate the outbreak of war. When the Soviet Union invades weak Angola; when it encourages Cuban adventures in Ethiopia; when it propels Vietnam to overthrow the régime in Cambodia; and when Russian regiments march into Kabul to overthrow three consecutive régimes in Afghanistan, and the West is constantly making concessions to the Soviet Union, all this reminds us of the West's endless concessions to Hitler.'[15]

Savimbi also had meetings at the Carlton Club and Reform Club, favourite haunts of top politicians, civil servants and intelligence officials. The meetings were chaired by Mr Edward Du Cann, MP, a director of Lonrho and chairman of the ruling Conservative Party's powerful 1922 Committee. Influential businessmen were present and a London newspaper revealed that a major West European channel of support for Savimbi was through a consortium of businessmen based in Paris.[16]

Many problems awaited Savimbi at home but, before he left, *The Times* of London – the newspaper beloved by the British Establishment – published an article by Lord Chalfont calling on the West to back UNITA. 'The very least the United States and its Western allies should now do is to make unequivocally clear their moral and political support for Dr Savimbi's cause,' wrote Chalfont. 'The very *best* they could do would be to supply him with some of the resources which he needs to win the war. The experience of Afghanistan has surely, if belatedly, removed any inhibitions in the West about arming and supporting those, anywhere in the world, who are fighting what are, in the last analysis, our battles.'[17]

* * *

While Savimbi was away South Africa launched massive raids into south-west Angola against SWAPO camps; reports of severe hunger among the peasant people of central Angola began to emerge; and trials were in progress which would result in the executions by the MPLA of many more UNITA followers.

The South African raids through June and July 1980 were conducted up to 80 kilometres deep into Cunene province. One report from the MPLA side estimated that 3,000 South African troops were engaged in the operations.[18] Apart from the South African desire to kill as many SWAPO guerrillas as possible, the raids also seemed designed to destroy the UN Namibian peace initiative which, if successful, nearly everyone believed would end in SWAPO coming to power in elections. The South Africans had just embarked on a new strategy of their own in Namibia, installing in power in Windhoek, under a South African administrator-general, a Namibian government called the Democratic

Turnhalle Alliance, composed of representatives of the major minority parties and all the tribal groups.

Lucio Lara alleged that it was Pretoria's aim to install UNITA in the proposed demilitarised zone as another means of undermining the United Nations initiative,[19] a theme taken up by the Angolan Foreign minister, Paulo Jorge: 'These South African aggressions are aimed at trying to discourage the Angolan people, party and government from their militant support for SWAPO. We also think these attacks, and particularly the June-July invasion, are aimed at trying to establish a zone in the south where UNITA can be installed. The idea is that after Pretoria accepts the demilitarised zone proposal, they will put their puppets there in order to force the UN to consider the UNITA presence and even to include UNITA in the negotiations. This is not accepted by the Angolan government, because UNITA doesn't represent anybody.'[20]

The commander of the MPLA's Cunene military region claimed that the June-July daily attacks had been just part of a pattern of constant incursions by South Africa throughout the first half of 1980. There had been two large-scale ground attacks and four parachute drops of special commandos; 34 aerial bombing or cannon attacks and 476 reconnaissance flights; and two long-range heavy artillery attacks. The South African troops had been concentrated heavily at 13 points along the frontier, and even after a withdrawal was announced at the end of July not all of the forces were, in fact, pulled out from Angola.[21]

The Cubans had not entered the fighting against the South Africans, wrote David Coetzee, a journalist with the pro-MPLA magazine *New African*. But the Cuban presence in the main towns was obvious: 'They are visible as medical orderlies, driving army Red Cross trucks, or in the Central Highlands in barracks converted from abandoned factories, idling away the afternoons playing baseball. In front of the main barracks in the town of Huambo they display a large slogan, a statement of Fidel's: "We will defend Angola as we will defend the whole of Africa."'[22]

*   *   *

The first indications of hunger on the Central Plateau came when the International Committee of the Red Cross (ICRC) announced in June 1980 that 50,000 peasants, mainly women and children, displaced by the intensifying war, had been greatly weakened by severe malnutrition.[23] Amazingly, this region, which had once been a cornucopia of grain and of Mediterranean and tropical fruits of all descriptions, which before independence had produced more foodstuffs than it could consume, now became a centre of food distribution for the starving.

The MPLA allowed journalists sympathetic to the régime to visit the Central Plateau where the ICRC had an initial budget of three million dollars to feed the people, with additional help from the European Economic Community.

Driving between Huambo and Bie, journalist Paul Fauvet noted abnormally large villages stretching for hundreds of metres along the sides of roads. In the towns there were many undernourished people in rags, cooking on patches of waste ground and living in derelict or unfinished buildings. The MPLA Commissars for Huambo and Bie provinces, Santana Petroff and Jamba ya Mina, claimed that the peasants were fleeing from areas where UNITA had 'resorted to terror to maintain control over tens of thousands of disillusioned peasants'.[24]

The problem of hunger was one which would grow through the 80s, and both Petroff and Jamba ya Mina were critical of the MPLA's central state machinery for failing to take decisive action to ensure food supplies to the Central Plateau. 'The inertia of the bureaucratic apparatus stands out in high relief,' wrote David Coetzee. 'Unless the government can provide the consumer goods and tools at the spot where the peasants need them in exchange for their surplus crops, they will have no incentive to produce that surplus, which is sorely needed. And if they do not solve this problem soon then UNITA may once again win an advantage.'[25]

*   *   *

Trials of UNITA activists alleged to have taken part in bombing attacks the previous year in Luanda and Huambo were in progress. Among the incidents cited in the Luanda trial before a Revolutionary Tribunal was a bomb attack in a fairground in which ten people were killed and an attack on a commuter train in which 17 people died.[26] Among the incidents cited at the Revolutionary Tribunal in Huambo was a bomb incident in a market place in which more than 150 people died.[27]

On 29 July 1980 sixteen members of UNITA sabotage cells in Luanda were sentenced to death. UNITA responded by issuing a statement saying that if the 'Luanda Sixteen' died, 50 of its MPLA prisoners would be immediately 'eliminated'.[28] And in another communiqué from the Political Bureau, UNITA said: 'These sentences of capital punishment are to be added to the long list of executions, arbitrary imprisonments, intimidations and other methods of repression utilised by the MPLA to impose law on a people deprived of its elementary human rights.'[29]

Citing the Charter of the Universal Declaration of Human Rights and the agreement reached at Alvor in 1975, UNITA appealed to the UN, the OAU, and Amnesty International to intervene 'in the safeguarding of democratic liberties' and to save the lives of the condemned men.[30]

On 5 August the MPLA announced that the 'Luanda Sixteen' had been executed. UNITA suspended its threat of immediate retaliatory execution of MPLA prisoners 'in the light of messages of sympathy and requests of clemency from international humanitarian organisations and friendly countries'. The movement began a 90-day period of mourning, but it warned that during this period any enemy soldiers taken prisoner were to be summarily executed.[31]

And a military offensive was launched in memory of the dead men. It began with a massive attack on the main fuel storage plant in Lobito, which UNITA said had been 'totally destroyed by explosive devices and other military actions' on the night of 10 August.[32] Admitting that at least two huge fuel tanks had been destroyed in the attack, the MPLA said more than 10,000 cubic metres of gasoline out of a total capacity at the Lobito plant of 22,500 cubic metres had been lost.[33]

UNITA blew up the central power plant of Huambo on 18

August and deprived the city of electricity for three days. Six days later nine of the members of the UNITA cells tried in Huambo were executed by firing squad.[34] On the same day UNITA ordered the immediate death by firing squad of 15 MPLA officers, ranging in rank from sergeant to lieutenant, for 'atrocities against defenceless civilians'.[35]

The executions had a ratchet effect, raising the level of violence in Angola to yet new levels. The MPLA government leaders said there was no longer any prospect of the Benguela Railway functioning normally until there was a settlement of the Namibian problem, and Commissar Petroff admitted that the 25 diesel engines once operating on the line had been reduced to five because of sabotage.[36]

*   *   *

UNITA prepared for a big push northwards from Luengue. First, UNITA forces captured the town of Rivungo, on the Zambian border, and on 20 August an attempt was repulsed by an MPLA motorised brigade of nearly 1,000 men to recapture the town of Savate. UNITA claimed to have killed 120 enemy soldiers at Savate and to have summarily executed ten soldiers, including the brigade's political commissar, in line with its decision about the period of mourning.[37]

On 11 September UNITA forces retook Mavinga. This time the intention was to hold the town permanently – and six years later, in 1986, MPLA forces had still not managed to return.

On 19 October an Antonov-26 attempted to bomb UNITA's landing strip at Luengue, which by then was being used as the rebels' main supply airstrip. The plane was hit by one of the ground-to-air missiles from the SAM-7 batteries protecting the airstrip. The crippled plane crashed several kilometres from Luengue, killing all the crew.

On 22 November another Antonov-26 was hit by SAM-7 missiles soon after take-off from Mpupa, an MPLA post under siege to the west of Luengue. It crash-landed and UNITA forces took as prisoners its stunned pilot and chief engineer. Both were Russians, and UNITA claimed they were members of the Soviet Air Force.

A UNITA statement said the prize captives demonstrated that the Soviet role in Angola was not confined to advising and training the MPLA. They were also participating in combat missions.[38]

* * *

In November 1980 Jimmy Carter was defeated by the Republican challenger Ronald Reagan in the American Presidential election. It would change Jonas Savimbi's fortunes once more for the better.

33

US Policy Shift Favours Savimbi

1981

'The best news since the beginning of the war of liberation five years ago (against the Cubans/MPLA),' said Savimbi of Ronald Reagan's inauguration in early January 1981 as President of the United States. 'The election of Reagan is our hope . . . for it signifies a telling blow against Soviet expansionism and for Cuban departure.'[1]

Reagan had pledged during his election campaign that he would attempt to persuade Congress to repeal the Clark Amendment so that US aid could be resumed to UNITA.

Savimbi's hand was also strengthened in January 1981 by the breakdown of UN-sponsored talks on the future of Namibia which had been going on in Geneva since the previous November. The Geneva talks were attended by South Africa, SWAPO, the United Nations, the 'Contact Group' of Western intermediaries, the US, Britain, Canada, France and West Germany, two of the five main anti-SWAPO parties in Namibia, and Zambia and other black Africa 'front line' states.

South Africa precipitated the breakdown of the conference, arguing that the UN was not behaving impartially between it and SWAPO. But at this time Pretoria had clear military superiority over SWAPO: UN partiality apart, South Africa simply saw no need in these circumstances to consider giving independence to Namibia while it could press, on the diplomatic front, for a withdrawal of Cuban troops from Angola as the price for its own withdrawal from Namibia. With no settlement of the problem in sight,

Savimbi was assured of continued South African support as he built up his forces.

A *Financial Times* correspondent who visited the SADF HQ for the central Kavango stretch of the Namibia-Angola border at Rundu concluded that the SADF itself was not considering any early solution to the Namibian problem. The military commanders at Rundu regarded the UN plan for the creation of a demilitarised border zone as impracticable. 'We can win this war,' Colonel Leon Martins, commander of the Kavango border section, told the *Financial Times* man. 'But if you allow the terrorists to come into your area, it would take 30 to 80 years. If you knock him out where he is – that is Angola – it will take 10 to 15 years.[12]

Back in Windhoek, the Namibian capital, Major-General Charles Lloyd, the SADF commander for Namibia, told the same reporter that strikes into Angola by his forces had crippled SWAPO in 1980 by inflicting 1,500 guerrilla deaths against 72 for the SADF. Estimating the remaining SWAPO strength at between 7,000 and 8,000, he said: 'Our object is to break the military force of SWAPO and its will to fight.'

* * *

In February 1981 the authors of an article on Savimbi entitled 'Reagan's Ally', in the magazine *The New Republic*, argued that a UNITA win in Angola was 'evidently within the realm of possibility'. It went on: 'It might serve notice to other countries that the wind might be beginning to blow from the West at long last.'[3]

The new US Secretary of State Alexander Haig indicated right from the beginning of the Reagan Presidency that the five-year-old US policy of withholding diplomatic recognition from the Angolan government would not be changed while Cuban troops remained in Angola. In mid-January 1981 Haig told the Senate Foreign Relations Sub-committee that he opposed recognition of the Luanda government 'so long as there are 20 mercenaries within their borders'.[4]

In late March Reagan announced that he would push ahead with his pre-election promise to persuade Congress to repeal the Clark Amendment. At this time Savimbi was again in Morocco, where he met a senior official from the US

State Department – probably deputy Assistant Secretary of State, Lannon Walker – to discuss an evolving US plan for Namibia and Angola.[5]

Just before the Walker-Savimbi meeting took place, a SWAPO communiqué said a delegation of six UNITA officials had met Alexander Haig, apparently in the United States. Haig had given the delegation an undertaking that the US would assist UNITA but that it would proceed cautiously to minimise the possibility of hostile domestic reaction in the US. The communiqué added that US personnel would visit UNITA territory to assess the movement's needs.[6] And on 29 March the *Sunday Telegraph* of London quoted diplomatic sources in Pretoria as saying three or four 'American military experts had made clandestine visits to [UNITA] guerrilla bases'. At the same time, South African military intelligence chiefs were making an unprecedented visit to Washington, where they were received by senior officials, including the US Ambassador to the United Nations, Mrs Jeane Kirkpatrick.[7]

Soon, details of the Reagan plan for the region, linking the independence of Namibia with a Cuban withdrawal from Angola, began to leak out. Administration officials believed that key African countries would have no choice other than to accept the plan, the *New York Times* reported in a front-page story from Washington. The newspaper said it had obtained access to a confidential Administration memorandum which said: 'African leaders would have no basis for resisting the Namibia-Angola linkage once they are made to realise they can only get a Namibia settlement through us, and that we are serious about getting such a settlement.'[8]

The starting point for the US Administration's thinking was that South Africa had to be coaxed into co-operation. UN-imposed sanctions, which were being called for by the majority of black African states, would not push South Africa to comply with demands to give Namibia its independence, the argument went: they would have the opposite effect and make South Africa more intransigent.

For the US this would mean in practice strengthening ties with South Africa, through symbols like official visits, which would end South Africa's pariah status; offering South

Africa more conciliatory – and, therefore, practically more feasible – terms for getting out of Namibia, using the prospect of a South African military withdrawal from Namibia as a lever for a Cuban withdrawal from Angola to be followed by an MPLA/UNITA power-sharing arrangement. Finally, the co-operation of black African states with all of this was to be secured with a promise of open elections in Namibia.

The new American proposals required agreement on a constitution for Namibia before elections were held under international supervision to pave the way for independence. The previous plan, put forward by the UN, envisaged an election for a constituent assembly which would then draft a constitution – the losers of the election under this system would thus also have lost the opportunity of making sure their rights were constitutionally protected.

The US policy was christened 'constructive engagement' because it involved South Africa as a recognised and legitimate participant in a general process of change in the southern and central African region, instead of as the accused in the dock.

The author of the memorandum obtained by the *New York Times* was Chester Crocker, the Professor of African Studies at Georgetown University, Washington, who had been nominated by Reagan as his Under-Secretary of State for African Affairs. Crocker was seen as intelligent but conservative by Carter/Kennedy-inclined liberal Democrats. But he was regarded as a dangerous liberal by the Republican right wing in Congress, who withheld confirmation of his nomination for several months.

Crocker was probably too cerebral for many of the right-wing Congressmen, and if they had read carefully his writings on southern Africa at the time they should have been able to see that his proposals for the region were by no means conventionally liberal. In the particular case of Angola, they spelled problems for the MPLA/Cubans for years to come.

In one article in particular he set down with great clarity the philosophy which would guide the Reagan Administration's policy on Angola and Namibia through the following years.[9] With the benefit of hindsight, Croker's article should have been compulsory reading for anyone interested in the Angola/Namibia problem.

On the problem of the closely interlocked conflicts, Crocker noted that, according to one school of thought, Namibia was at the top of the Western calendar, while the Angolan war was hardly on it at all. Somehow the Soviet-Cuban presence was legitimate or justified until Namibia was settled and UNITA defeated. But Crocker argued differently, presenting it less as his own view than as one held by many centrists and conservatives in America and Europe, as well as by the governments of China and most moderate and conservative Arab states.

'Angola is the logical focal point for policy,' he said. 'It is in Angola, after all, that anticommunist forces are effectively engaged in trying to liberate their country from the new imperialism of Moscow and its allies.

'This process should be encouraged with the aim of getting the Cubans out so that a genuine political reconciliation can take place. As for Namibia, while a settlement is important there, it will not by itself end the Angolan strife, because Savimbi is by no means the tool of South Africa. He could continue to operate with the active support of other African states and governments elsewhere. Accordingly, the West should back UNITA until such time as the MPLA is prepared to negotiate and to expel the communist forces from Angola. Namibia, according to this argument, is a separate and less important issue.'

Crocker, however, warned Washington about the dangers of being seen to back UNITA outright. It could produce an escalation of conflict and rule out the possibility of responding to frequent MPLA hints of a desire to reduce sharply their Soviet-Cuban ties.

He argued: 'The United States would serve its own best interests by admitting publicly the legitimacy of the UNITA struggle and maintaining the pressure for a departure by communist combat forces . . . We should identify with the desire of Angolans themselves to rid their land of foreign troops and the fighting they represent.'

So Crocker was arguing that it might be counter-productive to be seen to be supporting UNITA openly. He said nothing about the corollary that there might be advantages in encouraging, or persuading, or even paying others to back the Angolan insurgency. He made no comment upon the pros and cons of laundering American aid through third parties.

But one thing was sure. A very clever man with a low profile was taking up the poisoned chalice of southern Africa for the Reagan Administration. And he was a man with respect for the African continent as a whole, who did not see things in stark black and white, and who recognised that central and southern Africa were greatly rich and complex beyond the imaginations of many European and North American ideologists who saw the truth as simple. 'The region will be shaped by forces more substantial and concrete than journalistic conventions like *racist regimes* or *Marxist guerrillas*,' wrote Crocker.

* * *

Reagan and Crocker were good news for Savimbi – but there was also bad news. Members of UNITA's urban cells continued to pay the highest price if they were caught, as when 18 of them were sentenced to death in March 1981 for planting a bomb on a Luanda commuter train.[10]

Allegations began to be made of direct military co-operation between UNITA and certain SADF battalions based on the Namibia-Angola border, and in particular the 32nd or Buffalo Battalion. The 1,200-strong Buffalo Battalion was led by 25 white SADF officers, including at one time a Colonel Carpenter who, the MPLA alleged, had commanded South African troops during the 1975–76 invasion of Angola.[11] All the officers were South African, except one, Captain Christopher Clay, an American Vietnam veteran.[12] What he was now doing in Namibia was not made clear from accounts by journalists who met him.

The Buffalo Battalion's non-commissioned officers were mainly white mercenaries of Rhodesian, French, British, Portuguese and American origin. However, the ordinary soldiers were black Angolans who had formerly been in the FNLA and had sought refuge in Namibia after their movement's series of defeats between 1975 and 1978.

In 1980 two members of the Buffalo Battalion deserted, a British mercenary NCO and a black Angolan infantryman. They both alleged military collaboration between the SADF and UNITA.

The Briton, Trevor Edwards, became a mercenary soldier with the Rhodesian armed forces in 1978 and then signed a one-year contract with the SADF in March 1980. Edwards claimed, in January 1981, to a British newspaper that he had been a member of a 300-man force from the Buffalo Battalion that had driven 75 kilometres into Angola the previous May and stopped near Savate.[13] On 21 May 1980 the white officers blacked their faces and led their former FNLA troops in an attack on the MPLA battalion stationed there. The Buffalo Battalion took the town after losing ten FNLA and six white troops. 'There were no SWAPO at Savate,' said Edwards. 'It was a base for Angolan government soldiers and we knew that when we went in there.'

During the battle for Savate two UNITA representatives were at the Buffalo Battalion's companies' tactical headquarters, Edwards alleged. When the battle was over they walked into the town and claimed it for UNITA.

Edwards said the Buffalo Battalion often behaved with murderous brutality, sometimes killing civilians after they had been interrogated and taking Angolan soldiers back to their Namibian base at the western end of the Caprivi Strip for questioning: 'Sometimes you have to do it to the children to make the adults talk. There was a 12-year-old boy. We wanted to know what was going on. We wanted his mother to talk, so we tied him up like a chicken with his wrists up behind his back, strapped to his ankles. Then we played water polo with him, put him in this kind of dam and pushed him about, let him sink. Every so often we took him out. He wouldn't cry. He just wet himself. The mother didn't tell us anything. In the end we just left him in the water and he drowned. I just don't like that kind of thing.'

Private Jose Ricardo Belmundo, the FNLA deserter, gave his evidence on the Buffalo Battalion in Luanda to an 'International Commission of Inquiry into the Crimes of the Racist and Apartheid Regimes of Southern Africa'. The Commission was composed of MPLA sympathisers from East

Germany, Chile, France, Belgium and the United States.[14]

Belmundo, who had joined the FNLA in 1973, said he had deserted the Buffalo Battalion in January 1980 by crossing the Angolan border and surrendering to MPLA troops at Calai. He said the battalion's main operations area was Cunene Province, against SWAPO and MPLA targets. But he added: 'Whenever UNITA had operational difficulties it would contact South African military security. The South African security officials – for example, Colonel du Plessis – would call on 32 Battalion to organise a force to go in and get UNITA out of trouble. We would go and operate on behalf of UNITA in UNITA regions (in Cuando Cubango Province).'

Belmundo said Buffalo Battalion officers went on South African Air Force night flights to supervise the parachuting of food, weapons and other supplies to UNITA. Officers also gave instruction at UNITA camps inside Angola, particularly at Mucusso, just a few kilometres north-west of the Buffalo Battalion's central base at Bagani at the western end of Namibia's Caprivi Strip.

Savimbi denied the allegations by Belmondo and Edwards. Of the Englishman's claim that two UNITA soldiers had stood by to claim Savate in UNITA's name after 32 Battalion's attack, he said: 'It is too beautiful to be true, because if we wanted to take over a town after the South Africans have attacked it we are not going to send just two people.'

Neither Edwards' nor Belmundo's allegations could be trusted, said Savimbi. Recalling the desertion of the French mercenaries when the going became very rough in March 1976 (see Chapter 20), Savimbi said: 'It has become one of the principles of our organisation that mercenaries can become useless. Anyone who wants money put into his bank account before you take him into your war cannot allow himself to die because he has to go to enjoy that money you put in his bank. Always his preference will be to withdraw from serious combat.

'I don't believe the stories told by Edwards and Belmundo because a deserter is always a dangerous man. He will exaggerate for mercenary purposes or to ingratiate himself.'[15]

Far away from the scene, it was difficult for anyone to make sense of the claims and counter-claims in the conflict. So in June 1981, when I received an invitation from Savimbi to visit his territory in south-east Angola, I accepted. It was time to stop sifting through words and go back to see for myself at least a part of the truth.

34

Return to Angola

1981

The Zambezi had been crossed. Thousands of feet below stretched endless expanses of forest marbled by thick veins of savannah grasses. We were over Angola and somewhere down there was a black guerrilla army.

A thin, olive-green oblong appeared in the forest below. As we dipped and circled I could see dancers dressed in bright red and green, soldiers and a convoy of trucks.

We touched down on the sandy, grass-covered strip to the sound of music. The swaying dancers were singing in the rich descants and harmonies of the Bantu people of central and southern Africa: the music's spirit made the spine tingle. The words were propagandist, largely in praise of the big, full-bearded man with a general's three gold stars on his green beret who stood some 100 metres away, surrounded by aides.

Savimbi was waiting for us, carrying a silver-tipped ebony baton and wearing a dark green commando jacket and green trousers tucked into highly polished combat boots.

My journalist companion was Dick Harwood, Managing Editor of the *Washington Post*, a grizzled US Marine Corps veteran of Iwojima and a deeply experienced reporter who had covered Kennedy campaign trails and the Vietnam war. In addition the plane had brought several UNITA representatives from abroad, including Tito Chingunji, based in London, and Dr Jeremias Chitunda, based in Washington. While emotional reunions went on – much hugging and kissing on both cheeks – I observed some of the UNITA troops. They were much better equipped than when

I was last in Angola in 1976. They carried Soviet Kalashnikov AK-47 rifles, the classic guerrilla light weapon, and Soviet RPG-7 rocket launchers. There were Chinese 12.7 mm anti-aircraft guns along the strip and, most interestingly of all, there were SAM-7 ground-to-air missiles. UNITA's claim to have these simple but deadly weapons had been greeted with scepticism in the outside world. Harwood and I were the first reporters to see them.

The truck convoy – Polish Stars, Soviet Zils and VW Unimogs – had been unloading $US 40,000 worth of medical equipment and drugs from the plane. Savimbi got into his personal Land Rover with his bodyguard and we were assigned to Stars, sturdy, functional vehicles delivered by Poland to the MPLA and since captured by UNITA.

We bumped over deeply rutted tracks, gears grinding. In the last suffused orange glow of the day I could see water buck in the distance. Suddenly it was dark and the head-lights were switched on. If there was any possibility of attack by Cuban or government troops, the guerrillas didn't seem worried. The choristers continued to sing merrily and loudly on the back of the trucks.

Forty-five minutes later we sighted a camp fire. Across the track was a frontier-type pole: armed guards identified Savimbi, saluted and raised the gate. We entered an area where fires glowed every 100–150 metres in all directions. It was difficult to see people, but they were definitely out there because Dick and I could hear more singing and laughter. It was clear that the camp was spacious because we drove through it for another ten minutes before halting.

We were ushered to our huts. Mine was big and rectangular, a framework of tree poles covered with thatched elephant grass and built beneath overhanging tree branches. It was divided into two compartments. In one was a thatched bed, and in the other a thatched chair and an armchair and a writing table made from woven saplings. A wood fire burned on the sandy floor of the hut and there was a small paraffin wick lamp. Outside, by their own fire, sat two guerrillas, one cradling a Kalashnikov.

Hot water for washing arrived, followed by dinner, borne by two good-looking, well-built girl guerrillas. The menu:

thick and tasty rice, potato, tomato and onion soup, orange juice, strawberry jam between protein biscuits, black coffee.

A moment I'd been dreading arrived – a visit to a guerrilla loo. I had visions of hideous toilet arrangements. A guerrilla guard guided me through the murky undergrowth, and there was a splendid pit latrine – deep dug, covered by a thick layer of branches, twigs and sand with a small central hole, and surrounded by a thatched fence. UNITA obviously had efficient public health experts in its ranks.

Later, I sat for a while by my guards' fire. The night was magic. Overhead was an immense canopy of sparkling jewels; shooting stars made a celestial fireworks display. The moon came up – a huge, deep red disc, as though it had absorbed all the blood shed in this tragic land. Bourbon-slugging, hard-bitten old Dick later betrayed a sentimental side when he described it as 'a beauty to make the heart ache'.

I watched my guards prepare their own dinner. It was frugal: maize porridge and a few cubes of boiled meat cut from a hunk of dried, blackened antelope flesh they carried in their back-pack. It was swigged down with water from a tin hip-flask. Occasionally, they said, they varied the diet with fried grubs coated with wild honey.

The guerrillas slept under the stars by the fire. They spread their groundsheet and dug a little trench around it to deter some of Angola's many small crawling creatures. (I found a small, milk-white scorpion in one of my boots one morning.) Each man curled up clothed beneath his one blanket. Weapon and back-pack, with rolled groundsheet and blanket on top, were all the material wealth each guerrilla had in the world.

UNITA's was an unpaid volunteer army, offering only food, comradeship and a chance to die for a particular vision of Angola. Savimbi argued during our visit that he had more than 20,000 men under arms. In a British television documentary screened in early 1981, John Stockwell repeated his assertion that there were no more than 300 UNITA guerrillas, all poorly armed.

We would have to see.

* * *

The next morning, 26 June, was glorious: the air cool and as clear as crystal, the sky bright blue and cloudless. The first event was a meeting with Savimbi in a circular conference hut. From his big grass chair he briefed us on how he saw the political and military situation. We were just a few miles from Luengue, captured from government forces in June 1980, since when UNITA had pushed a lot further northwards. The more widely publicised fighting in Angola at that time between South African troops and SWAPO had taken place some 1,000 kilometres away in the south-west, Savimbi said.

UNITA's President asked us what we wanted to see. UNITA was claiming absolute control of territory the size of England as deep as 350 kilometres into Angola, so we asked to be taken to Mavinga, 250 kilometres inside Angola which both the government and UNITA were claiming to hold. We wanted also to see as many troops as possible; UNITA's claimed massive hauls of captured weapons; the movement's Soviet, Cuban, Portuguese and MPLA prisoners; its schools; its bush churches; its hospitals; and its collective farms.

All would be done said Savimbi. So we began.

*   *   *

Forty-eight hours later we were in Mavinga. We had inspected a newly-trained battalion of 700 troops *en route*, seen the wreckage of an Antonov-26 bomber shot down by one of UNITA's SAM-7s, and we had kept on moving through day and through night. The guerrillas had forged a snaking and twisting trail northwards over forest ridges, through savannah in river valleys and across fords. The Savimbi Trail, UNITA's equivalent of the Ho Chi Minh Trail, along which the Vietcong transported supplies to South Vietnam, penetrated more than 300 kilometres northwards into Angola from the Namibian border.

Dick and I each travelled in the cabs of Stars. Although we rarely exceeded 25 kilometres an hour, it was like riding bucking broncos as we constantly bumped over ruts and bounced off trees. It must have been hell, especially at night, for the thinly clothed guerrillas packed uncomfortably together on the open backs of the trucks. We were into the southern African winter, when night temperatures dip below freezing.

We had a number of breakdowns. The transmission blew on one truck and the fan belt snapped on another. When headlights were smashed against tree-trunks, cab lights were cannibalised to illumine the way dimly.

We began to get to know the guerrillas better. Jimmy Lois Muecalia, a brilliant young linguist, was our translator. As well as his tribal language and Portuguese, he spoke fluent English and French and passable Russian and Spanish – and yet he had never been out of Angola. Honorio and Chimoko were my personal bodyguards. Annabella, Linette and Elizet were the girls who washed our socks and did the cooking.

About 60 guerrillas were in the convoy. They came from Savimbi's élite 500-strong battalion of bodyguards. 'They would be ruthless with anyone who tried to kill President Savimbi,' said Jimmy. 'They have been trained to a point where they would die themselves rather than let the President be killed.' They looked efficient. At every halt they quickly but calmly formed skirmish perimeters with Kalashnikovs, mortars and grenade launchers. Most were scarcely out of their teens, so I assumed they had been recruited since the 1975–76 civil war.

Dick discovered that many of the guerrillas had interesting war names – Lonely, Gringo, Red Sun, Angola, Big Rat, Long Journey. Gringo was a popular name because in all the movies they had seen the gringos won the gunfights.

Our entry into Mavinga was like a clip from *High Noon*. No one stirred . . . because no one was there. To UNITA it was a precious jewel, a tangible symbol of its capacity to attack and defeat, in open country, a modern army of Angolan troops backed up by Cuban soldiers and Soviet logistical help. Later, Savimbi was to give us his version of the details of the battles for Mavinga.

Eventually dust stirred at the far end of the main street. Major Wenda Catata approached. He was commander of UNITA's 327 Battalion who were guarding the town. He invited us to inspect his troops, deeply entrenched beyond, but not inside, the town.

Mavinga had a useful airstrip. At one end of it were the

graves of MPLA soldiers who Major Catata said had died in the battles for the town. The ground was littered with spent munitions and there was a Star truck stuck in the crater blown by the land mine it had run over.

We photographed the troops, the wrecked buildings and the Mavinga town sign. Then it was back to our personal Stars for another body-bruising, all-night and all-day journey.

Eventually we reached a forest called Uantomba: troops lined the track for a couple of kilometres dancing, singing and waving Kalashnikovs and blazing wood torches in the air. I was barely conscious. It had been three nights and four days since I was last in a bed. I was shown to a dug-out hut – a deep pit covered by a grass cone. I realised from the dug-out that we must be in a combat area; then I fell into the deepest sleep of my life.

*   *   *.

I woke next morning to the sound of music and tramping feet. Squads and platoons were beginning their daily routine, marching and singing as they went. The soldiers were in fine fettle. Two months earlier they had been involved in the biggest of the battles for Mavinga: Savimbi claimed they had wiped out 500 MPLA troops.

A big parade had been arranged for this day – it was now June 29 – by the 1,400 men of 210 and 275 Battalions. It was to be addressed by N'Zau Puna and Lt.-Col. Demostenes Chilingutila, UNITA's chief field commander. Chilingutila had gained his expertise as an officer in the Portuguese Army fighting, among others, UNITA.

The marching, weapons drill, singing and dancing were spectacular. But the main event was a morality play. On the big, open parade ground Leonid Brezhnev, Fidel Castro and Agostinho Neto greeted each other in exaggerated fashion as *companeros* (brothers) before driving a devil's bargain. Brezhnev and Castro would send arms and men to Angola to drive out the UNITA *fantoches*. Neto would give them the country's diamonds, oil, coffee and fish in payment. In the next act Cuban soldiers arrived and began killing Angolan peasants – giving the soldiers full scope to display their acting talents – while in the forest UNITA was recruiting and training guerrillas. Finally, UNITA attacked and Brezhnev and Castro were driven from Angola.

Simplistic stuff, but it had the troops cheering and laughing deliriously.

It was time to move on again. We could either head south and see Savimbi's farms, schools, workshops, churches, Soviet prisoners, Cuban deserters and captured weapons; or we could go north with guerrilla companies, penetrating on foot behind Cuban and MPLA lines, sleeping in villages nominally under MPLA rule. 'The villagers receive the MPLA with songs during the day, but during the night they give information to UNITA,' said Lt.-Col. Chilingutila. 'We tell the local population to receive the MPLA, to say they are with them and that they no longer have anything to do with UNITA.'

The only Western journalist to have previously taken the northern option was the *Washington Post*'s courageous Leon Dash on his epic 1977 trip.

We took the southern option.

Ahead there still lay many amazing experiences, but I had begun to answer the question I went there with. I had already learned enough about Jonas Savimbi over the years to know that he would never give up his struggle. But did he have any real chance of winning against apparently daunting odds?

At only the half-way point of my trip, I was already astonished by the evidence of the organisation he had built up. In all the long years of struggle by Robert Mugabe's ZANU, the movement was never able to land planes in Rhodesia or move about in trucks, as UNITA does in Angola. Mugabe never led ZANU from bases in Rhodesia as Savimbi does UNITA from bases in Angola. Savimbi's attributes I was already aware of, but I had also grown to admire the personal qualities of the Africans I had been with over these few days – their remarkable hardiness, patience, humour, dedication, discipline, self-reliance and sheer joyousness.

We had already seen 3,000 well-armed troops. I didn't know whether UNITA had any hope of winning the war outright. But I had seen enough to be sure that the Cubans, Russians and MPLA could never win it either. And according to the textbooks of guerrilla warfare that is equivalent to defeat for the governing side.

35

Russians and Cubans

1981

From Uantomba we struck south-eastwards towards Savimbi's headquarters called Jamba, near Bambangando, about 80 kilometres north of the Namibian border and 50 kilometres from Zambia. The journey through immense stretches of forest and savannah seemed endless. The Portuguese called this region 'The Land at the End of the Earth', treating it as a great hunting reserve. There were herds of elephant, zebra and wildebeest. Ostriches ran beside us for kilometres at a time with their geese-sized chicks scurrying behind. The guerrillas shot some guinea fowl and a couple of small buck for the pot.

It was a couple of days before we saw other human beings. First, a Soviet-made petrol tanker, with a UNITA driver, passed in the opposite direction. Then in the distance, across a great savannah, we saw a red tractor ploughing. Jimmy Muecalia told us we were passing along the boundary of one of UNITA's collective farms. The tractor was preparing for the next maize crop. But we did not stop. We had an urgent appointment with UNITA's Soviet prisoners.

We stopped in late afternoon in a shady forest clearing containing scattered huts. The two heavily-bearded Soviets arrived just before dusk – by Polish Star, of course, one in the cab and the other on the open back. They had clearly not seen each other for some time because they exchanged affectionate slaps and conversed hastily as they stepped down from the truck surrounded by guards toting Kalashnikovs. We shook hands with the two Soviets and, after a quick photo session, we walked with them into one of the huts for an interview.

Mollaeb Kolya, then 39, a pilot, said that on 22 November 1980 he was at the controls of a Soviet-made Antonov-26 transport plane of the Angolan civil airline TAAG when it took off from Mpupa, 40 kilometres north of the Namibian border. Mpupa at the time was an MPLA base and Kolya had been ferrying troops between it and other MPLA outposts. (Mpupa had since fallen into UNITA's hands.) After take-off he climbed northwards. When the plane had reached 3,000 metres 'something' – a SAM-7 missile, said UNITA – hit the right outboard engine and part of the wing disintegrated.

Jimmy Muecalia did the translating. He had learned Russian while living with the Soviets throughout the first seven months of their captivity. Kolya said: 'I calculated we had ten kilometres before the plane hit the ground. I passed over some trees and put it down in high grass between the Cuito River and the forest.' He hurt his back in the crash-landing but, fearing an explosion, he managed to run from the burning wreckage. He lay dazed for some time but gained consciousness and went to the river to wash his face. He heard shooting and when he saw soldiers approaching he raised his hands.

Ivan Chernietsky, a 47-year-old aircraft engineer from Kiev, said he lay stunned after the crash for about four hours before he became aware of a group of Africans firing with automatic weapons. They took him prisoner and, with Kolya, he walked with the UNITA guerrillas and then travelled by truck before reaching his first place of captivity. Chernietsky said he and Kolya were employees of the Soviet Union's state airline Aeroflot, working on contract with TAAG. When the plane crashed it was taking 19 MPLA soldiers on leave from Mpupa. The soldiers appeared to have survived the crash and escaped capture.

Kolya said he was confident it was a civilian contract he had entered to come to Angola. 'In the Soviet Union I didn't know the war was continuing, so when I heard people in Luanda talking about the war I thought it was a trifle.' This evoked a splutter of rage from N'Zau Puna: 'You see what a liar he is.' Puna seemed determined to bludgeon us into his belief that both were military men well trained in the art of disinformation. We were unable to reach any conclusions about them, though Aeroflot is regarded in the USSR as an adjunct to the air force. Both handled our more loaded questions with dignity and aplomb. We interviewed each airman separately. But when asked their opinions of, for example, the morale of the Cubans or their own personal feelings about Angola they shrugged laconically and said these were questions that only 'specialists' could answer.

Within the limits of forest conditions, where the Soviets were living in elephant-grass huts, Kolya said he was being well treated. He missed his wife and two children in Moscow – though he was originally from Turkestan – and he missed being able to exchange ideas with friends, listen to the radio and read newspapers and books. He had no writing materials. Chernietsky, the more stoical of the two, said he had lived in Luanda for two years before the crash. He had made no friends among the Cubans because of language differences. In captivity he spent his time walking three kilometres twice a day from his hut to a nearby river and playing cards with his guards. He ate rice, macaroni, maize porridge, fish and antelope meat. Kolya said he believed the Soviet Union would initiate action to secure their release. Tears welled as he said: 'If I have to stay here for years I will die.' Asked what he was missing most, he laughed and said: 'Freedom.'

Kolya's and Chernietsky's chances of release looked slim. Later, Savimbi said they would be released only if the Soviet Union made an official, open request to UNITA acknowledging that the airmen were taken prisoner during a military action on Angolan territory.

*   *   *

The next morning two young Cuban soldiers were brought to the clearing. They were deserters, UNITA said. Neither of us found attractive the over-chumminess of one of the Cubans with his guards: it looked entirely like an attempt to play to the UNITA gallery; it made us highly suspicious of what might have been his true accounts of village massacres by Cubans.

Privates Miguel Edade, 21, and Angel Paulo Mojena, 19, said they had walked out of their base at Matale, the site of a major hydro-electric dam 500 kilometres north of the Namibian border, at midnight on 22 November 1980 for a pre-arranged meeting with a local woman who took them to the nearest UNITA base. They said they had deserted because Cuban soldiers in forward areas suffered food and clothing shortages. 'In Matale we had no spare trousers and some soldiers had no boots,' said Edade, the over-chummy one, beaming at his UNITA guards for approval.

Edade and Mojena said there were sharp differences between Cuban officers and other ranks. They said their 24-month tour of duty had been extended arbitrarily and indefinitely: they had been in the country for 26 months when they deserted. Officers, Edade said, did tours of 13-14 months and were sent home every six months for a month's leave. Both confirmed that Cuban Army units in Angola had withdrawn from frontline fighting since early 1980 and were now only giving logistics and command support.

Mojena alleged that in 1980 MPLA troops ran away from battles for Cuangar and Savate, the small towns near the Namibian border which UNITA claims were its first victories in its campaign to establish absolute control of south-east Angola. Mojena said the MPLA retreats were attempts to force the Cubans into battle against UNITA. The Cubans declined the challenge.

Edade, from Bajo Largo Las Mercedes in Cuba's Granma (formerly Oriente) Province, and Mojena, from Bartolomez Maso, Granma Province, both joined the Cuban Army on the same day, 14 August 1978. After only 19 days, 12 of them spent in military training, they were sailing for Angola on the troopship *13 March*.

Mojena, a 16-year-old student when he signed up, said a brother-in-law in the Military Commission assured him that his role in the Army would be as a teacher on an 'internationalist assignment'. When he arrived in Angola he was sent for another month's infantry training: he heard nothing again about teaching duties.

Both were posted with Cuba's 6259 regiment in Menongue from October 1978 to April 1980. In that period Edade estimated the Cuban death toll in the area as 37, while Mojena put it at 32, mainly in ambushes of convoys outside the town. There had been 'many' MPLA casualties and helicopters frequently left Menongue to recover dead and wounded from ambush sites. Both said they had been told they would be fighting South Africans in Angola. They had seen no action against white soldiers, but plenty against Africans.

Edade said that before it was decided to withdraw Cubans from frontline fighting he had taken part in attacks to destroy villages and crops and that local peasants, including women and children, had been killed. 'After one attack,' he said, 'the MPLA announced that 300 UNITA people had been captured, but they were just women, children and old men. MPLA morale is very low because many of the soldiers realise that killing Angolans is not correct. MPLA patrols advance, bombard with artillery, and report without evidence that they have destroyed UNITA bases.'

Edade claimed that on one occasion UNITA civilians had been taken up in a Cuban helicopter and pushed out by MPLA soldiers. Dick recalled that it was one of the favourite horror stories told about Americans in Vietnam when he was a correspondent there. He said it was apocryphal then and he guessed that Edade's story was apocryphal now.

Both men said they had come to hate Fidel Castro. They wanted to stay with UNITA: they did not want to seek asylum in any Western country.[1] We took some pictures of them posing with UNITA troops, Annabella, Elizet, Linette and some other women. As we left they were laughing and joking with their Angolan protectors.

36

Giant Cabbages and Forest Secretaries

1981

We were now nearing Savimbi's headquarters. After all we had seen, there were many questions we wanted to ask him. Like how did he finance his operation? And, more importantly, where did the South Africans fit in? That was the essential issue as far as Western politicians, interest groups and newspaper editors were concerned. The internal affairs of Angola and the fate of its people were of little more interest to them than those of a host of other black African nations which the West sees as doomed to endless destructive unrest and maladministration.

But before we met him there were still things we had to see.

* * *

En route, we stopped at the 'Resistance' agricultural collective farm. We walked through the main gate over a carpet of frangipani and rose petals: women lined the path, waving palm fronds and swaying gently as they sang songs of welcome. It's a custom I find delightful, and I was as moved by it in 1981 as when I first experienced it in Angola in 1975.

Captain Dario Catata greeted us. He was 'Director of the National Agricultural Plan', with a brief to make UNITA self-sufficient in food. In his first three-and-a half years Catata had built a network of collective and experimental farms, agricultural schools and advisory services for traditional peasant farmers. At the 'Resistance' collective Catata showed us stems from the recently harvested maize crop lying in great fields between the Luengue River and the forest edge. There were leopard spoor and hippo footprints in the mud of the fields. About six acres were given to tomatoes, peppers, onions, beans and tobacco. Catata cut a giant cabbage for us to eat with our next meal. He showed us pits where compost made of elephant and buffalo droppings, leaves and wood ash was maturing. There were seed beds raised above ground level on log platforms to minimise attacks by rodents and other pests.

Catata said the 'Resistance' collective – one of eight established to that date – had harvested 150 tonnes of maize that year from 54 hectares. The target for the next season was 350 tonnes using higher-yielding seeds on an expanded area of 100 hectares. The farm was jointly owned by local villagers and the UNITA military. The villagers gave one morning of labour each week in exchange for time on their private plots by the collective's tractor. Two villages of about 200 people each worked in co-operation with the 'Resistance'. The chief of one village, Kavanga Linguembe, a Nganguela, said he had brought his people from their tribal area 400 kilometres to the north in May 1980 after the MPLA began confiscating cattle and taking people to the town.

Attached to the collective was an agricultural school run by the Technical Director of the 'Resistance', Gusmao Chicosse, a former agricultural officer under the Portuguese. He had 19 students who had completed secondary science courses under the Portuguese and MPLA. They would train for three months before going out to establish new farms and service centres. Catata said there were four similar schools on other collectives. The collectives and service centres provided seeds, technical advice and, when available, fertilisers to the peasants for their private plots. Advice and seeds, said Catata, were also given to peasants and guerrillas in zones beyond those totally controlled by UNITA.

Catata claimed that UNITA would be totally self-sufficient in food by the end of 1981. Meanwhile, additional food came from neighbouring Namibia and Zambia. Impressive though UNITA's attempts were at developing previously uncultivated land, we had seen too little to be able to assess how realistic Captain Catata's forecast was.

Before we left the 'Resistance' we met seven Portuguese men with huge beards and long hair who had been prisoners of UNITA for up to four years. In captivity with them were eleven women and child relatives. These Lusitanian Rip Van Winkles had been captured from various places in MPLA-administered areas of central Angola. Senhor Jorge de Freitas, a 27-year-old shopkeeper, said the UNITA base he was taken to after capture was only 15 kilometres from his village, Que-Chikomba. 'We had never suspected it was there,' he said. 'I am sure that the local population had been in touch with UNITA all the time, otherwise the guerrillas could not have survived.' After the attack he and his family had been marched 1,000 kilometres to their present place of detention. Jorge was deeply worried about his four-year-old daughter, Iola Ximene, who needed a hernia operation. He was also concerned about her future education. 'There are four children in the camp. We are not teaching them. We are poorly educated people; we have no training.' He said he and his wife had thought of going to Portugal after Angola became independent, but his father-in-law had been in Angola for 34 years and did not want to leave. 'And, anyway, what was there to go to in Portugal? I had a daughter, and in Portugal I had nothing to give her. And so we stayed on because what little we had in the world was here in Angola.'

N'Zau Puna, present throughout the interview with the Portuguese, said they could go free tomorrow if either the Portuguese government or the International Committee of the Red Cross (ICRC) made an official request for their release and provided a plane to take them home. The Portuguese were pawns in a game UNITA was playing, in deadly earnest, for recognition of its cause. With Portugal siding firmly with the MPLA, things needed to be done to sow doubt in the minds of the former colonial rulers about the wisdom of their judgment. Senhor Antonio Nunes Neves (57), who had lived in Angola for 40 years, said the group was distressed that Portugal seemed to be doing little to secure their release. He went on: 'When the Polisario Front captured 15 Portuguese fishermen off the coast of Western Sahara (in early 1981), Portugal did its best for them and secured their freedom in 45 days – we have been here for 16 months, 28 months, four years, and for us Portugal is doing nothing.'

Towards the end of the interview one of the Portuguese asked N'Zau Puna if they could have a radio. They were desperate for sports news, and especially football results, from Portugal. Dick gave them the last of his cigarettes and promised to send them a radio when he returned home to Washington. We shook hands and left.

* * *

It was 10 p.m. when we reached the outskirts of Savimbi's camp, a kind of spreadeagled forest city, with strategic centres scattered several kilometres apart. We passed through gates and men, women and children lined the route singing and holding aloft blazing torches in the darkness. As our convoy passed they closed in and ran behind until there was a great phalanx of people bringing up the rear. At one gate, from whose arch a huge sign in English proclaimed 'Entering Free Angola', there was a ritual which upset Dick. A guard demanded that we hand over our passports. Dick envisaged a UNITA stamp being put in his passport which would complicate his future travel. The guard, after some persuasion by N'Zau Puna, agreed to leave our passports untouched.

We walked the last kilometre with singing people milling around us. As we washed and ate, the singing and dancing continued around our latest elephant grass homes. We went out to join the crowds later, and when we crawled into our sleeping bags in the early hours the party was still going on.

* * *

The next morning our first appointment was with 25-year-old Miss Anna Kulipossa. She had been sent by UNITA to Paris from 1977 to 1979 for advanced secretarial training. Savimbi's guerrilla state has administrators, and administrators need secretaries to type up officials' scrawled reports and to maintain records. It was Miss Kulipossa's revolutionary duty to produce these secretaries. We met her in the big grass hut which was her school. She was wearing a demure but smart Parisian suit and high heels. Under her watchful eye 20 African girls were learning to touch-type on ranks of typewriters, and in a separate compartment of the hut another four were unravelling the mysteries of a Roneo duplicator. During their six-month courses, Miss Kulipossa's girls were also studying shorthand, Portuguese, French and English.

*   *   *

We passed quickly through an adult literacy class and an open-air primary school before being taken to UNITA's hospital complex. We were asked to cover our filthy bush suits with sparkling white surgical gowns. We were also given gauze face masks. We were ushered into a mud hut. Inside a man lay covered by a sheet on an operating table lit by bulbs powered from a mobile generator of Soviet origin. The surgeon, dressed in white and wearing thin rubber surgical gloves, nodded to his anaesthetist to inject the patient. One of seven other assistants walked to a steriliser and removed a steaming towel wrap of surgical instruments.

Ninety minutes later, the surgeon removed the patient's appendix nodded his thanks to the anaesthetist and the rest of the team, and began stitching the wound.

Remarkably, none of the surgical team were qualified doctors. The surgeon, 50-year-old Martins Kayotela, had learned his skills over 20 years as a theatre nurse in a Protestant mission hospital in central Angola. He had been with Savimbi for part of the long march of 1976. The hospital director, Paulino Dungue, a male nurse, said UNITA had 21 other bush hospitals where operations were performed by surgeons with qualifications similar to Kayotela's. Dungue introduced me to UNITA's only qualified physician, Dr Adelino Manassas, a general practitioner who had been kidnapped from MPLA-held Huambo in 1979. Dr Manassas, 30, had a peculiar status. Though he had been working with the enemy, his skills were badly needed by UNITA. And though he was effectively a prisoner, he had real status in the hospital. He seemed to be on good terms with his captors-cum-colleagues. He said he badly missed his wife and two young children, with whom he had been able to exchange two letters through the ICRC.

* * *

Our next meeting was with the 'Menongue Eleven'. They were currently high in the UNITA pantheon of heroes. Sentenced by an MPLA court in Menongue on 17 March 1981 to be shot within 48 hours for terrorist activities, they escaped when fellow prisoners – UNITA activists serving life sentences – passed them spoons to dig through the brick and plaster walls of toilets adjoining their cells. They broke through at night into an unlit compound. They simply yanked up the bottom strands of the surrounding wire fence and went to a UNITA safe house, from where they were guided to one of the guerrilla camps in the forest outside the town.

The Eleven said that while holding jobs with the Government as teachers, male nurses and civil servants they had collected intelligence, distributed UNITA pamphlets, laid mines on tracks used by MPLA and Cuban vehicles, and planted bombs in the local military bakery, power station and radio station. All Eleven were members of the Nganguela tribe. Their spokesman, Jorge Cambinda, a 34-year-old primary schoolteacher, said few of the Eleven had known each other as UNITA sympathisers before they were arrested. They had operated in small, tight cells directed by forward UNITA military posts. Cambinda said it was no longer possible in Menongue to tell who were the real sympathisers of the MPLA. UNITA activists were under instruction to give an appearance of loyalty to the Government, and MPLA soldiers had on occasion helped the UNITA underground to place explosives. There was a deep level of frustration throughout the 25,000 population because of food shortages, long queues outside near-empty stores and poor health care by allegedly incompetent Cuban *medicos*. Cubans were occasionally found murdered on sidewalks, said Cambinda.

Another of the Eleven, a civil servant who had worked alongside Cubans, alleged that individuals had told him they were frustrated by their role in Angola. They had come unwillingly to the country and the mission was not the one that had been described to them in Havana – a war against white South African soldiers.

* * *

The next stop was UNITA's holy of holies – Savimbi's heavily fortified General Headquarters at the centre of the base. To enter the GHQ we passed through a big gate at which guards were constantly springing to attention. Before we were allowed to proceed telephone calls were made between the guard post and some internal control post deep in the GHQ. The telephone equipment was Russian, taken, UNITA said, from one of the MPLA towns they had captured. We were later shown the telephone exchange in a grass hut, run by a telephone engineer formerly with the MPLA telegraph department in Huambo.

The GHQ consisted of many giant huts spread hundreds of metres apart under the cover of trees. They were connected by paths made of gravel and duckboard and supplied with electricity from a captured Soviet generator and with water pumped from a tubewell to an overhead tank reservoir. The first hut we were ushered into contained one of the nerve centres of Savimbi's military operations. Young UNITA radio operators sat before banks of elaborate electronic equipment – most of it Soviet-made – monitoring every radio and telegraph communication passing between the enemy's major military centres. The operators jotted down the coded messages, and these were sent to another hut where code officers unscrambled them, working to some extent from captured enemy code books. Secretaries, graduates of Miss Kulipossa's academy, typed up the decoded messages. Savimbi quickly shared many of his enemy's closest secrets. His aides brought him summaries of significant intercepts throughout his working day, and during the night also if of sufficient importance. These he initialled before they were passed on for reading and initialling by other members of the High Command.

Among the enemy communication lines I noticed being monitored were those between Luena and Luanda, Cunene and Lubango, and Huambo and Luanda. In another hut about 25 young Angolans were receiving their training in telegraphic interception. Like so many UNITA fields of endeavour, the monitoring operation was a growing concern.

We were then introduced to Lt.-Col. Renato Mateus, UNITA's intelligence and ops chief, who guided us into his operations room, a giant green marquee. Here were intelligence officers studying captured enemy documents. Major Feliciano Huambo, fluent in Portuguese, Umbundu, English and French, was assessing documents from an MPLA helicopter shot down on 15 May 1981 at Via Vissati, 10 kilometres from Menongue. The identity card from the pilot's body showed he was a member of the Congo-Brazzaville Air Force, on loan to the MPLA.

Mateus's staff kept meticulous records, charts and maps of UNITA and enemy actions. Daily, fortnightly and monthly summaries of reported successes and failures were compiled and tabulated. Some reports came in by radio on the day of the action: others by far-flung guerrilla units took weeks or months to arrive. There was a system of spot checking the accuracy of reports. Mateus said his team drew up periodic assessments of the reasons for UNITA's successes and failures. His men were making careful studies of Angolan terrain from photographs, drawings and guerrilla reports. Draughtsmen were making precision drawings of enemy aircraft and captured weapons to enable UNITA troops and guerrillas to recognise them. Reference books on the library shelves included John Barron's *KGB*.

*   *   *

The following morning we were greeted by Colonel Mateus. He had assembled a great array of vehicles and weapons, said to have been captured in the battles for Mavinga, for us to inspect. There were 30 trucks – Polish Stars, Soviet Zils and Urals, and East German Ifas, for the most part, but also a French Berliet mobile workshop equipped with a stunning array of mechanical and electronic equipment. There was a Soviet BTR-152V armoured car, eight Soviet 76mm field artillery guns, a monster of a Soviet 122mm mortar, two

SAM-7s, fifteen Soviet 75mm recoilless cannons, eight Soviet 122mm rockets, fourteen Soviet 14.5mm anti-aircraft guns, more than 300 anti-personnel mines, radio communications equipment, several thousand rounds of ammunition of various calibres, more than 300 small arms, several documents, stacks of Angolan Government money, food and clothing.

Colonel Mateus said he had 120 trucks available for use, but there was a formidable maintenance problem. On most days there were 30 on the move and 90 either being serviced or awaiting service. There was a serious lack of spares, especially transmission parts, injection pumps and carburettors. Replacing smashed headlights was a problem, as we had seen on our journey to Mavinga. Some trucks could only be used in daylight. There was no lack of competent mechanics, but Mateus said he needed at least 500 trucks to be able to realise Savimbi's ambitious plans for a push into the heart of Angola.

*   *   *

Major Fonseca Santos, 41, a former technician in the Portuguese Army, welcomed us to his weapons maintenance workshop and school. Fifty technicians were restoring damaged weapons, mainly small arms, to working order. Most of the soldier-technicians had two years of secondary schooling: they were being trained by the Major and three other instructors for five months before being assigned as logistics specialists with guerrilla and regular units. Major Fonseca had a forge, carpentry workshop and metal workshop. He was awaiting the delivery by air of a \$US 20,000 lathe which would enable his team to rebore worn or damaged gun barrels. The forge was also producing spades, hoes, scythes and knives for the collective farms and for peasant agriculturalists.

The Major was supervising the construction of an underground repair shop which would be virtually invulnerable to air attack. He proudly showed off UNITA's first rocket. Adapted from a 76mm shell, fins had been added and its nose painted scarlet. It was just an entra-mural activity for the trainees, but Major Fonseca was immersely pleased that after being fired from a ramp over a 15-kilometre range it had landed within 10 metres of target.

* * *

For our spiritual welfare we were next taken to Protestant and Roman Catholic services in big wood and elephant grass churches.

The Protestant ceremony, attended by 300 people with worshippers overflowing into the open air, was conducted by the Reverend Sangendo Marcellino, a sombre man dressed in black cassock and white dog collar. I recorded his sermon delivered in Umbundu, and later had it translated by Canadians who had learned the language as missionaries in Angola. It was about Savimbi's politics as well as the Gospel, and sometimes the two were presented as synonymous.

'Thomas said he would not believe Jesus had risen from the dead unless he put his hands into his wounds,' said the Reverend Marcellino. 'The risen Jesus appeared again because of the doubts of Thomas. Ah friends (Dick and myself), before you actually saw the work of UNITA you were like Thomas. You had heard only about the work of UNITA but today you have seen it with your eyes, and you have touched our bodies and touched our leader, President Savimbi.'

The Rev Marcellino's theme was peace, but he had an unusual definition of the term. 'It's a word about which our leader has spoken many times,' he said. 'Peace comes with those who are able to fight. Our leader worked very hard to have all the political movements work together and build our country and have peace. But it proved impossible to do it that way. The power of the devil entered. Thus it was necessary for the people and the children to go into the forests to learn the work of shooting because peace comes with those who are able to fight.'

He recalled a time before he moved into the forest with UNITA when he was still running his church at Camundongo, near Bie, which was under MPLA control. 'We were having a baptismal service,' he said. 'While the service was in progress some cattle approached, and behind them were some UNITA troops. Some worshippers had to stand outside the church – as many of you are standing outside today – and when they saw the cattle and the troops behind them, they thought it was the enemy (the MPLA) coming with horses. They panicked, and those inside the church panicked too and fled, some jumping out of the windows. I was left with the baby I was baptising in my arms.

'From that time it was thought better that every time we worshipped someone should stay outside with guns. When we did that, those worshipping in the church had peace because those outside were those who knew how to shoot. That's why we trust in the words of our President who says "Peace comes with those who are able to fight."'

Little wonder that the Reverend Marcellino's texts were Matthew 10:34 and John 16:33. The former said: 'Do not think that I have come to bring peace on earth; I have not come to bring peace, but a sword.' And John: 'I have said this to you, that in me you may have peace. In the world you have tribulation; but be of good cheer, I have overcome the world.'

Outside, soldiers bearing Kalashnikovs joined in the prayers and singing, though they must have found the adaptations of rather dismal European hymns tame stuff compared with the vibrancy and joyousness of UNITA's own African anthems.

The Roman Catholic mass was even more sombre than the Protestant service. Though conducted by a black priest and catechists, all the authoritarian tradition of the Catholic Church in Portugal had been retained. The responses to the priest were made in Latin and only by the catechists, whose singing possessed sincerity and beauty. But the congregation of 200 were invited to say only the occasional Amen: all those wonderful rhythmic and tuneful voices were stilled, to their God's loss.

Just how deep the divide had been in Portuguese Angola between the state Catholic religion and the non-establishment Protestant beliefs brought by North Americans was illustrated when one of UNITA's Protestant-educated leaders leaned across and said to me:

'You know, this is the first time in my life I've been in a Catholic church.'

*   *   *

We were near the time when we would be able to discuss with Savimbi the implications of all we had seen. But first a mass rally had been laid on at the football ground, a cleared area between the forest and river. Several thousand people assembled, directed by UNITA's fledgling civil police force dressed in rather comic oversize bottle-green serge jackets and caps of the kind British railway porters wore half a century ago.

We were treated to some first-class marching by the newly trained 360 Battalion, jazzy drumming by its band, spectacular baton twirling by the drum major, karate and gymnastics, more singing and dancing and a snappy drill by the *alvorada* (boy scouts).

Then Savimbi rose to speak.

37

Luanda is our Destination

1981

Dressed in combat uniform, with his general's three stars on his beret and shoulder flashes, Savimbi stalked around the parade ground talking fast and energetically in the kind of booming voice Western politicians must have needed before the invention of the microphone. He gestured frequently, emphasising his points with his ebony walking stick. His command of his audience was absolute. When he nodded, the crowd agreed: rhetorical questions brought answers in unison: his jokes about the MPLA and Cubans brought whistles and cheers. Reminiscent of his enemy Fidel Castro's multi-hour orations to the faithful in Havana, Savimbi talked non-stop for three hours, switching between three languages – Portuguese, Ovimbundu and Chokwe – and by the end he was bathed in sweat. The speech was brief compared to some he has given – they can last for up to seven hours!

Savimbi's penchant for dramatic gesture came into play when he plunged into the middle of a platoon and emerged with his arm round the shoulder of a recruit barely 16-years-old. 'This young boy is away from his mother and father for the first time in his life,' he announced. 'He gets no pay in our army – only his food, uniform, rifle and the chance to fight for Angola's freedom. You officers must therefore not neglect his needs. You are now his mother and father. If you officers lack compassion for your men – and you know of some officers I have reduced to the ranks – this army could disintegrate, as you have seen on the MPLA side.'

The burden of Savimbi's speech was that UNITA's army

was going to reach Luanda and achieve final victory: 'Menongue – that is our starting point. Luanda is our destination . . . Let us make 1981 the year of the intensification of the war.' He warned that when they did reach Luanda they would be judged by the appearance they presented to the outside world: 'You must remember three principles – unity, compassion and efficiency. We insist that your authority originates in your compassion and your efforts at unity. The difference between us and the MPLA must not be in symbols but in our behaviour and in our lives.'

He told the new 360 Battalion, lined up in companies on three sides of the parade ground: 'Among our fellow countrymen are whites and *mesticos* and some are members of UNITA. Our unity, compassion and love must go beyond racial categories.' Referring to MPLA allegations that UNITA was a black racist movement, he said: 'As long as we maintain our present attitudes and standards of behaviour, it doesn't matter what is said outside. The truth will ultimately triumph.' But he added a few words of encouragement for 360 Battalion, who were black to a man: 'Many whites believe in the inferiority of the blacks. You must work and prove you can perform any task. Seeing what you have achieved in your months of training, I am happy and proud that UNITA is a fountain of young leaders: it will always be replenished.'

*   *   *

We had two interviews that evening with Savimbi that went on long into the morning around a giant log fire in the presence of all his available senior officers. It was with hindsight that I realised that in every interview I had ever conducted with Savimbi (except for the first time in Bie in September 1975) at least one of his senior colleagues had been present.

As we prepared to begin, Dick had a brush with an Angolan caterpillar. As he slipped on a jacket to fend off the sharp evening cold Dick began cursing and yelling. A big caterpillar with poisonous fur had got inside his sleeve and stung him badly. He had the jacket off rapidly and much of his arm was covered in a rash. A nurse rubbed the rash with alcohol and gave Dick a pill of some kind.

We could now move on to an even more painful and tricky subject – Savimbi's political albatross, his relations with South Africa, or, more specifically, with the South African military.

* * *

What follows is a distillation of the case he made:

Savimbi, not to our surprise, denied any military co-operation with South Africa. The war South Africa was waging in south-west Angola around N'Giva (Pereira D'Eca) against SWAPO was a separate issue from the widening conflict in south-east Angola between UNITA and the MPLA. If South African troops were involved militarily with UNITA, 'they will begin to be captured, for sure, and the MPLA will be able to produce them to the world as prisoners'.

But UNITA did enjoy cordial relations with South Africa along the 650 kilometres or so of common border the movement shared with Namibia: 'We cannot fight enemies on two fronts. We don't have any interest at all in having the South Africans come to bomb our areas: as long as they are in Namibia, we intend trying to maintain good relations with them.' UNITA obtained diesel fuel and other non-military supplies for Namibia in exchange for diamonds and other produce such as ivory. These contacts and trade were not anything for which UNITA needed to apologise. 'Black men with flat noses can hardly agree with a constitution based on racial discrimination, and we will say it all the time. But countries throughout this region have contacts with South Africa – Zambia, Zaire, Mozambique, Malawi, Botswana and even the MPLA in Angola. These countries make contact during the day; others do it at night, but there are contacts. We all feel and hope South Africa will change its internal policies, but meanwhile contacts will continue.'

He said the two places where UNITA traded across the border were military posts – Mucusso and Dirico, by my guess.

There were also mundane practical reasons for maintaining, at the very least, polite relations with the South

Africans. In the past, tribesmen of the Mkussu tribe on the Namibian side of the border would lose their cattle and accuse UNITA of stealing them. Sometimes Mkussu tribesmen on the Angolan side complained to UNITA that their cattle had been stolen and taken to Namibia. 'It was really necessary to have relations so that we could talk about these kind of problems.'

South Africa's relations with UNITA were not as close as the outside world imagined, Savimbi said. 'We are absolutely independent, and they don't trust us: we know that for sure.' From 1976 South Africa had still been intent on putting the FNLA into power in Angola, and had only turned its attentions towards UNITA from late 1978 onwards, after the FNLA had been cleared completely from southern Angola by the MPLA and Cubans. 'The truth is,' he told us, 'that the South Africans have never dropped the idea of rebuilding the FNLA: we have a lot of accurate information about their intent, even though they try to hide it from us.'

UNITA's SAM-7s were a source of friction with the South Africans, who wanted to know where the missiles were located because Pretoria's aircraft frequently flew in a line towards Menongue when attacking SWAPO bases in Angola. The South Africans had learned from their own intelligence sources about an MPLA C-130 transport plane shot down by a UNITA SAM-7 near Menongue on 16 May 1981. 'Immediately they contacted us and asked where we had our SAM-7s, but we would not tell them.'

But, we put it to Savimbi, no one in the outside world would believe that UNITA had captured and held on to Mavinga without help from South African forces. He conceded that UNITA had a credibility problem, and added: 'But I think it's important to be accurate.' What follows is his account of the battles for Mavinga, concentrating particularly on what was at that stage UNITA's biggest victory ever at the Lomba River in May 1981.

*   *   *

'We took Mavinga last 19 September (1980). An MPLA brigade of 2,000 guarded the town. We put in four battalions totalling about 2,500 men. First we attacked the command position about a kilometre north of the town, and then a position near the airstrip. Within four hours the MPLA were routed. They took heavy casualties and fled north. We had positioned a company of 200 men 20 kilometres to the north and they harassed the enemy as they retreated. We captured a number of 12.7mm anti-aircraft guns, some 122mm rockets, about 300 Kalashnikovs, and many trucks, including ambulances and a petrol tanker.

'They didn't try a counter-attack until March (1981). We beat that back, but the MPLA's big effort came in May. We knew it was coming, from our own radio interceptions and intelligence reports from inside Menongue. We established that a Cuban commander would direct the MPLA counter-attack. Then on 16 May, just as the offensive was about to begin, our guerrillas shot down an MPLA C-130 plane on its landing approach five kilometres from Menongue. Several Cubans died. The Cubans were furious with the MPLA for failing to secure the town's perimeter, and they withdrew from command of the Mavinga operation.

'We were happy when our radio intercepts showed that command had been passed to the MPLA's Lt.-Col. Mundo Rial. My High Command has studied carefully the tactical styles of all the enemy commanders – Cuban, Soviet and MPLA. There are at least two MPLA commanders, and one in particular, who are really brilliant and whom we respect. But this Mundo Rial, he is really a fool. He rarely had adequate reinforcements, and you know that if you can pin him down in a fixed position for five days he is lost.

'The attacking force of two MPLA brigades (2,500 men) left Cuito Cuanavale (about 150 kilometres north-west of Mavinga) after 16 May in a big truck convoy with about five armoured cars. On 21 May Chilingutila ordered a company of 200 guerrillas to test the strength of the MPLA column by harassing its flanks and inflicting casualties. MPLA officers sent radio messages to Mundo Rial, who was directing the operation from Menongue (about 400 kilometres north-west of Mavinga), asking for helicopters to evacuate the wounded. Mundo Rial replied that he would send helicopters the next day, but we intercepted his exchanges with

Luanda: he asked for helicopters and was refused. So we knew this man preferred to tell his soldiers lies rather than the truth. Those wounded men died where they had fallen.

'On 25 May one of our battalions (of 700 men) attacked the two MPLA brigades at the Lomba River (about 25 kilometres north-west of Mavinga). Chilingutila wanted to inflict casualties, assess the MPLA's morale, fix the column in one position and provide time to bring up another four of our battalions (2,800 men).

'In the course of the 25 May encounter, Mundo Rial made another fundamental error. He sent an open, non-coded order to his field commander to fight according to a Soviet military tactic known as 135. This enabled us to pinpoint the command post and supporting artillery. During that day's battle MPLA forces captured a UNITA sub-lieutenant who told them we were bringing up at least another three battalions of regular troops and several companies of guerrillas. (The sub-lieutenant was subsequently rescued by UNITA.) The MPLA commander, knowing he had no immediate reinforcements or air cover, asked for permission to withdraw to a safer position until he could be reinforced. By this time I had come northwards to direct our operation and the MPLA commander's thinking struck me as correct. But Mundo Rial ordered his field commander to advance: in fact, the commander did not move.

'We knew the presence of wounded on the ground from 21 to 25 May without evacuation would erode morale. When their commander did not move an inch and bunched all his forces within a five-kilometre perimeter we understood that their morale was very low and they were afraid. If they were planning any offensive they would have sent out patrols 15 kilometres deep, but they did nothing. I said let us now wait for 48 hours. If this man neither advances nor retreats, then he has no support from behind and we should just go for him. We waited. The MPLA forces did not move, and on 28 May our five battalions supported by guerrillas launched an assault. There was scarcely any resistance. Only at one time, when one of our cannon shells hit a truck load with 122mm rocket shells, did our forces believe the enemy was beginning to mount serious resistance. Troops took cover under the barrage, but they soon realised the shells were going up in the air and in all directions.

'From then onwards it was just a matter of pursuit; there was no resistance at all. They turned their backs and started to run. They were easy prey for our infantry; it was like shooting birds. We intercepted a radio message to Mundo Rial the day after the battle in which the field commander complained that soldiers had dropped individual weapons. Of his three leading battalions, the commander said one had not returned fire at all and another had stood and fired for only ten minutes.

'Our semi-regular battalions pursued the MPLA as they retreated, while guerrillas harassed the flanks under orders to kill those who resisted and take prisoner those who laid down their weapons.

'The first group of MPLA soldiers to arrive back in Cuito Cuanavale was only 130-strong out of the initial force of 2,500. Others straggled back for more than two weeks, according to our radio intercepts. It was a big success for us, but if you make such mistakes as Mundo Rial's you should wipe out a whole brigade. I always say it is more difficult to learn a lesson from a victory than a defeat, so we have been holding meetings since to analyse the battles. We believe we made mistakes. They were really in disarray, and with a little more daring and organisation we should have been able to press forward and take Cuito Cuanavale.

'Nevertheless, it was our biggest victory in one stroke, for the quantity and type of equipment captured and the number of enemy killed. They left their radio equipment for us and even left their codes on the ground. At the very least you would have expected them to destroy their codes.'

*   *   *

Some corroboration of Savimbi's account came from a couple of MPLA prisoners of war we interviewed in a camp near the UNITA HQ. They were a sad-eyed bunch, bare-footed and dressed in dark-grey dungarees. Of about 200 MPLA POWs UNITA claimed to hold, 30 were paraded before us. Dick selected two at random for interview.

Private Celestino Segunda, 23, a driver-mechanic in the

MPLA's 38th Brigade, escaped after the Battle of Lomba
River on 28 May. He wandered alone without a gun in the
surrounding forest until he was captured by UNITA guerrillas. Through a UNITA translator, Segunda said there had
been a fierce battle in which the MPLA had taken heavy
casualties and that the column had been attacked several
times in ambushes before 28 May. 'Even before we left Cuito
Cuanavale people were heavily demoralised,' he said. 'We
couldn't leave camp and nobody would tell us when or
where we were going to enter combat. When the order came
to go back to Mavinga there was a general feeling of frustration – no one really had the will to fight.'

Private Samuel Mario, 24, an artilleryman in the MPLA's
18th Brigade, was captured in the first Mavinga counter-
attack in March before he had fired a single round in real
battle. He said there were 'many, many casualties'. Food
was always very scarce. 'Morale was very bad because we
were not being told the truth at any time. There were lots of
troop movements and we were told we would be sent to
Luanda. No one told us we would be sent to Mavinga.'

*   *   *

The significance UNITA attached to the battles for Mavinga
is hard to overstate. Dick Harwood summed it up this way:
'They proved to the troops and their commanders that
they could function as a conventional army, not merely as
hit-and-run guerrillas fighting from ambushes. It proved
that they had the command structure, the logistics, the
communications and tactical skills to defeat forces with
superior equipment and air support . . . The battles also
proved that UNITA could not only take but hold an exposed
position in an area with heavy MPLA troop concen-
trations.'[1] Just as significant was the pivotal base Mavinga
provided for the intensifying push northwards by Savimbi's
forces. From Mavinga the Savimbi Trail extended another
130 kilometres northeastwards. Savimbi said there were
two small MPLA military outposts blocking its extension.
He believed these could be cleared soon, and then the Trail
and its network of branches could be extended at a rate of
80 kilometres a week through the thin undergrowth, with

an absolute minimum of trees being felled so there would
be maximum cover.

The extension of the Savimbi Trail was important if the
regular battalions were to be moved northwards to consoli-
date UNITA's hold on areas it had cleared of MPLA troops.
'With trucks we can take the semi-regular battalions
to within 50 kilometres of the objective. We could not
send them 300 kilometres on foot without food supplies
and other logistics, otherwise they would disintegrate
completely.'

Savimbi said his immediate objective was to extend the
Savimbi Trail as far as the Benguela Railway, 800 kilometres
inside Angola, and then push the battalions up to the
railway as well. On the way he would ignore towns like
Menongue, Cuito Cuanavale and Gago Coutinho. 'There
are vast gaps we can go through and, once we are through,
their forces will be so thinly spread over a vast area that we
are going to create havoc.'

* * *

We could not hang around to see whether Savimbi's offensive would prosper. It was time to leave. We said our
farewells, boarded our Stars and headed for the airstrip at
Luengue. We arrived on the night of 2 July, and before the
first light of morning we walked through the bush towards
the aircraft. It was a swish-looking Fokker Friendship. The
old Viscount which had brought us in flew its last journey
when it left Angola. Two of its four engines seized up on the
return flight, and the plane was broken up for spares and
scrap after it landed. Dick was pleased with the Fokker. He
had calculated he would be able to make it home in time for
the 4th of July and get down to his Delaware beach house
where his whole family – wife, sons, daughters and grand-
children – would all be assembled together for the first time
in years to celebrate American Independence Day.

It was not to be.

* * *

There was no moon and there were no lights on the runway,
just half-a-dozen paraffin lamps dimly marking the point

where it ended in the blackness of the forest. It was not a take-off to relish.

Dick and I claimed two of the half-dozen seats. Elsewhere, people sat on the floor and two seriously ill people were brought aboard on stretchers. The pilots ran up the engines to full power. The aircraft strained on the brakes and then, as they were released and the take-off run began, the under-carriage collapsed. The nose, right propeller and right wing ploughed into the earth runway, but the craft did not cartwheel. There was no fire, though fuel poured from the right engine. Another one hundred metres and it would have been very nasty.

Savimbi sent us a radio message assuring us that he would try to obtain another aircraft to take us out as soon as possible. But on the 4th of July, when Dick intended to be swigging iced beer on his Delaware beach in the bosom of his family, he was mooching around his jungle hut working out the theme of his articles on Angola for the *Washington Post*. After supper, Ernesto Mulato invited Dick and myself to a party. Troops from the local battalion had gathered around a magnificent bonfire in a forest clearing. The singing, dancing and poetry recitals began, and then Mulato stepped forward and read a proclamation in English. It concerned the 4th of July and what it meant to America and the world:

'We regret the circumstances in which you, Mr Richard Harwood, are celebrating this joyous day of yours, far away from your loved ones. But the values and ideals that have made your country the greatest on earth are the same values and ideals that bind us together – the struggle for freedom and liberty. We are therefore gathered here tonight, around this campfire, to share with you some moments of reflections and joy on your national holiday . . .'

It was a superb and thoughtful gesture by UNITA's people, not at all schmaltzy, though it brought tears to Dick's eyes. In his speech of thanks, Dick also thanked me, as a Briton, for having made America's 4th of July possible. Later he wrote that I hadn't seemed terribly amused by the remark, but I was greatly enjoying all the music and sentiment, and had long ago forgiven the Americans for cutting free from the apron strings of Old Mother Britain. A thought crossed my mind, as it had before in connection with Angola – a reflection that if the Poles were right to struggle for freedom from a totalitarian régime, as they were confidently doing then, who could really blame UNITA for struggling against an Angolan government modelled on much the same ideology as its Warsaw counterpart? And yet liberal people in the West who sympathised with the Poles had scant sympathy for the Angolan resistance, almost as though true freedom, true liberty were ideals that Africans should not aspire to because they were as yet too immature. It was an interesting paradox for a Briton to ponder on American Independence Day in the Angolan forest.

*   *   *

It took Savimbi nine days to find us another aircraft. It came in late one afternoon, an oil-stained, over-worked DC-4 which Dick pronounced the loveliest machine he had ever seen. The gossip was that the Italian-owned company, whose aircraft spent most of their flying time shuttling ivory and diamonds from remote parts of the African bush, had charged UNITA $US 60,000 – twice the normal rate – for our rescue.

At 3 a.m. we lurched and bumped down the pitch-black runway and then we were in the air and over the trees. Our hearts fell back from our mouths and later we crossed the Zambezi as the sun began to rise and we headed north towards the equator.

Somewhere back there Jonas Savimbi was planning his next moves.

38

South Africa Attacks Angola
1981

In mid-1981 officials at the UN still believed they would be called upon to deploy a 7,500-strong international force along the Angola-Namibia border when South Africa complied with the Contact Group's plans for a UN-supervised transition to independence for Namibia.[1]

The MPLA leadership desperately needed a Namibian settlement because they said Angola was being subjected to regular aggression from South Africa, and a crippling 50 per cent of the national budget was devoted to defence. 'Hundreds of trucks that should be used for health work, agriculture and education are being diverted for the war effort and our best youth is being conscripted to fight,' said Lucio Lara.[2]

But there was to be no respite for the MPLA.

* * *

On 23 August 1981 the SADF launched Operation Protea, a blitzkrieg attack on Angola's Cunene Province which surpassed in intensity the South African assault of June-July 1980 and the invasion of October 1975.

The South African Air Force attacked and destroyed radar stations and Soviet SAM-3 and SAM-6 missile sites which had recently been built in Cunene Province. Then three task forces in South African-built Eland heavy armoured cars, Ratel armoured personnel carriers and Buffel mine-protected troop carriers crossed the border to hit SWAPO camps concentrated in Cunene Province. In twelve days of intense fighting the South Africans thrust more than 150 kilometres into Angola; captured the towns of N'Giva (known before independence as Pereira D'Eca) and Xangongo (formerly Rocadas); killed about 1,000 SWAPO guerrillas and Angolan government troops; captured one Soviet sergeant-major and killed two senior Soviet Army officers; and seized nearly 4,000 tonnes of military equipment and arms.

Foreign correspondents taken to Oshakati military base in Namibia's Ovamboland, where the haul from Operation Protea had been assembled, reported seeing 13 Soviet tanks and 160 military vehicles, including armoured personnel carriers, mobile workshops, minelayers, petrol tankers, and 'Stalin Organ' multiple rocket launchers, millions of rounds of ammunition, crates of automatic weapons, some still unused and packed in grease, heavy mortars, 14.7mm Soviet anti-aricraft guns, recoilless cannon, portable SAM-7 anti-aircraft missiles, mines, and explosives.[3] One eye-witness reported seeing 280 brand-new Soviet trucks being driven into Windhoek by the SADF after the operation.[4]

The South Africans lost ten dead during Operation Protea, including two airforce men whose Alouette helicopter was shot down. To break into Xangongo, said South African Army Chief Lt.-Gen. Jannie Geldenhuys, the South African force had knocked out a Soviet T-34 tank and blasted Angolan troops out of an intricate network of bunkers and trenches devised and built under the supervision of Soviet advisers.

Further east, as South African units entered N'Giva, a convoy of 25 vehicles carrying Soviet advisers and SWAPO and MPLA officers left the town towards the north-east. The convoy was attacked first by South African jet fighters and then by ground troops. Only two vehicles escaped, and a Soviet non-commissioned officer, Sgt.-Major Nikolai Pestretsov, was taken prisoner. Next to him when he surrendered was the body of his wife, another Russian woman in uniform, and two Soviet Lieutenant-Colonels. Pestretsov was taken into captivity in South Africa.

Geldenhuys said his forces discovered that political prisoners in N'Giva's gaol had been shot dead by MPLA troops as the town came under attack. An elderly African was brought before reporters at Oshakati and he told them that MPLA soldiers had burst into the prison after the attack started and sprayed his cell with gunfire. His cell mates had been killed and he had been left for dead with head and stomach wounds.[5]

The General said Operation Protea had destroyed SWAPO's logistics system: he expected UNITA would capitalise on the situation to extend their 'buffer' zone from Cuando Cubango into Cunene.

Savimbi responded by declaring that UNITA supported independence for Namibia: 'It is a fundamental and inalienable right. It is also strengthened by the guarantee of free elections, internationally controlled. This is the question which has pitted the people of Namibia, the United Nations and South Africa against each other. Having recognised that Angolan territory is utilised as terrain for combats between South Africa and SWAPO, the situation prevailing in the southwest of our country concerns us profoundly, inasmuch as innocent Angolans are victims of these confrontations in which we are not engaged.'[6]

The MPLA, he said, was using Namibia to disguise the fact that it had not been elected and that it relied on Cuban and Soviet troops more to put down resistance by Angolans than to counter South Africa.

* * *

The Cubans were not involved in the fighting during Operation Protea, but they had ended their withdrawal into the bigger towns to take part in a big offensive against UNITA in central Angola. UNITA had learned this from documents recovered from a Soviet MI-8 helicopter shot down ten kilometres from Huambo on 17 July. Among nine Cubans found dead in the wreckage was a general, Tomaz Felichi.[7]

UNITA responded with a major offensive of its own. After fighting off a Cuban/MPLA motorised column to the north of Rito, a small town UNITA held in Cuando Cubango Province, Savimbi's semi-regular battalions, supported by guerrilla companies, struck north into Moxico Province and captured Lupire (19 September), Cassamba (16 November), Cangombe (21 December) and Ninda (27 December).[8]

These towns were all more than 350 kilometres inside Angola, and Cassamba was 650 kilometres to the north-east of Cunene Province, the focus of the MPLA-South African fighting. The fall of Cassamba showed there were two different wars being waged in Angola in different areas. Cassamba had another significance – it had been the scene of UNITA's disastrous baptismal guerrilla foray against the Portuguese back in 1966, and now, 15 years on, it had at last fallen to UNITA forces.

Though Savimbi tried to distance himself from Pretoria's war in Cunene, South Africa's Foreign Minister, Pik Botha, was evidently pleased with UNITA's progress. He said bluntly that there was no hope of the plan for Namibia being implemented while the Cubans remained in Angola. 'As long as they (the Cubans) are there Mr Savimbi will fight them,' he told foreign correspondents in Johannesburg. 'And there will be turbulence and a lack of peace and stability, and as long as that is there it doesn't matter what plan you evolve (for Namibia's independence), *you are not going to get it implemented*'.[9]

* * *

UNITA's probings northwards attracted little attention, but South Africa's assault into Cunene drew widespread international condemnation. In early September a UN Security Council resolution condemning the incursion was vetoed by the United States, which viewed with seriousness the proof produced by Pretoria of Soviet Army personnel in forward military areas in Angola. South Africa was ejected from the General Assembly debate on Namibia by a vote of 117 to 22.[10]

On the eve of the Security Council meeting Chester Crocker once more spelt out the Reagan Administration's determination that South African withdrawal from Namibia would only take place if it was matched by a Cuban withdrawal from Angola. 'We believe that movement on Namibia can reinforce movement toward Cuban withdrawal from Angola – and vice versa,' he said. 'Furthermore, we are convinced that a satisfactory outcome can only be based on parallel movements in both arenas.'[11] In the Security

Council the US veto revealed a serious split within the Western Contact Group on Namibia. Of the four other partners in the group, Britain abstained and France, West Germany and Canada voted with the majority to condemn South Africa.

The left-wing British weekly *New Statesman* perceptively noted that Pretoria had won a diplomatic victory that outweighed and would probably outlive any military gains it had made against SWAPO: 'Far from provoking the united condemnation of the five Western powers involved in seeking a negotiated rather than a military settlement in Namibia, Pretoria has driven a neat wedge straight into them and secured from the Americans what comes close to a public expression of sympathy for its standpoint.'[12] The casting of Washington's veto was front page news in South Africa, with one Johannesburg newspaper running the triumphant headline, 'Angola: US Protection for SA'.

Officially the SADF pulled out from Cunene at the end of Operation Protea on 4 September 1981. But by the end of the year the South Africans still had not fully withdrawn. The MPLA had lost control of some 35,000 square kilometres of Angolan territory in the south between the Cunene River and the Namibian border. Reuter's Lisbon correspondent Richard Wallis, visiting Luanda in December, quoted one 'reliable source with first-hand experience' in Cunene (possibly the ICRC, the only international organisation able to move between SADF and MPLA areas) as saying the region had become: 'a gigantic no-man's-land in which only a few inhabitants remained in ruined towns and where the civilian administration had completely broken down. The source said the only signs of South African presence he saw were occasional helicopter patrols. The Angolans have repeatedly said their troops could not penetrate the area without being bombed by Pretoria's air force.'[13]

South Africa had not only divided the Western Contact Group. Wallis noted that it had also driven a wedge between the MPLA and SWAPO, which arose from MPLA resentment that it had been left to face the full brunt of the South African incursion while SWAPO guerrillas hurriedly retreated beyond the range of the invaders. Following the invasion, a Portuguese newspaper[14] reported a number of 'serious incidents' when Cuban troops dispersed street demonstrations in Luanda against the presence of SWAPO. The rising tension was caused by the fact that SWAPO, along with the Cubans and MPLA leaders, had access to privileged food supplies (and fleets of Volvo trucks in which to transport them) at a time of chronic shortages in the Angolan capital. Quentin Peel, the *Financial Times*' southern Africa correspondent, reported from Luanda that the formal food distribution system had simply broken down and that prices had taken leave of reality, with one fish costing 4,000 kwanzas (about $US 100), the equivalent of an average monthly wage: 'Most people can get what they want, but only by endless queueing, or diligent searching, or having the right connections.'[15]

The South African invasion had other consequences. The number of Cuban troops in Angola had fallen to about 10,000 in September 1981, according to the CIA, but rose again by the end of the year to between 12,000 and 15,000.[16] In addition, the number of East German military advisers working with the MPLA, mainly in security and intelligence fields, had risen to 5,000.[17]

*   *   *

Towards the end of the year Savimbi received another invitation to visit the United States, where a government spokesman said he would be received at the State Department.[18] Savimbi arrived in the US on 28 November. The following day, the Angolan news agency ANGOP reported that Angola's only oil refinery, in Luanda, went up in flames. UNITA claimed responsibility for the attack, while the MPLA blamed South Africa. Petrofina, the Belgian company with a controlling interest in the refinery, said it would be out of operation for two months and cause a severe shortage of refined products.[19]

39

Savimbi Goes to Washington

1981–82

Savimbi's visit to Washington in December of 1981 was the outstanding diplomatic success of his career as a guerrilla leader up until that time. General Alexander Haig, the Secretary of State, assured him that ways and means would be found to bypass the Clark Amendment and help him by channelling funds through a third country.[1]

After his American visit, I visited Savimbi at his Rabat headquarters. There, in his office with pink bougainvillea outside trembling in the cool January breeze, he gave my newspaper an exclusive story about Washington's peace plan for Angola which – along with the parallel initiative for Namibia – would dominate news from southern Africa throughout 1982. It was significant that in Washington Savimbi had also been received by Chester Crocker, the architect of the Reagan Administration's southern African policy.

The first step in the American peace plan required Savimbi to release his two Soviet airmen prisoners in exchange for three Americans held by the MPLA, including two of the mercenaries sentenced to long jail terms in 1976 after being caught fighting with the FNLA. The prisoner exchange was to be accompanied by a cat's cradle of complex diplomatic initiatives to end the fighting in both Namibia and Angola. Negotiations involving high officials of several nations would take place in such cities as Mexico, Washington, London, Brussels, Paris, Zurich, Lisbon, Rabat, Pretoria, Dakar, Kinshasa and Brazzaville.

'We understood what the United States wanted to do, and

that they were firm on it,' said Savimbi. 'They wanted an independence settlement in Namibia, and also a withdrawal of the Cubans from Angola.' As part of the equation the MPLA government made its first offer of negotiations to UNITA in the six years the two movements had been fighting since independence. As a sign of good intent Savimbi said he was willing to halt UNITA attacks on the Benguela Railway – by now averaging one a day and causing a serious derailment every week – and permit it to operate uninterrupted for six months.[2]

The message for Savimbi was delivered to Lisbon on 14 January 1982 by Interior Minister Alexandre Rodrigues Quito, the senior MPLA negotiator on Namibia. From Lisbon, the message was taken to Savimbi in Rabat by Dr Leonardo Mathias, Portugal's Secretary of State for Foreign Affairs. It did not suggest where, or when, or at what level negotiations should open, but asked Savimbi for clarification on a number of issues should he be willing to consider negotiations.

Savimbi said that MPLA-UNITA contacts would be made through third-party intermediaries for the following two months, and he was sending his secretary for Foreign Affairs, Jeremias Chitunda, to Washington to co-ordinate contacts with the MPLA. Savimbi himself would delay his return to Angola until mid-February in case of further diplomatic developments. His hope was that middle-level UNITA and MPLA delegations would begin face-to-face meetings by April 1982. If they could mutually agree a negotiating framework – a formidable task in itself – talks could then move to a higher level.

The MPLA told Savimbi that one of the conditions for talks was that UNITA end its relations with South Africa. In his reply, through the Portuguese, Savimbi sought clarification. 'They are not being realistic,' he told me at the time. 'They themselves are buying food from South Africa and they have 30 South African technicians organising their diamond mines.'[3] He told the MPLA in his letter that the main obstacle to reconciliation was the Cuban presence in Angola.

UNITA's promised release of the Soviets in exchange for

the Americans represented a major concession to Washington, for Savimbi had hoped to use Kolya and Chernietsky to bargain for the release of some of his own followers imprisoned by the MPLA. In his meetings with Haig and Crocker, and also White House National Security Adviser William Clark and Under-Secretary of State for Political Affairs Walter Stoessel,[4] Savimbi was persuaded that he had to give way as part of the price for Washington's support on a Cuban withdrawal. And in return for American assurances of intent in securing a Cuban withdrawal, Savimbi gave a pledge that he would not obstruct Washington's parallel plans to bring Namibia to independence.

The MPLA, for its part, was seeking diplomatic recognition from Washington in return for its own co-operation in helping bring about a transition to independence in Namibia. The MPLA recognised that peace together with economic aid from the US would help rescue the Angolan economy from the parlous state into which it had fallen since independence. More than half of its foreign exchange was being consumed by defence, including payment for armaments and for Cuban, Soviet and East German personnel. Angola, which had once been a food exporting nation, was now importing it. Long queues at food shops were a common sight, and on the black market the exchange rate for the kwanza was 13 times that obtainable officially. So much money was being spent on arms that the country could not afford to buy spares to repair the thousands of rusting trucks. Water supplies in towns were erratic because of broken pumps. Few lifts worked, even in Luanda's smart office blocks. In central Angola the ICRC reported that hunger was spreading. There were the beginnings of popular disaffection because the élite of Angolan society, the MPLA rulers, had access to special shops from which workers and peasants were barred.[5]

The proposed withdrawal of the Cubans posed a difficult problem for the MPLA. Even if the South Africans simultaneously withdrew from Angola's borders, they still faced the problem of how to defend themselves against Savimbi. In a sense, the MPLA needed the South African threat: it provided an external validation for retaining Cuban troops who were needed even more importantly to contain internal insurrection.

Nevertheless, on 4 February Angola's Foreign Minister, Paulo Jorge, and his Cuban counterpart, Ididoro Malmierca, issued a statement in Luanda which was interpreted in Washington as a signal that the MPLA was ready to countenance the withdrawal of the Cubans. Havana and Luanda 'will analyse relaunching the programme of withdrawal of Cuban forces' once Namibia becomes independent and South African troops withdraw, 'which will considerably diminish the dangers of aggression against Angola,' said the statement. Havana would 'follow without hesitation any decision' made by Luanda on the Cuban expeditionary forces.[6]

The statement did not concede the 'parallelism' which the US was seeking and on which UNITA and the South Africans were insisting, but it clearly provided a real basis for negotiation.

* * *

The to-ings and fro-ings of everyone at this time will be analysed in minute detail by academics one day. For the time being, to illustrate the intensity of the diplomatic effort, it is worth listing the known meetings between key players in the drama between December 1981 and the beginning of February 1982:[7]

End of November 1981: Angola's President Eduardo dos Santos met President Abdou Diouf of Senegambia in Cape Verde and said he was willing to discuss a settlement with UNITA.

Early December 1981: Alexander Haig met Cuba's Vice-President Raul Castro in Mexico City, and then held talks with Savimbi in Washington.

12 December 1981: Portuguese Foreign Minister Goncalves Pereira suggested that a possible Cuban pull-out from Angola might be included in talks on the future of Namibia with the MPLA. At the same time President dos Santos offered to normalise Angola's relations with the US.

16 December 1981: Angola's Ambassador to Portugal, Adriano Sebastiao, said his country would talk to Savimbi if he severed links with South Africa.

1 January 1982: Angola's Foreign Minister Paulo Jorge met President Adbou Diouf and repeated dos Santos's assertion that the MPLA was considering offering negotiations to UNITA.

5 January 1982: Savimbi visited Diouf in Dakar and was given an account of the MPLA's thinking.

12 January 1982: In London Chester Crocker met Brand Fourie, the senior civil servant in the South African Foreign Affairs Ministry.

14 and 15 January 1982: Crocker met Paulo Jorge for secret talks in Paris and then again a week later in Kinshasa.

14 January 1982: Angolan Interior Minister Alexandre Rodrigues Quito arrived in Lisbon with a message for Portugal to pass on to Savimbi.

17 January 1982: Portugal's senior Foreign Ministry civil servant, Dr Leonardo Mathias, took Quito's message to Savimbi in Rabat.

15 January 1982: Angola's Defence Minister Pedro Maria Tonha Pedale met South African generals in Brazzaville, Congo. The South Africans included Lt.-Gen. Pieter van der Westhuizen, who, after Pieter Botha took over as South Africa's Prime Minister in 1978 from John Vorster, had become the country's intelligence supremo at the head of Military Intelligence (MI).[8] The MPLA asked the South Africans to ease military tension in areas of south-west Angola where it had been attacking SWAPO. The South Africans asked the MPLA to put pressure on SWAPO to keep a low profile while the Angola-Namibia diplomacy continued.

27 January 1982: Reuters and *The Economist* Foreign Report note US visitors between November 1981 and January 1982 to Rabat – the base for Savimbi during his foray outside Angola – were: Defence Secretary Caspar Weinberger; Weinberger's Assistant for International Security matters, Francis West; Deputy Defence Secretary

Frank Carlucci; the Deputy Director of the CIA, Admiral Bobby Ray Inman; President Reagan's special envoy, or 'troubleshooter', former Deputy CIA Director General Vernon Walters; and James Williams, Director of the defence Intelligence Agency (DIA).

4 February 1982: Paulo Jorge and Cuban Foreign Minister Ididoro Malmierca issued a joint statement in Luanda saying they would 'analyse relaunching the programme of withdrawal of Cuban forces'.

10 February 1982: Alexander Haig visited Lisbon, while Lt.-Col. Vitor Alves, spokesman for the Portuguese Council of State, held talks with the MPLA in Luanda.

* * *

At our January meeting in Rabat, Savimbi told UNITA's version of the 29 November 1981 attack on Luanda's oil refinery. It had been timed to coincide with Savimbi's arrival in the US. The sabotage team had three elements: a refinery employee who was a covert member of UNITA; a commander of an MPLA military platoon guarding the refinery who was also a covert UNITA man; and UNITA underground members in ordinary jobs in the capital. Six fin-tailed Soviet-made RPG-7 rockets had been sent by couriers from UNITA bases in central Angola to the cells in Luanda. The cell members were guided into the Petrofina petroleum complex at night by the refinery employee. The MPLA officer supplied four of the MPLA's own RPG-7 launcher tubes and the refinery worker indicated the most vulnerable targets.

'After the first explosion the MPLA troops started running away from the refinery instead of encircling it,' said Savimbi. 'Our people were able to leave easily because of the confusion. The refinery worker and the MPLA commander immediately left Luanda. They will reach our secure south-eastern bases by March.' The attack took place at 1 a.m.: Cuban troops arrived at 3 a.m., sealed off the area and started arresting passers-by. President dos Santos arrived at 4 a.m., and Security Minister Kundi Paiama at 7 a.m. The MPLA soon afterwards announced that Paiama, thought to be a rising star by Luanda-based diplomats, had been sacked because of the security failure. The MPLA also issued a statement saying that South African-trained white mercenaries had destroyed the refinery and that there was an 'unconfirmed possibility that the mercenaries came by submarine'. As evidence of Pretoria's involvement, Luanda daily newspapers carried photographs of a severed foot and tuft of scalp of a white man said to have died in the attack.[9]

The two contrasting versions of the attack again illustrate the difficulties of establishing precision about events in Angola. No reporters with UNITA had ventured beyond the movement's secure areas in the south-east, and no independent Western journalist on the MPLA side had been permitted to travel beyond Luanda unaccompanied.

Nowhere was the reporting more inadequate than when conveying developments in Angola's Central Highlands. Xan Smiley, in *The Times* of London, lamented: 'No Western observers – diplomats, journalists or businessmen – have more than the haziest idea what is happening in Angola's most important region . . . No journalist since independence in 1975 has been able to travel freely on the Central Plateau around the towns of Huambo and Bie, the most populous region and once the most productive agriculturally. It is the key to the whole country and the heartland of the largest tribe, the Ovimbundu.'[10]

What was clear was that life in the Central Highlands had been reduced to chaos and anarchy. Once the country's breadbasket, producing great surpluses of maize, wheat and vegetables, its people were now malnourished and there were no surpluses for the rest of Angola. In January 1982 Planning Minister Lopo do Nascimento said there would be severe food shortages for the rest of the year. Domestic food production had fallen by more than a quarter in 1981, he said, and imports would be restricted because of an acute shortage of foreign exchange.

Because the region was closed to most outsiders, the precise reasons for the disintegration of Angola's heartland were matters of speculation and controversy. The MPLA case[11] was that UNITA guerrillas were terrorising the peasants, confiscating their crops and forcing them to retreat from their fields either into the towns or deep into the forests. The MPLA had variously numbered these refugees from the Central Highlands at between 300,000 and 800,000. (The population of the Central Highlands is about 3.5 million out of a total Angolan population of approximately 6.5 million.)

Though the MPLA argued that UNITA bore responsibility for the heavy economic dislocation, at the same time they denied that UNITA had any significant support. They were nothing more than a 'handful of bandits', puppets of the South Africans. The daily attacks on the Benguela Railway were discounted as any evidence of support for UNITA: the MPLA said that great lengths of the railway ran through sparsely inhabited country which made it vulnerable to attack by small groups – and, anyway, many of the attacks were carried out not by UNITA but by South African commandos.

The UNITA version was a mirror image. Through 1979 to 1981 the Cubans/MPLA had reluctantly concluded they could never dissuade the population from feeding and protecting UNITA soldiers operating in the Central Highlands. The MPLA/Cubans had destroyed crops and villages to drive the peasantry into the towns in a kind of fortified settlements strategy: this involved the peasants living in huts grouped near the military barracks and working on plots close to the towns, thus depriving the insurgents of food and intelligence.

The only independent body of any significance trying to look after the peasants in the Central Highlands was the ICRC, which by December 1981 ran feeding centres for 60,000 people. But the young Swiss people who worked in the centres were in constant danger because the military convoys in which they travelled came under almost daily attack. In January 1982 a high-level ICRC delegation flew from Geneva to Rabat to ask Savimbi if a secret agreement could be reached to give their vehicles immunity from attack by his guerrillas.

Savimbi said the problem was that the Angolan Red Cross and the Scandinavian Red Cross used the same markings as the ICRC – and since these organisations were integrated into the MPLA's political effort they were subject to attack.

'But we agreed to give the ICRC the maximum freedom of movement possible,' said Savimbi. 'We guaranteed the total safety of ICRC planes. They agreed that ICRC trucks would not move in military convoys; and we agreed that when they moved by themselves they would not be attacked. But we could not give a total guarantee on trucks; mines do not discriminate.'

Savimbi was able to establish an intimate bond with the ICRC because his old professor at Lausanne University, Henri Rieben, had also taught several students who had become senior ICRC officials. But intimacy was no guarantee of harmony, and throughout the rest of 1982 the UNITA leader's relationship with the ICRC steadily deteriorated. So also did prospects of peace for Namibia and Angola.

40

The War Intensifies

1982

The first jolt to the peace process came in March when South Africa launched 'Operation Super', a helicopter-borne assault across the Angolan border against a new base that SWAPO had set up in the Cambeno Valley in Cunene Province. Inside a day 201 of some 250 young guerrillas lay lifeless, against three South African dead. Fifty tonnes of captured weapons were brought back to Namibia where journalists were told that the operation had been like a 'turkey shoot'.[1]

Nevertheless, until mid-year, the momentum for an Angola–Namibia settlement continued. A plan was accepted from the 'Contact Group' of Western nations who had proposed a three-phase transition to Namibian independence under UN supervision. It proposed:

* Agreement between the UN, South Africa and SWAPO on an electoral procedure.

* Agreement on the strength and composition of a UN force to be placed in Namibia and on the Angola-Namibia border after a ceasefire, and during the run-up to elections.

* A seven-month transitional period from the time of a ceasefire, involving the withdrawal of South African and SWAPO forces to designated bases, until the holding of UN-supervised elections which would be followed by independence.

South Africa and SWAPO reached accord on phase one, except for one SWAPO objection which it was agreed could be resolved later.

By June Pretoria was ready to accept the second phase and move to the final elections/independence phase, provided the Cubans simultaneously withdrew from Angola: 'That is the most important point in the whole settlement,' said the South African Prime Minister.[2] It was also the most difficult point. Indeed, it was insurmountable, although serious newspapers managed to suggest success was a mere hair's-breadth away. For example, *The Economist* said: 'A lot of problems have been solved. Only on one important point is there still disagreement: should a settlement be linked to the withdrawal of Cuban troops from Angola? "Yes," say the South Africans. "In no circumstances," say SWAPO, Angola and the neighbouring black states. "All right, not linked, but how about parallel?" say the Americans.

'In fact, the disagreement is not as deep as it sounds. Pretty well everyone, including the Angolans, agree that it is desirable for the Cubans to go home. The trick is the timing.'[3]

What *The Economist* did not explain was how to solve the MPLA's fundamental dilemma: Jonas Savimbi. Theoretically, once the South Africans withdrew 1,300 kilometres southwards from the Angola–Namibia border to the Namibia-South Africa border, there would no longer be any good external cause for the Cuban Army to stay in Angola. But Savimbi would remain, still fighting and relentlessly insisting that if the MPLA was demanding elections for the people of Namibia then it was illogical to deny elections to the people of Angola. The Cubans were needed to contain the MPLA's opponents, but how could the MPLA find a formula of diplomatic language to convince the international community that this had a basis in justice when the South African threat was gone?

What is surprising, with hindsight, is how long optimism was sustained through 1982 about a Namibian settlement, given that Prime Minister Botha's statements and actions demanded of the MPLA a concession it could not make . . .

unless, of course, Savimbi and UNITA could be eliminated in some way.

Botha took every opportunity of saying the Cubans must go. When Botha, accompanied by his intelligence chief, General van der Westhuizen, held a summit meeting with Kenneth Kaunda on 30 April 1982 he repeated the message to Savimbi's old friend, and introduced a new demand: the MPLA must negotiate with Savimbi and encompass UNITA into a government of national reconciliation. It was hardly a call from which Kaunda could demur: it was the stand he had taken in 1975–76 on what he had described as the highest of principles. And Botha was able to tell Kaunda that his strategy had full backing from Washington, whom Kaunda had asked to intervene in Angola back in April 1975.

As well as maintaining diplomatic pressure on the MPLA, Botha kept up the military pressure. With speculation rife in the South African and international press that a ceasefire between SWAPO and South Africa would be signed on 15 August 1982, the SADF launched yet another raid early that month deep into Namibia in which Pretoria announced that 314 SWAPO guerrillas had been killed. The new assault surprised even South Africans, for their government at first dismissed as 'blatant propaganda' Angolan allegations of a further major incursion into Cunene. What forced Pretoria's admission were the deaths of 12 SADF soldiers, none more than 22 years old, and three airmen, when the helicopter ferrying them to the battle zone was brought down by a SAM-7 missile. It was the highest casualty toll the South Africans had suffered in a single incident in more than 16 years of fighting in Namibia/Angola.[4]

Then, just as the bewildering optimism regained momentum about a possible ceasefire on 15 September, Prime Minister Botha made a particularly hardline speech to the congress of the Transvaal branch of the ruling National Party. Speaking in the political heartland of the party, and looking over his shoulder at the extreme right-wing Transvaal politician Dr Andries Treurnicht, who had broken away from the ruling party ealier in the year, Mr Botha said: 'The Government is not prepared, *nor will it ever be in future*, to implement any settlement plan for south west Africa

(Namibia) unless prior agreement is reached in terms of which Cuban forces must be withdrawn from Angola. If this position of the Government brings it into conflict with the UN or the international community at large, then we accept the consequences of such a conflict. Our position is that the presence of Cuban troops in any southern African country will constitute a threat to the interests of this country, and I wish to make it very clear that we shall not countenance such a presence.'[5]

It was at this congress that Botha won backing from the Transvaal members – the National Party's biggest provincial grouping – for his proposals for limited power-sharing with non-whites of mixed race or Asian descent but excluding blacks. The hard line against the Cubans in Angola was reinforced by the need to swing the majority of his very conservative party behind the reform plans, which were revolutionary in Afrikaaner terms.

A little earlier, in August, President Reagan wrote to President Nyerere, the doyen of the leaders of the black African front-line states, saying that an agreement on Namibian independence was conditional on the Cubans pulling out of Angola at the same time as the South Africans left Namibia. Without the parallel movement a 'fragile, historic opportunity will be lost,' said the American leader.[6] The US President's plea failed to convince the front-line leaders. When they met on 4 September they rejected linkage between Cuban withdrawal from Angola and independence for Namibia, and said the presence of Cubans in Angola was a bilateral issue between two independent states.[7]

That effectively ended the attempts to reach a settlement of the Namibia/Angola problem under UN auspices. A real-estate agent in Windhoek was told that his commission to find 50 houses for senior United Nations personnel had been withdrawn. Space booked on freight ships to take many tonnes of UN equipment to Namibia was cancelled. Brian Urquhart, the UN Under-Secretary-General, stopped taking journalists into his New York skyscraper map room to show them his plans for putting a multi-national force into Namibia.[8]

At the year's end Fidel Castro reinforced the deadlock

with a bitter speech to militiamen in Havana in which he denounced US foreign policy as fascist and said Cuban troops would remain in Angola for as long as the MPLA wanted them. Just four days earlier the CIA had said the Cubans had increased the number of their troops in Angola from about 20,000 early in the year to about 30,000 by December 1982. Speaking to his militiamen about the CIA allegations, Castro said: 'We are not going to say if the report is the truth or a lie. But if we did so we would be carrying out our duty in view of imperialist threats.'[9]

* * *

It was against this background, of apparent preparation for peace, constant South African military hammer-blows against SWAPO in Angola, that Jonas Savimbi continued his own war and his people suffered their own hardships.

In May another 12 members of UNITA's underground cells were sentenced to death by People's Revolutionary Tribunals and executed in Luanda and Lobito. In a statement, Savimbi said: 'UNITA vehemently protests the indiscriminate executions of its members by the MPLA minority régime. Due to the acquiescent silence of international human rights organisations such as Amnesty International, UNITA has no alternative but to intensify the fight for self-defence and to protect its members until the final victory.'[10]

This was not a fair attack on Amnesty, which had done more than any organisation to find out about, and publicise, death sentences imposed on dissidents in Angola – just as it had also with regard to opponents of the establishments in Namibia and South Africa. Without Amnesty there would have been no independent confirmation of the MPLA's severe actions against its own party dissidents, such as Nito Alves, and against UNITA. Privately, the Central Africa research desk at Amnesty's London headquarters said UNITA had been told of Amnesty's efforts to prevent death sentences in Angola from being carried out; but UNITA seemed 'unwilling or unable to adopt a more positive attitude towards us and has consistently failed to meet our requests for more information about the names of members of UNITA arrested or captured by the Angolan authorities'.[11]

The executions preceded the convening at Mavinga of UNITA's fifth policy-making Congress. Some 1,500 delegates trekked from across Angola to approve another major push northwards to begin from September. The semi-regular battalions would leave Mavinga and lay siege to towns like Gago Coutinho, which UNITA had lost back in 1976, at the beginning of the long march. Guerrilla groups and political commissars would begin expanding military activity into three provinces in the northern half of the country – Malange, Lunda and Cuanza Sul.

The establishment of permanent bases in the north was coupled with an appeal to members of more northerly tribes – such as the Kikongo, Kimbundu and Seles – to 'join UNITA in the struggle against Soviet-Cuban domination'.[12] The Congress, held from 26 to 31 July, ended with the publication of a manifesto, the Mavinga Declaration, which supported 'all measures leading to Namibian independence'. However, it called for the international community to draw a distinction between 'UNITA's struggle against the occupation of Angola by Soviet imperialism and its surrogates, and the conflict between the patriotic Namibians and the decolonising power which is the Republic of South Africa'.[13]

The Mavinga Declaration reinforced the South African and United States line that a Namibian settlement could only be achieved if there was a departure of the Cubans from Angola, 'leading to a peaceful settlement of the Angolan conflict'. It said the Contact Group-United Nations initiative had not led to any concessions by the MPLA in Angola. Instead, the government's drive against its opponents had intensified: the Mavinga Declaration noted that the Cubans had started an offensive on 2 July 1982 against UNITA positions 'using massive and lethal means, such as napalm and other substances, against defenceless civilian populations'.

The Cubans/MPLA overran UNITA-held towns at Baixo Longa and Vila Nova de Armada, to the south of Cuito

Cuanavale and within striking distance of such strategic UNITA strongholds as Mavinga and Luengue.

'Because of the talks going on (about Namibia's future) the enemy has increased the pressure on our forces. Up to the end of September the situation was very tough,' Savimbi told one journalist.[14]

There are no independent accounts of the offensive, but it appears to have lasted for more than three months and, according to UNITA communiqués, 5,000 Cuban and 12,000 MPLA troops were involved, backed by nearly 40 T-34 and T-62 tanks, seven MIG-21 and six Antonov-26 bombers, and 15 MI-8 and seven Alouette helicopters. Among UNITA strongholds bombed were Mavinga, Luengue, Ninda and Muie.[15] UNITA said that by 8 October, 400 of its soldiers had died in the offensive.[16]

The UNITA counter-offensive took place on propaganda and military fronts. The former involved the release in mid-September of 15 foreigners held by the movement, and then in mid-November the release of UNITA's two Soviet prisoners, Chernietsky and Kolya, in one of the most complicated prisoner exchanges in history. The first group released consisted of six Portuguese, three Brazilians, four Spaniards, an Argentine and a Swiss. Most were missionaries, priests, nurses and doctors working in outposts overrun by UNITA in various parts of central and southern Angola. Some had been forced to march hundreds of kilometres and had been held in bush bases for up to six months, except for one Portuguese who had been in captivity since July 1979. There were also two baby boys among the prisoners.[17]

Journalists crossed the River Cubango from Namibia into Angola to watch the official release ceremony. The site was 15 kilometres north of Mucusso, the small border post with Namibia which UNITA had held since 1977. One of their interesting revelations was that the site was a UNITA training and support base, obviously well known to the South Africans, who permitted the President of the South African Red Cross, Dr Pieter Smit, to cross the river and conduct the prisoners on their journey first to Johannesburg and then onwards to their homes in Europe and South America.

Colonel Bok Sapalalo told the correspondents that the prisoners had been taken to prevent them giving medical and other services to the MPLA – 'We had no intention of taking hostages. We only want to deprive the enemy of their services and then let them return to their own countries and people.' This was consistent with a theme that had been developed in the Mavinga Declaration calling on foreign workers to leave Angola because their security could not be guaranteed as the fighting continued to spread and intensify.

The farewell ceremonies were emotional, according to one correspondent: 'From the tearful embraces with their erstwhile captors, it was clear that the 15 had not been merely diplomatic about their insistence that they had been well treated. Some even called: "We shall be back" as the tin boats tilted away to the South West African bank.'[18]

Among the 15 was an ICRC nurse, 26-year-old Swiss girl Mary-Josée Burnier, who had been captured during a UNITA attack on a food relief convoy near Huambo on 25 May 1982.[19] Miss Burnier had walked more than 1,000 kilometres for 35 consecutive days with UNITA, but she was full of praise for her captors: 'They were kind and gentle. They could not have been more considerate.' But despite the Swiss girl's plaudits, relationships between the ICRC and UNITA deteriorated to a point where in October the ICRC suspended operations in central Angola because of the risks to its personnel.[20]

As well as the capture of Miss Burnier, ICRC relief columns suffered mine explosions and there were bomb attacks in March and July at its Bomba Alta orthopaedic centre in the suburbs of Huambo where people who had lost limbs during the war were fitted with artificial legs.[21] There were no casualties in the Bomba Alta attacks, but the ICRC was left in no doubt about UNITA hostility when a communiqué accused ICRC personnel of gathering intelligence for the MPLA. Savimbi said he was deeply indignant about the ICRC's 'connivant silence' about the MPLA's transformation of Protestant and Catholic missions at Chissamba, Camundongo, Chilesso, Dondi, Bunjei, Elende, Chinhama and Trapa into military bases. 'We have therefore decided to cease all contacts with the ICRC and we will not be responsible for whatever may happen to their personnel and facilities, because this organisation continues its stubborn presence in the war zones of UNITA.'[22]

At this stage the ICRC finally decided to call a halt to its activities, despite the fact that the number of people in the Central Highlands dependent upon it for daily feeding had grown to 120,000.[23]

*　　*　　*

The release of the two Soviet airmen had involved negotiations between seven different parties. As well as UNITA, representatives of the Soviet Union, the US, Zambia, Cuba, the MPLA and South Africa had been meeting each other on three continents for more than 18 months to arrange a swap which also involved three Americans imprisoned by the MPLA, a Russian soldier, a Cuban soldier and 94 MPLA soldiers held by South Africa, and the return of three bodies of South African soldiers killed by the MPLA/Cubans in Angola in exchange for the bodies of four Russians and one Cuban killed by the South Africans in Angola.

The exchange began in Jamba, where Chernietsky and Kolya were treated as honoured guests at a farewell dinner of impala stew before they were flown by the SADF to South Africa. They were photographed by journalists under giant banners depicting scenes from UNITA's war with the Cubans which bore the slogan 'Let's stop Soviet mad dreams'.[24]

The day after the prisoner and body swap had been completed, US Vice-President George Bush, on a seven-nation official visit to black Africa, said in Nairobi: 'The withdrawal of Cuban forces from Angola in parallel framework with South Africa's departure from Namibia is the key to the settlement we all desire. In the final analysis, it is also the surest way to guarantee Angola's long term security and independence. The United States wants an end to South Africa's occupation of Namibia. At the same time the United States wants an end to Angola's suffering and to the dangerous cycle of violence in the region. My government is not ashamed to state the US interest in seeking an

end to the presence of Cuban forces in Angola. Their introduction seven years ago tore the fabric of reciprocal restraint
between the US and the Soviet Union in the developing
world.'[25]

Zambia played a key role in the complex swap, which took
place at Lusaka Airport on 16 November and was supervised in its final stages by the ICRC. First a twin-engined
Red Cross plane flew in from Luanda and from it stepped
three Americans who had been imprisoned by the MPLA,
mercenaries Gustavo Grillo and Gary Acker, and civilian
pilot Geoffrey Tyler. Grillo and Acker had been sentenced to
30 and 16 years respectively in 1976 in the public trials of
white mercenaries caught fighting with the FNLA. Tyler
had been arrested and imprisoned in February 1980 after the
plane he had been flying, from Abidjan in the Ivory Coast to
Cape Town, landed on a road in south-west Angola after
developing engine trouble over the Atlantic.

A second Red Cross plane brought the bodies of the South
Africans into Lusaka from Luanda. The freed Americans
waited with US Embassy officials in the airport's international terminal until the arrival several hours later of the
Soviet, Cuban and Angolan prisoners and bodies in an
SADF C-130 transport plane.[26] The three Americans then
left on a flight for Paris *en route* to Washington, and the C-130
took the three South African bodies back to permanent
graves in their homeland. Soviet officials took custody of
Kolya, Chernietsky as well as another Russian, Sergeant-
Major Nikolai Pestretsov, taken prisoner by the SADF when
fleeing from N'Giva in August 1981. The Soviet officials also
received the four bodies of Russians killed at the same time
as Pestretsov was captured – including the Sergeant-Major's
wife.

The swap was above all a face-saver for the US and the
USSR. The Americans, embarrassed by the mercenaries'
incarceration in Luanda, had long sought their release.
Equally the Soviet Union felt humiliated by having its milit-
ary men in the hands of black African rebels and the South
African government. What Zambia gained from the role of
honest broker is difficult to say, but two days after the swap
George Bush arrived in Lusaka on one leg of his tour of

African countries considered to be of vital interest to the United States: the others were Senegal, Nigeria, Cape Verde, Kenya, Zimbabwe and Zaire. Zambia had its history of co-operation with Washington on Angola and a close insight into the continuing problems since much of its 1,300 kilometre border with Angola was now controlled by UNITA. MPs from the west of the country had told the Zambian Parliament that their constituents had to obtain passes from UNITA border offices in order to enter Angola to trade in fish and other items. They urged the government to explain who was considered the legitimate power in Angola. 'Zambians should be told of our stand,' said Mr John Kalenge, MP for Mwinilunga West. 'Who has authority in Angola? Is it UNITA? If Savimbi can serve us, then let us have him. It seems there are two governments there – in fact, three, because Cubans are also a government.'[26]

The release of the Soviet prisoners was followed a day later by the release, through Namibia, of Angola's Roman Catholic Archbishop of Lubango, Monsignor Alexandre dos Nascimento. He had been captured by UNITA soldiers a month earlier when he visited a mission station at Mongua, in Cunene Province. Released with the Archbishop were a French nun, a Dutch Catholic priest and three Angolan employees of the Angolan Red Cross who were also captured at Mongua. Four other Angolan Red Cross workers captured there chose to remain with UNITA.

* * *

Even as Savimbi was releasing his prisoners in an apparent gesture of conciliation, UNITA's military counter-offensive had begun in spectacular fashion. In its most important victory to that date, UNITA forces stormed Gago Coutinho (renamed Lumbala after independence) on 10 November, more than six years after Savimbi had been forced out of the town in the course of the long march. UNITA claimed 112 MPLA and 10 Cubans dead at Gago Coutinho; and 225 enemy captured, along with 43 enemy vehicles and more than 300 weapons. Two rebel soldiers were killed and six wounded, UNITA claimed.[27]

Gago Coutinho was 450 kilometres north of the Namibian

border. But in another attack, three days earlier, UNITA attacked the town of Calulo in Cuanza-Sul Province, 850 kilometres north of the border and only 220 kilometres south of Luanda. And at Calulo UNITA captured two Brazilian agricultural technicians, Senhor Alberto Gentil Pimenta and Senhor Alvaro da Cunha Oliveira.[28]

The MPLA said nothing about Gago Coutinho and Calulo. But it broke silence when UNITA claimed to have blown up the 350-metre-long Giraul River railway bridge, near Mocamedes, on the most southerly of Angola's three railways, the Mocamedes-Menongue line. UNITA said a specialist sabotage brigade had also destroyed a 400-metre road bridge across the river and killed 57 MPLA troops guarding the bridges.[29] The MPLA admitted the partial destruction of the bridges but alleged that the attack had been carried out by South African marines who were dropped offshore by a South African Navy vessel and moved one kilometre upriver in fibreglass launches.[30]

On 8 November UNITA claimed that one of its clandestine teams had blown up the MPLA's main assembly hall in Huambo; on 23 November it claimed to have captured Cangombe, near Gago Coutinho, when the MPLA abandoned it after a four-month siege; on 24 December UNITA forces penetrated the Huambo industrial suburb of Cuca, blew up two fuel-oil tanks, destroyed three giant sewing machines in a clothing factory and removed more than 3,000 bales of cloth; and on 24 December rebel troops shot down an Antonov-26 transport plane attempting to land at Lupire, near the major Cuban garrison at Cuito Cuanavale.[31]

On 24 December, also, UNITA said it had annihilated the MPLA's 16th Motorised Brigade while it was retreating the 120 kilometres from Lupire to Cuito Cuanavale, killing 263 MPLA soldiers and 32 Cubans. In that attack and others between 20 and 26 December UNITA claimed to have killed a total of 404 MPLA soldiers and 70 Cubans and to have moved into the northern coffee-growing province of Uige for the first time.[32]

The only independent report of the major UNITA push northwards came from a young AFP (French Press Agency) correspondent, Jean-Luc Porte, who persuaded the MPLA to let him visit Huambo at a time when French Foreign Minister Claud Cheysson and Development Minister Jean-Pierre Cot were making sympathetic gestures towards the MPLA.[33]

Porte reported: 'MPLA leaders here privately acknowledge that the situation has never been as bad. Ambushes have multiplied with the rainy season, and UNITA bands of 10 men have become units 100-strong. MPLA morale is further shaken by rumours that UNITA has infiltrated a number of government bodies. Basic commodities are now becoming scarcer round Huambo, once considered Angola's granary. Local people complain of the growing shortage of food and long queues form outside petrol stations. Cuts in the electricity and water supply – which is polluted – are frequent. 'UNITA is said to be trying to throttle Huambo economically because it cannot take the city by military means. The town is strongly defended, and I was told of "thousands" of Cubans camped on the outskirts.'[34]

An MPLA official told Porte that, in late November in the Huambo area, UNITA had attacked a supply convoy at Aquas Quentes and destroyed 21 trucks; launched a rocket attack on a convoy of petrol tankers near Vila Franca and killed 30 people; killed ten MPLA troops in an ambush at Chipiba; killed seven Cubans in a convoy near Cuma; and destroyed three Benguela Railway engines. In one of the railway attacks, between Lobito and Huambo, UNITA guerrillas had killed five people, stolen the goods being transported and set fire to the locomotive.

The move northwards clearly had great momentum, and when UNITA offered me the chance to be the first Western journalist to witness a major battle in Angola in more than 20 years of fighting, I accepted with alacrity. I would also become the first journalist to reach the Benguela Railway with UNITA since the civil war of 1975–76. I wanted a witness to the reality – so I invited another journalist to join me. Gwynne Roberts, a reporter/cameraman, had made remarkable films inside rebel territory in Kurdistan and Eritrea. In Angola he was to film our journey for the BBC's *Panorama* current affairs programme.

41

Into the Heart of Angola

1983

The white Angolan pilot of the old work-horse Viscount searched the forests and savannahs below, trying to locate landmarks which would guide him to Savimbi's airstrip at Luengue. The needle-thin target appeared suddenly on slightly elevated ground alongside a lush green river valley – for this was early January, in the middle of the rainy season – and soon we were landing. At first the thick bush lining the sandy runway appeared deserted, but then shadowy figures began to emerge carrying Kalashnikovs and RPG-7 rocket launchers.

The Viscount rolled to a stop, and as its doors opened we were hit by an explosion of sound: three African choirs, a pop group and a dance team competed against each other. Gwynne was stunned by the colour of it all. The singers and dancers were flanked by platoons of troops at unyielding attention. Big trucks – Soviet Urals and Polish Stars – began moving up to unload several tonnes of medicine and aviation fuel we had carried from our departure point, a black African capital where UNITA maintained a diplomatic-cum-logistics mission. Down the runway stood Savimbi surrounded by a phalanx of UNITA colonels and majors.

Our initial meeting with Savimbi was brief. It would be most profitable to talk to him after we had returned from the battle on the railway line. However, he was in especially ebullient form. He said his forces had advanced spectacularly over the previous six months: we would see the gains. He was confident of many other victories.

The object of the trip was simple. UNITA wanted to prove

that the big victories it had won were real, not just propaganda on paper, and that it exercised complete control over vast areas of the country. I wanted first-hand material for my newspaper and for my book.

With UNITA we would penetrate 800 kilometres into the very centre of the country, where we would witness an action on the Benguela Railway at a place yet to be disclosed. The journey there and back would be completed in a month, said Savimbi. It took two months, by which time we had covered 3,200 kilometres, more than 500 of them on foot.

*   *   *

From the airstrip we were driven to our huts in the base where I had waited with Dick Harwood for nine days after our aircraft crashed in 1981. Since my last visit, electric light had been installed, provided by a small diesel generator which chugged on through the night. We would see electric light in several bases: in 1981 electricity had been confined to Savimbi's General Headquarters at Jamba in the middle of the spectacular game reserve to the south-east of Luengue.

My experience had been that you meet unusual people in Angola. This occasion was no exception, and I wanted to speak to one of them – an English diamond merchant who had flown in with Gwynne and myself and half a dozen of UNITA's overseas representatives. The diamond merchant had come to buy UNITA diamonds, some panned from rivers and others smuggled out of mines in the north-east jointly run by the Angolan government and South Africa's Anglo-American company. He had also come to tell Savimbi that he had commitments from a group of West European businessmen of investments worth hundreds of millions of dollars should UNITA ever come to power. Money was also immediately available for Savimbi's struggle at rates of between 20,000 and 100,000 dollars per company – painless sidestakes by European fat cats against possible future shares in Angola's immense potential wealth.

The last we saw of the diamond merchant was as he changed in his hut from sweaty bush jacket and slacks into pinstripe suit, waistcoat, tie and white-starched collar for his jungle business meeting with Savimbi. He flew out again next morning after just 12 hours in Angola.

Our own work began that same morning with a briefing from UNITA's Chief of Staff, Demostenes Chilingutila, promoted to Brigadier since my last visit, and the Chief of Logistics, Colonel Bok Sapalalo, one of the survivors of the long march. Chilungutila, then 35, and Sapalalo, 28, represented different recruitment trends in UNITA.

Chilingutila, a stocky and muscled man, was formerly in the Portuguese Army in Angola and rose to the highest rank open to blacks: staff sergeant. An artillery specialist, he was at one time posted to eastern Angola operating against UNITA. Chilingutila joined UNITA after the Portuguese revolution of 25 April 1974. He was appointed Chief of Staff in April 1980, replacing Brigadier Samuel Chiwale, a veteran founder of the movement from the days when Chilingutila was part of the enemy.

Sapalalo was a bright high school graduate who, in the early seventies, *before* the Portuguese revolution, decided to join UNITA in the bush rather than go to university. Like many of his academic peers, he spoke near-fluent English though he had never lived in an English-speaking country. Sapalalo's left arm was missing below the elbow, blown off when a faulty anti-personnel mine that he was defusing exploded. At that time Sapalalo had been in charge of sabotage training.

The gist of the briefing by Chilingutila and Sapalalo was as follows: in the previous six months, since August 1982, UNITA had doubled the area of Angola under its total control in a series of fierce battles with the MPLA and Cubans which had gone almost entirely unreported and unregarded in the world press. The area, roughly equivalent in size to the United Kingdom, extended nearly all the way to the Benguela Railway. We would travel through that area. UNITA would show us battle sites and take us to towns captured from the MPLA that the government in Luanda had never publicly admitted losing. Last time I had visited Angola, Chilingutila's operational base was 200 kilometres inside Angola: this time I would find it 500 kilometres from Angola's southern border.

Beyond UNITA's 'area of control', and beyond what Chilingutila and Sapalalo described as its 'area of influence' where there was a great intensification of activities, guerrillas were pushing the boundaries northwards into an 'area of expansion'.

Within the 'area of influence', where the movement claimed control over the countryside and most of the villages, UNITA was concentrating attacks on economic targets. Particular objectives were the Mocamedes Railway and the one remaining regularly operational stretch of the Benguela Railway between Lobito and Huambo. Only one train every three months, with heavy troop escorts, was getting through to Menongue, at the end of the Mocamedes line 600 kilometres from the coast. The last train on the Benguela line to get through to Huambo from Lobito had arrived in September 1982 with an escort of 1,200 MPLA troops: but half of the train's consignment had been destroyed *en route* by 517 Battalion, one of two battalions of semi-regular troops established permanently north of the Benguela Railway.

UNITA now had several well-established guerrilla groups (as distinct from semi-regular soldiers) operating in the provinces of Cuanza Norte, Malanje and southern Luanda – that is, 400 kilometres north of the Benguela Railway and within 250 kilometres of Luanda. Many members of the Kimbundu, Seles and Songo tribes, traditional supporters of the MPLA in the pre-independence period, were now joining UNITA as guerrillas because of the parlous state of the Angolan economy.

UNITA had extended its 'area of expansion' in late 1982 into the far northern province of Uige, the Kikongo homeland of the practically moribund FNLA. UNITA political commissars had reached the province in November 1982 to begin recruiting support. UNITA guerrilla groups, salted with Kikongo tribesmen, had already moved into Uige ready to launch fighting on the new front.

The war had become so serious that the Cubans, having largely kept out of the fighting since 1980, acting only as military advisers and logistics organisers and defending the big towns, had re-entered the fray on a big scale in July 1982.

In addition to UNITA's semi-regular forces, organised in battalions 500 to 1,000 strong, and its guerrillas, operating in groups of 15 to 30 or in company strength of 120, a new type of unit had entered action in 1982. These were the 'Special Forces', roughly equivalent to the British SAS. These were tight-knit units, 45-strong, of well-proven soldiers trained intensively together for nine months in sabotage, hand-to-hand fighting and other military 'arts'. They kept strictly to themselves and were subject to iron discipline. Gwynne thought they looked very mean indeed.

We were given one of these units as a bodyguard for our journey – Special Force Gamboa, named after a UNITA hero who had died fighting the Portuguese. Lieutenant Bonaventura would be in command. In addition, a logistics team of 50 people was assigned to us under the command of Captain John Celas, a Kikongo who had also travelled with me in 1981. Brigadier Chilingutila was to press on ahead, and we would catch up with him at his field headquarters far to the north.

Meanwhile, as we prepared for departure, I asked if I could borrow a small knapsack so that I could keep my cameras near me. When it came I noticed some writing in ballpoint on the khaki canvas. It said: 'Natal Command – Lance Corporal Kuhn'. It was not a great surprise, though it was a timely reminder of one of the strange thumbs stuck in the Angolan pie. And I couldn't help wondering how I would explain the pack if, by mischance, we were ever picked up by an MPLA patrol.

*   *   *

We set out from Luengue in two giant Ural trucks. We were to travel along the Savimbi Trail to where it ended, 150 kilometres south of the Benguela Railway. Sitting up front in the Urals was hellish, though not quite as bad as in the Polish Stars in 1981 because now periodic rain showers kept down the dust. In fact, I developed a certain affection for these Soviet monsters. Mightily sprung, they ploughed on relentlessly over the roughest terrain, across fords and crude bridges, and up formidable slopes.

Within two days we were passing Mavinga, 250

kilometres inside Angola, where Dick and I had picked oranges in 1981. Then it had been the furthest point of our journey into Angola. Now it marked the virtual beginning of the trip.

After six days we reached a broad and beautiful waterway beaded on either side by magical lagoons, some small and others like giant lakes, each surrounded by tall, swaying papyrus reeds. This was a crucial point on UNITA's military logistics route. Unlike the smaller rivers to the south, the Cuando could not be forded or bridged. To get trucks to the war zone north of the Cuando River, the Chief of transport had set up a base on the mosquito-infested south bank where vehicles were completely dismantled to enable sections to be put aboard a small metal troop ferry, powered by outboard motor, and taken to a base on the north bank several kilometres upstream for reassembly.

The Chief of Transport, a 34-year-old white Angolan, Matos Leilinho, said it took eight days to get a Ural across the river from the time his men began to dismantle it to when it had been finally reassembled on the other side. A Star took three days and a British Land Rover 24 hours. The problem with the Urals was their complicated electrical system. Also at the Cuando River crossing was another white Angolan, Major Victor, who was in charge of UNITA's anti-aircraft defences. It was his job to distribute Soviet SAM-7 missiles, Soviet 14.5mm anti-aircraft guns and Chinese 12.7mm anti-aircraft guns to units throughout the country. To get them to such regions as the Central Highlands and further north, the guns were dismantled and carried on the backs and heads of guerrillas and porters. Major Victor also had to ensure that the missile and gun crews were trained and their weapons properly maintained. He was on an inspection visit to the Cuando crossing because it was a particularly vulnerable link in the logistics line. It had been regularly bombed, and the Major claimed that since July 1982 anti-aircraft defences at the crossing had shot down two MPLA Antonov-26 aircraft, two MI-8 assault helicopters and an Alouette reconnaissance helicopter.

We crossed the river in a rubber Zephyr boat, passing the metal ferry coming the other way carrying the chassis and back wheels of an East German 'Ifa' truck captured in fighting to the north of the Cuando. As we approached the logistics base on the north bank we saw a giant wooden frame which had been driven into the river bed near the bank. Over it hung a big chain and pulley for hoisting truck parts onto the seven-metre-long metal ferry. There was a warehouse, half-dug into the ground and covered by thatch, from which men were loading sacks of maize and drums of fuel onto a gigantic Soviet 'Kpaz' truck to be transported northwards. The 'Kpaz' and Urals and Stars at this base were riddled with bullet holes. They had been captured north of the Cuando when UNITA overran MPLA strongholds at Muie (May 1982) and Gago Coutinho (November 1982). It was in one of these 'aertex' Urals that we headed relentlessly northwards to Chilingutila's operations base camp at Kandende, in thick forest near the town of Muie.

Kandende was remarkable: there was electricity throughout, our huts were newly built of fragrant green grass and the beds were made up with beautifully laundered embroidered sheets. Bushcraft was in the sophisticated style of the Chokwe tribe, whose territory we had now entered. There were artistic little twirls in the roof thatch, and at the back of my hut there was a shower area where neatly peeled logs had been laid densely across a small pit so that your feet stayed clean while the water drained away after a dousing. Throughout the widely spread base ran arrow-straight paths, lined by fences made from tree logs stripped of their bark to expose the pink pith. The precision and discipline reminded me of the trim orderliness of Indian military cantonments, which contrast starkly with the civilian dirt and confusion around them.

Kandende gave only temporary respite from the punishment of travel with UNITA. Soon we were heading due east along a particularly hostile branch of the Savimbi Trail to one of UNITA's prize possessions, Gago Coutinho. The trail was forged through forest so dense with saplings that at times we were passing through a tunnel of greenery and over a surface made up entirely of knotted root systems that would test the endurance of any man or vehicle. We saw only a few small antelope and partridge-like francolin scuttering across the trail, but whenever we emerged from one of the tunnels there were always big eagles cruising the sky in search of prey.

One hundred and twenty kilometres had been covered in ten hours and darkness had fallen when we saw in the headlight beams a raised, tarred road. We were joining the main highway which runs for hundreds of kilometres along Angola's eastern border with Zambia. We had hit it at a point about ten kilometres south of Gago Coutinho. I began to sweat in sheer funk: earlier, UNITA officials had said they avoided using regular roads in areas formerly controlled by the MPLA because they had been comprehensively mined by UNITA guerrillas. Even more frightening were the crossings of two rivers by improvised wooden bridges which were barely wider than the Urals.

Passing through Gago Coutinho we saw in the headlights a series of Portuguese-style houses and buildings shattered by cannon and mortar shells. The town was eerily empty and we slept at a forest base five kilometres beyond it.

The next day began with a political rally. A company of semi-regulars performed some snappy drill, including a nice take-off of the rigid-backed marching style of Britain's Coldstream Guards. Then Chilingutila rose to address the local people. 'The fundamental difference between us and the MPLA,' he said in Portuguese, 'is that we do not want foreigners to come and rule the country. And, as you know, the MPLA brought the Cubans.' He promised that schools, hospitals and agricultural advisory centres would soon be established in the area. His speech was translated into Mbunda, the language of the small tribe of that name in the Gago Coutinho region, by Colonel Vicente Vihema, the local political commissar and himself an Mbunda.

Chilingutila said UNITA wanted people to move out of the MPLA-designed fortified hamlets around the town. 'We have come to stay and we will not leave again. Our forces are moving northwards. Come and discuss with us anything you want to. We must understand each other. And if your young people want to join FALA they will be welcome.' The elders and villagers had been well mobilised by UNITA's political organisers, cheer leaders and choral experts. There was much dancing and singing and everyone waved paper UNITA flags. Many seemed to be enjoying it; others were just going through the motions, as they presumably had also done under the MPLA. The village elders had stoic, enduring faces which seemed to contain much fundamental wisdom not lightly shared. They wore a bewildering array of old clothes and solar topees, and one wore a dinner jacket whose shiny lapels had faded with the passing years. Chilingutila, who measured each word and whose stern face broke occasionally into a warm smile, drew a rumble of approval from the old men when he said he would later hold a meeting restricted to the village elders. He went on: 'The MPLA has been teaching children not to respect their parents (more murmurs of approval). Children should not have guns put in their hands as the MPLA are doing with the Young Pioneers.[1] They should go to school.'

The importance of Gago Coutinho stemmed from the fact that the town controlled one of three access roads across Angola's 1,000 kilometres eastern border with Zambia. (The other two roads were to the north-east in Angola's Cazombo salient, jutting eastwards between Zaire and Zambia.) 'Kaunda knows this border is cleared,' Chilingutila told the rally. 'Kaunda is aware that UNITA is clearing the whole eastern border and that there is no alternative to dealing with us. You will be given UNITA passports so that you can go to trade in Zambia.'

Two important MPLA leaders in Gago Coutinho had been captured, said Chilingutila – Jose Chipoia, the local party leader, and Queen Lipito, a member of the Mbunda royal family who had become a deputy in Luanda to the MPLA Congress. Chipoia and Lipito were 'exchanging views with UNITA', said Chilingutila, and they would later be released.

We toured the wrecked town. There were people with bundles on their heads, bits and pieces collected from their homes in the MPLA's strategic hamlets – rows of mud huts beyond the former Portuguese villas and shops – to take back to their traditional villages. They looked bewildered, and one senior UNITA official admitted that 30 per cent of Angolans had no particular commitment to this war – they'll follow any side which is winning, wave the appropriate flags and, if necessary, stand on their heads for the latest group which comes bearing guns. That said, there seemed to be no doubt about the warmth with which another group of elders hugged Chilingutila, Gwynne and me.

Chilingutila described how UNITA had captured Gago Coutinho ten weeks earlier. It had been garrisoned by a brigade of 1,200 MPLA troops and a company of 90 Cubans. For several months beforehand, UNITA intelligence units gathered information by entering the town dressed as villagers and by talking to clandestine UNITA supporters, while guerrilla groups, varying in strength between 120 and 600, harassed its approaches. On the night of 7 November 1982, five battalions of semi-regular troops totalling 3,000 men moved into position: at first light they attacked the defenders in barracks and trenches at the airport and in other positions two kilometres away across a shallow valley around the whitewashed Protestant church. The battle was over in two hours. More than 200 were left dead, including 16 Cubans. Another 200, mostly ODP militiamen, surrendered. The rest of the enemy fled northwards. UNITA admitted only 12 of its own dead. Forty-three trucks, mostly Urals and Stars, had been captured along with more than 300 light and heavy weapons, including 14.5mm anti-aircraft guns.

The barracks and hangars at the airport had been punched full of holes by cannon and mortar shells: some buildings had collapsed completely. The wreckage of the Fokker Friendship shot up by MPLA MIG-fighters just before Savimbi abandoned the town, nearly seven years previously, still lay by the runway slowly rusting.

From one barrack I picked up a book of MPLA cartoons of Savimbi which, for all I knew, had been printed in the Soviet Union like much of the other literature on political ideology that had been left lying around. One cartoon showed Savimbi as a devil with blood dripping from exaggerated fangs as he bit into a black baby. As I showed the cartoons to Gwynne, a hand reached out and snatched them from my grasp. The hand belonged to Jorge Valentim, the former 'governor' of Lobito who had been sent into five years of internal exile for his mishandling of the city's affairs. The

African tradition is that a man deserves a chance to demonstrate that he has changed, and so Valentim had recently been reinstated to a position of responsibility as UNITA's Secretary of Information. Much to my dismay he had been assigned to accompany us on our travels and had already proved a crude, obstructive and unreliable propagandist. I demanded the return of the cartoons, and Valentim replied: 'I cannot allow my President to be seen like this. I know how Western journalists are.' From a man who continually accused the MPLA of spreading disinformation, this was ripe.

The conversation grew heated as we pointed out that the MPLA propaganda was laughably coarse and ridiculous and that anyway Savimbi had agreed there would be no restrictions on what we could cover. I told Valentim that I would make sure the incident was widely reported and that I would refer it to the highest level. 'With whom do you mean?' he asked. 'With your President,' I stormed self-righteously.

Chilingutila looked uneasy as Valentim and I faced up like fighting cocks in his wake, but with his limited command of English he probably did not understand what was happening. It was not the last that would be heard of the cartoon incident.

We returned to Chilingutila's Kandende base, toured the defensive trenches around its perimeter, saw piles of canned food (mainly Dutch, Brazilian and Portuguese), Soviet matches, MPLA T-shirts made in Cuba and weapons captured at Gago Coutinho. We visited the base hospital where men lightly wounded in the battle were recuperating. The more serious casualties had been sent south for treatment. The evening before our departure we were guests of honour with Chilingutila at a stunning concert in a floodlit wood and thatch amphitheatre with tiered seats for the troops. It was a show that would run for months if ever it hit Broadway or London's West End. There was a modern African ballet; a hilarious spoof on elders and their wives at a village dance, with soldiers cavorting in drag and others in greatcoats and boots several sizes too big for them; a karate display by a team in white bandanas and emerald shorts. An amazingly sensuous traditional dance by a wisp of a girl wowed the soldiers: they whistled and cheered as her navel vibrated and she glided towards Chilingutila, tipping her hat at him like some African Marlene Dietrich before contemptuously turning her quivering back on him. The resident troops of 333 Battalion sang in the rich harmonies and descants of Bantu Africa, and 'Mariko', an Angolan Sinatra clad in a green toga, crooned in English: 'The people of Angola have been sold as slaves to the Russians, Cubans and the East. When our hope was gone Doctor Savimbi showed us the way. The way was to the bush, to organise and to fight.' Most spectacular of all was the fire-eater in whose mouth embers glowed red hot as he sang and danced and bantered with the troops. Months later I asked Tito Chingunji how it was done without damaging the tongue or the delicate lining of the mouth. 'African magic,' Tito laughed.

* * *

We recrossed the Cuando, and spent a night on the southern bank before our waiting Urals headed north-westwards along the main Savimbi Trail to Lupire, the site of another major battle on Christmas Eve 1982. At the Cuando base, on 20 January, loud cheering and shouts of 'Good News' (incongruously in English, but pronounced Good-*ah* News) spread through the camp during the night. News had just been received by radio from Jamba that on 18 January UNITA's 517 Battalion had blown up the second largest dam in Angola, the Lomaoum, to the west of Huambo. Electricity to the city had been cut off. Thirty-three MPLA troops and 12 Cubans had been killed, and two Portuguese technicians had been captured and were being marched back to Jamba.

From Lupire the Savimbi Trail passed between the Cuban/MPLA-held posts of Cuito Cuanavale and Cangamba. It climbed up the watershed between the Cuanavale and Quembo Rivers onto the Central Plateau, more than 1,700 metres high, and ended at a base called Kweta. We began walking across the deep valleys and steep, forested hills of the plateau.

* * *

Savimbi had said the hike from the end of the Savimbi Trail to the railway would take two or three days. But we had already walked for seven when we arrived at Sandona – Savimbi's base during the fight against the Portuguese, and now an agricultural production centre – to be greeted by one of UNITA's brightest young officers, Colonel Ben-Ben Arlindo Pena. We walked with him for another two days before arriving at the forest headquarters of UNITA's military region 57. Now, said Ben, we were within 48 hours of the attack target on the Benguela Railway. The plan was for the local semi-regular battalion to wipe out the government garrison and reduce the town to dust. Angola's almost intangible war, fought beyond the view of Western reporters, was about to become very real.

42

The Battle for Cangonga

1983

At the headquarters of region 57, in dense forest just 60 kilometres south of the Benguela Railway, Colonel Ben-Ben Arlindo Pena introduced us to the UNITA battalion we would follow in their attack on an MPLA garrison.

The propaganda at the rally was powerful. Infant girls gently presented Ben, Gwynne and myself with bunches of wild flowers as a choir of 50 women sang a soft African lullaby. Then Battalion 017, their adrenalin pumping at the prospect of battle, launched into an electric song and dance routine.

'Cubans, if you hear a small noise you know UNITA has arrived. If you hear a second, you're dead,' said one song.

'Santos (Angola's President), you thought Angola would be easy to control: but now you're learning the truth,' said another. 'In 1976 we withdrew, but Savimbi knew where we were going and now it's the MPLA's turn to leave.'

The soldiers rolled on the ground during one particularly joyful chorus, and they sang: 'The day is coming when we will be able to return to our mothers and fathers, and everyone will be so happy.'

It was 8 February, the anniversary of the day seven years earlier in 1976 when Savimbi had ordered his forces to leave the towns and retreat into the forests in the face of the Cubans' slow but relentless advance through Angola. 'Those were dark days,' said Ben in his oration. 'Today we can see the light. After seven years we have passed through a hard school. We have been running a marathon, but from now on we begin to sprint. In 1983 many things will begin to change. Our forces crossing the Benguela Railway have the strength to crush the arrogance of the MPLA who say it is the South Africans they are fighting. We know, and you know, that it is the Angolan people they are fighting. We have learned to deal with the planes and armoured cars of the Cubans and the MPLA. What else have we to fear?'

On 9 February the attack force moved out – 520 semi-regular soldiers of Battalion 017 armed with B-1075mm cannons, 81mm mortars, RPG-7 anti-tank rockets and Kalashnikovs; the 45 soldiers of Special Force Gamboa; the 50-strong logistics team who had travelled with us from Luengue; a special unit of locally based explosives experts; a long chain of youths and women, some with children on their backs, carrying rifles, mines, mortar bombs and anti-tank rockets on their heads; and several hundred locally based guerrillas who joined us, here and there, after we had left the trucks and begun the march.

I was fascinated by the guerrillas. They were a different breed of military men. Their clothes were ragged and non-uniform and seemed like an extension of their skins. They walked alone, not in the orderly files of the battalion. In, and tied to, their knapsacks they carried all their worldly wealth, including their blankets made from beaten bark – for the ethos of the guerrilla was that he had to live off the country-side and not rely on supplies from logistics bases. As well as carrying their Kalashnikovs, they all sported big knives and village-made axes. When we passed the bole of a tree which had collected evil-looking green rainwater, one of the guer-rillas shocked the battalion soldiers when he drew a thin tube of wood from his matted hair and drank from the fetid-looking basin. He explained later that the water at the bottom of such pools was sweet, and all the guerrillas carried drinking tubes. The guerrillas' leader, Lt.-Col. Verissimo, was a huge man with a brilliant smile. He had been one of Savimbi's original guerrillas in 1966, and had refused all offers to live a 'soft' life with the semi-regulars. I thought I could see why. In 17 years as a guerrilla he had reached such a state of symbiosis with the forest that if he were to have fallen down he would have been indistinguishable from a toppled tree trunk.

We moved up to a small transit base 45 kilometres from the railway, and there Ben told us that the target was Cangonga, a small garrison town 130 kilometres west of Luena. A model, about the size of a badminton court, had been prepared by Lt.-Col Antonino Philipe, a reconnaissance specialist. He had reached the transit base a fortnight earlier to collate intelligence collected by his units over several months. The model utilised different coloured sands, ash, bark, moss and twigs to pick out buildings, approach roads and paths, surrounding hills and streams. There were several rows of concrete barracks, the railway station and a radio mast to the north of the rail line; immediately to the south of the line lay houses, shops and a Catholic church, and further south again was a red gravel airstrip. Sandwiching the garrison to the north and south were civilian strategic hamlets of tightly grouped mud and thatch huts. Ben strode to and fro across the model, pointing out zig-zag trench systems around the barracks and at each end of the airstrip. His plan was this:

As first light appeared in the east 100 infantrymen would launch a feint attack from the south, drawing the 300-strong MPLA garrison in their direction. The main attack by 300 UNITA troops would follow from the darkness in the west. The other 120 troops of Battalion 017 would be held in reserve. A company of more than 100 guerrillas would take positions to the west of Cangonga and another company to the east in case the MPLA tried to send a relief force, or to pick off enemy soldiers retreating from the beleaguered garrison.

But what about MIG aircraft and MI-8 helicopters at Luena? Surely they would be over Cangonga within minutes of learning of the attack? 'They won't come,' said Ben confidently. 'They know they got shot down by our anti-aircraft people. There is a Special Force unit near Luena with SAM-7s.' Surely some relief effort would be made when the MPLA garrison radioed that an attack had begun? 'There is no radio. A military train moving east from Cangonga borrowed it a few weeks ago. We attacked the train and captured the radio. It has not been replaced, according to our latest intelligence. They communicate by telephone, but our guerrillas will cut the wires just before the attack.'

We asked what would happen to the civilians in the town, and Ben replied in his usual direct manner: 'It will not be possible to avoid some deaths among them, but I have instructed my troops to do their best to keep civilian casualties low.'

On 10 February, at 5.30 a.m., we began the final day's march to Cangonga. It was a dramatic sight as three lines of troops streamed across river valleys and up into forest on the hills beyond. We stopped after three hours for a breakfast of cold rice and chicken. Tension rose suddenly as a succession of shots cracked out nearby. Ben hardly looked up from the chicken bone he was gnawing as he said calmly: 'It's probably an MPLA patrol doing some hunting.' How far away? 'A kilometre maybe.'

While Ben continued eating, Lt.-Col. Philipe and a major in charge of operations in Region 57 rapidly organised 30 guerrillas to shadow the patrol and, if necessary, kill them. Scouts moved to and fro giving reports to Ben as he sat against a fallen tree and completed his breakfast. The MPLA patrol was moving down a valley away from our resting place.

We stayed still for four hours as the guerrillas continued to watch the patrol, which was eventually established as having between five and ten men. They continued walking slowly down the valley, unaware of the presence of more than 1,000 of their enemy. Ben then instructed that they should be allowed to walk away from the danger: he did not want to attack them and take the risk that some might escape and raise the alarm before the coming battle.

Unwittingly the MPLA had won the first play in the battle for Cangonga. It began to pour with rain, and the enforced delay meant we had to move towards our final position before the town in pitch darkness. Without a moon, neither Gwynne nor I could see anything. Torches and matches were banned. Soldiers held our hands and guided us as we groped through undergrowth, skinned our shins on fallen trees, slithered down precipitous muddy slopes and waded waist-deep across rushing streams. We stopped at 10 p.m. and, sopping wet, climbed fully clothed into equally sopping sleeping bags, huddling together for warmth. It was a miserable, sleepless night, but as we lay still the battalion were being led to their attack positions by reconnaissance guerrillas. How they found their way through the wet blackness I'll never understand.

* * *

On 11 February at 3 a.m. a single rifle shot signalled to Ben that all his forces were in position. We began our final short hike to Cangonga. The rain had stopped. Just after 5 a.m. Ben gave radio orders to section officers of the battalion to begin the attack. We were about three kilometres south-west of the town when the mortar and cannon fire began. Huge flames shot up in the distance, outlining buildings. Then we began to hear the crackle of hundreds of Kalashnikovs.

Walking in strict single file along a path charted by reconnaissance guerrillas through a field of anti-personnel mines, we at last reached the Benguela Railway, crossed it to the north and began closing on the town from the west. The adrenalin pumped harder as we walked down the line towards Cangonga and its water tank on high steel supports came into view. Then as the staccato of the Kalashnikovs grew more persistent, and louder, we were pulled off into another mine-free route through the undergrowth and we finally entered Cangonga at the western end of the airstrip. To our right, huts surrounded by giant sunflowers were ablaze. To the left, a building that was clearly the MPLA's arsenal was burning and exploding periodically with great violence, prompting us to hit the ground in case flying shards of metal scythed us down.

As we walked along the strip UNITA officers urged us to keep moving and not stop to film and take photographs. The centre of the town was under UNITA control, but firefights were continuing in every direction amid the crumps and crashes of mortars and rockets. At the eastern end of the runway we stopped while Ben spoke with his field officers by radio. Then all hell broke loose. Concentrated firing came from huts about 30 metres to the right. Some MPLA soldiers had regrouped and launched a direct counter-attack against the command party. Gwynne stood filming in the direction of the firing before he was smashed to the ground in a mass rugby tackle by UNITA officers. He cursed them as they pinned him down. Ben, meanwhile, had quickly led me into long grass beyond the end of the runway. I did not need his command to get down: I was already trying to bury into the earth like some demented ostrich as bullets whooshed overhead and the arsenal erupted with increased fury.

Ignoring the danger, Ben strode upright throughout the counter-attack, shouting orders, while a section of our Gamboa Special Force bodyguard peeled off to deal with the MPLA soldiers who were invisible to me. The firing intensified as Ben led me, crawling, towards trenches near the whitewashed Catholic church. I dropped gratefully into one of the slits and moved along past crates of Soviet mortar shells newly wrenched open by the defenders. Then, rounding a bend, I saw a dead MPLA soldier. He was sprawled on his back in the shallow red earth, looking almost peaceful with a neat bullet hole in his forehead. While many of his comrades seemed to have run, he had paid a heavy price for his courage in standing and fighting. It all seemed too real to Gwynne when he caught the MPLA corpse in his viewfinder. He later recorded in his diary: 'Death had come instantly . . . I found it difficult to think that this soldier had been eating, sleeping, talking, or joking, all the things that one does in one's life, just one hour before, unaware that death stalked around him.'

From the trenches we moved into the church which had been stripped of pews and altar and was being used as a military barracks. The troops had been sleeping on the floor. Ripped from their slumbers as UNITA's attack began, the panicking soldiers had left their blankets and personal belongings behind in their flight. Jorge Valentim ranted tedious propaganda about how we were the first Western journalists to see how the MPLA desecrated and violated the sanctity of churches. I had no first-hand knowledge about the practices of the MPLA towards religion, but in this case UNITA's Information Secretary was talking nonsense. In wars churches have been used time and again as shelter for troops. Anyway, it was unlikely that a priest had been in Cangonga in recent years: when Portugal scuttled from Angola in 1975, most Portuguese priests scuttled too, leaving their black flocks to uncertain fates. And though the MPLA's constitution has anti-religious clauses, there were several Bibles in tribal languages among the abandoned possessions of the 'Marxist' soldiers.

It was a reminder of the danger of buying 'package deals' about any group in Africa: nothing on that continent is as straightforward close up as it seems from afar.

We moved across the centre of the town where the Special Force took possession of an 81mm mortar abandoned by the MPLA. Then, just past the modern school building, which was devoid of furniture or books, there were moments of horror.

Three UNITA soldiers appeared, dragging a body with the kind of respect normally accorded a stuck pig. The body moved and emitted a groan of agony: the MPLA soldier, a boy who was barely 18, had a gaping head wound which looked fatal. I shouted to the soldiers to put the boy down: he was dying. Though they understood no English, they responded by laying him face down in the dust. If it's true that any man's death diminishes one, then being witness to callous treatment of badly wounded fellow human beings makes one feel unclean. As journalists, we can claim we are only there to observe: but that cannot always be an excuse for inaction, for opting out of humanity. When the opportunity arose we asked Ben what his policy was towards enemy wounded. Those with slight wounds were treated and taken prisoner, he said. The badly wounded were left to die. What would happen to the wounded boy? 'We'll leave him.'

Gwynne and I decided we had to do something for the soldier. Roberts asked Ben if his wound could be treated, using the justified subterfuge that it would be good propaganda for UNITA to be seen caring for the enemy. A couple of hours later, when the action was less frantic, three male nurses went to work on the head wound in front of the cameras. A closer look showed that although the injury was serious it might not be fatal. We tried to discover the boy's name. He responded by raising his head momentarily and dropping it again with a terrible moan – he was concussed and frightened almost out of his mind. Ben gave us his guarantee that he would be taken care of and removed to a camp for prisoners: but despite several inquiries we received no further news of his fate.

Gwynne's personal diary caught the powerful emotions that overwhelmed him after he had seen the boy being dragged by the scruff of the neck and by his trousers, which had been pulled down around his knees: 'When I saw his face and head matted with blood seeping from a white wound onto his brown skin, pity swept through me and I was almost in tears as I filmed. This poor creature was in abject despair and terror. He groaned and, when he saw me filming, dropped his head and arms in humiliation. What had such a young lad done to deserve this – forced, possibly by poverty, to join the army? I felt sick at heart – half disgusted with myself for being there to film this, but also hating everyone for reducing a human being to such misery. And UNITA is not just the guilty party. America, Russia, France, East Germany, Saudi Arabia, Cuba, Zaire, South Africa, Zambia – the list is endless and includes Britain and West Germany – all share responsibility. Their interests have little to do with the good of the Angolan people.'

*   *   *

Meanwhile, the action at Cangonga continued. In the station-master's office the phone was off the hook: presumably an MPLA officer had made a futile effort to raise help.

UNITA soldiers ransacked the town for every possible useful item. The booty was heaped in piles in courtyards near the rail line – blankets, small Japanese generators, radios, rubber buckets, sewing machines, drinking bottles, uniforms, boots, Cuban carnival hats, cooking pots, bags. When one of the soldiers posed in the big blue carnival hat for a photograph, Ben sharply ordered him to remove it and replace it with his own military cap. Even the corrugated iron roofs of the barracks were stripped off to be taken away.

UNITA saboteurs began demolishing the town. The massive iron water tank that had fed the great steam engines was blown up. The wooden station-master's house disappeared in one mighty blast. A road petrol tanker exploded like a giant bomb, making us hit the deck again as big metal fragments hurtled overhead. Work began on destruction of the rail line. The Benguela Railway is single track, but sidings at Cangonga permitted trains to pass in opposite directions. Plastic explosives twisted them into grotesque shapes, ensuring that trains would not run over them again. The saboteurs ignored two long trains of goods wagons: they were empty and rusting and had clearly not moved for many months.

There was only a brief time to speak to some of the dazed civilians who had been rounded up to be taken to UNITA-controlled villages. A visit to the rows of whitewashed barracks showed that the MPLA troops had lived in Spartan conditions. Each individual barrack block was bare grey concrete on the inside with no furniture. Beds were blankets laid on straw mats. Their lamps were similiar to those of UNITA's soldiers – oil lamps fashioned from empty corned beef tins and cloth tape. In one barrack was a bowl of maize kernels a soldier had been sorting, and some kind of edible fungi spread out to dry on a grey cloth. One soldier had brightened his drab walls with coloured pencil drawings of flowers, and in the middle of them was a photo of the late President Neto above a caption praising solidarity with the Cubans.

Outside in the grass was a plastic holdall full of personal possessions – comb, mirror, African hair brush (metal-toothed, to cope with tightly curled and bushy hair), tooth-paste, arithmetic and general knowledge books published by the Luanda Ministry of Education, and exercise books. The grass around was pressed down where the fellow had cowered before running without his bag.

On the dirty concrete floor of the desolate schoolhouse were two badly wounded UNITA soldiers. One man's leg had been splinted after it had been shattered by mortar fragments. Another, immobile and almost entirely covered by a rain cape, lay dying: a male nurse said a mortar fragment had penetrated his ribcage. Elsewhere another UNITA soldier had died after being shot in the stomach.

After six hours in Cangonga we left with Colonel Ben, a platoon of 017 Battalion, our logistics men and the soldiers of Special Force Gamboa. We passed between burning huts as firefights between MPLA soldiers and their UNITA pursuers continued in far distant bush. Many soldiers in our column were leading goats and others had live ducks and chickens tied to their packs. Other soldiers would stay in the town for two or three days to complete the clearing-out operation and to reduce it to rubble.

It had been a day that was professionally exhilarating and, philosophically, profoundly sobering. A final analysis of the battle had to be made, but a deep weariness overcame us. It became almost impossible to put one foot in front of the other: we could not remember when we had last slept or eaten. For the time being only two things mattered – we had survived and we wanted to lie down. Ben halted the south-wards march after three hours and we fell immediately into deep sleep on the forest floor.

43

Aftermath

1983

After Cangonga we faced a return journey of more than 200 kilometres on foot and 650 kilometres by truck back down the Savimbi Trail. There was plenty of time to think about Cangonga and the significance of things we had seen in five weeks of travel.

First, the aftermath of the battle: Colonel Ben-Ben Arlindo Pena said 35 MPLA soldiers were confirmed killed and seven had been taken as prisoners. Two UNITA soldiers had died and six were wounded. The figures seemed plausible. The attack had been clinical in its efficiency. UNITA had amassed a force which far outnumbered the enemy and had struck by surprise from the forests. Ben said he had left several avenues of escape for the MPLA: 'It is always so in our attacks. If the enemy feel trapped they resist heavily and our casualties increase. In our kind of war we must keep our soldiers' morale high, so it is more important to keep our casualties light than to inflict heavy losses on the enemy.'

Nearly 600 civilians, including 200 children, had been rounded up from the town and brought to the forest bases. They would be distributed two or three families to a village in UNITA's 'area of control'. Political commissars would keep an eye on them until they were fully integrated, or 're-educated'. We spoke to the civilians. But though many of them told us they were UNITA supporters who had been taken to Cangonga against their wills, our conversations, through a UNITA interpreter, can have had little meaning. One man busily showed us a small photograph he said he had used on his UNITA membership card. Another poured out complaints about how bad the MPLA school was for his four children in Cangonga – and we had certainly seen for ourselves that it had no furniture or books and that all the washbasins were cracked and filthy. One woman claimed once to have belonged to LIMA, the UNITA women's movement. But how do European journalists on fleeting visits assess the real feelings of peasant people, caught up in a terrible war, whose language and culture and perspectives are so different? If any of the civilians were unhappy about being taken off to a new life in the forest, they were keeping quiet about it. And why not? In their situation, I'd wave the flag and sing the anthem of whichever movement was momentarily in control.

However, we'd got a crude, basic picture. The civilians looked bewildered rather than happily liberated. And no wonder. The MPLA rounds them up from the countryside and concentrates them in towns from where they can till the surrounding fields to feed the garrison. UNITA moves them out and scatters them around its areas where they learn a new line in political slogans. Of course, it's very easy and morally comfortable to sit on the fence and say each side is as bad as the other, and I know where I believe the best hope for the Angolan peasantry lies. But at the stage of warfare I've been describing above, the peasants are as helpless as chaff in the wind.

* * *

One happy outcome was that, despite Ben's prediction, there had been no civilian casualties. 'I was surprised,' he said. 'Normally the people move into the centre of the town and lie down, but here they fled quickly and we found them outside.' The MPLA garrison had been smaller than expected – 150 against intelligence assessments of 300. Prisoners under interrogation said a company had moved out of Cangonga to Luena a day or so before the attack. There had been no Cubans in the garrison. A column of 180 porters had moved into Cangonga to pick up the varied booty: but amongst it were only 30 or so enemy weapons. The big failure of the attack had been the destruction of the MPLA arsenal. 'The MPLA staged a resistance from that warehouse and my troops said they had to hit it with an RPG-7,' said Ben. 'I'm quite angry, because we needed the material for our stockpiles.'

The significance of the fall of Cangonga, said Ben, was that it would allow UNITA to punch a secure logistics line through to a semi-regular battalion and several companies of guerrillas who had already infiltrated 300 kilometres north of the Benguela Railway from the Cangonga area. One of the main military objectives Savimbi had set for 1983 was to push a corridor right up the centre of the country to where a salient of Zaire juts into north-central Angola. The destruction of Cangonga made even more distant the MPLA's fading dream of reopening the Benguela Railway to international traffic. Cangonga also had great propaganda value for Savimbi. He wanted outsiders to see and report that his soldiers were skilled and highly motivated and that they were striking successfully at MPLA targets deep in the heart of Angola. As a corollary, he wanted to demonstrate that a major war was in progress *among Angolans* about the future of their country. He wanted to counter MPLA allegations that all attacks against Cuban/MPLA posts were by South African forces and that UNITA were no more than a handful of *fantoches*.

* * *

For me there were other more personal and esoteric lessons learned, and satisfactions gained, from the journey to and from Cangonga, having little to do with the giant questions of military or economic strategy which concern men of power in the West and East. I had grown to like and admire (with some exceptions) the Angolans I had come to know in UNITA – and this must have had something to do with a quality of warmth and vivacity in Angolans in general, for people who have come to know Angola from a different perspective, that of the MPLA for example, report similar personal reactions to the country and its people.

Life in the forest and villages gave rise to completely new experiences and relationships. There was the rediscovery that existence in the forest could be a delight, not something to fear. The best time of the day usually came just before sunset when a halt was called to the 40-kilometre march. While I collapsed into a state of exhausted immobility, I watched Antonio, the UNITA guerrilla assigned to me as a batman, build my open-sided bivouac in an exhibition of speed and bushcraft which would have left Baden-Powell gasping. With his village-made axe he prepared the bed – a low earth table surrounding by a shallow channel to divert rainwater run-off – and swiftly chopped down saplings to form a frame for the bivouac. Antonio, who was perhaps 18 or 19, then tore thin strips of bark from the *chimwanji* tree to use as string to tie a sheet of canvas over the frame. The bed was completed with a 'mattress' of leaves, canvas and blankets. All was ready to settle down for the evening, and I first read Conrad's *Heart of Darkness* by the light of a fire that the guerrillas built and tended for us alongside the bivouac: 'The silence of the land went home to one's very heart – its mystery, its greatness, the amazing reality of its concealed life.'

By silence in Africa Conrad must have meant the absence of European city noise. Nightjars and cicadas called and chittered from dusk until dawn, and near rivers frogs made music like thousands of Tibetan bells. Beyond the bivouac the fires of the guerrillas glowed in every direction and there was laughter and talking. On clear nights the tropical sky was filled with the winking diamonds of other worlds, an awesome and humbling tapestry which somehow we never get time to gaze at in Europe. On other nights there would be powerful downpours, jets of rain passing the open side of the bivouac and hissing into the fire.

Though Antonio and I could only talk in pidgin Portuguese and three or four words of Ovimbundu, we communicated reasonably effectively with signs. Just as captors and hostages often become bonded, so journalists and guerrillas living together develop a close identity of interests. I was totally dependent on Antonio, and other members of UNITA's logistics team, for food, shelter and life itself. By the end I regarded him as a true brother and gave him the only gift I could offer, my Swiss penknife with all its gadgets.

Antonio was amazing. Whenever I began to slow down,

suffering from the pace of the march, he would be there waiting, straining under the 20 kilo load on his back and head. While I sank down at the end of the day, drained of energy, Antonio would lower his load and his Kalashnikov and immediately start preparing the bivouac and lighting the fire. Soon hot water would appear to bathe raw feet. Scalding, though not wonderfully appetising, coffee would be served. Nothing was too much trouble for him, and the memory of his kindness and concern is etched indelibly and will always influence my thinking about Africa.

* * *

Affection was lavished on children in the villages. They would be gently pushed forward to clutch our hands. In our column there were women with mortar shells, anti-tank mines and rifles on their heads and babies in cotton slings across their backs. During rest stops these babies would inevitably be placed in our arms amid much giggling by the women.

At one stage we were having to walk so far and fast that a *kipoia* was added to the column's equipment in case we broke down and needed to be carried. Despite temptation, I kept out of it, remembering clearly the fun everybody had on Independence Day in 1975 during the satirical *kipoia* sketch with the Portuguese *sahib*.

We were lucky to have a man of the calibre of Ben in overall charge of the operation. Considerate in his personal relations, intelligent, decisive, and brave in battle, Ben had no need to demand respect; he commanded it through the strength of his personality. He became a good friend.

Two memories of Ben stand out. The first is of him striding upright, purposefully directing the counter-attack when we came under MPLA fire on the airstrip at Cangonga. The second was one evening after the battle as we twiddled through various radio stations – the BBC, VOA, Radio Luanda. The dial hit Radio South Africa and a news-reader was saying that Foreign Minister Pik Botha had said South Africa was willing to *consider* giving aid to any anti-Soviet liberation movement in black Africa which asked. The statement was heavy with irony because the

South African government, without informing its own Parliament, was *already* aiding at least three movements, including UNITA. Ben collapsed in laughter at the absurdity
and duplicity of Botha's remark, and said: 'We're not even
having to *ask* them.'

We also benefited from Savimbi's health care planning.
Male nurses are attached to every UNITA military unit, and
Gwynne and I were given our own personal nurse, a gentle
man called Jacko. He tended my wounds with salves and
bandages when a tree, felled by our advancing truck, hit me
and gouged two deep channels of flesh from my arm. Jacko
dug *bitacoia* parasites from the soles of our feet with a
hypodermic needle. The *bitacoia* fly, common wherever
there is uncleared dirt in towns, burrows unnoticed into
your feet and lays its eggs. There the maggots grow large
and are first noticed as painful sores. Unless the white,
black-headed maggots are removed, your feet begin to rot.
The guerrillas reckoned we had picked up the *bitacoias* at
Cangonga, where the pumped water system had broken
down and pigs rooted among rotting garbage. Jacko doled
out vitamin and anti-diarrhoea pills and massaged our
aching calves with liniment when we thought we could
hardly march another step.

The *bitacoias* and occasional bouts of diarrhoea apart,
personal hygiene was not a great problem. Hundreds of
streams and rivers flow swiftly from the Angolan plateau
into various great African river systems. Clear, cool, sandy-
bottomed, and free of the debilitating *bilharzia* parasite common elsewhere in Africa, they are good sources of drinking
water and make excellent bathing pools. Among the best
times on our trip were those spent swimming with the
guerrilla leaders while clouds of yellow, blue, green and
orange butterflies fluttered over the stream banks.

Marching with UNITA we were able to see how Angola's
vast area and sparsely populated forests had helped the
rebels frustrate the Cubans and Soviets. I learned one day
how easily the soldiers could fade into the bush when I went
to a river to bathe. I thought I was alone, but as I began to
walk back, after dressing, some dozen soldiers rose from the
grass within metres of me carrying rifles and anti-tank

weapons. The members of Special Force Gamboa, assigned to protect me, had moved unseen and unheard into position with the stealth of leopards.

One evening, as we sat eating, Lieutenant Bonaventura, commander of Special Force Gamboa, demonstrated the gap that can exist between European and African perceptions. Bonaventura said something which made Ben, highly educated and well travelled, burst into laughter. 'The lieutenant wants to know how easily his platoon could infiltrate Britain,' said Ben. 'I tried to explain to him about customs, immigration officials, coastguard patrols, police, and that there was no forest.' Earlier, on the battlefield, Bonaventura's men had acted without regard for their own lives to protect ours. Now he had further endeared himself. I also grew to appreciate more fully the amazing singing and dancing of village Angola and to understand how Savimbi used these to motivate his followers. I had developed a real respect for black African cultural values. The rhythms, descants and harmonies made me – a musical illiterate – feel culturally degenerate. The dancing managed to be sensuous without being lewd: the consummate artistry of the women was achieved with the aid of buttock muscles which have presumably atrophied in Europeans.

It was plain before the end of the trip that, whatever happened to Savimbi and UNITA in the future, I would retain for ever affectionate memories of a people who defied the preconceptions of the outside world.

* * *

It was clear that UNITA was making other significant military gains. We had visited the site of the battle of Gago Coutinho, which gave Savimbi control of most of the border with Zambia and which the MPLA has since been unable to regain. Had we had more time, we could have visited a line of small towns UNITA had taken in the last nine months to the north of Gago Coutinho to a point about 30 kilometres south of Luena.

We had seen the victory at Cangonga and we also visited Lupire, the site of a bigger battle on Christmas Eve 1982. Lupire had been captured from the MPLA in January 1982. It was little more than a hilltop trading post. But it had a strategic value outweighing its size because it had an airstrip, commanded a view in all directions across the surrounding countryside, and was astride one of the main routes northwards from Mavinga to the Benguela Railway.

On 6 November 1982 the MPLA launched an offensive against Lupire from Cuito Cuanavale, 75 kilometres to the southwest of the hilltop, by the 1,800-strong 16th Motorised Infantry Brigade. The brigade's trucks were accompanied by four Cuban-manned armoured cars. Faced by an overwhelming enemy force, UNITA troops, commanded by Colonel Ben-Ben, made a tactical withdrawal from Lupire. But after the MPLA had arrived and dug in on the hilltop, UNITA laid ambushes along the dirt road to Cuito Cuanavale and surrounded Lupire with 1,800 semi-regular soldiers and 200 guerrillas. UNITA pumped into Lupire a steady rain of 60mm mortar shells. The MPLA force, cut off by road, had to be supplied entirely by air. Light Antonov-2 aircraft were used by the MPLA because UNITA's SAM-7 missiles were unable to lock onto their small engines. On 20 December the 16th Brigade unexpectedly began withdrawing in a 40-square-kilometre box formation. UNITA made a series of flanking attacks on the retreating forces between 20 and 24 December. It claimed to have badly mauled the 16th Brigade, killing 187 soldiers and destroying 17 trucks and a Soviet-made BRDM-2 armoured car while admitting 26 dead and 87 wounded of its own.

While we were in Angola an MPLA Defence Ministry statement said more than 300 UNITA soldiers had been killed in the battle for Lupire, which remained under MPLA control. Among the dead was a UNITA major with an important secret document in his mouth . . . 'He had tried to chew it up but had died before he was able to.'[1] The MPLA statement went on: 'By confronting a powerful counter-revolutionary force the 16th Brigade inscribed in letters of gold yet another heroic chapter in the history of the People's Armed Forces for the Liberation of Angola – the Lupire Campaign. There was one strike after another against the bandits. The few survivors fled in disarray, back to their bosses who had abandoned them to their fate. The (16th)

Brigade detachments had put the armed counter-revolution in Cuando Cubango Province out of action and in serious difficulties for a long time to come, and it would be hard for South Africa (*sic*) to mount another such operation in Cuando Cubango in the near future.'

Despite MPLA claims to control it, we stayed at a UNITA base on Lupire Hill on January 24 and filmed the UNITA battalion guarding its forested western flanks. It was still in UNITA hands when we returned on 20 February, after the battle for Cangonga. We inspected one of the Lupire battlefields. Angolan kwanza banknotes were scattered all over the grassy plain, and near a thick clump of trees stood a wrecked Soviet BRDM-2 armoured car which had been hit by two UNITA RPG-7 rockets. From it still seeped the sweet and hideous smell of death, and through the shell holes we saw the terrible remains of three soldiers who, according to UNITA, had been identified by MPLA prisoners as those of Cubans known as Captain Aguiar Gonzales, 'Vladimir', and Idale. The dead men haunted me, and some nights later I dreamed that one of the Cubans, almost beyond recognition as a human, showed signs of life. And there among the carnage was my wife taking his head gently in her hands, looking into his eyes and rubbing noses with him, willing him back to life.

* * *

Deep inside the country – in UNITA's 'area of influence' – there were other battles during our time spent with the rebels. On 17 January, as we were heading north along the Savimbi Trail, UNITA announced that it had blown up the second biggest dam in Angola, the Lomaoum, on the Catumbela River between the country's second and third-largest cities, Humabo and Lobito. A few days later, the MPLA confirmed on Luanda Radio that the dam, which supplied electricity to Huambo and Lobito, had been destroyed by 'Portuguese-speaking white mercenaries'. UNITA's story was that one of its semi-regular battalions, 517, based in mountains north-west of Huambo, had attacked the dam with the support of a company of 200 guerrillas and a 45-strong Special Forces platoon. The Special

Forces arrived in the area a week before the attack to collect information from villages sympathetic to UNITA. When the attack began at 4 a.m. on 17 January the Special Forces went straight to the house of the chief engineer, a Portuguese, and told him 2,500 kilos of explosives had been brought in to blow up the dam: he would live if he showed them where to place the charges and if, subsequently, the sluice gates collapsed and the turbines were destroyed. He complied, and was marched with his wife and daughter and four other Portuguese engineers to Jamba, from where they were sent home to Portugal through the auspices of the ICRC.

*   *   *

It had become clear to me that the MPLA faced an almost impossible task in its attempts to reoccupy UNITA's 'area of control'. Not only was the zone vast, but the rebels were highly motivated and had built up a sophisticated infrastructure. There was a network of party farms. Agricultural specialists provided villagers with seed and advised on farming techniques. UNITA trading officers bartered clothing and salt in exchange for villagers' surplus food and for ivory and animal skins. At a base south of Lupire we watched a trading session between the UNITA economic agent and about 40 representatives of the party from villages up to 300 kilometres away. They carried bags made of skins and crude village axes. Barefooted and dressed in ragged clothes, they had brought elephant and warthog tusks, balls of wild beeswax, and python, leopard and crocodile skins which they exchanged for trousers, shirts, blouses and brassieres which were stuffed into big black plastic bags for carrying back to the villages. UNITA officials said these items had ceased to be available since the MPLA had established a centralised state-controlled trading system and that the peasants did not want to trade their produce for kwanzas which had low purchasing power. The rate of barter exchange in the UNITA base was seven pieces of clothing for an elephant tusk and six for a leopard skin. The economic agent said UNITA had full-time workers in the Lupire area sifting streams for diamonds. In a good month they sometimes found 1,800 industrial quality diamonds.

Since UNITA's strategy was not to occupy towns it captured but merely to deny them to the MPLA by putting defensive forces beyond the perimeters, this made it a very elusive enemy. It puzzled me why the MPLA had not hit back with flexible guerrilla-style tactics instead of with big motorised columns, which got hopelessly bogged down as logistics lines became extended and UNITA declined to engage in head-on fights. In the 3,200 kilometres I travelled there was no evidence at all of attempts by government troops to harass the rebels' supply lines. Was this because of the MPLA's over-reliance on Cubans who could not 'swim like fishes' in Angola's black sea and be certain of the kind of support from the peasantry that is vital in any war against insurgents?

It was not a question which could be satisfactorily answered from the UNITA side. We hoped, however, that there would be other questions that *could* be answered once we got back to Jamba – such as whether there was any hope of reconciliation between Angola's warring factions and, if not, what the consequences would be for Angola?

But before we asked any questions we relaxed for a couple of days. We slept at Jamba between crisply ironed sheets in giant huts with electric light. We ate off English china in a mess where waiters served egg and chips, the tablecloths were sky blue, and the coffee came in silver pots. And there was welcome cool beer in cans imprinted with the exhortation 'Keep South Africa Tidy'.

We visited UNITA's big new underground operations room, where an immaculate young intelligence colonel gave us yet another military briefing. We watched the tough training programmes for the latest batches of recruits to the semi-regular battalions. We relaxed one evening at a variety show in a big floodlit arena. Crowds watched 50 women, dressed in sky blue jump suits and red kerchiefs, perform a modern African ballet and sing a stunning ballad which invited everyone to 'Advance With the Jaguar'. But where was Savimbi, the Jaguar to whom they referred? He had said he would meet us at his GHQ at the end of our journey to talk about the war he was waging.

It became clear that he was not there.

44

Savimbi Prepares for New Isolation

1983

Early one morning in late February we were awakened by
UNITA officers with the news that we would have to leave
the comforts of Jamba. We found Savimbi at the end of a
bruising six-hour truck journey at a miserable, mosquito-
infested base deep in bush country inhabited only by wild
game. Savimbi was in sombre mood.

He had sought solitude away from his General Headquarters so that he could work uninterrupted on a new military
strategy. Within the previous few days, he said, he had
received copies from UNITA's sources inside the Angolan
Foreign Ministry in Luanda of two documents which constituted an agreement between the MPLA and South Africa
that would impede the insurgency campaigns of both
UNITA and SWAPO.

The first document was a protocol agreement detailing
how talks between the MPLA and South Africa could be
conducted. The second was a provisional agreement on
troop pullbacks in Angola, signed on 8 December 1982 by
senior Angolan and South African Foreign Ministry officials
after a meeting at Sal Island in the Cape Verde Islands. The
talks were attended by Foreign Minister Pik Botha, Defence
Minister Magnus Malan and Hans van Dalsen, Director-
General of the Ministry of Foreign Affairs, for South
Africa. Angola was represented by Interior Minister
Alexandre 'Quito' Rodrigues, Deputy Defence Minister
Antonio dos Santos 'Ndalu' França, and Deputy Foreign
Minister Venacio de Moura. South Africa's Deputy Foreign

Minister, Brand Fourie, and Rodrigues and de Moura again flew to Sal Island on 23 February 1983 for what the MPLA described as 'a cordial meeting to exchange ideas'.[1]

As outlined by Savimbi, the proposed Angolan-South African agreement looked like a devils' pact. It provided for a ceasefire between South African and MPLA troops in Cunene Province and the withdrawal of the South Africans from south-western Angola into Namibia. The MPLA would be allowed to reoccupy their former military posts relinquished by the SADF. But, at the same time, Cuban forces allied to the MPLA would retreat to a line 320 kilometres north of the border with Namibia, and SWAPO would have to withdraw its bases beyond a line 480 kilometres north of the border. Joint MPLA-SADF commissions would monitor the ceasefire.

Savimbi declined to show us copies of the documents. He said there were clauses which, if publicised, would jeopardise the flexibility of UNITA's response. But he said it was implicit in the agreement that logistics support from South Africa to UNITA would be cut off. The South African-Angolan ceasefire would also free three MPLA motorised infantry brigades stationed near Cunene from defensive roles against the South Africans. 'Our friends (the South Africans) tell us nothing is happening between them and the MPLA,' said Savimbi. 'But the documents we have, and newspaper and radio commentaries, and the attitudes of MPLA officers we capture – who say that if there is a ceasefire the MPLA will make a big move against UNITA – give me the impression that there is something to prepare for. It would be a foolish thing on our side to sit down and think there will be no ceasefire between the MPLA and the South Africans.'[2]

Savimbi rated the chances of the implementation of the provisional MPLA-South African Accord at 50-50. 'We must be ready in case the ceasefire is implemented,' he said. 'If we make a correct analysis we can strike where we want, and the ceasefire will have a minimum effect on us. We have enough weapons and ammunition stockpiled to fight on for years. Our trucks will stop running because diesel supplies will be cut off. But, apart from that, nothing will be affected, absolutely nothing.'

The crucial thing was to be ready for anything. UNITA had been deserted by the South Africans before: 'The fact is that our friendship is something the South Africans can dispose of overnight. It is why we need to devise a strategy which ensures that we cannot become disposable material. If we can give a sign that we can win, we will not be disposed of. If we cannot give that sign, we will be disposed of. However, it will not be easy to sell out UNITA because there are many elements in this situation which are not controllable either by South Africa or the MPLA. In 1976 we had to disperse and accept that we might die. But in 1983 the situation is different. We don't have enough forces to make direct confrontations everywhere with the Cubans and the MPLA: if we did that, we would break our forces. We are confronted by 40,000 Cubans,[3] but if we avoid taking them on in fixed positions, if our activities force them to spread through the whole country, they are an obstacle we can overcome.'

Savimbi said that after he had worked out his new strategy, it would be presented to UNITA's Central Committee for approval. 'We have gone through more serious problems than today,' he said. 'Today other possibilities are open to us, but it is a problem of great concern. It is why we need to find an answer before there is a ceasefire between the MPLA and the South Africans. Part of the UNITA strategy would be an immediate intensification of military activities to undermine the Luanda-Pretoria accord. In a rare but unco-ordinated convergence of interest with UNITA, Savimbi said SWAPO had launched an offensive into Namibia in its own attempt to ruin the agreement. On 16 February a column of 1,500 SWAPO guerrillas had passed across the border from Angola into Namibia to the west of the Cubango River, he said. Soon, Willie van Niekerk, Namibia's Administrator-General, was announcing that the SADF had blunted SWAPO's biggest offensive in 16 years. He put the attacking force at about 700, broken into 14 groups of 50 men each.[4] By mid-March more than 200 of them had been killed.

*   *   *

The SWAPO–UNITA relationship needs a great novelist to do it justice, to trace all the twists, the regional and international developments, which transformed them from blood brothers in the fight against colonial rule into opponents across a Cold War divide of European origin. Savimbi's line in my earlier meetings with him was that UNITA had no quarrel with SWAPO. It supported SWAPO's desire to liberate Namibia, but not at the expense of UNITA and the continual denial of elections to Angolans. UNITA would never attack SWAPO, but would defend itself if attacked.

Savimbi had never previously admitted that UNITA had killed SWAPO guerrillas. This time, in the course of our conversation about the SWAPO conundrum, he did so. But he began with his explanation of the fundamental dilemma: 'SWAPO have a case. They want to liberate their country, as we want to liberate ours. They want elections to be held in Namibia, as we want elections to be held in Angola. They believe they would win those elections, as we believe we would win elections in Angola.

'We sympathise with SWAPO's desire to liberate their own country. The problem is that they are fighting from our country, not their own. If you fight from somebody else's country you have limitations. We had very good relations with SWAPO and we helped each other a lot up to 1975. From there we parted. I don't blame them. As the MPLA was in power in Luanda, SWAPO had to work with them. But we criticise SWAPO for becoming hostile to UNITA. We gave them their camps in southern Angola in 1975, so they should not have given in to MPLA requests to attack us. But they have attacked us, abducted our people, killed our cattle and taken our possessions. If they pass UNITA positions there is no trouble. But now they know that if they attack we will reply immediately.'

One such clash had taken place in March 1982: 'Three UNITA battalions in Cunene were attacked by 1,000 SWAPOs. The battle lasted six hours. SWAPO had more than 400 killed, and since then they have not tried to attack us again.' The probability must be that since the date of that interview with Savimbi (25 February 1983) there have been many other unrecorded clashes between UNITA and

SWAPO as the war has grown and as their military strate-
gies have, inevitably, become increasingly co-ordinated with
their respective benefactors.

*   *   *

As always, the conversation eventually drifted towards
UNITA's links with South Africa. I approached it with a
certain weariness since I had been through the ritual many
times before. I always expected Savimbi to sigh equally
wearily, but he never did. This time he shifted into a
comfortable position for a long discourse and said: 'Let us
go. It is not a problem we are afraid to discuss.'

So how did he justify the alliance?

He accepted help because there was a coincidence of
interests. It was not something new in international politics,
he said. Stalin's alliance with Hitler at the beginning of the
Second World War did not mean the Soviet leader had
wanted to embrace Nazism, and Churchill's subsequent
alliance with Stalin certainly did not mean that the British
people had approved of Communism. It was a question of
survival, and UNITA intended doing just that against a
régime imposed by Moscow.

'I am absolutely without remorse that I have dealings with
South Africa,' he said. 'They are the only real military and
economic power in this region, and every black African state
is trading with them, including the MPLA. And are those
people who criticise us going to say the MPLA has also made
a moral error if it now reaches agreement with South Africa?'

He did not expect armchair critics in the West to understand UNITA's policy towards South Africa. 'But do they
believe that black men like us approve of apartheid? Do they
think we want to import it to Angola? It is unthinkable.
Against whom would we apply it? Ourselves?

'My critics in the West are hypocritical. They say we
should not take aid from South Africa for our struggle. But
they will never give us aid themselves. They seem to be
asking us to commit suicide, to accept being crushed by
Cubans and Russians in our own country. We will not do
that. To avoid it, we have to take help from wherever it is on
offer.'

*   *   *

Savimbi said an invitation he had sent to the MPLA in December 1982 for talks had been rejected.[5] But he believed the two sides would eventually have to agree to some form of coalition government, to be followed by elections after three or four years. A coalition, he admitted, would be difficult because UNITA's political philosophy differed fundamentally from the MPLA's Moscow-style ideology. 'Policies for this country need to be rooted in our own culture,' he said: 'We want our languages, customs and traditions to be nurtured and cherished, not crushed or overwhelmed. Our identity comes from deep values developed in village society over many centuries. It is not something Marx took account of. Here in Angola we do not have an industrial society: 90 per cent of our people are peasant farmers. Marx himself spoke of the difficulty of applying his theories to "savages". I suppose it was people like us he was talking about.'

Savimbi spoke of his irritation with pro-Western labels pinned on him by international news agencies, forever trying to encapsulate truths in three words where three thousand are needed. UNITA was not fighting a civil war for the West: it was fighting for the majority of Angola's people. 'We are fighting to stop the Russians dominating Angola against the will of the people. We do not want to be an African Hungary or Czechoslovakia.'

If the West thought that it was in its interests to help UNITA, then the help would be welcome, said Savimbi. But he could not recall any guerrilla group since 1945 which had succeeded with Western assistance. The best ally in a guerrilla war was the Soviet Union, which gave unswerving military backing to its chosen friends. With Russia as an ally, UNITA would have no problem.

He laughed and said he had recently received a message from his friend of many years, the President of Zambia: 'Kaunda said he still agreed with our resistance, but gave us this warning: "The British, they like parties. The Americans, they like talking. But the Russians are professionals. I don't like the Russians, but I respect them because they do everything according to a plan." I read the message as an indication that he would like to support us, but that if we are relying on Western support we are on our own. Kaunda was saying we were brave and should go ahead even though we might have no one behind us.'

Savimbi said Western liberals were guilty of unconscious racism. Many of them argued for the continuation in Angola of a régime of a kind they would not tolerate for themselves. They also believed black Angolans were incapable of staging an effective resistance of their own.

'People in the West who sit and criticise UNITA don't understand what's going on in our country,' Savimbi said. 'They do not understand that our predicament is that we cannot lose this battle without also losing our destiny. The Cubans are killing our country, so we have to defend it as other peoples have defended themselves against invasions.

'We will go beyond the understanding of the West how to fight this battle because for us it is the battle for our physical and spiritual survival.'

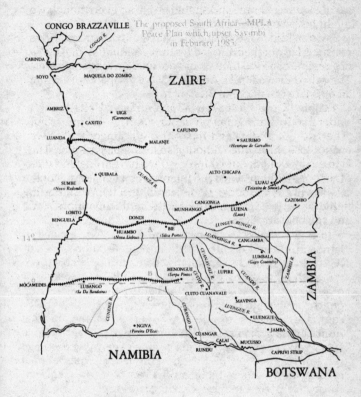

ANGOLA

The proposed South Africa—MPLA
Peace Plan which upset Savimbi
in February 1983.

A UNDER PROPOSED SOUTH AFRICAN—MPLA
  AGREEMENT, SWAPO GUERRILLAS WERE TO WITHDRAW
  BEHIND THIS LINE
B UNDER THE PROPOSED SOUTH AFRICAN—MPLA
  AGREEMENT, CUBAN TROOPS WERE WITHDRAWN
  BEHIND THIS LINE
C UNDER THE PROPOSED MPLA—SOUTH AFRICAN
  AGREEMENT, THERE WAS TO BE A CEASEFIRE IN THIS
  AREA

45

Brazilians

1983

UNITA's relations with the International Committee of the Red Cross, which had deteriorated through 1982, had by now been restored to the point where Savimbi declared them to be 'excellent'.[1]

In the third week of February, just before we arrived in Jamba at the end of our expedition, a delegation of senior ICRC officials held negotiations there with Savimbi. It ended with him signing the Geneva Convention on treatment of prisoners-of-war and with the ICRC delegation carrying out the first of a regular programme of inspections of POW camps established by UNITA. Apart from the obvious humanitarian dimensions, it represented a considerable propaganda coup for Savimbi to have been given official recognition by one of the most reputable international organisations. It strengthened his campaign to gain legitimacy for UNITA in the eyes of the world.

The move to mend relations had come from the ICRC, for the very good reason that it wanted to restore help to hungry peasants in the Central Highlands. Through UNITA's representatives abroad, the ICRC suggested that conciliation talks be held in Namibia or Zaire. 'We told them we were only prepared to meet them in Angola,' said Savimbi. 'They were reluctant to come to our areas and talk to us because of the resentment the government in Luanda might feel. We said we were not in a hurry; they were the ones who had the need because they had stockpiles of medicine and food in Huambo and Bie they wanted to distribute.'

Towards the end of 1982 the ICRC relented and sent a delegation to Jamba to talk with Savimbi. It was led by one of the ICRC's most senior operation directors, whose responsibilities included Angola. He was a fellow graduate of Savimbi's from the Department of International Law and Politics at Lausanne University. He brought with him letters to Savimbi from their old Professor at Lausanne, Henri Rieben.

The ICRC man had something of Savimbi's charisma. The two got on well, and together they worked out the details of an agreement which permitted the ICRC to recommence operations on the Central Plateau.[2] Savimbi agreed to instruct his commanders on a series of measures which would protect the lives of ICRC officials working in the war-hit areas of the Central Highlands. In return, Savimbi said, the ICRC agreed not to send people into the villages 'to propagandise the humanitarian work the ICRC is doing, to tell people to come into the towns because they were suffering and might die.' UNITA considered this to be direct political interference by the ICRC, because it involved attracting people away from places where UNITA had influence to strongly fortified MPLA areas. 'We said we would do nothing to obstruct the feeding of people who came into ICRC centres of their own free will.'

The ICRC acknowledged a complaint by Savimbi that an MPLA plane with Red Cross markings had bombed a UNITA position near Caluquembe, south-west of Huambo, a few months earlier. Together UNITA and the ICRC worked out a secret method which would enable UNITA commanders to recognise Red Cross markings which genuinely distinguished the ICRC planes from those used by the MPLA.

There was also a problem for Savimbi when ICRC personnel and other neutrals travelled with MPLA military convoys, regarded by UNITA as legitimate targets for attack. The problem was highlighted at the end of January 1983 when Savimbi admitted UNITA's responsibility for the killing of a Swiss missionary, a Roman Catholic priest, who died in his car when UNITA forces ambushed the MPLA convoy in which he was travelling near Huambo.

'If people move in military convoys, we cannot distinguish them from MPLA soldiers during an attack,' said
Savimbi. 'So we agreed with the ICRC that in future they
should travel alone, never in an MPLA convoy. I gave very
stern instructions to my commanders not to attack any
civilian car moving alone, and not only those of the ICRC.'

*   *   *

Flushed with the success of agreement with Savimbi, the
ICRC delegation which visited the POW camp asked if they
could take back to Europe UNITA's latest foreign hostages,
two Brazilian agricultural experts captured from an MPLA
state farm in Cuanza Sul Province on 30 October 1982.
Alvaro da Cunha, a 33-year-old agricultural surveyor from
Brazil's São Paulo Province, and Alberto Pimenta Filho, 43,
also a surveyor, from Minas Gerais Province, had arrived in
Angola in September 1980 and were due to return home
within a few days of the date of their capture.

Alberto described how they had been taken as prisoners:
'It was some time before four in the morning when I heard
shooting. It seemed to be coming from the house of the
MPLA soldiers: there were about 30 of them stationed on the
farm. I went to Alvaro's house and told him I thought we
were being attacked. The shooting got nearer and became
more intense, so we shut ourselves in the bathroom and put
out the light.

'The shooting lasted about 40 minutes. Then the guerrillas
came in and one of them discovered us. We asked them not
to shoot and said we were Brazilians. They told us no harm
would come to us, but we would have to do a lot of
marching. We started walking at 5.30 with about 500 UNITA
guerrillas and by midday my feet were bleeding. We were
greatly surprised by the attack. We had been told by the
MPLA that there was war in Angola, but only in the south
with South Africa. We heard of other attacks in the area, but
the MPLA always said it was just bandits. We walked for 44
days and travelled on trucks for another seven to reach
Jamba. We guess the journey was about 1,650 kilometres.
We stopped at a lot of UNITA bases on the way and met a lot
of people. We were surprised because we thought the war

was against South Africa, but all we met were Angolan guerrillas.'

Alvaro and Alberto had a contract with their employers in Brazil, a giant agricultural company called Prop. Profex, to develop the MPLA's state farm at Fazenda Longa. They had come with six colleagues to establish maize, soya bean and cassava plantations. The other six had returned home just before Alvaro's and Alberto's capture. The two men reck-oned it would be at least four years before Fazenda Longa began to show positive results. They had had trouble getting the Angolan labour force to work hard. 'Not that the Angolans are lazy people. On the contrary, they are good workers,' said Alberto. 'But their wages were low, inflation was high, and there was little to buy anyway. How can anyone work hard for good results in such conditions?'

They said they were being well cared for by UNITA. The biggest problem was boredom. They had only a few books and no radio in their hut and they spent most of their time playing cards with the soldier who kept guard over them with a sub-machine-gun. Their hope was that they would soon be released to rejoin their families in Brazil. Savimbi had other ideas. He turned down the ICRC delegation's request to take the Brazilians with them. He wanted Brazil's right-wing military dictatorship to know that UNITA was angry about its Angola policy.

'We only want the Brazilian government to recognise that there is a conflict in Angola and to stop lying to their own people,' said Savimbi. 'We want them to make clear that any Brazilian company that sends employees to Angola will be putting their lives at risk. We want an end to the blackout that the régime has imposed on news from Angola.'

Brazil, which shared with Angola a common language and Portuguese cultural past, was among the first countries to recognise the MPLA government in 1976. It had since become one of Angola's major trading partners, exporting railway engines, buses, trucks and foodstuffs. In April 1983 it gave Angola a 410 million-dollar credit line for the import of Brazilian food and manufactured goods.[3]

'I have no intention of releasing the Brazilians while the government prefers to do good business with the MPLA and hide from their own public what is going on here,' said Savimbi. 'Brazil has just unloaded twelve diesel locomotives for the Benguela Railway at Lobito. We had destroyed nearly all the diesels on the railway, and now Brazil has come to the MPLA's rescue for its own financial gain. Soon we will cripple all twelve of those locomotives. And if Brazilians are wise they will not come to Angola because they will be arrested by us.'

The previous year a Brazilian husband and wife, Protestant missionaries, had been among the bewildering array of foreigners captured during UNITA attacks and marched to Jamba before being released. Savimbi said another Brazilian had been captured just a few weeks earlier, on 30 January 1983, when UNITA forces overran a camp for political prisoners at Tari, near Quibala in Cuanza Sul Province. Amnesty International, confirming the attack and stating that UNITA had released about one hundred of the 300 to 400 inmates, said the MPLA called Tari a '*Campo de Recuperacao e Producao*' (Recuperation and Production Camp), where inmates worked in the fields, attended 're-education' classes, and were forbidden to send or receive letters.[4]

The Brazilian from Tari was anti-MPLA, said Savimbi. As soon as he reached Jamba he would be released in the hope that in Brazil he would give a different picture of what the MPLA was doing in Angola.

* * *

Alvaro and Alberto were, in fact, released without any publicity in June 1983 along with the Brazilian from Tari. Savimbi used the presence of the three Brazilians in Jamba as an opportunity to meet again with his old friend, Father Armando Cordeira, the Brazilian priest who had built the Silva Porto volleyball court with Savimbi and then given the determined young African a chance to study at his school before providing him with a Catholic scholarship to study medicine. Armando Cordeira had long since returned home to Brazil: he and Savimbi had not seen each other for a quarter of a century. It was therefore an emotional reunion when Cordeira flew into the airstrip at Luengue to take the three Brazilians home. Cordeira was given the status of a VIP by UNITA, as the celebrations went on for several days.

Though Cordeira's visit and the release of the Brazilians were never publicised by Savimbi, I found out about them by chance when I visited the home of a UNITA overseas representative in 1984. I rifled through photographs on the coffee table. One showed a small, grey-haired man embracing Savimbi with N'Zau Puna looking on. I asked who he was, and was told it was Cordeira. The rest of the story then emerged.

46

Important UNITA Gains

1983

Before we left Angola, Savimbi said there would be many other major actions through 1983. 'We are bound to do this because people are getting a little tired of the struggle. It has been a burden for them and they have suffered. I think UNITA would be asleep if it did not take the people's weariness into account.'[1]

But his next breakthrough came not on the battlefield, but on the diplomatic front. In West Germany, on 6 March 1983, the Christian Democrats led by Helmut Kohl won their first general election since the Social Democrats took power in Bonn in 1970. Kohl formed a government in coalition with the small liberal Free Democrat Party.

Just a fortnight earlier, in my conversation with Savimbi in Angola, he had told me: 'If the Christian Democrats win elections, it may be the best card UNITA has in its international struggle. We have contacts at the very highest level with the Christian Democrats, from Kohl and Strauss (Gerhard Strauss, the powerful leader of the Bavarian branch of the Christian Democrats) at the top.'[2]

For several months beforehand, while the Christian Democrats led an interim government following the resignation of the Social Democrat Chancellor Helmut Schmidt, the Christian Democrats had demonstrated that they were serious about giving support to UNITA, said Savimbi.

He did not elaborate on the nature of the support, which must have been clandestine. But on 29 March it became clear that the wind was blowing in UNITA's direction when the Kohl government said it would stop supporting SWAPO and reopen the West German consulate in Windhoek, the Namibian capital, which had been closed by the Social Democrats.[3] Thus the way was open for the new government to channel aid to Savimbi if it so chose. By 1985 UNITA had two permanent representatives in West Germany, one in Bonn and the other in Herr Strauss' power base, Munich. Savimbi had also assigned other members of his administration to the study of German.

* * *

On 12 March UNITA staged its most dramatic kidnapping yet of foreign hostages. At 5 a.m. the small town of Alto-Catumbela, built around a big paper pulp mill on the Benguela Railway 150 kilometres east of Lobito, was still asleep. So were most of the 550-man MPLA garrison. For several hours 1,500 UNITA semi-regular soldiers and guerrillas under the command of Lt.-Col. Alberto Kanhali had been moving into position. Artillery men set up mortars, whose tubes, base plates and shells they had carried on their backs. The sun had not risen when the first mortar shells began falling on Alto-Catumbela. Infantrymen moved in with their Kalashnikovs. By 10 a.m. the town had fallen and 86 foreigners living there had been rounded up. Sixty-six of them were Czechoslovaks, including 21 children and 17 women, and the other 20 were Portuguese.

The Czechoslovaks were technicians and managers at the pulp mill. Some of the Portuguese worked in the mill while others worked on the railway. Most of the Czechoslovak women were wives of the technicians, but one, Dr Rudeschkova, was a medical officer at the mill.[4] Alexander Ivan, a 53-year-old translator with the Czechoslovaks, recalled: 'We remained hidden inside our homes, but it was quite horrifying, particularly for the women and children. We could tell by the firing that we were surrounded. Our houses were shot to pieces, and we were very fortunate to emerge without a scratch. The guerrillas were very correct. They shook hands, told us who they were, and said we would be taken to the nearby mountains. There was no brutality.'

Few of the hostages had time to pick up spare clothes. Some had no footwear. By midday they had been shepherded into the mountains, which theoretically were rebel-free. 'Most of us had our families with us,' said Alexander Ivan. 'We would not have brought them to Angola if we had not thought it was safe. We were just civilians doing civilian jobs. But we saw conditions getting worse gradually, and restrictions were increased on the distance we could move from Alto-Catumbela. Always the MPLA told us the problem was purely a local one. But we are not stupid; we knew there were some big clashes going on around.'

From the mountains the hostages heard UNITA sappers blowing up the power plant, power lines, the mill's heavy machinery, marshalling sidings, railway points, three bridges, a locomotive and 36 trucks. While the destruction went on, the hostages began what would be a long and nightmarish march accompanied by more than 1,200 UNITA troops and porters. 'No one ever told us that we were prisoners,' said one of the Czechoslovaks. 'We thought that we would quickly return home.'

That hope was not borne out. They marched for two months in dreadful conditions. It was the wet season. They got soaked by torrential rain during the day, and had to sleep on sodden ground at night. Only the children, who included an 18-month-old toddler, had rudimentary groundsheets, made from small squares of plastic. The straggling column, several kilometres long and several kilometres wide, came under constant attempted attack by forces of the MPLA, which was deeply embarrassed by the UNITA coup against one of Luanda's East European allies. The MPLA deployed an estimated 6,000 Angolan and Cuban troops in an attempt to rescue the Czechoslovaks. But the Cubans withdrew their forces after two weeks, following appeals from Prague not to take actions which might endanger its citizens' lives.

More UNITA guerrillas joined the column to help fend off MPLA attacks. Illness struck the hostages: malaria, dysentery, pneumonia and earache. Stretchers were made to carry those who could not walk, six at first and eventually twenty. The number of porters was doubled to work in relays carrying the sick hostages. With the additional guerrillas and porters, the column grew to 2,000 in strength. When MIG planes and helicopters started bombing ahead of the column, it was divided into three to make interdiction by the government more difficult. The column was helped in its cat-and-mouse game by UNITA's communications centre in the south-east, which was monitoring government transmissions so that it could guide its people and their hostages past MPLA blockades. Food was basic; maize porridge shared by hostages, soldiers and porters. After 24 days salt ran out and also sugar for the bitter coffee carried by the guerrillas. Then, 39 days into their march, death struck the Czechoslovaks.

'Jeroslav Navratil was a handsome sportsman,' said Dr Rudeschkova. 'But he was living through the first and only big adventure of his life, and, without any warning signs that he was ill, he just lay down and died.' There was no time for his comrades to assist in the burial of Jeroslav Navratil, who was placed in the wet Angolan earth by the guerrilla rearguard. Dr Rudeschkova believes he was a diabetic without knowing it; the disappearance of sugar from the diet had killed him. Aware that the hostage death would damage their cause, UNITA withheld the announcement of Navratil's death until after all the hostages had reached Jamba in straggling groups, days apart, through May. (Just a few days before Navratil died, another UNITA supporter was executed by an MPLA firing squad. Tomas Pedro Vidro was sentenced to death in the coastal town of Sumbe formerly Novo Redondo by the Luanda Province People's Revolutionary Court for clandestine activities on behalf of UNITA.)[5]

Czechoslovak Prime Minister Lobomir Strougal appealed for help to the chairman of the OAU, Kenyan President Daniel Arap Moi, and to UN Secretary-General Javier Perez de Cuellar. Pope John Paul II appealed for the release of the surviving hostages: Savimbi responded by inviting the ICRC to provide transport home for the Czechoslovaks. At the end of June, foreign newsmen were invited to Jamba to watch UNITA's farewell ceremonies for the hostages. Thousands of people – the war wounded, bands and singers, the LIMA women's organisation, the youth movement, soldiers – paraded with banners to remind the departing Czechoslovaks where UNITA stood: 'Out with the Cubans'; 'Down with Soviet Expansionism in Africa and the World'; 'We Want Peace'. At the back of the parade ground were immense frescoes telling the history of UNITA and showing Soviet tanks and helicopters exploding into pieces. Everywhere were huge portraits of Savimbi. A big military parade featured infantrymen in impeccable marching order; Ural trucks mounted with Stalin Organs; and Soviet 120mm artillery pieces. Dr Rudeschkova, who had become the guardian angel of her fellow Czechoslovaks, stood near Savimbi. Suddenly her normally calm manner dissolved as she was overcome by tears. Correspondents watched Savimbi clasp her hand and talk to her privately while she regained her composure.

The ICRC refused to accept the hostages at the military parade. Instead ICRC representatives attended an evening ceremony in the arena where, a few months earlier, I had watched UNITA women singing 'Advance With the Jaguar'. There was an electric atmosphere as some of the hostages were lined up in the middle of the floodlit arena and the crowd sang UNITA anthems. Savimbi walked towards the group with the ICRC's Deputy Director for Africa, gestured towards the foreigners and said: 'They are yours.' 'Only the women and children?' asked the ICRC man. 'We will continue the discussion tomorrow,' said Savimbi.

After a long and heated debate in the Central Committee Savimbi had beaten back a demand by a hard-line faction that none of the hostages be released while there were UNITA prisoners held by the MPLA. Savimbi, aware that UNITA would be partly judged by the extent to which it respected human rights while waging war, persuaded the Central Committee that all 21 children, the 17 women and five of the men who were sick should be released. The remaining 20 men would be kept as hostages in future bargaining. The following day, when it was announced that some Czechoslovaks would not be returning home, there were scenes of high emotional intensity. The farewells were so traumatic, as the sick men, the women and children were taken away to be driven into Namibia, that UNITA officers tried to stop television cameramen from filming the departure.

From Namibia the 43 Czechoslovaks were flown to Johannesburg and then to Kinshasa, where they were met by Czechoslovak officials. They flew onward in a specially chartered Ilyushin jet of Czechoslovak Airlines and arrived in Prague on 1 July 1983.

To an extent, the release of the 43 was a triumph for Czechoslovak diplomacy. Its officials had worked mightily and they had engineered great exposure for the hostages' plight in the Western media to put pressure on Moscow to join the behind-the-scenes lobbying. But as soon as the women and children were released, the Prague government had lost the political game, for there was no longer an emotive pressure point which interested the Western press. The remaining 20 hostages were taken to a remote camp, several hours drive across rough tracks from Jamba, while UNITA began formulating conditions for their release. The eventual demand was for the freedom of a French doctor, Philippe Augoyard, imprisoned in Kabul after being captured while working with rebel Afghan tribesmen; the freedom of 36 UNITA political prisoners held in Luanda by the MPLA; and the release of the seven British mercenaries jailed by the MPLA since 1976.

Britain had long been seeking to extricate its seven mercenaries, and was disappointed when Angolan Foreign Minister Paulo Jorge did not make a gesture announcing their release during an official visit to Britain in February 1983. But London had no desire to endorse, or co-operate with, the UNITA demand. It wanted nothing to do with what it regarded as blackmail of a sovereign government, and there was no popular demand in Britain for action on behalf of the mercenaries, whose actions had been viewed with general distaste. Any leverage UNITA might have had on behalf of Augoyard disappeared when the Afghanistan government released the French doctor in early June without conditions.[6]

Savimbi continued to demand the release of his 36 followers imprisoned in Luanda, but there was no response from the MPLA. Savimbi had miscalculated his bargaining terms, and his hostages were therefore caught in limbo. Meanwhile, at their remote camp, the Czechoslovaks had few books and neither writing materials nor radio. The heat and rain which had oppressed them during their march was replaced in July and August by the freezing nights of the southern African winter when, to their amazement, ice formed on their washbowls.

They christened 14 August 1983 'Black Sunday'. On that day a UNITA official told them they should prepare for a stay of at least five years.

* * *

Munhango is a small but important town on the Benguela Railway. It had big railway engineering and repair workshops and it was a marketing centre for the many farmsteads in the surrounding area. Almost in the dead centre of Angola, it was also the birthplace of Jonas Savimbi.

In the cool morning darkness of 20 April 1983, UNITA semi-regular troops fanned out in the maize fields and among the mango and banana trees surrounding the government-controlled town of 8,000 people. They joined local guerrillas who had moved into position earlier to keep watch. The signal to attack came at 5 a.m. in the form of a rifle shot as the first faint glimmer of dawn showed on the horizon. A mortar barrage was launched from the east. Just before 5.30 a.m., more than 1,000 UNITA infantrymen swept in from the north with carefully controlled mortar fire pounding the ground ahead of them. The MPLA garrison of more than 400 men offered practically no resistance, and by 6 a.m. the government soldiers had either fled, been captured, or were dead. A light Antonov transport plane lay crumpled on the airstrip to the west of the town, hit by UNITA mortar fire as it prepared to take off.[7]

Colonel Ben-Ben Arlindo Pena led the attack. Foreign journalists were with him when he arrived at Munhango station and, incongruously, the telephone rang in the office.

It was a neighbouring station-master who wanted to find out about the explosions he had heard. 'Nothing is happening here,' said Ben. 'Everything is calm.' After putting the phone down Ben gave the order for the destruction of the town's infrastructure. Sappers began with the station itself and its radio installations. They moved on to steam locomotives in the workshop marshalling yards; the water tanks for the locomotives; and the switching points.

The attack on Munhango was – along with the attack I had witnessed on Cangonga – part of the months-long UNITA offensive to push thousands of troops far to the north of the Benguela Railway. On the way to Munhango, journalists with the UNITA force had passed through the flattened, crater-strewn ruins of Tempue (formerly Alto Quito) only days after the hill-top town, commanding a strategic route to the Central Highlands, had fallen to UNITA following a month-long siege. One of these journalists, Yves Loiseau, was told by Savimbi that 3,000 UNITA soldiers were now in the diamond mining province of Lunda in the northeast.[8] Some had reached the Zaire border there, and one group had even made a symbolic march 50 kilometres deep into Zaire. Not that they would have received a hostile reception, for both Loiseau and another French journalist, Edward Girardet, were told by Savimbi that French military advisers in Zaire had given UNITA officers specialised training in communications and anti-tank warfare. I, too, had been told by UNITA officers, during the march from Cangonga, that supply routes to the insurgents in Lunda had been opened up from Zaire.

Deep penetration of Lunda by UNITA posed a difficult problem for the MPLA, for the diamonds mined there were Angola's second-biggest foreign currency earner (after oil), bringing in more than 100 million dollars a year. However, diamond smuggling was losing Diamang, the state diamond company, another 60 million to 84 million dollars a year from its potential profits.[9] To help counter the smuggling the Minister of Mines and Industries, Lt.-Col. Bento Ribeiro, hired several former British Special Air Service (SAS) personnel to serve as mine police. The Britons, employees of a shadowy company called Defence Systems

International, were trained with their Angolan counterparts at a specialist school in Britain.[10]

The appointment of the Britons enraged both the Kremlin and Savimbi. When President dos Santos paid an official visit to Moscow on 16 May 1983 he was handed a report which accused the Britons of being spies. The report also demanded the arrest of Angolan investigators trying to uncover the full extent of a diamond smuggling scandal, in which many senior MPLA officials were involved. But the Minister of Planning, Lopo do Nascimento, defended the appointment of the Britons and accepted outside opinion that Angolan political and managerial interference, along with smuggling by MPLA officials, had reduced profits.[11]

Here among the diamond mines of Lunda was another Angolan paradox, another classical contradiction. Although South Africa was Angola's number one public enemy, a South African company, the famed De Beers, part of the Anglo American Company and Consolidated Goldfields group, largely ran Diamang and was a part-shareholder in the state-controlled company. One of De Beers' directors, Sir Philip Oppenheimer, flew regularly from Johannesburg to Angola with other executives to inspect the Diamang operation.[12]

Savimbi, despite his heavy dependence on South African support, was determined to create mayhem among the South African-run and part-owned mines.[13] He warned that his forces had orders to attack the 50 British security guards on sight, and if any were captured they would be treated as prisoners-of-war. He said some of the Britons were flying helicopters to trace smugglers, including UNITA 'economic agents' and soldiers. If caught, the mines police would be regarded as mercenaries in the same way as the Britons imprisoned by the MPLA in Luanda since 1976. 'If we find a French or a British technician, we let him go and say: "Please leave, we are going to attack,"' said Savimbi. 'But a man handling a gun – that's a different story.'[14]

Savimbi said he intended creating upheaval in Lunda Province so that some 700 foreign technicians working in the mines would leave. UNITA was also involved in diamond smuggling: 'Diamonds in the Lunda area are almost everywhere, and we're in a better position to know where they are,' said Savimbi. 'Some areas we know through the local population, others we've learned about from the Portuguese technicians who have returned home with their own maps and who are not working with the MPLA any more. They have passed this information to us.'[15]

How the smuggling network operated Savimbi would not describe, but he said: 'To get diamonds from up there to sell them to South Africa, that's a long way. But there is a shorter way – and we are part of that process.' With the Zaire border so close, Savimbi seemed to be suggesting that the diamonds were being channelled out through Kinshasa, and the *Washington Times*, reported: 'By gaining access to the Angolan borders with Zambia and Zaire, he [Savimbi] has opened new supply lines should his trade with South Africa across the Namibian border be cut off by a peace settlement.'[16]

Savimbi said that although MPLA officials had smuggling networks of their own, the biggest smugglers of all were the Cubans who 'were working for themselves'. This helped explain the appearance of Cuban diamonds on the Antwerp market although there were no known diamond mines on Cuba.[17]

* * *

The chaos in the diamond fields helped explain the extreme decrepitude into which Angolan cities had fallen under MPLA rule. A rare account came in the *New York Review of Books* from Xan Smiley, who managed to enter the country under the guise of a basketball correspondent with a black American team: 'Luanda's squalor is acute. Nearly every large building has broken windows, streets and sidewalks are pitted, rubbish is everywhere. Water pumps are frequently broken down, so that residential apartment blocks hurriedly vacated by the Portuguese often lack sanitation. Excrement lies stinking on staircases, even in fairly modern offices. There are practically no taxis, almost no functioning traffic lights.

'The biggest grumble of Luandans, as of all Angolans, is lack of food. Queues are everywhere. The black market in practically every essential and edible commodity flourishes, while the unofficial currency exchange rate – the journalist's shorthand for gauging a country's economic health – stands at about fifteen times the official one: close to Africa's record, ahead of Uganda and a little behind Ghana. The price of a cabbage or a couple of eggs sometimes exceeds the daily wage.

'Full-time MPLA party workers can buy essential goods in special shops, adding resentment to the ordinary worker's suspicion that Marxist egalitarianism does not extend to the new ruling class which preaches it most fiercely. Absenteeism is common because workers are constantly sloping off in search of food. Hungry workers doze on the job. The new party-licensed managerial class cites surprisingly old-fashioned reasons to explain low productivity, reckoned at about 20 per cent of pre-independence levels, hinting at "sabotage" or "workers' laziness".'[18]

*   *   *

In June 1983 a foreign journalist interviewed eight of the former inmates of the MPLA camp for political prisoners at Tari which had been overrun by UNITA forces on 30 January 1983. They had reached Savimbi's bases in the south-east with more than 50 other prisoners, including a Brazilian, a Zairean and six Portuguese, who had been held by the MPLA on charges of 'economic sabotage' or 'bourgeois attitudes'.[19]

Among the former inmates were Juan Francisco Cotingu, a bus driver from Huambo, and his wife, Marguerida. Cotingu was arrested in April 1980 and accused of being a UNITA sympathiser. At first, he was held in jail in Huambo where he said he was interrogated by the state security police, known familiarly as the DISA (*Direccao de Informaçao Seguranca de Angola*).[20] Cotingu said he was beaten with rifle butts. Cuban advisers working with the DISA often joined in his interrogation. Occasionally he saw East Germans, some in uniforms and others in civilian clothes, in the corridors. After four months he was sentenced to 20 years imprisonment and hard labour at Tari for collaborating with UNITA.

Several days after Cotingu's detention the police arrested Marguerida and accused her of collaboration for not having informed on her husband. In prison in Huambo she said she was stripped and beaten. 'They sprayed me with a hose and accused me of belonging to JURA (UNITA's youth movement). I was forced to stay naked. They gave me no covers to keep me warm at night and made me sleep on the cement floor. Two FAPLA came in and tried to rape me. At first I was able to resist, but for this they beat me badly.' She was joined by other women, also suspected of being members of JURA. Over three months they were all beaten and raped, Mrs Cotingu said. In the end, she was allowed to join her husband at Tari although she was not charged with any crime.

Armindo Rodrigues, a white Portuguese-born farmer who decided to stay in Angola after independence on his banana plantation near Benguela, was arrested by the MPLA in November 1980 and charged with harbouring UNITA sympathisers, something he did not deny. He spent 106 days in detention without trial before being sentenced to 20 years imprisonment and sent to Tari. During his time in detention without trial at Benguela he was interrogated by Cubans and East Germans as well as Angolans. 'Cubans would take ropes and semi-strangle prisoners to make them talk,' he said. Fellow inmates told him about courtyard executions, but he did not see any himself. The MPLA technique was to carry out interrogations at all hours of the day, using psychologically destabilising techniques such as refusing drinking water in hot weather and heavily salting food.

The former Tari prisoners said many people in the camp had been held without trial for up to six years. Others had been summarily sentenced by People's Revolutionary Tribunals without presenting evidence or allowing the accused a proper defence. However, conditions at Tari, a former sisal plantation operated as a state farm by the MPLA, were less unpleasant than the urban security centres that most of the prisoners had passed through. After working on the farm, the prisoners grew much of their own food on small private plots in their spare time.

The commandants at Tari were under direct orders from the Angolan Ministry of Security to 're-educate' political deviants, according to Mario-Antoine Cortez, Tari's chief of personnel and a member of the state security police, who was captured by UNITA. Three categories of prisoners were kept at Tari, he said: persons officially sentenced, those awaiting trial, and others detained without trial as security risks. There was public punishment for those who tried to escape, said the former prisoners. They were beaten with sticks or fists, and inmates were at times ordered to carry out the punishments on their fellows. Sometimes arms and legs got broken. People were forced to drink water mixed with petrol, or sometimes they were punished by being put in a wrecked car in the sun and forced to stay there for many days.

The political re-education programme had, in fact, virtually collapsed from 1981 because of lack of motivation among the camp personnel. 'Many guards had not been paid their salaries for months, and generally there was a "couldn't care less" attitude among them,' said Senhor Barata dos Santos, who had been serving a sentence for diamond smuggling after first being imprisoned without trial for almost two years. 'We also refused to co-operate during re-education lectures. We would talk back or ask irritating questions. So they finally gave up.'

Cuban and East German advisers did not participate in the running of Tari, but Soviet 'agricultural advisers' would occasionally inspect the centre. Cuban troops were stationed near the camp, but they made no attempt to intervene when UNITA overran it.

* * *

Through July and August 1983 UNITA's military push northwards intensified. On 1 July UNITA stormed another Benguela Railway town in an early morning attack. Again, the whole economic infrastructure of Cangumbe, 100 kilometres west of Luena, was destroyed by UNITA sappers before they retreated to their forest bases. UNITA claimed 57 MPLA dead in the battle against five of their own.[21] On 3 July UNITA staged its most dramatic assault in the northern half of Angola to that date. The 1,000-strong UNITA Ninth Brigade seized Mussende, 250 kilometres north of the railway. Mussende had particular strategic importance because it was the southern buffer point for Malanje, the second biggest city in the north, just 100 kilometres away by a narrow tarmac road. Consequently it was heavily defended and the attackers, by their own admission, did not have such an easy time as at Cangonga, Munhango and Cangumbe. According to the UNITA account (the MPLA maintained silence), the fighting lasted two-and-a-half hours and 248 MPLA soldiers were killed against 17 UNITA dead. About 1,300 civilians were taken from the town and distributed around UNITA-controlled villages and camps. UNITA claimed to have taken 37 MPLA prisoners and captured 3,000 mortar and rocket shells and 400 rifles. Additionally, it claimed that a Cuban company of 130 soldiers stationed at Mussende with the MPLA had been withdrawn by helicopter three days before the battle.[22]

Nine days after the Mussende battle, a trap was laid outside Mussende which led to the capture of a senior MPLA commander. The incident was described to me by a senior UNITA official:

'During the battle for Mussende we captured the MPLA's chief radio operator. He co-operated with our forces, and sent a message to the MPLA asking for helicopters to evacuate the wounded. Two MI-8 helicopters were sent to the place indicated, and members of one of our Special Forces were waiting there dressed in MPLA uniforms. They approached the helicopters after they landed. An officer stepped out and saluted and was immediately taken alive. The helicopters attempted to take off but they were shot down and the Cuban pilots killed.'[23]

The captured officer was Captain Jose Joaquim Gaspar, a Portuguese-born white Angolan, who was Chief of Staff of the MPLA's Seventh Military Region. UNITA leaders said he had just arrived in the Mussende area from Cabinda, where he had participated in an MPLA joint chiefs of staff meeting to plan offensives in the north against UNITA, and was now giving 'our forces important secret military information'.[24]

The Mussende action was quickly followed by a diplomatic coup. Four Members (Belgian, British, French and West German) of the European Parliament[25] paid a four day visit to Savimbi's liberated areas, and with Savimbi signed a joint communiqué which said the Parliamentarians 'shared with President Savimbi the opinion that UNITA is capable of controlling the whole of Angola, and that UNITA hopes to be able to negotiate with the Luanda government for a national reconciliation. The weight of UNITA's military success combined with full support from the civilian population gives legitimacy to the aims of President Savimbi to free his country from all foreign forces of occupation – Cubans, Soviets and East Germans. Both parties have agreed that the return of peace and independence to Angola holds the key to the peaceful transition to self-determination in Namibia and the re-establishment of lasting peace and security in southern Africa.'[26]

This provoked an outcry from the MPLA which said the politicians had 'violated the most elementary laws' by illegally entering a country with which each of their states had diplomatic relations. Savimbi had invited them so that he could 'crow about the crimes he is ordered to carry out by Pretoria against Angola'.[27] The MPLA accused them of entering Angola from Namibia with a South African military escort. Mr Luc Beyer de Rike, a Belgian Liberal Party Member of the European Parliament, said they could not disclose the route through which they had entered Angola, but he added: 'Among the many channels that exist, we have not taken that of the south.'[28] In fact, their route was probably the regular UNITA air link from Kinshasa.

Mr Beyer de Rike met the 20 remaining Czechoslovak hostages who, he said, were very distressed but in good health: 'They asked me to tell their ambassador (in Brussels) that it was necessary to try to reach a quick solution because they could not bear the terrible psychological tension. They were held in total ignorance of what was happening. When they were told of our visit, they thought the day of their release had arrived because they had been given neat clothes and different food.'

Beyer de Rike concluded that Savimbi's movement was 'a

fact that will be difficult to deny in any settlement in Angola as well as Namibia, the two problems being indissolubly linked'.

* * *

In late July UNITA demonstrated the value of the capture of the string of three railway towns, Cangonga, Munhango and Cangumbe. Along this central section of the Benguela Railway it pushed thousands of soldiers unhindered across the line into the provinces of the north-east. On 23 July UNITA's 12th Brigade overran Sautar, a small but important town controlling a main crossroads in the south of Malanje Province. In the battle for Sautar, UNITA claimed 58 enemy dead against six of its own.[29] Again, the MPLA said nothing about UNITA's claim. (I was to pass through Sautar's out-skirts less than five months later with a UNITA brigade.) But the MPLA did respond when, on 26 July 1983, UNITA said it had attacked a military train on the eastern outskirts of Luena carrying the 73rd Battalion of the MPLA's 21st Brigade, several Cuban soldiers and also some ODP mem-bers and their families. UNITA claimed 78 enemy dead and 319 wounded in the attack.[30]

The MPLA, in two communiqués, said the train had been blown up by a landmine, killing 50 and wounding 210. It said more than 50 of the dead and wounded were women and children and that the only two soldiers travelling on the ill-fated train were among the dead.[31]

Alarmed by the strength, frequency and wide spread of the UNITA offensive, President dos Santos told the MPLA's Central Committee that he was proclaiming a tough new internal defence law putting power and responsibility into the hands of regional military councils with martial law powers. The law gave dos Santos greater personal power, enabling him to decide which regions needed military coun-cils. In his address, he said councils were authorised to requisition 'property or persons' for the war effort and to 'try crimes against state security, economic sabotage, speculation and disobedience . . . as well as all crimes that harm or endanger the interests of collective defence and security'.[32]

The Angolan News Agency (ANGOP) said the law was necessary because imperialism refused to recognise that it had been beaten in Angola: 'Every day it perpetrates acts of aggression, vandalism and banditry against the territory and civilian population, spreading death, destruction and suffering while working for Pretoria's racist régime, mercenaries and other gangs of killers.'[33]

President dos Santos admitted UNITA's deep penetration of the north when, within weeks of taking his increased powers, he announced that he was setting up military councils in the northern provinces of Malanje and Lunda-Norte. In a speech in Malanje city[34] he said the councils were necessary to stem South African attempts to oust his government and put UNITA in power. He urged 'sacrifices, total engagement, revolutionary ardour and the mobilisation of all our energies and capacity for resistance to re-establish the conditions of peace and tranquillity which will permit us to build social well-being and happiness'.

Savimbi's response to dos Santos's new law was to deal the MPLA its biggest defeat in more than 20 years of warfare. But in the course of it his men suffered terrible losses.

47

Cangamba

1983

In the area that Savimbi now controlled there remained only two MPLA strongholds – Cuito Cuanavale and Cangamba.

Savimbi ruled out the possibility of taking Cuito Cuanavale. It was supplied by road from Menongue by hundreds of lorries and had a good airstrip which enabled the MPLA to put in plenty of supplies. 'There are Russians and Cubans there,' Savimbi said. 'They don't want to relinquish Cuito Cuanavale, because it is the bridgehead for any offensives they want to launch against us in the south-east. We don't have the means at present to take that town: it is very strong. What we have to do is harass it all the time.'[1]

Cangamba was different. I passed within 60 kilometres of it in February 1983 when returning by truck down the Savimbi Trail from Cangonga. Totally isolated, it had become a kind of Dien Bien Phu, defended heavily for morale and prestige rather than any good strategic reason.

Five hundred kilometres north of the Namibian border, Cangamba was defended by two MPLA brigades, the 44th and the 32nd – a total of 2,800 men. The 44th was a crack brigade, sent from Luanda to ensure that the government retained its foothold in UNITA territory. There were also two companies of Cuban troops (100 to a company) in the town, according to UNITA.[2]

Following the fall of Tempue to UNITA in April, all the MPLA's overland routes to Cangamba were severed. The surrounding territory was held by UNITA which was probing the town's perimeters with Special Forces. The MPLA was supplying its garrison by air from bases 300 kilometres away, an operation made difficult by UNITA SAM-7 missile teams around the town. To avoid the missiles the MPLA was using light Antonov-2 transport planes which arrived high over the town and made spiralling descents to the airstrip.

While I was in Angola, UNITA made it clear that it intended taking Cangamba before 1983 was out. Colonel Ben-Ben said the strangulation of the town had already begun and local people were leaving it because of food shortages. The force that attacked would have to be much bigger than the enemy garrison. And in February Savimbi had said: 'Cangamba is vulnerable. Around it we have four teams of SAM-7s, so it is difficult for them to supply. We have a big plan about it.'

*   *   *

It was another six months before the plan unfolded and the rebel assault began. And it was not on the pattern of a classic UNITA lightning dawn raid.

Savimbi amassed three brigades of semi-regulars, and many companies of guerrillas and platoons of Special Forces around Cangamba, slightly more than 6,000 attackers against the 3,000-strong enemy garrison. The siege began on 3 August with a big artillery barrage featuring some of the reconditioned Soviet 75mm artillery pieces captured in the battle for Mavinga three years earlier.

Then the poor bloody infantry were sent in, trying to find their way through minefields laid by the defenders. More than 100 of the UNITA infantrymen were to lose one or both legs before the battle of Cangamba was over. A special team from the Paris-based medical charity, Medicius Sans Frontières, arrived in Savimbi's territory to work on the rehabilitation of the crippled men.[3]

MIG-21 jets and MI-8 helicopters from Luena bombarded the UNITA attack forces. But by 11 August so many breaches had been made in the MPLA defensive minefields and trench systems that the more than 100 surviving Cubans, with their commanding lieutenant-colonel, were lifted out by helicopters.

On 14 August at 10 a.m. Cangamba was finally brought

under UNITA control. At the end of the biggest battle in more than two decades of civil warfare in Angola, 829 of the Cangamba garrison lay dead, some of them Cubans, and 328 had been captured. The rest fled northwards. In addition, a few days before, UNITA claimed to have killed 72 troops from two MPLA battalions which tried to recapture nearby Tempue for the government. UNITA said it had lost 63 men dead and 200 wounded in the Cangamba battle. Photographs were released of an Antonov plane sitting with its back broken by artillery fire on Cangamba's airstrip, and UNITA claimed also that its SAM-7 missiles and anti-aircraft guns had brought down five MIG-21 fighter-bombers and four helicopters. Some 2,300 weapons and 12 BRDM-2 armoured personnel carriers were captured, and 6,300 civilians were taken from the town and spread around UNITA areas.[4]

That was Savimbi's version of the battle for Cangamba, which no foreign reporters witnessed. The MPLA's story was different.

On the day that UNITA said it had captured the town, the MPLA announced in Luanda that it had beaten back a major assault by the enemy but that South Africa had rushed aid to UNITA, taking command of the offensive, putting 10,000 troops into southern Angola and bombing Cangamba until it had 'ceased to exist'. In defence of the town the MPLA killed 1,100 UNITA troops while 53 of its own had died. Three days after the UNITA announcement that Cangamba had fallen, the MPLA officially admitted that its forces had retreated, ostensibly to save civilian lives. After the retreat, helicopters landed there carrying South African regular troops, mercenaries and UNITA soldiers, the MPLA said.[5]

UNITA dismissed the MPLA version of the battle as a 'cheap disinformation campaign', denied that South African planes or troops had been involved, and invited press and ICRC representatives to visit the town and see that it had not been completely destroyed, as the MPLA alleged.[6] South Africa's defence chief, General Constand Viljoen, rejected the charges of South African military involvement and said the MPLA was trying to disguise UNITA successes.

The MPLA charged that South Africa had bombed

Cangamba with napalm. UNITA had made the same charge against the MPLA during the eleven-day assault on Cangamba, and it later released photographs of stacks of napalm bombs in the town with Soviet markings.

My own conviction – though far from absolute – is that the UNITA account was nearer the truth. At all stages, the MPLA *reacted* to UNITA accounts of the battle. If there had been a heavy South African involvement the MPLA would surely have alerted world opinion much earlier in the fighting, for it could have been sure of obtaining general condemnation of South African military actions so far inside Angola. And of the 1,100 enemy the MPLA claimed to have killed, it said all of them were UNITA guerrillas: not one was a South African.

Whatever the truth of the battle for Cangamba, there were no doubts about its consequences. UNITA had cleared from its midst a dangerous threat; some 6,000 of its forces had been freed from the siege to join other strike forces north of the Benguela Railway; UNITA's morale, already high after its series of 1983 victories, soared while that of the MPLA hit a new low.

But the scale of the battle meant that Angola's hidden war had entered a new and more serious stage, posing an acute problem for the MPLA's Cuban and Soviet allies. I wrote at the time: 'Soon Havana and Moscow will have to decide whether to advise its client to sue for peace or to send in more Cuban and Eastern-bloc troops to stem UNITA's advance.'[7]

48

Towards the Diamond Mines

1983

The response by Cuba and the Soviet Union to the MPLA defeat at Cangamba was to send yet more troops and weapons.

In late August Lucio Lara and Defence Minister Pedro Tonha were sent to Moscow by President dos Santos to request more weapons and advisers. In the first three weeks of September at least ten Soviet cargo ships unloaded arms, including modern Soviet-built T-62 tanks, in Luanda harbour. In October 40 Soviet military technicians arrived to strengthen air defences in Lubango, and 5,000 Cubans reinforced Havana's army in Angola, bringing its strength to more than 25,000.[1] UNITA claimed that among other Soviet weapons landed were 16 SAM-6 and SAM-8 missiles;[2] 24 helicopters; four naval patrol boats; and 20 mobile bridges.[3]

Savimbi's response was to launch UNITA's nearest attack to Luanda to that date. His forces overran the town of Calulo, about 200 kilometres south-east of the capital. The UNITA force killed two SWAPO guerrillas in Calulo and departed within 24 hours. With them they took food supplies and 27 hostages, including Brazilians, Spaniards, Portuguese, and 14 nuns and novices from the local Catholic mission.[4]

*   *   *

The war was becoming bigger, bloodier and more complex. I prepared to return to see for myself. I had been invited by Savimbi to become the first Western reporter to push north of the Benguela Railway and watch a battle in the diamond-mining province of Lunda, at the beginning of UNITA's rainy-season offensive. I decided also to make a television film and took with me a young Scottish cameraman, David Kane.[5]

* * *

Likuwa, UNITA's hospitality base near Luengue, had changed. The huts were bigger and more spacious. There was a special mess, where we were served a dinner of rice and antelope stew, washed down by lager beer from Namibia and good German white wine. But outside it was wild: a lioness had recently been shot after it had taken a UNITA soldier. As we went down to bathe in the exquisite clear water of a sandy-bottomed stream, a big herd of sable antelope burst out of the reeds. The rains were beginning to set in, and the sunset was breathtaking but soft – lots of mauve, purple and deep pink sky and, incongruously, green clouds.

The battlefields were also growing wilder. When UNITA overran Calulo and the nearby town of Mussende, American news media speculated excitedly about an impending drive towards Luanda that might bring down the MPLA.[6] But the government struck back hard. In a counter-offensive, from 5 September to 24 October, ten government infantry brigades supported by paratroopers, fighter planes, helicopters and more than 50 tanks retook Calulo and Mussende. The government said it killed 600 rebels in the counter-offensive: UNITA admitted 82 dead.[7] Whatever the true figures, it was an ominous prelude to the big UNITA offensive which Savimbi hoped would persuade the international community of his importance in the future of Angola and southern Africa. In his briefing before we headed north, Savimbi put a brave face on it, saying that as the MPLA was determined to defend the capital at all costs, it would have to give way elsewhere, especially in areas where UNITA now intended launching attacks.

The first major UNITA response to the government counter-offensive came on 8 November when an Angolan

Airlines Boeing-737 taking off from Lubango crashed 1,000 metres from the end of the runway, killing all 126 people aboard. UNITA said the plane, carrying army recruits and a company of the MPLA's Third Motorised Brigade to Luanda, was shot down by commandos of one of its Special Forces. The MPLA said the crash was due to technical failure, and that there were only two military officers aboard the plane.[8]

* * *

We pushed northwards aboard Ural trucks. After three days we were 50 kilometres north of Mavinga at a place called Kueyo, where within the last year UNITA had established a 200-hectare collective farm producing maize, sorghum, tobacco, beans and a variety of vegetables. By 12 November we had skirted the southernmost Cuban position, at Cuito Cuanavale, 300 kilometres north of the Namibian border, and were pushing up the valley of the Cuanavale River onto the Central Plateau. About 80 kilometres north of Cuito Cuanavale, we came upon a remarkable road bridge which UNITA engineers had constructed across the 40-metre-wide river since I was last there earlier in the year. It had enabled UNITA to open up an entirely new branch of the Savimbi Trail west of the Cuanavale towards the more densely populated areas of the Central Plateau. To enable trucks to get to the bridge, the engineers had laid roads made from tightly packed tree trunks across the swamps lining the river.

As earlier in the year, we were again escorted by a bodyguard of tough Special Forces, heavily armed and smartly dressed in navy-blue uniforms. Whenever an antelope or slender gazelle was spotted, one of their marksmen would fell it for that evening's supper.

In the ten months since I had witnessed the battle for Cangonga, the Savimbi Trail had been extended 120 kilometres northwards, so the trucks were now able to reach the Benguela Railway itself. We reached the line on 15 November, and that night, before we crossed the railway the following day at the beginning of a three-week march, UNITA announced that it had overrun an MPLA district capital at Cazombo, in the eastern salient of Angola which juts between Zambia and Zaire.[9]

Savimbi's offensive had begun.

* * *

We marched for 12 days, passing through entirely different countryside than I had experienced before in Angola. There were high, rolling hills topped by forest and gouged by cliffs and ravines clothed in curtains of delicate green ferns. Waterfalls tumbled 100 metres from plateau tops. Between the hills were wide valleys in which emerald grass was sprouting, brought on by the rains which were by now regularly drenching us. We stopped at villages where the people brushed our shoulders with palm leaves in traditional greeting and laid down carpets of green leaves for us to walk upon. An old friend, Colonel Smart Chata, a leader of the Chokwe tribe and UNITA's Secretary for Justice, met us in one village. Smart spoke beautiful, precise English, delivered with all the restrained, polite mannerisms of the best kind of English gentleman. So it was a surprise and a delight to see him transformed, or as his real self, as he addressed a rally in his native Chokwe – a full-blooded performance of incredible brio and body movements which politicians would get arrested for in Britain. We watched initiation dances for boys and girls. And we watched women pounding millet, singing a traditional tune to new, though hardly subtle, words: 'Cubans, you have to get out. Savimbi says so.' Smart said: 'We encourage people to maintain their culture, because our culture is what makes us Africans. At the same time, we incorporate that culture into our political structures.'

In one village, Sawanga, the people told us how in August 1982 the MPLA had occupied their settlement and 20 others in the area. The MPLA stayed for 15 days, during which time 70 people were executed to discourage customary support for UNITA. They had not returned since. The Sawanga chief gave each of us a warm hug, and dozens of people came to greet us in the *django*. We ate roast chicken and sliced baby turnips and chopped cabbage in salt and olive oil, a welcome change from the routine diet of boiled rice and canned sardines which induced regular bouts of diarrhoea. Later the villagers sang for us, comparing themselves, in their fight under Savimbi against the Cubans and Soviets, to the people of Israel being led out of Egypt. Then the old chief danced for us, in his traditional skirt and battered straw hat and underneath his tattered old umbrella of chiefly authority.

*   *   *

Travelling with us as interpreter was a new UNITA Secretary of Information, a delightful man called Jaka Jamba. Jaka was an intellectual whose Ph.D. had been based on some aspect of the life of Pascal. There, in the middle of 'darkest' Africa, I learned from Jaka one of the seventeenth-century French philosopher's greatest aphorisms: 'Le coeur a ses raisons que la raison ne connaît point.' (The heart has its reasons which reason does not know.) Jacka said it was his greatest wish, when peace came, to be a teacher of Angolan history. He picked up little orange fruits from the forest undergrowth and squeezed them to show us the rubber sap on which the great Angolan rubber boom was based at the turn of the century. The 30-year boom collapsed about 1910, but the profits it brought were enough to transform the way of life of the Ovimbundu: from shifting, subsistence agriculture they changed to intensive cash and barter cultivation.

*   *   *

One hundred and twenty kilometres north of the railway we entered the base camp of Brigadier Geraldo Nunda, the 31-year-old commander of UNITA's 'Northern Front'. Like many other UNITA bases I had seen, it was spread over many square kilometres. It had a football pitch, military parade ground, an open-air wood and thatch theatre, command and communications centre, and hospital, as well as the dug-out huts of the troops. Straight paths marked neatly by bark-stripped stakes linked the different parts of the camp. All the time, high overhead, droned Soviet-made Ilyushin and Antonov transport planes ferrying supplies from Luanda to Luena, in the east, where MPLA and Cuban troops were entirely cut off by road and rail as a result of UNITA military activities. Three battalions of semi-regular troops were at the base. They had crossed the Benguela Railway after UNITA won the battle for Cangonga on 11 February 1983. Within nine months the battalions had driven the MPLA from several small towns within striking distance of the base camp.

In the hospital wards – great wood and grass huts with beds made from reeds – we spoke to some of the men least severely wounded in the biggest Northern Front battle to that date for the Cuango River bridge. The 200-metre-long bridge crossed the Cuango, a big tributary of the mighty Congo, on the tar road from Luanda, the national capital, to Saurimo (Henriques de Carvalho), capital of the important north-eastern diamond mining province of Lunda, and the town of Luena (Luso) at the eastern end of the Benguela Railway.

Three hundred kilometres north of the Benguela Railway, and only 100 kilometres south of Angola's northern border with Zaire, the Cuango bridge had been destroyed in September, which accounted for the airlift we could see going on overhead from Luanda. During the battle for the bridge UNITA claimed to have shot down two MIG-21 jet fighters and two MI-8 helicopters. UNITA itself had taken heavy casualties: the several dozen men we saw had bullet and shrapnel wounds to arms, throats and jaws. They were all expected to recover and go back into battle. The most severely wounded had been carried south of the railway to more sophisticated hospitals run by Medicius Sans Frontières.

* * *

On 23 November a military rally was planned at the parade ground. SAM-7 missile teams assembled, and there were three Chinese 12.7mm anti-aircraft guns in place. The atmosphere at the base – far north into what outside analysts interpreted as MPLA/Cuban territory – was electric. But just as the rally got under way, a spectacular rainstorm began. Water plunged from the skies, heavy blankets of it which pounded the earth for three hours, accompanied by spectacular thunder and lightning. The rally was modified: the smartly kitted battalions still went through the drills, but the performers then crowded around the little grass pavilion in which we sat with Brigadier Nunda. Throughout the chilling, drenching downpour, they sang and danced non-stop, and rolled joyously in the mud, as if to say they were unstoppable.

* * *

On 24 November we moved out towards the target with the 2,000-strong brigade. We marched through the outskirts of the base, past dugouts where empty bullet packs were strewn around – fresh ammunition had obviously just been issued. The soldiers no longer wore their spick and span parade-ground uniforms: they were dressed in ragged, dirty clothes, rather as Wat Tyler's peasant army must have looked. On their backs and heads were mortar tubes, mortar shells, rocket launchers, rockets, machine-guns, maize flour, cooking pans and blankets. For a long time we walked along a disused road, which was disintegrating and becoming overgrown with creepers. We passed an abandoned settlement, stretched out along the road, where the houses were made of red laterite bricks. Nunda said it had been an MPLA outpost until it was cleared in a UNITA guerrilla operation in 1981. Now the houses were roofless and the walls were dissolving in the rain. That night we camped on a great hilltop, and when we heard the cry of babies we realised that we had with us women porters carrying their children in back-slings and weapons and ammunition on their heads.

On 25 November eight daylight hours were spent ferrying the brigade across the headwaters of the Cuango River by two inflatable rubber dinghies and two bark *pirogues* (native canoes). We swam in the swifter flowing river and admired a pathetic little baby monkey the brigade had picked up and was carrying as a mascot. A nurse dug a *bitacoia* parasite from my foot, and a barter deal was done with a herdsman for some of his cattle: they were slaughtered and transported across the river in big, bloody hunks for feasting on that night.

On 26 November we heard, on the BBC World Service, of the fall that day of the town of Andulo, 100 kilometres north of Bie, to a UNITA force. Eight Portuguese were killed in the crossfire and, according to later UNITA figures, 29 MPLA troops, three Cubans and five UNITA men were killed in the three-hour battle.[10]

On 27 November Brigadier Nunda told us his target – Alto Chicapa, a town of 5,000 people some 150 kilometres north of Luena. We met the intelligence team which had been entering the town for months beforehand. On the forest floor was a large-scale sand model of Alto Chicapa. The intelligence men pointed out an airstrip to the north-west, two water towers and the municipality's electric power generator. Barbed wire in good condition surrounded the barracks of the political police at the southern end of Alto Chicapa: barbed wire in a less healthy state protected the soldiers' barracks to the north. Defensive trenches were indicated on the model, along with a series of civilian houses for 4,000 people who, the intelligence men said, were UNITA supporters. The total enemy force was estimated at 700. They had two radios. The last convoy of supply trucks had visited the town seven weeks previously: villagers reported that MPLA morale was low because of poor food and clothing supplies. There had been desertions, and some MPLA soldiers traded clothes and bullets with the local population for food. There were no Cubans. The intelligence officers named all the top MPLA officers, the places where the troops slept (in the trenches), and the times at which they paraded and ate.

Nunda briefed us on his plan of attack. At 10 p.m., on the night before, UNITA soldiers would erect a rough wooden bridge across a small river to the north-west of Alto Chicapa. Two battalions, each of 600 men, would cross the bridge and get into position, one to attack from the west and the other from the north. The third battalion would be held in reserve. A 200-strong artillery unit would be placed to the west of the river. In addition, 150 locally-based UNITA guerrillas would harass MPLA soldiers who retreated southwards. There was a possibility of aerial intervention from MPLA airbases at Luena and Saurimo. For protection, the brigade was carrying SAM-7 missiles and 12.7mm anti-aircraft guns. But Nunda thought the battle would be so short that there would be no time to bring in aerial support. 'The morale of the enemy is very low, and in one hour everything will be over,' he said.

* * *

On 29 November we went with Brigadier Nunda across the river to the west of Alto Chicapa when the assault began at 5 a.m. Heavy mortars and cannons put down artillery fire. From our position, perhaps three kilometres away, we could see eucalyptus trees and the main tower of the hilltop town outlined against the first light from the rising sun. Then we heard the rattle of massed infantry rifle fire all over the hillside. At about 5.30 a white Vèry light was fired, a signal to the artillery to stop their bombardment, and by 5.40 the infantry fire also had stopped. We crossed the wooden bridge with Nunda and approached the town from the north where MPLA dead littered the scrub. We passed through a mud and thatch village near the centre of the town. Two huts were burning. There were no people around, only chickens and goats. When we reached the main street MPLA soldiers, bound and blindfolded, were already being interrogated by UNITA intelligence officers. Most of the garrison seemed to have fled southwards and eastwards before the attackers reached the centre, for no bodies were there.

While David filmed soldiers removing arms and useful materials and destroying the infrastructure, I wandered around Alto Chicapa. It had obviously once been a pleasant town, with fine Portuguese colonial-style bungalows, a hospital and a big restaurant where in past times travellers had perhaps stopped for a traditional Portuguese stew washed down by bottles of chilled *vinho verde*. But now there was scarcely any furniture in these buildings. There were no beds in the hospital wards, and the floor of one of them was covered in pools of black oil: in the clinic all the stuffing was coming out of the consulting couch and medicines were spread in jumbled piles all over the floor.

There had been no electricity recently in Alto Chicapa.

The generator, which would be dismantled and taken away by UNITA engineers, was in working order, but there was no fuel to drive it. Because there was no electricity, there was no water, which needed to be pumped up to the hilltop: as a result, all the town's toilets were unflushed, filthy and stinking. In the main street there was a municipal drinking fountain, and nearby an open-air swimming pool: both had long since ceased to function. In the houses, hospital and restaurant, wood fires had been lit on the floors. In many rooms empty cans of pork luncheon meat were scattered among skins of unripe mangoes and bananas: there was no evidence of any grain in the town. There were two East German trucks, but they had no wheels. None of the other bits of machinery around the town, with the exception of the generator, were in working order. It was a stark contrast with the efficiency of Savimbi's camps. The primary school was well stocked with Japanese and Czechoslovak pencils and attractive but propagandistic arithmetic textbooks. ('If it takes three bullets to kill two counter-revolutionaries, how many does it take to kill four?' asked on question.) Work had been going on, the exercise books showed. But the standard of the work, and of the teacher's marking, looked sadly low.

We spoke to some of the prisoners. To what they said needs to be attached all the caution necessary when hearing evidence from men frightened for their lives, as they surely were. But their evidence did seem to support that of our own eyes.

Sergeant Andre, the 22-year-old leader of an MPLA logistics platoon, said: 'We don't know why we're fighting, and the Cubans don't accept to stay here with us. And when they are in the town, we're in the trenches. They don't bring us food here because we have no Cubans or (East) Germans. This is why troops are deserting. There have been three desertions from my platoon, and maybe 120 altogether. They are leaving because of hunger, and often we survive by stealing. When the local population caught us stealing they sometimes attacked us with bows and arrows or guns.

'If we are wounded we are taken to hospital where the doctors are Cubans, and they amputate for the slightest wound. I saw many men with unnecessary amputations.

The Cubans don't usually go to the front to fight. They try to fight only where they can get diamonds.'

And Lieutenant Bazuka, the commander of the MPLA garrison, said: 'Relations between the Cubans and FAPLA (the MPLA Army) are very bad. They don't like to go to the front. They prefer to stay in the towns making love to our women. The FAPLA cannot get diamonds to sell, only the Cubans.'

* * *

Nunda said there had been much less resistance than expected. Partly, this was because there had been only 500 enemy troops in the town against the 700 suggested by the intelligence units. Twenty-five MPLA troops were killed and eleven captured. No UNITA troops were killed or even wounded. Among the dead were the commander of the local political police and the MPLA political commissar, a man named Bomba. Letters in the MPLA administration office showed that on 19 November poor Bomba had written to his superiors at Cucumbi, 80 kilometres to the north, saying the local population were behaving strangely and with a minimum of co-operation. He said he had received a letter from UNITA warning that he and the local battalions were targets: he was sure this meant UNITA was planning some action.

Compared with the earlier battle I had watched at Cangonga, Alto Chicapa was a complete walkover – a sledgehammer to crack a nut. Only a few weapons were captured – three 82mm mortars, two 75mm B-10 cannons and 53 Kalashnikov rifles – but Nunda was happy for strategic reasons. He could now push his brigade further north into Lunda Province. The main lesson he had drawn was from the low state of morale of the MPLA garrison: UNITA needed to intensify its propaganda to take advantage of this.

We left the Brigadier in Alto Chicapa, as he discussed with his officers the site of a new forward base for the brigade. 'Our troops were disappointed with the battle,' he said. 'They feel they were not really tested, and they want a new and bigger target soon. I'll have to decide on one.'

* * *

On the march back we met another battalion 'yomping' northwards to reinforce Brigadier Nunda on the Northern Front. It took us ten days to cover the 200 kilometres to the Benguela Railway at Munhango, where we were guided through minefields and saw, with considerable sadness, that after the battle there on 20 April 1983 UNITA had created a railway engine graveyard by firing anti-tank rockets into eight lovely old British-made double tender steam engines. 'Beyer, Peacock and Co. Ltd., Manchester, 1930' said the cast-iron logo on one of them. We comforted ourselves with ripe mangoes from the orchards around Munhango.

*   *   *

From Munhango it took four days on the trucks to get back to Luengue. We arrived at the same time as 36 Portuguese and Canadian hostages taken during the battle for Cazombo on 13 November. Fernando Moreira, a Portuguese shop-keeper who had worked in Cazombo for 12 years, said there had been 1,000 MPLA troops in the town. UNITA attacked at 7 a.m.: 'The firing lasted about an hour, but the MPLA lost the initiative after five minutes, and most of them started running towards Zambia.' (In fact, more than 300 MPLA soldiers and officials, including three district governors, registered themselves as refugees in north-west Zambia. They were flown back home from Ndola to Luena in an operation that the Zambian government tried to hide from the press.)[11]

A column of eight government trucks carrying weapons and food had arrived in the town the night before the attack, said Moreira. UNITA captured these along with several other trucks and four tractors, other big quantities of weapons and ammunition, and a warehouse stacked with rice, cooking oil, dried milk, tinned meat and soap.

Two Canadian missionary nurses, Nora Draper and Marion Wilson, had been led from Cazombo with 34 Portuguese on a 650-kilometre march to UNITA's main bases in the south-east. The missionaries had been taken by UNITA troops from the clinic outside Cazombo where they treated up to 1,000 poor peasant people each day. The

Canadians, freed by UNITA and flown to North America on Christmas Eve 1983, said they had not expected to be attacked, although they knew there were regular ambushes of MPLA convoys on roads to the north of Cazombo and earlier in the year all their own personal goods being delivered from Canada had been lost in a UNITA ambush. The Portuguese, however, said they knew from the local people that a big UNITA force was in the area and that an attack was imminent. One had even dug a trench in his garden in anticipation.

For UNITA the capture of Cazombo was of great importance. It secured control of the whole 1,100 kilometre Angolan frontier with Zambia, and it meant that more frontier posts could be opened through which Zambians would have to pass to trade with Angolans. In addition, Savimbi's people now controlled 150 kilometres of the Angolan border with Zaire, just opposite the area where Israeli military instructors had begun training the Shaba-based Kamanyola division of Zaire's army. From now onwards speculation would grow that Israeli military help was also coming UNITA's way.

* * *

Though the Canadians had quickly been returned home, the prospects for Rodolfo Esteves Lantegua of seeing his native Cuba within the immediate future were distinctly slim. We met him at a prisoner-of-war camp deep in the bush of south-eastern Angola, and he said he wanted us to convey, somehow, a message to Fidel Castro: 'I want to say I am here captured by UNITA, but I remain faithful to the ideals of the revolution and of Che. Only death will make me forget the revolution.'

Private Lantegua, 34, had been captured near Huambo on 23 February 1983 when two Africans he thought were MPLA soldiers asked him for a lift in the military truck he was driving. They were UNITA men.

Despite Lantegua's brave show of defiance, his spirits were low. 'My main problem is that there has been no word from my country. That makes me think. I don't understand why my state has not spoken out about my situation.' But

Lantegua added that he would rather stay a prisoner for 20 years than give up his revolutionary ideals. In 1986 he was still a prisoner of UNITA.

*   *   *

UNITA's 20 Czechoslovak hostages, left behind when their 43 relations and colleagues had been flown home the previous June, were less revolutionary in their ardour. Their spokesman, Alexander Ivan, a gentle man with courtly manners who spoke fluent English and Portuguese, said: 'We sometimes feel we are just pawns in a political game that is much bigger than us, and that humanitarian considerations do not come into it. We are rather pessimistic about our future. If we stay here indefinitely we fear that not all of us will return home, and those who do will not be worth much to their society or families.'

The Czechoslovaks were being held two to a hut, but with no communication permitted between the huts. They had no radios or writing materials, and few books: one had read V. S. Naipaul's *Among the Believers* several times. Their food was monotonous – soggy macaroni and tinned meat, with fresh antelope once a week, and no fruit or vegetables. Ten had had hepatitis and some had had malaria. One was operated on for a double hernia by a UNITA nurse. And another complained Schweik-like: 'My big problem is whether I'll come out with my last three teeth still intact.'

Alexander Ivan said: 'They are certainly not trying to torture us. But one official told me we were co-responsible for all the things that are happening in the civil war. He also told me that one of us had threatened to commit suicide, but I don't know who it can be because we are rarely allowed to gather together.'

On 16 December we flew out of Angola from Luengue, but before take-off I had a two-hour meeting with Savimbi and we discussed the Czechoslovaks. He said the terms for their release were now solely the freedom of 36 UNITA men imprisoned in Luanda and condemned to death by the MPLA. But his latest attempt to obtain a deal had failed: 'The International Red Cross went to Luanda last October and asked to see the 36 prisoners we had named. The MPLA failed to produce even one, so the conclusion has to be that they are dead. If they are dead we can produce more lists of people who have been arrested, and we will go on producing lists until the MPLA agrees to an exchange.'

The hostages had asked me for notepaper so that they could write Savimbi a letter. I gave the letter to Savimbi, and he read it to me: 'Please do all you can because now our situation becomes extremely difficult, and we want you to take an initiative to make the powers concerned move. If your efforts are successful we will be very grateful to you. The children of our land will be very grateful to you, and also it will bring you respect and admiration from the international community.'

Savimbi raised his eyebrows at this unlikely prospect of sudden international respectability, and sighed: 'All of them have signed the piece of paper. It is difficult. For the time being we must wait for information from the MPLA on what has happened to our first list of 36 prisoners. But in the end we have to think of some solution.'

*   *   *

Savimbi spelt out the aims of his offensive. It was a dual assault against Luanda Province, in the north-west, where the capital was situated, and against Lunda Province, in the north-east, where the diamond mines were. Additionally, UNITA intended that its units should push so far northwards that by March–April 1984 they would have reached Angola's northern border with Zaire.

The political aim remained that of forcing the MPLA into negotiations. 'But we have to advance militarily in order to persuade the MPLA to talk,' Savimbi said. 'We have positively identified a faction within the MPLA which wants to negotiate. That faction is willing to see the Cubans leave. It would solve the problem of Namibia, because the South Africans have said that they will leave when the Cubans leave, and more specifically it will solve the problems of the Angolans. That MPLA faction is growing stronger. Contacts are going on between us and them. Most of our contacts are made through Lisbon.'

Savimbi said the logic of a Cuban withdrawal was that the

South Africans would have no choice other than to leave Namibia. 'What excuse will they then give to the Americans when the Americans have achieved half their objective by achieving a Cuban withdrawal? The South Africans can be sure of the veto by the US in the UN against mandatory sanctions while the Cubans remain, but after they go the South Africans cannot depend upon it unless they fall in line with some of America's wishes.'

Savimbi asserted that some of the black African Front Line states recognised privately that a parallel withdrawal of Cuba from Angola and of South Africa from Namibia was necessary. 'They no longer believe Andrew Young's assertion that the Cubans are a stabilising factor in the region. Even though most of these states want to avoid formal linkage, they want to achieve a simultaneous solution of the problems in Angola and Namibia.'

In pushing northwards, Savimbi said he now had ten semi-regular battalions operating north of the Benguela Railway. But he emphasised that movements would be through the countryside, taking small towns, outposts, villages and isolating the MPLA/Cubans in the larger towns.

'We are preparing for the assault on the towns,' he said. 'There will come a moment when it is politically important to begin taking them, but we will have to pay a high price in lives.'

49

Operation Askari

1983–84

As UNITA's push northwards got under way, South Africa launched another major invasion of Angola. Operation Askari began on 6 December 1983 when a 10,000-strong SADF force crossed the border and began attacking targets in Cunene Province, supported by waves of Mirage and Impala fighter-bombers.

Ostensibly, Operation Askari was a normal early rains offensive to hit SWAPO in its Angolan bases before its guerrillas could begin their seasonal infiltration of northern Namibia. The South Africans, pouring across the border in armoured cars and armoured personnel carriers, took with them their new G-5 and G-6 155mm mobile artillery guns, deadly accurate from 40 kilometres, and claimed by the SADF hierarchy to be the most sophisticated artillery system in the world.[1]

General Constand Viljoen, the new Chief of the SADF, claimed success for the operation. His forces had penetrated deep into Angola and were holding territory as far north as the Tchamutete Heights, overlooking the town of Cassinga, 250 kilometres from the Namibian border; a total of 324 SWAPO troops and nearly 100 MPLA soldiers had been killed; one Cuban captured; 25 Soviet T-54 and PT-76 tanks destroyed; and a Soviet SAM-9 mobile missile system captured.[2]

However, the SADF itself gave few details of Operation Askari, which actually seems to have gone badly wrong at several stages, causing South Africa to begin a fresh assessment of the military threat posed by the quality of the renewed Soviet weapons build-up in Angola.

The first hitch had come in November 1983 when Soviet diplomats arranged a meeting with South Africa's Ambassador to the United Nations, Kurt von Schirnding, at New York's Algonquin Hotel. Soviet satellite reconnaissance had monitored the South African manoeuvres that would lead to Operation Askari. The Soviets told von Schirnding that beyond a certain point Moscow would not tolerate an SADF challenge to the MPLA/Cubans. Rules of engagement would be altered to permit battlefield contact with the SADF and there would be Soviet arms reinforcements for every South African escalation of the war: the MPLA would be given whatever support was needed to enable it to stay in power.

South African Foreign Minister Pik Botha said South Africa would not be intimidated by the Soviet threats, and Operation Askari went ahead – but not as originally planned. Military Intelligence chief, General van der Westhuizen, and Defence Minister Magnus Malan wanted an operation which would go all the way to Luanda, but the SADF chief, General Jannie Geldenhuys, and Prime Minister Pieter Botha knocked it down as operationally impossible.[3]

Operation Askari failed even in some of its modified aims. More than 1,000 of the 1,400-strong SWAPO force it sought to destroy was able to flee northwards to safety; it failed by a long way to achieve one of its operational options of capturing Lubango, site of an important provincial military headquarters; it failed to knock out what one senior South African Air Force officer described as 'the real juicy targets', the string of advanced missile sites between Mocamedes and Cuito Cuanavale, because South Africa's pilots realised they did not have the technical means to outwit the radar-guidance systems of the missiles which were manned by Soviet technicians.[4]

In addition, the MPLA armoured troops fought with more tenacity than expected. At a big battle for the town of Cuvelai, 200 kilometres inside Angola, two troop carriers were hit by tank shells and 21 South Africans died, a high loss by SADF standards which drew unfavourable domestic press comment about sons 'dying on distant battlefields' while the public had 'no independent means of assessing the facts of such operations'.[5]

Apparently chastened by the degree of resistance, Prime Minister Botha made an offer in mid-January to withdraw his forces from southern Angola by 31 January, provided the MPLA and SWAPO pledged not to take advantage of the withdrawal. The MPLA at first refused, but on 16 February 1984, in the capital of Zambia, the Lusaka Accord was signed by Foreign Minister Pik Botha and Angolan Interior Minister Alexander 'Kito' Rodrigues, under the watchful eyes of Kenneth Kaunda and Chester Crocker.

Peace, of a kind, had broken out. The Lusaka Accord, never published, provided for a phased withdrawal of SADF troops from the area of southern Angola they had occupied. The MPLA undertook to remove SWAPO from the area and ensure further that no Cuban or SWAPO troops entered the area in future. A Joint Monitoring Commission (JMC), comprising three SADF and three MPLA companies, would be set up to monitor the agreement and any violations. The headquarters of the JMC would at first be in Cuvelai, but it would move back in five stages towards the Angola-Namibia border.[6]

* * *

A month later, on 17 March 1984, the Lusaka Accord was followed by the signing by South Africa and Mozambique of the Nkomati Accord, another peace agreement, under which the two governments agreed to co-operate in a wide range of economic fields and to stop harbouring and training guerrilla movements opposed to their respective governments.

50

Savimbi Pushes On

1984

As peace, or at least the promise of it, descended elsewhere in the region, UNITA increased the momentum of its push northwards that had begun with the battles for Cazombo, Andulo and Alto Chicapa.

On my way back south from Alto Chicapa, Colonel Ben-Ben Arlindo Pena told me that for several months he had been concentrating his forces around the Benguela Railway town of Cuemba, shelling it and ambushing convoys as they. went in and out. He intended assaulting the town, but could not say when. He had to take into account the fact that the MPLA was expecting an attack and was steadily moving in reinforcements.

In fact, the siege of Cuemba was a feint for an attack on another town 100 kilometres to the west along the railway, Nova Sintra, which UNITA intelligence men studied for months while the fighting men left it entirely alone. Then two battalions under Ben-Ben's command moved up rapidly in a series of night marches, and UNITA overran Nova Sintra in a dawn attack on 24 January 1984. A Portuguese television team was with UNITA to record the action.[1] It was a classic use by UNITA of the weapon of surprise.

But an even more daring and elaborate military feint than Ben-Ben's at Cuemba-Nova Sintra was in progress on Brigadier Geraldo Nunda's Northern Front.

After I left him at Alto Chicapa, Nunda had very quickly found another target for his battle-hungry brigade. Cacolo, on the tar road across northern Angola from Luanda to

Saurimo, is about 100 kilometres north of Alto Chicapa. It was overrun by Nunda's brigade on 18 December 1983. Three missionary priests (a Pole, a Brazilian and a Filipino) and five missionary nuns (a Japanese, two Portuguese, a Spaniard and an Italian) were taken from the town and subsequently flown from Luengue by the ICRC to their native countries.

From Cacolo, right on the edge of the diamond mining areas of Lunda Province, the logic was that Nunda's next strike would be within the Lunda diamond fields. Logical, because Savimbi had openly stated it as his aim; because the fields were a long way from Luanda; and because 75 per cent of the country's diamond production was concentrated there. The other 25 per cent was located in one mine, Cafunfo, 250 kilometres north-west of Cacolo near the Zaire border.

Cafunfo was a most unlikely target. It was 1,100 kilometres from Savimbi's GHQ at Jamba; the British, Portuguese and Filipino expatriate workers there were protected by former members of the crack British SAS Regiment; and just the previous September the British Ambassador to Angola, Marrack Goulding, visited the mine and assured his compatriots there that UNITA was incapable of attacking it.[2]

On 23 February 1984 Nunda's 2,500-strong brigade – the three battalions with whom I had been at Alto Chicapa, plus the one I had seen 'yomping' northwards to join the Northern Front – overran Cafunfo. The fighting began at 5 a.m. and lasted only 50 minutes. According to foreign eyewitnesses, the MPLA offered little resistance and most of them fled. Twenty MPLA troops and eight Filipino miners were killed. Nunda's brigade marched off with 106 hostages – 16 Britons, four of them former SAS men; 40 Portuguese, including five women and four children; and 50 Filipinos, one of whom was carried all the way because of a bullet wound in his foot.[3] For 32 days the hostages trekked to the Benguela Railway. Another four days in trucks down the Savimbi Trail brought them to Jamba, where they were kept under armed guard.

Savimbi said the Filipinos and Portuguese would be freed unconditionally, but concessions from somewhere would

be needed to obtain the Britons' release. With the 36 UNITA
men detained in Luanda believed dead, there was no leverage there. And the MPLA now moved quickly to remove
another point of leverage and to put Britain in its debt –
within days of the Cafunfo raid, the release, asked for 28
times by the London government,[4] though never demanded by the British public, was announced by the MPLA of
the seven British mercenaries jailed since 1976 in Luanda.

UNITA had plenty of reasons to be angry with Britain.
Savimbi had warned London months beforehand that
Britons on contracts with the MPLA were likely to be killed
or taken prisoner as the war escalated. The response of the
Foreign Office Minister responsible for Africa, Mr Malcolm
Rifkind, was studiously to ignore UNITA, on the advice of
the ill-informed Ambassador Goulding. In November 1983
Rifkind visited Luanda, spoke of good prospects for bilateral
trade, and promised the MPLA that a high-level British
trade delegation would visit Angola early in 1984. 'We took
it very badly when Mr Rifkind went on TV and radio and
said UNITA was nothing,' said Savimbi.[5]

The British Overseas Trade Board team, led by Lord
Jellicoe, arrived in Angola in February 1984 on Rifkind's
business scouting mission. The Foreign Office's courting of
Luanda was made to look very sick. While the Jellicoe
mission was in Angola, UNITA was massing for the attack
on Cafunfo. And while Jellicoe and his British colleagues
were being wined and dined in Benguela Province, where
they emphasised how Britain could co-operate with the
MPLA in a wide range of fields, including telecommuni-
cations, the Angolan government was busy in nearby
Huambo executing by firing squad a young telecommuni-
cations worker, Isaias Nangolo. He had been sentenced for
passing information from government phone calls to
UNITA. Amnesty International, increasingly worried that
many defendants at Angolan political trials had been convicted on the basis of statements obtained under torture,
sent a message to President dos Santos expressing concern
that, contrary to rights under Angolan law, Nangolo had not
been allowed to appeal to a higher court.[6]

In an interview soon after the hostages reached Jamba,

Savimbi outlined his position: 'Even though we have taken the hostages, Britain has said it will never, ever, talk to UNITA. If that is its attitude, then the hostages will stay. They are in good hands, but if Britain does not talk we will keep them for a year or two, or however long it is necessary. The situation between Britian and ourselves is critical. Why does Britain, which is an old democracy, have such qualms about talking to UNITA when it rushed to recognise the Marxists in Luanda? It is totally ironic . . . Action will continue against British interests in Angola, unless they take heed of this warning. We are in a state of war and we cannot continue to allow them to give aid and assistance to our Soviet and Cuban-supported enemy.'[7]

*   *   *

Boosted further in confidence by the visit to Jamba in February 1984 of former US Secretary of State Alexander Haig, who assured Savimbi that Washington sought a regional peace solution that included UNITA,[8] and the visit three weeks earlier by two US State Department civil servants and US Republican Senator Steve Symms, UNITA embarked on one of its most ambitious assaults yet.

On 20 March a UNITA force of 5,000, comprising two brigades, attacked the coastal city of Sumbe (formerly Novo Redondo), the capital of Cuanza Sul Province some 150 kilometres north of Lobito. According to UNITA, nearly 300 of the defenders were killed in the attack; four Bulgarian and ten Portuguese technicians were taken hostage; several buildings were destroyed, including the provincial broadcasting station; and 1,200 UNITA sympathisers were released from the city jails.[9]

Western intelligence concluded that Sumbe was not an unqualified UNITA success. Among the weapons now being delivered by the Soviet Union to the MPLA were advanced MIG-23 fighter-bombers and armour-plated MI-24 helicopter gunships of the kind that were causing havoc among rebel tribesmen in Afghanistan and proving almost impossible to shoot down. Formations of these aircraft now entered the war and caught UNITA forces on open ground near Sumbe, inflicting heavy casualties, as shown by the

42 soldiers admitted dead by UNITA together with 103 wounded and seven missing. The MPLA version of the battle was probably near the truth, said these intelligence sources.

The MPLA's account said that UNITA, after initial success at Sumbe, retreated under great pressure. UNITA mortar teams on the forested hills behind the port had launched the attack, and UNITA infantrymen then swept into the town. The MPLA confirmed that UNITA captured Bulgarian and Portuguese technicians and that the city prison was attacked, 'resulting in the escape of 486 common law criminals who were serving well deserved sentences'. Equipment in the local agricultural college and Education Department warehouse was destroyed, and three senior members of the local MPLA administration were killed. But by mid-day government troops had forced the UNITA brigades to retreat to a coconut plantation outside the city. From then onwards the retreating UNITA columns came under constant attacks.[10]

* * *

At Cafunfo and Sumbe, UNITA had reached high points in its military drive northwards. From now onwards, the MPLA's MIG-23s, MI-24s and other sophisticated equipment from the Soviet Union would gradually change the course of the war. Savimbi's men would continue to achieve military successes, especially when operating in classical guerrilla formations, but henceforth a lot of energy and many lives would be expended in defending UNITA's south-eastern strongholds against an MPLA whose morale and hopes had been raised by the improved quality of its equipment and training.

* * *

After signing the Lusaka Accord, the MPLA, freed from direct military confrontation with South Africa, transferred three motorised infantry brigades from Cunene Province to Luena to prepare for a major offensive against UNITA. It began in May and ended in July. Little news was released of the offensive by either side, because the MPLA failed to reach its targets and because UNITA took unprecedented casualties in resisting the MPLA advance. 'By July both sides had fought each other to a standstill,' said one Western intelligence official. 'Many hundreds of UNITA and MPLA troops and some Cubans were killed.'

UNITA admitted privately to 300 of its men dead and 1,100 wounded in beating back a 15,000-strong government force backed by 200 tanks, MIG-23 fighter-bombers and MI-24 helicopter gunships. In one engagement at Leua, just east of Luena, the MPLA claimed to have killed 340 UNITA insurgents.[11]

During this period the prospects of an MPLA-UNITA political settlement seemed more remote than ever. President dos Santos emphasised that he was now looking for a military solution when he told a rally in June: 'We have no alternative but to liquidate UNITA.'[12]

The mass break-out of MPLA and Cuban motorised infantry from Luena towards Cazombo and Gago Coutinho was met by 16 UNITA battalions operating in concentrated, conventional positions. But when his men took terrible casualties from MIG-23 and MI-24 attacks, Savimbi ordered his commanders to break the battalions down into groups of 200 soldiers or less to launch incessant hit-and-run raids against the cumbersome and slow-advancing MPLA columns. The MPLA got to within a short distance of Cazombo, but on 27 July its badly mauled columns began retreating towards Luena.

Another MPLA offensive was launched in August towards Mavinga from Cuito Cuanavale, and towards Munhango from Luena. UNITA admitted to another 74 dead and 370 wounded before this offensive petered out in September.[13] In one period between 31 August and 12 September the MPLA claimed to have killed 300 UNITA soldiers.[14]

* * *

While the fighting intensified, and new foreign hostages were added to UNITA's haul, the 20 Czechoslovaks remained incarcerated in their remote bush camp in UNITA territory. But, unknown to them, negotiations for their release had begun on 25 January 1984 in the Brussels home of a Belgian journalist, Jean Wolf, who by chance knew both UNITA and Czechoslovakia well.

Three UNITA officials and the Czechoslovak Ambassador to Belgium, Mr Jaroslav Kvacek, began a series of negotiations which ended with a UNITA Central Committee member, Wilson dos Santos, visiting Prague from 5 to 8 May and signing with Czechoslovakia's Deputy Foreign Minister Stanislav Svoboda an agreement on the early repatriation of the hostages.[15] Newspapers in Prague announced the talks and said UNITA was fighting for a government of national unity in Angola – a far cry, *The Times* of London noted, from the usual description of UNITA as 'puppets backed by racist South Africa'.[16]

The terms of the deal were secret, but UNITA, on the insistence of South Africa and the US, was forced to turn down an early offer of weapons from Prague in exchange for the hostages. The deal did include a Czechoslovak commitment to withdraw its personnel from every part of Angola except Luanda and a promise to send a high government official to Jamba to receive the hostages on the day of their release.

But before Prague ate humble pie in Jamba, it was first the turn of Britain to do the same. Under another agreement whose essential details were kept secret, Britain sent Sir John Leahy, head of the African Department at the Foreign Office, to Jamba to receive the 16 British hostages from Cafunfo at a midnight ceremony on 12 May. Some of the more self-important Foreign Office officials regarded it as a humiliating and distasteful excursion. 'Opera bouffe in a jungle setting,' sniffed one.[17]

Sir John watched a military parade and held three hours of talks with Savimbi during his 48-hour stay, sleeping in one of UNITA's thatched guest huts. Savimbi asked Sir John to pass on a warning to the British government that other Britons working with the MPLA were at risk from UNITA activity in the north of Angola. And at the welcoming ceremony, he told Sir John: 'We seek peace in Angola and reconciliation, as we did in 1974. We shall firmly hold on to our arms and maintain our hearts open to dialogue.'[18]

The southern Africa correspondent of *The Times* of London noted that the British official, tight-lipped and uneasy on his arrival in Savimbi's 'lair', warmed to the UNITA leader's charm and that in his farewell speech he was fulsome in praise of Savimbi's 'great qualities of leadership and colourful style'. He said it had been suggested to him before he left Britain that it was degrading to have to go and beg for the release of British citizens. 'I have not had to beg for anything today, and if this is humiliation I can take a lot more of it,' he said to the cheering, singing and dancing Africans.[19]

One of the British hostages who left for London with Sir John told reporters: 'I'll bet we were the best-treated hostages anywhere in the world.' Another, referring to Marrack Goulding's assurances that Cafunfo was completely safe, said: 'We only stayed on because of those assurances. We now know, of course, that the advice was inaccurate.'[20]

*   *   *

In a bewildering exhibition of British Foreign Office merit judgement, Marrack Goulding was rewarded for his Angolan failure by being appointed Deputy Secretary-General of the United Nations. Poor Sir John Leahy, who had carried out the difficult task that UNITA at first demanded be performed by Malcolm Rifkind, was punished for the enthusiastic remarks he made during his stay at Jamba: he was quickly removed from his responsibilities for Africa in London and sent into distant exile as British High Commissioner to Australia.

*   *   *

It was Stanislav Svoboda himself, whose surname means 'freedom,' who came to Jamba to pay respects to Savimbi and take home the 20 remaining Czechoslovak hostages on 22 June 1984, fifteen months after they had entered captivity. One of the Czechoslovaks told reporters as he boarded the plane for Prague: 'We must be fair. We haven't been tortured or beaten or denied food, but it was hard to bear.'[21]

Before Mr Svoboda left with the hostages they signed

documents, like the British before them, promising never to return to Angola until the war was over.[22]

* * *

Despite the MPLA offensives in the south-east of the country, Savimbi's forces continued to strike suddenly in unexpected places. Among many attacks, the following were the most dramatic.

On 19 April 1984 a UNITA underground worker parked a truck containing 350 kilogrammes of explosives outside a hostel on Huambo's main street occupied by Cubans and Soviets. It blew up in the early evening, leaving more than 200 dead, including 37 Cuban officers and three Soviet lieutenant-colonels, according to UNITA, who said the operation was carried out with the co-operation of MPLA officers 'unhappy with the Cuban occupation of Angola'. The Soviet news agency Tass reported from Luanda that about 100 people, including women and children, had died in the 'monstrous crime' at Huambo: it did not mention Soviet or Cuban victims. And in a third version of the bombing, the Angolan Press Agency (ANGOP) said the booby-trapped truck had killed 24 people, including 'fourteen Cuban internationalists, all of whom had been working in education, health or construction'. ANGOP added: 'The criminals will be made to answer for their crime. We shall be harsh in administering revolutionary justice.' The official Havana daily, *Granma*, said that, as well as the 14 dead, 66 Cubans were wounded. 'Once again a group of self-sacrificing Cuban building workers offered their generous lives for the duty of helping in the economic and social development of other peoples,' said the newspaper.[23]

On 12 June UNITA attacked Quibala, 280 kilometres south-east of Luanda, and captured another clutch of foreigners – three American Protestant missionaries, two American businessmen, and six Colombian and Portuguese missionaries.[24] Quickly, the US State Department reached agreement with UNITA on the unconditional release of all the hostages, through the ICRC, as soon as they completed their 1,200-kilometre trek to Jamba.

On 18 June UNITA said it had attacked a train 180

kilometres from Luanda on the Luanda-Malanje line, killing 134 people. The MPLA confirmed the death toll, but accused UNITA of making cynical propaganda from an accident in which seven carriages were derailed and destroyed when the driver took a bend at 65 kilometres per hour instead of at the speed limit of 45 kilometres per hour.[25]

On 12 July UNITA launched its first raid into the oil-producing enclave of Cabinda. UNITA said it had destroyed an oil pipeline, killed 22 people and wounded 50. The MPLA said ten people had been killed; 200 metres of pipeline belonging to the US Gulf Oil Company had been destroyed; and 42,000 gallons of crude oil lost. UNITA said it planned to have a pioneer group of 250 soldiers permanently based in Cabinda by the end of 1984, and reports appeared saying Morocco, Israel, South Africa and the US were supplying UNITA with arms and ammunition for its attempted penetration of Cabinda from the Zairean port town of Matadi, at the mouth of the Congo River.[26]

On 27 July, said Lloyds of London, two ships, one East German and the other Angolan, had been badly damaged in Luanda harbour. UNITA claimed that its commandos had mined the ships, and Lloyds, which monitors all ship movements around the world, confirmed that the 5,650 tonne East German vessel *Arendsee* was half submerged after two mines destroyed her engine room. The 9,076 tonne Angolan ship *Lundoge* was being patched after a mine blew a hole in her side. UNITA said the *Arendsee* had discharged armoured cars and other military equipment at Lobito before sailing to Luanda: Lloyds confirmed that the vessel had discharged cargo at Lobito.[27]

On 28 September a UNITA commando Special Force penetrated the Lobito harbour area and destroyed seven diesel locomotives and the main railway signalling mechanism, an attack acknowledged by the MPLA only 15 months later at its second Congress in Luanda in December 1985.[28]

*　　*　　*

Throughout 1984, and despite the MPLA-Pretoria Lusaka Accord, Savimbi had an assured supply of weapons and other materials through and from South Africa. A US intelligence officer told me that in 1983 the rate of South African weapons deliveries to UNITA had tripled. And in December 1983 I had visited Savimbi's main logistic base near Luengue, which received the supplies, and saw that it had become a fantastic settlement. A dead straight avenue one kilometre long ran through the centre of it; the avenue was lined on either side by steel poles carrying electricity and telephone wires; huge timber, thatch and concrete warehouses bordered the avenue on either side; and work was in progress of the construction of a floodlit indoor basketball stadium.

The rate of delivery of South African supplies probably increased in 1984, and any lingering doubts about the existence of close relations between UNITA and South Africa were swept away on 14 September 1984 when Savimbi was the only black African leader to attend the inauguration of Prime Minister Pieter Botha as South Africa's new President. Botha's elevation coincided with the introduction of a new constitution which gave coloured and Indian politicians places in the South African Cabinet for the first time.

Even friends of Savimbi thought his visit to Cape Town was a political mistake. But his top aides said it had been considered carefully: Savimbi believed that *any* attempt to reform the political system in South Africa should be encouraged, and when he quietly visited the leaders of Kenya, Ivory Coast, Morocco, Togo and Zaire, they counselled him, in the aftershock of the Lusaka and Nkomati Accords, to go to the Cape Town ceremonies. They expected that Mozambique and other states like Malawi and Swaziland would be represented. In the event Savimbi found himself the sole African presence, and simply had to make the best of a bad job.

He had, anyway, already been in Cape Town in May 1984 for talks with Foreign Minister Pik Botha and Chester Crocker. It was assumed that the three men discussed ways of stepping up pressure on the MPLA to come to the negotiating table on the basis of parallel Cuban/South African withdrawals from Angola/Namibia.[29]

A practical demonstration of the pressure came in July when South Africa halted its withdrawal from Angola on the grounds that the MPLA was contravening the Lusaka Accord because SWAPO fighters were moving into areas vacated by retreating South African troops. There were also the first hints of a new South African demand – that not only was it necessary for Cuban troops to leave Angola to secure Namibia's independence, but the MPLA must agree also to enter a coalition government with UNITA. South African Law and Order Minister Louis Le Grange stepped up the pressure when he said the government had identified in Angola five separate training bases of the African National Congress (ANC), the outlawed political opposition to the white minority Pretoria government.[30]

*   *   *

President dos Santos gave signals of his willingness to negotiate when in October he sacked his hardline 'old guard' pro-Moscow Foreign Minister Paulo Jorge[31] and for the first time conceded the principle of 'linkage' – phased Cuban withdrawals in return for a South African withdrawal.

Dos Santos's offer emerged in a series of newspaper articles and leaks, beginning on 15 October, when, for the first time since coming to power, he gave an interview to an American journalist. Dos Santos told Jim Hoagland, foreign editor of the *Washington Post*, in Luanda, that Angola had shown flexibility and a sincere desire to achieve a regional settlement in secret proposals it had given to US envoys. Hoagland commented: 'The 90-minute interview was clearly designed to convey a sense of diplomatic opening towards the United States, which has refused to establish formal diplomatic relations with Angola. His remarks implicitly portrayed his revolutionary government as embarking on a new phase of diplomatic pragmatism, matching its decision to open up to foreign investment and trade with the West. Production by US and French oil companies here will provide Angola with more than 80 per cent of its $2 billion foreign exchange earnings this year.'

Dos Santo also told Hoagland that:

> Angola was prepared to live 'in an atmosphere of tolerance' with South Africa once Namibia was independent. Apartheid and white minority rule would then be treated as internal South African problems.

> The Reagan Administration should quickly establish diplomatic relations with Angola and open up opportunities for US investment and trade.

> The MPLA was prepared to offer an amnesty to followers of Savimbi, but not to the UNITA President himself and his top aides, who had betrayed Angola and betrayed Africa'. They would face certain death if they returned to Luanda.[32]

*   *   *

Dos Santos needed a settlement, Hoagland noted. Far from becoming the African Hanoi that Angolan revolutionaries dreamed would become a springboard for revolutionary challenge to white rule in South Africa and moderate régimes on its border, Luanda was the capital of a nation in chaos and ravaged by international intervention. 'Dreams lie broken in the desolate streets of Luanda, a city gripped by a continuing agony that contradicts the ideological victory that revolutionaries and liberals hoped for and that conservatives around the world feared,' wrote the *Washington Post* man. 'Mounds of rotting garbage drape the mile-long curb of the bayside promenade that the Portuguese lined with mosaic tile. Shops and businesses throughout this city of a million people are abandoned, their broken plate-glass windows replaced by boards or simply not replaced at all. At one pharmacy, a single bottle of shampoo sits amid empty shelves, a reminder of the collapse of the consumer economy here. Cuban soldiers in trucks and East German security personnel in jeeps bounce through Luanda's dusty streets regularly . . . There are no taxis in this town, leaving a visitor to rely on his feet and on the kindness of strangers – anyone with wheels. The only form of public transportation is a small number of buses that reel as hundreds of Angolans pile into and onto them.'[33]

Hoagland said that any hopes for reviving the economy after independence had been crushed under the weight of the centralised bureaucracy imposed on the country by the MPLA. 'A farmer found that to get a simple spare part for a tractor he had to submit a request to the Ministry of Agriculture in Luanda, which then had to pass it on to the Ministry of Planning, which would have to approve the foreign currency allocation for it. Coffee exports plummeted to ten per cent of the sales recorded during colonial time. Insecurity and theft in the diamond areas cut exports from 2.4 million carats in 1974 to one-fourth that figure today.'

And a *New York Times* correspondent who visited Huambo Province saw from his plane scores of abandoned villages surrounded by untilled fields. The head of the Institute of Agronomical Research in Huambo told him: 'Most of the countryside is now abandoned. The bandits rob or burn the harvests, and many of the peasants have to flee to the city for safety.'[34]

* * *

But when the dos Santos proposals were made public at the end of November, they were not attractive to South Africa. A 36-month gradual withdrawal was envisaged for the Cubans: but 5,000 would stay on permanently in the Luanda area and an unspecified number in Cabinda. The Cuban withdrawal would not begin until South Africa had removed all its forces, except for 1,500, from Namibia and United Nations troops had been established on the ground as a prelude to independence.[35]

South Africa responded by formalising its previously implied demand that Savimbi be given a key role in a transitional Angolan coalition government as part of any regional settlement. Pretoria also said the Cubans would have to leave Angola completely within three months, not six months, of the signing of any agreement.[36]

Savimbi himself demanded to be included in the complex negotiations. 'I do not want to rock the boat,' he said. 'I want to be *part* of it. We want the negotiators to recognise the elements which are making the MPLA more amenable – *we* are.' He went on: 'UNITA, while enjoying the sympathy of the United States of America and of the Republic of South Africa, is not of the view to accept being traded in for a fictitious withdrawal. UNITA will have to be a party to all negotiations whose objective will be to determine the future of Namibia and the corresponding withdrawal of the Cubans from our country.'[37]

At an Extraordinary Congress convened at Jamba from 2 to 9 November, UNITA recommitted itself to fight for multi-party elections in Angola, to launch an immediate major offensive in the Luanda region, and to release the last three foreign hostages it was then holding – the Bulgarians taken at the battle for Sumbe. The withdrawal of the Cubans must be *total*, said UNITA, and the 1975 Alvor Accord must still be the basis on which an Angolan government would be chosen.[38] In an attempt to shed the Marxist image some people had of the movement, UNITA also adopted new names for its Central Committee and Political Bureau. They became instead the Executive Committee and the National Committee.

On 25 November UNITA Special Force commandos destroyed 15 pylons and two electrical power sub-stations between Luanda and Cambambe, the hydro-electric dam which supplied power to the capital. Parts of Luanda were without electricity for several days. On 11 December another seven pylons between Cambambe and Luanda were blown up.[39]

The momentary prospects for peace were fading, and on the eve of New Year 1985 four UNITA underground workers were shot dead by an MPLA firing squad at Ndalatando, near Luanda, for 'crimes against the security of the State, treason, armed rebellion and economic sabotage'.[40]

51

The MPLA Strikes Back

1985

UNITA began 1985 with a series of attacks on targets in the north of the country, particularly in the provinces in the hinterland of Luanda city – Luanda Province itself, Cuanza Norte and Malanje. The MPLA banned free movement 30 kilometres from the capital, and ten MPLA brigades were moved from the south to reinforce the defence of the Luanda area. The main attacks were on electricity installations: the MPLA's 44th and 84th brigade were spread along the 160-kilometre length of the road from Luanda to the Cambamba hydro-electric power station to fend off assaults which regularly severed electricity supplies[1].

UNITA also claimed to have destroyed, on 22 February 1985, another train on the Luanda-Malanje line delivering arms to the MPLA's 81st Brigade based in Malanje: UNITA said it killed 38 enemy troops and carried off large quantities of weapons. On 27 February UNITA claimed to have shot down a Boeing-737 shortly after take-off from Lubango with several senior MPLA Army and State Security police aboard. And on 24 March another UNITA bomb in Huambo was said to have killed 11 Cubans and nine Bulgarians in the Hotel Almirante.[2]

These were just a few of many UNITA and MPLA claims and counter-claims whose truths were almost impossible to weigh, except as a general indication of the heavy scale of the fighting in a war still almost entirely hidden from the eyes of the outside world.

Two examples of stark contradictions in early 1985

concerned a UNITA attack on a small town, Calomboloca, just 55 kilometres southeast of Luanda, and an MPLA claim to have severely wounded Savimbi during a helicopter assault on UNITA's Jamba GHQ.

UNITA claimed to have killed 170 of the 420 MPLA troops guarding Calomboloca on 30 January, and to have destroyed two electricity sub-stations and the local railway station. The MPLA confirmed the attack, but said the casualties were entirely civilian, to which UNITA counter-responded: 'The MPLA calls any military action carried out by UNITA as an attack against the elderly, the women and children who seem to make up their armed forces.'

On 9 January the Angolan Press Agency, reporting from Luanda, said élite MPLA troops in helicopters had struck at Jamba with heavy air support. Savimbi was severely wounded. Two days later Savimbi met foreign correspondents at Jamba. He said reports of the attack and his wounding were MPLA propaganda, and he joked: 'I will die many times before I reach Luanda.'[3]

*　　　*　　　*

There was no disagreement about the most spectacular of the introductions to the new 1985 year in Angola. As the old year came to a close, UNITA launched yet another big attack on Cafunfo on 29 December. Once again, as in the previous February, Britons were captured and the hapless British Ambassador, Marrack Goulding, was caught unawares in Luanda. The scale of the fighting was terrible. When the MPLA finally reoccupied the town it was empty, except for hundreds of MPLA and UNITA corpses lying on the battlefield. The first task for the returning MPLA was to dig graves for the dead.

Three Britons, two Americans and 17 Filipinos were seized as hostages and released unconditionally, through the ICRC, on 14 March after they had completed the customary gruelling march to Jamba. They ate only cassava porridge, which one of them said looked 'like old wallpaper glue and tasted worse'. Two of the Britons said they were handled very roughly when they were captured in the early dawn hours of the attack. One, Mr John McMichael, a mine engineer, was fired on by machine-guns as he came out of his house with his hands raised: he thought he was certain to die before a UNITA officer halted the firing.

Incongruously, a Hercules C-130 transport plane of Transamerican Airlines of California landed on the Cafunfo airstrip in the middle of the battle. Thinking it was bringing MPLA troop reinforcements, UNITA forces opened fire with anti-tank rockets, killing the American pilot. The plane burned out on the runway, and the American co-pilot and engineer and the British loadmaster were taken as hostages. Here was another of those African contradictions that leave you wondering whether to laugh or cry. The Hercules was part of a fleet hired from Transamerican to shuttle equipment, food and oil between Luanda and the diamond mines because of the uncertain road and rail links. *The Times* of London said the fact that Transamerican was known to have CIA links was no barrier to us doing business with Luanda's pro-Soviet government. Former Vietnam war pilots lined up their planes, carrying American flags, in the queue for fuel at Luanda airport with Soviet Antonov troop carriers.[4]

Despite clear warnings the previous year that Britons working in Angola faced danger, Mr Rifkind, the British Junior Foreign Office Minister, rebuked Savimbi. 'The civil war is no justification for forcing hostages to undertake ordeals, such as a march,' he said. 'The taking of hostages does not win them any friends in the rest of the world and, if anything, damages their cause quite seriously.'[5]

Savimbi, aware that taking foreign hostages and releasing them unharmed, had boosted his international profile, countered: 'Foreign nationals still in Angola within the war zones should listen to our appeal and leave Angola.' He had earlier elaborated to *Le Monde* why it was a matter of principle for UNITA to exclude foreign contract workers: 'With the profits from oil and diamond exploitation by these foreigners, the MPLA is paying for their Cuban garrison. I cannot let this continue, and it would be good if the foreign oil companies at least stopped working against our interests. What I'm saying is not a threat, but a reminder, and people with good sense should take it into account.'[6]

The British Foreign Ministry still declined to warn its

citizens adequately of the dangers they might face in Angola.

On 9 May President dos Santos visited Lucapa, site of a big diamond mine in Lunda Province. At a rally he told residents: 'We came to verify the difficult conditions in which you, comrades, live, due to the war and due to obstacles to transporting food, medicines and raw materials. The situation remains difficult. Our main preoccupation in Luanda Norte is to solve its war problems. The UNITA bandits began infiltrating this province from the end of 1983. They are here to attack civilians, destroy houses, steal cattle and hamper diamond production. They are sabotaging the roads and railways to impede the transport of goods from Luanda and Lobito ports. They are ordered to carry out these operations by the South African racists. South Africa, as well as other imperialist powers, does not want our people to be totally independent.

'We have large quantities of salt in Luanda which are supposed to come this way. We have dried fish at Namibe which is supposed to come to this province. But the UNITA bandits sabotage the roads, bridges, and make it difficult for our people. Therefore, we must annihilate them first, so that we may bring salt, dried fish, oil, soap, and fuel to you.'[7] The next day UNITA guerrillas attacked a diamond mine at Luo, just to the south-east of Lucapa, and took with them a 34-year-old British engineer, Stephen Bowes. He was marched to Jamba and released two months later.[8]

*　　*　　*

On 17 April 1985 South African troops completed their withdrawal from Angola under the terms of the February 1985 Lusaka Accord. This coincided with an announcement from Pretoria that a government, called the Multi-Party Conference (MPC), made up of parties opposed to SWAPO, would be established in Namibia. The MPC, which was inaugurated in Windhoek together with a non-elected 62-seat National Assembly on 17 June, would ultimately be subject to South African authority. In defiance of the UN, there would be no South African troop withdrawal from Namibia. However, President Botha said he regarded the

MPC as only an interim arrangement for greater internal self-government until such time as there were 'realistic prospects of bringing about the genuine withdrawal of Cuban forces from Angola'.[9] And President Botha and Foreign Minister Pik Botha emphasised to Prime Minister Margaret Thatcher during a visit they paid to Britain that Western leaders would miscalculate badly if they concluded that South Africa had lost the will to force the Cubans out of Angola as a *quid pro quo* for Namibian independence.[10]

In just how adventurist a fashion South Africa was prepared to act in pursuit of that aim became clear on 21 May: the MPLA captured in Cabinda, 1300 kilometres north of the Namibian border, a South African Army reconnaissance commando, Captain Wynand Du Toit, and killed two of his colleagues, Sergeant Van Breda and Corporal Lie Benberg. In subsequent interrogation, which Pretoria alleged involved the use of torture and drugs, Captain Du Toit said the target for his nine-man team was the Gulf Oil installation at the small Cabindan town of Malongo. This plant produced 170,000 barrels of oil a day, or 65 per cent of Angola's total production. The team's mission was to plant 16 contact mines on oil storage tanks, pipelines and fire-fighting apparatus: if the mission had been successful, technicians estimated the cost to the tottering Angolan economy would have been nearly half a billion dollars. However, Captain Du Toit, Sergeant Breda and Corporal Benberg were discovered by an MPLA Army patrol as they hid in scrub near the perimeter of the Gulf Oil complex. Du Toit was wounded in the neck, shoulder and chest while the sergeant and corporal died. The rest of the team, carrying sub-machine-guns with silencers, short-wave radios and incendiary bombs, as well as the mines, escaped by two routes – aboard Zodia inflatable dinghies to a destroyer waiting off the coast, or through Zaire, where South Africa had made pre-arrangements.

During a three hour interview by Angolan and East European journalists, Captain Du Toit said: 'Our attack was to have been claimed by UNITA.' UNITA propaganda leaflets he was carrying were to have been left at the scene of the attack.

Pretoria declined to apologise for the raid. Its ambassador to the United Nations, Kurt von Schirnding, said the commando unit had been trying to obtain intelligence on ANC and SWAPO training bases in Cabinda and that Du Toit had been forced under duress to give false testimony. Though there was growing protest in the US about Gulf Oil's involvement with the MPLA, it was politically embarrassing for South Africa to be caught out attacking an American business enterprise. At the time MPLA Foreign Minister, Alfonso Van-Dunem Mbinda, emphasised that in repulsing the raid MPLA troops had saved American property and perhaps also the lives of some of the 128 US technicians based at Malongo.

Captain Du Toit's admission that he had been carrying UNITA propaganda caused major political discomfort to Savimbi. Du Toit said he had also taken part in a South African commando raid in 1982 to destroy the Giraul River bridge, near Mocamedes. Since its destruction had been claimed at the time by UNITA (see Chapter 40) this raised questions about what other UNITA 'successes' had been carried out by, or in co-operation with, the SADF.[11]

*   *   *

Embarrassment apart, the failure of South Africa's Cabinda adventure had practical consequences which raised the stakes still higher in southern Africa. Two days after Du Toit was paraded before the press and diplomatic corps in Luanda, Fidel Castro announced in Havana that he was prepared to send more Cubans to Angola if South Africa refused to give independence to Namibia.[12] Since South Africa was still only prepared to give independence to Namibia once all Cubans had left Angola, a classic diplomatic stalemate persisted.

By the end of 1985 Western intelligence agencies estimated that the Cuban troop presence in Angola had been raised to 31,000 compared with 25,000 at the beginning of the year. The Cubans were supported by 3,250 East German and Soviet personnel, mainly in operational planning, training, radar, anti-aircraft, advanced engineering and intelligence roles. UNITA claims that a North Korean brigade had entered the war with the MPLA were denied by Western intelligence.

Within six weeks of Castro announcing the despatch of more troops to Angola, the US Congress made a move which would enable Washington to increase its participation in the Angolan struggle on an official military basis . On 11 July the House of Representatives voted, one month after a similar Senate move, to repeal the Clark Amendment, thus ending the decade-old ban on US military aid to Angolan rebel movements.[13] Angola reacted angrily and broke off the low-profile talks which it had been conducting throughout the year with Washington. 'The repeal of the Clark Amendment will leave the US Administration and international imperialism free to openly and directly intervene in Angola and exercise political and military pressures on the Angolan state,' said the Angolan Foreign Ministry.[14]

UNITA, naturally, rejoiced. Its radio station, Voice of the Resistance of the Black Cockerel,[15] said of the Congressional move: 'Our country's situation has been enriched with new political developments . . . Now there is a possibility for the world's most powerful country economically and technologically to render more open assistance to our struggle.'[16]

At this time, the world's eyes were much less firmly fixed on Angola than on South Africa, where a year of unprecedented unrest among the powerless black majority had resulted in a thousand or more deaths in outbreaks of violence. But Angola now moved into a series of battles bigger and more costly of lives than anything its people had yet known. To coincide with a ministerial meeting in Luanda of the Non-Aligned Nations Movement from 2 to 7 September, the MPLA launched its biggest ever offensive against UNITA's liberated areas in east and south-east Angola. Eighteen MPLA brigades were assembled in Luena, Cuito Cuanavale and Menongue to attack rebel strongholds at Cazombo and Mavinga.

Four motorised infantry brigades set out from Luena at the beginning of August to cover 350 kilometres of bush country towards Cazombo. By 15 August another five motorised infantry brigades were moving up from Menongue to Cuito Cuanavale, from where they set out to conquer 120 kilometres of sandy scrub on the way to Mavinga.

The brigades were backed by the Angolan Air Force, modernised and re-equipped over the previous two years under a programme supervised by Iko Carreira, the Air Force commander. By September 1985 Western intelligence broadly concurred with South Africa's Military Intelligence in estimates of the MPLA's new air strength: 30 advanced MIG-23 fighter-bombers; 8 advanced Sukhoi-22 fighter-bombers; 50 MIG-21 fighter-bombers; 16 ageing MIG-17 fighter-bombers; 33 MI-24 helicopter gunships; 27 French Alouette assault helicopters: 69 MI-8 and MI-17 transport helicopters. Increasingly the planes were being flown by young Angolans trained in the Soviet Union, with back-up from Cuban and Soviet personnel. Eighty per cent of the country's combat pilots were estimated to be Angolan in 1985, against 40 per cent in 1982.

In all, Angola received more than one billion dollars worth of Soviet arms between January 1984 and August 1985, according to Western intelligence estimates. The MPLA's tank army was almost 500-strong by the time of the Cazombo-Mavinga offensives. It consisted of 30 modern T-62 tanks, 260 T-55s, 150 outdated T-34s and 50 amphibious PT-76s.

The quality of MPLA training had also improved. Five hundred-strong commando Special Brigades, trained through 1984–85 by former Portuguese counter-insurgency experts, had entered action in eastern Angola: the quality of food, facilities and uniforms for these new crack outfits showed a marked improvement on what the average MPLA soldier had come to expect.

Carreira's airforce had been restructured in such a way that the attacking infantry columns could expect improved logistics support as Antonov-12 and Antonov-26 transport planes flew in supplies to remote bush airstrips as they were secured by the advancing columns.

By 7 September the MPLA had reached the outer defences of both Cazombo and Mavinga. Both seemed certain to fall within days, as UNITA found itself unable to cope effectively with the constant attacks of MIG-23s, MIG-21s,

SU-22s and MI-24s. On 18 September Savimbi decided that one of the towns had to be sacrificed so that he could concentrate troops in an attempt to save the other.

Cazombo was abandoned. UNITA would try to preserve Mavinga, whose fall would give the MPLA a major airstrip to which aircraft could ferry materials for an assault on Jamba itself, described by a correspondent of the *Guardian* as the 'symbol of Luanda's inability to maintain control over the whole of the country'.[17] On 19 September the Angolan Defence Ministry announced that its forces had re-entered Cazombo, 22 months after UNITA had overrun the town and taken away the Canadian missionaries I had met in December 1983.

Meanwhile, in mid-September, South Africa launched another invasion of Angola. Twelve commando teams, each about 40-strong, crossed the border in pursuit of SWAPO guerrillas poised to infiltrate Namibia, said General Constand Viljoen, the SADF chief. The MPLA said, however, that South African forces were involved in direct actions against the columns advancing on UNITA's eastern strongholds. Soon they produced the body of a 22-year-old South African soldier, Lance-Corporal Hans Fidler, a medical orderly who was killed while treating wounded UNITA soldiers on the battlefields around Cazombo and whose body was taken to Luanda. Savimbi had always stressed that, following the events of 1975–76, a South African soldier would never again be captured fighting alongside his troops. Lance-Corporal Fidler was not, strictly speaking, a fighting man: but he was part of the SADF and the capture of his body by the MPLA began to expose the degree of UNITA–SADF co-operation. The political consequences for both UNITA and South Africa were bound to be great.

Soon the MPLA was accusing the South African Air Force of strafing its columns near Mavinga with Mirage fighter-bombers and Canberra bombers. On 30 September, for example, the Angolan Defence Ministry said more than eight South African planes shot down six MPLA helicopters near Mavinga and killed more than 50 of its troops. Between 1 and 3 October, said the Defence Ministry, there were three major South African air attacks, 'dozens of dead and wounded', and the shooting down of a MIG-21.

Despite a warning from Iko Carreira that UNITA would be making a costly strategic error if it made any conventional military stand, by 7 October Savimbi claimed to have stood firm at Mavinga and repulsed the MPLA offensive. The five brigades were retreating in disarray towards Cuito Cuanavale and being attacked all the way back. Soviet and Cuban officers with the defeated force had been helicoptered to safety.

Journalists visited one of the battlefields, just south of the Lomba River 25 kilometres from Mavinga. The *Financial Times* correspondent was able 'to verify the scale of material losses put by Dr Savimbi as 79 vehicles destroyed and 52 captured'.[18] The correspondent of *The Times* of London wrote: 'We must have seen at least 50 smashed trucks and the blackened hulks of a dozen or more Soviet-made armoured personnel carriers. In one small area some 20 Russian-made Zil trucks, one mounted with the multiple rocket launcher known as a Stalin Organ, had been destroyed. Near the Lomba River lay the twisted remains of an MI-25 helicopter. UNITA officers said it had been brought down by 120mm mortar fire as it tried to land and evacuate government soldiers.

'Many of the government units seem to have been taken by surprise, possibly suggesting the suddenness of an air strike. In one place a truck and an armoured personnel carrier had been hit. A soldier, his head half blown away, was still sitting in the back of the truck. Three other rotting corpses lay entwined beneath a haze of flies on the sand nearby and the bodies of two other soldiers lay further away, as if they had been cut down while running for cover.

'With or without direct South African intervention, it is fair to say that the further Luanda's ponderous armoured columns advanced through the clogging bush sand, the more exposed they became at the end of a tenuous supply line, whereas UNITA's more lightly armed infantry were fighting on home ground.'[19]

Savimbi denied any South African air or ground support in annihilating the MPLA Mavinga attack force. He

produced before Western correspondents a 22-year-old
MPLA pilot whose MIG-21 had been shot down by ground
fire near Mavinga on 5 October. Francisco Matamba, who
had trained for three years in the Soviet Union, said he
had flown 45 missions during the Mavinga campaign: not
once had he encountered South African warplanes, though
radar operators told him they had spotted South African
aircraft on their screens.

In the Cazombo and Mavinga campaigns, the MPLA
claimed to have killed more than 1,300 UNITA troops, while
UNITA itself admitted more than 450 dead and 2,000
wounded. UNITA claimed more than 2,300 MPLA dead in
the campaigns: the MPLA never published total figures of its
losses.

*   *   *

Though Savimbi denied South African involvement, it was
an open secret among the diplomatic and journalistic communities in Pretoria that the South African Air Force had
gone into action on UNITA's behalf at Mavinga and that the
SADF's 32 battalion was there on the ground with radar-
guided G-5 and G-6 artillery. The foray across the border
against SWAPO was seen more as an attempt to distract the
MPLA from its Mavinga attack than as an attempt to flush
out Namibian guerrillas.

The Cazombo and Mavinga offensives had put Savimbi
under the most extreme danger. If Mavinga had fallen, the
possibility of a successful attack on Jamba would have been
high. As it was, South Africa itself decided to come out
much more into the open about its relationship with
UNITA. On 20 September the Defence Minister, Magnus
Malan, said publicly for the first time that South Africa was
giving aid to UNITA 'of a material, humanitarian and moral
nature. Through our connections with UNITA we maintain
the interests of the free world on our subcontinent. We will
break our links with UNITA on condition that all foreign
forces are withdrawn from Angola.'

And on 2 October President Botha himself tacitly admitted that his military forces were helping UNITA inside
Angola. 'More Russians and more Russian weaponry are

being employed to destroy the resistance of the Angolan people, just like in Afghanistan,' he told the Cape Province Congress of his ruling National Party in Port Elizabeth. 'In the light of all this, the Government can hardly sit still.' He called on South Africa's neighbours and on African countries generally to join forces to expel all foreign troops from southern Africa. He said: 'Say to the Cubans "Go home" and say to the Russians "Go home", and the minute that happens I will be prepared to settle all our military forces inside South Africa.'[20]

*   *   *

While UNITA fought desperately against the MPLA at Cazombo and Mavinga, Savimbi kept guerrilla units active in the centre and north to maintain pressure on the government. On 11 November, the 10th anniversary of Angola's independence, their activities reached a dramatic peak in Benguela Province when virtually the whole provincial government was wiped out in an attack on a convoy of eleven vehicles protected by MPLA soldiers. Four provincial ministers were killed and four senior officials captured, including the Director of Internal Trade, who the previous year had entertained Lord Jellicoe and encouraged British businessmen to put their money into Benguela.

A fortnight later UNITA said it had shot down an Antonov-12 plane flying from Menongue to Cuito Cuanavale, resulting in the death of 10 Soviet military officials and 11 senior MPLA officers. The Angolan Defence Ministry confirmed the loss of the plane and the death toll, but said it had been shot down by the South African Air Force.[21]

*   *   *

The heavy losses suffered by UNITA at Cazombo and Mavinga concentrated minds in Pretoria and Washington. On 24 September South Africa sent Mr David Steward, a senior expert on Angola in the Foreign Ministry and a former ambassador to the United Nations, to Washington to press for American help for Savimbi. The summer repeal of the Clark Amendment was due to become law on 1 October.[22]

Soon US Representative Claude Pepper, a Democrat from Florida, and Representative Jack Kemp, a Republican with strong Presidential aspirations from New York, had jointly proposed a bill which would give $US 27 million of 'non-lethal' aid to UNITA. Commentators predicted it would find a majority in the House, almost exactly ten years after Congress had passed the Clark Amendment severing help to Savimbi. President Reagan gave private assurance that he backed the Pepper-Kemp initiative, but in an extraordinary public statement said he would prefer that the aid be channelled covertly rather than through Congress.[23]

In the final weeks of 1985 the US press was filled with intense debate on the pros and cons of resuming aid to UNITA. The forecasts were that the aid would be moving, through the CIA, by February 1986. Through all the weeks of the debate top UNITA and South African officials were in Washington, and some reports said that the US aid – including Stinger shoulder-fired missiles capable of hitting helicopters and low-flying jets, and Tow anti-tank missiles – had begun to flow before the world saw out 1985 at the Christmas and New Year festivals.[24]

Epilogue

'Since when do you have to agree with people to defend them from injustice?'

American playwright Lillian Hellman

* * *

Writing this interim conclusion of Savimbi's story in 1986 has been a sobering experience. When I decided some ten years ago that his story must be told it was because, having witnessed and reported Angola's independence war, I felt he had been betrayed, cheated and misrepresented by a wide variety of people and by historical circumstance. I believed then – and no evidence has since been presented to persuade me to change my mind – that he would have emerged as the Angolan leader with most support if the elections promised by Portugal had ever been held. Apart from that conviction, I always enjoyed his company: he has an ebullience, great intelligence, wide-ranging curiosity, a fund of fascinating stories and an easy charm which made it regrettable that a conversation ever had to end. Above all, I admired his courage when he decided, after all his allies had deserted him in the early months of 1976, to lead his people into the interior of Angola and find some way to fight on. No one gave him any chance of physical survival, let alone eventual success in securing the elections that might bring him to power. The lesson of history to that point was that any totalitarian movement which came to power with unreserved Soviet backing stayed there in perpetuity – as in Czechoslovakia, Poland, Hungary, for example. Vietnam, Cambodia and Laos had just fallen to Marxist-Leninist governments of various hues, and looked set to stay that way for generations. The Soviet invasion of Afghanistan had yet to come, along with the resistance it provoked which made Soviet ruthlessness look less invincible.

Savimbi had chosen what looked a probable death, and ignominy in the history books of the world, rather than surrender to a totalitarian takeover of his country by politicians who to this day have never tested their acceptability by democratic means. And the story of how this fate had overtaken him was far too complex to tell in one or two over-simplified, quickly disposable newspaper articles. Hence this book.

Well, Savimbi has survived. Not only that, but he has built up an army to fight the MPLA which is perhaps 60,000-strong, and that has been a remarkable achievement. And in 1986 the wheel of history came full turn and America resumed more-or-less open assistance to his movement. That, I am convinced, is right. But it is sobering because the price of the Angolan war, already high, will become infinitely higher.

The most obvious price has been the loss of countless thousands of lives, their souls ripped from their bodies by bullets with the markings of factories in a dozen or so countries more advanced – technologically – than Angola. It seems almost corny to lament such loss. It happens whenever there is war in a corner of the globe which seems remote and quaint to the 'civilised' people of Europe and North America. But the tragedy and the deaths are real nonetheless.

There has been a heavy price in living but mutilated bodies. Visit either side in the Angolan war and the large and growing numbers of limbless people is startling. Others abound with even more vital parts blown away or who have been hideously disfigured.

There is the heavy and immeasurable price of lost innocence. The MPLA holds power never legitimated by the people's choice. That should raise at least as many questions as the support Savimbi takes from South Africa. To what other depths do the MPLA feel justified in sinking when their power has to be maintained by helicopter gunships which mow down black Angolans who dissent, however wisely or misguidedly? What is just or legitimate about a government that in the last ten years has executed – judicially and extra-judicially – many hundreds of its black opponents and dissidents? The years following the unsuccessful coup attempt by Nito Alves in 1977 were the worst, but in 1985 at least 20 people were sentenced to death by military and people's tribunals and in 1984 at least 31. The precise number of people executed is particularly difficult to state in Angola because from the beginning of 1980 to April 1985 the MPLA made no public announcements when executions were carried out.

Of course, the loss of innocence applies also to UNITA. The truth about the extent of Savimbi's involvement with South Africa has emerged only slowly. Denials of involvement have given way to admittance of limited supplies of essentials such as petrol and diesel fuel, and finally to weapons and extensive co-operation. This dissimulation was necessary, I understand, for Savimbi would have received few plaudits and many brickbats from the world community for openly admitting his involvement with South Africa. His philosophy seems to have been: admit only as and when necessary, and then keep the admission within the tightest limits possible.

But, as anyone knows who has ever told a lie, it is a seductive form of behaviour. It helps avoid awkward confrontations: it gains advantages. Lying, like intimidation and ruthlessness, works. I see it in my present assignment as Europe correspondent of my newspaper: officials and politicians obfuscate and mislead through commission and omission. Savimbi has had to accept help from many Western and black African nations who demand as the price for that help his denial that it exists.

I have watched the process. When I first made contact again with Savimbi in 1980, he was open about some of the sources of his support. By the end of 1983, when I asked him where his help was coming from, he said it had been his policy to be candid about these matters: but it had got him into trouble with the countries involved, and now he regretted that he had to be more circumspect. I had flown into his territory from the capital of a black African country, X, which gave him a great deal of help but which I had promised not to name. I asked him the extent of the help he was now getting from X. He replied: 'We do not get any help from X.' Was he *sure* that he got no help from X? 'We do *not* get any help from X.' But we had flown in on his, Savimbi's, plane from X, hadn't we? 'I *cannot* say that I get any help from X.'

'We are not saints. We are making a war,' he told me on another occasion.

All that having been said, I have found UNITA reasonably honest with me in their dealings, and I have trusted them enough to travel 1,000 kilometres with them into hostile territory. Savimbi's top aides have been candid enough with me to say there are aspects of their struggle which cannot be told until long into the future (just as Britain, for example, classifies certain facts concerning government decisions and discussions for 30 years): and they laugh when they say I will have done well to get 70 per cent of the story right in view of the vast quantities of disinformation pumped out from all sides.

I labour this point because in the end the great untruths have been directed at Savimbi. And it was perhaps appropriate that Gabriel Garcia Marques, who after all had won the Nobel Prize for Fiction, should perpetrate perhaps the most blatant and damaging of these falsehoods.

Marques was recruited to write the semi-official account of the Cuban expedition to Angola. It is an extraordinarily boastful and sensationalistic piece of work, patronising and almost racist in tone as it relates the African adventure to the Cuban folks back home in a style reminiscent of Edgar Rice Burroughs' tales of Tarzan.

In one passage Marques laments the 'cultural backwardness' of the MPLA Africans the Cubans found themselves working among, and goes on:

'Old (African) superstitions not only complicated daily life, but also hindered the war effort. The Angolans had been convinced that the bullets would not penetrate white skin, they feared the magic of airplanes and refused to go into trenches because tombs were only for the dead . . . It was a dirty war in which (Cubans) had to watch out as much for snakes as for mercenaries, as much for cannibals as for cannonballs. A Cuban commander, in the midst of battle, fell into an elephant trap. Many times, especially in Cabinda, Cuban scouts felt betrayed by the primitive telegraph of the talking drums, whose thumping could be heard for as much as twenty miles away.'[2]

This is dreadful cliché-ridden rubbish. The line about cannibals is reminiscent of cartoons that used to be common in Europe of naked black men with bones through their noses standing round fires as white missionaries, complete with solar topees, simmered in giant cooking pots.

The Marques account may have been mere burlesque in parts, but some of his assertions, questionable though their accuracy was, have been repeated enough times to become incontrovertible truths in many minds.

His most important affirmation was to present as reality Fidel Castro's claim that 'on November 5 (1975) the Revolutionary Government of Cuba decided to send the first military units to Angola to support the MPLA'.[3] This was of fundamental historical importance, for it suggested that the Cubans arrived only in response to the South African invasion of Angola. Many people have since picked this up and run with it. During the debate in late 1985 and early 1986 on whether the United States should resume aid to Savimbi, many influential commentators used this fundamental 'fact' presented by Marques/Castro as the premise for their arguments. Jonathan Power of the *International Herald Tribune*, for example, urging the withholding of aid from Savimbi, wrote: 'The Cubans never set foot in Angola until the South Africans invaded Angola during its civil war.'[4]

This is quite simply false. And though John Marcum has written sagely: 'The foreign intervention and factional fighting that ensued in 1975 proved so chaotic and opportunistic that its exact sequence may remain forever arguable,'[5] such facts as we can be sure of show incontrovertibly that Cuban soldiers were in Angola with the MPLA in 1975 *before* there was any South African intervention. We have it on the word of Cuba's Deputy Prime Minister, Carlos Rafael Rodriguez, with details filled in by Wilfred Burchett, the

Australian Communist journalist who wrote sympathetically about the Chinese and the North Vietnamese and subsequently became close to the MPLA.

Rodriguez admitted to a group of correspondents in January 1976 that Cuba had sent 230 military advisers to Angola in May 1975 to train MPLA forces at Benguela, Cabinda, Henrique de Carvalho (Saurimo) and Salazar (Dalatando), near Luanda.[6] According to Burchett: '238 was the precise figure.'[7] John Stockwell says these advisers arrived in Angola as early as March, but even May 1975 was three to four months before the first South African instructors began training UNITA soldiers at Calombo, a disused Portuguese jail near Silva Porto (Bie).[8] All analyses suggest that these South African instructors began arriving in September 1975. The most reliable account is probably that of Stockwell, writing after he had resigned as chief of the CIA's Angolan Task Force and become an advocate of the Cuban/MPLA cause: 'In September the South Africans began to provide arms and training . . . First two, then twelve, then forty advisers appeared with UNITA forces near Silva Porto.'[9]

The Cuban instructors also arrived with the MPLA more than two months before the first American arms were delivered to Savimbi, according to Stockwell's account.[10] In other words, Cuban support to the MPLA began during the period when the Angolan transitional government was still functioning and months before UNITA began to receive its first backing from *either* South Africa *or* the United States.

Cuban military reinforcement of the MPLA did not end with the 238 men sent in May. According to John Marcum, 200 Cuban infantry instructors arrived in Luanda in August, again *before* any South African instructors had entered Angola to train UNITA. (But at about the same time, Marcum also notes, as a small group of South African troops took up position on the site of the South African-financed Cunene River hydro-electric project a few miles inside Angola. By the terms of an agreement for the construction of a series of dams along the Cunene, the South Africans had been previously permitted by the Portuguese to station a small force at the first 63-million-dollar dam site.)[11]

A decision to escalate Cuba's involvement further was made some time in August. Cuban troops and weaponry began to be embarked on ships for Angola from 7 September 1985.[12] The first ship may have reached Africa as early as 25 September 1975,[13] but of those which were positively identified the *Vietnam Heroico* was among the first to disembark at Porto Amboim, south of Luanda, on 4 October. Two other ships, the *Coral Island* and *La Playa de Habana*, disembarked on 5 and 12 October.[14] There were about 1,000 Cuban combat troops aboard these ships, along with armoured cars and military trucks. Among the soldiers who arrived on the *Vietnam Heroico* was Lieutenant Selso Caldez, subsequently captured by UNITA in early November and executed in March 1976 (see chapters 16 and 19).

These ships arrived *before* South Africa's Angolan invasion force crossed the border from Namibia some time between 14 and 23 October. The former is the date given in Robert Moss's semi-official account of the 1975 South African invasion: the latter is that given by Sean Macbride, the fiercely anti-South African former United Nations Commissioner for Namibia, in a secret memorandum of the UN headquarters in New York.[15]

There are various estimates of the number of Cuban troops who had reached Angola before Independence Day on 11 November 1975. These vary between 1,100 and 4,000. John Stockwell's figure of 2,800 may be the most trustworthy, in view of his pro-Cuban/MPLA sympathies.[16] What is clear is that this number of men could not have been mobilised and transported to Angola by that date if, as Gabriel Garcia Marques asserts and so many others have repeated, 'the Revolutionary Government of Cuba decided to send the first military units to Angola to support the MPLA' only on 5 November 1975.

Colin Legum, the London-based writer on Africa who has a long record of dogged opposition to the white régime in his native South Africa, wrote: 'The mobilisation and transport of such large numbers would require at least six weeks from the time the decision was taken. The Russian and Cuban contention that their military intervention was the result of South African intervention is clearly a *post facto* rationalisation, since they were seriously involved before March 1975, and they had already put their aid programme into its second phase by the beginning of October – fully three weeks before the South African army had crossed the frontier.

'One Cuban, taken prisoner by FNLA, gave details of his unit's arrival from Brazzaville in August 1975, almost two months before the South African army arrival.'[17]

In addition, the Soviet Union had begun its programme of arms deliveries to the MPLA in late August 1974, *eleven months* before the States began a much more limited delivery of arms to UNITA (see Chapters 1 and 11).

*   *   *

In the context of the continuing UNITA-MPLA struggle, *which* foreign weapons and armies came first to Angola is of basic significance. There may well be good reasons why the international community – including Western social and liberal democrats who would be aghast if a similar fate befell them – should abandon Savimbi and his UNITA followers to their fate in Angola. But it should not be on the basis of a towering falsehood. It should not be on the basis of a spurious premise designed to salve the consciences of those who do the abandoning.

My argument, with the civil war in Angola now being fought on a bigger scale than ever before, is starkly simple. The evidence is clear that while the MPLA participated in escalation of the war in 1974–75, Savimbi concentrated on trying to secure the elections, agreed by all parties to the conflict, which the Organisation of African Unity said UNITA would win (see Chapter 11). It is illustrative of the lack of natural justice in international law that the MPLA is now recognised as the legitimate government of Angola while members of UNITA are rebels beyond the protection of any law except that of natural survival.

*   *   *

Of course, the scene is more complicated when the FNLA is added to the picture. Chinese military instructors sent to the FNLA in June 1974, and the beginning of a flow of small CIA cash handouts to the same movement the following month, preceded the resumption of large-scale Soviet arms deliveries to the MPLA in August 1974. If you look for a point at which the whole terrible escalation of weapons deliveries and fighting began in Angola, following the overthrow of the Portuguese dictatorship on 25 April 1974, this is where you have to begin. It is what enabled the MPLA to legitimate its seizure of power as it received Eastern Bloc weapons, and Cuban and East German troop support, on a scale that the FNLA and UNITA would never subsequently enjoy.

It is the events of this period in mid-1974 which, I suppose, enabled Tanzania's President Julius Nyerere to say with less than strict accuracy in a BBC Radio interview almost two years later: 'The internal struggle (in Angola) had a lot to do with the Americans. The Americans were there well before November 11th (1975). The Cubans were not there. The original external intervention there was American and South African.'[18]

Hearing this kind of tendentious statement from an African statesman who once commanded wide international respect made me realise that analysis of the Angolan tragedy was less a matter of putting together a giant and difficult jigsaw puzzle than of examining a varied array of mud spats on a wall with no logical pattern. After all, was this not the Nyerere who had been instrumental in persuading the Chinese to help the FNLA in June 1974, who in a sense could be blamed for triggering the whole cycle, and who was therefore in a difficult position to condemn the Americans for following his lead a month later? Was this not the same Nyerere who by April 1975 had decided to train Savimbi's troops, and who by August 1975 had switched his support to the MPLA?

*   *   *

By early 1986 Angola and its civil war had become a lynchpin in the evolving saga of southern and central Africa. American right-wing Republicans eager to 'fight Communism' were preparing to restore aid to Savimbi, either overtly or covertly, to help him in his struggle against the MPLA,

Cubans, Soviets and East Germans. Liberal Democrats and some Republicans argued against such aid on the grounds that America might get sucked into an ever-escalating war and that it would find itself marked indelibly as an ally of South Africa. Pro-Savimbi Republicans retorted that doing nothing to help UNITA would reveal America as a fraudulent coward unprepared to help democratic movements against totalitarian régimes for fear of being misunderstood.

Neither side was very convincing. Savimbi needed the support of American 'anti-communists', just as he had little choice other than to accept the support of South Africa. 'No one can sincerely tell us that it would be better to be massacred by the Cubans rather than accept aid from South Africa,' he once told the French press. 'We want to live and we want our independence. To be promised the title of posthumous revolutionaries does not interest us.'[19] And in another interview after the MPLA had signed the Lusaka Accord with South Africa, he said: 'Lenin signed the Brest-Litovsk (which surrendered the Ukraine, Finland, the Baltic provinces, the Caucasus, White Russia and Poland to the Germans); Stalin the Nazi-Soviet Pact (in which Germany and the Soviet Union divided up central Europe between themselves); Machel the Nkomati Accord; dos Santos that of Lusaka. Today the men of Luanda dine with the South Africans, and together they chase SWAPO in Cunene. Who therefore can hope to come and give us lessons?'[20]

But though, for tactical reasons, Savimbi was presenting himself in the US in 1986 as the West's man in Africa, in my conversations with him he always rejected the simplistic 'pro-Western' label pinned on him by right-wing Americans and by news agencies – his was a *pro-Angola* fight, a fight for the right of people to choose their own government.

While Western conservatives exaggerated Savimbi's pro-Western sentiments to fit their prejudices and preconceptions of the region, liberals and progressives emphasised supposed conservative virtues in the MPLA to support *their* case for the Luanda government. In one of the more bizarre examples, the *New York Times* columnist Anthony Lewis quoted an unusual supporter for his argument that the United States should give diplomatic recognition to the

Marxist government in Angola. During a five-day visit to Luanda, Lewis met T. J. Fahey, an executive of the General Tire and Rubber Company of Akron, Ohio, which has a ten per cent stake in a state-owned Angolan tyre company. Fahey told Lewis: 'We are delighted to be here. They pay us meticulously – our fees and the salaries of our people. I'm just an old peddler, but I think it's a tragic mistake that we don't recognise Angola. Here is a country with incredible buying power and a need for every product on earth. I'm talking about America's commerical self-interest.'[21] Fahey's argument was a strange one for Lewis to make so much of, for he was putting the standard case of a capitalist travelling salesman. He would have argued the same way if he were selling tyres to South Africa, Chile, China, North Vietnam or the Central African Empire. Traders of this kind admired Mrs Indira Gandhi, during her suspension of democracy in India, and Mussolini for making their countries' trains run on time, and possibly also US Lieutenant Milo Mindbender, the wheeler-dealer in *Catch-22*, who defended the Germans he traded with clandestinely by saying: 'Maybe they did start the war, and maybe they are killing millions of people, but they pay their bills a lot more promptly than some allies of ours that I could name.'[22]

Lewis' prior record had shown an admirable concern with oppression and the denial of democratic rights under a variety of despicable régimes. If he had heard Fahey expressing similar views in Pretoria or Warsaw, the 'old peddler' would have been the target of Lewis' wrath.

It was strange that Lewis, in urging his government to embrace the MPLA, had nothing to say about the fact that the multi-party elections promised for Angola had never been held; that he did not point out that all opposition to the MPLA had been outlawed; and that he failed to record that in the six months on either side of his visit at least 43 Angolans were executed in their country's three main cities for their opposition to an autocracy they had not chosen.[23]

Just as curious as the adoption by Lewis, and a number of other leftist commentators, of the profit motives of right-wing capitalism to illustrate the respectability of the MPLA was their eagerness to demonstrate the dangerous leftist tendencies of Savimbi. Thus, Gerald Bender, a pro-MPLA professor of international relations at the University of California, quoted the American executive officer in Angola of Gulf Oil of Texas as saying: 'Savimbi would be the worst socialist of the lot and would be much harder to do business with than the MPLA.'[24] Executives of Gulf Oil, now part of the Chevron empire, have continued to emphasise that MPLA payments are prompt and that the royalty terms are among the most generous in the world. A number of liberals, including Representative Ted Weiss (Democrat, New York), said Savimbi's self-description as a 'Maoist' showed he was not a man to support[25] – in fact, Savimbi had said he admired Mao's theories of guerrilla warfare, because he had put them into practice and seen that they worked, but that he rejected Mao's economic theories, because time had shown that they did not work.

Western democrats go to the aid of beleaguered peoples much too rarely: but, in turning down Savimbi, there is the bonus of a *frisson* of moral righteousness. In the southern African region the ruthless determination with which the South Africans seek to apply apartheid is matched all too frequently by the blind fanaticism with which too many anti-apartheid campaigners are willing to sacrifice others in order to see apartheid crushed: the latter becomes a kind of racism of its own, as cruel in effect if not intent as the system it seeks to destroy. Its own absolutism sullies the principle for which it is fighting.

The need for one man-one vote, multi-party elections in Angola is as rarely heard from the lips of anti-apartheid campaigners as is the call for similar elections in South Africa from the American Right who have made themselves Savimbi's patrons.

It is, of course, much more difficult for liberal democrats to argue the case for liberty in Angola than it is in South Africa: the chances of being misunderstood are infinitely greater. The fact is that there are few easy cheers and back slaps to be won in calling for freedom in Angola. However, it is a pity that so many centre democrats flinch from analysing carefully what has happened in Angola simply because they fear their motives will be misinterpreted and abused.

Sometimes I have found the intolerance of white liberals in Britain towards some of my black UNITA acquaintances to be almost frightening. One lecturer I knew from Edinburgh University's Department of African Studies was a highly intelligent man who had left Rhodesia because he opposed its racial discrimination: he was tough on the whites of southern Africa, but also made rigorous critiques of the shortcomings of the newly independent black states. I thought he might like to meet a UNITA leader who was visiting me. 'No,' came the answer, 'I will never speak to those people.' N-E-V-E-R. It was an answer that shocked me because the young Angolan had packed more hardship into his 24 years than this white lecturer, despite all his principles, would ever know in his cushioned university existence. My black visitor had been imprisoned at the age of 15 by the Portuguese simply because some of his brothers were in the UNITA resistance: for six months of his two-year prison term he had been kept in solitary confinement in total darkness, living in his own excrement. When finally he was released, after the Portuguese revolution of April 1974, he was blind and did not recover his sight for many days; when he could see again he was terrified to discover that his once black skin had turned grey. Two of his brothers died fighting the Portuguese. Another died fighting the Cubans, and his sister was executed by the MPLA because her brothers opposed the régime. My visitor faced execution if he was ever caught in Angola, where he was in the forefront of the fight against the Cubans and he was an articulate interpreter of UNITA's difficult and complex history. At the very least, he had earned the right to be heard.

On southern Africa, Western liberal democrats have for too long applied moral logic with blinkers. They argue, rightly, for liberty and free elections in Namibia and the withdrawal of foreign forces, i.e. the South Africans. But they ignore the thorny logical concomitant that these sentiments raise, because if nothing less is good enough for the people of Namibia – and nothing less *is* good enough – why should anything less be good enough for the people of Angola?

My target here is the centre of the Western democratic

spectrum: the knee-jerk polarisation of the modern right and left has made reasoned argument at those poles almost redundant. If the far right backs UNITA for strategic reasons rather than in the interests of Angola's people, the far left equally ignores the people and supports the MPLA for reasons of ideological intolerance and hatred. In the absence of real analysis at those extremes, there is a need for the centre to provide it. Western liberals have tirelessly argued that Namibia's SWAPO guerrillas (and South Africa's ANC guerrillas) cannot be condemned for accepting support from Cuba and the Soviet Union because, for far too long, Namibia's black majority was unable to obtain sufficient support from a supine West. They, wisely, do not conclude that SWAPO will inevitably impose Marxist dictatorship because of the sources of its succour. Why, then, to extend the logic, condemn UNITA when, in its long-running campaign to gain free elections and the expulsion of foreign troops, it takes help from the only source from which it is available? In the absence of support from a power that is acceptable to their sensibilities, it is incumbent upon liberals to suggest some other realistic course of action than abject submission to what the liberal *Guardian* newspaper once admiringly described as the MPLA's declared goal of creating a fully-fledged Marxist-Leninist 'revolutionary democratic dictatorship.'[26]

The newspaper apparently failed to recognise the terrifying irony in the MPLA's self-description. It helped compound what was then my growing astonishment at the casual enthusiasm with which some Western liberals endorse as suitable for Africans political systems which they would rail against if imposed on their own societies. Or, as an American newspaper columnist once put it: 'A liberal is a person whose interests aren't at stake at the moment.'[27]

* * *

Some analysts believe the Angolan war may continue for another 30 years, with UNITA controlling the countryside and the MPLA the towns, while around them economic standards continue to fall and the death toll to rise. For a country which is beautiful and potentially very rich, and whose people are widely admired for their vivaciousness, such a prospect is monumentally futile.

All logic demands that the main protagonists, the MPLA and UNITA, reach an accommodation which allows some kind of power sharing, peace and the repatriation of foreign soldiers. That, of course, is easier said than done. Savimbi has offered the MPLA five years of coalition government with UNITA before Angola's first free election is held. But his condition is that all Cuban troops must first return home – without that, there would be no guarantee of safety for UNITA as it entered the main cities.

If South Africa withdraws from Namibia, and withholds support from UNITA, the MPLA has offered to retain only 10 to 12 thousand of the 31,000 Cuban troops that were estimated by Western intelligence to be in Angola at the end of 1985. There would be a total withdrawal of Cubans from the south, and those that remained in the country would be located only in Luanda Province and Cabinda.[28] Ostensibly they would provide protection for the capital and the oil wells against the South Africans, but it is clear that their real role would be to protect the two most important areas of the country from a UNITA onslaught. And once the South Africans had conceded Namibia's independence and withdrawn from the territory, there would be nothing to stop the MPLA reinforcing its Cuban garrison as soon as UNITA seemed likely to break through to the capital.

It looks like a circle that is impossible to break. But towards the end of 1985, at the five-yearly Congress of the MPLA, President dos Santos managed to oust Lucio Lara from the 13-man Politburo and Henrique 'Iko' Carreira from the 75-member Central Committee. Both men were strongly pro-Soviet and led the hard-line faction which opposed any form of conciliation talks with UNITA. Lara's dismissal was a surprise. For nearly 30 years Lara, the *mestico* son of a wealthy Portuguese sugar plantation owner, had been the movement's ideological expert: his permanent presence in the MPLA's top leadership seemed to be carved in tablets of stone. Carreira's downgrading was even more surprising, for, as head of the Air Force, he had supervised the rebuilding of the MPLA's air offensive power which had caused major problems for UNITA in 1984 and 1985. Both Lara and Carreira, along with several others removed from top positions, had been frequently referred to by US officials as 'obstacles' to the regional peace plans framed by Dr Crocker.[29]

Despite the suspension by the MPLA of talks with the US administration following the repeal of the Clark Amendment in the summer of 1985, President dos Santos showed further willingness to achieve a negotiated settlement by resuming negotiations with Washington in the autumn. Dr Crocker met senior Angolan ministers in Lusaka at the end of November 1985, and on 8 and 9 January 1986 he held two days of talks with President dos Santos in Luanda. No details of the proposals they exchanged were released, but the Angolan Press Agency (ANGOP) reported dos Santos as having told Crocker: 'In the event of new aggressions, Angola will solicit more aid from the international community and particularly from its traditional friends in the Soviet Union, Cuba and other socialist countries.'[30]

Dos Santos has shown his determination to negotiate only from a position of increasing military strength. Savimbi's aim is the same, as was seen when he journeyed to Washington in late January 1986 to obtain aid to purchase defensive weapons able to counter the increasing sophistication and numbers of weapons delivered to the MPLA.

The present level of the war is bad enough. It is estimated to have cost the country at least 20 billion dollars in destruction and in payments for arms and foreign troops.[31] A 900-million-dollar Soviet-Brazilian dam project on the Cuanza River cannot go ahead until a special 6,000-strong security unit has been trained to protect the workforce. The *Cuanza* currency unit sells at 1,500 to the dollar on the black market against the official rate of 30. In December 1985 a young MPLA military officer told the MPLA Congress: 'The war has become routine to us – every day there is fighting, every day dying, every day prisoners, every day UNITA boys giving up, every day peasants losing limbs.'[32]

Writer and former MPLA education minister Artur Lestana Pepetela has lamented: 'We were plunged into the East-West conflict and now we don't even know who we are. Every aspect of our lives is imbued with alienation and contradiction – black market vs. official planning, proletarian ideology in a rural society (only 12 of the 600 delegates to the MPLA's last Congress were rural peasants), pro-Soviet rhetoric while doing business with the West. Only peace will allow us finally to realise who we are and where we want to go.'[33]

If all the aggrieved parties could be brought to the negotiating table, maybe this agony could end. If the Cubans were to leave Angola, the South Africans would have no further excuse for staying in Namibia: in a very real sense, the Cuban involvement has delayed Namibian independence. If the Cubans and South Africans were to stage simultaneous and total withdrawals, the stage would not only be set for Namibian independence and elections in Angola, but in the general atmosphere of reduced tension there could be other important changes throughout the region. South Africa, freed of any possible military threat from Angola, might lose some of its siege mentality and experiment more boldly with racial reforms. Freed from the threat of spillover from Angola's war, there could be greater regional co-operation and progress. Zaire, a sleeping giant of a problem, might at last begin the massive programme of reform and development that its benighted people deserve: Zambia's disintegrating economy might at last pick up again with the reopening of the Benguela Railway: and in the general atmosphere of greater relaxation Zimbabwe's Robert Mugabe might feel able to demonstrate greater magnanimity towards his country's Ndebele minority.

This is the optimistic view, but the more realistic one might be that taken by Stephen Glover, an African specialist with the *Daily Telegraph*, after he had visited the Namibia-Angola border: 'My feeling is that barring miracles (and who would wish to?) the Cubans will not leave Angola. The South Africans will not leave Namibia, even if they fill the place with their surrogates. The war will go on and it will probably get worse. It may even turn out to be a big, quite famous war.'[34]

If the war intensifies, the international politics surrounding it and the foreign interests suffusing it will become even more complex. But, nevertheless, the central issue of Savimbi's war will remain simple and clear – that all the bloodshed and destruction was started by those who destroyed Angola's promised electoral process back in 1975. As well as surviving the Cuban/Soviet/MPLA attempt to wipe him out, Savimbi's remarkable achievement, in the face of great hardships, has been to keep this basic truism at the forefront of the debate. His unrelenting will to succeed has not surprised his old professor, Henri Rieben, at Lausanne University, whom I visited at his Centre for European Studies on the shores of Lac Leman in the summer of 1984. When I asked him if he was surprised that his erstwhile student from Angola had become such an important figure in African politics, Rieben answered: 'No, not at all. I think that every so often the world sees someone who is destined to be a man of his time. I recognised that special and rare quality in Jonas Savimbi even when he was just one student among others.'

I have decided to leave the last word on Savimbi with a gentle Scot who spent most of his working life as an eye doctor in India, giving sight to countless thousands of people at a mission hospital in Bihar. Since returning to Scotland, Dr Alastair King has been a leader of Amnesty International, and has been connected with campaigns that have secured the release from jails of Indian dissidents in South Africa, of black opponents of the Malawi régime, and of protestors against the abuse of psychiatry in the Soviet Union.

In a letter published in a newspaper, Dr King once said something I would never have dared say publicly myself. The letter, in which he was commenting on reports that battalions of the South African ANC (African National Congress) were fighting alongside the MPLA in Angola against UNITA, went:

'What a triumph for the makers of Soviet foreign policy that the two men whose influence they probably fear most in stemming the advance of Communism in southern Africa are now involved on opposite sides of a vicious and seemingly endless civil war.

'Jonas Savimbi of UNITA and Nelson Mandela of the

ANC are the two most potent forces for democracy and moderation in southern Africa today. The former, who should now by rights be part, if not head, of a freely elected government in Angola, has been fighting his lonely and bitter war against a Marxist dictatorship for the last ten years.

'Nelson Mandela, who should be leading negotiations with the South African government for the peaceful dismantling of apartheid, has now been imprisoned for over 20 years.

'The western democracies can only hang their heads in shame that such a situation (the military involvement of the ANC with the MPLA against UNITA) should ever have arisen. They abandoned Savimbi in his struggle for the freedom of his country to keep happy their relationships with the rest of black Africa. They kept quiet about Mandela and all that he stood for in order to maintain good trading relationships with white South Africa.

'Their continuing failure to recognise the importance of these two men and to take effective action in their support may eventually see fulfilled their apparent death-wish for democracy in southern Africa.'[35]

Brussels, 21 January 1986

Postscript

January 1986 to October 1987

'They don't seem to care about black Angolans killing other black Angolans with Russian aid. Does a black life mean less if taken by a black Angolan or Cuban than if by a white South African? Does the colour of the killer determine the degree of protest?' – Jonas Savimbi, to black American journalists, Washington DC, February 1986.

*   *   *

The sticky heat of the southern African summer had Jonas Savimbi's Jamba headquarters in its grip as he left in January 1986 to fly to Washington with 17 members of his Central Committee and his new wife, Anna Isobel Paulino. He had married Anna, his secretary for ten years, two months earlier at a Protestant ceremony in the bush. In the biting cold of the American capital's mid-winter he was received like a head of state. He met Ronald Reagan in the Oval Office at a time when the President was cancelling other appointments because of the Challenger space shuttle disaster. Afterwards there was the customary media interview for all Presidential guests of honour with the White House as a background. George Shultz received him at the White House and Caspar Weinberger greeted him at the Pentagon. Prime time television programmes allowed him to argue UNITA's case. Reuters published a fulsome profile and an interview in which Savimbi said his dream was to negotiate with Eduardo dos Santos an Angolan government of reconciliation and unity leading to free elections. He told the news agency that he was committed to a pluralist,

Western-orientated society, and added: 'I consider myself a democratic socialist.'

Savimbi arrived in Washington at the end of January secure in the knowledge that it was no longer a question of whether assistance would flow directly from the Americans, but simply a matter of when and in what form. On 12 November 1985 President Reagan had approved an initial programme of covert aid, including weaponry, worth at least $US 15 million for UNITA. Savimbi's role now was to reinforce supporters of that aid and win over critics.

By the time he left the US on 6 February, the *Washington Post* reported that Savimbi had support from the Reagan administration that 'appeared almost monolithic and a private assurance that lethal military aid will be speeding to him within weeks.'

Two months later the first reports appeared that 'Stinger' missiles had been delivered to UNITA through Zaire. The 'Stingers', hand-held ground-to-air missiles for use against low-flying assault aircraft, had never before been delivered to rebel groups. They were at least a generation ahead of the latest Soviet SAM-7s and gave UNITA the capability to attack the MPLA's MI-24 helicopter-gunships and MIG-23s which had caused many deaths among its followers during the previous year's fighting.

Having chosen 'covert' means to support Savimbi, Reagan did not need full Congressional approval for any programme conducted through the CIA. But he did want to avoid the kind of Congressional rebellion that had led to the Clark Amendment in 1976. Chester Crocker and George Shultz, the main Administration opponents of sending US military hardware to Savimbi, were therefore persuaded to appear before Congressional committees and pledge their support to the Reagan line.

Crocker, just five weeks after he had held talks with MPLA President dos Santos in Luanda, told the Senate Foreign Relations Sub-Committee: 'We intend to be supportive of UNITA in an effective and appropriate manner. This past year we have seen the MPLA government, strongly backed by Moscow and Havana, pursue an escalation (of the war). They failed. It is important in our view that they continue to fail.' The MPLA broke off contacts with Crocker, and it was to be more than a year before they were resumed.

Shultz told Senate Republicans that he too backed aid to UNITA, but would prefer it to be channelled 'covertly' rather than through a Congressional bill which would cause complications when it came to moving supplies through neighbouring black states. During his visit Savimbi argued that more important than South African help was the fact that 'twelve black African countries support us.' He declined to name them, though they certainly included Gabon, the Ivory Coast, Cameroon, Chad and Zaire.

Robert Dole, the Republican majority leader in the Senate, orchestrated Congressional support to give the President the political fallback protection he needed for the 'covert' programme. 'It will be just a matter of backing up the forklift in some warehouse, putting the weapons on an airplane and then trucking them in to Savimbi,' one Congressional backer of UNITA told the *Washington Post*.

It was a sweet moment for Savimbi. He had counselled his followers, during times when oblivion was a daily possibility, that, if they could only manage to survive, the dynamics of international politics would change around them. Now the only nation on earth which could provide effective help against the Soviets was committing political support and weaponry to UNITA. David Ottaway, African specialist on the *Washington Post*, wrote that 'Savimbi's time had come.'

*   *   *

One of the more bizarre consequences of the escalating war in Angola was the extension of the conflict to the plush chambers of public relations companies in Washington. Both the MPLA and UNITA hired prestigious lobbying firms to present their arguments to the capital's power-brokers. UNITA took on Black, Manafort, Stone and Kelly on a contract worth \$US 650,000 a year. The move was made at the urging of one of Savimbi's main bankrollers, the Saudi Arabian government. Black, Manafort had good relations with CIA Director William Casey. And Christopher J.

Lehman, a special assistant to President Reagan and, at 37, the younger brother of Navy Secretary John F. Lehman, left the White House to orchestrate the UNITA campaign for Black, Manafort.

The MPLA paid a similar amount to Gray and Co., another PR firm with close ties to the White House. Robert Gray, the firm's founder, had been chairman of Reagan's first inaugural committee. Furious right-wingers accused Gray of turning 'pink' as he appointed Daniel Murphy, a retired four-star admiral who had served as deptuy director of the CIA and as a top aide to Vice-President George Bush, to look after the MPLA's account. To the _Wall Street Journal_, Admiral Murphy explained the challenge of his presentational task with the Angolan government this way: 'Their image problem is that they're a bunch of Communists who have a bunch of Cubans there.' After years spent keeping his CIA eye on Communists, Admiral Murphy now advised MPLA representatives visiting the US to wear conservative suits and ties to contrast with Savimbi's preferred Mao-style suits and Guevara-type uniforms. Murphy also hired as his personal assistant a former employee of the Gulf Corporation, whose parent company, the San Francisco-based Chevron, exploits Angola's oil reserves and pays royalties which sustain the MPLA's war against UNITA.

* * *

While the firms fought on Washington's PR battlefields, braver men died in grimmer war zones as the conflict ground on in Angola. The communiqués of both sides spoke of heavy death and casualty tolls in countless encounters. Clashes between the MPLA and UNITA were now occurring at some place or other in Angola on a daily basis, unseen and little regarded by the world's press. UNITA continued trying to direct some operations against foreigners – from both East and West – working with the MPLA. A hostel housing Bulgarian contract workers in Benguela and a Cuban military barracks in Cuanza Sul province were among targets that UNITA claimed its Special Forces had destroyed. A bomb planted in a Huambo hotel killed several Cubans and Romanians.

Then, on 1 March 1986, came the biggest mass capture yet of foreigners by UNITA when its forces surrounded Andrada, the main MPLA diamond mining town in Lunda province, 1,000 kilometres north of Jamba. Among nearly 200 mineworkers captured, there were 100 Filipinos, 70 Portuguese, four Britons, two West Germans, two Romanians and a Canadian. The captives, who included 11 children and 25 women, two of them pregnant, were marched for 15 days into Zaire's Shaba province and left at a remote Methodist mission at a border village called Kapanga. The missionaries handed the foreigners to the ICRC, which arranged for them to travel to their home countries.

Describing the UNITA attack, John Sutherland, a Scot who was project manager at Andrada for the British-owned International Tractor Company (INTRACO), said everyone had been woken at about 4.30 a.m. on 1 March by mortar and heavy machine-gun fire. After two hours of fighting, the 800 MPLA troops guarding the mines had all fled. Most of the UNITA troops moved off immediately with the captives. But Mrs Anand Inamdar, a Canadian, was slightly wounded in the attack and was left in Andrada with 60 UNITA troops. In a television interview, she said she spent the following night with them – 'and there we were, all eating and barbecuing and music was going on.'

Keith Dyton, a Welsh mining engineer at Andrada, said the UNITA soldiers took with them the whole of the previous month's diamond production worth more than six million dollars. The soldiers carried from the mine anything that was portable and destroyed all remaining equipment and some buildings. The captured foreigners helped the UNITA soldiers to load big mine trucks with tinned food, rice and captured weapons and drive them beyond Andrade for depositing at underground stores in the forest. The soldiers also rustled about 1,000 cattle belonging to Diamang, the state diamond company. The captives heard MIG fighters of the Angolan Air Force searching for the UNITA column, but they were not troubled by MPLA ground forces. They eventually crossed the Cassai River, which forms the border with Zaire, by two rubber dinghies which shuttled people across nine at a time. The UNITA soldiers quickly faded back into Angola.

UNITA said the Andrada battle toll was 60 MPLA troops killed and several wounded against 19 UNITA troops killed and 30 wounded.

The attack inspired an interesting article by the *Guardian's* Jill Jolliffe, visiting Luanda, on the role played by several hundred Filipinos in the Angolan war. 'They are the latest model of Angola's mercenaries, the last civilians willing to drive truck supply convoys across battlefields,' she wrote. Their tasks, on contracts worth a mere $US 1,000 a month, involved driving the MPLA's only remaining civilian road transport in an attempt to reduce the huge backlog of containers of machinery, food and medical supplies stacking up on Luanda's wharves. (From Luanda, Lee Lescaze of the *Wall Street Journal* reported on 19 February 1987: 'Ships' crews watch each night as soldiers and civilians steal high percentages of the just-unloaded cargo.')

The Filipinos drove in convoys which stretched for five kilometres. The run to the diamond mines, in Lunda province, 1,200 kilometres east of Luanda, took 30 days. Each vast column included the Filipino's own enormous trailer-trucks, MPLA troop carriers and other military vehicles bristling with arms and anti-aircraft weapons. The military escort included Green Beret-style commandos under former Portuguese officers loyal to the 'Red Admiral' Rosa Coutinho who had returned to Angola on mercenary contracts.

The Filipinos had suffered surprisingly few casualties on the 'death runs' across Angola. One told Jolliffe that their charmed life owed something to an informal stand-off agreement they had with UNITA. 'When UNITA attacks, we hit the dust,' said a Manila man who had been driving in Angola for 15 months and had been attacked seven times. 'But they only go for the Angolans. They know we're just working for a living.'

Despite the Filipinos' cheerful bravery, only three land supply runs had got through to the diamond mines in the whole of 1985. The mines continued to depend on supplies by transport planes which also ran the risk of attack. A giant

Lockheed Hercules transport plane, leased to the MPLA by an Irish-owned enterprise, IAS Guernsey, was hit by SAM-7 missiles shortly after it took off on 10 February from the Dundo mining complex, near Andrada. The Canadian and American pilots managed to land the plane, though two of its four engines had been destroyed.

The tightening UNITA noose on Lunda province was wasting the diamond industry as a source of revenue for the MPLA. After the Andrada attack, INTRACO and another European company, the Luxembourg-based ITM, withdrew from the mines, just as the De Beers subsidiary, the London-based Mining and Technical Services, had pulled out the previous year. The MPLA's diamond exports were worth $US 234 million a year in 1980, the government's biggest foreign currency earner after oil. As UNITA intensified its attacks, production slumped to $US 56 million in 1984 and $US 32 million in 1985. In the first quarter of 1986 no diamonds were marketed, leaving Diamang, the state diamond company, without revenue and with costs of $US 4 million a month for the wages of 17,000 workers and to finance the air shuttle to the coast.

At the same time, UNITA's own share of diamond production steadily climbed. The diamonds were stolen during raids on MPLA mining centres, smuggled out of mines by underground members of UNITA and sieved from workings known to UNITA from old Portuguese mineralogical maps. In 1986 the UNITA mining team bought three frogmen's suits in Europe so that diamonds could be recovered from gravel at the bottom of Lunda province's deeper rivers. Oxygen tanks moved up regularly to Lunda on the backs of porters. Training of UNITA personnel in all aspects of the diamond trade began in 1983 and by 1986–87 was paying off handsomely, with profits swinging wildly between $US 50,000 and $US 4 million a month. In charge of the operation is a former guerrilla commander, Lt.-Col. Dias Vasconceles, who trained in Europe after UNITA had been swindled several times by European diamond dealers and middle men. Vasconceles now ensures that UNITA's diamonds fetch the full market rate. At Jamba he has diamond sorting lamps, sieves, electronic scales, diamond tweezers, head loops and diamond price grid charts. His team of 20 is in a constant process of training and is growing. Vasconceles himself makes up the packets of diamonds, according to the regulation practices of this most secretive of businesses, and takes them personally to Geneva and Antwerp to receive bids from Indian, American, Belgian and Israeli clients.

*	*	*

By April newspapers were anticipating another major dry season offensive by the MPLA against UNITA. At the beginning of the month the MPLA claimed to have shot down a South African Defence Force Hercules C-130 transport plane as it dropped supplies to UNITA troops near Andulo in Bie province. However, investigations by the International Air Transport Association (IATA) in Geneva discovered that the MPLA had shot down one of its own Hercules bearing the markings of Trans-Meridian, a British freight company which had gone out of business seven years earlier.

The scale of the Soviet re-supply operation for the planned offensive was formidable. Moscow even committed planes that were part of its strategic assets for any major conflict in Europe. These included several Ilyushin-76 transports and five of its total of 50 giant Antonov-22 'Cock' long-range, heavy-lift turboprop transports. From the ports of Luanda, Lobito and Namibe they airlifted to inland centres such as Menongue, Cuito Cuanavale and Luena T-62 and T-55 battle tanks, PT-76 amphibious tanks, and BTR-60 and BRDM-2 armoured personnel carriers. New SA-6, SA-8 and SA-13 air defence missile batteries and 'Flatface' and 'Barlock' anti-aircraft radar systems were also lifted in on a scale which would prove difficult for the South African Air Force to master. New MI-24 'Hind' helicopter-gunships and Mig-23 'Flogger' fighter-bombers were delivered in quantities which more than replaced those lost in the 1985 offensive. By the beginning of 1986 Western intelligence agencies estimated there were 27 MI-24s, 23 MIG-23s, 70 MIG-21s and 10 Sukhoi-22s in Angola. The MIG-21s were used for ground strikes while the MIG-23s, sometimes piloted by Soviets, provided air cover against

SADF planes. To back all this and other weapons – such as 22 MI-8 assault helicopters – the Soviet Union was also building a formidable maintenance and logistical support system.

In the 12 May 1986 edition of the magazine *West Africa*, the MPLA army deputy chief of staff, Roberto Monteiro Ngongo, admitted there were Soviet military both at the level of the MPLA's General Staff Headquarters and with the general staffs of all the military regions.

Ngongo was understating just how important Soviet involvement was. Western intelligence had noted the arrival in Angola in December 1985 of Soviet General Konstantin Shagnovitch to take overall control of all forces operating in the country on behalf of the MPLA, including the government's own troops. For Savimbi and for South Africa this was an ominous signal of Moscow's serious intent, for Shagnovitch was the highest ranking Soviet officer ever to have been posted on active service outside Europe or Afghanistan. The general, a counter-insurgency expert with skills honed fighting the Afghan guerrillas, was given the particular task of ensuring that future offensives against Savimbi's strongholds did not fail.

Shagnovitch was estimated to have about 950 fellow Soviets involved in command and training posts: these included General Mikhail Petrov, who later in 1986 was appointed first deputy on the Soviet Politburo in charge of counter-insurgency policy. Some 2,000 East German military men were deployed in the MPLA's intelligence and communication services.

By early April 1986 tanks and heavy artillery were gathered at Cuito Cuanavale and Luena ready for the offensive. Mechanised brigades and thousands of infantrymen were being deployed for the push.

In early May President dos Santos arrived in Moscow for his second official visit in three months. Meanwhile, Savimbi went to Cape Town to seek assurances on two fronts: first, on continued South African support for UNITA's fight; and, second, that South Africa had no intention of withdrawing from Namibia before all Cuban troops withdrew from Angola. Savimbi had been alarmed by an offer made by President Pieter Botha before the South African Parliament in March to begin pulling out of Namibia from 1 August 1986, '*provided* a firm and satisfactory agreement can be reached before that date on the withdrawal of the Cubans'. Botha assured Savimbi that the proviso was set in concrete, and Savimbi returned to intensify a counter-offensive that had been launched at the beginning of the year to harass the MPLA's supply lines. To underline his confidence, Savimbi paid another highly publicised visit to Munhango, in the dead centre of the country, with a West German television team and James F. Smith, a correspondent of the Associated Press. Smith got a shock when he found that the mighty dollar could not buy everything. At Munhango he offered to buy a UNITA private's military cap, and got the reply: 'What can I do with the money?'

Dos Santos came away from Moscow with assurances of continued Soviet commitment to the offensive. In mid-June a 10,000 tonne Soviet ship docked in Luanda with 100 heavy ground-to-air missiles aboard which were then airlifted to Luena by the Antonov-22s.

* * *

On 27 May, the MPLA offensive was launched on three fronts. Armour and infantry brigades began moving out, with close air support, towards key enemy positions. Two columns left Luena, one heading westwards towards Munhango and the other southwards towards Lumbala (Gago Coutinho). The third column set out from Cuito Cuanavale towards Mavinga and Jamba with the aim of cutting UNITA's logistics lifeline. Some 20,000 troops were involved overall, including battalions of Cuban infantrymen and Soviets at command level. The advance had begun later than in the previous year and it was noticeably more cautious, with greater efforts being devoted to securing rear bases and lines of supply. UNITA deployed large numbers of small guerrilla units to disrupt the MPLA's logistics. UNITA concentrated its heaviest defences around key water points, aiming to force the MPLA to bring in water by helicopter, as in the previous year.

The MPLA had made only limited progress by late July. Its

1st, 42nd and 54th brigades were beleaguered in Lucusse, about 80 kilometres to the south of Luena. The westwards push from Luena had enabled the MPLA to take Cangombe, about 60 kilometres away, but which had changed hands several times in the course of the war and was completely in ruins.

The most important push, from Cuito Cuanavale, had covered only 15 kilometres. It had been hampered by two main factors. First, UNITA units were heavily concentrated on the Bie to Menongue and the Menongue to Cuito Cuanavale roads, forcing the MPLA to fly in supplies. Second, UNITA had opened up another major military front in the far northwest of the country in the provinces of Zaire, Uige, Luanda and Cuanza Norte. The MPLA were forced to transfer three of the 22 brigades involved in the southern offensive to the northwest, where the Soviets began constructing a new military air base at Soyo on the Congo River estuary.

The mastermind of UNITA's northwestern operation was Colonel Antonio Dembo, the newly appointed Secretary for Military Mobilisation, a Kimbundu who from late 1985 established himself permanently in the Dembos forests to the northeast of Luanda. With his roots among the local people, Dembo now built on the work of earlier emissaries and developed UNITA's political and military network in the jungle-covered hills which had been the MPLA's most successful base area during the fight against the Portuguese.

Even further north, Dembo and his teams made great strides in winning over villages which had been traditionally loyal to the FNLA. These Kikongo people had in many ways endured worse hardships than any other Angolans. They suffered the corruption, inefficiency and narrow vision of their leader, Holden Roberto. And when the MPLA came to power the Kikongo were treated as second-class citizens by the victorious Kimbundu and *mesticos* of the Luanda-based MPLA, much as Robert Mugabe continued to heap indignities and death upon the 'losing' Ndbele in the Zimbabwe conflict. In the absence of any effective surviving FNLA organisation, UNITA was able to channel Kikongo resentment into support for its own resistance, and by July 1986 semi-regular UNITA battalions and guerrilla companies were operating in the most northwesterly provinces of Uige and Zaire. Recruits were making the 1200 kilometre overland journey to Jamba for training. Senior UNITA officers made frequent trips to the northwest to help Dembo develop the military and political campaigns. Establishing UNITA in the Kikongo homeland involved careful studies of local traditions: tape-recordings were made in the villages and sent back to the cultural unit at Jamba which is building up records of Angola's history and traditions, which have been mostly passed down from generation to generation by word of mouth. Nevertheless, Brigadier 'Ben-Ben' Arlindo Pena got a surprise when he trekked into Kikongo territory on a 'hearts and minds' foray and found that many of the local chiefs and their advisers were women. 'I quickly learned to take my hat off in their presence and talk to them as if they were my mother,' he said.

The most spectacular UNITA operation in the northwest came at dawn on 8 February 1986 when a force attacked the town of Camabatela, 200 kilometres northest of Luanda. UNITA claimed more than 200 MPLA dead, two MI-24 helicopters shot down, and an electrical station and 50 trucks destroyed. The MPLA admitted the attack, but described it as a 'massacre' of 107 men, women and children. ANGOP, the MPLA's news agency, said that UNITA attacked a bus nearby two days later and killed 12 passengers.

Through 1986 UNITA communiqués reported regular clashes in the northwest and officers enthusiastically reported back on how the thicker jungles and bigger hills of the region made guerrilla warfare easier than in central Angola. The UNITA officers found several old FNLA groups who had survived without any central command and who now joined up with UNITA. MPLA communiqués occasionally admitted the scale of UNITA's northwestern activities, as on 29 March when ANGOP said eleven 'UNITA counter-revolutionaries' were captured near the Zaire Province town of Mbanza Congo and paraded before the local population.

Nine days after the MPLA offensive began, ANGOP

announced that a South African patrol boat, armed with Israeli-made Scorpion missiles, had attacked Namibe and seriously damaged one Cuban and two Soviet ships, one of which sunk. The Soviet vessels were named as the *Kapitan Vislobokov* and *Kapitan Chirkov*. Two fuel storage tanks were also destroyed in the raid. The South African military maintained silence on the reports, but intelligence officials in Johannesburg told Anthony Robinson of the *Financial Times* that the attack on Namibe was just part of a clandestine South African military operation to disrupt MPLA supply routes to the main Angolan battle areas. ANGOP said the ships were carrying food, but since Namibe was a vital supply port for MPLA units attacking UNITA it is more likely that they were carrying military equipment.

* * *

By late July UNITA leaders were confident that they would again repulse the MPLA offensive. Despite the massive weaponry supplied by the Soviets, the MPLA advanced cautiously, suggesting that commanders were wary of UNITA's own upgraded weapons systems. And there were signs of eroding morale in MPLA ranks. The *Guardian's* Jill Jolliffe reported that streams of MPLA draft dodgers were crossing into Zaire and Zambia and that warrants for the capture of deserters were appearing in Luanda's daily newspaper.

But more significant was the opening of exploratory peace talks in London between UNITA's third ranking official, Tito Chingungi, the Permanent Secretary of the Central Committee, and the MPLA's foreign minister, Afonso Van Dunem. Several members of their delegations had been schoolmates together in Luanda before independence, which gave the talks a special poignancy. UNITA detected a real willingness among the MPLA delegation to set a framework for negotiations. The purge of hardliners from the MPLA at the December 1985 Congress had put pragmatists in the ascendancy in Luanda. But it was clear that no formula could be devised to enable Cuban and Soviet personnel to withdraw, without loss of face, before the dry season warfare gained full momentum and ran its course ahead of the arrival of the rains in October.

By mid-July UNITA's forces claimed to have brought down several MIG-23 and MIG-21 planes and MI-24 and MI-8 helicopters. Many tanks, armoured vehicles and trucks had been knocked out. Hundreds of men on both sides had died and many hundreds more were wounded. Then, in mid-August, a pre-emptive attack was made by 4,000 UNITA troops on Cuito Cuanavale, during which 12 radar installations were destroyed and two MIG-23 jets shot down. (The *Guardian*, 23 August 1986).

Few details of the raid emerged. But it did bring Shagnovitch's 1986 offensive to a halt. Some reports said South African ground and air forces had been involved in the six-day assault against Cuito Cuanavale, an impression reinforced by Savimbi's admission for the first time, to a Washington Post reporter, that South Africa had been involved in repulsing the MPLA's 1985 offensive. He told Patrick Tyler (*Washington Post*, 1 August 1986): 'I have no doubt in my mind that the South Africans see that if UNITA is crippled – or, let us take the extreme, wiped out – it will have a very negative impact on southern Africa.'

*   *   *

Just as important for UNITA as halting the MPLA offensive was a sudden acceleration in the non-stop deterioration of the Angolan economy. 'Our strategy is to raise the costs of the foreign occupation of Angola until the Cubans and Soviets can no longer bear the burden,' wrote Savimbi. 'A combination of rising military, financial and political costs will finally drive the imperialist forces from our shores.'

Between mid-1975 and mid-1986 world oil prices had plunged from a level of $25 a barrel to less than $10. On 19 February 1986 President dos Santos said that because of falling oil prices he was cutting the 1986 Angolan budget from three billion to $US 2.4 billion: more cuts would follow if there were further falls in the price of oil, which in 1985 had provided 90 per cent of Angola's export earnings. Dos Santos said that at least one-third of the MPLA's planned development programmes would have to be abandoned.

Many contracts with overseas companies would have to be cancelled or renegotiated. Foreign air travel, which in 1985 had cost the country $US 120 million, would be curtailed, especially for party members going on holidays and seeking medical treatment.

* * *

Meanwhile, UNITA intensified its international diplomacy and had mixed success. In Brussels senior UNITA officials held talks with Belgian Foreign Minister Leo Tindemans. But just along the road they were given the cold shoulder by the European Commission. Lorenzo Natali, the Commissioner for Third World aid who had emerged from the murky world of Italian Christian Democrat politics, ordered his officials not to meet UNITA delegates even though he regularly met opposition movements from other parts of the developing world. Commissioner Natali was clearly reluctant to ask himself why the MPLA was every bit as frightened of giving the vote to Angola's black citizens as the National Party was unwilling to give the vote to South Africa's black citizens.

The difference in attitudes between Tindemans and Natali mirrored the kind of European divisions Savimbi faced when he arrived on the continent in late October to visit the European Parliament, in Strasbourg, and Paris. He was received publicly in the French capital by the President of the National Assembly, Jacques Chaban-Delmas, and by Francois Léotard, Culture Minister and Secretary-General of the Republican Party, the minority party in the French centre-right coalition. Two hopefuls for the 1988 presidential contest, rightwinger Raymond Barre and socialist Michel Rocard, visited Savimbi privately. Rumours abounded that Prime Minister Jacques Chirac had also met Savimbi, but the UNITA leader refused to confirm it – 'That's for him (Chirac) to say,' Savimbi told *Le Monde* (28 October 1986). 'I can assure you there have been contacts with his representatives and they have promised to help us.'

Savimbi received scores of envoys from European governments, political parties and businesses at his hotel on the Avenue Kléber. Whatever gains he made were, as usual, on the basis of secretiveness. But mainly he learned that Western Europe's power citadels were more difficult to penetrate than the Oval Office of the White House. Complacent, clumsy and misguided diplomacy by Savimbi's envoys resulted in the cancellation of planned visits to London, Bonn, Brussels and The Hague. UNITA diplomats raised the stakes too high in each of these capitals, insisting that Savimbi be received at levels of government which the host nations found politically unacceptable.

Savimbi, however, made sufficient impact with his appeal to the West Europeans to help implement the 1975 elections to provoke Eduardo dos Santos into a hardline response.

On 11 November 1986, at a rally to mark the eleventh anniversary of independence, the Angolan president said: 'Recently references have been made to the so-called Alvor Accord. All Angolans know that this document lost its validity long ago. It has become obsolete and should lie in peace in our museum . . . Everybody knows that there is no true national liberation struggle in the world that does not have the direct or indirect support of the USSR or Cuba.'

Few Western newspapers recorded this oration at the funeral rites for Angolan liberty. Indeed, some UNITA critics in the West – themselves passionately committed to, and enjoying, the advantages of freedom – argued that democracy was a thin excuse for UNITA to wage civil war. The deputy foreign editor of *The Independent*, the new daily which has enriched British democracy, wrote brutally: 'A declared commitment to democratic pluralism in pursuit of western aid is rapidly becoming the last refuge of the scoundrel.'

*   *   *

Far away from the computerised newsrooms and the diplomatic manoeuvrings of the West, the guerrilla war in the Angolan countryside intensified until in mid-September 1987 the MPLA officially admitted for the first time that UNITA forces were active in most of the country's 18 provinces. In Luanda, Defence Minister Pedro Maria Tonha told Reuter's Central Africa correspondent, Pascal Fletcher, that UNITA guerrillas were active from Cabinda and Zaire provinces in the far north to Cunene and Cuando Cubango in the deep south. To fight the UNITA tide, new regional defence forces from the provinces were being recruited to help the regular army, said Tonha.

In the mood of growing MPLA frankness, Eduardo dos Santos said the war had cost 60,000 Angolan lives and made 750,000 of the country's 7.5 million people into refugees.

Defence Minister Tonha told Pascal Fletcher that many UNITA attacks were now being launched from across the Zaire border. Senior UNITA officials have always been highly sensitive about allegations of connections with Zaire, but they became more touchy than ever when the *New York Times* reported that the United States had begun to upgrade a Zairean air base near the Angolan border as a springboard for the airlift of arms to UNITA. James Brooke, the *New York Times* reporter who broke the story, was told before he left Zaire in late January 1987 that if he asserted a Zaire-UNITA relationship he would never again be granted a Zairean entry visa. The persistence with which senior UNITA officials in London, Lisbon, Washington and Paris sought to deny the Washington link with UNITA via Kamina suggested it was either totally false or very true indeed.

In Zaire, Brooke was the first Western reporter to visit camps run by the United Nations for people fleeing from the Angolan war. He noted that the refugees seemed to care little for the ideological divisions behind the war. At one camp, Kisenge, friends of Angolan exile Simão Segundo nodded assent as he said: 'The MPLA is the head and UNITA is the body – and one can't live without the other.'

* * *

In March 1987, Savimbi, under pressure from George Shultz, ever seeking a way of securing a relatively trouble-free Cuban withdrawal from Angola, offered to allow the Benguela Railway to reopen. By now, the line, once the finest in Africa, was in worse disarray than ever, as described by a correspondent for *The Independent* reporting from Lobito: 'About twice a month a train of nine engines and 65 wagons, 40 of them carrying maintenance equipment, leaves for Huambo (275 kms inland). It has a heavy military escort and pushes a truckload of sand in front of it to set off mines on the track. Huambo is a huge graveyard of wrecked engines and carriages. Beyond it, several bridges have been blown and the track is unusable.'

The US was anxious to provide an alternative route to the sea, bypassing South Africa, for the landlocked states of Zaire, Zambia and Zimbabwe. Savimbi said he was prepared to allow the railway to begin operating again provided the MPLA did not use it for military purposes and on condition that an international commission was established to supervise its use.

On 30 April 1987, a few days after Savimbi made his offer, Eduardo dos Santos, Kenneth Kaunda and Mobutu Sese Seko met in Lusaka and signed a declaration of intent to reactivate the Benguela Railway. The summit of the Angolan, Zambian and Zairean leaders was also attended by Viscount Etienne Davignon of the Société Générale, the Belgian company which now held 90 per cent of the shares in the former British-owned railway. Davignon's proposal was that the shareholdings in the railway be restructured with the Société Générale and the governments of Angola, Zaire, Zambia and Zimbabwe each taking a 20 per cent share of the stock.

Kaunda estimated that it would cost $280 million to rehabilitate the line and Davignon thought it could be operational again within two years. Both assessments seemed highly fanciful, but the plan had the kind of zest and originality which marked Davignon when he established a reputation as the most dynamic of European Commissioners while restructuring the European Community's troubled steel industries in the late seventies and early eighties. Davignon, and others, believed that cooperation on the railway could bring the MPLA and UNITA together for a single pragmatic purpose and perhaps lead to eventual political reconciliation. The Davignon Plan took its inspiration from Jean Monnet's pre-EEC European Coal and Steel Community, which ostensibly aimed to create cooperation in these spheres between France and Germany but was actually designed to so enmesh the economies of these traditional enemies that henceforth war between them would be unthinkable.

Sadly, the Davignon Plan for Angola did not achieve lift-off. The MPLA insisted on taking a 51 per cent share in the railway, which defeated Davignon's concept of an 'internationalisation' of the line. UNITA insisted it must have a representative on the supervisory commission: this was unacceptable to the MPLA, for it would amount to *de facto* recognition of UNITA, the beginning of a slippery slope towards *de jure* recognition.

The fragile lifeline towards peace was not grasped. Both sides instead prepared for more war.

*   *   *

Between mid-1986 and mid-1987, Western intelligence agencies estimated that Moscow sent one billion dollars worth of arms into Angola in preparation for the biggest government offensive yet against UNITA's southeastern strongholds – this brought to $4 billion the total Soviet military aid to the MPLA since 1977. General Shagnovitch planned a meticulous build-up and cautious advance towards Savimbi's airstrips at Mavinga, Luengue and Jamba from June 1987 onwards. Fuel, spares, ammunition and food were moved continuously from the rear to forward logistical dumps. Assisting him were General Petrov and General Ochoa, a Cuban air transport specialist.

William Claiborne of the *Washington Post*, visiting southern Angola on an MPLA-escorted trip, reported (9 July 1987): 'During one four-hour period last week at Lubango's airport, a constant stream of Soviet Aeroflot transport planes landed and their cargoes, including air-to-air missiles, were quickly unloaded by Cuban and Angolan troops . . . The scene at Luanda's airport was similar, with long lines of Aeroflot transports waiting on the taxiway for their turn to take off at intervals of only a few minutes.'

Earlier, at Cahama, near the Namibian border, Claiborne said he had been subjected to a lecture by a young MPLA officer, Captain Carlos dos Santos, on how his troops would not need Cuban or Russian help to drive the South African

Army out of Angola whenever it dared enter. Dos Santos asked the *Washington Post* man whether he could see any foreign faces around.

Claiborne's narrative continued: 'As he (the captain) stepped outside an officer's mess in this bomb-scarred southern Angolan town a car skidded to a halt in the dust and a Soviet officer, his face red with anger, barked an order to dos Santos to feed his troops at once. Then, warily eyeing several American journalists, the Russian roared away in a cloud of dust with a chastened dos Santos at his side. The brief episode underscored the sensitive relationship between the struggling Angolan Army and the estimated 950 Soviet advisers and 37,000 Cuban troops in this country . . .'

On the preparations for the offensive, *The Times* of London reported (4 July 1987): 'Air resupply of such towns as Cuito Cuanavale and Menongue provides the most striking reminder of Afghanistan, with Soviet-built Antonov transport planes spiralling down on to airstrips from great heights, spewing flares in an attempt to mislead the American anti-aircraft missiles which have recently proved so effective in UNITA hands.'

Simultaneously, Savimbi took moves to secure UNITA's position. There was a big UNITA counter-offensive in the north. On 13 May 1987 Reuter reported that MPLA troops had fought off a UNITA attack on Maquela do Zombo, in the far north near the Zaire border, during a visit to the town by President Eduardo dos Santos. UNITA said it had overrun a barracks and killed 29 government troops. The MPLA official account gave no details of casualties, but it said the 'suicidal and desperate' attack had been promptly repulsed.

In early September 1987 three Swedish hydroelectric technicians were seized by UNITA during an attack on an MPLA military convoy just 60 kilometres from Luanda. UNITA took special satisfaction in the capture of the Swedes, whose country was the leading Western supporter of the MPLA and which in its public statements of solidarity with the Luanda government described UNITA soldiers as 'terrorists'. Sweden, which was giving 22 million dollars in aid each year to the MPLA, faced tough negotiations with UNITA in gaining the release of its citizens, who were still in captivity at the time of writing.

To ensure continued South African back-up, as a complement to military aid from the US, Savimbi undertook a public visit to South Africa. To businessmen in Johannesburg the UNITA leader made a speech which some of his supporters in Europe and North America thought misjudged and damaging, but which was the *quid pro quo* requested by the South Africans for any potentially domestically unpopular military commitment that might be made against Shagnovitch's columns. According to the *New York Times*, Savimbi rebuked black leaders inside South Africa who refused to negotiate with President Pieter Botha. 'Why don't they talk?' Savimbi said. 'Someone who is running away from talking has something to hide.'

In Washington an intensive lobbying operation was undertaken by UNITA's six-man office. This resulted in a crucial 8–6 victory in the Intelligence Committee of the House of Representatives to continue providing US military aid to UNITA until 30 September 1988 on a covert basis. If the vote had been reversed, the issue would have come to the floor of the House, where UNITA supporters feared defeat because of the knock-on effect on dismay at disclosures about secret and illegal supplies of US arms to the Contra rebels in Nicaragua.

Senator Dennis DeConcini, a Democrat from Arizona, became a strong convert to UNITA's arguments for the need for elections in Angola. By a 94–0 vote he pushed a resolution through the Senate calling for peace and reconciliation in Angola. UNITA won over several other key Democratic Congressmen in a campaign designed to win support from liberals as well as from right-wingers. Representatives Dante Fascell and Claude Pepper and Senator Lawton Chiles became key Democratic proponents of UNITA, not least because of the large number of Cuban Americans living in their Florida constituencies who lobby strongly for Savimbi because of his fight with Fidel Castro. With help from such Congressmen Angola's Most Favoured Nation (MFN) status was repealed in the United States. This put the Angolan government on a similar tariff basis to other communist states trading with the US. Thus the tariff on Angolan oil imported to the US was more than tripled as a result of the MFN repeal.

But a move to block all trade between the US and Angola, which would have severely handicapped the Chevron oil operations in Angola, was defeated in the Senate. In this case a number of Republican supporters of UNITA voted against the embargo because they came from states where oil production equipment companies had important interests in Angola. Nevertheless, the public debate wearied Chevron and in 1987 it sold 20 per cent of its stake in Angola's oilfields to the Italian company Agip, a move which could presage a gradual sell-off of the rest of its interests in Angola.

Angola's oil had become a kind of affliction. While the oil brought in 90 per cent of the MPLA's foreign exchange, it also paid for the Sovet arms and Cuban soldiers which permitted the MPLA to continue seeking victory on Angola's battlefields rather than negotiating peace around a table.

Paul Betts, the *Financial Times* Paris correspondent, visited Luanda in September 1987 and was told by one Western businessman sharing his hotel: 'Despite its large oil revenues, or perhaps because of oil which has in many ways been a curse for the country by camouflaging the reality and enabling the government to finance the protracted war, the country has clearly reached the end of the road.'

Betts said Luanda, once known as the Rio de Janeiro of Africa, had totally broken down and become a city of refuse dumps on which almost naked children rummaged. Betts was directed to the French ambassador's residence by being told to turn right at a particularly big garbage pile. A few months earlier, Betts learned, 4,000 people had died of cholera in Luanda because of the collapse of sanitation services.

Betts' account of economic disintegration was mirrored by every Western correspondent who managed to gain entry into Angola in 1987. Richard Dowden of *The Independent* wrote (28 May 1987): 'Angola's internal economy is almost non-existent. The shops are empty and the fields and factories produce almost nothing.'

Africa Confidential noted (May 1987): 'Official rates of exchange and remuneration used by the government are out of line with reality by a factor of 5,000 per cent, which has a disturbing effect on every aspect of state planning and private life . . . In Huila, on the southern plateau, farm salaries are 17 months in arrears and the state farms are therefore being returned to private ownership . . . In central Angola, Huambo province has become the Beirut of Africa. The government builds by day and UNITA guerrillas destroy at night.'

As Luanda lurched through power and water shortages and many shops closed down permanently, the *Washington Post*'s Blaine Harden wrote (30 August 1987) that Angola's basic currency had become a can of beer – 'The standard way of making a living is to plot *esquemas*, schemes to get cans of beer to barter for water, fuel, clothing and food. Nearly everyone, it seems, is a schemer. Schemers shop in black markets. Three of the largest such markets in Luanda are called (roughly translated from the Portuguese): "Keep Your Mouth Shut", "Sorry, Senhor dos Santos", and "Prices Are So High, You Have To Trade Your Knickers".'

Against this background, the MPLA tried to move away from its policies of tight state control to a more market-based economy – in a sense, adopting the arguments UNITA had been making for years. Loss-making state enterprises were to be run down and private enterprise encouraged in trade, agriculture, transport and services. Membership of the International Monetary Fund would be applied for and a rescheduling of debt to Western creditors. At the same time Angola, which at independence was self-sufficient in food, appealed to the West for emergency aid to feed nearly two million of its people who were near starvation. *Time* magazine reported that it had been told by a Soviet diplomat in Luanda: 'This country needs Western investment. We have limits on what we can do.'

Despite its troubles, the MPLA made another attempt to overrun UNITA's bases in the southeast. Six brigades of soldiers, totalling about 20,000 men and made up mainly of

MPLA troops but including also Soviets and Cubans, began rolling towards Mavinga from Cuito Cuanavale in late September 1987 under the command of General Shagnovitch. The columns contained hundreds of tanks, armoured cars and trucks and were supported by helicopter gunships and jet fighter-bombers. By early October the biggest land battle in the history of Africa south of the Sahara was raging along the banks of the Lomba River just north of Mavinga. South Africa committed an unknown number of battalions to the battle and sent in several waves of Mirage fighter-bombers. As this book went to print, many thousands of men were dying in horrific warfare. Tanks, trucks and young men burned and planes and helicopters fluttered to the ground on the grim Lomba River battlefields, watched by uncomprehending village people who still revere the spirits who dwell in the stones and trees of a once barely disturbed wilderness.

The cost to the MPLA of the Lomba River losses are incalculable and raise questions that are impossible to answer at the time of writing. Will the dreadful losses in battle, combined with the nosedive of the economy, bring the MPLA to peace talks with its domestic opponents? Or will the Luanda government, with yet more help from Cuba and Russia and the oil income produced by Chevron, managed to gird itself for yet more offensives which drain its economy and bring death to its people?

The fear must be that the MPLA will be encouraged by the frightening ignorance of some 'respected' Western commentators on Angolan affairs. Flora Lewis of the *New York Times* could write blithely that UNITA was fighting 'in the first case for essentially tribal and, in the second, political reasons.' There was nothing to show, Ms Lewis argued, that UNITA constituted the desired 'democratic alternative.' She chose to overlook the fundamental truism that UNITA had had no chance to demonstrate whether or not it constituted a 'democratic alternative' because Angola's promised elections had been denied to the people. It was the sort of ill-informed bandwagon analysis that led Norman Podhoretz to despair in a *Washington Post* article at the 'vindictive satisfaction' with which Western commentators, enjoying the full fruits of democracy, made dismal forecasts about UNITA's future. He suspected that the reason they chose to disparage UNITA's resistance was because of 'the uneasiness inspired by the sight of people who reject the idea that peace is the overriding value and who, as the saying goes, would rather die on their feet than live on their knees. Discrediting such people may well be a way of evading the questions they implicitly raise.'

As the battles raged Savimbi was still pleading for the Western world to understand the nature of the struggle inside Angola. 'The moral case is clear,' he once wrote. 'UNITA is fighting for a free and independent Angola. We are fighting the Cubans and Soviets who would deny us our nation.

'Yes, UNITA receives aid from the Republic of South Africa, but it is hypocritical of the Soviets to claim that this means we somehow endorse the Pretoria government. We oppose apartheid. Fortunately, it is a dead ideology. It cannot be exported. The Lord did not ask our permission when he put Angola on the southwest coast of Africa. We need outside help, even if it has to come across the Namibian border. I would remind the Communists that Stalin's acceptance of war material from America and Britain during World War Two did not constitute an endorsement of liberal democracy on Stalin's part.

'We ask for your (Western) political and diplomatic support. We need you to insist at the United Nations and other international forums that the Cubans and Soviets leave Angola and that the promised elections be held.

'Do not underestimate the importance of your decision, for Angola is the Munich of Africa. Do not suppose that Zaire, Zambia, Botswana and Namibia will remain of the West when faced with an unopposed (Soviet) base in Angola. They will be forced to make their political accommodations with the Soviets just as most of Eastern Europe fell under Nazi political domination in 1938 without a shot being fired.

'That is why I say that UNITA is the key to Angola, Angola is the key to Africa, and Africa is the key to the West.

'I am not alone in this assessment. The Soviets agree.'

Notes

Notes on Prologue

1 Basil Davidson, *In the Eye of the Storm: Angola's People* (Penguin), p 290.
2 John Stockwell, *In Search of Enemies: a CIA Story* (Andre Deutsch), p 38.
3 For example, David Ottaway in the *Washington Post* of 27 December 1972.
4 Stockwell, *In Search of Enemies*, p 129.
5 Stockwell, p 139.
6 Stockwell, p 140.
7 Tchaka Zulu was an early nineteenth-century leader of the Zulu tribes of Natal, South Africa, who welded his followers into a great military power: Msiri established a powerful tribal kingdom in the late nineteenth century in what is now the Shaba province of Zaire: Jomo Kenyatta led a rebellion against the British and was first Prime Minister and then President of Kenya from 1964 until his death in 1978.
8 Stockwell, p 155.
9 Savimbi, in interview with author, Rabat, 19–21 January 1980.
10 Savimbi had been supplied with a Hawker Siddeley 125 executive jet by the British company Lonrho with two company pilots. While it was being serviced Lonrho hired the Danish Lear jet as a replacement.
11 Reuters, 22 September 1975.
12 Reuters, 22 September 1975.
13 Douglas Anglin and Timothy Shaw, *Zambia's Foreign Policy: Studies in Diplomacy and Dependence* (Westview Press, Boulder, Colorado), p 331.
14 Stockwell, p 162.
15 Stockwell, p 140.

16 Savimbi, in interview with author, London 4–5 July 1980.

Notes on Chapter 1
1 John Marcum, *The Angolan Revolution*, Volume 1: *The Anatomy of an Explosion (1950–1962)* (The M.I.T. Press, Cambridge, Massachusetts), p 5.
2 Lawrence W. Henderson, *Angola: Five Centuries of Conflict* (Cornell University Press, Ithaca and London), p 94.
3 John T. Tucker, *Angola: Land of the Blacksmith Prince* (World Dominion Press, London, 1933), p 16.
4 Henderson, *Angola: Five Centuries of Conflict*, pp 96–97.
5 H. Mark Roth and others, *Angola: A Country Study* (The American University, Washington DC), pp 36–37.
6 Marcum, *The Angolan Revolution*, Volume 1, p 104.
7 Henderson, p 120.
8 Marcum, *The Angolan Revolution*, Volume 1, p 20.
9 Henderson p 125.
10 Marcum, *The Angolan Revolution*, Volume 1, p 5.
11 Henderson, p 151.
12 Henderson, p 108.
13 Savimbi, in interview with author, Rabat, 19–21 January 1980.
14 Dr Henry Curtis MacDowell, 'Christian Patriot – Senhor Loth Malheiro Savimbi', written in 1973 for a missionary publication after the death of Loth Savimbi.
15 Savimbi, in interview with author, Rabat, 19–21 January 1980.
16 Dr Henry Curtis MacDowell, 'Christian Patriot, Senhor Loth Malheiro Savimbi'.
17 The full list of schools and churches founded by Loth Savimbi were: Munhango, Cubal, Ambandi, Sapessi, Chipeio, Jilinga, Belmonte, Katele-Kalucinga, Salvador-Mussende, Gumba, Chivinga, Lonhoha, Vila Alegre-Mungo, Vila Estrela, Mue-Cariango, Samaria, Bela Vista, Ekosa, Etumbuluko, Boa Esperanca, Florence and Lukata. This list was provided to the author in April 1985 by UNITA's policy-making Executive Committee. It

includes many schools founded after Loth Savimbi left employment with the Benguela Railway Company.

18 Savimbi, Rabat, 19–21 January 1980.
19 Savimbi, Rabat, 19–21 January 1980.
20 Savimbi, Rabat, 19–21 January 1980.
21 Henderson, p 25 and 51.
22 Savimbi, Rabat, 19–21 January 1980.
23 Savimbi, Rabat, 19–21 January 1980.
24 Savimbi, in interview with author, London, 4–5 July 1980.
25 Savimbi, London, 4–5 July 1980.
26 Savimbi, London, 4–5 July 1980.
27 Savimbi, Rabat, 19–21 January 1980.
28 The sisters Savimbi danced with were Judith and Victoria. In 1986, Judith, by then aged 53, was with her brother in his forest bases in Angola. Victoria died at the age of 16. Another sister, Isabel, died at the age of three months. Of two brothers, Vasco died aged three years and Abel, aged 59 in 1986, is with Jonas in UNITA-held areas of Angola.
29 Savimbi, London, 4–5 July 1980.
30 In 1957 Ghana had become the first black African nation to win independence from a European colonial master. Its first President, Kwame Nkrumah, dreamed of freeing and uniting Africa, and in 1958 he staged the All-Africn Peoples' Congress of liberation movement leaders in Accra, the Ghanaian capital. It was attended by Holden Roberto, future leader of the National Front for the Liberation of Angola (FNLA), and the Ghanaian press published articles which spoke of 'mass slavery in Angola' and of African resistance to the Portuguese regime: in fact, there was no resistance at this time.

Notes on Chapter 2

1 Margery Perham, *Colonial Sequence: 1949 to 1969* (Methuen, London), pp 175–176.
2 Margery Perham, letter to *The Times* of London, 10 May 1961.
3 Savimbi, in interview with author, Rabat, 19–21 January 1980.

4 V. Xavier Pintado, *Structure and Growth of the Portuguese Economy* (EFTA, Geneva, 1964), pp 12–13.

5 Agostinho Neto, *Sacred Hope*, translated from the Portuguese by Marga Holness (Tanzania Publishing House, Dar-Es-Salaam, 1974), p 1.

6 Savimbi, in interview with author, Rabat, 19–21 January 1980.

7 The wave of strikes organised by the PAIGC (African Independence Party of Guinea and Cape Verde) went on through 1958 and until 3 August 1959 when Portuguese soldiers at Pidiguiti, in Guinea-Bissau, opened fire on striking dockworkers and killed 50 of them. Another 21 strikers were imprisoned. This led to a decision by PAIGC Secretary-General Amilcar Cabral to switch emphasis from urban underground work to recruitment of the peasantry for a countryside-based guerrilla war. Cabral, an agronomist, had served earlier in the 'Portuguese Administration' in Angola and was keenly aware of the importance of bridging the inevitable gulf between intellectual and peasant, between urban modernist and rural traditionalist. To this extent, Cabral's philosophy matched that developed by Savimbi's UNITA, though the PAIGC continued to express its solidarity with the urban-based MPLA.

8 Savimbi, Rabat, 19–21 January 1980.

9 In Angola couples married in Protestant churches were registered by the colonial authorities as 'single' and their children as 'illegitimate'.

10 John Marcum, *The Angolan Revolution*, Volume 1, pp 111–112, 154–155; Savimbi, Rabat, 19–21 January 1980; note to author from UNITA's Executive Committee, April 1985.

11 Savimbi, Rabat, 19–21 January 1980.

12 Savimbi, Rabat, 19–21 January 1980.

13 Savimbi, Rabat, 19–21 January 1980.

14 Savimbi, Rabat, 19–21 January 1980.

15 Ismael Toure, head of the delegation of the newly independent Republic of Guinea, argued on 30 November 1959 before the United Nations General Assembly that Portugal's African territories were clearly non-self-

governing and that Portugal was bound by Article 73 of the UN Charter to report and answer to the UN on the rate of progress being made on preparing them for self-government. Holden Roberto, working incognito, was a member of the Guinean team.

16 Savimbi, Rabat, 19–21 January 1980.

17 The doctor was a member of a Dutch group of Moscow-oriented activists who had established an action committee to support the MPLA with money, publicity and propaganda. Based in Amsterdam, it was formally constituted in 1961 as the Angolan Action Committee.

18 Basil Davidson, *Africa in History* (Paladin Books, London), p 321.

19 The Scholarship came from a fund provided by US Protestant missionaries.

20 This would have granted France's African territories internal self-rule while binding them with Paris in a kind of loose federal system. Guinea opted for independence in 1958 outside the French Community. The French Community idea subsequently collapsed, but the next crop of French territories which became independent in 1960 – 14 in all, and excluding only Algeria (1962) and Djibouti (1977) – retained substantial financial and military links with Paris.

21 At independence the Belgians left the Congo (later renamed Zaire) with only one trained senior African civil servant. The Congo quickly collapsed into years of dreadful civil war, which the Portuguese helped stoke from Angola by supporting Moise Tshombe's secessionist rebellion in Katanga.

22 In a private note to the author (June 1985), Professor John Marcum commented: 'Some thin booklets with a "programme" did exist, produced in Ghana in 1959–60. Holden Roberto may very well not have had any with him, however. And the "programme" was rudimentary'.

23 Savimbi, Rabat, 19–21 January 1980.

24 Some writers, referring to this period of Savimbi's life, have said he was once a member of the MPLA. But he did not join; nor, though he considered it, did he join UGEAN.

25 Savimbi, Rabat, 19–21 January 1980.
26 After independence Kenyatta became one of Africa's most strongly anti-Communist leaders, often telling his people: 'Don't be fooled into looking to Communists for food.'
27 Jomo Kenyatta, *Facing Mount Kenya* (Secker and Warburg, London, 1938; Vintage, New York, 1962).
28 See Chapter 1.
29 Savimbi, Rabat, 19–21 January 1980.
30 Margery Perham, *Colonial Sequence: 1949 to 1969*, p 331.
31 Odinga and Mboya were both members of the minority Luo tribe. In 1969, Kenyatta, leader of the majority Kikuyu, imprisoned Odinga; and Mboya, regarded as the certain successor to Kenyatta as Kenyan President, was murdered in Nairobi by a Kikuyu gunman.
32 Savimbi, Rabat, 19–21 January 1980.
33 John Stockwell, *In Search of Enemies: A CIA Story* (Andre Deutsch), pp 236–237.

Notes on Chapter 3

 1 Rene Pelissier, 'Resistance et Revoltes En Angola (1845–1961)', Volume 3 (unpublished manuscript), p 1,225.
 2 Detailed, well researched accounts of the 4 February uprising appear in John Marcum's *The Angolan Revolution*, Volume 1, Chapter Four; Lawrence Henderson's *Angola: Five Centuries of Conflict*, Chapter Six; Richard Gibson's *African Liberation Movements*, Part Five (Oxford University Press, 1972); and the Rev. E. Edwin LeMaster's *I Saw the Horror in Angola*, published by *The Saturday Evening Post* on 12 May 1962.
 3 Savimbi, in interview with author, Rabat, 19–21 January 1980.
 4 The UPA revolt was infinitely more complex than can be conveyed in the space here. By far the most rigorous and outstanding account is that of John Marcum in Chapter Four, pp 130–158, of *The Angolan Revolution*, Volume 1.
 5 Frantz Fanon, *Black Skins, White Masks* (Grove Press, New York, 1967); *The Wretched of the Earth* (MacGibbon and Kee, London 1965). Roberto first met Fanon in

October 1958, when they attended the first All-African Peoples' Conference in Accra: subsequently they became friends.

6 Savimbi, in interview with author, Rabat, 19–21 January 1980.

7 Conversation between the author and Professor Henri Rieben at the European Research Centre, Lausanne University, May 1984.

Notes on Chapter 4

1 UGEAN also included liberation movements from other Portuguese colonial territories, but the movement was MPLA-dominated.

2 Among those who got scholarships were Tony Fernandes and Joseph Ndele, who went to Switzerland to study history and politics; Miguel N'Zau Puna, who studied agronomy in Tunisia; and Ernesto Mulato, who studied electrical engineering in London. All became close lieutenants of Savimbi when he established his own liberation movement, UNITA, in 1966.

3 Savimbi, in interview with author, Rabat, 19–21 January 1980.

4 The JUPA (Juventude-UPA) and LGTA (Liga Geral do Trabalhadores Angolanos).

5 The PDA drew its support from the Bazombo, a regional sub-tribe of the Bakongo.

6 Savimbi, Rabat, 19–21 January 1980.

7 John Marcum, *The Angolan Revolution*, Volume 1, p 254.

8 John Marcum, *The Angolan Revolution*, Volume 2; *Exile Politics and Guerrilla Warfare (1962–1976)* (The MIT Press, Cambridge, Massachusetts, 1978), p 87.

9 John Marcum, *The Angolan Revolution*, Volume 1, pp 213–214.

10 Basil Davidson, 'Unity in Angola?', *West African Magazine* (London), 14 December 1963, p 1,399.

11 John Marcum, *The Angolan Revolution*, Volume 2: *Exile Politics and Guerrilla Warfare (1962–1976)*, p 39 and p 119.

12 Savimbi, Rabat, 19–21 January 1980. (The FLN did in fact train some FNLA officers, but in Tunisia before Algerian independence in July 1962.)

13 Robert Davezies, *Les Angolais* (Editions de Minuit, Paris, 1965), p 211.

14 Robert Davezies, *Les Angolais*, pp 211–213.

15 Savimbi, Rabat, 19–21 January 1980.

16 Professor John Marcum argues that Savimbi was critical of Roberto for letting Chinese influence into the FNLA/GRAE at this time. This seems to stem from the widely reported opposition of Savimbi to the entry into the movement of the MPLA defector Viriato Da Cruz. Da Cruz was a hardline Marxist of the Maoist school. Savimbi's admiration of Mao was based on the Chinese leader's theories of, and practical achievements in, guerrilla warfare, not on his political theories. His opposition to Da Cruz was probably political and personal, and certainly did not mean he was opposed to practical collaboration with Peking.

17 Savimbi, Rabat, 19–21 January 1980.

18 FRELIMO (the Mozambique Liberation Front); SWAPO (the South-West African Peoples Organisation); ZAPU (the Zimbabwe African Peoples Union); ZANU (the Zimbabwe African National Union); ANC (the African National Congress); PAC (the Pan African Congress).

19 John Marcum, *The Angolan Revolution*: Volume 2, p 133.

20 Savimbi gave this account of his meeting with Guevara in his conversations with the author in Rabat, 19–21 January 1980.

21 If this was Guevara's judgement on the MPLA, it was somewhat harsh. Following his expulsion from Leopoldville, Neto had only been in Brazzaville for two months – scarcely long enough to have organised and launched a guerrilla warfare effort.

22 Boumedienne had given military training to about 20 FNLA officers in Tunisia in 1961. Had he perceived something then which would result in Algeria supporting the MPLA after he overthrew Ben Bella?

23 Guevara died on 11 October 1967. His death was deeply poignant. He believed he could rouse the tin miners of Bolivia, who were living in terrible poverty, to insurrection, but few supported him.

24 John Marcum, *The Angolan Revolution*, Volume 2, p 133.

25 John Marcum, *The Angolan Revolution*, Volume 2, p 134.
26 Savimbi, Rabat, 19–21 January 1980.
27 *Declaration de Monsieur Jonas Savimbi, Ministre des Affaires Etrangeres de GRAE* (Cairo, 16 July 1964, mimeograph). Reproduced widely elsewhere, including by the MPLA (document 44/64, Brazzaville, 17 August 1964), and by *Le Monde*, 22 July 1964).
28 John Marcum, *The Angolan Revolution*, Volume 2, pp 135–136.

Notes on Chapter 5

1 According to Savimbi, Neto wanted him to replace the existing MPLA Foreign Secretary, Luis de Azevedo, whom Neto described as ineffective and lacking understanding of international affairs. Azevedo had become Foreign Secretary after Mario de Andrade withdrew temporarily from political life in December 1962.
2 Savimbi, in interview with author, Rabat, 19–21 January 1980; John Marcum, *The Angolan Revolution*, Volume 2; *Exile Politics and Guerrilla Warfare (1962–76)*, (The MIT Press, Cambridge, Massachusetts, 1978), pp 161–162; Lawrence W. Henderson, *Angola: Five Centuries of Conflict*, (Cornell University Press, Ithaca and London, 1979), p 96.
3 John Marcum, *The Angolan Revolution*, Volume 2, p 172.
4 By 15 June 1964 the MPLA claimed that 150 of its partisans had been killed crossing Congo (Leopoldville) territory between Angola and Congo-Brazzaville. In May 1966 the MPLA reported that 32 of its militants had been killed in just one clash while crossing Congo (Leopoldville) territory.
5 Savimbi, Rabat, 19–21 January 1980.
6 Savimbi, Rabat, 19–21 January 1980.
7 Marcum, *The Angolan Revolution*, Volume 2, p 174.
8 *Courrier d'Afrique*, 21 April 1966.
9 Michael Wolfers and Jane Bergerol, *Angola in the Front Line* (Zed Books, London, 1983), p 161.
10 Interview with British journalist Mike Marshment in UNITA journal *Kwacha Angola* (special edition, London,

1972), p 15. There is some confusion among different writers as to which four countries in Eastern Europe Savimbi visited. The list here is based on information given to the author by UNITA's Executive Committee in April 1985. In North Vietnam Savimbi had a short meeting with one of his revolutionary heroes, General Vo Nguyen Giap, who successively and successfully commanded armies which defied Japanese, French and American armies. Giap's greatest victory was at Dien Bien Phu in 1954, which precipitated the collapse of French rule throughout Indonesia.

11 According to the *New York Times* of 25 September and 19 December 1975, Washington gave covert assistance to Holden Roberto from 1962 to 1969 as a 'fallback option' in case of Portuguese defeat: using Congolese and other channels this probably consisted of a modest supply of arms and money. With the advent in 1969 of the Nixon administration, the CIA 'deactivated' Roberto, though it left him on a $US 10,000 a year retainer for 'intelligence collection'.

12 Savimbi, Rabat, 19–21 January 1980.

13 Details provided to author in April 1985 by UNITA's Executive Committee.

14 David Martin and Phyllis Johnson, *The Struggle for Zimbabwe: The Chimurenge War* (Faber, London and Boston, 1981), p 11.

15 Letter of 21 September 1965 from Savimbi to 'the Missionaries of the United Church Board for World Ministries, New York.'

16 Richard Gibson, *African Liberation Movements: Contemporary Struggles Against White Minority Rule* (Oxford University Press, 1972), p 238.

17 The prison camp was part of the FNLA/GRAE's military complex at Kinkuzu in the Congo. A Bakongo businessman, Emmanuel Lamvu, described the prison camp as an 'African Buchenwald' after he escaped from it. In March 1977 Andre Kassinda, a dissident leader of the FNLA/GRAE labour movement, was executed in the camp.

18 Anibal de Malo.

19 Marcum, *The Angolan Revolution*, Volume 2, p 191.
20 The CONCP (Conferencia das Organizacoes Nacionalistas das Colonias Portuguesas), which at first grouped Soviet-leaning movements in the Portuguese colonies but later included other southern African movements.
21 Letter of 21 September 1965 from Savimbi to 'the Missionaries of the United Church Board for World Ministries, New York.'
22 They went to Cuba in October 1966 – Marcum, *The Angolan Revolution*, Volume 2, p 225.
23 *Le Monde*, 6–7 February 1966. This was a mortal blow to Da Cruz, who by now had joined the FNLA/GRAE. He flew into exile in China and devoted himself to his favourite pursuit, poetry. On 13 June 1973 he died in a Peking hospital after a long illness and years of political obscurity.
24 *Noticias* (Lourenco Marques) 14 May 1966.
25 Savimbi, Rabat, 19–21 January 1980.
26 Savimbi, Rabat, 19–21 January 1980.
27 Savimbi, Rabat, 19–21 January 1980.
28 *O Comercio*, a Luanda newspaper, said in its edition of 29 December 1966 that its figure, given the previous day, of 494 Teixeira de Sousa attackers dead and captured had been 'derived from an ambiguity'. Many of those listed as captured were simply villagers who had taken refuge in the town following the fighting.
29 Savimbi, Rabat, 19–21 January 1980.
30 Marcum, *The Angolan Revolution*, Volume 2, pp 191–192; *Le Monde*, 28 December 1966; *A Provincia de Angola* (Luanda), 28 and 30 December 1966.
31 Savimbi, Rabat 19–21 January 1980.
32 UNITA Executive Committee, April 1985.
33 Savimbi, Rabat, 19–21 January 1980.

Notes on Chapter 6

1 Savimbi, in an interview with the author, Rabat, 19–21 January 1980.
2 Moss, *Sunday Telegraph*, 1977.
3 As quoted in *China's African Revolution*, by Alan Hutchinson (Hutchinson, London, 1975), pp 247–248.

4 *Guerrilla Warfare*, by Mao Tse-tung, translated by Brigadier General Samuel B. Griffith (Anchor Press/ Doubleday, New York, 1978), p 93.

5 *Kwacha-Angola*, Volume 1, No. 3, December 1967.

6 Major Hoji Ia Henda and Dr Americo Boavida.

7 Richard Gibson, *African Liberation Movements*, p 223.

Notes on Chapter 7

1 Savimbi, in an interview with the author, London, 4–5 July 1980.

2 Savimbi in an August 1969 interview with British journalist Mike Marshment, published in *Kwacha-Angola*, 1972 ('Special Edition').

3 John Marcum, *The Angolan Revolution*, Volume 2, pp 182 –183.

4 UNITA military communiqué dated 10 September 1968, published in the November 1968 edition of *Kwacha-Angola*.

5 Marcum, *The Angolan Revolution*, Volume 2, pp 212 and 409.

6 Marcum, *The Angolan Revolution*, Volume 2, p 266.

7 Savimbi, London, 4–5 July 1980.

8 Savimbi, London, 4–5 July 1980.

9 Marcello Caetano, 'Address on Overseas Provinces', 28 November 1968 (Lisbon: Secretaria de Estado da Informacao e Turismo, 1970).

10 Marcello Caetano, statement on Angola, Luanda, 15 April 1969.

11 Savimbi, London, 4–5 July 1980.

12 Savimbi, London, 4–5 July 1980.

13 Savimbi, London, 4–5 July 1980.

14 Note to author from UNITA's Executive Committee, April 1985.

15 Savimbi, London, 4–5 July 1980.

16 Note to author from UNITA's Executive Committee, April 1985.

17 Savimbi, London, 4–5 July 1980.

18 Savimbi, London, 4–5 July 1980.

19 UNITA communiqué on the Second Congress.

20 Letter of 22 December 1969 from Mike Marshment to the Chairman of the OAU Liberation Committee, Dar-Es-Salaam. Copy in author's files.
21 Steve Valentine, *Times* of Zambia, 11 and 12 September 1969.

Notes on Chapter 8
 1 US National Security Study Memorandum 39.
 2 Douglas L. Wheeler and Rene Pelissier, *Angola* (Pall Mall Press, London, 1971), p 231.
 3 John Marcum, *The Angolan Revolution*, Volume 2, p 231.
 4 John Marcum, *Lessons of Angola*, Foreign Affairs, Volume 54, No. 3, April 1976, p 411.
 5 *Der Spiegel*, 15 June 1970.
 6 W. G. Clarence Smith, 'Class Structure and Class Struggles in Angola in the 1970s', *Journal of Southern African Studies*, 7 (1980), p 117.
 7 UNITA also alleged that chiefs were forced to surrender their younger wives to MPLA commanders.
 8 Agostinhino Neto, 'Angola: People in Revolution', *Tricontinental* (No. 12, May–June 1969), p 68.
 9 Richard Gibson, *African Liberation Movements: Contemporary Struggles Against White Minority Rule* (Oxford University Press, 1972), p 224.
10 Note to author from UNITA's Executive Committee, April 1985.
11 UNITA press statement, London, 7 December 1970; and UNITA war communiqué for July, August, September 1970.
12 The *Guardian*, 24 December 1970.
13 *The Times* of London, 3 October 1970. (Between 1970 and 1974 UNITA received 37,500 US dollars from the WCC; the MPLA 78,000 dollars; and the FNLA 60,500 dollars.)
14 Letter from Sietse Bosgra of 18 March 1971 to 'Angola Committee' supporters throughout Europe.
15 Sitte's account of his journey appeared in The *Observer* of London, 9 April 1972; the Zambia *Daily Mail*, 9 October 1971; and *Tages Anzeiger*, 5 October 1971.
16 The nineteenth-century Prussian general who was a brilliant strategist.

17 Marcum, *The Angolan Revolution*, Volume 2, p 201.
18 Savimbi, in an interview with the author, London, July 1980.
19 *The Times* of Zambia, 4 May 1971.
20 Zambia *Daily Mail*, 25 May 1972; *Le Soir*, Brussels, 21 March 1972.
21 Gaetano Pagano, *Visit to the MPLA and Their Liberated Areas* (International University Exchange Fund, Geneva, February 1975), p 15; Lawrence W. Henderson, *Angola: Five Centuries of Conflict*, p 226.
22 Marcum, *The Angolan Revolution*, Volume 2, pp 187–188.
23 Marcum, *The Angolan Revolution*, Volume 2, p 229.
24 Speech by Savimbi to the third UNITA Congress, 13–19 August 1973.
25 Leon Dash, 'The War in Angola', *Washington Post*, 23–26 December 1973.

Notes on Chapter 9

 1 Antonio de Spinola, *Portugal e o Futuro* (Lisbon, Arcadia, 1974).
 2 Lawrence W. Henderson, *Angola: Five Centuries of Conflict*, p 224.
 3 Dinis de Almeida, *Origens e evolucao do movimento de capitaes, subsidios para uma melhor compreensao* (Lisbon, Edicoes Sociais, 1977), p 206.
 4 *Provincia*, Luanda, 18 and 20 January 1984; *Report From Portuguese Africa* (editor: Michael Chapman), 4 January, 5 April and 11 May 1974.
 5 John Marcum, *The Angolan Revolution*, Volume 2, p 241.
 6 *Report From Portuguese Africa*, 5 May and 7 June 1974.
 7 Marcum, *The Angolan Revolution*, Volume 2, p 247.
 8 Reuters, Lusaka, 28 May 1974.
 9 Marcum, *The Angolan Revolution*, Volume 2, p 248.
10 *Afrique-Asie* (Paris), No. 61, 8 July 1974.
11 *O Seculo*, Lisbon, 9 August 1974.
12 *Kwacha-Angola*, June–August 1974.
13 Letter, 20 November 1984, to author from Michael Chapman (editor: *Report From Portuguese Africa*).
14 *Kwacha–Angola*, June–August 1974.

15 'Open Letter to the Militants,' signed by Daniel Chipenda, Lusaka, July 1973; Noticia, Luanda, 14 September 1974.

16 Marcum, *The Angolan Revolution*, Volume 2, p 211.

17 Note to author from UNITA's Executive Committee, April 1975.

18 Savimbi, in interview with author, Jamba, south-east Angola, 25 August 1985.

19 UNITA military communiqué, 27 January 1974.

20 *Kwacha-Angola*, June–August 1974.

21 Press statement made in Brussels by UNITA Foreign Secretary Jorge Sangumba, 29 August 1974.

22 Final communiqué, annual conference of UNITA, 20 July 1974.

23 Marcum, *The Angolan Revolution*, Volume 2, pp 245–246.

24 Marcum, *The Angolan Revolution*, Volume 2, p 246.

25 John Marcum, *Lessons of Angola*, Foreign Affairs, Volume 54, No. 3, April 1976, p 413.

26 Henry Kamm, reporting from Lusaka for the *New York Times*, 8 June 1974, at the time of a visit there by Portuguese Foreign Minister Mario Soares.

27 Marcum, *The Angolan Revolution*, Volume 2, p 248.

28 Marcum, *The Angolan Revolution*, Volume 2, p 252.

29 Savimbi in an interview with the author, London, 4–5 July 1980. (Professor John Marcum notes that since Chipenda came from the same Ovimbundu tribal group as Savimbi, the UNITA leader may have seen him as more of a direct rival in his own home 'constituency' than Neto).

30 Marcum, *The Angolan Revolution*, Volume 2, p 252.

31 Savimbi, London, 4–5 July 1980.

32 As told to the author and Reuter's manager for Africa, Shahe Guebenlian, in a meeting with Sikota Wina, member of the Central Committee of Zambia's ruling UNIP party, Lusaka, December 1975. Wina's story was subsequently confirmed to the author by senior Zambian intelligence officers, who said they had shown photos of the MPLA victims to Kaunda.

33 Bruno Crimi, *Trois Monologues*, Jeune Afrique, 14 September 1974, p 61.

Notes on Chapter 10
1 Final communiqué, annual conference of UNITA, 20 July 1974.
2 *diario De Noticias* and *O Seculo*, 29 October 1974.
3 John Marcum, *The Angolan Revolution*, Volume 2, p 244.
4 *Report from Portuguese Africa* (editor: Michael Chapman), 26 July, 14 August and 23 August 1974; Marcum, *The Angolan Revolution*, Volume 2, p 244.
5 *Zambia Daily Mail*, 16 November 1974.
6 *Report From Portuguese Africa*, 15 November 1974; *Zambia Daily Mail*, 16 November 1974; *Times of Zambia*, 16 November 1974.
7 *Zambia Daily Mail*, 18 November 1974.
8 *Diario de Luanda*, 27 November 1974; *Fraternité Matin*, Abidjan, 2 December 1974.
9 *Sunday News*, Dar Es Salaam, 10 December 1974.
10 *Daily News*, Dar es Salaam, 10 December 1974.
11 *The Times* of London, 19 and 20 December 1974; *Zambia Daily Mail*, and *Times of Zambia*, 20 December 1974; *Sunday Times* of London, 22 December 1974; *Trust* Magazine, Lusaka, May 1975.
12 James MacManus, The *Guardian*, 30 December 1974.
13 Reuters, Lusaka, 29 December 1974.
14 Colin Legum, *Africa Contemporary Record, Annual Survey and Documents, 1975–76* (Africana Publishing, New York).
15 Savimbi, in interview with author, Likua, Angola, 21 June 1981.
16 Marcum, *The Angolan Revolution*, Volume 2, pp 255–256.

Notes on Chapter 11
1 John Marcum, *The Angolan Revolution*, Volume 2, p 246.
2 Marcum, p 246.
3 David Martin, The *Observer*, 24 August 1975; Martin Meredith, *The First Dance of Freedom – Black Africa in the Postwar Era* (Hamish Hamilton, London, 1984), p 292.
4 British intelligence sources; also John Marcum, *The Angolan Revolution*, Volume 2, p 432; and Douglas G. Anglin and Timothy M. Shaw, *Zambia's Foreign Policy*

Studies in Diplomacy and Dependence (Westview Press, 1979), p 312.

5 Marcum, *The Angolan Revolution*, Volume 2, p 253.

6 Marcum, p 252; Robert Moss, *Sunday Telegraph* (London), 30 January 1977.

7 John Borrell, *The Observer*, 7 December 1974.

8 *Report From Portuguese Africa* (editor: Michael Chapman), 13 December 1974.

9 Marcum, p 253.

10 'Hearings Before the US Senate Sub-committee on Foreign Affairs,' 11 February 1976.

11 John Stockwell, *In Search of Enemies*, p 67.

12 Marcum, p 257.

13 Savimbi, in interview with author, Rabat, 19–21 January 1980.

14 Savimbi, Rabat, 19–21 January 1980.

15 Savimbi, Rabat, 19–21 January 1980.

16 Stockwell, *In Search of Enemies*, p 68.

17 Marcum, p 258.

18 *Report From Portuguese Africa*, 14 and 28 February 1975.

19 Jane Bergerol, *Financial Times*, 14 June 1975.

20 *Report From Portuguese Africa*, 25 April 1975.

21 David Martin, The *Observer*, 24 August 1975.

22 Savimbi, in interview with author, Jamba, Angola, 25 February 1983.

23 Anglin and Shaw, *Zambia's Foreign Policy*, p 329; Arthur Jay Klinghoffer, *The Angolan War: A Study in Soviet Policy in the Third World* (Westview Press, 1980), p 89; *The Times* of London, 7 January 1976, referred to Kaunda's April 1975 appeal to Ford 'to reverse what he considered to be a tide sweeping the MPLA to victory'.

24 Marcum, p 259.

25 Savimbi, Rabat, 19–21 January 1980.

26 Dr Bridgman, now a missionary in Zaire, in a letter to the author.

27 Savimbi, Rabat, 19–21 January 1980.

28 Contained in Dr Bridgman's letter.

29 Savimbi, Rabat, 19–21 January 1980.

30 Dr Bridgman, in a letter to the author.

31 Tony Hodges, *How the MPLA Won in Angola*, in Colin

Legum and Tony Hodges, editors, *After Angola: The War Over Southern Africa* (London, Rex Collings, 1976), p 50; *Report From Portuguese Africa*, 9 May 1975.

32 *Africa Development*, May 1975.
33 Barry Baxter, Gemini News Agency, in the *Times of Zambia*, 7 June 1975.
34 *Africa Development*, May 1975.
35 *Africa Development*, May 1975.
36 *Africa Development*, May 1975.
37 *Report From Portuguese Africa*, 9 May 1975.
38 *Financial Times*, 14 June 1975.
39 *Angola Report*, (editor: Michael Chapman), 13 June 1975; and Fola Soremekun, *Angola – The Road to Independence* (University of Ife Press, 1983), p 137.
40 Marcum, p 260.
41 Savimbi, Rabat, 19–21 January 1980.
42 *Times of Zambia*, 7 June 1975.
43 Savimbi, Rabat, 19–21 January 1980.
44 *Angola Report*, 25 July, 1 August and 8 August 1975.
45 Savimbi, Rabat, 19–21 January 1980.
46 Savimbi, Rabat, 19–21 January 1980.
47 Savimbi, Rabat, 19–21 January 1980.
48 Savimbi, Rabat, 19–21 January 1980.
49 Hodges, *How the MPLA Won in Angola*, p 53.
50 Marcum, p 262; Klinghoffer, *The Angolan War: A Study in Soviet Policy in the Third World*, p 65.
51 Savimbi, Rabat, 19–21 January 1980.
52 *Times of Zambia*, 3 August 1975.
53 Savimbi, Rabat, 19–21 January 1980.
54 *Zambia Daily Mail* and Reuters, Lusaka, 19 August 1975.

Notes on Chapter 12
1 As quoted by Douglas L. Wheeler and Rene Pelissier (Pall Mall Press Ltd., London, 1971), p 42.
2 Douglas Anglin and Timothy Shaw, *Zambia's Foreign Policy: Studies in Diplomacy and Dependence* (Westview Press, Boulder, Colorada), p 320.
3 Reuters, Lusaka, 20 August 1975.
4 Reuters, 24 September 1975.
5 John Stockwell, *In Search of Enemies*, pp 38 and 164.

6 Robert Moss, *Sunday Telegraph* (London), 30 October 1977.
7 Reuters, 26 October 1975.
8 Reuters, 29 October 1975.
9 Reuters, 29 October 1975.
10 Reuters, 5 November 1975.
11 Reuters, 5 November 1975.
12 Lawrence W. Henderson, *Angola–Five Centuries of Conflict*, p 154.
13 *Africa*, No. 52, December 1975, p 89.
14 *Angola Report* (editor: Michael Chapman), 3 October 1975.

Notes on Chapter 14
1 Jean Ziegler, *Les Rebelles–Contre L'Ordre du Monde* (Editions du Seuil, March 1983, p 259).
2 John Stockwell, *In Search of Enemies*, p 202.

Notes on Chapter 15
1 Robert Moss, the *Sunday Telegraph*, 6 February 1977.
2 As above.
3 As above.
4 Western intelligence officials, to author.
5 Robert Moss, the *Sunday Telegraph*, 13 February 1977. Dirk and Johanna de Villiers, *PW–A Biography of South African President P. W. Botha* (1985).
6 Savimbi, in interview with author, 4–5 July 1980.
7 Michael Wolfers and Jane Bergerol, *Angola in the Front Line* (Zed Books, London, 1983), p 23.
8 Professor Arthur Jay Klinghoffer, *The Angolan War: A Study in Soviet Policy in the Third World* (Westview Press, 1980), pp 82 and 95.
9 Robert Moss, the *Sunday Telegraph*, 13 February 1977.
10 Description of FNLA assault is based on accounts by Moss in the *Sunday Telegraph*; Stockwell in *In Search of Enemies* and Wolfers and Bergerol in *Angola in the Front Line*.
11 Note to author from John Marcum, author of *The Angolan Revolution*, Volume 1 and 2.
12 Dirk and Johanna de Villiers, *PW–A Biography of South African President P. W. Botha* (1985).

13 Gabriel Garcia Marques, in the *Washington Post* of 10 January 1977. Marques, the Colombian-born Nobel Prizewinner for Literature, has given the official Cuban account of Havana's involvement in the war.

14 *The Times* of London, 24 October 1975 and 23 June 1976, gives a figure of 1,100 to 1,500; John Stockwell gives a figure of 2,800 in *In Search of Enemies*; and Robert Moss gives a figure of 4,000 in his series of articles in 1977 in the *Sunday Telegraph*.

15 John Marcum, *The Angolan Revolution*, Volume 2, p 274; and John Stockwell, *In Search of Enemies*, p 232.

16 Robert Moss, the *Sunday Telegraph*, 30 January 1977.

17 Moss, *Sunday Telegraph*, 13 February 1977.

18 Moss, *Sunday Telegraph*, 13 January 1977.

19 Western intelligence officials, to author.

20 Stockwell, *In Search of Enemies*, p 232.

21 Algeria, Congo-Brazzaville, Guinea-Bissau, Guinea-Conakry, Malagasy Republic, Mali, Mozambique, Sao Tome and Somalia.

22 Western intelligence officials, to author.

23 Moss, *Sunday Telegraph*, 13 February 1977; Marcum, *The Angolan Revolution*, Volume 2, p 444.

24 Wolfers and Bergerol, *Angola in the Front Line*, p 42.

25 Stockwell, *In Search of Enemies*, p 215; Moss, *Sunday Telegraph*, 30 January 1977.

26 Wolfers and Bergerol, *Angola in the Front Line*, pp 27 and 39.

27 Lagos Radio External Service, 8 November 1975.

28 Savimbi at a press conference in Lusaka, 9 December 1975.

29 Stockwell, *In Search of Enemies*, p 227.

30 Stockwell, p 229.

31 Stockwell, p 230.

32 Stockwell, p 177.

33 Speech by Kaunda on 2 December 1975 at a Zambian Armed Forces seminar in Lusaka.

34 Castro speech to annual Congress of the Cuban Communist Party, as reported by Reuters, Havana, 21 December 1975.

35 This quote and those that follow directly are taken from

interviews with author and other foreign reporters in Lusaka on 9 and 11 December 1975.

36 The Luther King Library was part of the United States Information Service in Lusaka. Later, when it was clear that the MPLA was going to win, Young reversed his stand and called for US recognition of and reconciliation with Neto's administration.

37 London press conference, 19 November 1975.

38 Stockwell, *In Search of Enemies*, p 215.

39 *Washington Star*, 26 December 1975.

40 Moss, *Sunday Telegraph*, 13 February 1977.

41 *New York Times*, 7 February 1976.

Notes on Chapter 16

1 Savimbi, in interview with author, London, 4–5 July 1980.

2 Robert Moss, *Sunday Telegraph*, 13 February 1977.

3 South African Foreign Ministry officials, to author, August 1985.

4 *Tanzanian Daily News*, 18 December 1975.

5 *Zambia Daily Mail*, 7 January 1976.

6 Reuter, Johannesburg, 21 December 1975.

7 United States Information Service, 23 December 1975.

8 Reuter, Lusaka, 14 December 1975.

9 *Washington Star*, 30 December 1975.

10 *Christian Science Monitor*, 23 December 1975.

11 John Stockwell, *In Search of Enemies*, p 233.

12 Reuter, Havana, 21 December 1975.

13 Brand Fourie, to author, Johannesburg, 28 August 1975.

14 Robert Moss, *Sunday Telegraph*, 13 February 1977.

15 Douglas Anglin and Timothy Shaw, *Zambia's Foreign Policy: Studies in Diplomacy and Dependence* (Westview Press, Boulder, Colorado), p 332–333; *Rapport*, 15 February 1976.

16 Reuter, Lusaka, 28 January 1976.

17 Reuter, Lusaka, 31 December 1975.

18 *Zambia Daily Mail*, 8 January 1976.

19 Zambian Information Services Background 1/76, 13 January 1976 – full text of Kaunda speech.

20 Savimbi, in interview with author, London, 4–5 July 1980.

Notes on Chapter 17

1 Savimbi, interview with author, London, 4–5 July 1980.
2 Savimbi, interview with author, London, 4–5 July 1980.
3 Luis Rodriguez, a former Luanda newspaperman and BBC correspondent.
4 Max Hastings, *London Evening Standard*, 19 January 1976.
5 Savimbi, London, 4–5 July 1980; John Stockwell, *In Search of Enemies*, pp 177 and 185: Robert Moss, *Sunday Telegraph*, 6 February 1977.
6 Robert Moss, *Sunday Telegraph*, 6 February 1977.
7 Reuters, Lusaka, 20 January 1976.
8 Lawrence W. Henderson, *Angola–Five Centuries of Conflict*, p 257.
9 John Stockwell, *In Search of Enemies*, pp 193 and 234; John Marcum, *The Angolan Revolution*, Volume 2, p 439; *A Provincia de Angola*, 15 and 17 June 1975; *De Volksrant* (Amsterdam), 27 August 1975: Savimbi interview with author, Jamba, Angola, 25 August 1985.
10 This paragraph and subsequent ones are based on author's conversations with British intelligence officers in Africa. Many of the details were contained in Reuter despatches from 23 January 1976 onwards.
11 Reuters, Cape Town, 24 January 1976.
12 *Washington Post*, 3 February 1976.
13 *Newsweek*, 17 May 1976.
14 Michael Wolfers and Jane Bergerol, *Angola in the Front Line*, p 8.
15 John Kane-Berman, The *Guardian*, 21 April 1978.
16 *New York Times*, 7 February 1976.
17 Bernard Nossiter, *Washington Post*, 3 February 1976.
18 *International Herald Tribune*, 27 January 1976.
19 President Ford signed the Act on 9 February 1976 and made the comment at a White House breakfast with reporters. (*Philadelphia Inquirer*, 12 February 1976; Colin Legum and Tony Hodges, *After Angola: the War Over Southern Africa*, p 27). Not that the President was over-endowed with guts either – just a few months earlier he had refused to receive Soviet dissenter Alexander Solzhenitsyn at the White House because profitable grain sales were planned to the USSR and Kissinger was

about to make a visit to Moscow in pursuit of a SALT arms agreement.

20 *Washington Post*, 7 February 1976.

21 Savimbi, in interview with author, Luengue, Angola, 20 June 1981.

22 Reuter, Lusaka, 28 January 1976.

23 *Times of Zambia*, 30 January 1976; Reuters, Lusaka, 27 and 28 January 1976.

24 Stewart Dalby, *Financial Times*, 29 January 1976.

25 Legum and Hodges, *After Angola: The War Over Southern Africa*, p 27.

26 Stockwell, *In Search of Enemies*, p 233.

27 Most of Savimbi's comments in this sections were contained in Reuter despatches I filed on 8 and 9 February 1976.

28 Wolfers and Bergerol, *Angola in the Front Line*, p 56.

29 Reuters, Lusaka, 13 February 1976.

30 Jorge Sangumba, to correspondents in Lusaka, 13 February 1976.

31 *London Evening Standard*, 10 February 1976.

32 Kwacha Radio broadcast transcript, 13 February 1976.

33 Stockwell, *In Search of Enemies*, pp 216, 218 and 234.

34 Bruce Loudon, *Daily Telegraph*, 10 February 1976.

35 Stockwell, *In Search of Enemies*, p 235.

36 Savimbi, interview with author, Luengue, Angola, 25 February 1983.

37 *Christian Science Monitor* despatch from Kinshasa, 4 February 1976.

38 *New York Times* despatch from Kinshasa, 6 February 1976.

39 *Baltimore Sun*, 3 February 1976; *New York Times*, from London, 3 Feburary 1976; Stockwell, *In Search of Enemies*, p 224.

40 *Christian Science Monitor*, 4 February 1976.

41 The story was first broken on 8 February 1976 on America's NBC television network by its Kinshasa-based cameraman/correspondent Neil Davis, later to be killed in 1985 while filming an abortive military coup attempt in Thailand.

42 A grisly and morally sickening, and probably sometimes

exaggerated, account of the mercenary involvement with the FNLA is given by two of the former British mercenaries, Chris Dempster and Dave Tomkins, in *Fire Power*, (Corgi Books, London).

43 Robin Wright, *Christian Science Monitor*, 9 February 1976.
44 *The Times* of London, 7 January 1976.
45 Speech to the Zambian Parliament, 20 January 1976.
46 Zambian Information Services background paper, number 1/76, 12 January 1976, p 6.
47 University of Zambia Students' Union: *Statement on Angola issued on the occasion of a demonstration held by students of the University of Zambia in support of the MPLA on 15 January 1976*.
48 As reported in the *Zambian Daily Mail*, 26 January 1976.
49 Reuters, Lusaka, 26 January 1976.
50 The lower figure for student arrests comes from a *Zambia Daily Mail* report of 17 March 1976. The higher figure was given to the author by University of Zambia students.
51 Reuters, Lusaka, 6 February 1976.
52 Reuters, Lusaka, 14 February 1976.
53 Interavia ABC, 1977, p 708; Stockwell, *In Search of Enemies*, p 209.
54 Professor Arthur Jay Klinghoffer, *The Angolan War: A Study in Soviet Policy in the Third World* (Westview Press, Boulder, Colorado, 1980).
55 From author's own notes, but widely reported elsewhere at the time.
56 *New York Times*, 25 February 1976.
57 *Times of Zambia*, 24 and 25 February 1976.
58 *The Times* of London, 17 February 1976; *Rapport*, 16 February 1976.
59 Reuters, Lusaka, 25 February 1976.
60 *Zambia Daily Mail*, 18 March 1976. The Pearl Airways plane was allowed to leave after the dos Santos visit.
61 Reuters, Lusaka, 16 March 1976.
62 Reuters, Lusaka, 18 March 1976.

Notes on Chapter 18

1 Reuters, Lusaka, 4 February 1976. Sangumba was speaking to a group of foreign correspondents.

2 John Stockwell, *In Search of Enemies*, p 218.
3 During the university crisis, students made frequent phone calls to the Reuter office in Lusaka and sent letters. Relatives of the arrested foreign lecturers also made daily visits to publicise their plight.
4 Michael Wolfers and Jane Bergerol, *Angola in the Front Line*, p 58.
5 Douglas Anglin and Timothy Shaw, *Zambia's Foreign Policy: Studies in Diplomacy and Dependence* (Westview Press, Boulder, Colorado, 1979), p 332.

Notes on Chapter 19
1 *Daily Telegraph*, 10 February 1976.
2 UNITA communiqué, 5 March 1976.
3 Amnesty International, *Political Imprisonment in the People's Republic of Angola* (published March 1984), pp 4 and 24.
4 *Christian Science Monitor*, 2 March 1976; *Zambia Daily Mail*, 18 March 1976.
5 UNITA war communiqué, 3 March 1976.
6 Michael Wolfers and Jane Bergerol, *Angola in the Front Line*, p 57.
7 Martin Bell, *Newsnight*, BBC-2, 24 February 1976.
8 UNITA officials to author.
9 *Le Monde*, 18 February 1976.
10 Amnesty International, *Political Imprisonment in the People's Republic of Angola*, p 24.
11 Letter from Maria Goncalves de Freitas Christ to author, 18 October 1981.
12 *The Toledo Blade*, 11 March 1976.
13 Copyright, Kathryn Kane.

Notes on Chapter 20
1 Alan Palmer, *The Penguin Dictionary of Twentieth Century History*, (Penguin Books, London, 1979), p 244.
2 Most of the details in this account of the long march have come from long interviews by the author with Chingunji and Savimbi.
3 Anglin and Shaw, *Zambia's Foreign Policy*, p 338.

4 Anthony Mockler, *The New Mercenaries* (Sidgwick and Jackson, London, 1985), pp 167–168, 237.

Notes on Chapter 21

1 Transcript of March 1976 interview with Kaunda.
2 Douglas Anglin and Timothy Shaw, *Zambia's Foreign Policy: Studies in Diplomacy and Dependence*, p 338.
3 Joseph C. Harsch in the *Christian Science Monitor*, 29 April 1976.
4 A situation which had changed by the time of the US invasion of Grenada in 1984.
5 *New York Times*, 27 April 1976.
6 In June 1976 Kissinger held further talks on the future of southern Africa in Bavaria, West Germany, with South African Minister John Vorster.
7 *New York Times*, 21 May 1976.
8 *New York Times*, 28 April 1976.
9 *Le Point*, 24 April 1976.
10 *Le Monde*, 22 April; Irving Kaplan *Angola–A Country Study*, p 137; Reuters, Lisbon, 26 April 1976; *Zambia Daily Mail*, 27 April 1976; John Marcum, *The Angolan Revolution*, Volume 2, p 279.
11 UNITA press release issued in Lusaka in April 1976 under the title *Pinto D'Andrade Jailed and Tortured*.
12 Amnesty International, *Political Imprisonment in the People's Republic of Angola* (March 1984), pp 1 and 20.
13 *New York Times*, 22 May 1976.
14 Amnesty International, *Political Imprisonment in the People's Republic of Angola*, p 24.
15 Irving Kaplan, *Angola–A Country Study*, p 137.
16 John Stockwell, *In Search of Enemies*, p 137.
17 Robert Moss, the *Sunday Telegraph*, 13 February 1977.
18 Moscow Radio, 1 June 1976; *Christian Science Monitor*, 2 June 1976; *Observer* Foreign News Service, 9 June 1976.
19 *Baltimore Sun*, 5 June 1976.
20 Jonathan Randall, *Washington Post*, Kinshasa, 14 July 1976.
21 Savimbi, in interview with author, Rabat, 19–21 January 1980.

22 A shocking account of the mercenaries' behaviour and that of the MPLA commander who confronted them in war, Major Victor Correia Fernandes, is given by two mercenaries who escaped death or capture, Chris Dempster and Dave Tomkins, in their book about the mercenary debacle in Angola. Entitled *Firepower* (Corgi, London, 1978), it makes sickening but salutary reading.

23 David Martin, *Observer's* African correspondent, writing in the *Zambia Daily Mail* of 10 June 1976.

24 Amnesty International, *Political Imprisonment in the People's Republic of Angola*, p 16.

25 When Gearhart was captured by the MPLA he had been in Angola less than a week and had not fired a shot.

26 The *Guardian*, 10 July 1976; Irving Kaplan, *Angola – A Country Study*, p 137; Reuters, Luanda, 29 June 1976.

27 *Sunday Telegraph*, 20 February 1977.

28 Dial Torgerson of the *Los Angeles Times*, writing from Luanda, 20 June 1976. Torgerson died in a helicopter accident while on a reporting assignment in Honduras eight years later.

Notes on Chapter 22

1 As quoted by K. S. Karol in *Guerrillas in Power–The Course of the Cuban Revolution* (Jonathan Cape, London, 1971), p 173.

2 Savimbi, in interview with author, Rabat, 19–21 January 1980.

3 From personal diary of Luis Rodrigues, a Portuguese journalist who made a nine month journey on foot into Savimbi's territory in 1976.

4 Author's interviews with Chilingutila and Pena in February 1983 and December 1983.

5 Savimbi, in interview with author, Likua, Angola, 20 June 1981.

6 Vakulukuta brought the Cuanhamas into UNITA at the beginning of the seventies, after he had graduated from the University of Grenoble, France. But, of course, before that there were already close ties between UNITA and SWAPO.

7 In a personal note to the author, Professor Marcum wrote that the Soviet Union had long pressed SWAPO to sever ties with UNITA. SWAPO was party to a Soviet initiative at Khartoum in January 1969 which brought six African liberation movements, including the MPLA but excluding the then 'pro-Chinese' UNITA, together into formal association. Though the MPLA and SWAPO lobbied together as part of the 'Khartoum group' at international conferences and meetings of international organisations, SWAPO continued its intimate bilateral ties with UNITA.

8 *New York Times*, 9 November 1976.

9 *Los Angeles Times*, Luanda, 18 June 1976.

10 Acronym for the Popular Armed Forces for the Liberation of Angola (FAPLA), the MPLA army. UNITA's army is called the Armed Forces for the Liberation of Angola (FALA). Unless it is unavoidable, this book tries to avoid confusion and complication by simply using the terms 'MPLA army' and 'UNITA army'.

11 UNITA official statement, 31 October 1976.

12 Personal diary of Luis Rodrigues.

13 Reuter report from Oshakati, Namibia, 11 November 1976.

14 *New York Times*, 9 November 1976.

15 Reuters, Oshakati, 11 November 1976.

16 *The Times* of London, 9 November 1976.

17 *New York Times*, Huambo, 3 June 1976.

18 Personal diary of Luis Rodrigues.

Notes on Chapter 23

1 Savimbi, as quoted by Leon Dash in the *Washington Post* of 13 August 1977.

2 Unless otherwise stated, the scource for all material in this chapter is Leon Dash's account of his 4 October 1976 to 22 May 1977 Angola journey which appeared as a seven-part series in the *Washington Post* from 7 to 13 August 1977.

3 UNITA press release in New York of 18 October 1976, entitled 'Fidel Castro's Troops Continue to Kill and Maim the People in Angola.'

4 Savimbi, in interview with author, Rabat, 19–21 January 1980.
5 Most of the MPLA administrators at this time were *mesticos* or white Portuguese who had opted for Angolan citizenship.

Notes on Chapter 25
1 Portuguese for 'spy'.
2 Tito Chingunji, in interview with author, Edinburgh, October 1980.
3 Savimbi, interview with author, Rabat, 19–21 Jan 1981.
4 See Chapter 21.

Notes on Chapter 26
1 Irving Kaplan, *Angola: A Country Study*, pp 137–8; Martin Meredith, *The First Dance of Freedom*, pp 345–6.
2 Savimbi, interview with author, Rabat, 19–21 January 1980.
3 Savimbi, interview with author, London, 4–5 July 1980.
4 Savimbi, interview with author, London, 4–5 July 1980.
5 Savimbi, interview with author, Rabat, 19–21 January 1980.
6 Author's conversations with Savimbi in 1980 and 1981, and with other UNITA officials.
7 Savimbi, interview with author, Jamba, Angola, 1 July 1981.
8 Gerard Chailland, *The Struggle for Africa – Conflict of the Great Powers* (Macmillan Press, London, 1982), pp 104–109.
9 *Los Angeles Times*, 30 January 1976.
10 Chailland, *The Struggle for Africa*, p 107.
11 Chailland, *The Struggle for Africa*, p 109; David Dansoko, *Angola: the Secret War*, in *Jeune Afrique* of 27 January 1985.
12 *Jeune Afrique*, 27 January 1985.
13 Savimbi, interview with author, London, 4–5 July 1980.
14 Irving Kaplan, *Angola: A Country Study*, p 140.
15 John Marcum, *The Angolan Revolution*, Volume 2, p 227.
16 Savimbi, interview with author, Jamba, Angola, 1 July 1981.

17 Irving Kaplan, *Angola: A Country Study*, p 140.
18 Savimbi, interview with author, Likua, Angola, 20 June 1981.
19 Savimbi, interview with author, Likua, Angola, 20 June 1981.
20 *Angola Church News*, Volume 1, Number 7, Summer 1983, p 3.
21 From a personal memo to the author from Professor John Marcum.
22 Interview with Savimbi, and also a private letter from Dr Burgess to the author.
23 Savimbi, interview with author, Likua, Angola, 20 June 1981.
24 Letter to author from Dr Burgess.
25 Letter to author from Dr Burgess.
26 Savimbi, interviews with author, Rabat, 19–21 January 1980, and Likua, Angola, 20 June 1981.
27 Letter to author from Dr Burgess.
28 In visits to Angola from 1981 onwards the author has met and interviewed Catata and many of the nurses, engineers, teachers and administrators who deserted from MPLA territory to UNITA.
29 This section on the Alves coup is based on accounts by Marcum, *The Angolan Revolution*, Volume 2, p 445; Kaplan, *Angola: A Country Study*, pp 138–140; Amnesty International's *Political Imprisonment in the People's Republic of Angola*, of March 1984; and Michael Wolfers' and Jane Bergerol's *Angola in the Front Line*, pp 85 to 99. The official account by the surviving MPLA factions of the coup attempt is well stated in Wolfers' and Bergerol's work, and also an official report of 12 July 1977 by the MPLA Political Bureau entitled 'Informacao do Bureau Politico Sobre a Tentativa de Golpe de Estado de 27 de Maio.'
30 From a personal memo to the author from Professor John Marcum.
31 Wilfred Burchett, *Southern Africa Stands Up* (Urizen Books. New York, 1978) p 121.
32 Wolfers and Bergerol, *Angola in the Front Line*, p 98.
33 Kaplan, *Angola: A Country Study*, p 142.

Notes on Chapter 27

1 Savimbi, in interview with author, Jamba, Angola, 1 July 1981.

2 Savimbi, in interview with author, Jamba, Angola, 1 July 1981.

3 Savimbi, in interview with author, Jamba, Angola, 1 July 1981. (Holden Roberto appeared at the World Affairs Council in San Francisco in September 1984, where he said to Professor John Marcum that both South Africa and France were now aligned against him and were supporting UNITA).

4 Colin Legum, *The Western Crisis Over Southern Africa* (Africana Publishing Company, New York and London), pp 181–185.

5 Savimbi, in interview with author, Rabat, 19–21 January 1980.

6 From a personal memo to the author from Professor John Marcum.

7 Irving Kaplan, *Angola: A Country Study*, p 141; Colin Legum, *The Western Crisis Over Southern Africa*, pp 183–184.

8 Savimbi, in interview with author, Rabat, 19–21 January 1980.

9 Savimbi, in interview with author, London, 4–5 July 1980.

10 Savimbi, in interview with author, London, 4–5 July 1980.

11 The *Sunday Times* of London, 10 September 1978.

12 *Africa Confidential*, 14 February 1979.

13 Savimbi, in interview with author, Rabat, 19–21 January 1980.

14 Colin Legum, *The Western Crisis Over Southern Africa*, pp 183–184; Irving Kaplan, *Angola: A Country Study*, p 141.

15 Martin Meredith, *The First Dance of Freedom*, pp 345–346.

16 Young made the remark on the CBS TV programme *Who's Who*, on 25 January 1977.

17 Wolfers and Bergerol, *Angola in the Front Line*, p 221.

18 Paulo Tuba, the director of Roberto's 'cabinet', and Pedro Vaal Hendrick Neto, who was the FNLA's deputy

head of foreign affairs, settled in Boston, Massachusetts.
19 Savimbi, in interview with author, Rabat, 19–21 January 1980.
20 *Political Imprisonment in the People's Republic of Angola*, Amnesty International (March 1984), p 26; UNITA press release, December 1978.
21 Savimbi, in interview with author, Rabat, 19–21 January 1980.

Notes on Chapter 28

1 Savimbi, in interview with author, Rabat, 19–21 January 1980.
2 Edward Girardet, writing in the *Christian Science Monitor*, 31 May 1983.
3 Savimbi, in interview with author, Rabat, 19–21 January 1980.
4 *Christian Science Monitor*, 31 May 1983.
5 As reported in the *Guardian*, 11 May 1978.
6 The *Guardian*, 22 December 1978.
7 *African Confidential*, 13 February 1980, Volume 21, No. 4.
8 Savimbi, in interview with author, Rabat, 19–21 January 1980.
9 Dirk and Johanna de Villiers, *PW–A Biography of South African President P. W. Botha* (1985).
10 The 'black unit' Ms. Lewis refers to could either be a battalion of bushmen who, according to West European businessmen who provide UNITA with funds, often work in co-operation with UNITA forces, or it could be the 32 Battalion, made up of former members of the Chipenda FNLA Squadron. The bases of both battalions are in the Caprivi Strip in Namibia, near the Angolan border.
11 According to a report by Amnesty International ('Political Imprisonment in the People's Republic of Angola' – 1984), sixteen UNITA members were executed in the capital in August 1980 for the 1979 bombings. UNITA retaliated by executing 15 government soldiers held prisoner, whom it said had been condemned to death by an 'Angolan People's Resistance Tribunal'.

12 International Committee of the Red Cross sources, and author's own observations during journeys north of the Benguela Railway with UNITA forces in late 1983.

13 Tito Chingungi, who by 1986 was a Brigadier and number three in the UNITA hierarchy as Permanent Secretary to the Executive Committee (as the Central Committee was renamed in November 1984).

14 Savimbi, in interview with author, Rabat, 19–21 January 1980.

15 Tito Chingungi was the source for this information.

16 Savimbi, Rabat, 19–21 January 1980.

17 Savimbi, Rabat, 19–21 January 1980.

18 MPLA battalions are smaller than UNITA battalions, which consist of 500 to 800 men, depending on the range and number of specialist support troops attached to a battalion for an action.

19 Savimbi, Rabat, 19–21 January 1980.

Notes on Chapter 29

1 Savimbi, interview with author, Rabat, 19–21 January 1980.

2 Nyerere is popularly known by his Swahili title of 'Mwalimu', which means 'teacher'.

3 *New York Times*, 8 November 1979, with added detail from Savimbi in interview at Jamba, Angola, 25 August 1975.

4 *The Times* of London, 7 July 1980.

5 *Daily Telegraph*, 17 December 1979.

6 I have not seen any evidence that the findings, if any, of the inquiry were ever published.

7 Memo to author from Professor John Marcum.

Notes on Chapter 31

1 *Newsweek*, 12 November 1979.

2 *New York Times*, 8 November 1979; *Newsweek*, 12 November 1979.

3 *Newsweek*, 12 November 1979.

4 Savimbi, in interview with author, Rabat, 19–21 January 1980.

5 *Chicago Tribune*, 7 November 1979; *News World*, 6 November 1979.
6 *New York Times*, 8 November 1979.
7 A week earlier a Dutch newspaper had reported scenes of weeping parents at Brazzaville, capital of Congo-Brazzaville, as 1,200 children aged 10 to 15 prepared to fly out of the country, without parental sanction, for training as a future civilian and military élite.
8 *New York Times*, 22 November 1979.
9 *National Catholic Register*, December 1979.
10 Savimbi, Rabat, 19–21 January 1980.
11 Savimbi, Rabat, 19–21 January 1980.

Notes on Chapter 32
1 Savimbi, in interview with author, London, 1 July 1981.
2 Savimbi, in interview with author, London, 4–5 July 1980.
3 Colin Legum in *Diplomacy of Power–Soviet Armed Forces as a Political Instrument*, chapter 13 entitled 'Angola and the Horn of Africa', p 605. (Published in 1981 by the Brooking Institute – editor: Stephen Kaplan).
4 *The Economist Foreign Report*, 12 December 1979.
5 *The Times* of London, 18 January 1980.
6 Amnesty International, *Political Imprisonment in the People's Republic of Angola* (March 1984), p 26.
7 UNITA communiqué, 'The Voice of the Angolan Resistance,' No. 3/80, 28 March 1980.
8 UNITA communiqués No. 3/80, 28 March 1980, and No. 4/80, 8 April 1980.
9 *Daily Telegraph*, 17 April 1980.
10 Savimbi, interview with author, Jamba, Angola, 1 July 1981; UNITA communiqué No. 5/80, 17 April 1980.
11 *Los Angeles Times*, 29 May 1980.
12 Decision of UNITA's Central Committee, meeting in extraordinary session from 29 February to 2 March 1980.
13 Savimbi, London, 4–5 July 1980.
14 *Anti-Apartheid News*, November 1980.
15 Institute of Strategic Studies, 7 July 1980.
16 *Sunday Times*, 13 July 1980.

17 *The Times*, 7 July 1980.
18 *New African*, September 1980.
19 David Coetzee, Gemini News Service, 'The Real Aims of South Africa's Raids into Angola', 12 August 1980.
20 'Agony on Angola's Central Plateau', by Paul Fauvet, in *Africa*, No. 109, September 1980.
21 Ginette Cot, writing from MPLA territory in *Afrique-Asie*, 1 September 1980.
22 David Coetzee, 'Angola—The Longest War', *New African*, September 1980.
23 *Bulletin of the International Committee of the Red Cross*, No. 53, 4 June 1980.
24 *Africa*, No. 109. September 1980.
25 Coetzee had grasped the kernel of the truth, but in its entirety it was more complicated than that. With the departure of the Portuguese, sales of agricultural produce in the commercial sector collapsed. Transport became scarce as Portuguese left with their trucks, or with vehicle keys; most of the skilled mechanics, who were Portuguese, had left. UNITA, and also the MPLA, added an insecurity factor, Finally, the over-centralisation and dogmatic policies of the MPLA compounded the problems.
26 *Guardian*, 1 August 1980.
27 *Afrique-Asie*, 1 September 1980.
28 UNITA communiqué, No. 11/80, 29 July 1980.
29 UNITA communiqué, No. 12/80, 4 August 1980.
30 UNITA communiqué, No. 12/80, 4 August 1980.
31 UNITA communiqué, No. 13/80, 7 August 1980.
32 UNITA communiqué, No. 14/80, 11 August 1980.
33 *Afrique-Asie*, 1 September 1980.
34 *Le Monde*, 26 August 1980; *Daily Telegraph*, 26 Agust 1980.
35 UNITA communiqué, No. 15/80, 25 August 1980. The 15 MPLA dead were named as Sub-Lt Jose Maria; Sgt Kisua Jacinto; Sub-Lt Pedro Tiragem; Sub-Lt Chico Joao Belo; Sgt Augusto Daniel Seco Seco; Political Commissar Joao Sahinga; security official Mario Pinto Jaime; Sub-Lt Necas; Sgt Zenza Dipombo; Lt Domingos Pedro; Sgt Antonio N'Jila; Sgt Jose Ngongo; Sgt Bento Joao Domingos; Sgt Alberto Zange; Sgt Estavao Eduardo.

36 *Guardian*, 15 July 1980; *New African*, September 1980.
37 UNITA communiqué, No. 15/80, 25 August 1980.
38 UNITA communiqué, No. 19/80, 2 December 1980.

Notes on Chapter 33

1 *L'Express*, Paris, 16 January 1981.
2 Quentin Peel, in the *Financial Times*, 12 February 1981.
3 Arnaud de Borchgrave and Michael Ledeen in the February 1981 edition of *The New Republic*.
4 *International Herald Tribune*, 24 January 1981.
5 *The Times* of London, 26 March 1981; *Washington Post*, 29 March 1981; Reuters, Washington, 6 April 1981.
6 A SWAPO communiqué issued in London, 7 March 1981.
7 *Financial Mail*, Johannesburg, 20 March 1981.
8 *New York Times*, 1 June 1981.
9 'Southern Africa – A US Policy for the 80s', by Chester Crocker with Mario Greznes and Robert Henderson, in *Africa Report*, January–February 1981.
10 *Guardian*, 11 March 1981.
11 Statement by Private Jose Ricardo Belmundo to an 'International Commission of Inquiry into the Crimes of the Racist and Apartheid Regimes of Southern Africa' in Luanda from 30 January to 2 February 1981.
12 *Daily Telegraph*, 10 March 1981.
13 *Guardian*, 29 January 1981.
14 *Afrique-Asie*, 1 September 1980; transcripts from the Luanda 'International Commission of Inquiry,' 30 January–2 February 1981.
15 Savimbi, interview with author, Jamba, Angola, 1 July 1981.

Notes on Chapter 35

1 Mojena and Edade were still with UNITA at its Jamba headquarters in 1986. They had jobs there driving trucks between different parts of the spread-eagled base.

Notes on Chapter 37

1 Richard Harwood, the *Washington Post*, 21 July 1981. This was part of a richly descriptive seven-part series which

appeared in the *Post* from 19 to 25 July 1981 under the general title: *Angola – A Distant War*.

Notes on Chapter 38
1 *The Times* of London, 16 June 1981.
2 *Guardian*, 29 July 1981.
3 Christopher Munnion, the *Daily Telegraph*, 16 September 1981; *The Times* of London, 4 September 1981.
4 Mr Don Brunette, the Prosecutor-General of Namibia, to the author in August 1985.
5 *Daily Telegraph*, 16 September 1981.
6 UNITA special communiqué, 27 August 1981.
7 UNITA communiqué No. 6/81, 22 July 1981.
8 Savimbi, in interview with author, Rabat, 18 January 1982.
9 Robert Weller, of the Associated Press, reporting from Johannesburg, 1 September 1981.
10 *The Times* of London, 7 September 1981; Reuter and Associated Press, 4 September 1981.
11 *Financial Times*, 1 September 1981.
12 *New Statesman*, 4 September 1981.
13 Reuter despatch from Luanda, 17 December 1981.
14 *O Dia*, Lisbon, 28 September 1981.
15 *Financial Times*, 14 September 1981.
16 *Washington Post*, 3 December 1981.
17 Richard Wallis, Reuter despatch from Luanda, 18 December 1981.
18 *New York Times*, 4 December 1981.
19 The *Scotsman*, quoting agency despatches, 2 December 1981.

Notes on Chapter 39
1 *Observer*, 24 January 1982.
2 The *Scotsman*, 20 January 1982.
3 The Diamond Trading Company, part of South Africa's Anglo American De Beers empire, had three directors on the board of Diamang, Angola's 77 per cent state-owned diamond production company – *Financial Times*, 14 September 1981.

4 In Washington in December 1981.

5 *Financial Times*, 14 September 1981; *New York Times*, 23 July 1982; *The Times* of London, 17 August 1982; Bulletin of the International Committee of the Red Cross, September 1982.

6 *International Herald Tribune*, 8 February 1982; Alan Cowell of the *New York Times* reporting from Luanda in July 1982. (A previous programme for Cuban withdrawal was announced in April 1976 but was never implemented).

7 The *Scotsman*, 20 January 1982; *The Times* of London, 20 January 1982; *Spectator*, 13 March 1982; Richard Wallis, of Reuters, reporting from Luanda, 17 December 1981; *Africa Confidential*, 14 April 1982; *Economist Foreign Report*, 25 December 1981, 28 January 1982 and 29 April 1982; Marc Delteil, of Reuters, reporting from Rabat, 27 January 1982.

8 MI, under Pieter Botha, had gained the primacy once enjoyed in the South African intelligence establishment by the Bureau of State Security (BOSS), which had been downgraded and renamed the National Intelligence Service (NIS).

9 *International Herald Tribune*, 14 December 1981; *New York Times*, 18 July 1982.

10 *The Times* of London, 30 October 1981.

11 Among examples of the case for the MPLA are those argued by Jonathan Steele in the *Guardian*, 2 March 1981; Paul Fauvet, *Africa*, September 1980; and David Coetzee, *New African*, September 1980.

Notes on Chapter 40

1 *Newsweek*, 29 March 1982.

2 *Guardian* and *The Times* of London, 18 June 1982.

3 *The Economist*, 2 October 1982.

4 *The Times* of London, *Rheinische Post*, and the *East London Daily Dispatch*, 12 August 1982; *Newsweek*, 23 August 1982; *International Herald Tribune*, 27 August 1982; *Economist*, 11 September 1982.

5 *International Herald Tribune* and *The Times* of London, 15 September 1982; *South Africa Digest*, 17 September 1982.

6 *Observer*, 17 October 1982; *Economist Foreign Report*, 14 October 1982.
7 *International Herald Tribune*, 6 September 1982.
8 *Newsweek*, 23 August 1982; *Daily Telegraph*, 24 November 1982.
9 George Gedda, Associated Press, 9 December 1982; *Guardian*, 13 December 1982.
10 Amnesty International Newsletter, Vol. XII, No. 8, August 1982; UNITA communiqué, 29 May 1982.
11 Private letter from the International Secretariat of Amnesty International, 15 July 1982.
12 The Mavinga Declaration, 31 July 1982.
13 The Mavinga Declaration, 31 July 1982.
14 *New York Times*, 5 December 1982.
15 Muie, 150 kilometres north of Mavinga, had fallen to UNITA on 9 April 1982, according to UNITA communiqué No. 2/82 of 18 April 1982.
16 UNITA communiqués of 1 and 15 October 1982.
17 *Daily Telegraph*, 20 September 1982.
18 Christopher Munnion, *Daily Telegraph*, 20 September 1982.
19 *International Review of the Red Cross*, No. 230, September –October 1982.
20 Special ICRC Bulletin for 1982.
21 *International Review of the Red Cross*, No. 230, September –October 1982; Reuter, Lisbon, 11 October 1982.
22 Special communiqué of the Political Bureau and Central Committee of UNITA, 26 October 1982.
23 Special ICRC Bulletin for 1982.
24 Joseph Lelyveld, *New York Times*, 16 November 1982.
25 *Washington Post*, 17 November 1982.
26 *Times* of Zambia, 6 March 1982.
27 Reuter, Lisbon, 10 November 1982; UNITA communiqué No. 12/82, 9 November 1982; Associated Press, 11 November 1982.
28 As above.
29 UNITA special communiqué, 15 November 1982; Associated Press, from Johannesburg, 15 November 1982.
30 Angolan National News Agency, 13 November 1982.

31 UNITA communiqués of 11 November and 28 December 1982.
32 *New York Times*, 30 December 1982; UNITA communiqué, 28 December 1982.
33 Cot, a suave French socialist who takes particular care about the cut of his suits, had suggested the possibility that French troops might 'guarantee the territorial integrity of Angola' if Cuban troops left. Savimbi replied: 'Perhaps Cot is ready for French troops to take the same consequences as the Portuguese and Cubans?'
34 *The Times* of London, 3 December 1982; *O Jornal de Noticias*, 2 December 1982.

Notes on Chapter 41
1 The Young Pioneers are the MPLA's élite political youth brigade. Modelled on similar organisations in the Soviet Union, they parade in neat uniforms with red neckerchiefs.

Notes on Chapter 43
1 Angolan Press Agency (ANGOP) report, 6 January 1983.

Notes on Chapter 44
1 Angolan Press Agency (ANGOP), Luanda, 26 February 1983.
2 Author's interview with Savimbi at bush camp in southeastern Angola, 25 February 1983, the origin of all Savimbi quotes in this chapter.
3 Savimbi said the Western media argued there were 18,000 to 25,000 Cuban troops in Angola. He argued that UNITA had 'firm' evidence that there were 30,000 Cuban troops in the country and 10,000 other Cuban personnel.
4 *Africa Confidential*, Volume 24, No. 6, 16 March 1983.
5 Probably through the Portuguese Foreign Ministry.

Notes on Chapter 45
1 Savimbi, in interview with author, south-east Angola, 25 February 1983.

2 The author has talked to the official involved. His identity is not revealed to avoid jeopardising his ability to carry out his ICRC humanitarian tasks.

3 ANGOP (Angolan Press Agency), 19 April 1983. The credit was announced at the end of a two-week visit to Brazil by Angolan Planning Minister Lopo do Nascimento.

4 Amnesty International's *Political Imprisonment in the People's Republic of Angola* (March 1984), p 21.

Notes on Chapter 46

1 Savimbi, in interview with author in south-east Angola, 25 February 1983.

2 As above.

3 *Guardian*, 30 March 1983.

4 The account of the capture and march of the Czechoslovak hostages is based on several sources: the author's own interview with 20 of the hostages in December 1983; Yves Loiseau's graphic story in *Le Matin*, 2 July 1983; and the *Observer* of 17 April 1983 and 8 May 1983.

5 *Jornal De Angola*, 10 April 1983.

6 The *Scotsman*, 4 June 1983.

7 Based on accounts of the Munhango attack by Yves Loiseau in *Le Matin*, 2 July 1983; and by Edward Girardet in the *Christian Science Monitor*, 31 May 1983, and the *Economist*, 30 July 1983.

8 On 10 May 1985, President dos Santos confirmed Savimbi's claim to have pushed UNITA forces into the north of Lunda Province in 1983 when he said in a radio address: 'Dear comrades, our main preoccupation in Lunda Norte Province is to solve its war problems. The UNITA bandits are trained in South Africa. Armed elements began infiltrating this province from the end of 1983. They are here to attack the civilian population, destroy houses, steal cattle and hamper diamond production.' BBC monitoring service of a speech in Portuguese by dos Santos on the Luanda domestic radio service.

9 *Observer*, 24 July 1983.

10 *The Times* of London, 6 June 1983 and 14 October 1983.
11 *The Times* of London, 6 June 1983.
12 *The Times* of London, 14 October 1983.
13 As well as largely running Diamang, De Beers also marketed the company's diamonds through the De Beers London-based subsidiaries, Mining and Technical Services, the Diamond Trading Company, and the Central Selling Organisation.
14 Gwynne Roberts, *Scotsman*, 1 July 1983.
15 *Scotsman*, 1 July 1983.
16 *Washington Times*, 10 June 1983.
17 Antwerp diamond traders, to author.
18 *New York Review of Books*, 17 February 1983.
19 Edward Girardet, *Christian Science Monitor*, 3 June 1983.
20 The DISA was, in fact, disbanded in 1979 after allegations of abuses and corruption were made against it by Neto. But its two successor organisations, under the Ministries of State Security and the Interior, continued to be known colloquially under the old name.
21 UNITA communiqué No. 33/83, 2 July 1983.
22 UNITA communiqué No. 34/83, 5 July 1983.
23 Tito Chingungi, then London representative of UNITA.
24 UNITA communiqué No. 35/83, 13 July 1983.
25 Luc Beyer de Rike, Liberal Party, Belgium; Elmer Brock, Christian Democrat, West Germany; Sir James Scott Hopkins, Conservative Party, United Kingdom; Olivier D'Ormesson, Christian Democrat, France.
26 Joint communiqué, 16 July 1983.
27 Angolan Press Agency (ANGOP) commentary, 5 August 1983.
28 *Le Monde*, 22 July 1983.
29 UNITA communiqué No. 37/83, 25 July 1983.
30 UNITA communiqué No. 39/83, 31 July 1983.
31 ANGOP reports from Luanda, 28 July 1983 and 5 August 1983.
32 *The Times* of London, 1 August 1983, and the *Washington Post*, 6 October 1983.
33 ANGOP report from Luanda, 31 July 1983.
34 ANGOP report from Luanda, 5 September 1983.

Notes on Chapter 47

1 Savimbi, in interview with author, south-east Angola, 25 February 1983.
2 Author's conversations with Colonel Ben-Ben Arlindo Pena, February 1983.
3 Author's conversation with Dr Rony Brauman, President of Medicius Sans Frontières, 16 December 1983.
4 *Guardian* and *Daily Telegraph*, 16 August 1983; UNITA communiqué signed by Jonas Savimbi, 14 August 1983; UNITA communiqué No. 42/83, 18 August 1983; Glen Frankel, *Washington Post*, 6 October 1983.
5 *Scotsman*, 16 August 1983; *The Times* of London, 1 September 1983; Reuter despatch from David Reid in Lisbon, 17 August 1983.
6 UNITA communiqué No. 42/83, 18 August 1983; *The Times* of London, 18 August 1983. (The first foreign newsmen to describe and photograph Cangamba were a Portuguese television team in February 1983.)
7 *Scotsman*, 18 August 1983.

Notes on Chapter 48

1 *Washington Post*, 6 October 1983; Godwin Matatu, reporting from Luanda, in edition 147 of *Africa* magazine for November 1983; *Newsweek*, 10 October 1983.
2 The SAM-6 has a range of about 55 kilometres and is employed against aircraft at high altitudes. The SAM-8 is designed to take on low-flying attacks.
3 UNITA communiqué, No. 50/83, 6 November 1983.
4 *Washington Post*, 6 October 1983; *Newsweek*, 19 September 1983.
5 The film was shown on the BBC *Newsnight* programme in early January 1984, and also on the CBS network in the United States as well as in West Germany, Sweden and Japan.
6 *Newsweek*, 19 September 1983; *Washington Post*, 6 October 1983.
7 *Scotsman*, 4 January 1984.
8 *Guardian*, 9 and 11 November 1983.
9 UNITA communiqué No. 53/83, 15 November 1983.

10 *Focus on Africa*, BBC World Service, 26 November 1983; UNITA special communiqué, 28 November 1983.
11 *Times of Zambia*, December 1983; *Afrique-Asie*, No. 362, 2–15 December 1985; Savimbi, in interview with author, Likua, Angola, 16 December 1983.

Notes on Chapter 49
1 *Economist*, 30 March 1985; *Guardian*, 13 January 1984; James Adams, *Israel and South Africa: The Unnatural Alliance* (Quartet Books, London); *The Times* of London, 10 January 1984.
2 *Daily Telegraph*, 30 January 1984; *Financial Times*, 9 January 1984; *Sunday Times*, Johannesburg, 8 and 15 January 1984; *Rapport*, 15 January 1984; *Pretoria News*, 13 January 1984; Major-General G. L. Meiring, officer commanding South-West Africa Territory Force, writing in the July issue of *Strategic Review*, published by the University of Pretoria's Institute for Strategic Studies.
3 *Economist*, 30 March 1985; *Financial Times*, 5 January 1984; *Washington Post*, 5 January 1984.
4 *Economist*, 30 March 1985; *The Times* of London, 10 January 1984; *Guardian*, 9 January 1984.
5 *Star*, Johannesburg, 9 January 1984; *Economist*, 30 March 1985.
6 Associated Press report from Pretoria, 23 January 1984; Major-General Meiring, in the July issue of *Strategic Review*; *Economist*, 30 March 1984.

Notes on Chapter 50
1 Led by reporter Jose Manuel Barata-Feyor of the Portuguese TV (RTP) documentary series, *Grande Reportagem*.
2 *Daily Telegraph*, 2 April 1984.
3 *Daily Telegraph*, 2 April 1984.
4 *Scotsman*, 29 February 1984.
5 *Spectator*, 14 April 1984; *Daily Telegraph*, 2 April 1984.
6 Amnesty International Weekly Update Service 09/84, 1 March 1984; Angolan Press Agency (ANGOP) report from Benguela, 22 February 1984; ANGOP report from Huambo, 22 February 1984.

7 *Daily Telegraph*, 2 April 1984.

8 *Noticias de Portugal*, 13 March 1985.

9 UNITA communiqué No. 2/84, 26 March 1984.

10 *Jornal de Angola*, 10 April 1984.

11 ANGOP, Luanda, 25 May 1984.

12 President dos Santos, in speech at a mass rally in Namibe, 15 June 1984.

13 Declaration of the Extraordinary Congress of UNITA, 9 November 1985.

14 ANGOP, Luanda, 27 September 1985. (UNITA claims to have killed more than 2,000 enemy troops in the May-July and August-September offensives. Since no outsiders saw the fighting, these figures are only useful to indicate that very heavy fighting did take place).

15 The agreement was signed in Prague on 8 May 1984.

16 *The Times* of London, 23 June 1984.

17 *The Times* of London, 17 May 1984.

18 *The Times* of London, 14 and 17 May 1984.

19 *The Times* of London, 17 May 1984.

20 *The Times* of London, 14 May 1984; *Daily Telegraph*, 2 April 1984.

21 Reuters, Johannesburg, 22 June 1984.

22 *The Times* of London, 23 June 1984.

23 Tass, Luanda, 21 April 1984; ANGOP, Huambo, 23 April 1984; Granma, Havana, 25 April 1984; UNITA Communiqué No. 10/84, 20 April 1984.

24 UNITA communiqué No. 15/84, 14 June 1984.

25 ANGOP, Luanda, 21 June 1984; ANGOP, Ndalatando, 25 June 1984; UNITA communiqué No. 19/84, 20 June 1984.

26 UNITA communiqué No. 24/84, 15 July 1984; ANGOP, Luanda, 14 July 1984; ANGOP Cabinda, 16 July 1984; *Africa Confidential*, Volume 25, No. 15, 18 July 1985; *Africa Confidential*, Volume 25, No. 23, 14 November 1985.

27 UNITA special communiqué, 29 July 1984; author's conversation, 1 August 1984, with Lloyds Intelligence Department, Colchester, England.

28 UNITA special communiqué, 1 October 1984; Second Ordinary Congress of MPLA-Workers' Party, Luanda, 2–9 December 1985, Central Committee report on the Politico-Military situation.

29 *Observer*, 5 August 1984.
30 *Guardian*, 3 and 27 July 1984; *Le Monde*, 3 August 1984.
31 *Guardian*, 23 October 1984; *Le Monde*, 24 October 1984.
32 *Washington Post*, 15 October 1984.
33 *International Herald Tribune*, 14 November 1984.
34 James Brooke, reporting from Huambo for the *New York Times*, 31 December 1984.
35 The dos Santos proposals were contained in a message handed to UN Secretary-General Javier Perez de Cuellar in New York on 20 November 1984 by Elisio de Figueiredo, Angola's Ambassador to the UN.
36 *Daily Telegraph*, 26 November 1984.
37 *New York Times*, 12 November 1984. *Observer*, 16 December 1984.
38 Declaration of the Extraordinary Congress of UNITA, Jamba, 9 November 1984.
39 UNITA communiqué No. 44/84, 26 November 1984; UNITA communiqué No. 48/84, 18 December 1984.
40 *Guardian*, 31 December 1984.

Notes on Chapter 51

1 *Diario De Lisboa*, 2 April 1985; UNITA communiqués No. 2/85, 18 January 1985, No. 3/85, 23 January 1985, No. 4/85, 30 January 1985, No. 11/85, 25 March, No. 12/85, 28 March 1985; *Africa Confidential*, Volume 26, No. 4,13 February 1985.
2 UNITA communiqués No. 6/85, 26 February 1985; No. 7/85, 4 March 1985; No. 10/85, 24 March 1985.
3 ANGOP, Luanda, 9 January 1985; Reuters, Jamba, Angola, 13 January 1985, UNITA communiqué No. 4/85, 30 January 1985.
4 *The Times* of London, 2 January and 15 March 1984; *The Times* of London, 14 October 1983; Reuter and Associated Press, Jamba, 14 March 1985; *Daily Telegraph*, 3 January 1985.
5 *Guardian*, 2 January 1985.
6 *Scotsman*, 15 March 1985; *Le Monde*, 20 March 1984.
7 Luanda Radio Home Service, 10 May 1985.

8 *Sunday Times* (London), 12 May 1985; *The Times* of London, 13 May 1985.

9 South African Press Association, 18 April 1985; *Johannesburg Star*, 17 April 1985; *Guardian*, 17 June 1985; *Scotsman*, 18 June 1985; *The Times* of London, 23 June 1985.

10 *Africa Confidential*, Volume 25, No. 12, 6 June 1984.

11 *Scotsman*, 24, 25, 30 May, 22 June 1985; *The Times* of London, 24 May 1985; *Observer*, 26 May 1985; *The Sunday Times* (London), 26 May 1985; *Afrique-Asie*, July 1985.

12 *Financial Times*, 31 May 1985.

13 *Observer*, 14 July 1985.

14 *New York Times*, 15 July 1985.

15 Located in South Africa, according to the BBC Monitoring Service, which listens in to rebel radio stations around the world.

16 Voice of the Resistance of the Black Cockerel, 28 July 1985.

17 Victoria Brittain, *Guardian*, 19 September 1985.

18 Anthony Robinson, *Financial Times*, 9 October 1985.

19 Michael Hornsby, *The Times* of London, 9 October 1985.

20 The account of the Cazombo-Mavinga campaigns and their consequences are culled from many sources. These include my own interview with Savimbi at Jamba on 25 August 1985 as the MPLA columns approached Cazombo and Mavinga; various MPLA and UNITA communiqués; *Sunday Times* (London), 15 and 29 September 1985; *Guardian*, 18, 19, 20 September, 2 and 9 October, 1985; *Daily Telegraph*, 20 September, 2 and 9 October 1985; *Scotsman*, 21 September, 1 and 2 October 1985; *Washington Post*, 10 October 1985; *Observer*, 13 October 1985; *Newsweek*, 21 October 1985; *Washington Times*, 13 November 1985.

21 UNITA communiqués No. 14/85, 20 November 1985, and No. 63/85, 26 November 1985; ANGOP, Luanda, 25 November 1985.

22 *Daily Telegraph*, 25 and 28 September 1985; *Guardian* and *The Times* of London, 24 September 1985.

23 *Washington Post*, 2 and 11 November 1985; *New York Times*, 25 November 1985.

24 *Economist Foreign Report*, 15 December 1985.

Notes on Epilogue
1 Amnesty International, International Secretariat, January 1986.
2 The 8,000-word Marques account was originally published in an official Cuban publication, *Proceso*, in January 1977. It was also serialised in three issues of the *Washington Post*, 10–12 January 1977, under the title *Cuba in Africa: Seed Che Planted*. This had a certain irony in view of the encouragement Guevara had given Savimbi to fight from permanent guerrilla bases in Angola.
3 Made in a Castro speech at Conakry, Guinea, and reported in *Granma Weekly Review*, 28 March 1976.
4 *International Herald Tribune*, 4 December 1985.
5 John Marcum, *Africa Notes* (The Georgetown University Centre for Strategic and International Studies), No. 52, 20 December 1985.
6 *Granma Weekly Review*, 2 May 1976; Barry A. Sklan, *Cuba: Normalization of Relations*, Issue Brief No. IB75030, Congressional Research Service, Library of Congress (3 March 1976), 23.
7 Wilfred Burchett, *Southern Africa Stands Up* (Urizen Books, New York, 1978), p 34.
8 John Marcum, *The Angolan Revolution*, Volume 2, p 269; John Stockwell, *In Search of Enemies*, p 258.
9 John Stockwell, *In Search of Enemies*, p 185.
10 John Stockwell, *In Search of Enemies*, p 58.
11 John Marcum, *The Angolan Revolution*, Volume 2, pp 268–273.
12 Arthur Jay Klinghoffer, *The Angolan War: A Study in Soviet Policy in the Third World*, p 112.
13 Robert Moss, *Sunday Telegraph*, 30 January 1977.
14 Robert Moss, *Sunday Telegraph*, 30 January 1977; Jorge Dominguez, *Cuba: Order and Revolution* (Belknap Press of Harvard University Press, 1978), pp 354–355; John Stockwell, *In Search of Enemies*, p 170.
15 Document sdg/smcb of 2 November 1975 from Sean Macbride to UN Secretary General Kurt Waldheim; Robert Moss, *Sunday Telegraph*, 6 February 1977.
16 John Stockwell, *In Search of Enemies*, p 231.
17 'The Role of the Western Powers in Southern Africa', by

Colin Legum, in *After Angola: The War Over Southern Africa* (London, Rex Collings, 1976), pp 21 and 40.

18 Nyerere made his remarks in a BBC World Service interview in April 1976. Replying to them on 27 April, during a visit to Zambia, Henry Kissinger said: 'I know we did not do anything on a substantial scale in Angola until there was massive Soviet and Cuban intervention.'

19 *Tribune*, Paris, 11 September 1982.

20 *Jeune Afrique*, 29 August 1984. There were several press reports after the Lusaka Accord of MPLA and South African forces killing SWAPO dissidents in Cunene.

21 *New York Times*, 23 January 1981.

22 *Catch-22* by Joseph Heller (Jonathan Cape, London, 1962).

23 *Amnesty International*, 'Political Imprisonment in the People's Republic of Angola' (London, March 1984).

24 Gerald Bender, 'Angola: Left Right and Wrong', in *Foreign Policy*, No. 43, Summer 1981 (Carnegie Endowment for International Peace, New York).

25 Congressman Ted Weiss *Newsletter*, 6 November 1985.

26 *Guardian*, 2 March 1981.

27 Willis Player of the *San Diego Tribune*.

28 President Eduardo dos Santos in an interview with Jim Hoagland, foreign editor of the *Washington Post*, 29 October 1985.

29 *Guardian*, 14 December 1985. Two other hard-line leaders removed from the Politburo were Ludi Kissassunda, a former Chief of Security under Neto, and Henrique Santos Onambwe, Minister of Industry and a former security officer.

30 *International Herald Tribune*, 10 June 1986.

31 President Eduardo dos Santos, quoted in the *Christian Science Monitor*, 3 February 1984.

32 *Guardian*, 20 December 1985.

33 *Christian Science Monitor*, 11 February 1984.

34 Stephen Glover, *Daily Telegraph*, 18 November 1982.

35 *Scotsman*, 19 September 1985.

Index